New Developments in Environmental Sociology

Wherever possible, the articles in these volumes have been reproduced as originally published using facsimile reproduction, inclusive of footnotes and pagination to facilitate ease of reference.

For a list of all Edward Elgar published titles visit our site on the World Wide Web at www.e-elgar.com

New Developments in Environmental Sociology

Edited by

Michael R. Redclift

Professor of International Environmental Policy
King's College, University of London, UK

and

Graham Woodgate

Lecturer in Environmental Studies
Institute for the Study of the Americas, University of London, UK

An Elgar Reference Collection
Cheltenham, UK • Northampton, MA, USA

Published by
Edward Elgar Publishing Limited
Glensanda House
Montpellier Parade
Cheltenham
Glos GL50 1UA
UK

Edward Elgar Publishing, Inc.
136 West Street
Suite 202
Northampton
Massachusetts 01060
USA

A catalogue record for this book is available from the British Library.

ISBN   1 84376 115 7

Printed and bound in Great Britain by MPG Books Ltd, Bodmin, Cornwall

This book is dedicated to the memory of Fred Buttel who, more than anyone, helped to establish and define the field of environmental sociology, and to whom we all owe an enormous debt.

Contents

Acknowledgements

The editors and publishers wish to thank the authors and the following publishers who have kindly given permission for the use of copyright material.

American Sociological Association for articles: David John Frank, Ann Hironaka and Evan Schofer (2000), 'The Nation-State and the Natural Environment Over the Twentieth Century', *American Sociological Review*, **65** (1), February, 96–116; Frederick H. Buttel (2000), 'World Society, the Nation-State, and Environmental Protection: Comment on Frank, Hironaka, and Schofer', *American Sociological Review*, **65** (1), February, 117–21; David John Frank, Ann Hironaka and Evan Schofer (2000), 'Environmentalism as a Global Institution: *Reply to Buttel*', *American Sociological Review*, **65** (1), February, 122–7.

Battelle Press for excerpt: Sheila Jasanoff and Brian Wynne (1998), 'Science and Decisionmaking', in Steve Rayner and Elizabeth L. Malone (eds), *Human Choice and Climate Change*, Volume One: The Societal Framework, Chapter 1, 1–7, 74–7, references.

Blackwell Publishing Ltd for excerpt: Éric Darier (1999), 'Foucault and the Environment: An Introduction', in Éric Darier (ed.), *Discourses of the Environment*, Chapter 1, 1–33, references.

Elsevier for excerpts and articles: Marina Fischer-Kowalski and Helga Weisz (1999), 'Society as Hybrid Between Material and Symbolic Realms: Toward a Theoretical Framework of Society-Nature Interaction', in Lee Freese (ed.), *Advances in Human Ecology*, Volume 8, 215–51; Joseph Murphy (2000), 'Ecological Modernisation', *Geoforum*, **31**, 1–5, 7–8; Arthur P.J. Mol (2000), 'The Environmental Movement in an Era of Ecological Modernisation', *Geoforum*, **31**, 45–56; Joseph Murphy and Maurie J. Cohen (2001), 'Consumption, Environment and Public Policy', in Maurie J. Cohen and Joseph Murphy (eds), *Exploring Sustainable Consumption: Environmental Policy and the Social Sciences*, Volume 1, Chapter 1, 3–11, references; Allan Schnaiberg, David N. Pellow and Adam Weinberg (2002), 'The Treadmill of Production and the Environmental State', in Arthur P.J. Mol and Frederick H. Buttel (eds), *The Environmental State Under Pressure*, Research in Social Problems and Public Policy, Volume 10, 15–32; Bianca Ambrose-Oji, Tim Allmark, Peter Buckley, Bindi Clements and Graham Woodgate (2002), 'The Environmental State and the Forest: Of Lookouts, Lumberjacks, Leopards, and Losers', in Arthur P.J. Mol and Frederick H. Buttel (eds), *The Environmental State Under Pressure*, Research in Social Problems and Public Policy, Volume 10, 149–69.

Koninklijke Van Gorcum BV for excerpt: Terry Marsden (2003), 'Conclusions: Rural Development as "Real" Ecological Modernisation?', in *The Condition of Rural Sustainability*, Chapter 12, 237–55, references.

Oxford University Press for excerpt: John S. Dryzek (1997), 'Leave it to the People: Democratic Pragmatism', in *The Politics of the Earth: Environmental Discourses*, Chapter 5, 84–101, references.

Polity Press for excerpt: Alan Irwin (2001), 'Society, Nature, Knowledge: Co-constructing the Social and the Natural', in *Sociology and the Environment: A Critical Introduction to Society, Nature and Knowledge*, Chapter 7, 161–87, notes, references.

Routledge for excerpts: Arturo Escobar (1996), 'Constructing Nature: Elements for a Poststructural Political Ecology', in Richard Peet and Michael Watts (eds), *Liberation Ecologies: Environment, Development, Social Movements*, Chapter 2, 46–68; Sarah Whatmore and Lorraine Thorne (1997), 'Nourishing Networks: Alternative Geographies of Food', in David Goodman and Michael J. Watts (eds), *Globalising Food: Agrarian Questions and Global Restructuring*, Chapter 11, 287–304; Noel Castree and Bruce Braun (1998), 'The Construction of Nature and the Nature of Construction: Analytical and Political Tools for Building Survivable Futures', in Bruce Braun and Noel Castree (eds), *Remaking Reality: Nature at the Millenium*, Chapter 1, 3–42; David Demeritt (1998), 'Science, Social Constructivism and Nature', in Bruce Braun and Noel Castree (eds), *Remaking Reality: Nature at the Millenium*, Chapter 8, 173–93; Margaret FitzSimmons and David Goodman (1998), 'Incorporating Nature: Environmental Narratives and the Reproduction of Food', in Bruce Braun and Noel Castree (eds), *Remaking Reality: Nature at the Millenium*, Chapter 9, 194–220.

Sage Publications Ltd for excerpts and article: Steven Yearley (1996), 'Rethinking the Global', in *Sociology, Environmentalism, Globalization: Reinventing the Globe*, Chapter 5, 142–51, references; Frederick H. Buttel (2000), 'Classical Theory and Contemporary Environmental Sociology: Some Reflections on the Antecedents and Prospects for Reflexive Modernization Theories in the Study of Environment and Society', in Gert Spaargaren, Arthur P.J. Mol and Frederick H. Buttel (eds), *Environment and Global Modernity*, Sage Studies in International Sociology 50, Chapter 2, 17–39; Peter Dickens (2001), 'Linking the Social and Natural Sciences: Is Capital Modifying Human Biology in Its Own Image?', *Sociology*, **35** (1), 93–110.

Taylor and Francis, Inc. (http://www.taylorandfrancis.com) for article: Riley E. Dunlap and William R. Catton, Jr. (2002), 'Which Function(s) of the Environment Do We Study? A Comparison of Environmental and Natural Resource Sociology', *Society and Natural Resources*, **15**, 239–49.

Taylor and Francis Ltd (http://www.tandf.co.uk/journals) for article: Andrew Blowers (1997), 'Environmental Policy: Ecological Modernisation or the Risk Society?', *Urban Studies*, **34** (5–6), 845–71.

University of Chicago Press for article: John Bellamy Foster (1999), 'Marx's Theory of Metabolic Rift: Classical Foundations for Environmental Sociology', *American Journal of Sociology*, **105** (2), September, 366–405.

White Horse Press for article: Michael Redclift (2001), 'Environmental Security and the Recombinant Human: Sustainability in the Twenty-first Century', *Environmental Values*, **10** (3), 289–99.

John Wiley and Sons Limited for article: Joseph Huber (2000), 'Towards Industrial Ecology: Sustainable Development as a Concept of Ecological Modernization', *Journal of Environmental Policy and Planning*, **2**, 269–85.

Zed Books Ltd for excerpts: Wolfgang Sachs (1999), 'Globalization and Sustainability', in *Planet Dialectics: Explorations in Environment and Development*, Chapter 8, 129–55, references; Jon Barnett (2001), 'Environmental Security for People', in *The Meaning of Environmental Security: Ecological Politics and Policy in the New Security Era*, Chapter 9, 122–38, references.

Every effort has been made to trace all the copyright holders but if any have been inadvertently overlooked the publishers will be pleased to make the necessary arrangement at the first opportunity.

In addition the publishers wish to thank the Marshall Library of Economics, Cambridge University, the Library of the University of Warwick and the Library of Indiana University at Bloomington, USA for their assistance in obtaining these articles.

Introduction

Graham Woodgate and Michael Redclift

Sociological engagement with nature and the environment has come a long way since the 1960s, when sociologists began responding to early episodes of environmental degradation, seeking to elucidate the sociological components of natural resource use regimes. In the 1970s, disruption of oil supplies and the publication of the Limits to Growth report prompted research and debate about the failure of 'development' to meet the needs of the poor, more generalised processes of natural resource decline and the social character of limits to growth (e.g. Hirsch, 1977). This research suggested that, while nature might set ultimate biophysical limits to economic progress, social structure and market dynamics set more immediate limits to growth. Almost half a century later, virtually the entire range of social sciences has become involved in attempts to elucidate the complex nature of human interactions with(in) nature. Some of the subsequent writing in this field, which bridges several disciplines and bodies of literature, was published in *The International Handbook of Environmental Sociology* (Redclift and Woodgate, 1998).

During the last decade or so, environmental sociology and the 'boundary studies' with which it is associated (rural sociology, ecological and environmental economics, environmental anthropology, geography and political science) have sought to address a series of issues drawn from both 'real world' situations and the elaboration of post-structural and post-modern theory. On the one hand, tacit concern with environmental issues has grown internationally; and particularly within the context of 'globalisation' and the agendas of the anti-globalisation movement, which were made so evident in 1999 at the 'Battle in Seattle'. On the other hand, the political incorporation of approaches that were once considered eccentric or radical, such as the routine use by governments of environmental indicators and environmental accounting, have served to develop the methodological base from which market economics can be 'environmentalised'. At the same time, neither approach has proved fully equal to the important task of assessing the effects, both material and ideological, of both social opposition to global environmental changes *and* their formulation in policy discourses. This task – to critique approaches such as Ecological Modernisation within a context of increasing 'global' agreements – has been left to authors who focus on scientific and policy uncertainties, and to scholars in political science and international relations. Their work constitutes a critique of both scientific knowledge and its cultural and political manifestations.

The articles we have selected suggest that many of the concerns of the earlier volume continue to be important, such as metabolism and the nature/culture dichotomy. Not surprisingly, however, other matters have increasingly come into view: the concern with the state and the environment, for example, and the coming to fruition of a post-structural political ecology, that seeks to combine structural and cultural perspectives, by emphasising the centrality of the (human) subject, while refusing to ignore the materiality of the (environmental) problem. The 'environment', always a difficult and ambiguous category, has been set upon by the wolves of globalisation and 'the cultural turn', competing both for our intellectual attention and our academic loyalty. We believe that environmental sociology is benefiting from their carnivorous appetites.

Part I

The article by Riley Dunlap and Bill Catton with which this collection begins provides a comparison of natural resource sociology and environmental sociology as established and practised in the USA.[1] Having traced the historical and institutional roots of the two sub-disciplines, Dunlap and Catton go on to compare the two in terms of the subject matter they deal with and their relation to policy making. They conclude by suggesting that, while there may be considerable overlap between the two fields of endeavour, in contrast to the more empirical and policy-oriented character of natural resource sociology, environmental sociology has tended to be more theoretical, with particular attention being paid to the application and modification of mainstream theory.

Dunlap and Catton's assessment is reflected in the content of this book. Part I reproduces some of the more stimulating recent publications concerning social theory and the environment. Following Dunlap and Catton, the book continues with an essay from Fred Buttel (Chapter 2), in which he sets out to explore the relevance of classical sociological theory to contemporary environmental sociology. Buttel briefly reviews the ways in which the classical works of Marx and Engels, Durkheim, and Weber provide import points of departure for sociological understandings of environmental issues, noting that despite a tendency towards a 'radically sociological outlook, it by no means completely neglected the biophysical world'. This is illustrated by exploring the fortunes of classical concepts, theories and social imperatives in contemporary environmental sociology. In this respect Buttel concludes 'as much as environmental sociologists have been critical of the shortcomings of classical theory, their work has tended to have very definite affinities with many of the concepts, methodological principles, and presuppositions of the classical tradition' (Buttel, 2000, p. 23).

In the second half of the essay, attention is turned to theoretical developments within environmental sociology, including Schnaiberg's 'treadmill of production', a broad spectrum of work on the social construction of environmental problems and the growing attention being paid to European theories of reflexive and 'ecological modernisation' (EM). All of these developments are represented in this volume.

Schnaiberg's important contribution to Environmental Sociology was unaccountably missing from the earlier volume we edited (Redclift and Woodgate, 1997). In this volume we have made partial reparation. His later work, on the treadmill of production, is outlined in the chapter by Schnaiberg, Pellow and Weinberg (Chapter 3), taken from Arthur Mol and Fred Buttel's (2002) edited collection on *The Environmental State Under Pressure*. The notion of the 'environmental state' captures the contradictory position of the modern state in terms of its mandates of fostering economic development and social welfare at the same time as maintaining healthy and satisfying environments. Schnaiberg *et al.* utilise the 'treadmill of production' model to establish the context in which the environmental state has to operate. In contrast to ecological modernisation theory,[2] the treadmill of production model suggests a far more pessimistic outlook on the prospects for sustainable development. According to Schnaiberg and colleagues, EM theory appears to have a rather limited application, representing the behaviour of some cutting-edge industries, particularly in Europe, but with less relevance to the wider industrial economy especially as experienced in the USA. Notwithstanding Schnaiberg's reservations about the general applicability of EM theory, interest in the framework and its practical application with respect to public policy continues to grow. Given the extent and diversity of the EM literature, we decided to bring together a sample of such works within a separate section of the book, following the broader theoretical scope of Part I.

Part I continues by returning to classical foundations for environmental sociology with an article from John Bellamy Foster (Chapter 4), in which he explores Marx's theory of metabolic rift. In this piece Foster sets out to undermine the prevailing notion that the classical tradition has little by way of insight to offer contemporary environmental sociology. Foster notes that, to date, most efforts to identify relevant aspects of Marx's work have focused on his early philosophical writing. In contrast, Foster directs our attention to his later work on political economy, particularly in respect of the impact of capitalist industrialisation in agriculture. Stimulated by the work of the early agricultural chemists such as Liebig and Davy and especially Liebig's later critique of capitalist agriculture, Marx developed his theory of metabolic rift, to explore the impacts of capitalist development on the underlying conditions of production. Marx claimed that capitalist development of both industry and agriculture created a rift in the metabolism between society and nature as successive cycles of agricultural production depleted soil nutrients and removed them from the rural spaces of production to urban centres of consumption. Central to this theoretical construct is the concept of '*stoffwechsel*' or social-ecological metabolism, which Marx used to describe the human relationship to nature through the labour process.

Foster is critical of those environmental sociologists who have suggested that classical scholars such as Marx have little to offer to contemporary environmental sociology. He does point out, however, that with the death of Lenin, a keen supporter of ecological research and conservation, ecological thought was repressed as bourgeois and largely excised from the institutionalised tenets of Marxism. This problem of appropriation may go some way to explaining why so many environmental sociologists have failed to identify any really significant Marxist contributions to our contemporary understanding of environmental issues. This is in marked contrast with the situation reviewed in the earlier volume, in which one contributor argued, 'Marxism can offer profound insights into the way in which societies relate to the environment' (Woodgate, 1997, p. 9 referring to Dickens's chapter, in Redclift and Woodgate, 1997). Foster also points to what he calls the 'definitional problem' that has restricted environmental sociological interest in classical theory. In particular he refers to the idea, advanced by Catton and Dunlap (1978), that despite the diversity in mainstream sociological theory, it is all fundamentally anthropocentric in character, part of the human exemptionalist paradigm.

Peter Dickens provides Chapter 5, with an essay in which he uses Marx's theory of subsumption to reveal a new way in which social theory can be linked to biology, Dickens's essay draws on recent developments in biology and epidemiology to demonstrate how 'complex combinations of genetically-determined predispositions and capitalist social relations are responsible for important features of contemporary social stratification and well-being' (2001, p. 93). Dickens's analysis leads him to claim that capitalism is reconstructing human biology in its own image. To develop our understanding of biology–society relations, Dickens emphasises the need to monitor on-going work by natural scientists related to the complex processes by which 'biological-cum-social classes' are being made, while remaining alert to emergent internal contradictions to the logic of the processes by which capital is modifying our human biology.

In uncovering some of the historical roots of sociological concern with nature, and employing suitable concepts and theories in the analysis of contemporary socioenvironmental issues, works such as those of Buttel, Foster and Dickens are creating opportunities for important new contributions to environmental sociology. The concept of metabolism has already begun to be explored in greater detail.[3] While this may help us to understand the material aspects and ecological sustainability of nature–society interaction, it is also important to incorporate an understanding of the role of culture and social construction in mediating socioenvironmental relations.

With this project in mind, Chapter 6 by Marina Fischer-Kowalski and Helga Weisz seeks to construct a theoretical framework, which portrays society as a material–symbolic hybrid. The aim of this piece, reflecting the authors' interdisciplinary institutional setting, is not simply to construct a more complete sociological model, but to move toward an epistemological framework that is accessible to both natural and social sciences. At its core, the framework relies on two key processes: 'socioeconomic metabolism' and the 'colonisation of natural processes'. According to Fischer-Kowalski and Weisz, the colonization of natural processes refers to 'the intended and sustained transformations of natural processes by means of organised social interventions'. Colonizing interventions cause change in biophysical processes, but to do so they must be 'culturally conceived of, organised and monitored; [colonization] must "make sense" in the world of communication' (1999, p. 234). The framework assumes that culture and nature are dichotomous, and attempts to construct an interface between the two. If society (or the cultural sphere of causation) can influence the structure and function of natural systems, and natural systems (or the natural sphere of causation) can produce similar effects on the structure and functioning of society then, argue the authors, there must be a third realm. Thus the depiction of society as a material–symbolic hybrid rests on the coincidence of the material and symbolic realms within 'real' worlds, inhabited by 'real' people, their artefacts, codes and other living and inert matter.

The Fischer-Kowalski and Weisz article represents an attempt by critical realist sociologists to counter claims that societies and their interactions with nature can be reduced to systems of symbolic communication, while at the same time seeking to incorporate the 'cultural turn' within their framework of understanding. Whether or not their efforts are considered fruitful will depend on the perspective of the reader: they have certainly made a contribution to coevolutionary theory.

Chapter 8 reproduces an extract from the work of Éric Darier, who turns in the perhaps unlikely direction of Michel Foucault (especially given the frequently repeated idea that Foucault 'detested nature') as a source of inspiration for environmental sociology, A brief review of his life's work, however, reveals a wealth of stimulating concepts to enrich environmental sociology. especially with respect to the analysis of environmental discourses (in their widest sense): the power/knowledge relationship, the normalisation/resistance dialectic, governmentality and biopower, to name but a few.

The influence of Foucault is clearly evident in Arturo Escobar's (1996) work on post-structural political ecology (Chapter 7), when he says that there cannot be a materialist analysis, which is not, at the same time, a discursive analysis. For Escobar, post-structural political ecology is 'a theory of the production of social reality which includes the analysis of representations as social facts inseparable from what is commonly thought of as "material reality"' (1996, p. 46).

There is a growing body of work from the environmental social sciences, including many of the articles and chapters collected together within the covers of this book, which reflects on the increasing difficulty of maintaining the ontological division between nature and society. Alan Irwin's recent book, *Sociology and the Environment* (2001), comes at the problem from the opposite direct to Fischer-Kowalski and Weisz. Rather than a realist attempting to weave elements from constructionist sociology into his understanding of society–nature interaction, Irwin is a constructionist attempting to deal with the materiality of social life. In the body of the book, Irwin considers 'sustainability discourse', 'the risk society thesis' and 'the sociology of scientific knowledge' (SSK) as alternative lenses through which to view and interpret contemporary concern with environmental issues. Not surprisingly, Irwin suggests that despite the innovative contribution that Beck's Risk Society thesis has made to a structural understanding of our environmental concern, insufficient attention is paid to the processes through which environmental discourses are constructed and mediate our relationships with nature.

Irwin's response to this problem, presented here in Chapter 9, is to develop the notion of 'co-construction', prefigured in the work of other such as Haraway (1991), Beck (1992), Demeritt (1996) and Dickens (1992). Co-construction refers to the idea that human beings are not the only actors involved in social construction. It represents a constructionism that while epistemologically anti-realist, does not take the further step of suggesting ontological relativism. Thus, co-construction 'captures the dual process of the social and the natural being varyingly constructed within environmentally related practices and particular contexts' so that the social and the natural are better understood as *'actively generated co-constructions'* (Irwin, 2001, p. 173, emphasis in original): 'social and environmental problems draw upon the same nature–culture nexus and, as such, are co-constructed within environmental and sociological discussion' (p. 174).

Irwin's work on co-construction is particularly stimulating for those of us from the more realist traditions that have been working on the idea of the 'coevolution'[4] of nature/society. This is not the place for exploring in depth the possible synergy to be gained from linking together the notions of coevolution and co-construction, but such work holds great potential.

Part II

Given the rapidly expanding interest in ecological modernisation (EM) in academia and beyond, Part II of this collection brings together several essays which provide a flavour of the range of issues that are being addressed from an EM perspective. The first, (Chapter 10), is an extract from Joseph Murphy's editorial introduction to a special issue of *Geoforum* (**31**), in which he surveys the development of EM theory since the 1980s. Although Murphy identifies a number of weaknesses in the EM literature, he concludes his short review by suggesting that the real strength of EM theory lies in its attempts to 'move beyond the conflictual relationship that is often assumed to exist between the economy and the environment'.

An essay from Joseph Huber (Chapter 11) follows Murphy's piece. Huber is considered by some to be the founding father of EM theory. In the essay reproduced here, he seeks to elucidate the pursuit of sustainable development from an EM perspective. His article analyses 'sufficiency' and 'efficiency' as alternative strategies for achieving sustainable development. The sufficiency strategy has been adopted by many environmental NGOs, and seeks to prompt enlightened publics to limit their material desires. It also promotes the contraction of the global free-market economy and a more equitable distribution of increasingly scarce natural resources. In contrast, 'efficiency' is a discourse of industry and business, which looks to efficiency gains in the use of energy and materials in production to allow for further economic growth towards a more ecological form of modernisation. Huber identifies good reasons for both these courses of action but suggests that in isolation, or indeed in tandem, they fall short of a sustainable response to the current ecological challenge. It is in this context that he suggests a third discourse, which he calls 'consistency'. Consistency points toward an industrial metabolism that is consistent with nature's metabolism. The transformation of environmentally unadapted industrial structures towards a consistent industrial metabolism 'implies major or basic technological innovations not just incremental efficiency-increasing change and minor modifications of existing product chains' (2000, p. 270).

In an article which picks up on both the intellectual and policy implications of global environmental change, Andrew Blowers provides the next chapter (Chapter 12) in this section on ecological modernisation. Blowers investigates two opposing perspectives on the relationship between environmental and social change. Ecological modernisation is characterised as developing out of a 'liberal, pluralist and reformist' perspective, in stark contrast to Beck's risk society thesis: 'a radical perspective which stresses conflict, inequality of power and revolutionary change' (1997, p. 846). Blowers links these intellectual traditions with ideological positions: EM is related to a shallow environmentalism, which recognises environmental constraints to economic development, while the risk society is linked to deep ecologism, demanding fundamental changes in social organisation and behaviour.

In terms of political action and policy, Blowers introduces the notion of 'defining moments' of social change, in which the EM perspective represents a *'moment of transition* as society continues to pursue the project of modernisation while taking due care and attention of environmental constraints'. From the risk society perspective, the contemporary historical point in time demands revolutionary change and may thus represent a *'moment of transformation'* (p. 847, original emphasis). In developing these arguments, Blowers sets the context for evaluating the strengths and weaknesses of these competing discourses and assessing the prospects for future change.

The final article in Part II of the book comes from Arthur Mol (Chapter 13), another of the key figures associated with the development of EM theory. In 'The Environmental Movement in an Era of Ecological Modernisation', Mol undertakes an analysis of the changing character of environmental nongovernmental organisations (NGOs) and considers their importance to wider processes of ecological modernisation. Since the emergence of the modern environmental movement in the 1970s, Mol claims that, within Europe at least, faced with counter movements, fragmentation, global coordination, a widening of single-issue foci and fading grassroots links, the overall dominant ideologies, strategies and positions of environmental NGOs have changed dramatically. The direction of these changes has been towards a more pragmatic engagement with science, industry, the state and relevant supra-state organisations, in the pursuit of their environmental objectives.

Part III

In Part III of the collection we have chosen a selection of articles that dwell on the problem of developing and implementing environmental policy that is more culturally relevant and sensitive to the realities of public concern. It should come as no surprise then that the work incorporated into this section of the book draws heavily on social constructionism.

The section begins with an excellent, concise yet incisive, review of what the authors call 'analytical and political tools for building survivable futures'. In the introduction to their book *Remaking Reality: Nature at the Millenium*, Noel Castree and Bruce Braun (Chapter 14) explore three theoretical traditions which provide valuable analytical tools for understanding the contemporary construction of nature: Marxist political economy, post-structural political economy and the emerging field of science and technology studies. This structure represents a step-wise approach to developing a framework for analysing the construction of nature. The Marxist approach focuses on nature's material transformation in the course of the development of capitalist production, while the post-structuralist turn in political economy brings in questions of representation and framing. Finally science and technology studies are introduced to broaden the focus from culture and discourse in social construction, to the networks of social, technical, discursive and organic elements that are implicated in the making and remaking of 'nature', such that what counts as 'nature' and indeed 'society' always has multiple dimensions.

This collection includes three extracts from Braun and Castree's *Remaking Reality*. The extract from their introduction is followed in this volume by David Demeritt's piece on science, social constructivism and nature (Chapter 15), while Margaret FitzSimmons and David Goodman's contribution is included in Part V on Agriculture, Food and Sustainable Rural Development as Chapter 27. Demeritt's essay represents a move to the realist–relativist middle ground, following an analysis of forms of social constructivism.[5] The 'artifactual constructivism' to which Demeritt adheres, whilst epistemologically anti-realist, does not take the additional step of proposing ontological relativism and thus provides a space in which erstwhile realists and relativists can meet. Indeed, as we have already noted, there is more than a passing resemblance to the content and conduct of debates surrounding coevolution and co-construction. Material–symbolic hybrids are co-constructed in the course of society/nature coevolution. Richard Norgaard, who has been developing his coevolutionary perspective for some 20 years, would be equally at home with the case study of silvicultural versus ecological forestry presented by Demeritt in his explication of co-construction.

Chapter 16 was written by Sheila Jasanoff and Brian Wynne in their contribution to Volume One of the influential *Human Choice and Climate Change*. In their chapter, Jasanoff and Wynne draw on several decades of social science research into scientific knowledge and policy making to 'show why initial assumptions about how to study and respond to climate change have proved inadequate' (p. 3). Their analysis reveals how the technical knowledge deemed appropriate for policy interventions is not exclusively a production of the scientific community, but rather 'a sociotechnical hybrid whose authority depends on active communication and collaboration among multiple cultures … each of which possesses its own distinctive resources for producing and validating knowledge' (p. 74). In the context of climate change and other global environmental issues, however, the negotiated hybrids which emerge from the scientific–bureaucratic nexus risk generating expectations that cannot be met, leading to loss of public faith in the institutions of science and public decision making and the prescriptions for environmental remediation that they propose. In concluding their essay, the authors suggest that such outcomes may in part be avoided by 'the patient construction of communities of belief that provide legitimacy through inclusion rather than exclusion, through participation rather than mystification, and through transparency rather than black boxing' (p. 77).

The final chapter in Part III, Chapter 17, is a short extract from the introduction to *Exploring Sustainable Consumption*, co-edited by Maurie Cohen and Joseph Murphy (2001). The volume is important in addressing the imbalance in attention paid to production and consumption in terms of promoting sustainable development: as Murphy and Cohen put it: 'For the past two centuries, and particularly during the last thirty years, solving environmental problems has been construed as a producer responsibility and consumers have been placed at a distance from the assignment of culpability' (p. 4). The extract included in this volume critiques the 'levers, knobs and dials' approach to public policy analysed by Jasanoff and Wynne. The atomistic ontology of such mechanistic, instrumentalist approaches to policy seems to suggest that 'society itself is not really part of the picture at all' (p. 11). The overall aim of their book is thus to integrate 'the conventional view of consumption as the material throughput of resources ... with an understanding of the political, social and cultural significance of these practices' (p. 5).

Part IV

Despite the existence of champions and detractors of processes of globalisation, most commentators have come to accept that this most recent stage of capitalist development represents a double-edged sword for the environment. As Beck (1998) has suggested, the multiple dimensions of globalisation cannot be understood as a unified phenomenon unless they are first understood individually and in terms of their inter-relationships. In this vein, Beck distinguishes between the ideology of 'globalism': a kind of liberalism writ large, which reduces – through monocausal economistic methods – the multidimensional character of globalisation to the single dimension of the economy, and 'globality', a term which he employs to refer to a perceived and reflexive 'world society', structured by social relations that are neither integrated in the politics of the nation state nor determined or even determinable by the politics of the nation state.

The first essay in Part IV, Chapter 18, is taken from Wolfgang Sachs 1999 volume, *Planet Dialectics*. The extract traces the history of economic globalisation, placing particular emphasis on the last 30 years or so since we were first presented with the image of the Earth photographed from the moon in July 1969. According to Sachs, 'symbols are the more powerful the more meanings they are able to admit. They actually live on ambivalence. ... The photograph of the globe contains the contradictions of globalisation' (p. 129). The key contradiction upon which the article dwells, is that between the 'physical limits' of the Earth, highlighted by the planet's isolation in space and 'economic expansion', symbolised by our inability to distinguish political boundaries when the planet is viewed from afar. 'The two narratives of globalisation – limitation and expansion – ... fight it out in both the arena of theory and the arena of politics. The outcome of this struggle', suggests Sachs, 'will decide the shape of the new century' (p. 131).

The extract from Sachs, which in Beck's terminology dwells in most detail on the phenomenon of 'globalism', is followed by the concluding chapter from Steven Yearley's book *Sociology,*

Environmentalism, Globalization (1996), which focuses more on what Beck has labelled 'globality'. Yearley's argument in Chapter 19 is that global environmental problems are 'global' because they have been socially constructed as such. He notes that many social movements claim that their projects are globally beneficial, but that the environmental movement distinguishes itself in three important ways: its close ties to science, its practical claims to international solidarity and its capacity to provide an alternative to industrial capitalism. Nevertheless, he remains critical of attempts to portray environmentalism as intrinsically global in character.

The next three articles in this collection are linked together. The debate is set in motion with Chapter 20 by David Frank, Ann Hironaka and Evan Schofer, published in the *American Sociological Review*, which challenges the idea that contemporary increases in environmental protection activities practised by nation states are the result of domestic processes prompted by environmental degradation and economic affluence. The alternative explanation proposed by the authors suggests a more top-down process, in which increases in environmental protection activities are associated with blueprints for such activity drafted in world society that are translated at national 'receptor sites' such as scientific institutions, before being transmitted to domestic actors, by whom they are encoded into national policy.

Frank, Hironaka and Schofer employ event history to discern the causal processes that advance or retard the rate of specific environmental events among nation states. Their statistical analysis supports their key hypotheses. The article is followed by a critical comment from Fred Buttel and a subsequent response by Frank, Hironaka and Schofer, both of which are reproduced in this volume as Chapters 21 and 22, respectively. While Buttel welcomes the contribution that the original article makes to debate, he identifies what he sees as a number of critical shortcomings in their argument, including the following: first, while their data do portray a diffusion of organisational forms, there is no evidence that such diffusion affects practical outcomes. Second, in dismissing domestic influences, they ignore import antecedents of both domestic and international environmental policies. Third, their representation of the diffusion of environmentalism as essentially free from conflict is inaccurate, as is their lack of attention to contradictions between environmental and other global institutions. In their reply to Buttel, Frank *et al.* tackle each of his criticisms by extending the same analytical techniques and rhetorical devices as they employ in their original article. The debate is likely to continue!

With the rise in our appreciation of critical issues of resource scarcity and environmental degradation at both national and global levels, age-old security concerns have expanded to include a new focus. In his book *The Meaning of Environmental Security* (2001), an extract from which is presented as Chapter 23, Jon Barnett explores the institutionalisation of environmental concerns within national and international security establishments. However, as Barnett clearly portrays, the notion of environmental security that has emerged from this process is unlikely to make any meaningful contribution to the environment or indeed human security.

> The principal failings of environmental security as presently conceived can be summarised as follows: it propagates the environmentally degrading security establishment; it talks in terms of, and prepares for, war; it defends the environmentally destructive modern way of life; and it ignores the needs and desires of most of the world's population. In short, at present, environmental security secures the processes that destroy the environment and create insecurity for the many for the benefit of the few (p. 122).

Such rhetoric strikes a particularly resonant note at the time of writing, post-9.11.2001 and after the military defeat of Iraq by a 'coalition' of forces, led by the United States. It is still unclear whether 'security', environmental or human, has been increased by this invasion and the subsequent 'liberation' of the Iraqi people.

In response to this contemporary conception of environmental security Barnett's article thus seeks to reformulate the concept in terms of human rather than 'national' security and peace rather than aggression. It is followed by Chapter 24 by Michael Redclift, which picks up on some of the issues identified by Peter Dickens in Part I of this book, shedding light on the implications of recent developments in biology and particularly what he terms the 'new genetics', for notions of environmental security. He concurs with Barnett that security needs to be refocused at the human scale, but concludes that, in the future, notions of sustainability and security need to become more cognisant of changes in 'our' nature that result from genetic manipulation, as well as environmental change.

Michael Redclift's chapter is followed by an extract from an important new book that attempts to identify alternative political regimes to liberal democracy, more suited to our current concern with environmental sustainability: John Dryzek's *The Politics of the Earth* (1997). The extract we have chosen for Chapter 25 undertakes an analysis of liberal democracy, not as a set of institutions, but as a way of apprehending problems: what Dryzek calls 'democratic pragmatism' and defines as 'more or less democratic problem solving constrained by the structural status quo' (p. 84).

Chapter 26 comprises another piece from Arthur Mol and Fred Buttel's book, *The Environmental State Under Pressure* (2002). In 'The Environmental State and the Forest', Bianca Ambrose-Oji and colleagues provide an analysis of the social dynamics of a globally sponsored biodiversity conservation project in the West African state of Cameroon. The chapter focuses on the role of the environmental state in terms of its contradictory role in fostering capital accumulation, while maintaining its legitimacy. The state's legitimacy is preserved, both locally and internationally, by protecting local people's access to the ecological capital required for sustaining rural livelihoods and conserving what is conceived as a globally important centre of biodiversity. Of particular interest in this chapter is the critical analysis it provides of local participation, considered by many a *sine qua non* in achieving sustainable rural development.

Part V

The final section of the book delves more deeply into issues surrounding agriculture, food and sustainable rural development. It begins with our final extract from Braun and Castree's *Remaking Reality* (2000), which sees Margaret FitzSimmons and David Goodman redressing a longstanding shortcoming of social theory in terms of its ability to tackle environmental issues head on and its avoidance of the specific agency and materiality of nature. They argue for a 'focus on *incorporation* – as metaphor and process – as a useful way of bringing nature into the body of social theory and, more literally, into the social body of living organisms, including ourselves' (p. 104, original emphasis).

An assessment of potential contributions from environmental history, and various threads of Green Marxist thought, to a more appropriate theoretical framework for the analyses of agriculture, food and rural development issues, provides the backdrop for their own analysis and a useful introduction to the remaining chapters of this volume.

Linking back to the debate on globalisation at the beginning of Part IV, the next two chapters in Part V examine the opportunities for crafting sustainable rural livelihoods offered by alternative food and agriculture networks. Chapter 28 by Sarah Whatmore and Lorraine Thorne (1997) employs actor network theory to examine fair trade networks, which aim to ensure that rural producers in less industrialised countries receive a fair share of the final value of their products, when sold in the retail outlets of highly industrialised nations. Graham Woodgate *et al.* follow this with Chapter 29 prepared for a European Union-sponsored workshop on alternative food and agriculture networks.

The chapter examines the political economy and ecology of various alternative production systems, including organic agriculture, permaculture and biodynamic agriculture. Having assessed the content and trajectories of these alternative rural production strategies, the focus shifts from the structural properties of such systems to the range of actors – individual, institutional, biotic and geophysical – which may be enrolled in the particular livelihood and lifestyle strategies of rural producers and consumers. The chapter concludes by examining the extent to which recent changes to the European Common Agriculture Policy might encourage conditions for more sustainable rural development options to emerge, and flourish. Finding little solace in regional policy provision, the authors offer an agenda for further research and academic engagement with practical action.

The final contribution to this volume is taken from Terry Marsden's new book *The Condition of Rural Sustainability* (2003). The book is divided into three parts; the first examines the impact of agro-industrial development on rural livelihoods, food quality and the environment, highlighting negative impacts in all spheres. In Part two Marsden goes on to examine the institutional response of the European Union to the negative impacts of agricultural industrialisation in terms of what has been called post-productivist agriculture, in which environmental and social objectives are raised above the traditional concern with increasing the economic efficiency of agricultural production. Part three of his book examines alternatives to both agro-industrial and post-productivist strategies, which he summarises as 'Agrarian rural development as a form of ecological modernisation'. In the extract that we have chosen for Chapter 30, Marsden summarises the three approaches to sustaining rural development and assesses the prospects for the future. His contribution to this volume rounds off, in this respect, some of the academic discourse referred to at the beginning; by exploring both the discourses of environmental policy and their material embodiment in a changed countryside and a changed nature.

Acknowledgements

The editors wish to acknowledge the helpful comments and suggestions on a draft contents for this book provided by: Karl-Werner Brand, Riley Dunlap, Marina Fischer-Kowalski, Bernhard Glaeser, Joseph Huber, Alan Irwin, Richard Norgaard and Steven Yearly.

Notes

1. For a more detailed account of the fortunes of environmental sociology since the late 1970s, see Dunlap (1997).
2. EM theory portrays a generally optimistic outlook on the prospects for 'sustainable development' as capitalist enterprises respond to market signals for more 'environmentally friendly' products and production processes.
3. See, for example, the edited collection from Robert Ayers and Udo Simonis (1994) and Marina Fischer-Kowalski (1997).
4. For one of the most detailed accounts of the coevolutionary perspective see Norgaard (1994). Briefer introductions to coevolutionary theory may be gained from Redclift and Woodgate (1994), Norgaard (1997) or Woodgate and Redclift (1998).
5. Within environmental sociology the terms constructionism and constructivism are used interchangeably.

References

Ayers, Robert and Udo Simonis (eds) (1994), *Industrial Metabolism: Restructuring for Sustainable Development*, Tokyo, New York and Paris: United Nations University Press.

Beck, Ulrich (1992), *Risk Society: Towards a New Modernity*, London: Sage.

Beck, Ulrich (1998), ¿*Qué es la Globalización? Falacias del Globalismo, Respuestas a la Globalización*. Barcelona: Paidós.

Catton, William and Riley Dunlap (1978), 'Environmental sociology: a new paradigm', *American Sociologist*, **13**, 41–9.

Demeritt, David (1996), 'Social theory and the reconstruction of science and geography', *Transactions of the Institute of British Geographers*, **21**, 484–503.

Dickens, Peter (1992), *Society and Nature: Towards a Green Social Theory*, Hemel Hempstead: Harvester Wheatsheaf.

Dunlap, Riley E. (1997), 'The evolution of environmental sociology: a brief history and assessment of the American experience', in Michael Redclift and Graham Woodgate (eds), *The International Handbook of Environmental Sociology*, Cheltenham, UK and Northampton, MA, USA: Edward Elgar, 1–39.

Fischer-Kowalski, Marina (1997), 'Society's metabolism: on the childhood and adolescence of a rising conceptual star', in Michael Redclift and Graham Woodgate (eds), *The International Handbook of Environmental Sociology*, Cheltenham, UK and Northampton, MA, USA: Edward Elgar, 119–37.

Haraway, Donna (1991), *Simians, Cyborgs and Women: The Reinvention of Nature*, London: Free Association Books.

Hirsch, Fred (1977), *Social Limits to Growth*, London and New York: Routledge and Kegan Paul.

Meadows, D.H., Meadows, D.L., Randers, J. and Behrens, W. (1972), *The Limits to Growth*, London: Pan Books.

Norgaard, Richard (1994), *Development Betrayed: The End of Progress and a Coevolutionary Revisioning of the Future*, New York and London: Routledge.

Norgaard, Richard (1997), 'A coevolutionary environmental sociology', in Michael Redclift and Graham Woodgate (eds), *The International Handbook of Environmental Sociology*, Cheltenham, UK and Northampton, MA, USA: Edward Elgar, 158–68.

Redclift, M. and Woodgate, G. (1994), 'Sociology and the environment: discordant discourse?', in Michael Redclift and Ted Benton (eds), *Social Theory and the Global Environment*, New York and London: Routledge, 51–66.

Redclift, M. and Woodgate, G. (1997), *The International Handbook of Environmental Sociology*, Cheltenham, UK and Northampton, MA, USA: Edward Elgar.

Woodgate, Graham and Michael Redclift (1998), 'From a "sociology of nature" to environmental sociology: beyond social construction', *Environmental Values*, **7**, 3–24.

Part I
Social Theory and the Environment

[1]

Society and Natural Resources, 15:239–249, 2002
Copyright © 2002 Taylor & Francis
0894-1920/2002 $12.00 + .00

Which Function(s) of the Environment Do We Study? A Comparison of Environmental and Natural Resource Sociology

RILEY E. DUNLAP
WILLIAM R. CATTON, JR.

Department of Sociology
Washington State University
Pullman, Washington USA

Natural resource sociology and environmental sociology have different historical roots, organizational identities, institutional bases of support, and scholarly orientations, yet both share a common concern with understanding the environmental bases of human societies. Differences as well as similarities between the research foci of the two fields are illustrated by distinguishing between three fundamental functions that ecosystems serve for human societies: supply depot, waste repository, and living space. While natural resource sociologists pay relatively greater attention to the supply depot function (ecosystems as the source of natural resources), their work inevitably touches on the other two functions as well and therefore is not necessarily narrower in focus than that of environmental sociologists. Yet, despite their common concerns, the differing bases of support, orientations, and clienteles for the two fields suggest that there is good reason for both to retain their separate identities.

Keywords ecosystem functions, environmental sociology, living space, natural resource sociology, supply depot, waste repository

It is not immediately clear that natural resource sociology and environmental sociology constitute two distinct fields, and it could plausibly be argued that they are more appropriately seen as two terms referring to the same thing—sociological interest in environmental/natural resource issues (Buttel 1996). Clearly, people who call themselves natural resource sociologists and those who call themselves environmental sociologists have much in common. They see environmental/resource issues as significant matters deserving attention, and specifically as topics worthy of sociological investigation. Thus, both natural resource and environmental sociologists depart considerably from the larger discipline of sociology with its near total

Received 20 September 2000; accepted 5 July 2001.
This article is a revision of a paper presented at the 8th International Symposium on Society and Resource Management, Western Washington University, Bellingham, Washington, June 2000. We are indebted to William Folkman for information on the history of the Rural Sociological Society's Natural Resources Research Group.
Address correspondence to Riley E. Dunlap, Department of Sociology, Washington State University, Pullman, WA 99164-4020, USA. E-mail: dunlap@wsu.edu

neglect of nonsocial factors such as natural resources and environmental degradation (Catton and Dunlap 1980).

But despite these commonalities, there do appear to be differing emphases between natural resource and environmental sociology, as noted by both Field, Luloff, and Krannich (2002) and Buttel (2002) in their contributions to this symposium. The purpose of this article is to explore these differences from another perspective. We first look at the differing roots of these two fields, paying special attention to how they became institutionalized in organizational settings and how their roots and institutional bases continue to influence both fields. Then we turn to an examination of the differing functions that ecosystems play for human societies in an effort to clarify more substantive differences, particularly predominant foci of research, between the fields. We conclude with observations as to why we think it is logical for natural resource sociology to continue as a distinct field separate from the arguably more encompassing field of environmental sociology.

Historical and Institutional Roots

To understand the difference between natural resource sociology and environmental sociology it is important to look to their roots. Natural resource sociology is largely a product of the Rural Sociological Society (RSS), where it was institutionalized via the Natural Resources Research Group (NRRG), whereas environmental sociology is mainly a product of the American Sociological Association (ASA), where it was institutionalized via the Section on Environmental Sociology (now the Section on Environment and Technology). A closer look at the historical formation of these two groups provides insights into the differing emphases and orientations of those who call themselves natural resource sociologists and those who label themselves environmental sociologists.

Although "man–land" relations and thus natural resources have always been a major focus of rural sociology,[1] what has become the NRRG began when William Folkman—a sociologist working for the U.S. Forest Service—proposed formation of an RSS committee on the "Sociological Aspects of Forestry Research" in 1963. The committee was organized at the 1964 RSS meeting, and quickly became an RSS "research committee." The committee was concerned with "human problems in relation to the forest and related natural resources," and the first year discussed five major problem areas: (1) indiscriminate burning, (2) indiscriminate cutting, (3) grazing and protection of forest species from animals, (4) flood control, and (5) recreational use.

By the 1965 RSS meeting the group had become the "Research Committee on Sociological Aspects of Natural Resource Development," with Wade Andrews and others bringing in a strong concern with water resources to complement the focus on forest resources. A key concern from the outset was to foster interaction between sociologists and natural resource agencies and managers. For example, the minutes of the 1966 meeting describe a presentation by George Jemison, Deputy Chief in Charge of Research, U.S. Forest Service, as follows:

> Dr. Jemison pointed out that foresters' attitudes toward the work of social scientists are changing. More and more, foresters are recognizing that social scientists have a contribution to make relative to the "people problems" associated with forestry. This change in attitudes has to a large extent been brought about by opportunities for two-way conversations between indi-

viduals in the two disciplines. Additional opportunities need to be created to expand this two-way conversation.

The minutes continued by discussing the possibilities for obtaining research grants to conduct studies that would prove useful to the U.S. Forest Service.

For the 1967 RSS meeting the committee organized three sessions including papers dealing with forest fire prevention, various aspects of outdoor recreation, and water resources, and a similar set of themes appeared in the 1968 sessions as well. By 1969 there were sessions on "Interdisciplinary Methodologies in Natural Resources Research," "Theory in Natural Resources Research," and "Applications of Social Science Research to Policies in Natural Resource Management." Subsequent efforts by the committee yielded the important volume, *Social Behavior, Natural Resources and the Environment* (Burch et al. 1972), which includes chapters on an even broader range of resource and environmental topics (see Field and Burch 1988 for a more detailed assessment of the field).

This brief overview of the formation of the NRRG exemplifies several characteristics that still apply to the sociology of natural resources today. First, there is a concern with issues and problems surrounding human use and management of natural resources, giving the field a strong applied orientation. This orientation is strengthened by a second characteristic, that of strong relations with natural resource agencies and personnel. Indeed, reflecting past successes in demonstrating the utility of a sociological approach for providing insight into resource management problems, nowadays there are more natural resource sociologists currently employed in government agencies—and more interaction between those in academic positions and such agencies—than in the early decades of the field. Finally, and related to the prior points, is the fact that natural resource sociologists often appear to be involved in various ways with policymaking and implementation—far more than is typical for sociology in general. If there is a down side to any of this, it might be that the strong emphasis on applied and policy-relevant work often sets the intellectual agenda of natural resource sociology, with the result that theoretical concerns may be given short shrift (see recent volumes of this journal for a good sense of the kinds of work currently being done by natural resource sociologists).

The field of environmental sociology has a somewhat more diverse intellectual history, but it clearly took root and began to grow with the formation of the ASA Section on Environmental Sociology. Ironically, however, its institutionalization began with an equally applied orientation. In 1973, in response to a resolution from the ASA Business Meeting, the Council of the American Sociological Association authorized formation of a committee "to develop guidelines for sociological contributions to environmental impact statements." Appointed in early 1974, the "Ad Hoc Committee on Environmental Sociology" (as it was strategically labeled by its chair, C. P. Wolf) rapidly developed a network for distribution of its newsletter that provided both the impetus and the organizational basis for formation of its successor—the ASA Section on Environmental Sociology. Organized at the 1975 ASA meeting (with Bill Catton elected the first chair), and officially recognized by ASA in 1976 when it attained the requisite 200 members, from the outset the section drew members with a wide range of interests well beyond impact assessment.

Energy issues, particularly concerns with shortages and conservation, were a major focus of papers and sessions in the early years of the ASA section, while work on environmentalism (from analyses of the environmental movement to studies of environmental attitudes) was also a popular theme. There was also a strong emphasis on studies dealing with housing and the built environment, as part of an explicit effort to make the section open to all sociologists interested in the environment— ranging from "built" to "natural" environments. A vast array of other concerns, ranging from natural hazards to ecological theory, were also represented in the section (Dunlap and Catton 1979). This eclectic orientation of environmental sociology has continued over the years. Studies of local environmental contamination and resulting grass-roots environmental action, and the emergence of concerns with environmental justice, became prominent in the 1980s, and risk analyses and global environmental change became major emphases in the 1990s (see Buttel 1987; Dunlap 1997). Although all of these topics have been the subject of considerable empirical research, there has also been an increase in theoretical work over the past two decades. Indeed, while a good deal of work in environmental sociology is applied and/or atheoretical, the field seems to be paying increasing attention to theory, particularly efforts to apply and adapt mainstream theories such as various political economy, modernization, and cultural theories, to environmental analyses (see, e.g., Dunlap et al. 2002; Spaargaren et al. 2000).

In short, natural resource sociology and environmental sociology, despite overlap in both subject matter and personnel, clearly have differing roots and orientations. The former has a stronger applied orientation, in part because much of the work is done by or for natural resource agencies, and as a result it has often proven policy relevant. The latter encompasses a far wider variety of foci, ranging from applied to highly theoretical, but has seldom produced findings that feed into policymaking. Yet its theoretical orientation is beginning to provide strong connections to "mainstream" sociology, making environmental sociology less peripheral to the larger discipline than in years past. Both fields seem to have experienced international growth, although our sense is that environmental sociology is the more popular term and emphasis throughout the rest of the world, as environmental sociology sections have been formed within the national sociological associations of several other nations, and the International Sociological Association's Research Committee on Environment and Society (RC 24) has played a crucial role in fostering international interchange and collaboration among environmental sociologists (see Dunlap 1997).

Three Functions of the Environment

Instead of trying to examine the wide variety of research conducted in each of the two fields, it may be more useful to look at the basic subject matter of both fields in order to discern differing emphases between them. To do this we need to step back and examine the fundamental ways in which human societies relate to the biophysical environment. As ecologists increasingly point out, nature performs many services for human beings (Daily 1997). At the risk of oversimplicity, we can sort these numerous services into three general types of functions that ecosystems serve for *Homo sapiens* and all living species (Dunlap 1994).

First, the environment provides us with the resources necessary for life, ranging from air and water to food to materials needed for shelter, transportation, and the vast range of economic goods we produce. Human ecologists thus view the environment as providing the "sustenance base" for human societies, and we can also think of it as a "supply depot." Some resources such as forests are potentially renewable, while others like fossil fuels are nonrenewable or finite. When we use resources faster than the environment can supply them, even if they are potentially renewable (such as clean water), we create resource shortages or scarcities (Catton 1980).

Second, in the process of consuming resources, humans, like all species, produce "waste" products; indeed, humans produce a far greater quantity and variety of waste products than do other species. The environment must serve as a "sink" or "waste repository" for these wastes, either absorbing or recycling them into useful or at least harmless substances. When land was sparsely populated and utilization of resources was minimal, this was seldom a problem. Modern and/or densely populated societies generate more waste than the environment can process, however, and the result is the various forms of "pollution" that are so prevalent worldwide.

Like other species, humans must also have a place to live, and the environment provides our home—where we live, work, play, travel, and spend our lives. In the most general case, the planet Earth provides the home for our species. Thus, the third function of the environment is to provide a "living space" or habitat for human populations. When too many people try to live in a given space the result is over-crowding, a common occurrence in many urban areas, and some analysts suggest that the entire planet is now overpopulated by human beings, although efforts to determine the number of people the earth can support have proven to be contentious (Cohen 1995).

When humans overuse an environment's ability to fulfill these three functions, "environmental problems" in the form of pollution, resource scarcities and over-crowding and/or overpopulation are the result. However, not only must the environment serve all three functions for humans, but when a given environment is used for one function its ability to fulfill the other two is often impaired. Such conditions of functional competition often yield newer, more complex environmental problems (Table 1; see Dunlap 1994 for a more detailed analysis).

TABLE 1 Three Functions of the Environment

Supply depot: Source of renewable and nonrenewable natural resources such as air, water, forests, fossil fuels, etc. that are necessary to sustain human societies. Overuse results in "shortages" of renewable resources such as clean air and water and in "scarcities" of nonrenewable resources such as fossil fuels.

Waste repository: A "sink" that absorbs the waste products of human life, including industrial production. Exceeding the ability of ecosystems to absorb wastes creates"pollution," which may harm humans and other living beings and eventually lead to the disruption of entire ecosystems.

Living space: The "home" for humans and other living beings, including not only our housing, but where we work, play, and engage in other activities (e.g., our transportation systems). Overuse of this function results in crowding and congestion, and in the destruction of habitats for other species.

Conflict among functions: Using an ecosystem for one function may impair its ability to fulfill one or both of the other two adequately, as when a waste site makes an area unsuitable as living space and/or pollutes natural resources such as groundwater. Recent evidence of human-induced "global environmental change" (such as global warming and ozone depletion) suggests that humans may be overusing the global ecosystem, impairing the earth's ability to fulfill all three functions for *Homo sapiens*.

Competition among environmental functions is obvious in conflicts between the living-space and waste-repository functions, as using an area for a waste site typically makes it unsuitable for living space. Similarly, if hazardous materials escape from a waste repository and contaminate the soil, water, or air, the area can no longer serve as a supply depot for drinking water or for growing agricultural products. Finally, converting farmland or forests into housing subdivisions creates more living space for people, but means that the land can no longer function as a supply depot for food or timber (or as habitat for wildlife).

Understanding these three functions provides insight into the evolution of environmental problems, or the problematic conditions created by human overuse of the environment. In the 1960s and early 1970s, when awareness of environmental problems was growing rapidly in the United States, primary attention was given to air and water pollution and litter—problems stemming from the environment's inability to absorb human waste products—and the importance of protecting areas of natural beauty. The "energy crisis" of 1973 highlighted the dependence of modern industrialized nations on fossil fuels and raised the specter of resource scarcity in general. The living-space function came to the fore in the late 1970s when it was discovered that a neighborhood in Niagara Falls, NY, was built on an abandoned chemical waste site that had begun to leak toxic materials. Love Canal came to symbolize problems created by using an area first as a waste repository and then as living space (Dunlap 1994).

New environmental problems continually emerge as the result of humans trying to make incompatible uses of given environments. Global warming is an excellent example. It stems primarily from a rapid increase in carbon dioxide in the earth's atmosphere produced by a wide range of human activities, especially burning fossil fuels (coal, gas, and oil), wood, and forest lands. This buildup of CO_2 traps more of the sun's heat, thus raising the temperature of the earth's atmosphere. While global warming results from overuse of the earth's atmosphere as a waste site, the resulting warming may produce changes that make our planet less suitable as a living space (not only for humans, but especially for other life). A warmer climate may also affect the earth's ability to continue producing natural resources, especially food supplies.

These examples of how human activities are harming the ability of the environment to serve as our supply depot, living space, and waste repository involve focusing on specific aspects of particular environments (e.g., a given river's ability to absorb wastes without becoming polluted). However, it is increasingly recognized that the health of entire ecosystems is being jeopardized as a result of growing human demands being placed on them. An ecosystem is an interacting set of living organisms (animals and plants) and their nonliving environment (air, land, water) that are bound together by a flow of energy and nutrients (e.g., food chains), and can range in size from a small pond, to a large region such as the Brazilian rainforest, to the entire biosphere—the earth's global ecosystem (Freese 1997). Technically, it is not "the environment" but "ecosystems" that serve the three functions for humans—and for all other living species.

Exceeding the capacity of a given ecosystem to fulfill one of the three functions may disrupt not only its ability to fulfill the other two, but also its ability to continue to function at all. As a recent U.S. Environmental Protection Agency (EPA) report noted, "Ecological systems like the atmosphere, oceans, and wetlands have a limited capacity for absorbing the environmental degradation caused by human activities. After that capacity is exceeded, it is only a matter of time before those ecosystems begin to deteriorate and human health and welfare begin to suffer" (U.S. EPA

Science Advisory Board 1990, 17). Human overuse of ecosystems thus creates "ecological disruptions" that become "ecological problems" for humans. As more and more people require places to live, use resources, and produce wastes, it is likely that ecological problems will worsen and that new ones will continue to emerge.

The notion that human societies face "limits to growth" was originally based on the assumption that we would run out of food supplies or natural resources such as oil, but nowadays it is recognized that the ability of ecosystems to fulfill any of the three necessary functions can be exceeded. Ozone depletion, for example, stems from exceeding the atmosphere's limited ability to absorb chlorofluorocarbons (CFCs) and other pollutants. Thus, it is not the supply of natural resources per se, but the finite ability of the global ecosystem to provide us with resources, absorb our wastes, and still offer suitable living space (which, as we have seen, are interrelated) that constrains human societies (Dunlap 1994). The emergence of problems such as ozone depletion, climate change, species extinction, and rainforest destruction are indications that modern societies may be taxing the limits of the global ecosystem (see, e.g., Vitousek, et al. 1997; Wackemagel and Rees 1996).

The emerging image of humans relative to the global ecosystem is depicted by a comparison of Figures 1a and 1b, which are intended to illustrate the changed relationship between humans and the global ecosystem in recent decades. Figure 1a makes two primary points: First, the three competing functions of the environment did not greatly interfere with one another in the not-too-distant past (circa 1900), as there was generally a supply of new resources and lots of open territory in much of the world when one area became crowded, polluted, or stripped of resources; and second, the total amount of human demand (for living space, resources, and waste absorption) was within the carrying capacity of the global ecosystem. In contrast, Figure 1b shows that a greater portion of the ecosystem is now being used for each function; that these functions overlap and therefore conflict with one another much more than in the past; and—perhaps—that their growth has exceeded the earth's carrying capacity (represented by the areas lying outside of the rectangle). While the question of carrying capacity is difficult to resolve (Freese 1997), it is clear that humans are having an unprecedented impact on the global ecosystem (Vitousek et al. 1997).

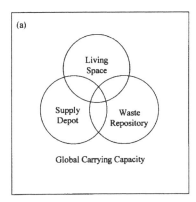
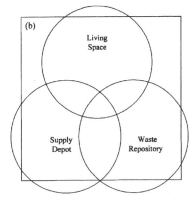

FIGURE 1 Competing Functions of the Environment. (a) Situation circa 1900. (b) current situation?

Implications for the Two Fields

This brief overview of contemporary ecological problems reveals how dramatically the subject matter of *both* natural resource sociology and environmental sociology has changed over the course of both fields' short existence. What seemed like fairly discrete, bounded, and intellectually manageable resource/environmental problems have evolved in the past three decades to far more complex and ambiguous problematiques—posing unforeseen challenges to both fields. The overview also provides us with a means of making rough comparisons between the subject matter and research emphases of both fields.

The major difference between the fields may initially seem merely to be the narrower focus of natural resource sociology. Its very name implies a preoccupation with the supply depot function, whereas all three functions fall within the purview of environmental sociology. Yet despite a primary concern with natural resources, particularly problems regarding their use and management, it is unfair to argue that natural resource sociologists ignore the other two functions. Indeed, most efforts to understand natural resource use and management inevitably touch on the living space and/or waste repository functions as well. For example, problems with fisheries often arise not just from overharvesting, but from pollution and loss of fish habitat. Likewise, the loss of farm land is typically due to urban sprawl, forest production may be impacted by acid rain, and timber harvesting affects recreational uses. In short, nowadays it is difficult to deal with natural resource issues without considering more than simply the supply and management of such resources.

While the field of environmental sociology includes all three functions within its purview, most environmental sociologists tend to specialize in aspects of the environment that deal with one or perhaps two functions. A particularly popular topic the past couple of decades has been the actual and potential contamination of neighborhoods and towns by toxic and other hazardous wastes. Such work focuses on problems surrounding the waste-repository function, especially when use of an area for a waste site creates conflicts with living-space needs. At a more macro level, growing attention is being given to tropical deforestation, particularly the pressures to increase living space and farm land that give rise to deforestation in less developed nations. Perhaps the closest that environmental sociologists come to examining issues related to all three functions is via studies of global environmental change, although even here individual projects tend to focus on issues such as the primary causes of CO_2 emissions and other fairly narrow research questions.

Thus, although the purview of environmental sociology is quite broad, covering all three functions that the environment serves for humans, and that for natural resource sociology tends to be more narrowly focused on the supply depot function, the actual breadth of specific research projects in the two fields likely differs only modestly. Furthermore, while natural resource sociologists have often focused on localized resource issues (Buttel 2002; Field et al. 2002), the reality of a globalizing economy makes it increasingly difficult to ignore the international dimensions of resource use and management (see, e.g., Wackernagel and Rees 1996). Consequently, although environmental sociology may currently focus relatively more attention on national and global issues, the future may see less difference in the geographical foci of work in the two fields as both pay growing attention to the global dimensions of resource and environmental problems and policies.

Some might argue that since natural resource sociology tends to concentrate on a portion of the intellectual pie comprising the focus of environmental sociology, it ought to be considered a subset of the larger field. While plausible at first blush, such a position ignores important realities that argue for the continued existence of natural resource sociology as a distinct field—at least in terms of its organizational base, personnel, and orientation. There is obviously a strong clientele for the work done by natural resource sociologists, as government agencies and other organizations seek useful knowledge for the solution of natural resource problems. Agencies such as the U.S. Forest Service want researchers who are knowledgeable about forest resources, can participate in interdisciplinary research teams, and can deliver policy-relevant research products. A similar pattern exists for fisheries, wildlife, water resources, minerals, farmland, and most other natural resources. It makes sense, therefore, for sociologists to specialize in the study of these various natural resources so that they can bring a sociological perspective to bear on issues that were once thought to have solely technical solutions. Furthermore, as is obvious from the International Symposia for Society and Resource Management, the strong agency–academic base for natural resource sociology has created a unique situation in which both academics and agency personnel trained in a range of other disciplines have, by dint of firsthand experience, become practicing natural resource sociologists (conducting surveys, designing public participation programs, doing social impact assessments, etc.)—creating a positive-sum situation for the field.

With the possible exception of environmental justice researchers and the U.S. EPA, environmental sociologists have been far less successful in cultivating clienteles (or being cultivated by clienteles) for their work. Some progress in demonstrating the utility of sociological work seems to have been done in the case of risk analysis, and efforts continue to show the relevance of our discipline for efforts to understand and mitigate global environmental change. Yet the pattern of institutionalized support for sociological research that exists in many resource agencies does not yet seem to be as strong in the U.S. EPA and the diverse set of other federal and state agencies responsible for protecting the quality of the nation's environment.

We therefore expect that natural resource sociology will continue to be a vital area, receiving strong support in terms of research funding, and that the same will be true for environmental sociology, albeit for different reasons. Environmental sociology is stimulated by societal attention to environmental problems, student interest, and sheer intellectual interest—especially on the part of younger cohorts of sociologists who have been raised in an era when environmental problems are of obvious societal significance and thus seem worthy of intellectual attention. The rapid growth of international interest in environmental sociology has been especially notable the past decade or so, and is having a substantial impact on the field—particularly in the form of increased emphasis on applying mainstream theoretical perspectives to environmental issues.

The continued vitality of each fields can only benefit both, and we look forward to continuing dialog between practitioners of both (in many cases via individuals with one foot planted firmly in each field). Environmental sociologists can benefit from the strong empirical orientation and emphasis on policy relevance apparent in much of natural resource sociology, while natural resource sociologists may find the increasing theoretical sophistication of environmental sociology potentially useful. The growing scale and complexity of ecological problems, and heightened societal recognition of the fact that they are ultimately "people problems," call for collaborative efforts and mutual learning among all sociologists interested in resource and environmental issues.

Note

1. Because of this historical legacy, some natural resource sociologists felt environmental sociologists were "reinventing the wheel" with their call for greater attention to the environmental bases of social life (e.g., Dunlap and Martint 1983). Such a charge by Field and Johnson (1986), made during the Reagan era when both sociological and societal interest in the environment had waned compared to the prior decade (Dunlap 1997), led to a spirited defense of the need for environmental sociology by Dunlap (1986). Fortunately, the ensuing 15 years have seen both natural resource and environmental sociology become securely established fields of inquiry. As this symposium hopefully indicates, one consequence of this increased security is less defensiveness and impetus toward "turf wars" between natural resource and environmental sociologists.

References

Burch, W. R., Jr., N. H. Cheek, Jr., and L. Taylor, eds. 1972. *Social behavior, natural resources, and the environment.* New York: Harper and Row.

Buttel, F. H. 1987. New directions in environmental sociology. *Annu. Rev. Sociol.* 13:465–488.

Buttel, F. H. 1996. Environmental and resource sociology: Theoretical issues and opportunities for synthesis. *Rural Sociol.* 61:56–76.

Buttel, F. H. 2002. Environmental sociology and the sociology of natural resources: Institutional histories and intellectual legacies. *Society Nat. Resources*

Catton, W. R., Jr. 1980. *Overshoot: The ecological basis of revolutionary change.* Urbana: University of Illinois Press.

Catton, W. R., Jr., and R. E. Dunlap. 1980. A new ecological paradigm for post-exuberant sociology. *American Behavioral Scientist* 24: 15–47.

Cohen, J. E. 1995. *How many people can the earth support?* New York: Norton.

Daily, G. C., ed. 1997. *Nature's services: Social dependence on natural ecosystems.* Washington, DC: Island Press.

Dunlap, R. E. 1986. Environment, ecology, and agriculture revisited: Ancestor worship and the dangers of disciplinary myopia. *The Rural Sociologist.* 6:304–314.

Dunlap, R. E. 1994. The nature and causes of environmental problems: A socio-ecological perspective. In *Environment and development*, ed. Korean Sociological Association, 45–84. Seoul, Korea: Seoul Press.

Dunlap, R. E. 1997. The evolution of environmental sociology. In *The international handbook of environmental sociology*, eds. M. Redclift and G. Woodgate, 21–39. Chelterham, UK: Edward Elgar.

Dunlap, R. E., F. H. Buttel, P. Dickens, and A. Gijswijt, eds. 2002. *Sociological theory and the environment.* Boulder, CO: Rowman & Littlefield.

Dunlap, R. E., and W. R. Catton, Jr. 1979. Environmental sociology. *Ann. Rev. Sociol.* 5: 243–273.

Dunlap, R. E., and K. E. Martin. 1983. Bringing environment into the study of agriculture: Observations and suggestions regarding the sociology of agriculture. *Rural Sociol.* 48: 201–218.

Field, D. R., and W. R. Burch, Jr. 1988. *Rural sociology and the environment.* Greenwich, CT: Greenwood Press.

Field, D. R., and D. R. Johnson. 1986. Rural communities and natural resources: A classical interest. *The Rural Sociologist.* 6:187–196.

Field, D. R., A. E. Luloff and R. S. Krannich. 2002. Revisiting the origins of and distinctions between natural resource sociology and environmental sociology. *Society Nat. Resources.*

Freese, L. 1997. *Environmental connections.* Suppl. 1 (Part B) to *Adv. Hum. Ecol.* Greenwich, CT: JAI Press.

Spaargaren, G., A. Mol, and F. H. Buttel, eds. 2000. *Environment and global modernity.* London: Sage.

U.S. Environmental Protection Agency Science Advisory Board. 1990. *Reducing risk: Setting priorities and strategies for environmental protection.* Washington, DC: U.S. EPA.

Vitousek, P. M., H. A. Mooney, J. Lubchenco, and J. M. Melillo. 1997. Human domination of Earth's ecosystems. *Science* 277(25 July):494–499.

Wackernagel, M., and W. Rees. 1996. *Our ecological footprint: Reducing human impact on the earth.* Philadelphia: New Society.

[2]

Classical Theory and Contemporary Environmental Sociology: some reflections on the antecedents and prospects for reflexive modernization theories in the study of environment and society

Frederick H. Buttel

Introduction

Sociology has long had something of an ambivalent relationship to the classical tradition, even if this is seldom explicitly acknowledged. On the one hand, the continued importance of the classical tradition in formal terms can be gauged by the fact that classical theory remains a core requirement in most undergraduate and graduate sociology programs throughout the Western world. A PhD-holding sociologist would be considered incompetent if s/he did not know the basics of the sociologies of Marx, Weber, and Durkheim, and the meaning of concepts such as false consciousness, traditional domination, or organic solidarity. Essentially every text on sociological theory makes the claim that classical sociology has very strongly influenced the development of the sociological discipline, and that classical theory is still highly relevant to the sociological enterprise (a typical recent example being Morrison, 1995). One frequently encounters claims that virtually all important sociological notions – even the ideas of contemporary postmodern theorists – were 'anticipated' by the classical theorists (Hughes et al., 1995).

At the same time, the typical sociologist in the world today would be very unlikely to consult, much less devote serious study to, the *Grundrisse, Capital, Suicide, Division of Labor in Society, Economy and Society*, or *The Protestant Ethic and the Spirit of Capitalism* during a typical workday (or a typical work-year, for that matter). Pieces of classical sociological scholarship are rarely cited in the contemporary sociological research literature. Many influential sociological theorists such as Anthony Giddens (1987: Chapter 2) have claimed that the contexts and assumptions of nineteenth century classical theory are no longer relevant to the late twentieth century, and that progress in social theory will require jettisoning the classical sociological tradition. Some sociologists now go so far as to say that by the 1940s, the 'classical project' – the development of sociological abstraction aimed at addressing moral and political problems – had undergone 'dissolution' (Wardell and Turner, 1986). And it becomes harder every year to convince our students they need to study classical theory when *Grundrisse, Capital, Suicide, Division of Labor in Society, Economy and Society,* and *The Protestant Ethic and the Spirit of Capitalism* are not in prominent places on our own bookshelves.

The ambivalence about the relevance and influence of the classical tradition has been of particular importance in environmental sociology. It is useful to recall that the works of the initial exemplars of environmental sociology were anchored almost entirely in mid-century normal science – e.g., the neo-Ogburnianism of Fred Cottrell (1955), the functionalism of Walter Firey (1960), the unexceptional attitude studies of outdoor recreation groups and general environmental public opinion studies (Burch et al., 1972), the rural-community sociology of natural resources (Burch and Field, 1988), and so on. Whether or not one feels that this relatively ordinary proto-environmental sociology was strongly conditioned by the classical tradition, it is clear that what separated it from mainstream sociology in 1970 was not its theoretical or methodological commitments per se. Rather, the mere fact that Cottrell, Firey, and others found environmental-ecological matters to be interesting independent and/or dependent variables was the crucial difference between 1950s and 1960s proto-environmental sociology and so-called mainstream sociology.[1] In every other major respect proto-environmental sociology from the 1950s through the early 1970s was indistinguishable from 'mainstream' sociology.

Indeed, even the most central works of the first stage (from Earth Day until approximately 1975) of modern environmental sociology in North America (e.g., Burch, 1971; Burch et al., 1972; Klausner, 1971) were not particularly rebellious about either mainstream sociology or the classical tradition. In these early days of environmental social science the principal voices of theoretical defiance on behalf of the environment were *not* those of environmental sociologists. Instead, non-sociologists such as Walter Prescott Webb (1952), Richard G. Wilkinson (1973), and Murray Bookchin (1971) were the most visible or influential social science scholars who criticized mainstream inquiry for its lack of attention to the environment.

But when environmental sociology began to gather momentum during the mid – to late – 1970s, its major preoccupations came to include explaining why Western sociology had ignored the biophysical environment and what kinds of modifications of sociological theory would be required to reflect the importance of the biosphere and biophysical forces in social structure and social life. This second stage of the development of (North American) environmental sociology consisted of the elaboration of what I have earlier (Buttel, 1986) referred to as the 'new human ecology', and what Dunlap and Catton have referred to as the 'new ecological paradigm'. Integral to the new human ecology was a certain hostility toward mainstream sociology, as well as the desire to build a new sociological theory in which biophysical variables would play a definite and central role. The most central figures in the new human ecology were, of course, Dunlap and Catton. Dunlap and Catton were not the first sociologists to criticize the classical tradition for its neglect of the biophysical environment or to see mainstream and environmental sociology/social science in 'paradigmatic' terms. But in their late 1970s and early 1980s writings Dunlap and Catton articulated the notion of 'paradigm' with the ecological critique of classical sociological theory with exceptional clarity and persuasiveness (e.g., Catton, 1976; Catton and Dunlap, 1978; Dunlap and Catton, 1979; Dunlap and Catton, 1983). There is scarcely a significant text in environmental sociology today that fails to cite one or more of these early works by Dunlap and Catton as having provided the template for modern environmental sociology.

Put most succinctly, Catton and Dunlap and several other pioneers of 1970s and early 1980s environmental sociology (e.g., Cotgrove, 1982) made three key arguments about environmental sociology and sociological theory. First, it was argued that modern sociology was strongly influenced by the 'social facts' injunction and the 'exceptionalism/exemptionalism' of the classical theorists. Second, it was held that mainstream classical and contemporary sociology, despite its apparent diversity, essentially constitutes a unitary (exemptionalist) paradigm, while environmental sociology is a distinct – and a competing or alternative – paradigm. Finally, it was argued that one of the key tasks of environmental sociology is to demonstrate to mainstream sociologists that a sounder sociological theory must be built from some of the core premises of environmental sociology (e.g., the principle that societies and biophysical environments exist in reciprocal interaction with each other).

It is arguably the case that while the second and third aspects of the Dunlap-Catton agenda are not so central anymore to the field of environmental sociology, the first posture – critique of the fundamental exemptionalism of the classical tradition, and the assertion of its irrelevance to environmental sociology – remains an article of faith within North American (and to a considerable, but lesser, extent in European) environmental-sociological circles (Dickens, 1992; Martell, 1994). Put somewhat differently, the core of North American environmental sociology – or, in other words, the new human ecology – has tended to be formed in *opposition or in response* to mainstream sociology and/or the classical tradition.

In this chapter I will employ the issue of the ir/relevance of the classical tradition to a meaningful environmental sociology as a vehicle for making some observations on the historical development of environmental sociology, and on the role that two versions of 'reflexive modernization' theory are playing, and could play, in this field. I will begin by exploring some of the insights and blinders that the classical tradition has bequeathed to the contemporary cadre of environmental sociologists. I will conclude that this is a very mixed legacy – that environmental sociology needs some of the tools that were initially developed by the classical theorists, but that the overall thrust of the classical tradition was to downplay ecological questions and biophysical forces. I will then make some comments on the historical development of environmental sociology and the role of the classical tradition and its mid-twentieth century legacies in that development. Finally, I will focus on three relatively new theoretical perspectives in environmental sociology: social constructivism and two versions of reflexive modernizationist thought – namely, 'risk society' and 'ecological modernization' theories. I will identify some strengths and weaknesses of each. As I will suggest later, ecological modernizationism is unlikely to become the dominant theory in the field, but it raises particularly critical issues for the field, and with modifications has significant synthetic potential for making environmental sociological theory both comprehensive and empirically useful.

Classical sociology and the environment

Each of the major classical theorists can be seen to have developed or elaborated one or more theoretical premises or methodological injunctions that can be regarded as exemptionalist or unconducive to considering biophysical factors as independent or dependent variables. Durkheim, for example, is well known for his 'social facts' injunction – the notion that the role of sociology is to explain or account for 'social facts', while employing (exclusively) other social facts as explanatory factors. Durkheim's social facts injunction was propounded to distinguish sociology from psychology and biology, and to distance it from utilitarianism. Marx's relentless critiques of Malthus were intended to distinguish historical materialism from the oversimplifications of Malthusian population/food arithmetic. Weber could not have been more emphatic about the fact that sociology is a discipline in which evolutionary reasoning, and any other styles of reasoning from biology and the natural sciences, must be rejected because societies and natural systems have qualitatively different dynamics.

Craig Humphrey and I (Buttel and Humphrey, 1987) have argued elsewhere, however, that there is, in a certain sense, *a classical environmental sociology*. Elements of environmental sociology have roots deep in nineteenth century social thought. Not only did Marx, Durkheim, and Weber incorporate what we might regard as ecological components in their works, they did so from a variety of standpoints. Among the multiple ecologically relevant components of their works are materialist ontologies (in the case of Marx and Engels), biological analogies (Durkheim), use of Darwinian/evolutionary arguments or schemes (Marx, Durkheim, Weber), and concrete empirical analyses of resource or 'environmental' issues (Marx, Weber).

Classical environmental sociology

Marx and Engels worked from a materialist ontology, which should be understood to mean not only a structural/non-idealist posture and an emphasis on the conditions of production and labor, but also an understanding that, in principle, the predominance of the sphere of production and social labor cannot be understood apart from nature. This is particularly clear if one reads the early 'philosophical' works by Marx (those published in 1844 or earlier), in which the notions of 'nature' and the material world are employed frequently, and in a non-deterministic or dialectical manner (Parsons, 1977). It is thus no accident that contemporary works in environmental sociology that are explicitly neo-Marxist (e.g., Dickens, 1992) tend to draw inspiration disproportionately from the works of the early Marx. But while the work of the young Marx was quite ecological in some respects, this does not imply that the later work of Marx (and Engels) was devoid of references to nature and the natural world.[2] Marx and Engels, for example, frequently referred to the penetration of capitalism as a cause of massive air pollution and other threats to the health and welfare of workers, and to the need for political economy to treat relations between society and nature (Dickens, 1992; Parsons, 1977). Parsons (1977) and Burkett (1996) have noted how Marx was fascinated by agronomy and the biology of agricultural production, and in *Capital*

Marx often used agronomic examples to demonstrate the role of nature in social production. Burkett (1996), in his elegant defense of Marx against claims that his methodology is unecological, makes particular note of the fact that Marx's analysis of modes of production includes not only class (or people-people) relations but also the relations of material appropriation (people-nature relations). Marx and Engels' schema positing the contradictory development of class societies and the revolutionary transformation from one mode of production to another contains an evolutionary component based on Darwin's work (Lopreato, 1984). But as I will note later, environmental social science theories have tended to incorporate one (and sometimes both) of two constitutive elements: a materialist outlook, and an emancipatory orientation. Thus, among the reasons for the particular relevance of the young Marx to environmental sociology is that Marx's work prior to 1945 or so tended to reflect both materialist and emancipatory postures.

Like Marx, Durkheim also set forth a modified evolutionary schema and relied heavily on metaphors from Darwinian evolution and organismic biology. While Durkheim questioned Spencer's argument that evolutionary change led to continuous progress, his theory was based on an evolutionary view of social change (Turner, 1994). The master direction of change was from primitive societies with a low division of labor to modern societies with a complex division of labor. Durkheim, however, differed from Spencer in emphasizing the disruptive qualities of change. The transition from primitive to modern societies was accompanied by anomie and a breakdown of social solidarity and regulation. While Durkheim anticipated that modernizing societies ultimately would exhibit new, more effective organic solidarity, he regarded the establishment of adequate integration and solidarity to be problematic.

Durkheim freely used biological concepts in presenting his theories of social evolution and solidarity, as is evident in the concept of organic solidarity. *The Rules of Sociological Method* (1895) referred to various types of societies along the continuum from traditional to modern as 'species' or 'societal species'. Moreover, his most famous work, *The Division of Labor in Society* (1893), set forth the major elements of a theoretical perspective that has come to be known as (classical) human ecology. The *Division*'s famous schema for explaining the transition from mechanical to organic solidarity was rich in imagery about population density, resource scarcity, and competition for survival that bears a strong resemblance to more modern notions of human ecology.

A final classical theorist widely considered to be among the most influential in Western sociology was Max Weber. While Marx and Durkheim largely assumed that there was some knowable *a priori* direction of social change, Weber firmly rejected the theoretical viewpoint that there was a unilinear course of societal development. Social change was determined by shifting constellations of subjective, structural, and technological forces that ultimately were rooted in human motivations and history. Moreover, Weber (1922) was an outspoken opponent of Social Darwinism, and he frequently stressed how social science differed from biological sciences and that the methods and concepts of the former must be different than those of the latter. Weber's work thus has been taken to be the first decisive break from nineteenth century evolutionism anchored in biological analogies (see Sanderson, 1990; Burns and Dietz, 1992; Dietz and Burns, 1992, for comprehensive overviews of 'social evolutionism'). Interestingly, Weber's works that most clearly reflect the break with biological analyses are those such as *The Agrarian Sociology of Ancient Civilizations* and his *General Economic History*, in which material on the impacts of social structures on natural resources or the impact of natural resources on social organization is most prominent.

The multiple respects in which Weber's work can be seen to accommodate an environmental or human-ecological dimension can be most dramatically illustrated by contrasting the neo-Weberian environmental sociologies of Patrick West (1984) and Raymond Murphy (1994). These two scholars draw on what might be regarded as entirely different 'corners' of Weber's work. According to West (1984), from Weber's historical sociology of religion and his empirical research on ancient society one can distill a human ecology that is rich and provocative for contemporary environmental sociology. Weber's historical and comparative method rested on environmental factors playing casually important roles at times in history. Weber treated environmental factors as interacting in complex casual models, and they 'frequently affect complex societies through favoring the "selective survival" of certain strata over others' (West, 1984: 232). It is arguably the case that Weber's (probably unintended) use of Darwinian imagery was truer to Darwin's theory than was that of Spencer and others. Thus, for West, the relevance of Weber's work to environmental sociology is not only that Weber analyzed concrete instances of struggles over resources (e.g., control of irrigation systems), but also that Weber's causal logic was essentially a Darwinian one that still has the potential to help build bridges between sociology and the ecological sciences.

While West's (1984) account of Weber's sociology of environment and natural resources is anchored in Weber's comparative macro-historical sociology, Murphy (1994) has developed a Weberian environmental sociology based largely on a completely different literature – Weber's concept of rationalization and his ideal-types of rationality and orientations to action drawn primarily from *Economy and Society* (1968). Murphy (1994) argues that rationalization and the expansion of formal rationality have involved tendencies to an ethic of mastery over nature (or the 'plasticity' of the relationship between humans and their natural environment), to the quest for technologies to realize this mastery, and to a lack of attention to human threats to the environment. Similar to Weber's notion of charismatic authority, Murphy suggests that the ecological irrationalities caused by rationalization will stimulate social movements that aim at 'de-rationalization' or 're-rationalization' of modern institutions.

Classical tradition in contemporary environmental sociology

Before proceeding to discuss some of the more significant recent trends in environmental sociology, it is useful to begin by noting some of the historical tendencies of environmental sociology from a classical sociological perspective. Two sets of observations deserve mention here. First, environmental sociology has tended to have affinities with two different – and, in some respects, contradictory – components of the classical tradition. On the one hand, environmental sociology has tended to be materialist – in its stress on the natural world and the material substratum of human life – and objectivist – in its stress on the negative consequences of science and technology and its endorsement of the project of the ecological and environmental sciences. On the other hand, environmental sociology has been sympathetic with the emancipatory or liberatory impulse as articulated by ecology movements of various stripes. The most creative and influential works in the field have aimed to incorporate both materialism and emancipation and to synthesize the two outlooks. Materialism, objectivism, and the emancipatory impulse are amply represented in the significant corners of the classical tradition. Emancipation, for example, is a key theme in the philosophical works of the 'young Marx' as well as in Weber's work on charismatic authority.

Several other aspects of the classical tradition have reinforced environmental sociology's affinities with it. Scholars such as Swingewood (1991) have stressed that the nineteenth century classical tradition was essentially pessimistic in that it stressed the negative social implications – anomie, alienation, the 'iron cage' and disenchantment – of bourgeois society. Giddens (1987) has likewise stressed the fact that the classical tradition was preoccupied with changes in the economy and in the structure of production as the prime movers in shaping social change in modern societies. It is significant that mainstream environmental sociology has tended to be a relatively pessimistic sociology (because of its being anchored in arguments about the intrinsic tendencies to environmental degradation) and has stressed the importance of the economy and the structure of production. It is thus no accident that as much as environmental sociologists have been critical of the shortcomings of classical theory, their work has tended to have very definite affinities with many of the concepts, methodological principles, and presuppositions of the classical tradition.

It is useful to conclude this discussion of classical sociology and the environment with a few observations, some of which depart in some respects from conventional wisdom on the topic. One must indeed recognize the radically sociological (and thus the 'exemptionalist') standpoint of Marx, Weber, Durkheim, Simmel, and other nineteenth and early twentieth century classical thinkers. As will be noted later, one of the characteristics of the sociological project as it emerged from the key figures of nineteenth century thought was that a sociological explanation is more elegant to the degree that its underlying concepts abstract beyond the natural world. But while classical theory did tend toward a radically sociological outlook, it by no means completely neglected the biophysical world. We need to recognize that the 'exemptionalism' of the classical tradition can be exaggerated, and thus the neglect of the biophysical environment in twentieth century sociology cannot be accounted for only by the 'exemptionalism' of the classical tradition. Indeed, as stressed several times earlier, a large share of the contemporary environmental sociological theory literature has been explicitly anchored in the works of one or more classical theorists. One of the ironies of modern environmental sociology is that while there is often ritualistic criticism of Marxism for its neglect of the environment, neo-Marxism is perhaps the most pervasive influence on environmental sociology across the world today. This is not surprising, however, when we consider Marxism's materialism, its critical posture toward bourgeois society, its focus on the economy and productive institutions, and its compatibility with social – emancipatory position – postures with which environmental sociology has long had strong affinities.

The lack of attention to the environment in sociological inquiry has arguably had as much or more to do with the historical conditions of the establishment of sociology, especially the imperative to distinguish sociology from other natural and social science disciplines (especially psychology, biology, and economics), and also the reaction against Social Darwinism and geographical-environmental determinism. In addition, the lack of attention to the environment was as much a reflection of Western culture – of its Enlightenment influences, its consumerism, its having been mesmerized by the 500-year boom, its colonial and postcolonial expansionism, and so on – as it was a prescription from the classical theorists. In fact, at mid-century classical theory was much more 'ecological', or much more likely to recognize the materiality (Buttel, 1996) of social life, than was main-stream sociology. The dominant forms of sociology at mid-century – Parsonian functionalism, post-industrial society theory, logic of industrialization theory, modernization theory, pluralism – were arguably far less cognizant of the natural world than were the perspectives of Marx, Durkheim, Weber, Simmel, Tönnies, and so on.

The classical tradition should by no means be seen as above criticism, however, both for sociology at large (see, for example, Giddens, 1987) as well as for its role in guiding environmental sociology. There are clearly some definite limitations of classical theory for understanding the environment. Interestingly, among the limitations of the classical tradition for understanding the environment are two shortcomings – its Eurocentricity and innocence about globalization – that it shares with much contemporary environmental sociology.

The theoretical development of North American environmental sociology

To the extent that the classical tradition can be regarded as exemptionalist or unecological, I consider the exemptionalism of the classical theorists to have been a necessary step in the development of a nondeterministic sociological tradition. This is to say, the classical tradition represented the liberation of social science from a series of reductionisms and chauvinisms – of biological analogies, utilitari-anism, the German (neoclassical economics) analytical school, psychology, clericalism, nationalism, and so on. Overcoming these reductionisms and preju-dices enabled the development of an overarching or encompassing social science discipline which would be able to accommodate a variety of explanatory schemes and methods, and explore a variety of empirical problems.

Likewise, I believe that we need to be respectfully critical of 1970s and 1980s North American environmental sociology as having been a necessary, but incom-plete, step in the development of thought about societal-environmental relations. I believe that North American environmental sociology should be seen as a point of departure, rather than as an end-point for a period of 'normal science', primarily on account of the fact that this literature was developed as much in reaction to mainstream sociology and in metatheoretical terms as it was developed as a source of specific hypotheses to explain societal-environmental relations.

Though the underlying strategy for promulgating a new ecological paradigm in sociology was not often clearly articulated, the pioneers of North American environmental sociology can be seen to have reacted to, and to have striven to influence, mainstream sociology by employing three major arguments. First, the authors of the major works in environmental sociology tended to stress documenting the seriousness of the environmental crisis (e.g., Catton, 1980; Catton and Dunlap, 1978; Schnaiberg, 1980), albeit by relying primarily on secondary litera-ture such as popularized treatments of ecology by persons such as Paul Ehrlich and Barry Commoner. This tendency remains very strong today (e.g., Benton, 1996a; Murphy, 1997). Second, these major works tended to theorize about how and why the regular or customary institutional dynamics of modern industrial societies – market processes, capitalist relations, industrial relations, urbanization, political democracy and corporatist structures, social norms and cultural values, science and technological innovation – have tended to involve *intrinsic or necessary trends to environmental degradation and crisis.*[3] Third, while the overall stress of these theories was to explain degradation, and thus was essentially pessimistic, at the same time these theories all held out hope that these dynamics can and would be negated or overridden through public value change and/or environmental move-ment mobilization. Thus, the public value change and the environmental move-ment were portrayed as being a rational and necessary response to the environ-mental crisis, and social policy change resulting from movement mobilization and pressure was seen to be the principal mechanism of environmental improvement (e.g., Milbrath, 1984; see also the discussion in Yearley, 1996).

Catton and Dunlap have articulated particularly clearly each of these three rationales for a specialized field of environmental sociology and for why these premises should be reflected in mainstream sociology. During the early years of North American environmental sociology, Catton (1976, 1980) documented in particularly comprehensive fashion the ominous implications for the human species of ongoing trends toward environmental destruction. In so doing, he showed that the core institutions of contemporary industrial societies were devel-oped during a period of (apparent) abundance – the '500-year boom' dating from the heyday of mercantilism and the beginnings of capitalism – though Catton has hastened to stress that much of this abundance was ephemeral because it was based on past or future 'ghost acreage'. Catton suggested further that these institutions have persisted up to this day and have had remarkable momentum and inertia. Dunlap and Catton (1994) have also stressed the continuing force of the 'dominant Western world view' among publics in terms of how this world view props up the institutional practices portrayed in Catton's earlier work (e.g., Catton, 1976). Finally, Dunlap and Catton (1994) have developed very strong arguments about why environmentalism is a progressive force that should be supported by the social science community.

Allan Schnaiberg's environmental sociology (Schnaiberg, 1980; Schnaiberg and Gould, 1993), probably second only to Dunlap and Catton's in its influence throughout North America, has likewise been anchored in a conceptualization of the very powerful momentum behind environmental destruction. Schnaiberg has argued that the environmental crisis is due primarily to there being a very strong tendency to an environmentally destructive 'treadmill of production'. By treadmill of production, Schnaiberg means that the competitive character of capitalism and the imperative for states to underwrite private accumulation while dealing with the social dislocations of private accumulation combine to virtually compel private and public policies and practices that lead to exponential, capital-intensive, envi-ronment-degrading economic growth. Thus, the actions of private firms and state managers, as well as consumer-citizens and labor groups, all combine to reinforce the treadmill character of industrial accumulation. Schnaiberg has also portrayed the environmental movement as the principal countervailing social mechanism for societies to improve their environmental performance (Gould et al., 1996).[4]

There are certain shortcomings of the predominant conceptualizations of environment-society relations in the North American environmental sociology literature, however. One limitation of the traditional North American environmental sociology literature is that it has devoted far more attention to theorizing environmental degradation than to theorizing environmental improvement (see Buttel, 1996). As obvious as this limitation may seem, it needs to be recognized that shifting to a stress on environmental improvement is by no means unproblematic. Since environmental sociology's justification within the larger discipline is that it is better able than mainstream sociology to recognize why environmental problems are serious, getting worse, and could imperil human survival, the sub-discipline has historically had something of a self-interest in emphasizing degradation and crisis over improvement. Further, degradation is relatively easy to theorize because one can draw on historical as well as contemporary data in order to show how various institutional ensembles affect environmental degradation processes. The historical instances of environmental improvement (or of structures and processes of environmental improvement with contemporary relevance), however, are far fewer than those of degradation. Also, environmental improvement processes are very likely more subtle and more complex phenomena than are environmental degradation processes; while there are arguably some overarching institutional processes that lead to degradation, improvement is not likely to be so constituted. For these and other reasons, the traditional North American literature has not devoted a great deal of attention to improvement processes – and to the degree that improvement is discussed it is presumed that environmental movement mobilization resulting in state policy change is the master process.

A second shortcoming of the North American environmental sociology literature is that it has arguably overestimated the coherence of environmental movements, and exaggerated the degree to which environmental improvement will ultimately derive from environmental movement mobilization. For example, there has by no means been a strong association between environmental movement mobilization and environmental legislation in the US. Despite the growth of US environmental movements since the early 1970s, these groups have had very few major accomplishments since then. Virtually all of the landmark US environmental legislation – the National Environmental Policy Act, the Clean Water Act, the Toxic Substances Control Act, the Endangered Species Act, and so on – was passed in the early 1970s or earlier. Since the mid-1970s, the best this growing movement could do was to engage in rear-guard actions to preserve as much of this legislation as possible. Further, much of the environmental improvement that has actually occurred since the mid-1970s has been due to market-induced conservation, behavioral changes, technological advances, and responses to civil-legal incentives that discourage exposure to civil litigation on nuisance and liability grounds (Mol, 1995). Finally, there are now numerous critiques of modern environmentalism's track record in selecting issues and tactics that can lead to broadly shared environmental improvements (see, for example, Gottlieb, 1994; Sachs, 1993). Thus, North American environmental sociology has stood in need of revision. I will now turn to three relatively new environmental-sociological frameworks to which many sociologists have turned to complement the perspectives of the pioneering 'new human ecologists'.

The debate over social constructionism

Social constructionism – or, more broadly, the 'cultural turn' of sociology and environmental sociology – has been highly controversial, arguably more so than has been justified. While much has been made between the apparent debate between Dunlap/Catton (1994) and myself (Buttel, 1992; Taylor and Buttel, 1992) on this matter, I do not regard this debate as being particularly fundamental to the field. I suspect that the only truly significant difference between my perspective on the social construction of environmental knowledge and concepts and that of Dunlap is that I see environmental science as being less coherent, and as exhibiting a greater level of diversity and controversy, than he does. Further, it is my observation that there is a fairly strong consensus in the field that neither an unquestioning realist posture toward environmental knowledge nor a radical relativist posture is 'sustainable' within sociology, much less environmental sociology (see Freudenburg et al., 1995, for a related argument).

Social constructionism and related discourse-analytic scholarship (e.g., Hajer, 1995; Hannigan, 1995; Lash et al., 1996; Wynne, 1996; Yearley, 1996) have played a useful role in environmental sociology. But its utility has not been in making environmental sociology a branch of the sociology of scientific knowledge (SSK), i.e., in casting doubt on the degree to which global warming claims or global environmental knowledge are a faithful reflection of the realities of the natural world. Indeed, relativization of environmental science or global environmental change has in general not been, nor should it be, the major goal of social constructionist environmental-sociological studies. Rather, their purposes have been to make several important points. First, a one-sided realist account of environmental science and knowledge – which environmental sociology often comes perilously close to embracing – is just that – one-sided, and inconsistent with any reasonable sociological perspective which must take into account both 'structure' and 'agency', and the material and the symbolic. Even from a realist perspective, any concept such as global environmental change must be regarded as an abstraction which, if it proves to be a good one, will help to illuminate the processes of the natural world but in so doing will obscure others; and such an abstraction should be regarded as being important only on a provisional basis until its validity can be established through repeated replications and experiments. Second, environmental-scientific discourses matter. Interpretive-discursive sociologies of environmental knowledge claims, environmental risks, environmental ideologies, and environmental politics can contribute a great deal to environmental sociology by illuminating how and in what ways discourses are structured and renegotiated. These interpretive sociologies are not intrinsically inconsistent with structural or materialist views from more mainstream quarters of environmental sociology (as Hajer, 1995, masterfully demonstrates). Third, it is critical for environmental sociology to recognize the crucial role that the scientization of protest, social movements, and politics is playing (Buttel, 1992). In other words, while not detracting from the fact that scientific knowledge tends to more or less mirror the realities of the natural world, the crucial role of science often lies in how it is 'represented' and how it is employed within social movements, interest groups, regulatory agencies, epistemic communities, international organizations and 'regimes', and so on. Scientific knowledge thus often tends to be enmeshed with social symbols, political ideologies and discourses, social movement 'frames'. How this occurs makes an enormous difference in terms of environmental policy and politics.

In addition to social constructionist perspectives on the relations between environmental knowledge/science and environmental movement, some scholars (DuPuis and Vandergeest, 1995; Goldblatt, 1996; Hannigan, 1995) have strived to take the social constructionist agenda a step or two further, mainly by bringing the tools of cultural sociology into environmental sociology. In most such instances, the relativization of environmental knowledge is not a major or even a minor goal. Doing so, in fact, is a fairly mindless, trivial exercise. Further, several scholars from otherwise mainstream sociology have begun to enter the terrain formerly known as environmental sociology by applying cultural-sociological tools to phenomena such as environmentalism, ecology movements, green parties, and so on (MacNaughten and Urry, 1995). With environmental sociology becoming more important to the mainstream of the discipline because of their own initiatives rather than ours strikes me as being much more positive than negative.

Reflexive modernization, ecological modernization, and environmental sociology

Over the past half dozen or so years environmental sociology in the advanced countries has been very appreciably reshaped by the application of a second set of theories developed in Northern Europe, primarily for application to phenomena such as green parties, ecology movements, the relationships between science and environmental movements, industrial ecology, and so on. While these theories are in a sense quite diverse, they all tend to see environmental improvement as being as or more important to explain than environmental degradation. Each also embraces the notion that there are ongoing complex changes in the social values and behaviors deriving from environmental degradation and crisis. Each of these theories also tends to downplay the role of certain forms of environmentalism, especially radical, 'expressive' environmentalism, in environmental improvement. In my view, two of these emerging traditions in environmental sociology – risk society and ecological modernization theories – are playing particularly important roles in rectifying some of the shortcomings of North American environmental sociology. These two theories are both built around Ulrich Beck's (and, more recently, Anthony Giddens') concept of reflexive modernization (see Beck et al., 1994, and the commentary by Goldblatt, 1996).

Beck's notion of reflexive modernization is very closely linked to his theory of the transformation from 'industrial society' to 'risk society'. His concept of reflexive modernization is based on the notion that the further the process of 'simple modernization' (essentially capitalist rationalization and industrialization, undergirded by science and technological development) proceeds, 'the more the foundations of industrial society are dissolved, consumed, changed and threatened'

(Beck, 1994: 176). Modernization is seen to have led to a set of risks and hazards that not only threaten current generations, but might also prejudice the quality of life, and possibly the very survival, of future generations. For Beck, the 'ecological crisis', the risks of mega-accidents such as Bhopal and Exxon Valdez, the environmental risks of recombinant DNA and genetic engineering, the personal risks entailed by medical high technology, and the declining capacity of states to regulate directly the production practices that give rise to these risks are examples of the outcomes of simple modernization. The growing public recognition of these hazards and risks is one of the two principal precipitants of 'reflexive modernization', and ultimately of the risk society. The other major precipitant of reflexive modernization is the decline of parliamentary institutions, the individuation of politics, the decline of class, and the growing role of 'subpolitics'.

At one level, one can think of reflexive modernization as being both 'reflex' and 'reflection'. The 'reflex' or structural component of reflexive modernization essentially holds that the risks and hazards generated by modernization, or by industrial society, call the central institutions of society (science, the legal system, parliamentary democracy, the market economy) into question. The 'reflection' or more actor-centered component of reflexive modernization includes the 'freeing' of actors relative to social classes and other social-structural categories, the consequent construction of new identities and roles, and the formation of new social movements around these new identities and concerns about risks. In particular, the trend in the advanced societies has been for their citizens to scrutinize science, technology, and scientific institutions by making moral claims to rationality that are equal to those of modern science. 'Reflexive modernization', says Beck (1992: 14) 'means not less but more modernity, a modernity radicalized against the paths and categories of the classical industrial setting'.

The second major stream of work flowing from reflexive modernization is that of ecological modernization theory. The link between reflexive modernization and ecological modernization is less direct than it is to the theory of the 'risk society'. Some proponents of ecological modernization (Spaargaren and Mol, 1992) are actually quite critical of how Beck has applied reflexive modernization to risk society theory. But most sociological proponents of ecological modernization strongly concur with the two constituent notions of reflexive modernization: first, human and institutional choices are not simply the reflections of master-structural forces of capitalism, industrialization, and so on; and second, the solutions to environmental problems will lie in a progressive modernization of societies (rather than in the 'de-modernization' or 'counter-modernization' that is advocated within radical environmentalism).

As Mol (1995: Chapter 3) and Hajer (1995) have stressed, there are several different streams of thought within ecological modernization. Mol shows that Karl Polanyi's (1957) work can in some sense be seen as a precursor to ecological modernization. Most sociologists who work in the field, however, grant that the notion was most systematically developed by the German social scientist, Joseph Huber (see Mol's, 1995, summary of Huber's work). In contrast to the predominant thrust of mainstream US environmental sociology having been devoted to explaining environmental degradation, ecological modernization theory grew out of social research, environmental movement involvement, and ecological research on practical, non-utopian means of achieving environmental improvement. Among the principal claims of ecological modernization is that under conditions of state-and-society regulated market capitalism, which have become dominant since at least World War II in OECD countries in particular, contemporary capitalist enterprises have proved to be able to accustom themselves to ecological constraints to a certain extent up to now, without being deprived of favorable production conditions, new markets, or growing profits. In addition, environmental protection and reform has proved to be a profitable market for the expanding eco-industry. Consequently, there is reason to believe that – in economic terms – the incorporation of nature as the third force (in addition to capital and labor) of production in the capitalist economic process has become an increasingly feasible proposition (Mol, 1995: 41).

The heart of ecological modernization theory is a relatively optimistic view of the potentials for technological change to lead to solutions for environmental problems. In particular, it is argued that, at least in some societies, the socioeconomic influences on technological R&D and industrial technology choice will over time tend to lead to improvement in the efficiency of conversion of raw materials into finished products and to reduction in the quantity and toxicity of the waste stream from industry. Huber's work essentially incorporated an evolutionary neo-Schumpeterian view of long cycles of technological innovation. Other ecological modernizationists such as Mol (1995) and Spaargaren (1996) tend to stress a more contextual approach based on (1) the specificities of national and local regulatory and policy regimes, and (2) the social and physical nature of the sectors, products, and production processes involved.

Ecological modernization theory also holds a distinctive posture on the role of state environmental policy. Much mainstream environmental sociology has theorized that the traditional bureaucratic-capitalist state has performed poorly in terms of environmental protection. By contrast, many ecological modernizationists have argued that new trends in the structure of states (including the decline of 'command-and-control' environmental regulation and the concomitant 'modernization' of the state) are actually stimulating environmental 'self-regulation' within civil society via legal mechanisms (e.g., civil liability law), economic mechanisms (market-induced efficiency and environmental policy incentives), and citizen-movement pressures.

Those familiar with Northern Europe will recognize that risk society theory seems to be an apt portrayal of the rise of the German Green Party and other radical environmental movements in Germany. Ecological modernization theory also seems strongly consistent with many of the restructurings and technological trends in industry (and the consumption sphere) in Germany, The Netherlands, and elsewhere in the region.[5]

As risk society and ecological modernization theories have become more influential, they have been subjected to several criticisms.[6] Some of these criticisms have been directed at the larger reflexive modernization perspective. For example, these theories have been criticized from the perspective of developing countries because they tend to be Eurocentric and lack generalizability to most societies in the world. It has long been recognized that modernizationist theories of social change are not very useful in understanding developing-country dynamics. Many of the assumptions of modernization theories have limited applicability to low-income countries, and this is no less the case with reflexive modernization perspectives. Other theories have been specific to either risk society or ecological modernization theory. Some of the typical criticisms of risk society theory, for example, stress its quasi-constructivist conceptualization of technological and ecological risks, and note that in most societies the pervasiveness of public preoccupation with such risks is far less than portrayed in Beck's scholarship (see, for example, Murphy, 1994).

Perhaps the most problematic aspect of risk society theory is its being anchored in the notion of the 'equality of risk' – that regardless of one's class one cannot be exempt from or escape large-scale hazards and risks. The equality of risk is seen by Beck as contributing to the demise of social class and as facilitating new forms of subpolitics across traditional class lines. It is apparent, however, that to the degree that there is an equality of risk in the countries of Northern Europe this is because social inequality and residential segregation are less there than in the laissez-faire capitalist societies such as the US, and very substantially less than in most developing countries.[7] In most societies in the world today, in fact, there is relatively little 'equality of risk'. If anything, 'environmental inequality' (Szasz and Meuser, 1997) is the rule rather than the exception. And environmental inequality is not confined to the low-income countries of the South. For example, the US environmental justice movement, which arose from the civil rights movement to seek redress for the *inequalities* of exposure to environmental hazards along racial and class lines – has been a crucial innovation in American environmentalism. Environmental justice – the notion that all persons have a right to a clean environment as an entitlement of citizenship – may well be a strategy with considerable applicability to environment quality (and social justice) efforts in developing countries. At a minimum, environmental justice-oriented thinking in the international environmental movement could play a significant role in constraining institutions such as the World Bank to presume that it is a socially acceptable policy to encourage and facilitate movement of heavily polluting and toxic-producing production processes to the South. Likewise, Murphy (1994), recognizing the highly unequal distribution of the costs and benefits of environmental extraction and destruction across social groups in North America, has anchored his acclaimed environmental sociology treatise in the notion of 'environmental classes' – a concept that is premised on the inequality of risk, hazards, access to resources, consumption capacity, and other environmental processes.

Of the two reflexive-modernization-related theories, ecological modernization has proved to be the most influential in relatively mainstream environmental-sociological circles. Among the reasons for its influence is that it is (1) a particularly affirmative response to the imperative for environmental sociology to be socially useful and to be able to shed light on possibilities for environmental improvement, and (2) an apt portrayal of the culture, processes, and political structures of state-induced environmental reforms in much of the West (Hajer, 1995). Ecological modernization has thus risen to prominence in the field very rapidly. A good indicator of its influence is that Mol's (1997) paper in the recent Redclift and Woodgate's (1997) anthology on environmental sociology is one of the few chapters that is built around advocacy for a particular theoretical approach. Further, several of the chapters in the Redclift and Woodgate anthology devote considerable attention to ecological modernization.

The ecological modernization approach is much more likely to have lasting influence on environmental sociology than will risk society theory. But while ecological modernization has received growing attention in environmental sociology, it has also begun to receive criticisms. Here I will briefly discuss some of these criticisms and evaluate them along with ecological modernization's current and potential strengths.

The most significant criticisms of ecological modernization are three-fold. First, there is the matter of its having been based on the Northern European experience, and its concomitant lack of generalizeability. Thus, it has been argued that ecological modernization processes as depicted in the ecological modernization literature are premised on the existence of social and political institutions that can provide strong signals to industries and consumers that pro-environmental behavior is expected, and that the absence of environmentally sound behavior would result in costly public or private sanctions. This is not to say that in the OECD countries outside of Northern Europe, and especially in the newly industrializing countries of the developing world, there is an absence of forces pushing in this direction. Indeed, virtually all countries, including those in the South, have environmental laws and regulations on the books. There also exist customary social relations and practices (e.g., common property regimes) that serve to conserve resources (Lipschutz and Mayer, 1993). But across the world today the absence of state environmental-regulatory powers, including the inability to provide incentives to induce pro-environmental practices in civil society, is a widespread phenomenon (Lipschutz, 1996).

A second criticism of ecological modernization and related approaches (e.g., notions of industrial ecology and environmental Kuznets curves) is that the types of environmental reforms that are seen as progressive (e.g., pollution control and source reduction in the Dutch chemical industry (Mol, 1997)) tend to involve relatively little decrease in the human toll on environmental resources. As Bunker (1996) has stressed, despite global improvements in the efficiency of the use of materials over the past two decades, aggregate consumption of minerals and other raw materials has continued unabated.

A third and related criticism (e.g., by Blühdorn in this volume) is that ecological modernization as a theory and discourse can serve to legitimate a political culture of environmental policy-making that basically absolves industrial corporations and other agents of environmental destruction of their responsibilities, and serves to ignore how the 'modernization' of the state is contributing to growing inequalities of wealth and power within countries and across the world-system. Furthermore, Blühdorn has also been critical of how reflexive modernization theories in general tend to dismiss the significance and the potential long-term efficacy of 'radical' environmentalism.

These criticisms are serious, but ecological modernization's potential contributions are also very significant. The many advantages of reflexive-modernization-based approaches to environmental sociology suggest that it will be well worth the effort to address their shortcomings. Ecological modernization has the potential to temper the pessimism and the lack of attention to concrete processes of environmental improvement that has tended to be endemic to the materialist core of environmental sociology. Ecological modernization also avoids falling victim to a presumption of the 'equality of risk', and can be complemented by incorporating concepts such as Murphy's (1994) notion of 'environmental classes'. As I note below, ecological modernization potentially can add a comparative dimension, building on some of the insights of Hajer (1995). A more comparative ecological modernization perspective can help it to address its Eurocentricity and lack of generalizeability. Perhaps most importantly, ecological modernization theory suggests provocative hypotheses, the resolution of which will help to make environmental sociology a stronger empirical science.

While this is not the time or place for laying out an improved version of ecological modernization theory, I will sketch some notes about possible avenues for enhancing the contribution of ecological modernization and related approaches. First, instead of (at least implicitly) presuming that there is a common type of political culture and state structure that is most conducive to ecological modernization, ecological modernization scholars could begin with a comparative perspective. Thus, while ecological modernization is the prevailing discourse of environmental politics in much of the West, this is by no means the case in other societies and national states. This observation could lead to interest in comparative analysis of political cultures of environmental reform; further, to the extent to which there is diffusion of these political cultures through globalization processes – a project that Mol has already initiated in his contribution to this volume – ecological modernization could be explored in a broader world-systemic perspective.

It also strikes me that ecological modernization and its notions of political modernization and its appropriation of notions such as 'issue advocacy coalitions' are highly compatible with another new and rapidly growing area of sociological scholarship: the work of Peter Evans (1995, 1996) on 'embedded autonomy' and 'state-society synergy'. Evans' concepts are highly relevant to environmental sustainability issues, as is evidenced by the fact that his most recent research interest has been in urban sustainability and 'livable cities' in the South (Evans, 1998). Evans' concepts of embedded autonomy and state-society synergy can also provide much of the framework for deepening the comparative project of ecological modernization research. Evans' work represents an effective response to the need for a realistic model of states and power relations which is not innocent of coercion and domination, while at the same time it is able to identify salient respects in which states can have positive impacts on, and through, civil society processes. Evans' (1998) observations on the role of state-society synergy at the sub-national level also demonstrate how political cultures and configurations which have little in common with those depicted by Mol (1997) for the Netherlands can have positive impacts on environmental improvement in the South.

In addition to the need for a more comparative approach to ecological modernization research, it is also necessary for its practitioners to address the various literatures, such as those on postmodernization and development studies, that raise profound questions about modernization theories. Ecological modernization theories have yet to take account of some of the observations from the three or so decades of critique of modernization theory in development studies. Modernization theories of all kinds need to address the tendency to the teleological presumption that there are essentially common paths of development and change that all national societies must inevitably traverse.

I opened this paper by saying that ecological modernization is unlikely to become the dominant theory in environmental sociology. In part, this is because of some of its weaknesses, as just discussed. But beyond these weaknesses, it is arguably the case that ecological modernization has several characteristics – an optimistic view of the potential for environmental reform and 'ecological restructuring' and thus certain 'exemptionalist' overtones, skepticism about the role of radical environmentalism, and a lack of attention to stressing explanations for environmental degradation – that cause it to be viewed with some amount of suspicion in environmental sociological circles. These very characteristics of ecological modernization, however, cause it to be a provocative challenge to received wisdom in environmental sociology.

Conclusion: further theoretical exhortations

I have strived to advance a perspective on theory in environmental sociology that is appreciative of the continued relevance of the classical tradition but which is prepared to recognize the many shortcomings of classical social theory. The classical theorists' works can always be read in two different ways – as being hopelessly dated works that do not have much to say about an epoch that departs so much from that of the nineteenth century, and as a continuing source of insights and methodological approaches that are applicable to almost any empirical problem we might come up with. My guess is that environmental sociology will always essentially consist of a set of perspectives which have definite lineages to the classical theorists while also having an ecological-material ontology of some sort (e.g., a notion of 'ghost acreage', treadmill of production, ecological modernization) superimposed on them. Another aspect of classical theory that is very positive for environmental sociology is that which Wardell and Turner (1986) have referred to as the 'classical project'. The future of environmental sociology may well lie in whether it is able to restore the 'classical project' of uniting sociological abstraction with a meaningful role in addressing moral and political issues.

It is my view that environmental sociology broadly construed has continued to stray from the new human ecology or materialist core that predominated in the late 1970s and 1980s. A number of theoretical views that may be regarded in one respect or another as 'exemptionalist' – social constructivism, risk society, critical theory, and ecological modernization – have appropriated some of the turf formerly occupied by the new human ecology. On the whole, this has been a positive development. I feel that environmental sociology has been more than capable of assimilating these divergent views while avoiding environmental sociology becoming reduced to answering the question of how and why 'ecology' has come to be culturally significant. Environmental sociology is strong and well established enough that it can tolerate, and even thrive within, theoretical pluralism. The diversification of the field is opening up avenues of theoretical innovation and synthesis that were not present a decade ago (Buttel, 1996). Further, this more diversified theoretical base is increasing the opportunities for environmental-sociological theory to be integrated more closely into concrete empirical research. The overall trends thus strike me as being very positive.

The reflexive modernization-related frameworks portrayed above have been particularly creative responses to some of the limitations of the traditional North American environmental-sociological literature. They permit serious analysis of

environmental improvement and take a less singular and utopian view of environmental movements than is typical of much of environmental sociology. They allow
that citizen-actors are not just passive recipients of the overarching forces of
modernity/modernization, and that they can themselves affect the 'modernization'
process. Reflexive modernization theories recognize that it is possible that modernization can be 'turned back on to itself' in order to address the problems which
it has itself created. Risk society theory, along with related interpretive, constructivist, and discourse-analytical theories (e.g., Hajer, 1995; Lash et al., 1996), has
particular strengths in helping us to recognize that while there are social-structural
forces that facilitate solutions to environmental problems, there also needs to be
a sounder conceptualization of the multiple (and contradictory) processes by which
these forces can become reflected in institutional practices and social behaviors
(see especially Hajer, 1995). Most importantly, these theories – particularly
ecological modernizationism – raise important questions and suggest areas of
research that will be of relevance to environmental sociology as a whole.

Notes

1. It is striking to me that the first major work of contemporary (post-Earth Day) environmental sociology, Burch's *Daydreams and Nightmares* (1971), reflects the eclectic (or
   agnostically respectful) posture toward the classics which I see in ascendance in environmental sociology and which I believe is the most appropriate orientation toward the
   classics.
2. Also, two of the most influential recent neo-Marxist environmental sociology anthologies, by O'Connor (1994) and Benton (1996b), include contributions that derive largely
   from the work of the late Marx (particularly his *Grundrisse* and the three volumes of
   Capital).
3. The emphasis on the inherent or intrinsic tendency to environmental destruction or
   degradation should also be seen as one of the principal ways in which environmental
   sociologists distinguished their work from that of the neo-Durkheimian 'human ecologists'. Among human ecology's central concepts were those of adaptation and equilibrium, which implied a tendency for social institutions over time to come into symmetry
   or stability with respect to environmental resources. Mainstream North American environmental sociology practitioners thus tended to regard human ecology as having a benign or unrealistic view of the stresses humans were placing on the natural environment, and an overly optimistic assessment of the capacity of institutional processes for
   responding to environmental problems (Buttel and Humphrey, 1987).
4. Note that I am not disagreeing about the fundamental importance of 'environmental
   movements'. My concern is that one cannot theorize the role of environmental movements in dealing with ecological issues apart from the contradictory roles of states in
   this process. That is, while environmental conservation and protection are directly or
   indirectly state-regulatory practices and the role of states in a societal division of labor
   is to 'rationalize', states face conflicting imperatives (accumulation [or the responsibility for satisfactory aggregate economic performance] and legitimation) and formidable
   pressures from various groups in civil society (especially capital) that cause them to be
   internally conflicted over or very reluctant to invoke environmental protection policies
   and practices.
5. Note, though, that most ecological modernization research focuses on the production
   sphere, particularly heavy-industrial production. Spaargaren (1996: Chapter 6) has ar-

gued that its principles should also apply to consumption, and he has sketched out a schema for understanding the ecological modernization of household consumption.

6. Despite their common rooting in notions of reflexive modernization, there are very significant differences between risk society and ecological modernization theories. Risk society theory is far more 'apocalyptic' than ecological modernization theory. Ecological modernization theory tends to find states up to the task of making possible environmental improvement, whereas risk society theory is much more skeptical. While neither risk society nor ecological modernization theory has much use for the claims of radical environmental groups, risk society theory has a far more positive view of 'subpolitics' and new social movements than does ecological modernization theory. As Mol (1995: 48) puts the matter, 'subpolitics hardly emerge as an option in ecological modernization theory'.

7. The lack of residential and spatial segregation in Northern Europe does lead to a certain equality of risk vis-à-vis hazards such as industrial accidents and toxic wastes. This relative equality of risk as depicted by Beck is largely made possible by the fact that Northern European welfare-statist institutions place a floor under wages, and thus level class differences in income and living standards. The working and dominant classes of Northern Europe are far less residentially and spatially segregated than is the case in the developing world, and even in the US.

Bibliography

Beck, U. (1992), *Risk Society*. Beverly Hills, CA: Sage.

Beck, U. (1994), The reinvention of politics: towards a theory of reflexive modernization, in: U. Beck et al. (eds), *Reflexive Modernization*. Cambridge: Polity.

Beck, U. (1995), *Ecological Politics in an Age of Risk*. Cambridge: Polity.

Beck, U., A. Giddens and S. Lash (eds) (1994), *Reflexive Modernization*. Cambridge: Polity.

Benton, T. (1996a), Marxism and natural limits: an ecological critique and reconstruction, in: T. Benton (ed.), *The Greening of Marxism*. New York: Guilford, pp. 157-183.

Benton, T. (ed.) (1996b), *The Greening of Marxism*. New York: Guilford.

Bookchin, M. (1971), *Post-Scarcity Anarchism*. Berkeley: Ramparts.

Bunker, S.G. (1996), Raw material and the global economy: oversights and distortions in industrial ecology. *Society and Natural Resources*, 9: 419-430.

Burch, W.R., Jr. (1971), *Daydreams and Nightmares*. New York: Harper & Row.

Burch, W.R., Jr., N.H. Cheek and L. Taylor (eds) (1972), *Social Behavior, Natural Resources, and the Environment*. New York: Harper & Row.

Burch, W.R., Jr. and D.R. Field (1988), *Rural Sociology and the Environment*. Westport, CT: Greenwood Press.

Burkett, P. (1996), Some common misconceptions about nature and Marx's critique of political economy. *Capitalism-Nature-Socialism*, 7: 57-80.

Burns, T.R. and T. Dietz (1992), Cultural evolution: social rule systems, selection, and human agency. *International Sociology*, 7: 259-283.

Buttel, F.H. (1986), Sociology and the environment: the winding road toward human ecology. *International Social Science Journal*, 109: 337-356.

Buttel, F.H. (1992), Environmentalization: origins, processes, and implications for rural social change. *Rural Sociology*, 57: 1-27.

Buttel, F.H. (1996), Environmental and resource sociology: theoretical issues and opportunities for synthesis. *Rural Sociology*, 61: 56-76.

Buttel, F.H. and C.R. Humphrey (1987), *Sociological theory and the natural environment*. Paper presented at the annual meeting of the American Sociological Association, Chicago, IL, August.

Catton, W.R., Jr. (1976), Why the future isn't what it used to be (and how it could be made worse than it has to be). *Social Science Quarterly*, 57: 276-91.

Catton, W.R., Jr. (1980), *Overshoot*. Urbana: University of Illinois Press.

Catton, W.R., Jr. and R.E. Dunlap (1978), Environmental sociology: a new paradigm. *The American Sociologist*, 13: 41-49.

Cotgrove, S. (1982), *Catastrophe or Cornucopia*. Chichester: Wiley.

Cottrell, F. (1955), *Energy and Society*. New York: McGraw-Hill.

Dickens, P. (1992), *Society and Nature*. Philadelphia: Temple University Press.

Dietz, T. and T.R. Burns (1992), Human agency and the evolutionary dynamic. *Acta Sociologica*, 35: 187-200.

Dunlap, R.E. and W.R. Catton, Jr. (1979), Environmental sociology. *Annual Review of Sociology*, 5: 243-73.

Dunlap, R.E. and W.R. Catton, Jr. (1983), What environmental sociologists have in common (whether concerned with 'built' or 'natural' environments). *Sociological Inquiry*, 53: 113-35.

Dunlap, R.E. and W.R. Catton, Jr. (1994), Struggling with human exemptionalism: the rise, decline and revitalization of environmental sociology. *The American Sociologist*, 25: 5-30.

38   Environment and Global Modernity

DuPuis, E.M. and P. Vandergeest (eds) (1995), *Creating the Countryside*. Philadelphia: Temple University Press.

Evans, P. (1995), *Embedded Autonomy*. Princeton: Princeton University Press.

Evans, P. (1996), Government action, social capital, and development: reviewing the evidence on synergy. *World Development*, 24: 1119-1132.

Evans, P. (1998), *Liveable cities?* Unpublished manuscript. University of California, Berkeley: Department of Sociology.

Firey, W. (1960), *Man, Mind, and Land*. New York: Free Press.

Freudenburg, W.R., S. Frickel and R. Gramling (1995), Beyond the nature/society divide: learning to think about a mountain. *Sociological Forum*, 10: 361-392.

Giddens, A. (1987), *Social Theory and Modern Sociology*. Stanford, CA: Stanford University Press.

Giddens, A. (1994), *Beyond Left and Right*. Stanford, CA: Stanford University Press.

Goldblatt, D. (1996), *Social Theory and the Environment*. Boulder, CO: Westview Press.

Gottlieb, R. (1994), *Forcing the Spring*. Washington, DC: Island Press.

Gould, K.A., A. Schnaiberg and A.S. Weinberg (1996), *Environmental Struggles*. New York: Cambridge University Press.

Hajer, M. (1995), *The Politics of Environmental Discourse*. New York: Oxford University Press.

Hannigan, J. (1995), *Environmental Sociology*. London: Routledge.

Hughes, J.A., P.J. Martin and W.W. Sharrock (1995), *Understanding Classical Sociology*. London: Sage.

Klausner, S.A. (1971), *On Man in His Environment*. San Francisco: Jossey-Bass.

Lash, S., B. Szerszynski and B. Wynne (eds) (1996), *Risk, Environment and Modernity*. London: Sage.

Lipschutz, R.D., with J. Mayer (1996), *Global Civil Society and Global Environmental Governance*. Albany: State University of New York Press.

Lipschutz, R.D. and J. Mayer (1993), Not seeing the forest for the trees: rights, rules, and the renegotiation of resource management regimes, in: R.D. Lipschutz and K. Conca (eds), *The State and Social Power in Global Environmental Politics*. New York: Columbia University Press.

Lopreato, J. (1984), *Human Nature and Biocultural Evolution*. Boston: Allen & Unwin.

MacNaughten, P. and J. Urry (1995), Towards a sociology of nature. *Sociology*, 29: 203-220.

Martell, L. (1994), *Ecology and Society*. Amherst: University of Massachusetts Press.

Milbrath, L. (1984), *Environmentalists: Vanguard for a New Society*. Albany: State University of New York Press.

Mol, Arthur P.J. (1995), *The Refinement of Production*. Utrecht: Van Arkel.

Mol, A.P.J. (1997), Ecological modernization: industrial transformations and environmental reform, in: M. Redclift and G. Woodgate (eds), *The International Handbook of Environmental Sociology*. London: Edward Elgar, pp. 138-149.

Morrison, K. (1995), *Marx, Durkheim, Weber*. London: Sage.

Murphy, R. (1994), *Rationality and Nature*. Boulder, CO: Westview Press.

Murphy, R. (1997), *Sociology and Nature*. Boulder, CO: Westview Press.

O'Connor, M. (ed.) (1994), *Is Capitalism Sustainable?*. New York: Guilford.

Parsons, H.L. (ed.) (1977), *Marx and Engels on Ecology*. Westport, CN.: Greenwood Press.

Polanyi, K. (1957), *The Great Transformation*. Boston: Beacon.

Redclift, M. and G. Woodgate (eds) (1997), *The International Handbook of Environmental Sociology*. London: Edward Elgar.

Sachs, W. (ed.) (1993), *Global Ecology*. London: Zed Books.

Sanderson, S.K. (1990), *Social Evolutionism*. Oxford: Basil Blackwell.

Schnaiberg, A. (1980), *The Environment*. New York: Oxford University Press.

Schnaiberg, A. and K.A. Gould (1993), *Environment and Society*. New York: St. Martin's Press.

Spaargaren, G. (1996), *The Ecological Modernization of Production and Consumption*. PhD thesis. Wageningen: Wageningen Agricultural University.

Spaargaren, G. and A.P.J. Mol (1992), Sociology, environment, and modernity: ecological modernization as a theory of social change. *Society and Natural Resources*, 5: 323-344.

Swingewood, A. (1991), *A Short History of Sociological Thought. Second Edition*. New York: St. Martin's Press.

Szasz, A. and M. Meuser (1997), Environmental inequalities: literature review and proposals for new directions in theory and research. Manuscript. University of California, Santa Cruz: Board of Studies in Sociology.

Taylor, P.J. and F.H. Buttel (1992), How do we know we have global environmental problems? Science and the globalization of environmental discourse. *Geoforum*, 23: 405-416.

Turner, J.H. (1994), The ecology of macrostructure, in: L. Freese (ed.), *Advances in Human Ecology, Vol. 3*. Greenwich, CT: JAI Press, pp. 113-138.

Wardell, M.L. and S.P. Turner (1986), Introduction: dissolution of the classical project, in: M.L. Wardell and S.P. Turner (eds), *Sociological Theory in Transition*. Boston: Allen Unwin, pp. 11-18.

Webb, W.P. (1952), *The Great Frontier*. Boston: Houghton Mifflin.

Weber, M. (1922/1968), *Economy and Society*. Berkeley: University of California Press.

West, P.C. (1984), Max Weber's human ecology of historical societies, in: V. Murvar (ed.), *Theory of Liberty, Legitimacy and Power*. Boston: Routledge & Kegan Paul, pp. 216-234.

Wilkinson, R.G. (1973), *Poverty and Progress*. New York: Praeger.

Wynne, B. (1996), May the sheep safely graze? A reflexive view of the expert-lay knowledge divide, in: S. Lash et al. (eds), *Risk, Environment, and Modernity*. London: Sage.

Yearley, S. (1996), *Sociology, Environmentalism, Globalization*. London: Sage.

[3]
THE TREADMILL OF PRODUCTION AND THE ENVIRONMENTAL STATE

Allan Schnaiberg, David N. Pellow and
Adam Weinberg

THE INITIAL LOGIC OF THE TREADMILL

The *treadmill of production* (TOP) is a concept first introduced in 1980 by
Schnaiberg, arising from two observations. First, a major change appeared in
the impact of production processes upon ecosystems in the last half of the 20th
century. Second, social and political responses to these impacts were quite
variable and volatile. While some people rebelled against this modern production
system, others embraced new technologies as their best hope for solving
environmental problems.[1]

Ironically, we have returned to this theoretical ambivalence at the end of the
twentieth century. Among environmental sociologists, proponents of ecological
modernization (EM) have postulated that there is a growing independence, or
'emancipation,' of the ecological sphere from the political and economic spheres
in state and industry policy-making (Mol, 1995; Spaargaren & Mol, 1992).
Thus, within each of the spheres, there are significant environmentally-induced
institutional transformations, which leads firms to employ new technologies to
reduce environmental impacts of production. Contrarily, our own model falls
within the range of political economy perspectives that view recent political
and economic trend as minimizing – and often undermining – progress on both
the social and ecological goals. Proponents of political economy models urge

The Environmental State Under Pressure, Volume 10, pages 15–32.
ISBN: 0-7623-0854-0

16   ALLAN SCHNAIBERG, DAVID N. PELLOW AND ADAM WEINBERG

increased mobilization and opposition to socially and ecologically oppressive actions by state and private sector actors.

In this paper, we outline the model of the treadmill as a political-economic context for the so-called *environmental state*. Contrary to many assumptions of ecological modernization theory, we find that economic criteria remain at the *foundation* of decision making about the design, performance and evaluation of production and consumption. This primacy of economic criteria still tends to overshadow most, if not all, ecological concerns. Further, the state also shares this orientation, despite its own political interests, and often cedes a great deal of power to private sector actors. We view this as highly problematic for creating conditions for sustainability and ecological responsibility.

Schnaiberg argued that one major element of change in the U.S. production system during the Post World War II era was the changing status of workers, moving from a working to a middle-class, albeit within a society still marked by considerable poverty (Rubin, 1996; Reich, 1992). Workers gained new income and occupational opportunities through the post-1945 expansion of production and trade. In three books, Schnaiberg and his collaborators outlined a new production system that had changed its relation to the environment in two fundamental respects (see Schnaiberg, 1980; Schnaiberg, Watts & Zimmermann, 1986; Schnaiberg & Gould, 1994):

- First, modern factories needed greater material inputs. The modern factory was capital-intense, and hence, more energy was needed to run machinery. Likewise, the machinery was designed to vastly increase production levels, thus requiring far more raw materials. This feature of this new production system helped explain why ever-greater levels of *withdrawals* from eco-systems were required. These ecological withdrawals led to one set of environmental problems, natural resource depletion.
- Second, modern factories used many more chemicals in the new production processes. The modern factory used new "efficient" energy/chemical intensive technologies to transform raw materials into finished products. Thus, workers were increasingly engaged in managing energy and chemical flows, and directing their flows through the complex machinery, to create marketable products. This feature led to a second set of environmental problems, pollution – which Schnaiberg termed *additions* to the ecosystem.

In a later series of empirically-grounded works (Gould, Schnaiberg & Weinberg, 1996; Schnaiberg, 1994; Gould, 1991, 1992, 1993; Weinberg, 1997a, b; Weinberg, Schnaiberg & Pellow, 1996; Gould, Weinberg & Schnaiberg, 1995), this earlier concept of the treadmill was further elaborated, as Schnaiberg was joined by a succession of students, including: Gould, Weinberg and Pellow. Together they depicted a political economy driven by the following goals:

1. **Economic expansion**. Economic expansion is generally viewed as the core of any viable social, economic, or environmental policy. Economic expansion is thought to increase the profits that corporate managers and their investors require for capital outlays. Workers are believed to benefit from these outlays because they lead to increased production, which creates new local employment opportunities. Capital outlays also lead to higher levels of productivity, a precondition for rising wages. Government agencies need to ensure that national production generates sufficient profitability to: (a) induce investments by capital owners; (b) provide enough additional market values to maintain a level of wages adequate to sustain consumer demand; and, (c) generate enough tax revenue to cover the state's social expenditures. Governments believe that tax revenues from the accelerating treadmill will rise more rapidly than citizen demands. Thus, government officials and agencies increasingly share a stake in the economic expansion of the private sector.

2. **Increasing consumption**. If economic growth is to come about through increased production of the amount of goods, consumers need to have the disposable income to purchase the goods. Therefore the state, along with private capital, works to make low-interest loans available to consumers for the purchase of homes and other items. This ensures a continued cycle of production and consumption.

3. **Solving social and ecological problems by speeding up the treadmill**. Social and ecological problems are thought to be best solved "through the market." Thus, there is an untenable, almost magical, sense that any type of economic expansion will reduce social and ecological problems. Poverty will be reduced by a growing economy because there is an expanded job base and increased wages at the bottom. A growing economy also supports government social expenditures (for education, housing, and other needs of the poor) and provides the source of funding for technology development that could address environmental ills.

4. **Economic expansion via large firms**. Economic expansion is seen as fostered primarily through the growth of large firms, the Fortune 500 or "core firms." Large firms are thought to be the driving engine of the economy. Their growth creates the most demand for jobs, and it creates secondary demand for supplies, which fuels the growth of smaller entrepreneurial firms. The wages paid to the large labor pools provide consumption capacity among consumers who keep mainstreet American

18   ALLAN SCHNAIBERG, DAVID N. PELLOW AND ADAM WEINBERG

merchants in business. The earlier popular slogan "What's good for General
Motors is Good for America" captures this thinking.

5. **Alliances among capital, labor, and governments**. The post-1945 political
economy was largely held together by an implicit contract. Private capital's
need for a reliable labor force aided in the development of strong trade unions
that could collectively bargain for wage increases and safer working conditions. Workers' need for jobs and their general satisfaction with unprecedented
material gains led to a "no strike" pledge with management. The state played
its part by expanding public education in order to produce a higher quality
labor force, while also expanding consumer credit to make sure that domestic
demand for goods kept pace with the increase in production.

Throughout these papers, we noted that as early as the 1960s in the United
States, the treadmill had already begun to undergo significant changes (Gordon,
1996; Reich, 1992; Rubin, 1996). With increasing international competition,
investors and managers became concerned about the existing pact between
management and labor, which ensured a relatively high rate of return to workers,
as workers accommodated the treadmill. In part this reallocation of profits had
occurred because of rising rates of unionization, and the growing agreements
between unions and investors/managers. However, beginning in the mid-to-late
1960s, and increasingly in the 1980s and 1990s, managers began to undermine
unions. Their tactics ranged from union-busting, to mobility from unionized to
non-unionized areas within the United States (e.g. from north to south), and
then increasingly to off-shore production facilities. The state did nothing to
prevent these shifts, and indeed accepted the argument that higher corporate
profits would lead to further national economic expansion.

With the growth of global investment and production patterns in recent
decades, these anti-labor trends have accelerated sharply. Among other
indicators, there has been well over a 50% decline in union membership in the
United States, frequently and inaccurately attributed merely to changes in
the composition of the workforce, from blue collar to white collar. Yet most
de-unionization has in fact been the result of union busting campaigns
(Bluestone & Bluestone, 1994). To some extent, the earlier form of the treadmill
had followed the "high road" to development (Harrison, 1994), allowing workers
a greater share of material gains. But after the 1960s the treadmill began to
shift to the "low road", in which labor costs were to be reduced to ensure higher
profits. Arising from this shift, negative ecological and social outcomes emerged.
We noted that this shift can be attributed to a convergence of technological and
political changes that made it possible for firms to act on their historical desire
to minimize labor costs.

First, ever more of the production process shifted to energy- and chemical-intensive forms, using these elements to replace human labor and simpler machinery. Second, a smaller share of the work force was involved in the production process, much as had happened in earlier decades within agricultural production. For example, in Chicago's Ford Motor Company Plant on the city's Southeast Side, production workers were downsized from over 5000 to under 2500 in a decade. In Dearborn, Michigan's River Rouge Ford plant, the reductions were even more dramatic. Third, those workers remaining in the plants were increasingly deskilled, relying on automation for the execution of many tasks previously done by human beings (Edwards, 1979). Again, the state was passive with regard to these changes, in part because of the growing involvement by firms in campaign financing, which escalated substantially (Beeghley, 1995). Moreover, the corporate-framed ideology of modernization, "growing world competitiveness", and "free trade" rationalized these shifts as well.

Yet the state became caught in a double bind. With increasing displacement of the labor force from production, there were growing demands for social safety nets, to cushion displaced workers and their families. Under these pressures, the U.S. state moved in an uncritical fashion to further support the expansion of the treadmill, now under the rubric of "free trade." Implicit in this statement was the hope that the new accelerated treadmill would resolve the very community problems that the previous state of the treadmill had created.

"But the old communities implied safety and stability that the new corporate communities cannot offer. They provided continuity and relationships across the generations, rules that didn't change no matter how often we broke them, and leaders, trusted men and women, who had the interests of the community at heart. The continuity is gone, the rules keep changing, and somehow the downsizing captains of today's corporations are one's idea of trusted community elders" (Longworth, 1998, p. 112).

SOCIAL vs. ECOLOGICAL ELEMENTS OF THE TREADMILL

Two forms of a "treadmill" emerged in this new system. As firms made more products using more efficient technologies, they also garnered rising profits, which could be invested in still more productive technologies. This suggested a kind of *ecological treadmill*. Profits were thus invested in new technologies that would support still greater production expansion. This expansion required greater inputs (raw materials and energy) and hence greater withdrawals of natural resources. It also led to greater additions (toxic chemical pollution and other forms of liquid and solid waste). The implications of this model were that ecosystems were increasingly becoming used as sources of raw materials and as "sinks" for toxic wastes, thereby increasingly degrading ecosystems while enhancing profit levels.

A second form of the treadmill was *social*. After each cycle of production, a growing share of profits was allocated to upgrading the technological "efficiencies" of the firm. Workers (in some ways analogous to ecosystems) were helping to sow the seeds of their own displacement. By generating profits in one cycle, they would help set in motion a new level of investment in labor-saving technology, ultimately leading to their removal from the production process (Rifkin, 1995).[2] Despite these trends, some workers gained opportunities in this process, as skilled technological workers (Wellin, 1997).

Moreover, as this treadmill expanded, it created new sources of revenue for governments. Some of this revenue was used to give displaced workers social and economic compensation (e.g. income supplements and alternate employment). Thus, there were losses and some gains as the treadmill expanded, replacing earlier forms of production, natural resource utilization, and employment.

In its initial formulation, therefore, the treadmill was more than a model for ecological impacts of production. Inherent in its logic was a necessary and simultaneous shift in social relations in production, and social relations between producers and other institutions. Thus, from its inception, the treadmill's focus has been both *within the firm* and *within the society in which the firm is embedded*. This is a primary distinction between the theory of the treadmill of production and the theory of ecological modernization. Moreover, a core of this differentiation between models is the emphasis within the treadmill model of **social distributional** features. Social distributional features of the treadmill include the changing nature of the workforce, the relationship between social inequality and environmental quality, the growing autonomy of firms from control by local and national governments, and the growing dependency of governments on treadmill organizations for fiscal and political support. So for example, in recent decades, the rising tide of global investments and geographic shifting of production has intensified competitive pressures on ever more workers in industrial societies (Longworth, 1998), leading to down-sizing and increasing bifurcation of global labor forces, outsourcing of production, and a decline in real wages for more workers (Rifkin, 1995). Furthermore, ecological risks within communities and workplaces have increased markedly (Erikson, 1994), while nation-states have ceded significant policy-making authority to corporate-run global trade organizations.

In a series of recent works, we have used empirical data on recycling (Weinberg, Pellow & Schnaiberg, 2000; Pellow, Schnaiberg & Weinberg, 2000; Schnaiberg, Weinberg & Pellow, 1998), green businesses (Weinberg, 1998;

Pellow, 1999; Gould, 1999), and social movements (Pellow, 2000; Weinberg, 1997) to make sense of these changes. Considering recycling programs in the U.S., it becomes clear how the practice of substituting larger forms of physical capital for human labor had permeated every aspect of this industry. From billing and accounting, to collection, processing, labeling and shipping, the recycling industry has wholeheartedly adopted labor-saving technologies, robotics, and expert systems. The commodification of recycling also fundamentally represented a failure of the environmental movement, which had earlier emphasized its use-value potential. Additionally, the anticipated employment and revenue gains for communities and governments never materialized and when municipalities contracted with private industry, the same trends prevailed. Furthermore, despite recycling's local image, markets for post-consumer waste are much more volatile and global in scope than previously expected. This double-bind that governments face is a typical dynamic produced by the modern treadmill of production. We address this topic further in the following section.

GOVERNMENT ENVIRONMENTAL POLICIES AND THE CONSTRAINTS OF THE TREADMILL

From a conceptual perspective, we might characterize an "environmental state" as encompassing the following feature: whenever it engaged in economic decision-making, considerations of ecological impacts would have equal weight with any considerations of private sector profits and state sector taxes. Put this way, most industrialized nation-states fall far short of this standard. Indeed, it is increasingly true that any **environmental policy-making** is subject to more intensive **economic** scrutiny, while economic policies are subject to less and less environmental assessment (Daynes, 1999; Soden & Steel, 1999)[3].

One way of expanding our example of the government double-bind in recycling is to consider the broader limits to state environmental protection policies. The brief outline of the central tenets of the treadmill noted previously indicates that unlimited expansion of treadmill production is a goal of treadmill proponents. Therefore, it would appear that **any** state environmental protection is experienced as a form of **scarcity**, which limits treadmill producers from reaching their desired state of indefinite expansions of production or profits. In like manner, at first blush all **firms** embodying ecological modernization appear as countercases for the diffusion of the treadmill logic, as such firms hypothetically are equally concerned with environmental and economic goals.

Two features of the American political-economic landscape affirm the tensions inherent in state environmental policy-making. The first is that generally, treadmill organizations resist environmental regulation with all their substantial means

22   ALLAN SCHNAIBERG, DAVID N. PELLOW AND ADAM WEINBERG

at their disposal. For example, prior to the advent of recycling regulations and programs, container firms fought all forms of "bottle bills", spending perhaps U.S. $50 million opposing such bills, and succeeding in about 2/3 of the states. Yet even these bottle bills were only indirectly constraining firms. Legislation did not directly mandate a refillable container, but only the imposition of a deposit on all containers. Yet refunding mechanisms for the deposit put some cost burdens on non-refillable container manufacturers and/or users. Thus, in recent years in New York state, bottlers have refused to repurchase stockpiled refunded containers. They have let these accumulate at brokers and large retailers, seeking thereby to mobilize opposition to the bottle bill system. For the remaining 2/3 of states, container manufacturers and bottlers have simply encouraged recycling, and have kept feedstock prices low, and labor costs for refilling containers also low.

Second, where direct resistance against any environmental legislation becomes infeasible, under pressures from environmental NGOs, firms first dilute the legislation to minimize its impacts on their operations. Then they wait for opportunities to further lighten their regulatory load, whenever the political climate shifts and/or NGOs are elsewhere engaged. In the recycling arena, this has been commonplace. Affected industries have continuously shifted their campaigns to avoid mandatory direct controls on their production and distribution activities. All U.S. government regulations have avoided mandating firms with a "life cycle" responsibility for their own generation of post-consumer wastes, as has occurred in some European states. Instead, governments had introduced fairly weak mandates for firms, requiring higher "recycled content" of their production. Firms have responded by including post-production waste recycling (a standard economic practice for decades) as part of post-consumption recycling.

On a broader level, the major types of state environmental policies have been largely restricted to regulating ecological additions (pollutions of various types). They have largely avoided regulating ecological withdrawals (depletions of various ecosystems). There is some confusion over this, because American environmental legislation has also included some protection of specific ecosystems – e.g. regulating logging in national parks, in old-growth areas, for example. But even in these cases, which represent a rather small share of national and state environmental legislation, there is no prohibition of the general treadmill expansion into a variety of **other** ecosystems. That is, the most the state has done is to restrict this expansion in a small set of publicly-owned lands, to protect a limited range of ecosystems. The same is true for other legislation such as the Endangered Species Acts, which has put somewhat ineffective controls over specific habitats of a small number of particular species.

Yet is leaves unprotected all manner of national and transnational habitats to resource extraction – and even to certain "protective" extractions from delicate ecological reserves, such as oil fields in the Alaskan Reserves. Thus, in general, the state has allowed private firms to extract a great deal of ecological withdrawals on publicly-owned lands.

After spending many years analyzing political and social conflicts around environmental policies, we are nonetheless startled to realize how very limited a role the state has played in protecting natural habitats in the United States and throughout the world, especially the developing world. It sometimes appears to us that treadmill organizations and their states have accepted a tradeoff: permit firms relatively unlimited access to the world's biotic and mineral reserves, and the states are politically permitted to tinker with "end-of-pipe" controls over a limited range of pollutants, to maintain their political legitimacy with other constituents.

Treadmill organizations seem to be arguing: do not attempt to control national and global expansion of production, through limiting economic access to ecosystems, or we will undermine your agencies. Perhaps the most interesting case is in global warming, where states **appear** to be moving into the atmospheric "habitat" and restricting expansion of the treadmill. Neither the Rio UNCED ("Earth Summit") nor the Kyoto ("Climate Change") conferences have actually undermined the expansionism of the treadmill, though, especially within the United States, but also even within Europe. This is because, for the first time, national governments, under the auspices of transnational organizations such as the United Nations, having begun to consider regulations that still **indirectly** restrain treadmill expansion. And while expressions of accommodation and good will seem present, treadmill organizations are nonetheless baulking at these national and transnational efforts.

A more recent example is the President's Council on Sustainable Development (PCSD).[4] The PCSD was an effort by U.S. Vice President Al Gore to bring private sector, federal government, and NGO leaders together to move forward on an ecological modernization agenda. From 1993–1999, the PCSD was a central hub of environmental activity for the Clinton Administration. Two major reports were issued (PCSD, 1993, 1999) which outlined a vision and an action plan. This culminated in a May 1999 National Town Meeting in Detroit, where private sector and federal officials committed to implement parts of the action plan. The following observations about the PCSD are most relevant to the treadmill model:

(1) Whereas the early efforts had fairly impressive participation by the private sector, this was short-lived. For example, by 1999 the Metropolitan and

24   ALLAN SCHNAIBERG, DAVID N. PELLOW AND ADAM WEINBERG

Rural Strategies Task Force had no active private sector participation, despite being the task force charged with deal with urban and rural forms of sustainable economic development. Numerous participants commented to us that private sector representatives were initially active because they feared that the Vice President would push for a series of ecologically-motivated policies, as articulated in his book (Gore, 1992). When it became clear the PCSD would not have broad support within the administration to make sweeping changes, the private sector saw no need to continue its participation. In other words, when the threat disappeared, so did the private sector. The other side of this observation is our conclusion that the environmental movement's hope for meaningful reform from the PCSD was dependent upon the private sector's involvement. Ultimately, movement participants had no power to ensure that either the private sector or the state would participate in good faith and implement any final recommendations.

(2) The PCSD was part of Vice President Gore's *reinventing government* initiative. One early idea was to re-focus major federal policy around ecologically-sound production. There was some discussion of the possibility that the U.S.DA's Extension Service would become a sustainable development entity. Those early efforts to emancipate the environment within federal agencies met with fierce and consistent opposition. Their efforts were stymied and many of the key players moved on to other jobs.

(3) Two types of actions *have* been carried out. First, some of the action items have been implemented. However, they are primarily federal programs that required no private sector support. They are also issues that have broad political appeal. For example, "smart growth" has become a popular initiative. Following the logic of the treadmill, we note that smart growth is a weak environmental project. It has broad support from urban mayors who want reinvestment, suburban communities that want to contain congestion, and private sector actors that want the federal government to pay for their urban infrastructure needs. It is basically a gift from the federal government to powerful urban actors, who are concerned about economic and political needs.

Second, there is an coalition of federal extensions working together in a Sustainable Development Extension Service (SDEN). They are currently working on a series of innovative projects in Burlington, Vermont. However, the initial goal of revised SDEN has been reduced to a minuscule effort that exists alongside the more traditional massive extension service. Thus, even where there are innovative efforts they usually exist alongside identical programs pushing non-sustainable forms of production. One participant from a major federal agency involved in natural resource protection commented at a meeting:

"*You* take for granted that there is support for sustainable development. *I* have to go back and be able to make a strong case for these ideas. There is tremendous opposition. People are not going to just act because it seems like a good idea to protect the environment. There are a lot of other constituencies out there."

(4) Finally, we note that the term "sustainable development" has been dropped by the Vice President in the campaign in favor of the concept of *livability*. A group of major foundations had agreed in the summer of 1999 to help move forward some of the actions proposed in the last PCSD report. The initiative is called the *Livability Campaign*. The proposed Rural Sustainable Development Network is now called the *Rural Livability Project*. Our informants within the federal agencies commented that, the Administration felt that there was considerable hostility towards anything environmental (from the Republican congress especially), while there was insufficient support from any constituency powerful enough to get legislation passed or to get the Vice President elected. Hence a strong environmental agenda would most likely become an election obstacle, but was not likely to become a source of campaign strength. Thus, projects were reframed around "quality of life" issues, in hopes of attracting suburban constituencies, who are perceived to be substantially more powerful than environmentalists.

We believe that cases like the PCSD and U.S. recycling practices challenge two of the major tenets of ecological modernization theory: that the environment has been emancipated from the economic sphere, and that the environmental movement is a major political force. Neither of these claims holds up in the current U.S. administration, as environmental policy-making has continued to be written within an economic framework and where the participation of environmental organizations continues to be open to constant challenge. In a recent empirical assessment, Daynes states, "Even though it was clear that Bill Clinton was quite serious about the environment and quite unafraid to confront the most controversial issues, the 'politics of the moment' frequently interfered with the administration's environmental focus" (1999, p. 265). Daynes goes on to argue that the political opposition to anything that disrupts private sectors actors and their agendas has been too great for the administration to combat, especially in the aftermath of 1994 mid-term elections. He concludes that "the roles most commonly used (by the President to push for environmental reforms) were the roles that are traditionally the weakest" (1999, p. 300).

We find that the treadmill model has much more explanatory power with regard to the above dynamics. Specifically, the treadmill is premised on the

argument that the major motives behind environmental policy-making are economic, and that the environmental movement – which, like all social movements,
is driven by use values – is competing in a fierce struggle against powerful actors
in biased political and social arenas to get competing agendas acknowledged.

THE "ONLY" PERSPECTIVE OF THE
TREADMILL, VERSUS THE "FULLY" PERSPECTIVE
OF ECOLOGICAL MODERNIZATION

In a 1994 book (Schnaiberg & Gould), we outlined an evaluation problem that
is inherently political, and one that will perhaps help us understand the differences between the treadmill and ecological modernization theories in viewing
the modern "environmental state." Briefly put, our argument was that there are
two ways of evaluating any change in state (or firm) actions. One uses the *past*
as a guide, and sees any positive change as "fully" moving from a negative
past to a *more*-positive present. The other sees "only" a limited amount of
change, comparing the present status to a *future* goal to be desired.

From the latter perspective, the state has actively or passively permitted the
treadmill to achieve its current practices, which are inherently *un*sustainable on
both ecological and social dimensions. Unsustainability is an outcome of this
current economic and political arrangement (Schnaiberg, 1980, 1982, 1986a,
1994; Schnaiberg & Gould, 1994; Gould, Weinberg & Schnaiberg, 1993;
Weinberg, 1995; Weinberg & Gould, 1993; Gould, Schnaiberg & Weinberg,
1996; Pellow, 1994). In terms of the criterion for "the environmental state"
outlined above, it is clear that we have "only" moved in very small increments
towards this goal, of making economic considerations on a parity with ecological
protection.

Conversely, from the standpoint of some ecological modernization theorists,
firms (under pressures or encouragements from their states and NGOs) have
moved "fully" beyond their earlier dismissal of ecological costs of their
profitable activities. The firms now take **some** ecological factors into some
account in **some** of their planning and activities. Moreover, since the state has,
over the past 25 years, incorporated **some** consideration of ecological outcomes
for **some** economic policies, there has been "fully" some movement away from
a strictly *economic synthesis* of the societal-environmental dialectic (Schnaiberg,
1980, Schnaiberg & Gould, 1994).

Tacitly or explicitly, some of these arguments by ecological modernization
theorists seem to suggest that, if this ecological modernization is permitted to
continue, we will achieve some ideal sustainable end-state. But, they argue, this
will occur through processes of supra-industrialization, not through processes

of de-industrialization (as might be shared by some theorists of the treadmill such as us). And states should encourage these forms of super-industrialization, to delink natural resources form economic development.

We will close with some difficulties we observe with projecting this end-state from the evidence accumulating from ecological modernization analyses.

CONCLUSION: WHY THE TREADMILL SEES ECOLOGICAL MODERNIZATION AS ONLY A SMALL CHANGE IN THE ECONOMIC STATE

Our analysis of the role of the state within the treadmill stresses the typical practices of economic organizations, their autonomy relative to the state, and their regulation by the state. Governments have (until the recent growth spurt) been increasingly restricted by policies promulgated by coalitions driven by reproducing the treadmill. As a result, ever more profitable corporations are now "generously" endowing local governments, schools and universities, and public broadcasting with "public support" ranging from motor vehicles to environmental curriculum. And also as a result, government regulation is increasingly curtailed around many environmental policies.

For example, Weinberg (1994) presented findings about how weakly the Illinois government supported citizen access to toxic substance data that the state collected under the Community Right to Know provisions of the Superfund Amendments and Reauthorization Act of 1986. Attending the session was a sociologist who worked for the Illinois Environmental Protection Agency – who affirmed Weinberg's findings. Moreover, he noted that, although the agency was mandated to receive these corporate toxic waste inventory statements, there were no personnel assigned to do anything to help communities get access to and understand these technical documents. Since firms understood this *de facto* unregulated situation, they were under few constraints in preparing these documents, and relatively few constraints in handling their toxic waste by-products. Thus, Kirsch finds in his work in Massachusetts that "establishing the State Department of Environmental Quality Engineering had the opposite effect of its creators' intentions. Instead of providing an umbrella that could monitor industrial effects on the environment, the agency tied up complaints regarding potential hazards. . . . There was no direct monitoring of the environment" (1998, pp. 108–109).

Why do our treadmill analyses seem to differ so broadly from those of ecological modernists? Part of the answer is a methodological one – the differences lie in: (1) sampling approaches, and (2) projections for future change. We will touch on these next.

28   ALLAN SCHNAIBERG, DAVID N. PELLOW AND ADAM WEINBERG

Sampling Differences

The tendency for EM theorists is to sample "best practice" industries. This makes sense given the research orientation, which is to look for change and try to theorize the processes and significance. However, it makes it hard to distinguish between an "epidemic of reports" and a "report of an epidemic" of EM transformations. We experienced a similar example of purported innovations in community energy policies while serving on a National Research Council panel (Stern & Aronson, 1984). The panel was initially informed about "hundreds of communities" that had innovated to reduce energy use after the "oil crises" of the 1970s. Later, we discovered that there had only been two such communities – Davis, California, and Seattle, Washington – but that their "success" generated *hundreds* of media and scientific reports. Ironically, even for these two communities, there had been little evaluation of how these changes affected social distributional features of the cities.

This gives us further pause when we consider that EM may actually be a substitute for governmental attention to *other* dimensions of sustainable development – e.g. corporate innovations may have been paid for by regressive taxes on employees and/or communities in which the companies are embedded. Numerous public sector and private sector conferences are organized and task forces convened to extol the increased "greening" of production. But such developments are more cost-effective than capital-intensive changes of production technologies, and still cheaper than maintaining both social equity and environmental protection, as sustainable development practices are intended to do. Our experiences with the President's Council for Sustainable Development affirm this. While the participants were actively engaged in seeking sustainable development, the Council itself was a political shadow play, designed in part to boost the visibility of the Vice-President and presidential candidate Albert Gore – and it is now defunct.

Furthermore, the units being sampled may be inappropriate for the broader inferences of ecological modernization. For example, the apparent "decoupling" of economic development from energy consumption and other natural resource inputs may be misleading. The relocation of ever more industrial production abroad under globalization, while retaining profits in industrial countries, may separate ecological and economic outcomes of firms as **geographic networks** of production.

Moreover, firms may be increasingly outsourcing much of the negative aspects of production. Firms may have different roles within **commodity chains**, in which material transformations are tracked from initial ecological resources to final products and wastes. Thus, for example, recycling programs in cities are actually the outcomes of decisions made by container producers, consumer product manufacturers, and their trade associations.

Projections of Future Changes – The Negative

In some ways, EM examines the "cutting edge" of changes in corporate structure. It assumes that these changes will eventually diffuse into other corporate entities and actions. But instead, EM cases may simply represent a "creaming" of a program of ecological incorporation into production practices. This concept arose in projecting early rates of success in public programs. Initially, many innovative public programs have a high and positive selection rate. But this means that the early period has "creamed" or culled from the potential population of adopters. The remainder of the population has been negatively selected, to eschew the program. Thus, the early adoption rates will not be sustained by later groups encountering the program. Indeed, it is not yet clear whether enough time has elapsed so that EM cases have had a time series of evaluations, to examine whether early changes in the same firms had been institutionalized, in changing market conditions. Our recycling study was carried out in that arena of change, precisely because at least a decade had elapsed since communities had been incorporating recycling practices. Thus we could see whether these changes, even if once **attained**, could be **sustained**. And indeed, we found that many were not sustained even for a decade (Weinberg, Pellow & Schnaiberg, 2000).

Projections of Future Changes – The Positive

Even where we find change, we believe the treadmill to be a more persuasive model of the political economy of environmental problems and protection. Firms continue to push for higher profit margins to the neglect of both social equity and ecological concerns. Those firms that do make ecological improvements fall into one or more of the following categories: (1) firms were forced by regulation or social movement action to make improvements; (2) they made improvements only when their economic bottom line would be secure; or (3) they achieved the *appearance* of improvements through "creative accounting" or misreporting. Ecological modernization theorists tend to view such "improvements" as evidence that environmentalists are a powerful 'third force' in negotiating these changes (Mol, 2002), and as part of a trajectory toward an end state of sustainability. We challenge both of these claims. We find that economic criteria remain at the *foundation* of decision making processes. Further, the state also shares this orientation, despite its own political

30   ALLAN SCHNAIBERG, DAVID N. PELLOW AND ADAM WEINBERG

interests, and often cedes a great deal of power to private sector actors. Thus, we believe that political economy models in general, and the Treadmill in particular, continue to have strong explanatory power with their starting assumptions on conflict and politics, and the general dynamics of capitalism.

NOTES

1. Schnaiberg's earliest work (1973) delved into the components of the "environmental movement." He identified four different forms of environmental groups: cosmetologists, meliorists, reformers, and radicals. Each of the groups perceived the causes of environmental problems in quite different ways. The groups also differed in their views of the severity of environmental problems Thus, they offered quite different remedies for *environmental protection*.

2. There is an emerging case study literature on this topic, as it played itself out in the United States in the 1970s and 1980s. Thus, Dudley (1994) documents how Chrysler closed its Kenosha plant, even when workers had the highest productivity rate of any facility, so that jobs could be transferred to higher technology facilities that required fewer workers. Wellin's (1997) study was a particularly informative ethnography of a food manufacturer undergoing automation. Workers shared their special knowledge of intricate production processes with management, with a promise that they would share in the increased profits associated with rising productivity. At the end of this cycle, a small share of workers did indeed gain new positions in the control of operations, but the bulk of workers found themselves in more deskilled positions, with a net loss of status (see also Besser, 1996; Kirsch, 1998).

3. This was clearly true under Reagan and Bush, who had a Council on Competitiveness to ensure that no policy would negatively impact economic opportunities (Daynes, 1999). Under Clinton, many environmentalists assumed this would change. The Council was abolished by Executive Order. However, economic criteria have continued to dominate policy decesions. Even the Council on Environmental Quality (CEQ), which was suppose to be one of the main vechiles to role back the Reagan assault has "continue(d) to decline and its role in policy making is minimal at best" (Soden & Steel, 1999, p. 332).

4. Two of the authors (Weinberg and Pellow) were active in the PCSD, serving as Task Force members. Additionally, Weinberg helped prepare papers, meetings, and reports. The information in this paper derives from their experiences with the PCSD.

REFERENCES

Beeghley, L. (1996). *The Structure of Social Stratification in the United States* (2nd ed.). Boston: Allyn & Bacon.

Bluestone, B., & Bluestone, I. (1994). *Negotiating the Future: a Labor Perspective on American Business.* New York: Basic Books.

Daynes, B. (1999). Bill Clinton: The environmental presidency. In: D. Soden (Ed.), *The Environmental Presidency.* Albany, NY: SUNY Press.

Dudley, K. M. (1994). *The End of the Line. Lost Jobs, New Lives in Post-industrial America.* Chicago: University of Chicago Press.

Edwards, R. (1979). *Contested Terrain: The Transformation of the Workplace in the Twentieth Century.* New York: Basic Books.

Erikson, K. (1994). *A New Species of Trouble.* New York: W. W. Norton.

Gordon, D. (1996). *Fat and Mean: The Corporate Squeeze of Working Americans and the Myth of Managerial "Downsizing".* New York: The Free Press.

Gore, A. (1992). *Earth in the Balance.* Boston: Houghton Mifflin.

Gould, K. (1991). The sweet smell of money: Economic dependence and local environmental political mobilization. *Society and Natural Resources, 4,* 133–150.

Gould, K. (1992). Putting the (w)r.a.p.s on public participation: Remedial action planning and working-class power in the Great Lakes. *Sociological Practice Review 3*(3), 133–139.

Gould, K. (1993). Pollution and perception: social visiability and local environmental mobilization. *Qualitative Sociology, 16*(2), 157–178.

Gould, K., Weinberg, A. S., & Schnaiberg, A. (1995). Natural resource use in a transnational treadmill: International agreements, national citizenship practices, and sustainable development. *Humboldt Journal of Social Relations, 21,* 61–93.

Gould, K., Weinberg, A., & Schnaiberg, A. (1993). Legitimating impotence: Pyrrhic victories of the environmental movement. *Qualitative Sociology, 16,* 207–246.

Gould, K., Schnaiberg, A., & Weinberg, A. (1996). *Local Environmental Struggles: Citizen Activism in the Treadmill of Production.* New York: Cambridge University Press.

Harrison, B. (1994). *Lean and Mean: The Changing Landscape of Corporate Power in the Age of Flexibility.* New York: Basic Books.

Kirsch, M. (1998). *In the Wake of the Giant: Multinational Restructuring and Uneven Development in a New England Community.* Albany, NY: SUNY Press.

Longworth, R. (1998). *Global Squeeze: The Coming Crisis for First-world Nations.* Chicago: Contemporary Books.

Mol, A. P. J. (1995). *The Refinement of Production: Ecological Modernisation Theory and the Chemical Industry.* Utrecht: van Arkel.

Mol, A. P. J. (2002). *Ecological modernisation and the environmental state* (this volume).

Pellow, D. (1994). Environmental justice and popular epidemiology: Symbolic politics, hidden transcripts. Paper Presented at the Annual meetings of the American Sociological Association. Los Angeles, CA. August.

Pellow, D. (1998). Bodies on the line: Environmental inequalities and hazardous work in the U.S. recycling industry. *Race, Gender & Class, 6,* 124–151.

Pellow, D. (1999). Framing emerging environmental movement tactics: mobilizing consensus, de-mobilizing conflict. *Sociological Forum, 14,* 659–683.

Pellow, D. (2000). Putting the ecological modernisation thesis to the test: Accounting for recycling's promises and performance. *Environmental Politics,* forthcoming.

Pellow, D., Schnaiberg, A., & Weinberg, A. S. (1995). Pragmatic corporate cultures: Insights from a recycling enterprise. *Green Management International, 12,* 95–110.

President's Council on Sustainable Development (1994). *Education for Sustainability.* Washington, D.C.: United States Government Printing Office.

President's Council on Sustainable Development (1999). *Towards a Sustainable America: Advancing Prosperity, Opportunity, and a Healthy Environment for the 21st Century.* Washington, D.C.: United States Government Printing Office.

Reich, R. (1991). *The Work of Nations: Preparing Ourselves for 21st Century Capitalism.* New York: Knopf.

Rifkin, J. (1995). *The End of Work: The Decline of the Global Labor Force and the Dawn of the Post-market Era.* New York: G. P. Putnam's Sons.

Rubin, B. A. (1996). *Shifts in the Social Contract: Understanding Change in American Society.* Thousand Oaks, CA: Pine Forge Press.

Schnaiberg, A. (1980). *The Environment: From Surplus to Scarcity.* New York: Oxford University Press.

Schnaiberg, A. (1982). Did you ever meet a payroll? Contradictions in the structure of the appropriate technology movement. *Humboldt Journal of Social Relations, 9,* 38–62.

Schnaiberg, A. (1994). The political economy of environmental problems and policies: Consciousmness, conflict, and control capacity. In: L. Freese (Ed.), *Advances in Human Ecology* (Vol. 3, pp. 23–64). Greenwich, CT: JAI Press.

Schnaiberg, A., & Gould, K.. (2000 [1994]). *Environment and Society: The Enduring Conflict.* West Caldwell, New Jersey: Blackburn Press.

Schnaiberg, A., Weinberg, A. S., & Pellow, D. N. (1998). Politizando la rueda de produccion: Los programmas de reciclaje de residuos solidas en Estados Unidos. [Politicizing the treadmill of production: Reshaping social outcomes of efficient recycling.] *Revista Internacional de Sociología,* 19–20 (January-August), 181–222.

Soden, D., & Steel, B. (1999). Evaluating the environmental presidency. In: D. Soden (Ed.), *The Environmental Presidency.* Albany, NY: SUNY Press.

Spaargaren, G., & Mol, A. P. J. (1992). Sociology, environment, and modernity: Ecological modernisation as a theory of social change. *Society and Natural Resources, 5*(4), 323–344.

Stern, P., & Aronson, E. (Eds) (1984). *Energy Use: The Human Dimension.* New York: W. H. Freeman.

Weinberg, A. (1997a). Local organizing for environmental conflict: Explaining differences between cases of participation and non-participation. *Organization and Environment, 10*(2), 194–216.

Weinberg, A. (1997b). Power and public policy: Community right-to-know and the empowerment of people, places, and producers. *Humanity and Society, 21,* 240–257.

Weinberg, A. (1998). Distinguishing among green businesses: Growth, green and anomie. *Society and Natural Resources, 11,* 241–250.

Weinberg, A. (1994). Citizenship and natural resources: From rights in theory to rights in practice. Paper presented at the annual meetings of the American Sociological Association. Los Angeles, CA. August.

Weinberg, A., & Gould, K. (1993). Public participation in environmental regulatory conflicts: treading through the possibilities and pitfalls. *Law and Policy, 15,* 139–167.

Weinberg, A., Schnaiberg, A., & Pellow, D. (1996). Sustainable development as a sociologically defensible concept: From foxes and rovers to citizens. In: L. Freese (Ed.), *Advances in Human Ecology* (Vol. 5, pp. 261–302). Greenwich, CT: JAI Press.

Weinberg, A., Schnaiberg, A., & Gould, K. A. (1995). Recycling: Conserving resources or accelerating the treadmill of production? In: L. Freese (Ed.), *Advances in Human Ecology* (Vol. 4, pp. 173–205). Greenwich, CT: JAI Press.

[4]

Marx's Theory of Metabolic Rift: Classical Foundations for Environmental Sociology[1]

John Bellamy Foster
University of Oregon

This article addresses a paradox: on the one hand, environmental sociology, as currently developed, is closely associated with the thesis that the classical sociological tradition is devoid of systematic insights into environmental problems; on the other hand, evidence of crucial classical contributions in this area, particularly in Marx, but also in Weber, Durkheim, and others, is too abundant to be convincingly denied. The nature of this paradox, its origins, and the means of transcending it are illustrated primarily through an analysis of Marx's theory of metabolic rift, which, it is contended, offers important classical foundations for environmental sociology.

CLASSICAL BARRIERS TO ENVIRONMENTAL SOCIOLOGY

In recent decades, we have witnessed a significant transformation in social thought as various disciplines have sought to incorporate ecological awareness into their core paradigms in response to the challenge raised by environmentalism and by what is now widely perceived as a global ecological crisis. This transformation has involved a twofold process of rejecting much of previous thought as ecologically unsound, together with an attempt to build on the past, where possible. This can be seen as occurring with unequal degrees of success in the various disciplines. Geography, with its long history of focusing on the development of the natural landscape and on biogeography (see Sauer 1963), was the social science that adapted most easily to growing environmental concerns. Anthropol-

[1] I would like to express my gratitude to Joan Acker, Paul Burkett, Michael Dawson, Michael Dreiling, Charles Hunt, John Jermier, Robert McChesney, Fred Magdoff, Harry Magdoff, John Mage, David Milton, Robert O'Brien, Christopher Phelps, Ira Shapiro, Paul Sweezy, Laura Tamkin, and Ellen Meiksins Wood for creating a climate of intellectual exchange and support without which this work would not have been possible. I would also like to express my gratitude to the *AJS* reviewers, all of whom contributed in positive ways to this article. Direct correspondence to John Bellamy Foster, Department of Sociology, University of Oregon, Eugene, Oregon 97403. E-mail: jfoster@oregon.uoregon.edu

Environmental Sociology

ogy, with a tradition of investigating cultural survival and its relation to ecological conditions (see Geertz 1963; Milton 1996), also adjusted quickly to a period of greater environmental awareness. In other social science disciplines, significant progress in incorporating ecological ideas has been made, yet with less discernible effect on the core understandings of these fields. Economics, which was able to draw on the theoretical foundations provided by A. C. Pigou's *Economics of Welfare* (1920), has seen the rapid development of a distinctive, if limited, approach to environmental issues focusing on the internalization of "externalities"—making "environmental economics . . . one of the fastest-growing academic sub-disciplines throughout the industrial world" (Jacobs 1994, p. 67). As a relatively atheoretical field, political science has had little difficulty in incorporating environmental issues into its analysis of public policy, its focus on pluralist interest groups, its social contract theory, and more recently its emphasis on rational choice (Dryzek 1997)—though the pragmatic character of most political science in the United States, together with the lack of a strong Green political party and the absence of a clear connection between identification with environmental causes and voting behavior, has kept the politics of the environment on the margins of the discipline.

In sociology too, dramatic progress has been made, as seen by the rapid growth of the subfield of environmental sociology in the 1970s and again (after a period of quiescence) in the late 1980s and 1990s (see Dunlap 1997). Nevertheless, sociology is perhaps unique within the social sciences in the degree of resistance to environmental issues. An early barrier erected between society and nature, sociology and biology—dividing the classical sociologies of Marx, Weber, and Durkheim from the biological and naturalistic concerns that played a central role in the preclassical sociology of the social Darwinists—has hindered the incorporation of environmental sociology within the mainstream of the discipline, according to an interpretation repeatedly voiced by prominent environmental sociologists over the last two and a half decades (Burch 1971, pp. 14–20; Dunlap and Catton 1979, pp. 58–59; Benton 1994, pp. 28–30; Murphy 1994, pp. ix–x; Beck 1995, pp. 117–20; Buttel 1996, pp. 57–58; Murphy 1996).

Hence, until recently "there has . . . been general agreement among environmental sociologists that the classical sociological tradition has been inhospitable to the nurturing of ecologically-informed sociological theory" (Buttel 1986, p. 338). "From an environmental-sociological point of view," Buttel (1996, p. 57) has argued, "the classical tradition can be said to be 'radically sociological,' in that in their quest to liberate social thought and sociology from reductionisms, prejudices, power relations, and magic, the classical theorists (and, arguably more so, the 20th century interpreters of the classical tradition) wound up exaggerating the auton-

American Journal of Sociology

omy of social processes from the natural world." Likewise, Benton (1994, p. 29) has observed that "the conceptual structure or 'disciplinary matrix' by which sociology came to define itself, especially in relation to potentially competing disciplines such as biology and psychology, effectively excluded or forced to the margins of the discipline questions about the relations between society and its 'natural' or 'material' substrate." "Sociology," according to one prominent environmental sociologist, "was constructed as if nature didn't matter" (Murphy 1996, p. 10). Such marginalization of the physical environment was made possible, in part, through the enormous economic and technological successes of the industrial revolution, which have long given the impression that human society is independent of its natural environment (Dunlap and Martin 1983, pp. 202–3). This is seen as offering an explanation for the fact that "sociological work on resource scarcity never appeared in the discipline's top journals" in the United States (Dunlap 1997, p. 23; also Dunlap and Catton 1994, p. 8).

Modern sociology in its classical period, according to the prevailing outlook within environmental sociology, was consolidated around a humanistic worldview that emphasized human distinctiveness in relation to nature. This has been referred to by some as the old "human exemptionalist paradigm" in contrast to the "new environmental paradigm," which rejects the anthropocentrism supposedly characteristic of the former view (Catton and Dunlap 1978; Dunlap and Catton 1994). With respect to Durkheim, for example, it has been argued that the social constituted a distinct reality, relatively autonomous from the physical individual and from psychological and biological pressures (Benton and Redclift 1994, p. 3; Dunlap and Catton 1979, p. 58). "The thrust of Durkheim's and Weber's methodological arguments," according to Goldblatt (1996, p. 3), "was to cordon off sociology from biology and nature, rejecting "all forms of biological determinism"; while Marx's treatment of such issues, though considerable, was largely confined to the "marginal" realm of agricultural economics.

In the language of contemporary environmentalism, then, sociology is a discipline that is "anthropocentric" in orientation, allowing little room for consideration of society's relation to nature, much less the thoroughgoing "ecocentrism" proposed by many environmentalists. It is rooted in a "socio-cultural determinism" that effectively excludes ecological issues (Dunlap and Martin 1983, p. 204). For Dunlap and Catton (1994, p. 6), sociology needs to shed "the 'blinders' imposed by [human] exceptionalism" and to acknowledge "the ecosystem dependence of all human societies."

One result of this problem of theoretical dissonance is that environmental sociology, despite important innovations, has continued to have only a

Environmental Sociology

marginal role within the discipline as a whole. Although an environmental sociology section of the American Sociological Association was launched in 1976, it did not have the paradigm-shifting effect on sociology that leading figures in the section expected. Neither was sociology as a whole much affected by the rise of environmental sociology, nor did environmental issues gain much notice within the profession. As one leading practitioner of environmental sociology observed in 1987, "The discipline at large has handily withstood the challenges to its theoretical assumptions posed by environmental sociologists" (Buttel 1987, p. 466).

Where the core sociological discipline has been most ready to acknowledge environmental issues is in the area of environmental movements. There the literature has rapidly expanded in recent years through the growth of the environmental justice movement, concerned with the impact of environmental degradation on distinct sociological groupings, conceived in terms of race, class, gender, and international hierarchy. But this literature owes much more to social movement theory than to the environmentalist challenge to traditional sociological conceptions.

One way in which environmental sociologists have sought to address this problem of what are generally perceived as barriers within classical sociology to any consideration of the physical environment is by reaching out to the preclassical social Darwinist tradition: thinkers such as Malthus and Sumner (Catton 1982). Recently, however, there has been a great deal of research within environmental sociology directed not at circumventing the main classical sociological theorists but at unearthing alternative foundations within the classical literature, neglected in later interpretations. For example, an impressive attempt has been made by Murphy (1994) to establish a neo-Weberian sociology by applying Weber's critique of rationalization to the ecological realm and developing an "ecology of social action." Järvikoski (1996) has argued that we should reject the view that Durkheim simply neglected nature, choosing to address instead Durkheim's social constructionism with respect to nature, while examining how society fit within the hierarchical conception of nature that he generally envisioned. Others have stressed Durkheim's use of biological analogies and the demographic basis that he gave to his social morphology of the division of labor and urbanism, which seemed to foreshadow the urban-oriented human ecology of Park and other Chicago sociologists (Buttel 1986, pp. 341–42). The most dramatic growth of literature in relation to classical sociology, however, has centered on Marx's ecological contributions, which were more extensive than in the other classical theorists, and which have spawned a vast and many-sided international debate, encompassing all stages of Marx's work (e.g., Schmidt 1971; Parsons 1977; Giddens 1981; Redclift 1984; Clark 1989; Benton 1989; McLaughlin 1990;

369

American Journal of Sociology

Mayumi 1991; Grundmann 1991; Eckersley 1992; Perelman 1993; Hayward 1994; Harvey 1996; Burkett 1997; Foster 1997; Dickens 1997; O'Connor 1998).

Significantly, this growing literature on the relation of classical sociological theorists to environmental analysis has caused some of the original critics of classical sociology within environmental sociology to soften their criticisms. Buttel, one of the founders of the subdiscipline, has gone so far as to suggest that, despite all of their deficiencies in this respect, "a meaningful environmental sociology can be fashioned from the works of the three classical theorists" (1986, pp. 340–41). We now know, for example, that Weber, writing as early as 1909 in his critique of Wilhelm Ostwald's social energetics, demonstrated some concern over the continued availability of scarce natural resources and anticipated the ecological economist Georgescu-Roegen in arguing that the entropy law applied to materials as well as energy (Martinez-Alier 1987, pp. 183–92). Durkheim's analysis of the implications of Darwinian evolutionary theory—as we shall see below—pointed toward a complex, coevolutionary perspective. Nevertheless, the widespread impression of rigid classical barriers to environmental sociology continues to exert its influence on most environmental sociologists, leaving them somewhat in the state of the mythical centaur, with the head of one creature and the body of another, unable fully to reconcile their theoretical commitment to classical sociology with their environmental sociology, which demands that an emphasis be placed on the relations between society and the natural environment.

The following will focus on addressing the seemingly paradoxical relation of classical sociological theory and environmental sociology by centering on the work of Marx, while referring only tangentially to the cases of Weber and Durkheim. It will be argued that neglected but crucial elements within Marx's social theory offer firm foundations for the development of a strong environmental sociology. In contrast to most treatments of Marx's ecological writings, emphasis will be placed not on his early philosophical works but rather on his later political economy. It is in the latter that Marx provided his systematic treatment of such issues as soil fertility, organic recycling, and sustainability in response to the investigations of the great German chemist Justus von Liebig—and in which we find the larger conceptual framework, emphasizing the metabolic rift between human production and its natural conditions.[2]

It may seem ironic, given Marx's peculiar dual status as an insider-founder and outsider-critic of classical sociology (not to mention his repu-

[2] The issue of sustainability, or the notion that basic ecological conditions need to be maintained so that the ability of future generations to fulfill their needs will not be compromised, is the leitmotif of most contemporary environmental thought.

Environmental Sociology

tation in some quarters as an enemy of nature), to turn to him in order
to help rescue sociology from the embarrassing dilemma of having paid
insufficient attention to the relation between nature and human society.
Yet, the discovery or rediscovery of previously neglected features of
Marx's vast intellectual corpus has served in the past to revitalize sociology in relation to such critical issues as alienation, the labor process, and,
more recently, globalization. The irony may seem less, in fact, when one
considers that there already exists "a vast neo-Marxist literature in environmental sociology, and [that] there are few other areas of sociology today that remain so strongly influenced by Marxism" (Buttel 1996, p. 61).

In constructing this argument around Marx, an attempt will be made
to comment more broadly on the paradox of the existence—as we are now
discovering—of a rich body of material on environmental issues within
classical sociological theory, on the one hand, and the widespread perception that the classical tradition excluded any serious consideration of these
issues, and itself constitutes a barrier inhibiting the development of environmental sociology, on the other. Here two hypotheses will be advanced
arising out of the treatment of Marx. First, the apparent blindness of classical sociological theory to ecological issues is partly a manifestation of
the way classical sociology was appropriated in the late 20th century. This
can be viewed as *the appropriation problem.* Second, environmental sociology's critique of classical traditions has itself often been rooted in an
overly restrictive conception of what constitutes environmental theorizing, reducing it to a narrow "dark green" perspective (as exemplified by
the deep ecology tradition).[3] This can be thought of as *the definitional
problem.*

THE DEBATE ON MARX AND THE ENVIRONMENT

It is a sign of the growing influence of environmental issues that in recent
years numerous thinkers, from Plato to Gandhi, have had their work re-
evaluated in relation to ecological analysis. Yet it is in relation to Marx's
work that the largest and most controversial body of literature can be
found, far overshadowing the debate over all other thinkers. This literature (insofar as it takes environmental issues seriously) has fallen into four
camps: (1) those who contend that Marx's thought was antiecological from

---

[3] Environmentalists sometimes use the terms "dark green" and "light green" to refer
to the same division as that between "deep ecology" and so-called "shallow ecology."
In both cases, the nature of the distinction is the same: between what is thought of
as an "anthropocentric" perspective versus a more "ecocentric" one—though such distinctions are notoriously difficult to define. For a sympathetic account of deep ecology,
see McLaughlin (1993).

371

beginning to end and indistinguishable from Soviet practice (Clark 1989; Ferkiss 1993); (2) those who claim that Marx provided illuminating insights into ecology but ultimately succumbed to "Prometheanism" (protechnological, antiecological views)—a corollary being that he believed that environmental problems would be eliminated as a result of the "abundance" that would characterize postcapitalist society (Giddens 1981; Nove 1987; Redclift 1984; Benton 1989; McLaughlin 1990; Eckersley 1992; Deléage 1994; Goldblatt 1996); (3) those who argue that Marx provided an analysis of ecological degradation within agriculture, which remained, however, segregated off from his core social analysis (O'Connor 1998); and (4) those who insist that Marx developed a systematic approach to nature and to environmental degradation (particularly in relation to the fertility of the soil) that was intricately bound to the rest of his thought and raised the question of ecological sustainability (Parsons 1977; Perelman 1993; Mayumi 1991; Lebowitz 1992; Altvater 1993; Foster 1997; Burkett 1997).

Some of the sharpest criticisms of Marx from an environmentalist standpoint have come from leading sociologists (both non-Marxist and Marxist), particularly in Britain. Giddens (1981, p. 60) has contended that Marx, although demonstrating considerable ecological sensitivity in his earliest writings, later adopted a "Promethean attitude" toward nature. Marx's "concern with transforming the exploitative human social relations expressed in class systems does not extend," Giddens writes, "to the exploitation of nature" (1981, p. 59). Similarly, Redclift (1984, p. 7) has observed that for Marx the environment served "an enabling function but all value was derived from labor power. It was impossible to conceive of a 'natural' limit to the material productive forces of society. The barriers that existed to the full realization of resource potential were imposed by property relations and legal obligations rather than resource endowments." More recently, Redclift and Woodgate (1994, p. 53) have added that, "while Marx considered our relations with the environment as essentially social, he also regarded them as ubiquitous and unchanging, common to each phase of social existence. Hence, for Marx, the relationship between people and nature cannot provide a source of change in society. . . . Such a perspective does not fully acknowledge the role of technology, and its effects on the environment." Finally, Nove (1987, p. 399) has contended that Marx believed that "the problem of production had been 'solved'" by capitalism and that the future society of associated producers therefore would not have "to take seriously the problem of the allocation of scarce resources," which meant that there was no need for an "ecologically conscious" socialism.

Marx thus stands accused of wearing *blinders* in relation to the following: (1) the exploitation of nature, (2) nature's role in the creation of value,

(3) the existence of distinct natural limits, (4) nature's changing character and the impact of this on human society, (5) the role of technology in environmental degradation, and (6) the inability of mere economic abundance to solve environmental problems. If these criticisms were valid, Marx's work could be expected to offer no significant insights into problems of ecological crisis and indeed would itself constitute a major obstacle to the understanding of environmental problems.

In contrast, an attempt will be made to demonstrate here, in the context of a systematic reconstruction of Marx's theory of metabolic rift, that these ecological blinders are not in fact present in Marx's thought—and that each of the problems listed above were addressed to some extent in his theory. Of more significance, it will be contended that Marx provided a powerful analysis of the main ecological crisis of his day—the problem of soil fertility within capitalist agriculture—as well as commenting on the other major ecological crises of his time (the loss of forests, the pollution of the cities, and the Malthusian specter of overpopulation). In doing so, he raised fundamental issues about the antagonism of town and country, the necessity of ecological sustainability, and what he called the "metabolic" relation between human beings and nature. In his theory of metabolic rift and his response to Darwinian evolutionary theory, Marx went a considerable way toward a historical-environmental-materialism that took into account the coevolution of nature and human society.

MARX AND THE SECOND AGRICULTURAL REVOLUTION: THE METABOLIC RIFT

The Concept of the Second Agricultural Revolution

Although it is still common for historians to refer to a single agricultural revolution that took place in Britain in the 17th and 18th centuries and that laid the foundation for the industrial revolution that followed, agricultural historians commonly refer to a second and even a third agricultural revolution. The first agricultural revolution was a gradual process occurring over several centuries, associated with the enclosures and the growing centrality of market relations; technical changes included improved techniques of crop rotation, manuring, drainage, and livestock management. In contrast, the second agricultural revolution (Thompson 1968) occurred over a shorter period (1830–80) and was characterized by the growth of a fertilizer industry and a revolution in soil chemistry, associated in particular with the work of the great German agricultural chemist Justus von Liebig.[4] The third agricultural revolution was to occur still

---

[4] Thompson (1968) designates the second agricultural revolution as occurring over the years 1815–80, that is, commencing with the agricultural crisis that immediately followed the Napoleonic Wars. I have narrowed the period down to 1830–80 here in

American Journal of Sociology

later, in the 20th century, and involved the replacement of animal traction with machine traction on the farm and the eventual concentration of animals in massive feedlots, together with the genetic alteration of plants (resulting in narrower monocultures) and the more intensive use of chemical inputs—such as fertilizers and pesticides.

Marx's critique of capitalist agriculture and his main contributions to ecological thought have to be understood in relation to the second agricultural revolution occurring in his time. For Marx, writing in *Capital* in the 1860s, there was a gulf separating the treatment of agricultural productivity and soil fertility in the work of classical economists like Malthus and Ricardo, and the understanding of these problems in his own day. In Marx's ([1863–65] 1981, pp. 915–16) words, "The actual causes of the exhaustion of the land . . . were unknown to any of the economists who wrote about differential rent, on account of the state of agricultural chemistry in their time."

The source of the differential fertility from which rent was derived was, in the work of Malthus and Ricardo in the opening decades of the 19th century, attributed almost entirely to the natural or absolute productivity of the soil—with agricultural improvement (or degradation) playing only a marginal role. As Ricardo (1951, p. 67) observed, rent could be defined as "that portion of the produce of the earth, which is paid to the landlord for the use of the original and indestructible powers of the soil." These thinkers argued—with the presumed backing of natural law—that lands that were naturally the most fertile were the first to be brought into production and that rising rent on these lands and decreasing agricultural productivity overall were the result of lands of more and more marginal fertility being brought into cultivation, in response to increasing demographic pressures. Further, while some agricultural improvement was possible, it was quite limited, since the increases in productivity to be derived from successive applications of capital and labor to any given plot of land were said to be of diminishing character, thereby helping to account for the slowdown in growth of productivity in agriculture. All of this pointed to the Malthusian dilemma of a tendency of population to outgrow food supply—a tendency only countered as a result of vice and misery that served to lower fecundity and increase mortality, as Malthus emphasized in his original essay on population, or through possible moral restraint, as he was to add in later editions of that work.

order to distinguish between the crisis that to some extent preceded the second agricultural revolution and the revolution proper, for which the turning point was the publication of Liebig's *Organic Chemistry* in 1840 followed by J. B. Lawes's building of the first factory for the production of synthetic fertilizer (superphosphates) a few years later.

374

Environmental Sociology

Classical Marxism, in contrast, relied from the beginning on the fact that rapid historical improvement in soil fertility was possible, though not inevitable, given existing social relations. In his "Outlines of a Critique of Political Economy," published in 1844, a young Friedrich Engels was to point to revolutions in science and particularly soil chemistry—singling out the discoveries of such figures as Humphry Davy and Liebig—as constituting the main reason why Malthus and Ricardo would be proven wrong about the possibilities for rapidly improving the fertility of the soil and thereby promoting a favorable relation between the growth of food and the growth of population. Engels (1964, pp. 208–10) went on to observe that, "To make earth an object of huckstering—the earth which is our one and all, the first condition of our existence—was the last step toward making oneself an object of huckstering." Three years later in *The Poverty of Philosophy,* Marx (1963, pp. 162–63) wrote that at "every moment the modern application of chemistry is changing the nature of the soil, and geological knowledge is just now, in our days, beginning to revolutionize all the old estimates of relative fertility. . . . Fertility is not so natural a quality as might be thought; it is closely bound up with the social relations of the time."

This emphasis on historical changes in soil fertility in the direction of agricultural improvement was to be a continuing theme in Marx's thought, though it eventually came to be coupled with an understanding of how capitalist agriculture could undermine the conditions of soil fertility, resulting in soil degradation rather than improvement. Thus in his later writings, increasing emphasis came to be placed on the exploitation of the earth in the sense of the failure to sustain the conditions of its reproduction.

Liebig and the Depletion of the Soil

During 1830–70 the depletion of soil fertility through the loss of soil nutrients was the overriding environmental concern of capitalist society in both Europe and North America, comparable only to concerns over the growing pollution of the cities, deforestation of whole continents, and the Malthusian fears of overpopulation (Foster 1997; O'Connor 1998, p. 3). In the 1820s and 1830s in Britain, and shortly afterward in the other developing capitalist economies of Europe and North America, widespread concerns about "soil exhaustion" led to a phenomenal increase in the demand for fertilizer. The value of bone imports to Britain increased from £14,400 in 1823 to £254,600 in 1837. The first boat carrying Peruvian guano (accumulated dung of sea birds) unloaded its cargo in Liverpool in 1835; by 1841, 1,700 tons were imported, and by 1847, 220,000 (Ernle [1912] 1961, p. 369). European farmers in this period raided Napoleonic battlefields such

American Journal of Sociology

as Waterloo and Austerlitz, so desperate were they for bones to spread over their fields (Hillel 1991, pp. 131–32).

The second agricultural revolution associated with the rise of modern soil science was closely correlated with this demand for increased soil fertility to support capitalist agriculture. In 1837, the British Association for the Advancement of Science commissioned Liebig to write a work on the relationship between agriculture and chemistry. The following year saw the founding of the Royal Agricultural Society of England, viewed by economic historians as a leading organization in the British high-farming movement—a movement of wealthy landowners to improve farm management. In 1840, Liebig published his *Organic Chemistry in Its Applications to Agriculture and Physiology,* which provided the first convincing explanation of the role of soil nutrients, such as nitrogen, phosphorous, and potassium, in the growth of plants. One of the figures most influenced by Liebig's ideas was the wealthy English landowner and agronomist J. B. Lawes. In 1842, Lawes invented a means of making phosphate soluble, enabling him to introduce the first artificial fertilizer, and in 1843, he built a factory for the production of his new "superphosphates." With the repeal of the Corn Laws in 1846, Liebig's organic chemistry was seen by the large agricultural interests in England as the key to obtaining larger crop yields (Brock 1997, pp. 149–50).

In the 1840s, this scientific revolution in soil chemistry, together with the rise of a fertilizer industry, promised to generate a faster rate of agricultural improvement—impressing many contemporary observers, including Marx and Engels, who up to the 1860s believed that progress in agriculture might soon outpace the development of industry in general. Still, capital's ability to take advantage of these scientific breakthroughs in soil chemistry was limited by development of the division of labor inherent to the system, specifically the growing antagonism between town and country. By the 1860s, when he wrote *Capital,* Marx had become convinced of the contradictory and unsustainable nature of capitalist agriculture, due to two historical developments in his time: (1) the widening sense of crisis in agriculture in both Europe and North America associated with the depletion of the natural fertility of the soil, which was in no way alleviated, but rather given added impetus by the breakthroughs in soil science; and (2) a shift in Liebig's own work in the late 1850s and early 1860s toward an ecological critique of capitalist development.

The discoveries by Liebig and other soil scientists, while holding out hope to farmers, also intensified in some ways the sense of crisis within capitalist agriculture, making farmers more acutely aware of the depletion of soil minerals and the paucity of fertilizers. The contradiction was experienced with particular severity in the United States—especially among farmers in New York and in the plantation economy of the Southeast.

Environmental Sociology

Blocked from ready access to guano (which was high in both nitrogen and phosphates) by the British monopoly of Peruvian guano supplies, U.S. capitalists spread across the globe looking for alternative supplies. Nevertheless, the quantity and quality of natural fertilizer obtained in this way fell far short of U.S. needs (Skaggs 1994).

Peruvian guano was largely exhausted in the 1860s and had to be replaced by Chilean nitrates. Potassium salts discovered in Europe gave ample access to that mineral, and phosphates became more readily available through both natural and artificial supplies. Yet prior to the development of a process for producing synthetic nitrogen fertilizer in 1913, fertilizer nitrogen continued to be in chronically short supply. It was in this context that Liebig was to state that what was needed to overcome this barrier was the discovery of "deposits of manure or guano . . . in volumes approximating to those of the English coalfields" (quoted in Kautsky [(1899) 1988], vol. 1, p. 53).

The second agricultural revolution, associated with the application of scientific chemistry to agriculture, was therefore at the same time a period of intense contradictions. The decline in the natural fertility of the soil due to the disruption of the soil nutrient cycle, the expanding scientific knowledge of the need for specific soil nutrients, and the simultaneous limitations in the supply of both natural and synthetic fertilizers, all served to generate serious concerns about present and future soil fertility under capitalist agriculture.

In upstate New York, increased competition from farmers to the west in the decades following the opening of the Erie Canal in 1825 intensified the concern over the "worn-out soil." In 1850, the British soil chemist, James F. W. Johnston, whom Marx (Marx and Engels 1975a, vol. 38, p. 476) was to call "the English Liebig," visited the United States. In his *Notes on North America,* Johnston (1851, pp. 356–65) recorded the depleted condition of the soil in upstate New York, comparing it unfavorably to the more fertile, less exhausted farmlands to the west. These issues were taken up by the U.S. economist Henry Carey, who in the late 1840s and 1850s laid stress on the fact that long-distance trade, which he associated with the separation of town from country and of agricultural producers from consumers ([1847] 1967a, pp. 298–99, 304–8), was the major factor in the net loss of nutrients to the soil and in the growing soil fertility crisis. "As the whole energies of the country," Carey wrote of the United States in his *Principles of Social Science,* "are given to the enlargement of the trader's power, it is no matter of surprise that its people are everywhere seen employed in 'robbing the earth of its capital stock'" ([1858–59] 1867, p. 215; also Carey [1853] 1967b, p. 199).

Carey's views were to have an important impact on Liebig. In his *Letters on Modern Agriculture* (1859), Liebig argued that the "empirical agri-

377

culture" of the trader gave rise to a "spoliation system" in which the "conditions of reproduction" of the soil were undermined. "A field from which something is permanently taken away," he wrote, "cannot possibly increase or even continue equal in its productive power." Indeed, "every system of farming based on the spoliation of the land leads to poverty" (1859, pp. 175–78). "Rational agriculture, in contrast to the spoliation system of farming, is based on the principle of restitution; by giving back to the fields the conditions of their fertility, the farmer insures the permanence of the latter." For Liebig, English "high farming" was "not the open system of robbery of the American farmer . . . but is a more refined species of spoliation which at first glance does not look like robbery" (1859, p. 183). Echoing Carey (1858), Liebig (1859, p. 220) observed that there were hundreds, sometimes thousands, of miles in the United States between the centers of grain production and their markets. The constituent elements of the soil were thus shipped to locations far removed from their points of origin, making the reproduction of soil fertility that much more difficult.

The problem of the pollution of the cities with human and animal wastes was also tied to the depletion of the soil. In Liebig's (1863, p. 261) words, "If it were practicable to collect, with the least loss, all the solid and fluid excrements of the inhabitants of the town, and return to each farmer the portion arising from produce originally supplied by him to the town, the productiveness of the land might be maintained almost unimpaired for ages to come, and the existing store of mineral elements in every fertile field would be amply sufficient for the wants of increasing populations." In his influential *Letters on the Subject of the Utilization of the Municipal Sewage* (1865) Liebig argued—basing his analysis on the condition of the Thames—that organic recycling that would return the nutrients contained in sewage to the soil was an indispensable part of a rational urban-agricultural system.

Marx and the Metabolic Rift

When working on *Capital* in the early 1860s, Marx was deeply affected by Liebig's analysis. In 1866, he wrote to Engels that in developing his critique of capitalist ground rent, "I had to plough through the new agricultural chemistry in Germany, in particular Liebig and Schönbein, which is more important for this matter than all the economists put together" (Marx and Engels 1975a, vol. 42, p. 227). Indeed, "to have developed from the point of view of natural science the negative, i.e., destructive side of modern agriculture," Marx was to note in *Capital*, "is one of Liebig's immortal merits" ([1867] 1976, p. 638). Far from having ecological blinders with regard to the exploitation of the earth, Marx, under the influence of Liebig's work of the late 1850s and early 1860s, was to develop a systematic critique of capitalist "exploitation" (in the sense of robbery, i.e., failing to maintain the means of reproduction) of the soil.

Marx concluded both of his two main discussions of capitalist agriculture with an explanation of how large-scale industry and large-scale agriculture combined to impoverish the soil and the worker. Much of the resulting critique was distilled in a remarkable passage at the end of Marx's treatment of "The Genesis of Capitalist Ground Rent" in *Capital*, volume 3, where he wrote:

> Large landed property reduces the agricultural population to an ever decreasing minimum and confronts it with an ever growing industrial population crammed together in large towns; in this way it produces conditions that provoke an irreparable rift in the interdependent process of the social metabolism, a metabolism prescribed by the natural laws of life itself. The result of this is a squandering of the vitality of the soil, which is carried by trade far beyond the bounds of a single country. (Liebig.) . . . Large-scale industry and industrially pursued large-scale agriculture have the same effect. If they are originally distinguished by the fact that the former lays waste and ruins the labour-power and thus the natural power of man, whereas the latter does the same to the natural power of the soil, they link up in the later course of development, since the industrial system applied to agriculture also enervates the workers there, while industry and trade for their part provide agriculture with the means of exhausting the soil. (Marx 1981, pp. 949–50)

Marx provided a similar and no less important distillation of his critique in this area in his discussion of "Large-scale Industry and Agriculture" in volume 1 of *Capital:*

> Capitalist production collects the population together in great centres, and causes the urban population to achieve an ever-growing preponderance. This has two results. On the one hand it concentrates the historical motive force of society; on the other hand, it disturbs the metabolic interaction between man and the earth, i.e. it prevents the return to the soil of its constituent elements consumed by man in the form of food and clothing; hence it hinders the operation of the eternal natural condition for the lasting fertility of the soil. . . . But by destroying the circumstances surrounding that metabolism . . . it compels its systematic restoration as a regulative law of social production, and in a form adequate to the full development of the human race. . . . All progress in capitalist agriculture is a progress in the art, not only of robbing the worker, but of robbing the soil; all progress in increasing the fertility of the soil for a given time is a progress toward ruining the more long-lasting sources of that fertility. . . . Capitalist production, therefore, only develops the techniques and the degree of combination of the social process of production by simultaneously undermining the original sources of all wealth—the soil and the worker. (Marx 1976, pp. 637–38)

In both of these passages from Marx's *Capital*—the first concluding his discussion of capitalist ground rent in volume 3 and the second concluding

American Journal of Sociology

his discussion of large-scale agriculture in volume 1—the central theoretical construct is that of a "rift" in the "metabolic interaction between man and the earth," or in the "social metabolism prescribed by the natural laws of life," through the removal from the soil of its constituent elements, requiring its "systematic restoration." This contradiction is associated with the growth simultaneously of large-scale industry and large-scale agriculture under capitalism, with the former providing agriculture with the means of the intensive exploitation of the soil. Following Liebig, Marx argued that long-distance trade in food and clothing made the problem of the alienation of the constituent elements of the soil that much more of an "irreparable rift." As he indicated elsewhere in *Capital* (vol. 1), the fact that "the blind desire for profit" had "exhausted the soil" of England could be seen daily in the conditions that "forced the manuring of English fields with guano" imported from Peru (1976, p. 348). Central to Marx's argument was the notion that capitalist large-scale agriculture prevents any truly rational application of the new science of soil management. Despite all of its scientific and technological development in the area of agriculture, capitalism was unable to maintain those conditions necessary for the recycling of the constituent elements of the soil.

The key to Marx's entire theoretical approach in this area is the concept of social-ecological metabolism (*Stoffwechsel*), which was rooted in his understanding of the labor process. Defining the labor process in general (as opposed to its historically specific manifestations), Marx employed the concept of metabolism to describe the human relation to nature through labor:

> Labour is, first of all, a process between man and nature, a process by which man, through his own actions, mediates, regulates and controls the metabolism between himself and nature. He confronts the materials of nature as a force of nature. He sets in motion the natural forces which belong to his own body, his arms, legs, head and hands, in order to appropriate the materials of nature in a form adapted to his own needs. Through this movement he acts upon external nature and changes it, and in this way he simultaneously changes his own nature. . . . It [the labor process] is the universal condition for the metabolic interaction [*Stoffwechsel*] between man and nature, the everlasting nature-imposed condition of human existence. (Marx 1976, pp. 283, 290)

Only a few years before this, Marx had written in his *Economic Manuscript of 1861–63* that "actual labour is the appropriation of nature for the satisfaction of human needs, the activity through which the metabolism between man and nature is mediated." It followed that the actual activity of labor was never independent of nature's own wealth-creating potential, "since material wealth, the world of use values, exclusively consists of

Environmental Sociology

natural materials modified by labour" (Marx and Engels 1975*a*, vol. 30, p. 40).[5]

Much of this discussion of the metabolic relation between human beings and nature reflected Marx's early, more directly philosophical attempts to account for the complex interdependence between human beings and nature. In the *Economic and Philosophical Manuscripts* of 1844, Marx had explained that, "Man *lives* from nature, i.e., nature is his *body*, and he must maintain a continuing dialogue with it if he is not to die. To say that man's physical and mental life is linked to nature simply means that nature is linked to itself, for man is a part of nature" (1974, p. 328; emphasis in original). But the later introduction of the concept of metabolism gave Marx a more solid—and scientific—way in which to depict the complex, dynamic interchange between human beings and nature, resulting from human labor. The material exchanges and regulatory action associated with the concept of metabolism encompassed both "nature-imposed conditions" and the capacity of human beings to affect this process. According to Hayward (1994, p. 116), Marx's concept of socio-ecological metabolism "captures fundamental aspects of humans' existence as both natural and physical beings: these include the energetic and material exchanges which occur between human beings and their natural environment. . . . This metabolism is regulated from the side of nature by natural laws governing the various physical processes involved, and from the side of society by institutionalized norms governing the division of labor and distribution of wealth etc."

Given the fundamental way in which Marx conceived of the concept of metabolism—as constituting the complex, interdependent process linking human society to nature—it should not surprise us that this concept enters

---

[5] Marx highlighted the methodological importance of the concept of "material exchange [*Stoffwechsel*] between man and nature" in his *Notes on Adolph Wagner*, his last economic work, written in 1880 (1975, p. 209). As early as 1857–58 in the *Grundrisse*, Marx had referred to the concept of metabolism (*Stoffwechsel*) in the wider sense of "a system of general social metabolism, of universal relations, of all-round needs and universal capacities . . . formed for the first time" under generalized commodity production (1973, p. 158). Throughout his later economic works, he employed the concept to refer both to the actual metabolic interaction between nature and society through human labor, and also in a wider sense to describe the complex, dynamic, interdependent set of needs and relations brought into being and constantly reproduced in alienated form under capitalism, and the question of human freedom that this raised—all of which could be seen as being connected to the way in which the human metabolism with nature was expressed through the organization of human labor. Marx thus gave the concept of metabolism both a specific ecological meaning and a wider social meaning. It makes sense therefore to speak of the "socioecological" nature of his concept.

American Journal of Sociology

into Marx's vision of a future society of associated producers: "Freedom, in this sphere [the realm of natural necessity]," he wrote in *Capital* (volume 3), "can consist only in this, that socialized man, the associated producers, govern the human metabolism with nature in a rational way, bringing it under their own collective control rather than being dominated by it as a blind power; accomplishing it with the least expenditure of energy and in conditions most worthy and appropriate for their human nature" (1981, p. 959).

Just as the introduction of the concept of "metabolism" allowed Marx to provide a firmer, scientific grounding for his ideas, so the central position that this concept came to occupy in his theory encouraged him to draw out some of its larger implications. The term "metabolism" (*Stoffwechsel*) was introduced as early as 1815 and was adopted by German physiologists in the 1830s and 1840s to refer to material exchanges within the body, related to respiration (Bing 1971; Caneva 1993). But the term was given a somewhat wider application (and therefore greater currency) in 1842 by Liebig in his *Animal Chemistry,* the great work that followed his earlier work on the soil, where he introduced the notion of metabolic process (in the context of tissue degradation). It was subsequently generalized still further and emerged as one of the key concepts, applicable both at the cellular level and in the analysis of entire organisms, in the development of biochemistry (Liebig [1842] 1964; Brock 1997, p. 193; Caneva 1993, p. 117).

Within biological and ecological analysis, the concept of metabolism, beginning in the 1840s and extending down to the present day, has been used as a central category in the systems-theory approach to the relation of organisms to their environments. It refers to a complex process of metabolic exchange, whereby an organism (or a given cell) draws upon materials and energy from its environment and converts these by way of various metabolic reactions into the building blocks of proteins and other compounds necessary for growth. The concept of metabolism is also used to refer to the regulatory processes that govern this complex interchange between organisms and their environment (Fischer-Kowalski 1997, p. 120). Leading system ecologists like Odum (1969, p. 7) employ "metabolism" to refer to all biological levels, beginning with the single cell and ending with the ecosystem.

Recently, the notion of metabolism has become what Fischer-Kowalski (1997, pp. 119–20) has called "a rising conceptual star" within social-ecological thought, as a result of the emergence of cross-disciplinary research in "industrial metabolism." For some thinkers, it offers a way out of one the core dilemmas of environmental sociology raised by Dunlap and Catton (1979) and Schnaiberg (1980), which requires a way of envisioning the complex interaction between society and nature (Hayward 1994, pp. 116–

17; Fischer-Kowalski 1997). Further, the concept of metabolism has long been employed to analyze the material interchange between city and country, in a manner similar to the way in which Liebig and Marx used the concept (Wolman 1965; Giradet 1997). Within this rapidly growing body of literature on social-ecological metabolism, it is now well recognized that "within the nineteenth-century foundations of social theory, it was Marx and Engels who applied the term 'metabolism' to society" (Fischer-Kowalski 1997, p. 122).

Indeed, environmental sociologists and others exploring the concept of "industrial metabolism" today argue that just as the materials that birds use to build their nests can be seen as material flows associated with the metabolism of birds, so similar material flows can be seen as part of the human metabolism. Fischer-Kowalski has thus suggested "considering as part of the metabolism of a social system *those material and energetic flows that sustain the material compartments of the system*" (1997, pp. 121, 131; emphasis in original). The tough question, however, is how such a human metabolism with nature is regulated on the side of society. For Marx, the answer was human labor and its development within historical social formations.

MARX AND SUSTAINABILITY

An essential aspect of the concept of metabolism is the notion that it constitutes the basis on which life is sustained and growth and reproduction become possible. Contrary to those who believe that he wore an ecological blinder that prevented him from perceiving natural limits to production, Marx employed the concept of metabolic rift to capture the material estrangement of human beings in capitalist society from the natural conditions of their existence. To argue that large-scale capitalist agriculture created such a metabolic rift between human beings and the soil was to argue that basic conditions of sustainability had been violated. "Capitalist production," Marx ([1861–63] 1971*b*, p. 301) wrote, "turns toward the land only after its influence has exhausted it and after it has devastated its natural qualities." Moreover, this could be seen as related not only to the soil but to the antagonism between town and country. For Marx, like Liebig, the failure to recycle nutrients to the soil had its counterpart in the pollution of the cities and the irrationality of modern sewage systems. In *Capital* (volume 3), he observed: "In London . . . they can do nothing better with the excrement produced by 4 1/2 million people than pollute the Thames with it, at monstrous expense" (1981, p. 195). Engels was no less explicit on this point. In addressing the need to transcend the antagonism between town and country, he referred, following Liebig, to the fact that "in London alone a greater quantity of manure than is produced by

American Journal of Sociology

the whole kingdom of Saxony is poured away every day into the sea with an expenditure of enormous sums" and to the consequent need to reestablish an "intimate connection between industrial and agricultural production" along with "as uniform a distribution as possible of the population over the whole country" (Engels [1872] 1975, p. 92). For Marx, the "excrement produced by man's natural metabolism," along with the waste of industrial production and consumption, needed to be recycled back into the production, as part of a complete metabolic cycle (1981, p. 195).

The antagonistic division between town and country, and the metabolic rift that it entailed, was also evident at a more global level: whole colonies saw their land, resources, *and soil* robbed to support the industrialization of the colonizing countries. "For a century and a half," Marx wrote, "England has indirectly exported the soil of Ireland, without as much as allowing its cultivators the means for making up the constituents of the soil that had been exhausted" (1976, p. 860).

Marx's view of capitalist agriculture and of the necessity of cycling the nutrients of the soil (including the organic wastes of the city) thus led him to a wider concept of ecological sustainability—a notion that he thought of very limited practical relevance to capitalist society, which was incapable of such consistent rational action, but essential for a future society of associated producers. "The way that the cultivation of particular crops depends on fluctuations in market prices and the constant change in cultivation with these prices—the entire spirit of capitalist production, which is oriented towards the most immediate monetary profits—stands in contradiction to agriculture, which has to concern itself with the whole gamut of permanent conditions of life required by the chain of successive generations" (Marx 1981, p. 754).

In emphasizing the need to maintain the earth for "successive generations," Marx captured the essence of the contemporary notion of sustainable development, defined most famously by the Brundtland Commission as "development which meets the needs of the present without compromising the ability of future generations to meet their needs" (World Commission on Environment and Development 1987, p. 43). For Marx, the "conscious and rational treatment of the land as permanent communal property" is "the inalienable condition for the existence and reproduction of the chain of human generations" (1981, pp. 948–49). Indeed, in a remarkable, and deservedly famous, passage in *Capital* (vol. 3), Marx wrote, "From the standpoint of a higher socio-economic formation, the private property of particular individuals in the earth will appear just as absurd as the private property of one man in other men. Even an entire society, a nation, or all simultaneously existing societies taken together, are not owners of the earth, they are simply its possessors, its beneficiaries, and

Environmental Sociology

have to bequeath it in an improved state to succeeding generations as *boni patres familias* [good heads of the household]" (1981, p. 911).

This took on greater significance near the end of Marx's life, when, as a result of his investigations into the revolutionary potential of the archaic Russian commune (the Mir), he argued that it would be possible to develop an agricultural system "organized on a vast scale and managed by cooperative labor" through the introduction of "modern agronomic methods." The value of such a system, he argued, would be that it would be "in a position to incorporate all the positive acquisitions devised by the capitalist system" without falling prey to the purely exploitative relation to the soil, that is, the robbery, that characterized the latter (Marx and Engels 1975a, vol. 24, p. 356). Marx's absorption in the literature of the Russian populists at the end of his life, and his growing conviction that the revolution would emerge first within Russia—where economic, and more specifically agricultural, abundance could not be assumed—forced him to focus on agricultural underdevelopment and the ecological requirements of a more rational agricultural system.[6]

Marx and Engels did not restrict their discussions of environmental degradation to the robbing of the soil but also acknowledged other aspects of this problem, including the depletion of coal reserves, the destruction of forests, and so on. As Engels observed in a letter to Marx, "the working individual is not only a stabaliser of *present* but also, and to a far greater extent, a squanderer of *past*, solar heat. As to what we have done in the way of squandering our reserves of energy, our coal, ore, forests, etc., you are better informed than I am" (Marx and Engels 1975a, vol. 46, p. 411; emphasis in original). Marx referred to the "devastating" effects of "deforestation" (Marx and Engels 1975a, vol. 42, p. 559) and saw this as a long-term result of an exploitative relation to nature (not simply confined to capitalism): "The development of civilization and industry in general," Marx wrote, "has always shown itself so active in the destruction of forests that everything that has been done for their conservation and production is completely insignificant in comparison" ([1865–70] 1978, p. 322). He lamented the fact that the forests in England were not "true forests" since "the deer in the parks of the great are demure domestic cattle, as fat as London aldermen"; while in Scotland, the so-called "deer-forests" that were established for the benefit of huntsmen (at the expense of rural laborers) contained deer but no trees (1976, pp. 892–93). Under the influence of Darwin, Marx and Engels repudiated the age-old view that human beings were at the center of the natural universe. Engels expressed "a

[6] On this later phase of Marx's analysis, in which he addressed the agricultural concerns of the Russian populists, see Shanin (1983).

American Journal of Sociology

withering contempt for the idealistic exaltation of man over the other animals" (Marx and Engels 1975*b*, p. 102).

Some critics attribute to Marx an ecological blinder associated with an overly optimistic faith in the cornucopian conditions supposedly made possible by the forces of production under capitalism. In this view, he relied so much on the assumption of abundance in his conception of a future society that ecological factors such as the scarcity of natural resources were simply nonexistent. Yet whatever Marx may have thought in his more "utopian" conceptions, it is clear from his discussions of both capitalism and of the transition to socialism that he was far from believing, as Nove (1987, p. 399) contends, "that the problem of production" had already been "solved" under capitalism or that natural resources were "inexhaustible." Rather, capitalism, as he emphasized again and again, was beset with a chronic problem of production in agriculture, which ultimately had to do with an unsustainable form of production in relation to natural conditions. Agriculture, Marx observed, "when it progresses spontaneously and is not *consciously controlled* . . . leaves deserts behind it" (Marx and Engels 1975*b*, p. 190; emphasis in original). Within industry too, Marx was concerned about the enormous waste generated and emphasized the "reduction" and "re-use" of waste—particularly in a section of *Capital* (volume 3), entitled, "Utilization of the Refuse of Production" (1981, pp. 195–97). Moreover, he gave every indication that these problems would continue to beset any society attempting to construct socialism (or communism). Hence, although some critics, such as McLaughlin (1990, p. 95), assert that Marx envisioned "a general material abundance as the substratum of communism," and therefore saw "no basis for recognizing any interest in the liberation of nature from human domination," overwhelming evidence to the contrary (much of it referred to above) suggests that Marx was deeply concerned with issues of ecological limits and sustainability.

Moreover, there is simply no indication anywhere in Marx's writings that he believed that a sustainable relation to the earth would come automatically with the transition to socialism. Rather, he emphasized the need for planning in this area, including such measures as the elimination of the antagonism between town and country through the more even dispersal of the population (Marx and Engels [1848] 1967, pp. 40–41) and the restoration and improvement of the soil through the recycling of soil nutrients. All of this demanded a radical transformation in the human relation to the earth via changed production relations. Capitalism, Marx wrote, "creates the material conditions for a new and higher synthesis, a union of agriculture and industry on the basis of the forms that have developed during the period of their antagonistic isolation" (1976, p. 637). But in order to achieve this "higher synthesis" in a society of freely associated producers, he argued, it would be necessary for the associated producers to "govern the human metabolism with nature in a rational way"—a requirement that raised fundamental challenges for postcapitalist society (1981, p. 959; 1976, pp. 637–38).

Another ecological blinder commonly attributed to Marx is that he denied the role of nature in the creation of wealth by developing a labor theory of value that saw all value as derived from labor, and by referring to nature as a "free gift" to capital, lacking any intrinsic value of its own (Deléage 1994, p. 48; Churchill 1996, pp. 467–68; Georgescu-Roegen 1971, p. 2). Yet this criticism is based on a misunderstanding of Marx's political economy. Marx did not invent the idea that the earth was a "gift" of nature to capital. This notion was advanced as a key proposition by Malthus and Ricardo in their economic works (Malthus 1970, p. 185). It was taken up later on by the great neoclassical economist Alfred Marshall (1920) and persisted in neoclassical economics textbooks into the 1980s. Thus, in the 10th edition of a widely used introductory economics textbook, we discover the following: "Land refers to all natural resources—all 'free gifts of nature'—which are usable in the production process." And further on we read, "Land has no production cost; it is a 'free and nonreproducible gift of nature' " (McConnell 1987, pp. 20, 672). Marx was aware of the social-ecological contradictions embedded in such views, and in his *Economic Manuscript of 1861–63* he attacked Malthus repeatedly for falling back on the "physiocratic" notion that the environment was "a gift of nature to man," while ignoring how this was connected to the definite set of social relations brought into being by capital (Marx and Engels 1975a, vol. 34, pp. 151–59).

To be sure, Marx agreed with liberal economics that under the law of value of capitalism nature was accorded no value. "The earth . . . is active as agent of production in the production of a use-value, a material product, say wheat," he wrote. "But it has nothing to do with producing the *value of the wheat*" (1981, p. 955). The value of the wheat as in the case of any commodity under capitalism was derived from labor. For Marx, however, this merely reflected the narrow, limited conception of wealth embodied in capitalist commodity relations and in a system built around exchange value. Genuine wealth consisted of use values—the characteristic of production in general, transcending its capitalist form. Hence, nature, which contributed to the production of use values, was just as much a source of wealth as labor. "What Lucretius says," Marx wrote in *Capital* (1976, p. 323), "is self-evident: *nil posse creari de nihilo,* out of nothing, nothing can be created. . . . Labour-power itself is, above all else, the material of nature transposed into a human organism."

It follows that "labour," as Marx stated at the beginning of *Capital,* "is not the only source of material wealth, that is, of the use-values it pro-

American Journal of Sociology

duces. As William Petty says, labour is the father of material wealth, and the earth is its mother" (1976, p. 134). In the *Critique of the Gotha Programme,* Marx criticized those socialists who had attributed what he called *"supernatural creative power* to labour" ([1875] 1971*a,* p. 11; emphasis in original) by viewing it as the sole source of wealth and disregarding the role of nature. Under communism, he argued, wealth would need to be conceived in far more universal terms, as consisting of those material use values that constituted the basis for the full development of human creative powers, "the development of the rich individuality which is all sided in its production as in its consumption"—expanding the wealth of connections allowed for by nature, while at the same time reflecting the developing human metabolism with nature ([1857–58] 1973, p. 325).

Marx therefore set himself in opposition to all those who thought the contribution of nature to the production of wealth could be disregarded, or that nature could be completely subordinated to human ends regardless of their character. Commenting in the *Grundrisse* on Bacon's ([1620] 1994, pp. 29, 43) great maxim that "nature is only overcome by obeying her"— on the basis of which Bacon also proposed to "subjugate" nature—Marx replied that for capitalism the theoretical discovery of nature's "autonomous laws appears merely as a ruse so as to subjugate it under human needs, whether as an object of consumption or a means of production" (1973, pp. 409–10).

For Engels too, it was clear that to construct a society built on the vain hope of the total conquest of external nature was sheer folly. As he wrote in *The Dialectics of Nature* ([1874–80] 1940, pp. 291–92), "Let us not, however, flatter ourselves overmuch on account of our human conquest of nature. For each such conquest takes revenge on us. . . . At every step we are reminded that we by no means rule over nature like a conqueror over a foreign people, like someone standing outside nature—but that we, with flesh, blood, and brain, belong to nature, and exist in its midst, and that all our mastery of it consists in the fact that we have the advantage of all other beings of being able to know and correctly apply its laws."

For Marx, "the human metabolism with nature" was a highly dynamic relationship, reflecting changes in the ways human beings mediated between nature and society through production. Engels and Marx read *The Origin of Species* soon after it appeared in 1859 and were enthusiastic supporters of Darwin's theory of natural selection. Marx (1976, p. 461) called Darwin's book an "epoch-making work," and in January 1861, Marx wrote a letter to the German socialist Ferdinand Lasalle stating that Darwin had dealt the "death blow" to " 'teleology' in the natural sciences" (Marx and Engels 1975*a,* vol. 41, pp. 246–47). Marx expressed no reservations about Darwin's fundamental theory itself—not even with regard to

Environmental Sociology

Darwin's application of the Malthusian "struggle for existence" to the world of plants and animals—yet he was sharply critical of all attempts by social Darwinists to carry this analysis beyond its proper domain and to apply it to human history. Unfortunately, some critics have viewed his cautionary notes in this respect as criticisms of Darwin himself.[7]

Darwin's evolutionary theory led Marx and Engels to what would now be called a "cautious constructionism" (Dunlap 1997, pp. 31–32). For Marx, human evolution, that is, human history, was distinct from evolution as it occurred among plants and animals, in that the natural evolution of the physical organs of the latter, that is, "the history of natural technology," had its counterpart in human history in the conscious development of the "productive organs of man in society" (technology), which helped establish the conditions for the human mediation between nature and society via production (Marx 1976, p. 493). Marx was of course aware that the Greek word organ (organon) also meant tool, and that organs were initially viewed as "grown-on" tools of animals—an approach that was utilized by Darwin himself, who compared the development of specialized organs to the development of specialized tools (see Pannekoek 1912; Darwin [1859] 1968, pp. 187–88).

Engels was later to add to this an analysis of "The Part Played by Labour in the Transition from Ape to Man" (Engels 1940, pp. 279–96). According to this theory (verified in the 20th century by the discovery of *Australopithecus*), erect posture developed first (prior to the evolution of the human brain), freeing the hands for tools. In this way, the human (hominid) relation to the local environment was radically changed, altering the basis of natural selection. Those hominids that were most successful at toolmaking were best able to adapt, which meant that the evolutionary process exerted selective pressures toward the development of the brain, eventually leading to the rise of modern humans. The human brain, according to Engels, evolved then through a complex, interactive process, now referred to as "gene-culture evolution." As biologist and paleontolo-

---

[7] Marx and Engels's complex relation to Darwin's work—which neither denied a relation between society and biology nor reduced one to the other—may also have something to say about why they never utilized the term "ecology," coined by Darwin's leading German follower Ernst Haeckel in 1866, the year before the publication of volume 1 of *Capital*. Although the concept of ecology only gradually came into common usage, Marx and Engels were very familiar with Haeckel's work and so may have been aware of his coinage of this concept. Yet, the way that Haeckel, a strong social Darwinist, originally defined the term was unlikely to have predisposed them to its acceptance. "By ecology," Haeckel had written, "we mean the body of knowledge concerning the economy of nature . . . in a word, ecology is the study of all those complex interrelations referred to by Darwin as the conditions of the struggle for existence" (Golley 1993, p. 207).

American Journal of Sociology

gist Stephen Jay Gould has observed, all scientific explanations of the evolution of the human brain thus far have taken the form of gene-culture coevolution, and "the best nineteenth-century case for gene-culture coevolution was made by Friedrich Engels" (Gould 1987, pp. 111–12). The analysis of Marx and Engels thus pointed to coevolution (Norgaard 1994), neither reducing society to nature, nor nature to society, but exploring their interactions. Indeed, the view that "nature reacts on man and natural conditions everywhere exclusively determined his historical development," Engels observed, "is . . . one-sided and forgets that man also reacts on nature, changing it and creating new conditions of existence for himself" (1940, p. 172).

The key to the metabolic relation of human beings to nature then is technology, but technology as conditioned by both social relations and natural conditions. Contrary to those who argue that Marx wore an ecological blinder when it came to envisioning the limitations of technology in surmounting ecological problems, he explicitly argued in his critique of capitalist agriculture, that while capitalism served to promote "technical development in agriculture," it also brought into being social relations that were "incompatible" with a sustainable agriculture (1981, p. 216). The solution thus lay less in the application of a given technology than in the transformation of social relations. Moreover, even if the most advanced technical means available were in the hands of the associated producers, nature, for Marx, sets certain limits. The reproduction of "plant and animal products," for example, is conditioned by "certain organic laws involving naturally determined periods of time" (1981, p. 213). Marx reiterated the Italian political economist Pietro Verri's statement that human production was not properly an act of creation but merely "the reordering of matter" and was thus dependent on what the earth provided (1976, p. 132). The human interaction with nature always had to take the form of a metabolic cycle that needed to be sustained for the sake of successive generations. Technological improvements were a necessary but insufficient means for the "improvement" in the human relation to the earth. For Marx, human beings transformed their relation to nature but not exactly as they pleased; they did so in accordance with conditions inherited from the past and as a result of a complex process of historical development that reflected a changing relation to a natural world, which was itself dynamic in character. Redclift and Woodgate (1994, p. 53) are therefore wrong when they say that Marx wore blinders in relation to the coevolution of nature and society, viewing the human relation to nature as an "unchanging" one. Engels began his *Dialectics of Nature* with a dramatic description of the historic defeat of 18th-century conceptions of nature in which the natural world existed only in space not in time; "in which all change, all development of nature was denied" (1940, p. 6).

390

Environmental Sociology

BEYOND THE APPROPRIATION AND DEFINITIONAL PROBLEMS

The foregoing suggests that Marx's analysis provides a multilayered and multivalent basis for linking sociology (and in particular the classical tradition of sociology) with environmental issues. Yet, if this is so, why has this concern with ecological issues not found a strong echo in the Marxist tradition throughout its development, and why has our understanding of Marx so often excluded these issues? Why has environmental sociology, which is concerned directly with these questions, been so slow to acknowledge Marx's importance in this respect? The first question relates to what we referred to at the beginning of this article as "the appropriation problem," the second to what was labeled "the definitional problem."

The Appropriation Problem

Marx's reputation as an ecological thinker was no doubt affected by the fact that, as Massimo Quaini (1982, p. 136) has pointed out, he "denounced the spoliation of nature before a modern bourgeois ecological conscience was born." Nevertheless, Marx's ecological critique was fairly well-known and had a direct impact on Marxism in the decades immediately following his death. It came to be discarded only later on, particularly within Soviet ideology, as the expansion of production at virtually any cost became the overriding goal of the Communist movement. The influence of Marx's critique in this respect can be seen in the writings of such leading Marxist thinkers as Kautsky, Lenin, and Bukharin.

Kautsky's great work, *The Agrarian Question,* published in 1899, contained a section on "The Exploitation of the Countryside by the Town" in which he held that the net external flow of value from countryside to town "corresponds to a constantly mounting loss of nutrients in the form of corn, meat, milk and so forth which the farmer has to sell to pay taxes, debt-interest and rent.... Although such a flow does not signify an exploitation of agriculture in terms of the law of value [of the capitalist economy], it does nevertheless lead . . . to its material exploitation, to the impoverishment of the land of its nutrients" (Kautsky 1988 [1899], p. 214).[8] Arguing at a time when the fertilizer industry was further developed than

---

[8] In saying there was no exploitation of agriculture in law of value terms, Kautsky was arguing that transactions here, as in other areas of the economy, were based on equal exchange. Nonetheless, he insisted that "material exploitation" (related to use values) was present insofar as the soil was being impoverished. Marx too argued that the soil was being "robbed" or "exploited" in the latter sense and connected this to the fact that the land under capitalism was regarded as a "free gift" (as Malthus had contended) so that the full costs of its reproduction never entered into the law of value under capitalism.

American Journal of Sociology

in Marx's day, Kautsky discussed the fertilizer treadmill resulting from the metabolic rift:

> Supplementary fertilisers . . . allow the reduction in soil fertility to be avoided, but the necessity of using them in larger and larger amounts simply adds a further burden to agriculture—not one unavoidably imposed by nature, but a direct result of current social organization. By overcoming the antithesis between town and country . . . the materials removed from the soil would be able to flow back in full. Supplementary fertilisers would then, at most, have the task of enriching the soil, not staving off its impoverishment. Advances in cultivation would signify an increase in the amount of soluble nutrients in the soil without the need to add artificial fertilisers. (Kautsky 1988, vol. 2, pp. 214–15)

Some of the same concerns were evident in Lenin's work. In *The Agrarian Question and the "Critics of Marx,"* written in 1901, he observed that, "The possibility of substituting artificial for natural manures and the fact that this is already being done (partly) do not in the least refute the irrationality of wasting natural fertilisers and thereby polluting the rivers and the air in suburban factory districts. Even at the present time there are sewage farms in the vicinity of large cities which utilise city refuse with enormous benefit to agriculture; but by this system only an infinitesimal part of the refuse is utilized" (1961, pp. 155–56).

It was Bukharin, however, who developed the most systematic approach to ecological issues in his chapter on "The Equilibrium between Society and Nature" in *Historical Materialism* his important work of the 1920s. Cohen (1980, p. 118) has characterized Bukharin's position as one of " 'naturalistic' materialism," because of its emphasis on the interaction between society and nature. As Bukharin wrote,

> This material process of "metabolism" between society and nature is the fundamental relation between environment and system, between "external conditions" and human society. . . . The metabolism between man and nature consists, as we have seen, in the transfer of material energy from external nature to society. . . . Thus, the interrelation between society and nature is a process of social reproduction. In this process, society applies its human labor energy and obtains a certain quantity of energy from nature ("nature's material," in the words of Marx). The *balance* between expenditures and receipts is here obviously the decisive element for the growth of society. If what is obtained exceeds the loss by labor, important consequences obviously follow for society, which vary with the amount of this excess. (Bukharin 1925, pp. 108–12)

For Bukharin, technology was the chief mediating force in this metabolic relationship between nature and society. The human metabolism with nature was thus an "unstable equilibrium," one which could be progressive or regressive from the standpoint of human society. "The productivity of labor," he wrote, "is a precise measure of the 'balance' between

Environmental Sociology

society and nature." An increase in social productivity was seen as a progressive development; conversely, if the productivity of labor decreased— here Bukharin cited "the exhaustion of the soil" as a possible cause of such a decline—the relationship was a regressive one. Such a decline in social productivity resulting from an ill-adapted metabolic relation between society and nature could, he argued, lead to society being "barbarianized" (1925, pp. 77, 111–13).

Thus the whole "process of social production," Bukharin (1925, p. 111) wrote, "is an adaptation of human society to external nature." "Nothing could be more incorrect than to regard nature from the teleological point of view: man, the lord of creation, with nature created for his use, and all things adapted to human needs" (1925, p. 104). Instead, human beings were engaged in a constant, active struggle to adapt. "Man, as an animal form, as well as human society, are products of nature, part of this great, endless whole. Man can never escape from nature, and even when he 'controls' nature, he is merely making use of the laws of *nature* for his own ends" (1925, p. 104). "No system, including that of human society," Bukharin (1925, p. 89) insisted, "can exist in empty space; it is surrounded by an 'environment,' on which all its conditions ultimately depend. If human society is not adapted to its environment, it is not meant for this world." "For the tree in the forest, the environment means all the other trees, the brook, the earth, the ferns, the grass, the bushes, together with all their properties. Man's environment is society, in the midst of which he lives; the environment of human society is external nature" (1925, p. 75). Indeed, human beings, as Bukharin emphasized in 1931, need to be conceived as "living and working in the biosphere" (1971, p. 17).[9]

Other early Soviet thinkers connected to Bukharin demonstrated a similar concern for ecological issues. Komrov (1935, pp. 230–32) quoted at length from the long passage on the illusion of the conquest of nature in Engels's *Dialectics of Nature* and went on to observe that, "The private owner or employer, however necessary it may be to make the changing of the world comply with the laws of Nature, cannot do so since he aims at profit and only profit. By creating crisis upon crisis in industry he lays waste natural wealth in agriculture, leaving behind a barren soil and in mountain districts bare rocks and stony slopes." Similarly, Uranovsky

---

[9] In referring to the "biosphere," Bukharin drew upon V. I. Vernadsky's *The Biosphere*, first published in 1922, which was one of the great works in ecological science of the 20th century and was extremely influential in Soviet scientific circles in the 1920s and early 1930s. Vernadsky was "the first person in history to come [to] grips with the real implications of the fact that the Earth is a self-contained sphere" (Margulis et al. 1998, p. 15). He achieved international renown both for his analysis of the biosphere and as the founder of the science of geochemistry (or biogeochemistry) (Vernadsky [1922] 1998).

American Journal of Sociology

(1935, p. 147) placed heavy emphasis, in a discussion of Marxism and science, on Marx's research into Liebig and "the theory of the exhaustion of the soil."[10]

Burkharin's ecological work and that of those associated with him was a product of the early Soviet era. The tragedy of the Soviet relation to the environment, which was eventually to take a form that has been characterized as "ecocide" (Feshbach and Friendly 1992; Peterson 1993), has tended to obscure the enormous dynamism of early Soviet ecology of the 1920s and the role that Lenin personally played in promoting conservation. In his writings and pronouncements, Lenin insisted that human labor could never substitute for the forces of nature and that a "rational exploitation" of the environment, or the scientific management of natural resources, was essential. As the principal leader of the young Soviet state, he argued for "preservation of the monuments of nature" and appointed the dedicated environmentalist Anatolii Vasil'evich Lunacharskii as head of the People's Commissariat of Education (Enlightenment), which was put in charge of conservation matters for all of Soviet Russia (Weiner 1988a, pp. 4, 22–28, 259; Weiner 1988b, pp. 254–55; Bailes 1990, pp. 151–58). Lenin had considerable respect for V. I. Vernadsky, the founder of the science of geochemistry (or biogeochemistry) and the author of *The Biosphere*. It was in response to the urging of Vernadsky and mineralogist E. A. Fersman that Lenin in 1919 established in the southern Urals the first nature preserve in the USSR—and indeed the first reserve anywhere by a government exclusively aimed at the scientific study of nature (Weiner 1988a, p. 29; Bailes 1990, p. 127). Under Lenin's protection, the Soviet conservation movement prospered, particularly during the New Economic Policy period (1921–28). But with the early death of Lenin and the triumph of Stalinism in the late 1920s, conservationists were attacked for being "bourgeois." Worse still, with the rise of Trofim Denisovich Lysenko, as an arbiter of biological science, "scientific" attacks were launched first on ecology and then genetics. By the late 1930s, the conservation movement in the Soviet Union had been completely decimated (Weiner 1988b, pp. 255–56).

The disconnection of Soviet thought from ecological issues, from the 1930s on, was severe and affected Marxism in the West as well, which

[10] Uranovsky was one of the first scientists to be arrested, in 1936, in the Stalinist purges (Medvedev [1971] 1989, p. 441). Accompanying Bukharin as a member of the Soviet delegation to the Second International Conference of the History of Science and Technology, London 1931, was also the brilliant plant geneticist N. I. Vavilov (one of the greatest figures in the history of ecological science), founder and first president of the Lenin Agricultural Academy, who applied a materialist method to the question of the origins of agriculture with the support of early Soviet science (Vavilov 1971). Like Bukharin and Uranovsky, he fell prey to the Stalinist purges.

between the 1930s and the 1970s tended to ignore ecological issues, though there was a revival of interest in this area in Marxism as well with the renewal of environmentalism following the publication of Rachel Carson's *Silent Spring* in 1962. To be sure, when Western Marxism had first emerged as a distinct tradition in the 1920s and 1930s, one of the major influences was the Frankfurt School, which developed an ecological critique (Horkheimer and Adorno 1972). But this critique was largely philosophical, and while it recognized the ecological insights in Marx's *Economic and Philosophical Manuscripts,* it lost sight of the ecological argument embedded in *Capital.* Hence, it generally concluded that classical Marxism (beginning with the later Marx) supported a "Promethean" philosophy of the straightforward domination of nature. Not until the 1960s and 1970s did a more complex interpretation begin to emerge in the writings of the thinkers influenced by the Frankfurt tradition (Schmidt 1971; Leiss 1974). And it was not until the late 1980s and 1990s that scholars began to resurrect Marx's argument on soil fertility and organic recycling (Perelman 1988; Hayward 1994; Foster 1997; Fischer-Kowalski 1997). Much of the renewed emphasis on Marx's (and Liebig's) treatment of soil fertility and its ecological implications has come from agronomists and ecologists concerned directly with the debates around the evolution of soil science and the struggles over agribusiness versus organic agriculture (Mayumi 1991; Magdoff, Lanyon, and Liebhardt 1997; Gardner 1997).

It is scarcely surprising, then, that interpretations of Marx within sociology, and environmental sociology in particular, have been affected by an "appropriation problem." Sociologists in general tend to have little knowledge of volume 3 of Marx's *Capital,* where his critique of capitalist agriculture (and of the undermining of soil fertility) is most fully developed, and while these issues were well-known to the generations of Marxist thinkers who immediately followed Marx, they largely vanished within Marxist thought in the 1930s. Even today, treatments of Marx's relation to ecology that purport to be comprehensive focus on his early writings, largely ignoring *Capital* (Dickens 1992). This appropriation problem had important ramifications. It left the appearance that there were no explicit linkages between human society and the natural world within classical Marxism, thus facilitating the notion that there was an unbridgeable gulf between classical sociology and environmental sociology.

Analogous appropriation problems might be raised with respect to the other classical theorists. Martinez-Alier (1987, pp. 183–92) has argued that Weber's important essay on Ostwald's social energetics has also been neglected; indeed it has yet to be translated into English. This has left the false impression that Weber had nothing to say in this area. Durkheim discussed the sociological origins of the classification of nature within what he called the "first philosophy of nature," and related this to modern

American Journal of Sociology

scientific evolutionism. He also commented in profound ways about Darwinian evolutionary theory, the indestructibility of matter, the conservation of energy, and so on (Durkheim and Mauss 1963, pp. 81–88; Durkheim [1893] 1984, pp. 208–9; Durkheim [1911–12] 1983, pp. 21–27, 69–
70). The systematic character of his more naturalistic thinking has never
been properly addressed, and works like *Pragmatism and Sociology,* in
which he presents some of his more complex views in this regard, have
generally been ignored. Nevertheless, it is clear that his analysis pointed
toward a complex, coevolutionary perspective. "Sociology," he wrote, "introduces a relativism that rests on the relation between the physical environment on the one hand and man on the other. The physical environment
presents a relative fixity. It undergoes evolution, of course; but reality
never ceases to be what it was in order to give way to a reality of a new
kind, or to one constituting new elements. . . . The organic world does
not abolish the physical world and the social world has not been formed
in contradistinction to the organic world, but together with it" (Durkheim
1983, pp. 69–70).

The Definitional Problem

Along with the appropriation problem, which deals with how received
sociology has been affected by the selective appropriation of the classical
tradition, there is also the definitional problem, which stands for the fact
that sociology's (specifically environmental sociology's) failure to address
the classical inheritance in this regard is at least partly due to overly narrow, preconceived definitions as to what constitutes genuinely environmental thought.

Here a major role was assumed by the contrast, drawn by Catton and
Dunlap (1978), between the "human exemptionalist paradigm" and the
"new environmental paradigm." All of the competing perspectives in sociology, such as "functionalism, symbolic interactionism, ethnomethodol-
ogy, conflict theory, Marxism, and so forth" were seen as sharing a common trait of belonging to a "human exceptionalist paradigm" (later
renamed "human exemptionalist paradigm"), and thus the "apparent diversity" of these theories was "not as important as the fundamental anthropocentrism underlying *all* of them" (Catton and Dunlap 1978, p. 42).
The human exemptionalist paradigm was depicted as embracing the following assumptions: (1) the existence of culture makes human beings
unique among the creatures of the earth, (2) culture evolves much more
rapidly than biology, (3) most human characteristics are culturally based
and hence can be socially altered, and (4) a process of cultural accumulation means that human progress can be cumulative and without limit.
The habits of mind produced by this human exemptionalist paradigm,

396

Environmental Sociology

Catton and Dunlap (1978, pp. 42–43) argued, led to an overly optimistic faith in human progress, a failure to acknowledge ecological scarcity, and a tendency to neglect fundamental physical laws such as the entropy law.

For Catton and Dunlap, this "human exemptionalist paradigm," which encompassed nearly all of existing sociology could be contrasted to what they termed the "new environmental paradigm" emerging from environmental sociology, which was based on the following assumptions: (1) human beings are one of many species that are interdependently connected within the biotic community; (2) the biotic community consists of an intricate web of nature, with complex linkages of cause and effect; and (3) the world itself is finite, there are natural (physical, biological) limits to social and economic progress (1978, p. 45). In contrast to the "anthropocentrism" that characterized the human exemptionalist paradigm, the new environmental paradigm represented a shift toward what is now called an "ecocentric" point of view in which human beings are seen as part of nature, interconnected with other species and subject to the natural limits of the biosphere.

Ironically, the chief problem with this contrast between the human exemptionalist paradigm and the new environmental paradigm is that, even while emphasizing environmental factors, it tended to perpetuate a dualistic view of society versus the physical environment, anthropocentrism versus ecocentrism, and thus easily fell into the fallacy of the excluded middle (or a false dichotomy). There is a tendency in this view to see any theory that emphasizes socioeconomic progress or cultural accumulation as thereby "anthropocentric" and opposed to an "ecocentric" perspective, which seeks to decenter the human world and human interests. Nevertheless, logic suggests that there is no reason for such a stark opposition, since there are numerous ways in which sociology can embrace a concern for ecological sustainability without abandoning its emphasis on the development of human culture and production. Moreover, extreme ecocentrism runs the risk of losing sight of the sociological construction of much of the "natural world." Although classical sociology may have been anthropocentric to some extent in its focus on socioeconomic advance and its relative neglect of external nature, it was not necessarily antiecological (in the sense of ignoring natural limits) insofar as it acknowledged ecological sustainability as a requirement of social progress. The current preoccupation with sustainable development and coevolutionary theories within environmental discussions suggests that there have always been complex views that attempted to transcend the dualisms of humanity versus nature, anthropocentrism versus ecocentrism, socioeconomic progress versus natural limits.

Marx in particular has been criticized for being "anthropocentric" rather than "ecocentric" in orientation and hence outside of the framework of green theory (Eckersley 1992, pp. 75–95). Yet this kind of dualistic

American Journal of Sociology

conception would have made little sense from his more dialectical perspective, which emphasized the quality (and sustainablilty) of the *interaction*
between society and its natural conditions. It is the commitment to ecological sustainability, not the abstract notion of "ecocentrism," which most
clearly defines whether a theory is part of ecological discourse. Moreover,
a comprehensive *sociology* of the environment must by definition be coevolutionary in perspective, taking into account changes in both society
and nature and their mutual interaction.

CONCLUSION: THE ELEMENTS OF ENVIRONMENTAL SOCIOLOGY

The burden of argument in this article has been to demonstrate, using the
case of Marx, that it is wrong to contend that classical sociology "was
constructed as if nature didn't matter" (Murphy 1996, p. 10). A central
claim of this article, backed up by logic and evidence, has been that each
of the six ecological blinders commonly attributed to Marx—namely his
alleged inability to perceive (1) the exploitation of nature, (2) nature's role
in the creation of wealth, (3) the existence of natural limits, (4) nature's
changing character, (5) the role of technology in environmental degradation, and (6) the inability of mere economic abundance to solve environmental problems—are in fact wrongly (or misleadingly) attributed to him.
The point of course is not that Marx provided definitive treatments of all
of these problems but rather that he was sufficiently cognizant of these
issues to elude the main traps and to work the vitally important notion
of the "human metabolism with nature" into his overall theoretical framework. Hence his work constitutes a possible starting point for a comprehensive sociology of the environment. No doubt some will still insist, despite the argument presented above, that Marx did not place sufficient
emphasis on natural conditions, or that his approach was too anthropocentric, more along the lines of utilitarian-conservationism that genuine green
radicalism. Some will still say that he in fact never entirely renounced
economic development despite his insistence on a sustainable relation to
the earth. But the evidence regarding his concern with ecological issues—
particularly the crisis of the soil as it was perceived in the mid-19th century—is too extensive, and too much a part of his overall critique of capitalism, to be simply disregarded. Marx certainly argued *as if nature mattered*, and his sociology thus takes on a whole new dimension when
viewed from this standpoint.

Just as Marx translated his early theory of the alienation of labor into
more material terms through his later analysis of exploitation and the degradation of work, so he translated his early notion of the alienation of
nature (part of the Feuerbachian naturalism that pervaded his *Economic
and Philosophical Manuscripts*) into more material terms through his later

398

Environmental Sociology

concept of a metabolic rift. Without the latter concept, it is impossible to understand Marx's developed analysis of the antagonism of town and country, his critique of capitalist agriculture, or his calls for the "restoration" of the necessary metabolic relation between humanity and the earth, that is, his basic notion of sustainability. Marx's response to Liebig's critique of capitalist agriculture was coupled, moreover, with a sophisticated response to Darwin's evolutionary theory. What emerges from this is a historical materialism that is ultimately connected to natural history; one that rejects the crude, one-sided traditions of mechanical materialism, vitalism, and social Darwinism that existed in Marx's day. Yet, at the same time, Marx avoided falling into the trap of Engels's later "dialectical materialism," which, ironically, drew too heavily on both Hegel's *Logic* and his *Philosophy of Nature,* abstractly superimposing a despiritualized Hegelian dialectic (i.e., conceived in purely logical terms, divorced from Hegel's self-mediating spirit) on top of what was otherwise a mechanical view of the universe. Instead, Marx provides, as we have seen, a cautious constructionism, fully in tune with his own practical materialism, which always emphasized the role of human praxis, while remaining sensitive to natural conditions, evolutionary change, and the metabolic interaction of humanity and the earth.

Marx's main contribution in this area was methodological. He saw "the economic formation of society" as part of a process of "natural history" and struggled within his critique of political economy to take account of both natural conditions and the human transformation of nature (1976, p. 92). In the process, he applied a dialectical mode of analysis not to external nature itself (recognizing that the dialectic had no meaning aside from the self-mediating role of human beings as the agents of history) but rather to the *interaction* between nature and humanity, emphasizing the alienation of nature in existing forms of reproduction and the contradictory, nonsustainable character of the metabolic rift between nature and society that capitalism in particular had generated. Moreover, Marx conceived this metabolic rift not simply in abstract terms but in terms of the concrete crisis represented by the degradation of the soil and by the problem of human and animal "wastes" that engulfed the cities. Both were equal indications, in his analysis, of the metabolic rift between humanity and the soil, reflected in the antagonism of town and country.

The way in which Marx's analysis prefigured some of the most advanced ecological analysis of the late 20th century—particularly in relation to issues of the soil and the ecology of cities—is nothing less than startling. Much of the recent work on the ecology of the soil (Magdoff et al. 1997; Mayumi 1991; Gardner 1997) has focused on successive, historical breaks in nutrient cycling. The first such break, associated with the second agricultural revolution, is often conceived in essentially the same

American Journal of Sociology

terms in which it was originally discussed by Liebig and Marx and is seen as related to the physical removal of human beings from the land. This resulted in the failure to recycle human organic wastes back to the land, as well as the associated break in the metabolic cycle and the net loss to the soil arising from the transfer of organic products (food and fiber) over hundreds and thousands of miles. It was these developments that made the creation of a fertilizer industry necessary. A subsequent break occurred with the third agricultural revolution (the rise of agribusiness), which was associated in its early stages with the removal of large animals from farms, the creation of centralized feedlots, and the replacement of animal traction with farm machinery. No longer was it necessary to grow legumes, which had the beneficial effect of naturally fixing nitrogen in the soil, in order to feed ruminant animals. Hence, the dependence on fertilizer nitrogen increased, with all sorts of negative environmental consequences, including the contamination of ground water, the "death" of lakes, and so on. These developments, and other related processes, are now seen as related to the distorted pattern of development that has characterized capitalism (and other social systems such as the Soviet Union that replicated this pattern of development, sometimes in even more distorted fashion), taking the form of a more and more extreme metabolic rift between city and country—between what is now a mechanized humanity and a mechanized nature. Similarly, the ecological problem of the city is increasingly viewed in terms of its metabolic relationship to its external environment (focusing on the flows of organic nutrients, energy, etc.) and the ecological distortions that this entails (Wolman 1965; Giradet 1997; Fischer-Kowalski 1997; Opschoor 1997).

The fact that Marx was able to conceive a sociological approach that pointed to these developments when they were still in their very early stages represents one of the great triumphs of classical sociological analysis. It stands as a indication of how sociology could be extended into the ecological realm. It reinforces the view that ecological analysis, devoid of sociological insight, is incapable of dealing with the contemporary crisis of the earth—a crisis which has its source and its meaning ultimately in society itself.

It is not just Marxist sociology that is in a position to draw on Marx's insights in this respect, which are sociological as much as they are Marxist. Moreover, other paradigms within classical sociology have much more to contribute to the analysis of the natural environmental context of human social development than is commonly supposed. There is no doubt that Weber and Durkheim were both concerned in their own ways with the metabolic interaction between nature and society. Although systematic investigations into the work of Weber and Durkheim in this respect still

Environmental Sociology

have to be undertaken, it is not to be doubted that embedded in their sociologies were important insights into ecological problems. When Weber wrote at the end of *The Protestant Ethic and the Spirit of Capitalism* of a civilization characterized by "mechanized petrification" that might continue along the same course—that of formal or instrumental rationality—"until the last ton of fossilized coal" was burnt, he was suggesting the possibility of a wider social and environmental critique of this civilization (Weber [1904–5] 1930, pp. 181–82). Likewise, Durkheim's discussions of Darwinian theory and its implications for social analysis pointed the way toward a sociological understanding of the coevolution of nature and society. In the cases of Weber and Durkheim—as in Marx—we may surmise that an appropriation problem, coupled with a definitional problem, has hindered the appreciation of the way in which their sociologies took natural conditions into account.

Today, even among leading environmental sociologists who criticized the classical traditions of sociology for failing to take into account the physical environment, there is a dawning recognition that these classical traditions have proven themselves to be resilient in the face of challenges of environmental sociologists and are open to reinterpretation and reformulation along lines that give greater weight to ecological factors. Dunlap points to the emergence, in recent years, of "'greener' versions of Marxist, Weberian and symbolic interactionist theories" (1997, p. 34). Ironically, it is coming to be recognized that the problem of "human exemptionalism," that is, the neglect of the physical environment, may have been less characteristic of classical sociology than it was of the sociology that predominated after World War II—during a period when the faith in technology and the human "conquest" of nature reached heights never before attained, only to lead to disillusionment and crisis beginning with the 1960s. Developing an environmental sociology as an integral part of sociology as a whole thus requires that we reach back into past theories in order to develop the intellectual means for a thoroughgoing analysis of the present. For environmental sociology the crucial issue today is to abandon the "strong constructionism" of most contemporary sociological theory, which tends to view the environment as simply a product of human beings, and to move toward a more "cautious constructionism" that recognizes that there is a complex metabolic relation between human beings and society (Dunlap 1997, pp. 31–32, 35; Dickens 1996, p. 71). Surprisingly, this is turning out to be an area in which the classical sociology of the mid-19th and early 20th centuries still has much to teach us as we enter the 21st century—a century that is bound to constitute a turning point for good or ill in the human relation to the environment.

American Journal of Sociology

REFERENCES

Altvater, Elmar. 1993. *The Future of the Market.* London: Verso.
Bacon, Francis. (1620) 1994. *Novum Organum.* Chicago: Open Court.
Bailes, Kendall. 1990. *Science and Russian Culture in an Age of Revolutions.* Bloomington: Indiana University Press.
Beck, Ulrich. 1995. *Ecological Enlightenment.* Atlantic Highlands, N.J.: Humanities Press.
Benton, Ted. 1989. "Marxism and Natural Limits." *New Left Review* 178:51–86.
———. 1994. "Biology and Social Theory in the Environmental Debate." Pp. 28–50 in *Social Theory and the Global Environment,* edited by Michael Redclift and Ted Benton. New York: Routledge.
Benton, Ted, and Michael Redclift. 1994. "Introduction." Pp. 1–27 in *Social Theory and the Global Environment,* edited by Michael Redclift and Ted Benton. New York: Routledge.
Bing, Franklin C. 1971. "The History of the Word 'Metabolism.' " *Journal of the History of Medicine and Allied Sciences* 26 (2): 158–80.
Brock, William H. 1997. *Justus von Liebig.* Cambridge: Cambridge University Press.
Bukharin, Nikolai. 1925. *Historical Materialism: A System of Sociology.* New York: International.
———. 1971. "Theory and Practice from the Standpoint of Dialectical Materialism." Pp. 11–33 in *Science at the Crossroads.* London: Frank Cass.
Burch, William. 1971. *Daydreams and Nightmares.* New York: Harper & Row.
Burkett, Paul. 1997. "Nature in Marx Reconsidered." *Organization and Environment* 10 (2): 164–83.
Buttel, Frederick. 1986. "Sociology and the Environment." *International Social Science Journal* 109:337–56.
———. 1987. "New Directions in Environmental Sociology." *Annual Review of Sociology* 13:465–88.
———. 1996. "Environmental and Resource Sociology." *Rural Sociology* 61 (1): 56–76.
Caneva, Kenneth. 1993. *Robert Mayer and the Conservation of Energy.* Princeton, N.J.: Princeton University Press.
Carey, Henry. 1858. *Letters to the President on the Foreign and Domestic Policy of the Union.* Philadelphia: M. Polock.
———. (1858–59) 1867. *Principles of Social Science,* vol. 2. Philadelphia: J. B. Lippincott.
———. (1847) 1967a. *The Past, the Present and the Future.* New York: Augustus M. Kelley.
———. (1853) 1967b. *The Slave Trade Domestic and Foreign.* New York: Augustus M. Kelley.
Catton, William. 1982. *Overshoot.* Urbana: University of Illinois Press.
Catton, William, and Riley Dunlap. 1978. "Environmental Sociology: A New Paradigm." *American Sociologist* 13:41–49.
Churchill, Ward. 1996. *From a Native Son.* Boston: South End.
Clark, John. 1989. "Marx's Inorganic Body." *Environmental Ethics* 11:243–58.
Cohen, Stephen. 1980. *Bukharin and the Bolshevik Revolution.* Oxford: Oxford University Press.
Darwin, Charles. (1859) 1968. *The Origin of Species.* Middlesex: Penguin.
Déléage, Jean-Paul. 1994. "Eco-Marxist Critique of Political Economy." Pp. 37–52 in *Is Capitalism Sustainable?* edited by Martin O'Connor. New York: Guilford.
Dickens, Peter. 1992. *Society and Nature.* Philadelphia: Temple University.
———. 1996. *Reconstructing Nature.* New York: Routledge.
———. 1997. "Beyond Sociology." Pp. 179–92 in *International Handbook of Environ-*

Environmental Sociology

mental Sociology, edited by Michael Redclift and Graham Woodgate. Northampton, Mass.: Edward Elgar.

Dryzek, John. 1997. *The Politics of the Earth*. Oxford: Oxford University Press.

Dunlap, Riley. 1997. "The Evolution of Environmental Sociology." Pp. 21–39 in *International Handbook of Environmental Sociology*, edited by Michael Redclift and Graham Woodgate. Northampton, Mass.: Edward Elgar.

Dunlap, Riley, and William Catton. 1979. "Environmental Sociology." Pp. 57–85 in *Progress in Resource Management and Environmental Planning*, vol. 1. Edited by Timothy O'Riordan and Ralph D'Arge. New York: John Wiley & Sons.

———. 1994. "Struggling with Human Exceptionalism." *American Sociologist* 25 (1): 5–30.

Dunlap, Riley, and Kenneth Martin. 1983. "Bringing Environment into the Study of Agriculture." *Rural Sociology* 48 (2): 201–18.

Durkheim, Émile. (1911–12) 1983. *Pragmatism and Sociology*. Cambridge: Cambridge University Press.

———. (1893) 1984. *The Division of Labor in Society*. New York: Free Press.

Durkheim, Émile, and Marcel Mauss. 1963. *Primitive Classification*. Chicago: University of Chicago Press.

Eckersley, Robyn. 1992. *Environmentalism and Political Theory*. New York: State University of New York Press.

Engels, Friedrich. (1874–80) 1940. *The Dialectics of Nature*. New York: International.

———. 1964. "Outlines of a Critique of Political Economy." Pp. 197–226 *The Economic and Philosophic Manuscripts of 1844*, edited by Dirk J. Struik. New York: International.

———. (1872) 1975. *The Housing Question*. Moscow: Progress.

Ernle, Lord. (1912) 1961. *English Farming Past and Present*. Chicago: Quadrangle.

Ferkiss, Victor. 1993. *Nature, Technology and Society*. New York: New York University Press.

Feshbach, Murray, and Arthur Friendly, Jr. 1992. *Ecocide in the U.S.S.R.* New York: Basic.

Fischer-Kowalski, Marina. 1997. "Society's Metabolism." Pp. 119–37 in *International Handbook of Environmental Sociology*, edited by Michael Redclift and Graham Woodgate. Northampton, Mass.: Edward Elgar.

Foster, John Bellamy. 1997. "The Crisis of the Earth." *Organization and Environment* 10 (3): 278–95.

Gardner, Gary. 1997. *Recycling Organic Wastes*. Washington, D.C.: Worldwatch.

Geertz, Clifford. 1963. *Agricultural Involution*. Berkeley: University of California Press.

Georgescu-Roegen, Nicholas. 1971. *The Entropy Law in the Economic Process*. Cambridge, Mass.: Harvard University Press.

Giddens, Anthony. 1981. *A Contemporary Critique of Historical Materialism*. Berkeley and Los Angeles: University of California Press.

Giradet, Herbert. 1997. "Sustainable Cities." *Architectural Design* 67:9–13.

Goldblatt, David. 1996. *Social Theory and the Environment*. Boulder, Colo.: Westview.

Golley, Frank. 1993. *A History of the Ecosystem Concept in Ecology*. New Haven, Conn.: Yale University Press.

Gould, Stephen Jay. 1987. *An Urchin in the Storm*. New York: W. W. Norton.

Grundmann, Reiner. 1991. *Marxism and Ecology*. Oxford: Oxford University Press.

Harvey, David. 1996. *Justice, Nature and the Geography of Difference*. New York: Blackwell.

Hayward, Tim. 1994. *Ecological Thought*. Cambridge, Mass.: Polity.

Hillel, Daniel. 1991. *Out of the Earth*. Berkeley and Los Angeles: University of California.

American Journal of Sociology

Horkheimer, Max, and Theodor Adorno. 1972. *The Dialectic of Enlightenment.* New York: Continuum.
Jacobs, Michael. 1994. "The Limits to Neoclassicism." Pp. 67–91 in *Social Theory and the Environment,* edited by Michael Redclift and Ted Benton. New York: Routledge.
Järvikoski, Timo. 1996. "The Relation of Nature and Society in Marx and Durkheim." *Acta Sociologica* 39 (1): 73–86.
Johnston, James. 1851. *Notes on North America.* London: William Blackwood & Sons.
Kautsky, Karl. (1899) 1988. *The Agrarian Question,* 2 vols. Winchester, Mass.: Zwan.
Komarov, V. L. 1935. "Marx and Engels on Biology." Pp. 190–234 in *Marxism and Modern Thought.* New York: Harcourt, Brace.
Lebowitz, Michael. 1992. *Beyond Capital.* London: Macmillan.
Leiss, William. 1974. *The Domination of Nature.* Boston: Beacon.
Lenin, V. I. 1961. *Collected Works,* vol. 5. Edited by Victor Jerome. Moscow: Progress.
Liebig, Justus von. 1859. *Letters on Modern Agriculture.* London: Walton & Maberly.
———. 1863. *The Natural Laws of Husbandry.* New York: D. Appleton.
———. 1865. *Letters on the Subject of the Utilization of the Metropolitan Sewage.* London: W. H. Collingridge.
———. (1842) 1964. *Animal Chemistry or Organic Chemistry in its Application to Physiology and Pathology.* New York: Johnson Reprint.
Magdoff, Fred, Less Lanyon, and Bill Liebhardt. 1997. "Nutrient Cycling, Transformations and Flows." *Advances in Agronomy* 60:1–73.
Malthus, Thomas. 1970. *Pamphlets.* New York: Augustus M. Kelley.
Margulis, Lynn, et. al. 1998. Foreword to *The Biosphere,* by V. I. Vernadsky. New York: Copernicus.
Marshall, Alfred. 1920. *Principles of Economics.* London: Macmillan.
Martinez-Alier, Juan. 1987. *Ecological Economics.* Oxford: Basil Blackwell.
Marx, Karl. (1847) 1963. *The Poverty of Philosophy.* New York: International.
———. (1875) 1971*a. Critique of the Gotha Programme.* Moscow: Progress.
———. (1861–63) 1971*b. Theories of Surplus Value,* pt. 3. Moscow: Progress.
———. (1857–58) 1973. *Grundrisse.* New York: Vintage.
———. 1974. *Early Writings.* New York: Vintage.
———. 1975. *Texts on Method.* Oxford: Basil Blackwell.
———. (1867) 1976. *Capital,* vol. 1. New York: Vintage.
———. (1865–70) 1978. *Capital,* vol. 2. New York: Vintage.
———. (1863–65) 1981. *Capital,* vol. 3. New York: Vintage.
Marx, Karl, and Friedrich Engels. (1848) 1967. *The Communist Manifesto.* New York: Monthly Review.
———. 1975*a. Collected Works.* New York: International.
———. 1975*b. Selected Correspondence,* edited by S. W. Ryazanskaya. Moscow: Progress.
Mayumi, Kozo. 1991. "Temporary Emancipation from the Land." *Ecological Economics* 4 (1): 35–56.
McConnell, Campbell. 1987. *Economics.* New York: McGraw Hill.
McLaughlin, Andrew. 1990. "Ecology, Capitalism, and Socialism." *Socialism and Democracy* 10:69–102.
———. 1993. *Regarding Nature.* Albany: State University of New York Press.
Medvedev, Roy. (1971) 1989. *Let History Judge.* New York: Columbia University Press.
Milton, Kay. 1996. *Environmentalism and Cultural Theory.* New York: Routledge.
Murphy, Raymond. 1994. *Rationality and Nature.* Boulder, Colo.: Westview.
———. 1996. *Sociology and Nature.* Boulder, Colo.: Westview.
Norgaard, Richard. 1994. *Development Betrayed.* New York: Routledge.
Nove, Alec. 1987. "Socialism." Pp. 398–407 in *The New Palgrave Dictionary of Eco-*

Environmental Sociology

nomics, vol. 4. Edited by John Eatwell, Murray Milgate, and Peter Newman. New York: Stockton.

O'Connor, James. 1998. *Natural Causes.* New York: Guilford.

Odum, Eugene. 1969. "The Strategy of Ecosystem Development." *Science* 164:262–70.

Opschoor, J. B. 1997. "Industrial Metabolism, Economic Growth and Institutional Change." Pp. 274–86 in *International Handbook of Environmental Sociology,* edited by Michael Redclift and Graham Woodgate. Northampton, Mass.: Edward Elgar.

Pannekoek, Anton. 1912. *Marxism and Darwinism.* Chicago: Charles H. Kerr.

Parsons, Howard, ed. 1977. *Marx and Engels on Ecology.* Westport, Conn.: Greenwood.

Perelman, Michael. 1988. "Marx and Resources." *Environment, Technology and Society* 51:15–19.

———. 1993. "Marx and Resource Scarcity." *Capitalism, Nature, Socialism* 4 (2): 65–84.

Peterson, D. J. 1993. *Troubled Lands.* Boulder, Colo.: Westview.

Pigou, A. C. 1920. *The Economics of Welfare.* London: Macmillan.

Quaini, Massimo. 1982. *Marxism and Geography.* Totowa, N.J.: Barnes & Noble.

Redclift, Michael. 1984. *Development and the Environmental Crisis.* New York: Methuen.

Redclift, Michael, and Graham Woodgate. 1994. "Sociology and the Environment." Pp. 51–66 in *Social Theory and the Global Environment,* vol. 1. Edited by Michael Redclift and Ted Benton. New York: Routledge.

Ricardo, David. 1951. *Principles of Political Economy and Taxation.* Cambridge: Cambridge University Press.

Sauer, Carl. 1963. *Land and Life.* Berkeley: University of California Press.

Schmidt, Alfred. 1971. *The Concept of Nature in Marx.* London: New Left.

Schnaiberg, Allen. 1980. *The Environment.* Oxford: Oxford University Press.

Shanin, Teodor. 1983. *Late Marx and the Russian Road.* New York: Monthly Review.

Skaggs, J. M. 1994. *The Great Guano Rush.* New York: St. Martin's.

Thompson, F. M. L. 1968. "The Second Agricultural Revolution, 1815–1880." *Economic History Review* 21 (1): 62–77.

Uranovsky, Y. M. 1935. "Marxism and Natural Science." Pp. 136–74 in *Marxism and Modern Thought.* New York: Harcourt, Brace.

Vavilov, N. I. 1971. "The Problem of the Origin of the World's Agriculture in the Light of the Latest Investigations." Pp. 97–106 in *Science at the Crossroads.* London: Frank Cass.

Vernadsky, V. I. (1922) 1998. *The Biosphere.* New York: Copernicus.

Weber, Max. (1904–5) 1930. *The Protestant Ethic and the Spirit of Capitalism.* London: Unwin Hyman.

Weiner, Douglas. 1988*a. Models of Nature.* Bloomington: Indiana University Press.

———. 1988*b.* "The Changing Face of Soviet Conservation." Pp. 252–73 in *The Ends of The Earth,* edited by Donald Worster. New York: Cambridge University Press.

Wolman, Abel. 1965. "The Metabolism of Cities." *Scientific American* 213 (3): 179–90.

World Commission on Environment and Development. 1987. *Our Common Future.* New York: Oxford University Press.

[5]

Sociology Vol. 35, No. 1, pp. 93–110. Printed in the United Kingdom © 2001 BSA Publications Limited

Linking the Social and Natural Sciences: Is Capital Modifying Human Biology in Its Own Image?

Peter Dickens
Faculty of Social and Political Sciences
University of Cambridge

ABSTRACT Social science has long fought shy of the natural sciences. Meanwhile, concerns with the environment, health and the new genetics are creating a need for systematic links to be made between these disciplines. This paper suggests a new way in which social theory can be linked to biology. Recent developments in biology point to the importance of considering organisms in relation to their environment. And work in epidemiology stresses the links between the infant-development, health in later life and the well-being of future generations. Complex combinations of genetically-determined predispositions and capitalist social relations are responsible for important features of contemporary social stratification and well-being. The paper is informed by critical realist epistemology and Marx's theory of the subsumption. Such a fusion leads to a key assertion. Capital tends to modify the powers of human biology in its own image.

KEYWORDS biology, the body, critical realism, health, social theory.

Biology and the social sciences: the challenge

A decade ago Benton (1991) argued that there are four main reasons why an alliance between the natural and social sciences should be attempted. Feminism and gay liberation clearly raise very important questions as the biological or social bases to gender or homosexuality. 'The politics of health' raises similar issues. The social science literature in this area is largely based on statistical correlations and people's understandings of their circumstances. An understanding of the causal mechanisms involved in people's well-being remains severely under-conceptualised. Under-standing environmental degradation also surely entails a fusion between the social and natural sciences. There can again be no escape from what Benton (1991) called 'the enormously complex web of biological, chemical and physical interactions' involved. Debates over animal rights and animal welfare also raise major question-marks over the society/biology dichotomy. The supposed divide between humans on the one hand and animals on the other can no longer be left unproblematised. Underlying human behaviour and development are causal mechanisms similar to those in the non-human world. The recent transmission of *spongiform encephalopathy* from cows to humans particularly posed these continuities in a catastrophic way. It attacked the human mind, that very part of human beings which supposedly makes them distinct from other species.

There is therefore an extremely strong case for developing the social sciences in ways which make them reflect on-going and rapidly developing interactions between society and the causal powers of nature. The urgency for a realignment of these separate spheres is just as great now as it was ten years ago and the forms of politics discussed by Benton are just as strident as ever. Furthermore, biology has become a decreasingly monolithic discipline and it is now becoming clear which versions are likely to be useful in making an effective fusion between the natural and social sciences.

A fifth ground for exploring biology–society relations: and problems of explanation

A fifth reason for sociologists now taking biology seriously has been the very rapid rise of the new genetics and its promises for future human well-being. The problem is that of explanation. Take the following press report:

> CRACKING THE CODE OF HUMAN LIFE
>
> UNRAVELLING THE SECRETS OF CHROMOSOMES WILL CHANGE THE FACE OF RESEARCH INTO CURES AND TREATMENTS OF ILLNESSES FOR YEARS TO COME
>
> In human terms, the fact that chromosome 22, the second smallest of the human chromosomes, carries genes linked to schizophrenia, chronic myeloid leukaemia and a trisomy 22, the second commonest cause of miscarriages, as well as genes involved in congenital heart disease, mental retardation, breast cancer and cataracts, offers hopes for vast improvements in the way diseases and medical conditions are treated for hundreds of years.
>
> [*Guardian*, 2 December 1999]

Note the phraseology. A chromosome is said to carry genes 'linked' to schizophrenia and other diseases. Other genes are 'involved in' congenital heart disease. The 'fact' of these links and involvements 'offers hopes for vast improvements'. But what explanatory claims can be made here? A small number of illnesses, such as Huntington's and cystic fibrosis, are indeed acquired by largely genetic means (Marteau and Richards 1996). But for the great mass of diseases with connections to specific alleles the actual level of risk is small and highly variable between individuals. A disease such as Huntington's is therefore a 'freak' in these terms. And even with Huntington's the age of onset is very variable, suggesting other extra-genetic processes may be at work. The connections between genes and illnesses are therefore far more complex than the publicity surrounding the human genome project might suggest. It is not at all clear, for example, whether such illnesses are a product of a number of gene combinations or of relations between the human body and the external social or even natural environment. Words such as 'linked' and 'involved in' seem at first sight to be saying much but in explanatory terms they are saying rather little.

At this point we can advance an alternative approach to understanding. Critical realism views the world as 'a stratified open system'. It offers ways of exploring the relations between different areas of knowledge such as social theory and biology. It sees the social, biological and indeed physical world as an open system with multiple causes underlying outcomes. It nevertheless asserts that there are relatively enduring structures and causal mechanisms in both nature and society. Entities, such as human bodies, are seen as having latent powers of ways of acting and they combine with one another and with contingent circumstances to produce what is experienced and observed. Thus contingent factors, such as the particular kind of society in which a human being develops, may well be important in terms of how generative structures, mechanisms and tendencies operate in practice. Finally, critical realism is 'critical' in the sense that it questions the theories and social practices which it studies (Bhaskar 1979; Sayer 2000).

All this is a far cry from the supposedly 'scientific' accounts of the implications of the human genome project. It is extremely difficult to establish the causal links between particular genes and particular illnesses. If we are looking for the most significant underlying causes of most human illnesses we would be well advised to start adopting a different explanatory strategy.

A very similar point can be made regarding the connection between genes and 'IQ' or cognitive capacities. Note the following press-cutting:

SCIENTISTS DISCOVER GENE THAT CREATES HUMAN INTELLIGENCE

By Roger Highfield, Science Editor

The first gene that influences human intelligence has been found by scientists, a discovery with huge social and educational implications. The research could herald the development of genetic tests to target potential high-flyers, pave the way to IQ-boosting drugs and will raise fears that embryos that lack smart genes could be aborted. The gene, believed to be the first of many that contribute to normal intelligence, has been found after a six-year search by a team headed by Prof. Robert Plomin of the Institute of Psychiatry at London ... The find marks the first piece of the puzzle of how genetic contributes to human intellect, compared with influences such as education and upbringing.

[*Daily Telegraph*, 31 October 1997]

The discoveries made, however, are much less dramatic than this cutting suggests (Plomin *et al.* 1994; Plomin 1999; Chorney *et al.* 1998). Plomin and his colleagues do claim to have found a link between a gene (IGF2R) and a high level of intelligence as measured by *g*, a capacity for complex mental work first invented by Spearman. But, as they themselves point out, this only accounts for a small proportion of genetic influences on *g*. And most individuals with high *g* levels do not even have the particular form of the gene (the 'allele') associated with high *g* levels.

Clearly the possibility of certain kinds of intelligence being genetically inherited cannot be wholly ruled out. But major problems of explanation again arise. Correlation, even if it is found, is not the same thing as explanation. It is extremely unlikely that there is a gene 'for' such a complex capacity as 'intelligence'. Indeed, there are no genes 'for' anything. Some mutations of some genes in rare instances produce a disease such as Huntington's. But genes code protein and this usually has multiple functions in the body. A similar point arises in connection with IQ. Whatever inherited influences there may be in IQ, they stem from interactions between a large number of variations in a large number of genes. Plomin's work itself shows that no alleles are associated with more than 1 per cent variance in IQ scores. In short, scientific endeavour is a long way from discovering a gene that 'creates human intelligence'.

The scale to which explanation must surely shift is that of interactions between genes within the human genome. It must also turn to the relationships between the organism and its environment. Particularly significant here are the 'homeobox' clusters of genes producing proteins which activate thousands of other genes in the organism (Robertis *et al.* 1990; Erwin *et al.* 1997; Gehring 1998). Homeobox genes are profoundly enduring structures, referred to by some biologists as 'God Genes'. They have existed for around one billion years and are conserved in all animals and plants. They lay down the basic components and ground plan for all animals; a head, back and thorax, for example, as well as eyes, brain-structure and appendages such as paws, fins or wings. And within the organism these genes are consistently found in the same spatial relations to the 'paralogous' genes deriving from gene duplication rather than common descent. To put all this in realist terms, the causal powers of growth and development are still genetic but the explanation has now shifted to relations between complexes of genes within the organism. Furthermore, a basic underlying structure (one deriving from broadly shared and largely unchanging functions) has developed variations in relation to specific environmental contexts. Some variations in appendages have allowed, for example, faster swimming, speedier running or better grasping. Still others have enabled the development of mental capacities or 'intelligence' in human beings and perhaps in other animals. But, again, such development of intellectual capacities was based, and is still based, on an originally small number of genes (Wills 1993).

Recent tendencies: social constructionism and reductionism

Meanwhile, contemporary social theory's understanding of 'embodiment' has over recent years been increasingly subjected to postmodernist and post-structuralist thought. This largely denies the genetic, corporeal and physical reality of the biological body. The result, in Williams's terms, is that bodies are 'radically reconfigured as fluid, multiple, fragmented and dispersed' (1999:798):

> The body, in short, is everywhere and nowhere today: the more it is talked about and studied, the more elusive it becomes; a fleshy organic entity and a natural symbol of society; the primordial basis of our being-in-the-world and the discursive product of disciplinary technologies of power/knowledge; an on-going structure of lived experience and the foundational basis of meaning, imagination and reason; the wellspring of human emotionality and site of numerous 'cyborg' couplings; the physical vehicle of personhood and identity and the basis from which social institutions, organisations and structures are resisted or reproduced.

But, as Turner (1984) has written, 'for the individual and the group, the body is simultaneously an environment (part of nature) and a medium of the self (part of culture)' (pp. 38–9; see also Shilling 1997). Social theory has excelled at recognising the body as the medium of the self but not as part of nature. It thereby reproduces the dualism between mind and body, culture and nature, which has long bedevilled Western culture.

Benton's original paper insisted on a 'cautious' welcome of biology into social theory. His plea for caution stemmed from his concern with biological reductionism. His concern was partly with neo-Darwinism and the reduction of the biological organism (its structure and behaviour) into its genetic fragments (Dawkins 1989). As is now well known, sociobiology attempted to explain social behaviour, including that of humans, in terms of the copying and reproduction of genes. Even at the time Benton was writing such a view was under fierce attack. One criticism, coming from some biologists themselves, concerned Dawkins's attempt to treat genes as autonomous. Reproduction involves new gene *combinations*, and these (as distinct from the copying of genes) are likely to be a powerful source of variation.

Biological reductionism nevertheless still thrives. Evolutionary psychology, for example, is a rapidly-growing and fashionable field of intellectual endeavour. It stands at the opposite end of the spectrum from the strong social constructionism practised by many social theorists. While the latter denied the reality of biology altogether, evolutionary psychology promotes biology to the exclusion of all forms of social understanding. One of its chief exponents is Pinker (1997). He describes the mind as: 'a neural computer, fitted by natural selection with combinatorial algorithms for causal and probabilistic reasoning about plants, animals, objects and people. It is driven by goal states such as food, sex, safety, parenthood, friendship, status and knowledge' (1997:524). This type of psychology is therefore another kind of fundamentalism, one which attempts to explain almost all forms of behaviour from our evolutionary inheritance. Clearly human beings and their behaviour must in some sense be a product of evolution, but this work attributes almost any kind of practice (including altruism, selfishness, the killing of step-children by step-parents and an enduring preference for savannah-style landscapes) to our phylogeny and our genetically inherited 'hard-wiring.' (Curry *et al.* 1996). Evolutionary psychology is 'sociobiology sanitised'; a re-packaging with some of its most outrageous claims (including its sexism) toned down (Dusek 1999). But it signally fails adequately to address the criticisms which Gould and Lewontin (1979) and others originally had of sociobiology. Despite the pleas of Pinker and others to the contrary, evolutionary psychology continues to produce a continuous stream of *post hoc*, non-testable and non-falsifiable 'just-so stories'. It also ignores the fact that many features of organisms are by no means straightforward products of our evolution. A number of the evolved characteristics of humans and other animals have become used and adapted in new ways. The general consciousness of human beings is clearly a product of evolution. However, it can by no means be assumed that such consciousness necessarily evolved for humans in such a way as to leave humans 'selfish', 'altruistic' or 'sexist'. Therefore the 'reading off' of such behaviours from our evolutionary inheritance is a misconstrued and misleading project. But again most damaging from a social theorist's viewpoint is the attribution by evolutionary psychology of virtually all forms of social and power relations to genetics and our evolutionary inheritance. Ways of overcoming the Cartesian dualism between body and mind certainly need to be found, but reducing mind to biology is not the right way of going about this complex task (Benton 1999).

So the original arguments mounted by Benton in favour of sociology taking biology seriously have hardly gone away. Furthermore, as this paper will shortly suggest, the recent arrival of new forms of Social Darwinism and recent assertions regarding the link between human biology and human intellectual capacities lend new and further urgency to the creation of an improved link between biology and social theory.

Biology and society: recognising the organism in context

Developments within feminism seem at first to offer some of the most productive ways forward. On the one hand, embodiment has long been central to feminism; and this work has been extremely important in terms of understanding how the body is signified, lived and controlled (see, for example, Price and Shildrick 1999). On the other hand, this work still largely eschews the biological body; largely, no doubt, in recoil from biological reductionism and essentialism. The outcome is that, while the body is central to feminist theory it remains largely studied through a cultural lens; its interior processes and its development remain missing. As Birke (1999:46) puts it: 'Human development – the process of becoming human as we enter the world, or of becoming an adult as we grow – seem to be missing from feminist insistence on "lived bodies" or social constructionism'. Alternative concep- tualisations of the body tend to be more attractive to feminist biologists such as Birke (see also Hubbard 1990). Benton alluded to these in drawing attention to traditions in biology which could allow much improved relations between social theory and the life sciences. He argued that 'a *variety* of philosophical resources exists, not just for rethinking the relationships among the life-science disciplines, but also for establishing non-reductive conceptual links between the life- and human-sciences' (1991:17, Benton's emphasis).

These alternative approaches give particular emphasis to the organism and its environment. They have become more mainstream since the time Benton's paper was published. The problem of explanation is now less one of biology and sociology failing to communicate. Rather, it is defining and eventually linking those relatively well-established areas of biology and social theory which are broadly compatible. In the case of biology, holistic, non-reductionist, approaches in fact go back a long way. Benton mentioned early twentieth-century biologists such as Haldane and Whitehead. In our own era we could mention the highly influential figure of Waddington. He and later authors such as Wills (1993) and Maynard Smith (1998) suggest that organisms grow not only in relation to their physical and social environment but through realising their new genetically-based potentials.

Note that this approach to ontogeny, or lifetime-development of organisms, is compatible with the organism-centred approach to phylogeny, or the long-term evolution of species outlined in the earlier 'homeobox genes' discussion. Both are different sides of the same coin. Lifetime-development depends on genetic information accumulated over millions of years of evolution and long-term evolution depends on developmental changes in successive generations. Both also give special emphasis to interactions between organism and environment (Oyama 1985).

The above forms of biology offer in general terms the possibility of a liaison between the natural and social sciences. In particular, they allow recognition of the organism developing within particular contexts or types of society. But we must now elaborate on precisely how this liaison should be put into effect. Development *in utero* and during the earliest stages of childhood turn out to be key meeting-points.

Understanding cognitive capacities: a developmental perspective

Over a century ago Darwin's cousin, Francis Galton, used identical twins to test the extent to which IQ is a product of heredity or environment. The assumption was that if the twins turned out to have similar levels of intelligence this could be accounted for by the children sharing some inborn characteristics. Today identical twins are still very frequently used for this type of study, the idea being to find two such twins who are separated at birth and brought up by two different adoptive families. If their level of IQ remains similar despite their different upbringings then an obvious conclusion is that the similarity is due to the fact that have exactly the same genotype. If their IQ level is different, then the explanation is assumed to be environmental. On the face of it recent studies seem to confirm the conclusion that genetic similarity is a powerful predictor of IQ level. Thus experiments by Bouchard *et al.* (1990) suggest that genes are responsible for between 60 and 70 per cent of variation in IQ.

In *The Bell Curve* (Herrnstein and Murray 1994) this study was used to develop the argument that IQ is substantially inherited; that people with high IQs are breeding their own kind and people with low IQs are doing the same, albeit on a larger scale. The result is an increasingly polarised society, made up of a 'cognitive elite' on the one hand and what Daniels *et al.* term a 'cognitive peasantry' on the other. In what Hernnstein and Murray believe to be a meritocratic society it is the dull (and rapidly growing) peasantry which is losing out in the competition for jobs in an economy increasingly based on the capacity to handle knowledge. According to *The Bell Curve*, therefore, human society is part of the natural order. It is largely a product of innate, genetically-acquired, qualities.

However, more recent work has challenged such conclusions on the basis of twin studies (Daniels *et al.* 1997; Devlin *et al.* 1997). First, these authors re-examined the data from a number of studies of identical twins who had been reared apart. Furthermore, they explored data from two hundred studies of IQ correlations between different types of relatives. They made the common-sense observation that twin studies necessarily emphasise the role that genes have to play. But as twins marry different people and pass their genes to the next generation, the twins' genes encounter a wholly different genetic context. Some of these genes' effects will change or even disappear. The genes from different parents will start combining with one another and create unpredictable results.

The above processes place a considerable question-mark over *The Bell Curve's* explanation of self-inflating 'cognitive elites' and 'underclasses'. Genes are obviously inherited but it is wrong to conclude, as did Herrnstein and Murray, that IQ is therefore genetically inherited. Such a conclusion is unwarranted by the state of biological knowledge. Furthermore, there is evidence that people are quite capable of significantly increasing their IQ levels over their lifetimes. Finally, a review carried out by the American Psychological Association (Neisser *et al.* 1996) shows that employers are increasingly looking for people with a range of skills other than simple 'IQ'. A premium is now being placed on, for example, interpersonal skills, 'personality' and what Goleman (1996) calls 'emotional intelligence'.

A second challenge concerns the importance of the uterine 'environment'; the earliest experiences and relationships of the developing child. Again, experiments with twins proved helpful. Dizygotic or fraternal twins are the result of the fertilisation of different eggs by different sperm in the same mother. Their genetic 'similarity' is therefore the same as that of normal siblings born at different times. Nevertheless, fraternal twins still demonstrate a higher heritability of IQ than non-twin siblings who have been raised together. These differences are well documented and they are usually attributed to the fact that non-twin siblings are born at different times and are therefore raised under somewhat different conditions. But Daniels *et al.* show that the higher heritability of IQ amongst fraternal twins might not be a product of genes at all, but a product of their shared intrauterine environment. Statistical analysis (using models which incorporated or did not incorporate the effect of uterine environment) provided the closest 'fit' to the data. Their conclusion is that only about one-third of the similarity in IQs can be linked to their genes. This is a far cry from the 60 to 80 per cent suggested by Herrnstein and Murray.

So the genetically-based conclusions of *The Bell Curve* are, to say the least, premature (see also Devlin *et al.* 1997). While genes *per se* may have a role to play, other factors are important in determining levels of intelligence. Specifically, the very earliest phase in a child's development is especially important. As Daniels *et al.* point out (1997:58): 'Brain growth occurs during both the prenatal and perinatal period, with substantial growth occurring *in utero* and the majority of brain development completed by age one'. But, while rejecting the purely genetic argument, the significant point is that biology and society are combining to affect levels of intelligence. As Daniels *et al.* stress, much of the brain's growth takes place while the baby is still *in utero*. Pregnant mothers' excessive alcohol consumption, drug-use, smoking cigarettes, and eating poor diets are closely linked to the intellectual impairment of their children (Reinisch *et al.* 1995; Olds *et al.* 1994; Rush *et al.* 1980; Pagliaro and Pagliaro 1996). Daniels and his colleagues are not sociologists but their discussion leads directly into areas where sociologists have distinctive views. It is important not to adopt uncritically the stereotype surrounding problem drug-use, alcohol-intake and poor diet. Such problems are spread across the social spectrum. But such practices are indeed concentrated amongst the unemployed and those with few material resources. Furthermore it has been shown that over 40 per cent of people with these problems are the children of one or more adults with the same problems, poor people having inadequate diets and engaging in excessive alcohol-consumption, drug-use and cigarette consumption. Recent work on 'problem' drug-users suggests that the problem is indeed increasingly prevalent amongst the unemployed and those with few material resources (Das Gupta 1990; Kandall 1996).

In short, we appear to be coming back to something resembling *The Bell Curve* thesis, but from a wholly different direction. Genes themselves are having a relatively small effect on intelligence and hence social stratification. But social or class position can have significant effects on human biology, and on the development of generations of children and on their cognitive capacities. Note again that 'biology' has shifted away from mechanistic assumptions about genes *per se* and towards the causal powers of organisms, albeit genetically-inherited causal powers. We can take this point further by turning to the impacts of the earliest stages of development on later life.

Understanding well-being: the significance of pre-natal development

Recent research also offers important explanations of how ill-health is passed on within families. It offers significant clues as to how an underclass of relatively unhealthy people may be in the process of creation and reproduction. Again, complex combinations of biological and social processes are involved, genes *per se* receiving relatively small explanatory weight.

Epidemiological work strongly suggests that a pregnant mother gives an unwitting 'weather-forecast' to her unborn child, signalling via the uterus the kind of world into which her child is to be born (Barker 1998). This is a well-recognised effect in non-human mammals but it has so far received little attention in twin studies. Children from poor backgrounds, it now appears, are being biologically designed 'to make the best of a bad job' (Bateson and Martin 1999:111). Their blood-flow, metabolisms and production of hormones lead to altered bodily structures and functions. In evolutionary terms they are thereby made 'well-adapted' to their environment. As a result they are more likely to suffer from illnesses such as chronic bronchitis and cardiovascular disease. Furthermore, their lives are likely to be shorter than average.

Most importantly, 'weather-forecasts' are passed on from one generation to the next, the capacity of a woman to nourish her fetus being in part determined by that woman's own intrauterine experience. Thus the effects of her mother's environment are transmitted to her own child. We can therefore envisage a possible biological mechanism contributing to the reproduction of an 'unfit' underclass over the long term; generations of people being not only born into poor circumstances but biologically 'designed' for such circumstances. They not only suffer ill-health and early death themselves but pass on these afflictions and fates to future generations. Studies of marriage patterns shows that mating takes place between people from similar social and educational backgrounds(Lampard 1992; Prandy and Bottero 1998). This tendency must further widen the gap between the developmental endowments of the better and worst off.

Paradoxically, however, a child also suffers if he or she is born into conditions to which they are *not* well-adapted. As long as an individual remains undernourished in post-natal life its glucose–insulin metabolism is adequate. But if, for example, a child whose mother has been starved is born into a world with high levels of sugar in food, this results in an increased predisposition to diabetes. This is known as 'non-insulin dependent diabetes'. People who have retained a traditional lifestyle in, for example, rural Africa or the highlands of Papua, New Guinea, experience low levels of non-insulin dependent diabetes or avoid this problem completely. Populations in Europe, North America and the western Pacific societies, by contrast, are much more affected. In the latter case up to one-third of the population is afflicted by this problem. Similar outcomes have been found amongst populations who have undergone rapid migration. Ethiopian Jews transferred to Israel during a recent famine in Ethiopia are a case in point. After only four years 9 per cent of those under 30 years had developed non-insulin-dependent diabetes (Barker 1998).

We are witnessing here the failure of those least 'fit' for their environment. But of course there is a world of difference between the above accounts and those of, say, Herbert Spencer or *The Bell Curve*. This epidemiological work incorporates the environment itself having direct major effects on human well-being. It insists on the social as well as the biological causes of illness and short lives.

Human development and post-natal experience

However, the significance of early development for later well-being extends well beyond the pre-natal stage. Piaget and his followers described and theorised the mental development of children from their earliest age (for a recent discussion, see Sylva 1997). It is a process of transition from a dependence on thought based on immediate experience to one in which powers of abstraction are used to interpret the world and solve problems. These general changes in adolescent reasoning are accompanied by, and reflected in, the formation of personality, the construction of sexual identity and, more generally, the creation of self in relation to others (Kohlberg 1969). Such development, according to Piaget, is continued into later stages of individual's life. The individual emerges from the 'egocentrism' of childhood to recognise the needs and levels of knowledge of others (Cox 1980).

Piaget's work has been much developed. General patterns of infant development differ according to the cultures in which they develop. Children in Western capitalist societies are quickest to grasp abstract ideas separated from their context (Buck Morss 1982). To put this in critical realist terms, it is modern capitalist society which particularly promotes and develops a child's potential for abstract thought. Nonetheless, Piaget's work on ontogeny of the human body continues to be highly regarded and it suggests an important way in which the concerns of biology (specifically, the causal mechanisms underlying development) can again be linked with the more conventional concerns of sociology with social relations and the formation of human identity.

There is now, however, a further fast-growing literature again showing that the social relations a child experiences in infancy, childhood and adolescence strongly affect how he or she develops in later life (see, for example, Keating and Hertzman (eds.) 1999; Keating and Miller 1999; Marmot and Wadsworth (eds.) 1997; Montgomery *et al.* 1996; Montgomery *et al.* 1997). Thus emotional stability, educational performance, cognitive capacities and social mobility have all been demonstrated to be closely related to how a child has developed in the home, school and wider society. As Keating and Miller put it, following their survey of the literature (1999:232): 'it is already clear that these findings are consistent with the notion that early experience becomes biologically embedded, especially during sensitive periods, and has pervasive and enduring effects on later development'. Such a perspective clearly again places a massive question-mark over arguments that such capacities or incapacities are genetically hard-wired into the human population. And once more it turns towards forms of explanation based on the causal powers and propensities of human beings in relation to their environment.

The above work on early childhood therefore largely supplants attempts to explain well-being and intelligence simply in terms of either 'genes' or 'environment'. The arguments in this new approach all take human *development*, and its implications for later well-being, as a common starting-point. The debates centre on precisely how the life-course affects later illness and life-expectancy. Are discrete events in early life responsible for problems in adulthood? Are such problems the product of cumulative social processes during the life-course? Or are they, as we might expect, a combination of both such processes? Discrete events in early life indeed combine with shocks during the life to affect levels of health in adult life (Power and Hertzmann 1999). It seems clear that both such shocks are most likely to be experienced, however, by working-class people. It is they who are most subject to the classic risk factors generating later ill health. These include under-nutrition and other adverse circumstances affecting development, such as poor housing conditions, parental divorce and low levels of education during childhood. Note that the implications of this work for public policy are much more significant than that recognised by Herrnstein and Murray. For cognitive capacities and for health and well-being of all sorts, it is clear that interventions at the very earliest stages of a child's life could well bring very important benefits.

How does the realist perspective as outlined above relate to contemporary excitements with plastic, bionic, virtual and interchangeable bodies? (Williams 1997) Clearly it is important to examine how the body is socially constructed and how identities are made and remade via the body. But the central research task here must be to recognise the interplay between such constructions (more accurately, construals) and the corporeal reality to which they are linked. As Williams puts it in his discussion of human disability, 'diversity and difference ... are rooted in real impaired bodies' (1999:811). They are, to use his words, 'organically moored'. The causal mechanisms and emergent properties of human bodies are, to coin a phrase, the material base on which the ideological superstructures surrounding human biology are formed. None of this is to argue that such construals are unimportant. They remain central because they clearly influence how illnesses, levels of intellectual ability and so forth are interpreted by the particular kinds of society in which they develop. And they are of key importance in determining health strategies, education policies and research-funding.

The subsumption of human biology to capital?

It seems clear that the deliberate genetic modification of foetuses will shortly take place. This will enable the elimination of genes which are believed to predispose people to certain illnesses. As suggested earlier, the range of afflictions which can be treated in this way is likely to be limited. Later, these practices may even be extended in an attempt to improve intelligence, appearance, athleticism and behaviour (Silver 1998; Dejevsky 1999). Sociologists and others will be interested to learn that geneticists in Alabama claim to have found a 'perfect husband' gene which disposes rats (non-human 'rats', that is) to be monogamous (Connor 1999). The social and political implications of such developments may or may not be far-reaching. They are perhaps best explored by science-fiction movies such as *Bladerunner*, human genetics there being used by a ruling class to create an underclass of slaves and soldiers with strictly limited lifespans.

The implication of the work reported in this paper, however, is that processes of biological modification analogous to those outlined in such films are already under way; and without the intervention of malevolent geneticists working for trans-national corporations. Furthermore, the relations between society and biology are complex and dialectical. Some of the causal processes work in exactly the opposite way to that suggested by *The Bell Curve*. The genetically induced causal powers of human organisms are being influenced by society rather than society being a direct product of genes. At the same time, the embedding of biology into social structure (resulting in, for example, intergenerational reproduction of people predisposed to illness and short lives) also feeds back into social structure. There is a biological basis to an underclass but it is not the one offered by *The Bell Curve* (Dickens 2000).

Missing from Benton's original paper calling for closer links between biological theory and the social sciences was some relatively clear and theoretically informed suggestion as to precisely what might be expected from such a fusion. Marx's theory of subsumption, radically extended beyond his original conception, offers a plausible understanding of what may be taking place. He lays out his theory of the 'formal' and 'real' subsumption of labour to capital in *Capital*, Volume 1. The 'formal' process is 'the direct subordination of the labour to capital, irrespective of the state of the former's technological development' (1976:1034). 'Real' subsumption is the thoroughgoing transformation of labour processes and the relations of production under distinct social and technological conditions. 'Real' subsumption, therefore, alludes to workers losing their autonomy. Their work is governed by the movements of the capitalist's machine. Seen in the wider context of Marx's historical materialism, the subsumption of labour to capital is the process by which human *internal* nature is changed while social relations are made to transform *external* nature into the things people need.

Marx's original analysis of 'de-skilling' has now, for course, been considerably discussed and developed (Braverman 1974; Hales 1980). The process in the sphere of paid work consists of taking 'knowledges' out of a given labour process and placing them in the possession of a distinct set of workers sometimes referred to as 'mental' workers. But such a transfer is a preliminary to transforming such 'knowledges' and re-embodying them in new labour processes. Such segregation of a distinct ruling class charged with managing mental labour has a long history. It has been especially significant to the rise of capitalism. An important prelude to such processes is the segregation of popular scientific knowledge from the science of the laboratory or field-station. Changes during the late eighteenth and early nineteenth centuries were especially significant (Drouin and Vensude-Vincent 1996; Outram 1996; Secord 1996; Shteir 1996). It was during this era when that what Shteir refers to 'a deepening divide between the generalist and the specialist' developed (p. 151). Understanding de-skilling has been extended by, amongst others, feminist writers. Mies and Shiva (1993) are amongst those who have shown how in developing countries the separation and subordination of certain kinds of work systematically relegates certain kinds of labour such as domestic work or child-care to unpaid women.

The suggestion of this paper, however, is that such subsumption may be taking an even more radical form than that suggested by recent commentators. Capital, in conjunction with the various forms of biological predispositions outlined earlier, may over the long term have been shaping human biology in its own image. Thus the genetically endowed propensities for human beings to develop, grow and die have been harnessed or incorporated by capital to make distinct classes of people. The epidemiological work outlined above implies that feedback loops are being set up which are creating real biological differences between classes. More 'holistic' forms of biology lend support to the possibility of such developments. The early and pioneering work of Waddington (1957) on fruit flies pointed not only to the robustness of organisms to environmental change (and their capacity for changing the form of their development as a result of environmental change) but, even more importantly, the transmission of certain kinds of characteristics to future generations. This is not a case of Lamarckian transmission of *acquired* characteristics between generations. Rather, it is the realisation of existing genetic potential within organisms resulting from environmental shocks. In such ways, and over time, organisms adapt to their environment. The implication is, of course, that different potentials could be realised under different social-cum-environmental circumstances.

Understanding biology-society relations: ways forward

The developmental perspective emphasised in this paper raises three new questions for interdisciplinary research. First, social scientists need to continue monitoring on-going work by biologists, epidemiologists and others on the complex processes by which biological-cum-social classes are being made. Secondly, there is growing evidence from animal studies that some acquired characteristics can after all be passed on to future generations. Complex feedbacks are occurring between somatic cells (those not usually transmitting genetic information) and germ cells (those giving rise to sperm and egg and thus transmitting genetic information to future generations). Acquired resistance to certain diseases is probably being passed on to later generations via the germ line. Possibly, therefore, some people are not only making themselves resistant to disease but are *genetically* transmitting such resistance to future generations. Increasing life-spans in affluent Western societies may be important here. On the one hand, they allow more scope for acquired tolerances to be transmitted to the germ-line and taken up by later generations. On the other hand, longer lifespans may allow somatic faults more time to be transmitted to the germ-line (Steele *et al.* 1998). The subsumption of labour by capital may therefore be taking place via the modification of the germ-line. Note that this understanding still crucially relies on recognising processes both within the genome as a whole and between the genetically constituted organism and its environment.

Third, social science must remain alive to emergent contradictions. For example, the question of fetal growth and its impact on later health has not so far been raised in debates over the new reproductive technologies. Low-income women are most likely to be used as surrogates (Rowland 1992). As we have seen, however, levels of nutrition and other factors mean that the fetuses of such women may particularly suffer from short and relatively unhealthy lives. As regards human development and cognitive capacities, the continuing creation of groups of people with well-enhanced capacities for handling abstract ideas may in some sense be good for the management of capitalist social relations, but it may be bad for the maintenance of harmonious human relations. It may also be bad for the effective management of the environment, a process which entails constant movement between abstraction and engagement with concrete detail. Thus the concentration of intellectual capacities within self-reproducing elites may be counter-productive, and 'the cognitive peasantry' may have a better idea of how to behave towards one another and to the surrounding environment.

These are all matters on which biologists and social scientists should now be working together. They are likely to be amongst the central areas of social and political conflict in the twenty-first century.

ACKNOWLEDGEMENTS
Special thanks to David Barker, Berth Danermark, Jenneth Parker, Martin Richards, Angela Ryan, Richard Wilkinson and three anonymous referees.

REFERENCES
Barker, D. 1998. *Mothers, Babies and Health in Later Life.* London: Churchill Livingstone.

Bateson, P. and Martin, P. 1999. *Design for Life*.London: Cape.

Benton, T. 1991. 'Biology and Social Science: Why the Return of the Repressed Should be Given a (Cautious) Welcome. *Sociology* 25:1–30.

Benton, T. 1999. 'Evolutionary Psychology and Social Science.' *Advances in Human Ecology* 8:65–98.

Bhaskar, R. 1979. *The Possibility of Naturalism*. Brighton: Harvester.

Birke, L. 1999. 'Bodies and Biology', in J. Price and M. Shildrick (eds.) 1999, op. cit.

Bouchard, T., Lykken, D., McGue, M., Segal, N. and Tellegen, A. 1990. 'Sources of Psychological Differences: The Minnesota Study of Twins Reared Apart'. *Science* 250:346–53.

Braverman, H. 1974. *Labor and Monopoly Capital*. New York: Monthly Press.

Buck-Morss, S. 1982. 'Socio-Economic Bias In Piaget's Theory and Its Implications for Cross-Cultural Studies', in S. Modgil and C. Modgil (eds.), *Jean Piaget: Consensus and Controversy*. London: Holt, Rinehart and Winston.

Chorney, M., Chorney, K., Seese, N., Oliver, M., Daniels, J., McGuffin, P., Thompson, L., Detterman, D., Benbow, C., Lubinski, D., Eley, T. and Plomin, R. 1998. 'A Quantitative Trail Locus Associated with Cognition Ability in Children'. *Psychological Science* 9:159–66.

Connor, S. 1999. '"Perfect Husband" gene discovered'. *Independent*, 18 August.

Cox, M. 1980. *Are Young Children Egocentric?* London: Batsford.

Curry, D., Cronin, H. and Ashworth, J. (eds.) 1996. 'Matters of Life and Death'. *Demos Quarterly* 10.

Daniels, M., Devlin, B. and Roeder, K. 1997. 'Of Genes and IQ', in B. Devlin, S. Fienberg, D. Resnick and K. Roeder (eds.), *Intelligence, Genes and Success*. New York: Springer-Verlag.

Das Gupta, S. 1990. 'Extent and Pattern of Drug Abuse and Dependence', in H. Ghose and D. Maxwell (eds.), *Substance Abuse and Dependence*. London, Macmillan.

Dawkins, R. 1989 (2nd edn). *The Selfish Gene*. Oxford: Oxford University Press.

Dejevsky, M. 1999. 'Psst! You Want a Smart Kid?' *Independent*, 5 August.

Devlin, B., Daniels, M. and Roeder, K. 1997. 'The Heritability of IQ'. *Nature* 388:468–71.

Dickens, P. 2000. *Social Darwinism*. Buckingham: Open University Press.

Drouin, J-M. and Bensaude-Vincent, B. 1996. 'Nature for the People', in N. Jardine, J. Secord, and E. Spary (eds.), *Cultures of Natural History*. Cambridge: Cambridge University Press.

Dusek, V. 1999. 'Sociobiology Sanitized: Evolutionary Psychology and Gene Selectionism'. *Science as Culture* 8:129–69.

Erwin, D., Valentine, J. and Jablonski, D. 1997. 'The Origin of Animal Body Plans'. *American Scientist*, March-April. http://www.amsci/articles/9/articles/Erwin-1.html

Gehring, W. 1998. *Master Control Genes in Development and Evolution*. New Haven: Yale.

Goleman, D. 1996. *Emotional Intelligence*. London: Bloomsbury.

Gould, S. and Lewontin, R. 1979. 'The Spandrels of San Marco and the Panglossian Paradigm.' *Proceedings of the Royal Society B* 205:581–98.

Hales, M. 1980. *Living Thinkwork*.London: CSE Books.

Herrnstein, R. and Murray, C. 1994. *The Bell Curve*. New York: Free Press.

Hubbard, R. 1990. *The Politics of Women's Biology*. London: Rutgers.

Kandall, S. 1996. *Substance and Shadow*. Cambridge, Mass.: Harvard University Press.

Keating, D. and Hertzman, C. 1999. *Developmental Health and the Wealth of Nations*. New York: Guilford.

Keating, D. and Miller, F. 1999. 'Individual Pathways in Competence and Coping', in D. Keating, and C. Hertzman, 1999, op. cit.

Kohlberg, L. 1969. 'Stage and Sequence: The Cognitive Developmental Approach to Socialisation, in D. Goslin (ed.), *Handbook of Socialisation Theory and Research*. Chicago: Rand McNally.

Lampard, R. 1992. 'An Empirical Study of Marriage and Social Stratification'. Unpublished doctoral dissertation, University of Oxford.

Marmot, M. and Wadsworth, M. (eds.) 1997. 'Fetal and Early Childhood Environment: Long-Term Health Implications'. *British Medical Bulletin* 53:(1).

Marteau, T. and Richards, M. 1996. *The Troubled Helix.* Cambridge: Cambridge University Press.

Marx, K. 1976. *Capital. Vol. 1.* Harmondsworth: Pelican.

Maynard Smith, J. 1998. *Shaping Life: Genes, Embryos and Evolution.* London: Weidenfeld and Nicholson.

Mies, M. and Shiva, V. 1993. *Ecofeminism.* London: Zed Books.

Montgomery, S., Bartley, M., Cook, D. and Wadsworth, M. 1996. 'Health and Social Precursors of Unemployment in Young Men in Great Britain'. *Journal of Epidemiology and Community Health* 50:415–22.

Montgomery, S., Bartley, M. and Wilkinson, R. 1997. 'Family Conflict and Slow Growth'. *Archives of the Diseases of Childhood* 77:326–30.

Neisser, U., Boodoo, G., Bouchard, T., Boykin, A., Brody, N., Ceci, S., Halpern, D., Loehlin, J., Perloff, R., Sternberg, R. and Urbina, S. 1996. 'Intelligence Knowns and Unknowns'. *American Psychologist* 51:77–101.

Olds, D., Henderson, C. and Tatelbaum, R. 1994. 'Intellectual Impairment in Children of Women Who Smoke Cigarettes in Pregnancy'. *Pediatrics* 93:221–7.

Outram, D. 1996. 'New Spaces in Natural History', in N. Jardine, J. Secord and E. Spary (eds.) op.cit.

Oyama, S. 1985. *The Ontogeny of Information.* Cambridge: Cambridge University Press.

Pagliaro, A. and Pagliaro, L. 1996. *Substance Use among Children and Adolescents.* New York: Wiley.

Pinker, S. 1997. *How the Mind Works.* Harmondsworth: Allen Lane/Penguin Press.

Plomin, R., McClearn, G., Smith, D., Vignetti, S., Chorney, M., Chorney, K., Benditti, C., Kasarda, S., Thompson, L., Detterman, D., Daniels, J., Owen, M. and McGriffin, P. 1994. 'DNA Markers Associated with High Versus Low IQs: The Quantitative Tract Loci (QTL) Project. *Behaviour Genetics* 24(2):107–18.

Plomin, R. 1999. 'Genetics and General Cognitive Ability'. *Nature* (forthcoming).

Power, C. and Heertzman, C. 1999. 'Health, Well-Being and Coping Skills', in D. Keating, and C. Hertzman, 1999, op. cit.

Prandy, K. and Bottero, W. 1998. 'The Use of Marriage Data to Measure the Social Order in Nineteenth-Century Britain'. *Sociological Research Online* 3, 1.

Price, J. and Shildrick, M. (eds.) 1999. *Feminist Theory and the Body.* Edinburgh: Edinburgh University Press.

Reinisch, J., Saunders, S., Mortensen, E. and Robin, D. 1995. 'In Utero Exposure to Phenobarbitol and Intelligence Deficits in Adult Men.' *Journal of the American Medical Association* 274:1518–25.

Robertis, E., Oliver, G. and Wright, C. 1990. 'Homeobox Genes and the Vertebrate Body Plan'. *Scientific American,* 263(1):26–32.

Rowland, R. 1992. *Living Laboratories.* London: Lime Tree.

Rush, D., Stein, Z., Sussex, M. and Brody, N. 1980. Chapter in D. Rush, M. Stein and M. Sussex (eds.), *Diet in Pregnancy.* New York: Liss.

Sayer, A. 2000. *Realism and the Social Sciences.* London: Sage.

Secord, A. 1996. 'Artisan Botany', in N. Jardine, J. Secord and E. Spary (eds.), op. cit.

Shilling, C. 1997. 'The Undersocialised Conception of the Embodied Agent in Modern Sociology.' *Sociology* 31:737–54.

Shteir, A. 1996. *Cultivating Women, Cultivating Science.* Baltimore, Md: Johns Hopkins Press.

Silver, L. 1998. *Remaking Eden.* London: Weidenfeld and Nicholson.

Steele, E., Lindley, R. and Blanden, R. 1998. *Lamarck's Signature.* St. Leonards: Allen & Unwin.

Sylva, K. 1997. 'Critical Periods in Childhood Learning'. *British Medical Journal* 53(1):185–97.

Turner, B. 1984. *The Body and Society.* Oxford: Blackwell.

Waddington, C. 1957. *The Strategy of the Genes.* London: Allen & Unwin.

Williams, S. 1997. 'Modern Medicine and the "Uncertain Body": From Corporeality to Hyperreality?' *The Social Science of Medicine* 45(7):1041–9.

Williams, S. 1999. 'Is Anybody There? Critical Realism, Chronic Illness and the Disability Debate'. *Sociology of Health and Illness* 21(6):797–819.

Wills, C. 1993. *The Runaway Brain.* London: Flamingo.

Biographical note: PETER DICKENS is Senior Research Fellow, Faculty of Social and Political Sciences, University of Cambridge. He is also Fellow and Director of Studies in Social and Political Sciences, Fitzwilliam College. He has written widely on urban sociology, environmental sociology and the links between the natural and social sciences.

Address: University of Cambridge, Faculty of Social and Political Sciences, Free School Lane, Cambridge, CB2 3RQ.

[6]

SOCIETY AS HYBRID BETWEEN
MATERIAL AND SYMBOLIC REALMS
TOWARD A THEORETICAL FRAMEWORK OF
SOCIETY-NATURE INTERACTION

Marina Fischer-Kowalski and Helga Weisz

ABSTRACT

We approach an understanding of society-nature interactions by proposing an epistemological framework accessible for both natural and social sciences. The framework focuses on the mutual dependencies of symbolic/cultural and biophysical processes that are relevant for societal dynamics, thus linking social and economic development to environmental change. We begin with a description of three overall models of society-nature interactions, as proposed by scientists from three different disciplines whose theoretical concepts have substantially influenced our own approach. We then proceed to our own model, starting with a description of two key processes of society-nature interactions: *socioeconomic metabolism* and *colonization of natural processes*. Socioeconomic metabolism refers to flows of materials and energy between society and nature. Colonization of natural processes refers to the deliberate and sustained transformation of natural processes using various forms of intervention such as planting, application of agrochemicals, consolidation of

Advances in Human Ecology, Volume 8, pages 215-251.
ISBN: 0-7623-0567-3

farmland, changes of water regimes, breeding, or genetic engineering. Based on this, we sketch an epistemological framework that allows for a concept of society-nature interactions that is consistent with both a social systems framework and a natural systems framework, respecting the complexity on both sides. Finally, we discuss the implications of this understanding of society-nature interaction for social theory.

INTRODUCTION

In order to achieve an adequate understanding of contemporary environmental problems and, even more, of "sustainable development," it is essential to focus on society-nature interactions. This requires a common epistemological basis that can serve as a bridge between the social and the natural sciences and that presents itself as accessible for both sides. This demands sufficiently complex notions of both society and natural systems.

The difficulty inherent in such a task is essentially twofold. First, it carries with it the long tradition of Western dualistic epistemology and, in particular, the classic problem of Cartesian dualism; that is, how can the material and the symbolic interact?[1] We believe that modern systems theory, in particular, the theory of open, self-organizing, but operationally closed systems (cf. Maturana and Varela 1975; Buckley 1968), offers a solution to this epistemological dualism.

Second, we have to deal with a dualism between philosophies of science, namely, between the natural and the social sciences. This introduces the well-known problems associated with interdisciplinarity.[2] Apparently, all approaches aiming at conceptualizing society-nature interactions struggle with this challenge. From its beginnings, human ecology has tried to assemble various related approaches from different disciplines and rearrange them within a new paradigm (Young 1974). Likewise, ecological economics attempts to describe the interdependencies between economic systems and ecosystems (Georgescu-Roegen 1971; Daly 1973; Boulding 1966).

What is the problem with this dualism between the philosophies of science? With a certain amount of overstatement, one can say that the mainstream social sciences leave us conceiving of society or the economy as highly complex units to be explained solely by their internal mechanisms. These complex units are seen as surrounded by an undifferentiated "environment" largely irrelevant for the system's dynamics. The natural sciences generally exhibit the complementary view. There, natural systems are viewed as highly complex units with many interdependencies and, at the same time, human agency is described by a single-actor-model of very low complexity ("humans" causing "disturbances"). Most certainly, it is this dualism with which we must cope.

Thus, what we are seeking is a conception of society-nature interactions that would not be reductionistic in either direction—one that would be, in other words, neither "naturalistic" nor "culturalistic." What criteria should be applied to judge success for such a project? One set of criteria would refer to the explanatory value of our approach. Does it help to understand how—given the preconditions of biological evolution—human societies could be so successful as to allow the human species to become so dominant on this planet? And, is our approach useful in attaining an understanding of the major features of different modes of subsistence[3] and the transitions between them?

A realistic theory of society-nature relations must be applicable to a wide range of historical conditions and long-term mutual feedbacks between society and nature. It has to allow for placing social change into a natural history framework and for considering the time perspective. Finally, the theory must be able to provide a conceptual framework for understanding contemporary "environmental problems" and help to adequately structure empirical data about society-environment interactions. It must conceptually allow for an anthropogenic environmental crisis; that is, it must take into consideration the possibility of biophysically relevant interactions between symbolic (cultural) systems and the material world that are historically variable and that are not compensated for by natural adaptation. This implies a conception of cultural evolution beyond anthropological adaptationism.

We begin here with a description of three overall models of society-nature interactions, as proposed by scientists from three different disciplines: Stephen Boyden, human ecologist; Maurice Godelier, cultural anthropologist; and Rolf Peter Sieferle, historian. Their theoretical concepts have substantially influenced our own approach. We then proceed to our own model, starting with a description of two key processes of society-nature interactions: *socioeconomic metabolism* and *colonization of natural processes.*[4]

Finally, we work to complete the circle and sketch an epistemological framework linking our theory to the issues presented in this introduction: How can society-nature interactions be conceptualized in a manner consistent with both a social systems and a natural systems framework, respecting the complexity on both sides? What can be deduced from this understanding of society-nature interactions for social theory?

We proceed by tracing our own history as a team, which began with the endeavor to describe societies' "pressures on the environment." We chose a path of gradually increasing theoretical integration and seem to have ended up posing a quite fundamental challenge to traditional social science perspectives on society.

THREE MODELS OF SOCIETY–NATURE INTERACTION: BOYDEN, GODELIER, AND SIEFERLE

Boyden's Human Ecological Model

In his book *Biohistory: the Interplay Between Human Society and the Biosphere*, Stephen Boyden (1992) sketches a basic conceptual framework of the interrelationships between the biosphere and society on the one hand, and between humans and society on the other. Boyden's model has an important and uncommon feature: the distinction between the material and the symbolic world (in Boyden's terms, biophysical realities and abstract culture) overlaps with the distinction between human society and nature (see Figure 1). Ecologically based concepts commonly picture biosphere and society (or, more often, the "anthroposphere") as concentric circles, with one being part of the other. Boyden's use of the term biosphere refers especially to ecosystems and does not include those material elements incorporated under the general heading of "human society." According to Boyden, human society comprises abstract culture, humans, and their activities/artifacts. However, abstract culture is a realm of its own:

> It is necessary to draw attention to the important distinction in this model between *biophysical actualities* and *cultural abstractions*. Cultural abstractions are those abstract aspects of human situations comprising *culture* itself, including beliefs, assumptions, attitudes, and values, and *cultural arrangements*, such as the economic system, political organisation, and institutional structures (Boyden 1992, p. 97).

Artifacts belong to the realm of human society, and they are placed between the biosphere and humans. There are four interrelations between humans and biosphere: biometabolism, technometabolism, other impacts, and an indirect relation via artifacts. Biometabolism, according to Boyden, refers to the "material inputs and outputs, and the throughputs of energy, of human organisms themselves," while technometabolism "is defined as the inputs and outputs of human populations of materials and energy which are due to technological processes" (Boyden

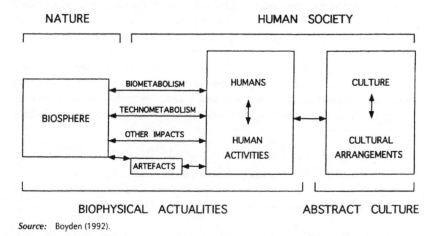

Source: Boyden (1992).

Figure 1. Society-Nature Interrelationship According to Boyden

1992, p. 72).[5] Humans and their artifacts exist as amphibians between the two realms. Humans are viewed as biological organisms on the one hand, and as "individual humans" on the other; they are the bearers of sociocultural "human activities" (farming, mining, traveling, etc.).

Although Boyden developed an interdisciplinary model with remarkable social science orientation, he nevertheless places culture within a *biological* evolutionary framework. He remarks about *the emergence of human culture:* "As the anatomical changes were taking place in our ancestors..., something else was happening of tremendous significance. This was the evolutionary emergence of the *human aptitude for culture*, and hence the emergence of culture itself" (Boyden 1992, p. 74).

According to this text, there is no major qualitative difference between the biological evolution of an attribute of the species, as an individual capability of each member ("human aptitude for culture"), and the evolution of elaborate symbolic systems. The weight of the argument is based upon the individual organism. As Boyden sees it, culture is not an emergent feature of social systems but is, rather, the summation of genetically transmitted aptitudes such as the ability to invent symbols, which finally leads to spoken language. "Language is an accumulative phenomenon, the consequence of very small contributions made by a very large number of people over a very long time" (Boyden 1992, p. 74). The aptitude for culture as understood by Boyden also comprises the ability to learn the meanings of symbols (this ability, however, can also be found in other animals, especially mammals) and use them in communication, as well as "the tendency to be sensitive to, to accept and absorb the messages transmitted from the cultural environment" (Boyden 1992, p. 75).

Society–Nature Interrelations as a Driving Force of Social Change: Godelier

One key element of Maurice Godelier's work is a commitment to the tradition of Levi-Strauss. This can be seen, for example, in the privileged position that the notion "pensée" has in his work.[6] *Pensée*—or, in the common English translation, *mind*—refers to a reality *sui generis* and is irreducible to individual consciousness. Consequently, Godelier devotes much attention to cultures and their self-organizing patterns.[7] For Godelier, humans are not just individual representatives of a species; he always relates human activities to culture and society.[8]

Another key element is Godelier's attempt to reformulate the relationship between infrastructure and suprastructure, as well as, within the Marxist tradition, the dialectics of means of production and modes of production. This twofold theoretical commitment enables him to avoid a naturalist or materialist reductionism and to avoid instrumentalizing culture merely as a tool for adaptation. Likewise, there is enough Marxist influence in Godelier's thinking to lead him to search for the consequences of the material conditions of the appropriation of nature for society's mode of organization and, in turn, to search for the consequences that modes of organization have for modes of appropriation of nature—even if he considers this a methodologically difficult task.

In the introduction to *The Mental and the Material*, Godelier formulates his core hypothesis, thereby establishing a bridge between cultural anthropology and world history:

> *Human beings have a history because they transform nature.* It is indeed this capacity which defines them as human. Of all the forces which set them in movement and prompt them to invent new forms of society, the most profound is their ability to transform their relations *with* nature by transforming *nature itself* (Godelier 1986, p. 1).

This way of looking at history relates to the Marxist tradition, but it transcends it in an ecological, or coevolutionary, direction. The classic reading of Marx leads to a discussion of changing "modes of appropriation of nature"[9] through the development of new means of production. Godelier's reading stresses the fact that human appropriation of nature modifies nature, and this modified nature in turn stimulates social change. Godelier thus deviates from common social science by viewing nature as historically variable, not as static—and his core hypothesis attributes societies' historical dynamics to a feedback process from nature. So, according to Godelier, the dynamic force in human history is not so much the dialectics of the "means of production" and "modes of production" with nature as an external element—something to be appropriated—but is instead the very interaction between social and natural relations itself.

Godelier distinguishes among several types of materiality, depending on the degree of interconnectedness with human society:

> First, there is that indefinite part of nature which still remains outside the direct or indirect sway of mankind, but never ceases to affect it: the climate, the nature of the subsoil, etc. [The examples given by Godelier would nowadays need to be questioned.] Secondly, there is that part of nature which has been transformed by human intervention, but indirectly, without the latter's agents having either intended or anticipated the consequences of their action. [Examples given are erosion and changes in vegetation due to the repeated use of bush fires; here, we would tend to use the term "anthropogenically influenced."] Thirdly, there is of course that part of nature which has been directly transformed by human beings and cannot thereafter be reproduced without their attention, energy and labor. [Examples given are cultivated plants and domestic animals. In our terminology, as discussed below, we would call this type of materiality "colonized."] Parts of nature transformed by human beings for their own use in the process of producing their material conditions of existence: . . . tools and weapons made out of wood, stone, etc., constitute so many external organs extending the reach of the human body and adding their powers to its. [We would term these "artifacts."] Then there are all those elements of nature which, detached from it by human action, serve in either their original form or after transformation as material support for the production of social life in all its dimensions. [Examples given are shelters and other buildings—here, we also would speak of artifacts, thereby using a similar definition of this term as Boyden.] The boundary between nature and culture, the distinction between the material and the mental, tend moreover to dissolve once we approach that part of nature which is directly subordinated to humanity—that is, produced or reproduced by it (domestic animals and plants, tools, weapons, clothes). Although external to us this nature is

not external to culture, society or history. It is that part of nature which is transformed by human action and thought. It is a reality which is simultaneously material and mental. It owes its existence to conscious human action on nature.... This part of nature is appropriated, humanized, becomes society: it is history inscribed in nature (Godelier 1986, p. 4).

As with Boyden (and Marx), Godelier's core distinction between the material and the mental is not identical with the distinction between natural and societal. Material reality differs from mental (or symbolic, or *idéel*) reality, but society encompasses both. Thus, Godelier's categories very much resemble those of Boyden. Society, then, according to Godelier, is constituted by the coupling of a set of mental or symbolic elements, and a certain set of material elements.[10] Thus, Godelier's distinctions can easily be connected to Boyden's basic model of society-nature interrelations. What both do not demonstrate, however, in our judgement, is a perspective on complex evolving systems.

Complex Systems and Cultural Evolution According to Sieferle

Sieferle (1997a) tackles the problem that he calls the cultural evolution of the society-nature interrelationship. He is interested in how human societies and human cultures can acquire sufficient functional independence to potentially destroy the natural conditions of their own persistence despite being a product of natural evolution. Sieferle takes up the key elements of Boyden's model and develops it in accordance with Luhmann's theory of social systems.

Sieferle's model encompasses three elements: Nature (N), human Population (P), and Culture (C). N stands for nature in the sense of an ecologically ordered system. Nature comprises all material elements of reality except for human beings. Nature can be characterized as a self-organizing system, able to generate certain states of low entropy and maintain them over longer periods of time. P stands for human Population in the sense of humans' specific biological features. Population constitutes the interface between Nature and Culture. It performs as a carrier of information with respect to Culture, and as a carrier of physical functions with respect to Nature. It acts as a transformer of (symbolic) information into (material) functioning and vice versa. C stands for Culture and is the "assembly of information stored in the human nervous system or on other information carriers" (Sieferle 1997a, p. 38). Culture in and of itself is an autopoietic system, consisting of recursive communication and differentiated into various subsystems.[11]

For analytical purposes, Nature and Population can be looked upon as jointly making up a human ecological system; that is, the human population as a physical aggregate can be seen as being part of nature and entertaining certain material exchanges with (other) natural aggregates. Such a human ecological system could be analyzed by purely natural science methods. This approach, nevertheless, would fail to take account of the specific feature of human populations: that they

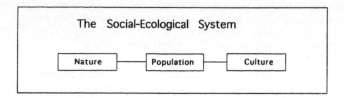

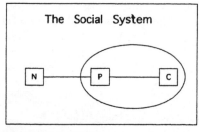
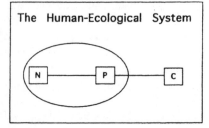

Source: Sieferle (1997a).

Figure 2.   Socioecological Interdependencies

are guided by an extrasomatic cultural system. To ignore this feature would be to reduce humans to being just one species with some particular genetic attributes among millions of other species. Such an abstraction might make sense for certain purposes, but it would provide a highly incomplete picture.

Likewise, Population and Culture can be looked upon as a system. Together they constitute what Sieferle calls the social system or society (see Figure 2). According to Sieferle, both elements are indispensable; neither can there be a purely symbolic, nonmaterial human society, nor can there be a human population without a cultural system. The Population serves as the physical carrier of information for Culture, and it serves as the carrier of physical functions. There can be no contact between Culture and Nature unless mediated by Population. Culture cannot "experience" Nature unless through Population, and Culture cannot influence Nature unless through Population. Nevertheless, the relationship between Population and Culture should not be interpreted as an instrumental one; neither can Population be viewed as "an instrument" of Culture, nor can Culture be viewed as "an instrument" of Population. They are functionally interdependent but far from being completely in control of one another. Population cannot control Culture, nor can Culture control Population.

Sieferle then proceeds to describe the interactions between the three elements under consideration. For the interaction between Nature and Population he distinguishes two interrelations. One is *biological*: the organisms that make up Population draw certain energetic and material inputs from Nature, and they produce certain outputs. They experience the impacts of temperature, atmospheric gases, or aggressive microorganisms. This biological exchange between Population and Nature affects both elements.

The second interaction between Nature and Population that Sieferle describes is a *technological* one. Population expends physical labor on elements of Nature, creating and maintaining artifacts. Sieferle considers not only buildings and machines, fields and forests, but also animals and plants under human control (or even genetically altered by humans) to be artifacts. These artifacts interact with other elements of Nature; they act upon them as an irritation to which the rest of Nature will show adaptive reactions—adaptations that alter the whole impact-profile of Nature, including the factors subject to biological exchange processes.

There is a symbolic interrelation between Population and Culture. Population acts as a carrier of functions for Culture; it transforms information, orders, and images into physical actions. It acts as Culture's one and only "organ of sense." Population represents its experiences symbolically and relates them in ways corresponding to specific subsystems of Culture: as scientific insight, social conflict, economic price, aesthetic complaint, and so forth. Sieferle stresses that the organization of these representations does not "mirror" processes in Nature; they are part of a different set of interrelations. Thus, changes in Nature may act upon Culture via the experiences and representations of Population by causing an irritation, to which Culture may react in many different ways. A "causal" reaction—that is, a reaction directed toward the origin of the irritation—is only one possibility and, as Sieferle states, not even the most likely one. Culture is therefore not, as ecological anthropology sometimes sees it, an adaptive instrument developed by Population to handle Nature. The relationship between Population and Culture is more complicated and more fragile.

> Since Culture cannot exist without Population, the evolutionary minimum condition of Culture
> is to provide Population with a behavior repertoire that permits survival. Ultimately, it must
> not irritate the interrelation between Population and Nature to a degree that Population would
> no more be able to support and pass on Culture. It is difficult, though, to identify this boundary
> condition in any specific case" (Sieferle 1997a, p. 53, our translation).

As in Boyden's model, Sieferle positions humans as members of two worlds. Referring to their physical properties, their bodies, they are part of material reality, and as carriers and communicators of information, they are part of the symbolic reality of Culture. Beyond this formal similarity, there is a substantial difference between Sieferle's and Boyden's concepts of culture. According to Sieferle, culture is an emergent property of systems of communication, functioning by its own self-referentiality, whereas for Boyden, culture originates from an individual "aptitude for culture" or from value orientations.

SOCIOECONOMIC METABOLISM

We will now take a closer look at the kind of society-nature interaction which Marx was the first to term "metabolism between man and nature." The basic question we address concerns the degree to which material and energetic processes that fit under the label "metabolism" may provide a useful understanding of the interrelation of society with nature. Our critical discussion begins with a brief review of various traditions dealing with such a notion.[12] In contemporary approaches to industrial metabolism or material flow analysis, which originated a decade ago, the various social science traditions that utilize this concept are typically not reflected. However, an epistemological consideration of the early attempts to apply the concept of metabolism to society are especially fruitful, for they provide a rich source of ways to bridge social and natural sciences. Subsequently, we will try to unfold our notion of socioeconomic metabolism and apply it to various modes of human subsistence up to contemporary industrial metabolism and its relation to prosperity.

Concepts of Metabolism in Sociology

Marx and Engels used the notion of a metabolism between man and nature in conjunction with the basic, almost ontological, description of the labor-process.

> The labor-process ... is human action with a view to the production of use-values, appropriation of natural substances to human requirements; it is the necessary condition for effecting exchange of matter between man and nature; it is the everlasting nature-imposed condition of human existence, and therefore independent of every social phase of that existence, or rather, is common to every such phase" (Marx 1990 [1867], p. 183).

Marx's and Engels' notion of metabolism was influenced by the contemporary biological concept of metabolism as portrayed in popular writings by physiological materialists such as Moleschott (1857).[13] Nineteenth-century biology described metabolism as an exchange of matter between an organism and its environment, rather than as cellular biochemical conversions, as modern biology does. Marx and Engels did not use this notion in a metaphorical sense only; they mean to imply a material exchange relation between humans and nature, a mutual interdependence beyond the widespread and simplistic idea of humans "utilizing nature." The notion points to a fundamental material interrelatedness on an anthropological level, but it is not used as a tool to analyze capitalist society. In their writings, there exists no such idea as accumulation of capital having to do with the appropriation of the accumulated "wealth" of nature (e.g., fossil fuels). Appropriation as a basis for capital accumulation is always—and is only—the appropriation of surplus human labor, as Martinez-Alier (1987, pp. 218-224) points out. In other contexts, Marx uses the expression "societal metabolism" as an analogue to describe the exchange of commodities and the relations of production within society (see Schmidt 1971, p. 92).

The application of concepts of natural sciences to society was not unusual in early sociology.[14] In contrast to contemporary concepts of socioeconomic metabolism, which stress the material aspect of metabolism, early social scientists focused on the energetic aspect. Herbert Spencer stated in his *First Principles* in 1862, that the process of societal progress and the differences in stages of advancement among societies relate to the amount of available energy. Societal progress is based on energy surplus. It is energy surplus in the first place that enables social growth, and thereby social differentiation, by providing space for cultural activities beyond basic vital needs (Spencer 1880).

Wilhelm Ostwald, winner of the 1919 Nobel Prize in chemistry, had a somewhat similar contribution to make. Referring to the second law of thermodynamics, he argued that minimizing the loss of free energy is the objective of every cultural development (Ostwald 1909). Thus, according to Ostwald, one may deduce that the more efficient the transformation from crude energy into useful energy, the greater a society's progress. For Ostwald, the increasing of efficiency has the characteristics of a natural law affecting every living organism and every society. He stresses that every society must be aware of the energetic imperative *(Energetischer Imperativ)*: "Don't waste energy, use it" (Ostwald 1909, p. 85). Additionally, Ostwald was one of the few scientists of his time sensitive to the limitations of fossil resources. According to him, a sustainable economy must use exclusively solar energy.[15]

Sir Patrick Geddes, cofounder of the British Sociological Society in 1902, sought to develop a unified calculation based upon energy and material flows and capable of providing a coherent framework for all economic and social activity (Geddes 1997 [1884]). He called for the emancipation of the economy from its monetary basis in favor of an economy of energy and resources. In four lectures at the Royal Society of Edinburgh, Geddes developed a type of economic input-output table in physical terms. Beginning with the sources of energy as well as the sources for materials used, Geddes shows how energy and materials are then transformed into products in three stages: the extraction of fuels and raw materials; manufacture; and transport and exchange. Between each of these stages there occur losses that must be estimated. The final product might then be surprisingly small in proportion to the overall input (Geddes 1997 [1884]). Geddes appears to have been the first scientist to approach an empirical description of societal metabolism on a macroeconomic level.

Frederick Soddy, another Nobel laureate in chemistry, also turned his attention to the energetics of society but did so with an important twist. He saw energy as a critical limiting factor of society and, thus, was one of the few social theorists sensitive to the second law of thermodynamics (Soddy 1912, 1922, 1926). Similarly, Werner Sombart (1919, II, p. 1137) in his analysis of late-eighteenth-century development at least recognized the social relevance of energy. The scarcity of fuel wood was, in his view, at that time seriously threatening the advance of capitalism altogether. In the mid-1950s, Fred Cottrell (1955) again raised the idea that available energy limits the range of human activities. According to him, this is one of the reasons why pervasive social, economic, political, and even psychological change accompanied the transition from a low-energy to a high-energy society.

Summarizing briefly, the concept of metabolism as applied to society appears to be not completely alien to the traditions of social theory. However, for the development of sociology as a discipline, these more or less sweeping energetic theories of society remained largely irrelevant. In contrast to sociology's "founding fathers," modern sociologists seldom refer to natural parameters as either causes or consequences of human social activities, and they almost never did so before the advent of the environmental movement. Neither the system-oriented nor the interaction-oriented U.S. traditions, nor the "materialist" Marxist traditions revived in the 1960s, dealt with possible physical properties of society and society-nature interaction (see Dunlap and Catton 1979 for a focus on the American literature). Some of the well-known French sociologists such as Michel Foucault (1977) and Pierre Bourdieu (1985) at least summoned the human body onto the sociological stage, so to speak, as did the German sociological theorist Norbert Elias (1994). Investigating the work of other major European macrosociological theorists, such as Jürgen Habermas (1984) and Niklas Luhmann (1984, 1989, 1997), one searches in vain for concepts referring to the material dimensions of the society-nature interaction.

Insights for Socioeconomic Metabolism from Anthropology

The origin of cultural anthropology (as in the works of Morgan 1963 [1877]) was, similar to that of sociology, marked by evolutionism—that is, by the idea of universal historical progress from more "natural" or "barbarian" to more "advanced" and "civilized" social conditions. Then, however, cultural anthropology split into two directions, one more functionalist, the other more culturalist.[16] The functionalist tradition is one from which contributions to societal metabolism could be expected; functionalism did not, as was the case in sociology, turn toward economics and distributional problems, but retained a focus on the society-nature interface. In effect, several conceptual clarifications and rich empirical material on societies' metabolism can be gained from this research tradition, which Orlove in his critical review (1980) terms ecological anthropology.

Leslie White, one of the most prominent anthropologists of his generation and an early representative of the functionalist tradition, rekindled interest in energetics. For White, the vast differences in the types of extant societies could be described as social evolution, and the mechanisms propelling it were energy and technology. "Culture evolves as the amount of energy harnessed per capita and per year is increased, or as the efficiency of the instrumental means (i.e. technology) of putting the energy to work is increased" (White 1949, p. 366). A society's level of evolution, he thought, can be assessed mathematically as product of the amount of per capita energy available and the efficiency of its conversion. So, in fact, this was a metabolic theory of cultural evolution, however unidimensional and disregarding of environmental constraints it may have been.[17]

Julian Steward's method of cultural ecology (Steward 1968) paid much attention to the quality, quantity, and distribution of resources within the environment. In the early comparative study "Tappers and Trappers" (Murphy and Steward 1955), for example, two cases of cultural (and economic) change are presented, in which tribes traditionally living from subsistence hunting and gathering (and some horticulture) completely change their ways of living as a consequence of changing their metabolism. The authors analyze this as being an irreversible shift from a subsistence economy to dependence upon trade. Translating this analysis into the terms of metabolism (a concept the authors do not apply), the following transformations took place: (1) the substitution of a metabolism based upon exchange with other societies for a metabolism based upon the natural environment, whereby these cultures became "primary producers" or "extractors" in a social division of labor on a grander scale; and (2) the substitution of certain new materials and sources of energy for traditional ones, the former being produced and distributed by completely different mechanisms on a completely different spatial scale. These changes in metabolism contribute to the transformation of numerous social and cultural features of these communities.

Several analyses of metabolism have been produced by authors grouped together by Orlove (1980) as "neofunctionalists": Marvin Harris, Andrew Vayda, and Roy Rappaport. The followers of this approach, according to Orlove, "see the social organization and culture of specific populations as functional adaptations which permit the populations to exploit their environments successfully without exceeding their carrying capacity" (Orlove 1980, p. 240). The *unit* maintained is a given population. Sociological functionalists would point to the maintenance of a particular social order instead. In contrast to biological ecology, neofunctionalists in anthropology treat adaptation not as a matter of populations but as a matter of cultures. Cultural traits are units which can adapt to environments and which are subject to selection. In this approach, human populations are believed to function within ecosystems as other populations do, and the interaction between populations with different cultures is put on a level with the interaction between different species within ecosystems (Vayda and Rappaport 1968).

This approach has been very successful in generating detailed descriptions of food-producing systems (Anderson 1973; Kemp 1971; Netting 1981) and in offering solutions to apparent riddles of bizarre habits and, thereby, attracting much public attention (Harris 1966, 1977; or Harner's famous analysis of Aztec cannibalism, Harner 1977). The functionalist tradition of cultural anthropology, although it did not apply the concept of metabolism explicitly, revealed rich empirical material to be interpreted in terms of socioeconomic metabolism. However, by conceiving of culture merely as functional adaptations to the natural environment, these approaches severely underestimated the emergent properties of social systems. It is, indeed, the autopoietic character of culture which allows for a social development far beyond adaptationism.[18]

Socioeconomic Metabolism as a Biological Analogy

Metabolism originated as a biological concept. It describes the chemical conversion of material and energy by organisms to sustain reproduction:

> To sustain the processes of life, a typical cell carries out thousands of biochemical reactions each second. The sum of all biological reactions constitutes metabolism. What is the purpose of these reactions—of metabolism? Metabolic reactions convert raw materials, obtained from the environment, into the building blocks of proteins and other compounds unique to organisms. Living things must maintain themselves, replacing lost materials with new ones; they also grow and reproduce, two more activities requiring the continued formation of macromolecules (Purves et al. 1992, p. 113).

The attempt to apply this concept to a unit beyond the level of organisms—to a human society or community—in a more than merely metaphorical manner, must lead to serious considerations.[19] We address this by the deduction of some general preconditions from the biological concept that could serve as a guideline for its applicability to other units. What are these preconditions?

Expressed more abstractly, the biological concept of metabolism refers to a complex, dynamic system ("organism") consisting of highly interdependent compartments ("cells," "organs"). This system reproduces its compartments and thereby itself as a whole, materially and energetically, by means of a highly complex self-organizing process (called metabolism) which the system seeks to maintain in widely varying environments. Metabolism requires certain energetic and material inputs from the environment, and it returns these to the environment in a different form. If the system cannot maintain its metabolism, it "dies" or, more abstractly, ceases to exist in its present form.

Summarizing, we can define four general preconditions:

1. The unit is a highly integrated system, consisting of functionally interdependent compartments;
2. The metabolism of the system comprises the metabolisms of its compartments;
3. The law of conservation of mass (the sum of energetic and material inputs to the system equals the sum of outputs, plus changes in stock) applies to the system as a whole and to each of its compartments; and
4. The unit depends upon the processes called metabolism and seeks to maintain them under varying environmental conditions.

Can these preconditions be met for an entity like a human society or community?

Let us begin by considering the nature of these functionally interdependent "compartments" of society that require a continuous energetic and material flow for their reproduction. If we pick up Godelier's basic argument, we may consider societies as settings to organize the reproduction of human populations. If this is so, the primary material compartment of any society will be (the bodies of) its population. This population can be accounted for in numbers and in mass, and each member of the population requires a certain material and energetic metabolism. The biological metabolic demand of the population will depend on the number of humans considered to be members of the population of this society,[20] on their body weight,[21] on their reproduction rates, on their working hours, and on the energy spent per working hour. It will also depend slightly on climate and other environmental circumstances. Without having done very indepth research, we have estimated this metabolic demand at about seven metric tons of freshwater, four-and-a-half metric tons of air, and about one metric ton of biomass per year. The range of variation should not be too great. If it makes sense at all to look at human communities and societies as organizations serving human survival, they will, in effect, sustain a metabolism that at least equals the sum of the biological metabolisms of their human members.

What else should be considered as "material compartments" of society? As we show in more detail at the end of this paper, this question has to be handled both from a cultural perspective (addressing which objects other than human bodies a society considers as "belonging" to itself), and from a biophysical perspective (addressing which nonhuman material elements society indeed reproduces—that is, tries to keep in a certain state—through its organized activity). Which objects these are will depend upon mode of subsistence and technology. Again following Godelier, one must consider *cultivated plants, livestock, and domestic animals*. It makes a fundamental difference whether a society survives by hunting and gathering or whether it cultivates plants and keeps animals and must organize the conditions of their metabolism. How much the metabolism of plants or animals is provided for by society may be a matter of degree. Cattle may roam about and receive no more than occasional food, salt, and water (as in some parts of Australia) or they may be kept in stables and have most of their lives regulated by the farmer's hands. A tree may simply have been planted and then grow all by itself, or it may be continuously looked after, watered, fertilized, cut, and protected from competition. Operationally, the dividing line between those living beings that make up physical compartments of society and those that do not is always fuzzy and open to discussion. But, once something is considered to be maintained as a material compartment belonging to society, *all* of its metabolism becomes part of society's metabolism, according to the second precondition above. Keeping plants and animals changes society's metabolism—even if the human population breathes, eats, and drinks much the same as before (which, however, is not very likely).

Similar considerations apply to *human-made and maintained technical structures*. The critical element of the definition, again, is "maintained." Human-made structures that are not deliberately maintained decay and become renaturalized. This refers not only to all kinds of artifacts such as tools, machines, durable consumer goods, but also to built infrastructure such as houses, roads, dams, or sewers. The maintenance of such objects requires a constant flow of energy and materials[22] (and human labor), as with a living being. The flow of energy and materials has to be socially organized, and it adds to society's metabolism. Ceteris paribus, the more objects a society needs, owns, and seeks to maintain, the larger will be its metabolism.

Continuing these considerations directly leads to meeting precondition 3: inputs will equal outputs, plus changes in stock (that is, growth or decrease of the compartments themselves). This is equivalent to respecting the physical law of conservation of mass and energy.

And what about precondition 4? Does it make sense to claim that a society seriously depends upon its metabolism—as specified above—and seeks to maintain it under changing environmental conditions? Does a society depend on the maintenance of its population? Is human metabolism (as biological metabolism) dependent upon the maintenance of agricultural crops and animal livestock? And does this again depend on the maintenance of certain tools and infrastructures? And, finally, in what way does society's metabolism itself influence or change the environmental conditions it depends upon?

The most convenient way to deal with these questions is to discuss them historically, which we endeavor to do below. We will pick up the discussion of precondition 1, which appears to be the most difficult to judge and which we consider the most critical, in the concluding section.

MODES OF SUBSISTENCE AND THEIR CHARACTERISTIC METABOLIC PROFILES

By *characteristic metabolic profile* of a society (community), we mean the total energetic turnover and the total material turnover, classified by type of material (such as water, air, biomass, minerals, etc.), of this community or society per year, divided by the size of its population. This metabolic profile will be highly variable according to the mode of subsistence. Picking up this notion from Adam Smith, we distinguish three modes of subsistence: hunter and gatherer societies, agrarian societies, and industrial societies. The pressures exerted upon the environment, qualitatively and quantitatively, will substantially depend on the mode of subsistence.

If we think of hunters and gatherers, the only "material compartment" of those communities we have to consider are the people themselves. Other than their biological metabolism, they will use wood for making fire, hunting tools, and digging sticks, and they will use (a very small amount of) firestone for other tools, and maybe they will use some forage for dogs.[23] Thus, the characteristic metabolic profile of hunter and gatherer societies will be very similar to (and just slightly exceed) the biological metabolic demand of their population. Clearly, hunter and gatherer societies must maintain their metabolism under varying environmental conditions. If they fail to sustain their populations, they will either literally die out or undergo severe cultural change.

How do hunter and gatherer societies modify their environments in ways that might threaten the maintenance of their metabolism? The main problem seems to be the overexploitation of resources.[24] Many cultural regulations in hunter and gatherer societies can be functionally interpreted as defenses against ecological overexploitation, such as various practices limiting offspring, or the cultivation of a preference for idleness (see Sahlins 1972). In principle, however, such societies do not create pollution problems for themselves. Since all materials are extracted from current biospheric cycles, and the population density cannot exceed the limits set by locally available nutrition, the metabolic output of such societies should be easily absorbed and reconverted by their local environments.

As soon as societies start to control the reproduction of their biological resources—that is, as soon as they start colonizing their environments, such as by breeding livestock, growing crops, or paving roads—they acquire a quite different metabolic profile. It must not only contain water, air, and nutrition for humans, but also cover the needs of the livestock. Beyond that, there is an increased material demand for artifacts and infrastructure: tools for agriculture, containers and buildings for storage, means of transport, fortifications and weapons against possible robbery of the now stored and accumulated riches, and so on. According to our estimates from various sources (see Table 1), the per capita metabolic input of agrarian societies, both in terms of matter and energy, exceeds that of hunter and gatherer societies by about three- to tenfold. This increase in metabolism is not to be equated with increased prosperity. Colonization allows for an increase in population density because it secures a higher and more constant input flow from a given area (e.g., storage); but, while under hunter and gatherer conditions practically the whole metabolism of a community is dedicated to the direct needs of its human members, colonizing practices require a considerable amount of material infrastructure that does not directly benefit human needs, yet adds to the scale of metabolism. In fact, members of agrarian societies with a metabolic rate well above that of a hunter and gatherer society (both in material and in energetic terms) may be much less well-nourished and lead a much less comfortable life (Sieferle 1997b, p. 71).

As with hunter and gatherer societies, it seems obvious that agrarian societies seek to maintain their metabolic profile under varying environmental conditions. They seek to maintain their crops, livestock, and houses, even at the price of human lives. If this maintainance is not possible, biological, social, and cultural reproduction is threatened.

What, then, are the typical effects of an agrarian mode of subsistence upon its environment? What problems for their own metabolism do they tend to create? Agrarian societies try to establish control over resource flows by means of colonization. While still area-dependent in energetic terms, agrarian societies have to provide for the reproduction of key resources. There typically occurs an overexploitation of noncolonized resources such as woods, grasslands, or freshwater reserves. In addition, the specific risks of colonizing practices themselves may in the long run reduce the resource base (such as through salination of irrigated land or erosion). Another difficulty seems to arise from overly high rates of reproduction, inherent in the agrarian mode of subsistence. While many cultural regulations are directed at reducing reproduction (such as chastity rules and restricted access to marriage, or human sacrifice and infanticide), the high workload associated with colonizing activities acts as a constant pull toward having more children for labor (Harris 1991, p. 95). As a consequence, resource scarcity is an endemic feature of agrarian societies.

What about the output side; are there pollution problems? Since the characteristic metabolic profile of agrarian societies, in qualitative terms, still contains mostly materials directly extracted from local biospheric cycles,[25] pollution problems may occur mainly as a consequence of the regional concentration of people. Problems of hygiene are more common than problems of toxicity. As Crosby (1986) demonstrated, urban settlements provided breeding grounds for microbes to an extent that had been previously unthinkable.[26]

Table 1 attempts a quantitative comparison of the characteristic metabolic profiles of hunter and gatherer societies, an example of an agrarian society (Törbel, Switzerland, in 1875), and an average of contemporary industrial societies for which there exist data on a national level. Törbel, at that time a small agrarian village in Switzerland, was investigated in an indepth study by Netting (1981), which allows an estimate of its metabolic profile. A comparison of the examples for the three modes of subsistence yields a three- to fivefold increase in the scale of metabolism from one mode of subsistence to the other, in terms of both materials and energy.

Table 1. Characteristic Metabolic Profiles for Three Modes of Subsistence

	Hunter and Gatherer Societies	Agrarian Societies	Industrial Societies
Energetic input in GJ/capita.year	10-20	approx. 65	250
Material input in t/capita.year	approx. 1	approx. 4	19.4

Source: Hunter and gatherers: own estimates based on Harris (1991); for agrarian society: Netting (1981); for industrial societies: Fischer-Kowalski and Hüttler (1999) based on data on Germany, Japan, The Netherlands, and the United States from Adriaanse et al. (1997) and data on Austria from Schandl (1998), Fischer-Kowalski and Haberl (1998).

The increase of metabolic scale from hunters and gatherers to agrarian societies is mainly a consequence of the different amounts of biomass required. As we have explained above, this is due to the changing socioeconomic status of animals. For hunters, animals are booty (and subsequently food, clothes, tools, etc.). The food that animals require comes from natural cycles. For farmers, animals are live-stock—socioeconomic property. They must be fed, fenced, and housed, in order for their products to be used for human nutrition and their strength for performing physical labor. All the materials required for this must, as explained above, be considered as part of the socioeconomic metabolism. As an Alpine village, Törbel particularly depends on livestock. Milk and cheese make up the most important part of the human diet in this agricultural example. A more vegetarian agrarian culture could be expected to live on a much smaller biomass input.[27] Of course, agrarian societies also use minerals and other materials, but the amount is very small and does not show on the scale of Table 1. Had we used a more urban agrarian example, their proportion might have been somewhat higher.

The increase in metabolic rate between agrarian and industrial society is mainly due to new components: fossil energy carriers and considerable amounts of minerals and metals.[28] This does not imply, however, that less biomass is needed. The per capita input of biomass remains more or less the same. In terms of material metabolism, the five countries averaged to represent a *characteristic metabolic profile of industrial society* are fairly similar (Adriaanse et al. 1997, Hüttler et al. 1998).

As far as is known from the data, the scale of material and energetic metabolism has more or less steadily increased over many decades and is still increasing even in the most prosperous economies (Adriaanse et al.1997; de Bruyn 1997; Berkhout 1998). In industrial societies, the core problem does not seem to be population growth but growth in energetic and material metabolism. Industrial societies not only seek to maintain their metabolism; they seem to strive to increase it.

This tendency has become a target for political programs aimed at a more sustainable future. The most common and well-known one, although not labeled in the framework of metabolism, is the set of international agreements on the reduction of global carbon dioxide emissions (first highlighted in the Agenda 21 agreed in Rio de Janeiro in 1992). While carbon dioxide emissions are not toxic, they still represent one of the most imminent threats to the global climate and can only be checked by reducing the input of carbon in society's metabolism (usually for combustion). This is a good illustration of the new type of environmental problems generated by industrial metabolism. The abundant use of fossil fuels has made resource scarcity a minor problem, whereas the scale of metabolism generates wastes and emissions that present new, global problems on the output side.

There exist various policy approaches that have a direct bearing on the notion of industrial metabolism and its reduction. They can be assembled under the heading of "delinking economic and material growth," with more or less ambitious goals (e.g., Schmidt-Bleek 1994 on the "Factor 10 Club"; Weizsäcker et al. 1995 plead for a factor 4 reduction). Several estimates show that currently there is no more than a relative delinking, where material growth slows down compared to economic growth in monetary units but not in absolute scale (see de Bruyn 1997; Berkhout 1998; Hüttler et al. 1998).

COLONIZATION OF NATURAL PROCESSES

The concept of socioeconomic metabolism provides a clear and integrated analytical framework for various environmental issues that were previously treated separately. It has helped to create a new paradigm of environmental dynamics beyond the all too one-sided attention upon toxins and pollution, and it has directed attention to the fact that input and output are but two sides of the same process. At the same time, it was precisely this growing realization of society's metabolism as key to operationalizing the "sustainability" of society-nature interactions that demonstrated to us its limitations as a concept. Issues such as loss of biodiversity, potential hazards connected with genetic engineering, or environmental degradation caused by different forms of land use, could not be addressed within this paradigm. It seemed obvious that society's interventions in natural processes could not be reduced to metabolic exchanges and that interconnected changes in both the environment and social structures can be observed that have at best a very indirect connection to metabolic changes. These considerations suggested a new concept: *colonization.*

Colonization refers to the intended and sustained transformation of natural processes, by means of organized social interventions, for the purpose of improving their utility for society. The concept of colonization provides a theoretical framework for both biophysical and cultural analyses, focusing on the mutual dependencies between the two. For something to be a colonizing intervention, it must be causally effective in changing some biophysical process; it must make a difference in the world of matter. Likewise, it must be culturally conceived of, organized, and monitored; it must "make sense" in the world of communication.

The term colonization derives from the Latin word *colonus,* which means "peasant" and refers to the cultivator of the soil. Considering the outstanding importance of historical and contemporary agrarian colonization, such a denotation seems appropriate.[29] We can analyze, for example, agriculture as a set of colonizing interventions, linking social objectives to the changing of biophysical processes. Agriculture means the elimination of the original flora of an area by clearing vegetation, weeding, and applying herbicides; the changing of physical soil parameters through plowing, drainage, and irrigation; the changing of chemical soil parameters through fertilization, crop rotation, and fallow; successful action against competitors for food, through their elimination or decimation; and building fences, setting up scarecrows, and applying pesticides. Finally, the crops are changed through breeding, which is to say, through colonizing interventions

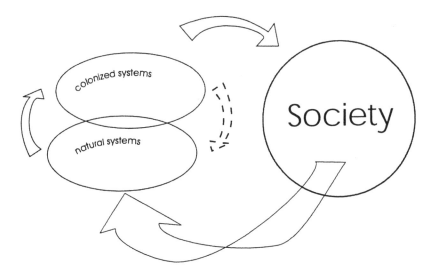

Figure 3. How Colonizing Interventions Work

into the process by which crop populations evolve. If the original wild crops were allowed to remain, the agricultural effort would not be worthwhile.

Societies have to invest considerable effort in increasing the productivity of biomass digestible for humans. Considering the complexity of the affected natural systems, however, it appears that with all their many interventions, societies actually control only a few parameters. The rest is left to the internal dynamics of the natural systems themselves (see Figure 3).

One central aspect of colonization is intention. Following Swenson's (1997, pp. 3, 37) definition of intentional dynamics, we can state that intention is "end-directed behavior prospectively controlled or determined by meaning or information about paths to ends" (as contrasted to behavior determined by local potentials, such as water flowing down a slope). Intention marks the main difference between "anthropogenically influenced" and "colonized." Traces of past or present human activity, or anthropogenic influence, may be found everywhere in natural systems. To say that something is anthropogenic is to do nothing more than to attribute a certain causal influence on the present state of some natural system to previous or ongoing processes in which humans are or were involved. This tells nothing about the cultural side of the process.

In the framework of world history, the origin of colonization is described as the neolithic revolution, involving the transition from a hunter-gatherer to an agrarian mode of subsistence. The intention of agricultural effort is to change nature. This implies taking on a prospective responsibility for the reproduction of biological resources.

Natural systems are usually more fragile in the colonized state than in the uncolonized state. Agrarian ecosystems are a good example. They must be maintained in an early state of ecological succession to maximize productivity, and the favored uniformity of plants must be defended against food competitors. Bred animals and cultivated plants reproduce their favorable phenotype over generations only with maintenance work. In order to ensure the reproduction of their needed properties, they must be isolated from their wild relatives, and possible mates need to be carefully selected. Only permanent effort can stabilize the preferred features of the colonized systems.

Essential cultural structures originate from colonization. To perform a wide range of colonizing activities, societies must engage in corresponding organizing efforts. Although the respective cultural manifestations may be highly diverse, there are certain relevant social structures that are manifest in all colonizing societies. Work/labor, sedentary ways of life, anticipation of the future, planning, and innovation are all immediate necessities of agrarian modes of subsistence. Labor and technological innovation dramatically gain in cultural importance. Societies that usually do not take responsibility for the conditions required to reproduce their biological resources only increase the exploitation of these resources when improving their technologies or increasing their labor input. Under conditions of colonization, however, returns may in fact be raised. Population densities reached by agrarian societies are made possible by increased area productivity and there is a tendency towards high rates of human reproduction because children are socially important in their function as needed labor. In addition, rights of disposal over nature gain a completely new dimension. Only those who can safely expect to harvest the returns will invest sustained and prospective effort.

The transition from agrarian to industrial societies, then, is fuelled by a metabolic innovation, namely, the transition from an energy system based on solar input to one based on fossil fuels. At first, colonizing strategies focus on new tools and infrastructure. It is only in the twentieth century—due to the industrialization of agriculture and, subsequently, the development of genetic engineering as well as other methods of modern biotechnology—that a qualitative leap occurs in comparison to agrarian modes of colonizing living systems.

By and large, colonization seems to be an irreversible process for both natural and social systems. Colonized systems never revert to their original state once particular forms of utilizing these systems are abandoned. Alpine pastures are one example. Since abandoning them would lead to soil erosion, in some cases their utilization continues despite the fact that it is unprofitable. This is also true for social processes of development. One will hardly find an example of the reversion of an agrarian society to a society of hunters and gatherers. Hence, societies which gradually take over responsibility for the conditions of reproducing their biological resources will increasingly become dependent upon their colonized systems.

Accordingly, societies and their natural environments enter into a process of mutual conditionality, which may best be termed coevolution (cf. Vasey 1992;

Norgaard 1997; Sieferle 1997b). Processes of coevolution cannot be easily observed and analyzed. They unfold over long periods of time and are typically twisted by a wealth of other processes as well. Coevolution is a heuristic concept, but there is a conspicuous lack of elaborate concepts applying evolutionary thinking to issues of cultural evolution. In order to develop a nonreductionist conception of coevolution which is adequate in terms of evolutionary thinking, one needs first of all a sufficiently exact concept of systems. We must begin with the fact that evolution is only possible at the systems level.[30]

Both natural and social systems must be conceived of as highly complex, dynamic, and autopoietic. The essential criterion which determines systems is that they are capable of maintaining a permanent difference between themselves and their environments. This difference may be defined in paralled for both populations and social systems as the totality of all mutually related genetic reproduction on one hand, and as the totality of all mutually related communicative reproduction on the other. If one subscribes to a modern understanding of evolution, the properties of systems like these can never be understood as purely adaptive, as mere adjustment to the environment. Instead, adaptation is always just one minimal condition of systems' stabilization.

This conception of systems may provide fruitful points of departure for the understanding of coevolution. Let us address the issue by investigating the temporal dynamics of colonization, first with reference to natural systems and, second, with reference to social systems.

Since natural systems are so complex, scientific theories are necessarily incapable of fully capturing the complexity. This implies that even the most modern colonization technologies transform but few natural parameters compared to the total number of parameters operating in the system (if this number is countable at all, it must be higher by a factor several times the power of 10). The rest is left to the self-regulative capacity of the natural systems. Referring again to crop farming, one can say that neither the photosynthesis of plants nor their metabolism, nor transport processes within plants nor the biochemical processes which are responsible for their growth and reproduction, are socially controlled. The vast complexity of natural systems renders the concept of their "total colonization" almost absurd.

Natural systems must accommodate interventions, a process which will never be completely predictable due to the complexity and the intrinsic dynamics of natural systems. As a result, societies always run the risk that the colonized systems will no longer provide the required services. The vulnerability of overbred domestic animals, monoculture harvest failures, as well as the increased probability of flooding due to specific forms of water management, can serve here as examples. These undesired consequences of colonizing interventions force the societies in question to design new solutions. Modern societies typically react by means of additional colonizing interventions: Domestic animals are treated with antibiotics, monocultures are sprayed with pesticides and herbicides, and so forth. This leads, in turn, to ever new problems, such as health problems due to residuals in food, economic problems that result from the declining quality of biological raw materials and the increasing effort required to process them industrially, harvest losses due to herbicides, water supply problems due to contamination, and more.

With respect to the internal operations of societies, other features come to be significant. Colonization is regularly connected with work, technological know-how, and social bargaining processes concerning rights of disposal. Increasingly, colonization is also connected with decision processes concerning the application of colonizing techniques, as well as with money. This leads to a completely different way of considering problems of risk. Whenever societies enter into a process of permanently increasing control over natural processes and, consequently, become dependent on the effectiveness of their colonizing techniques, they risk affecting the internal functioning of the societies themselves. Increased responsibility for the conditions of reproducing the life-supporting functions of natural systems is purchased at the expense of expenditures of social resources such as work, time, and money, which probably grow disproportionally. Risk, then, means to approach the limits of social organizing capacity.

In our view, this represents a new research problem: What social resources are tied up in colonizing activities, and how does this allocation of resources influence social development? The following case study serves as an example of how these theoretical considerations may shape empirical studies.

Biosphere 2

In 1991, the doors of a 1x3 hectares glass arch in the desert of Arizona closed behind four men and four women. Together with 3,800 species of plants and animals, which had been brought into the glass house from all over the world, the eight "Bionauts," as they called themselves, took part in a survival experiment in this materially closed second Biosphere. The goal of the experiment was to demonstrate how far technical control over life-supporting ecosystem processes can go.

We analyzed this enclosure experiment with respect to many parameters, one of them being colonization efficiency. The basic idea was that Biosphere 2 seemed to have realized the future of colonization on a laboratory scale. In this respect, the results were unambiguous. In the small world of Biosphere 2, where social control over natural processes was so much tighter than anywhere else, a loss of control quickly threatened life. There was dramatically less time and space available to absorb and correct problems, compared to the real biosphere. Changes in natural processes immediately had effects on the small group of humans.

Several parameters were estimated, including: (1) requirement of human labor for colonization, (2) energy consumption, (3) energy costs, and (4) human nutrition. Estimates gave the following results: In spite of infinite access to energy and information, the Bionauts had to spend approximately 75% of their time to preserve the life-supporting systems. The energy needed to maintain the whole artificial ecosystem was 28.000 Gigajoules (GJ) per person per year, which is one thousand times higher than the average per capita energy consumption of an industrial society like Austria. Calculated at average energy rates in the United States, the energy costs would have been U.S. $4 million (Odum 1996), which sounds even more enormous if we consider that U.S. energy rates are comparably low.[31]

Still, all eight persons were permanently undernourished. On average, every Bionaut lost 16% of his or her body weight during the two years of enclosure (Roy et al. 1996). Despite the enormous expense of energy, information, and human labor, the available nutrition energy could not be raised above 2.9 GJ per person and year, which is far below the biological demand of 4.6 GJ. From a social-ecology point of view, we can assume that Biosphere 2 created a society whose colonization efficiency corresponded to that of a medieval agrarian society, whereas the metabolic profile, being 1,000 times above that of a contemporary industrial society, reached that of a postindustrial society far in the future.

Conclusions for a Socioecological Understanding of Risk

To further develop the concept of colonization, a more elaborate socioecological concept of risk is required. In a recent paper on metatheoretical foundations of risk analysis, Rosa (1998, p. 17) distinguishes four separate stages: (1) risk identification, (2) risk estimation, (3) risk evaluation, and (4) risk management. From our considerations regarding society-nature interaction, we might add a fourth stage of risk analysis, one concerned with the questions of *risk generation*. The starting points of our considerations are the environmental historical approach of Müller-Herold and Sieferle (1998) and the systems theory approach of Luhmann (1993,1997).

Müller-Herold and Sieferle show that the dynamics of increasing social risks caused by colonization is a phenomenon which did not originate within industrial societies but is a consequence of the coevolutionary process between society and nature. It can be traced directly to colonization. Müller-Herold and Sieferle denote this process as a risk spiral. Through a new definition of the term risk, Luhmann offers the possibility of connecting technological and sociological risk approaches, which is especially fruitful for the colonization concept. Luhmann defines risk as a possible future benefit or damage which can be attributed to a decision. He defines danger, on the other hand, as a possible future damage which cannot be attributed to a decision but occurs as an exogenous event. Based upon this, the evolution of the society-nature relationship can be described as a transformation process, in the course of which societies gradually transform dangers into risks. The tool of this transformation is colonization (for Luhmann, "technique"), and the whole process must be considered irreversible. Thus, colonization can be conceived as a process which generates social rather than environmental risks. Luhmann describes the linkage between technique and social risks as "structural linkage" (*strukturelle Koppelung*). He writes:

> that means: in all contemporary operations social communication must presume technique and must rely on technique, because alternatives are not at disposal in the problem-horizons of operations. The time required to replace a given technique by introducing regressive developments would be exceedingly high and the factual consequences would be serious to such an extent and unpredictable in detail, that a shift to alternative paths of development virtually can be excluded" (Luhmann 1997, p. 532, our translation).

Continuing with this reasoning, one could ask what will happen if societies continue on their current path of development. The time required to do so might also become exceedingly high and the factual consequences serious to such an extent that a perpetuation of the current path of development would prove to be virtually impossible. This would mean that societies gradually transform dangers into risks until the organizing capacity of society is exceeded and, eventually, risks are retransformed into dangers (see also "dangers of second order" in Lau 1989; Beck 1995).

SOCIETY AS A SYMBOLIC-MATERIAL HYBRID: AN ATTEMPT AT THEORETICAL INTEGRATION

What are the consequences for social theory of the concepts discussed above? How can they be integrated into a comprehensive, general model? We begin with Sieferle's systemic interaction model and develop our model on the basis of his preliminary assumptions concerning evolutionary theory and on the dichotomy between "culture" and "nature." We assume that culture (conceived as system of recursive human communications) and nature (conceived as systems of the material realm) are dichotomous, and we attempt to construct a kind of interface between these two realms. We assume that society is, in fact, capable of influencing natural systems and, in turn, that natural systems exert an influence on society. Hence, there must exist a sphere comprising moments of both realms. The dynamics of this sphere, then, underlies both the system of social regulations functioning by way of communication (cultural exchange) and the system of biophysical regulations functioning by way of flows of material and energy (natural exchange). Therefore, the sphere in question is capable of both cultural and natural exchange.

To analyze this complex in more detail, let us first look at it from the point of view of systems theory. For a given culture—that is, a particular social system—other cultures and the material world are both part of the environment. From the point of view of a culture, it is possible only to determine the degree to which these environments are relevant for itself. There are some parts of the environment with which the system maintains intensive interactions, whereas it hardly interacts with other parts. A cultural system can only reproduce itself if it is capable of maintaining exchange with its relevant environments. At the same time, it must maintain the difference between itself and the environment. Therefore, we must postulate a cultural sphere which transcends the mere symbolic system of communications. Culture may—and must—regulate parameters of the environment in order to be able to reproduce itself. Hence, the cultural sphere—or, to be more precise, the cultural sphere of causation (*kultureller Wirkungszusammenhang*)—is the result of the operative performance of culture; that is, it is steered by culture and refers to those interactions with the environment which are essential for its reproduction. Industrial societies, for example, derive their dynamics from an exponentially growing consumption of materials and energy. In order to maintain this flow of resources, they adapt the intensity with which they colonize natural environments accordingly.[32] Consequently, we may argue that this sphere, in which the cultural and the material world overlap, originates from a process of interaction that appropriates and integrates parts of the natural world into the cultural sphere of causation, thus establishing cultural control over parts of the material environment. Cultural control is determined by the cultural system, which describes certain material environments (organisms, objects, territories) as pertinent to itself, as its "own," and displays a high density of regulation in its treatment of these environments. The operation of cultural control, however, is also materially effective in that it does indeed change the material environment.

Sieferle defines society as the unity of population and culture. According to this understanding, humans are cultural-natural hybrids. Human action and human experience are invariably characterized by the fact that cultural as well as natural moments are inseparably interlaced. In the words of Sieferle:

> Society is ... essentially symbolic-immaterial communication which, however, can only function if certain preliminary material conditions are met. At least "people" must exist as a material substrate or "interface" of communication processes, serving as carriers of information and social functions. The effects exerted by these people on the rest of nature (by means of work or metabolism), however, are real (Fischer-Kowalski and Sieferle 1998, p. 53, our translation).

In our model, we distinguish a natural sphere of causation from a cultural sphere of causation (see Figure 4). We agree with Sieferle that humans, as communicators and living beings, are the core of the intersection of the two spheres. However, we also believe that it is both theoretically appropriate and empirically fruitful to entertain a wider conception of the intersection between cultural and natural spheres of causation. The natural sphere of causation comprises the totality of the material world; the cultural sphere of causation is defined as the sphere influenced by recursive communication which, in its core, is constituted by a cultural system (culture).

Culture generates some form of self-understanding, according to which certain segments of the material world are considered as parts "belonging" to this system. This applies to humans but also to domesticated animals and possibly to cultivated plants as well as to artifacts. These elements are segregated from "residual

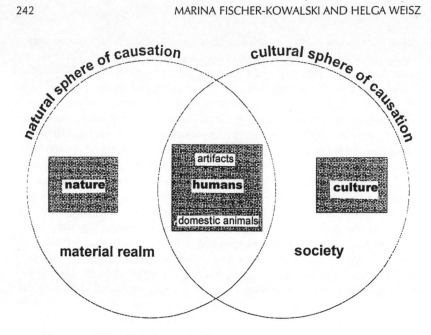

Figure 4.   The Interaction between Cultural and
Natural Spheres of Causation

nature" because their reproduction is to a high degree culturally regulated and controlled. This is exactly what determines the overlapping zone between cultural and natural spheres of causation. Society, therefore, may be described as an organized set comprising a cultural system and those material elements accorded preferential treatment by the cultural system.

With this conception of society, the delimitation of societies becomes historically variable. Each cultural system claims that it is made up of certain humans as well as of material elements, which are considered to belong to it. The cultural system claims a certain legitimacy to dispose of these elements which, as a general rule, is also acknowledged by other cultural systems. There are variants and gradations; for example, with respect to the citizens belonging to a nation-state, it is possible to distinguish among full citizens, the residential population, people having legal capacities, or people who just happen to live in a certain territory at a certain time. The state claims certain rights of disposal over all these concerned groups. To be human, then, is at the same time too much and too little a criterion to determine membership in a particular society. Given these restrictions, what can be said with respect to the other material elements of society?

As a general rule, there exists a cultural distinction between "subjects" and "objects" that privileges humans vis-à-vis other material elements.[33] What is typical under these conditions is that elements of the material world over which these "subjects" exert certain rights of disposal (in the form of property rights or rights of use) are also culturally defined as "belonging" to society. It is possible to reach somewhat different forms of delimitation if one defines these elements not by legal rights of disposal but according to economic principles of valuation. In this case, objects either belong to the realm of goods or they do not. To sum up, this implies that culture defines certain rules of assignment between elements of the material world and elements of the cultural system—rules that articulate and express rights of disposal over these elements as well as the extent to which they may be classified as "belonging" to the system in question. These rules are acknowledged by other cultural systems to a greater or lesser extent. In this way, cultural systems define some kind of material "court" which is fenced off from the rest of the material world. The exact delimitation of this frontier, however, is necessarily imprecise.

What does it mean, then, to say that a cultural system regulates the reproduction of certain material elements? This can be discussed with reference to the concept of metabolism which, in a heuristic sense, promises to be extremely helpful but also requires careful operational elaboration.[34] Speaking of metabolism, one must first have adequate knowledge of the (materially delimited and finite) system that is to be reproduced. Only then is it possible to assess the material and energetic flows required for the maintenance of the system in question. The paradigm of metabolism largely follows economic reasoning, and economics is concerned with the material flows within society as far as they manifest themselves in the form of monetary flows. The empirical description of socioeconomic metabolism describes a physical economy in which the internal material flows of society are conceptualized in close correlation with monetary flows—and, if one wants to interpret these material flows economically, this correlation is even more necessary. The physical description of material flows, however, goes beyond the corresponding monetary description in two respects. On one hand, it is necessary to consider material flows between societies and nature and, on the other hand, the model must satisfy the law of conservation of mass.[35] This permits the identification of an area of intersection that does not include just humans but domesticated living beings as well. It is this sphere which must be reproduced by way of metabolism in order to maintain a specific mode of subsistence. Since interactions between cultural and natural systems are always mediated by human beings, human bodies are of particular relevance in this metabolic process. Maintaining a particular social formation such as an industrial society, however, would be impossible without the artifacts properly belonging to the social formation in question. It is by way of these artifacts that society generates particular instruments of perception, of intervention in natural processes, and of communication which far exceed the possibilities incorporated in human bodies themselves.

Therefore, society would be constituted by the systemic relation between a particular culture (whichever way this may be differentiated internally), a particular

244   MARINA FISCHER-KOWALSKI AND HELGA WEISZ

human population, and the material artifacts (inanimate as well as living) that it considers to belong to itself (cultural relation), and which it produces and reproduces (as a material relation). The precise notion of a system (that is, a unit that is able to reproduce a difference between itself and its environment) does not, however, apply to this concept of society. This means society can no longer be conceived of as a system, but rather as a unit that has historically variable and imprecise material delimitations. Only now can we return to the question raised above, whether the preconditions that apply to the concept of metabolism are met by a unit like a society. Operationally, we think that it can be applied and that it is useful in a more than metaphorical way, although the theoretical preconditions we proposed cannot be fully met.

According to this theory, the material world would consist of innumerable material elements (ordered in whichever way) and of countless feedback control systems which, to varying extents, are influenced (and have already been influenced) culturally—including the human bodies themselves as well as the most diverse human artifacts. This implies that human societies cannot be portrayed simply as subsystems of the biosphere, although we have no reservations against conceiving both cultural and natural systems as offsprings of biological evolution. Human societies, however, cannot be reduced to cultural systems; that is, they cannot be reduced to systems of symbolic communication which are subsystems of a universe of information or meaning. In our understanding, human societies are irreducible hybrids between a natural, material world and a cultural world of recursive communication.

ACKNOWLEDGMENTS

The authors wish to thank the team Social Ecology in Vienna for parenting this theoretical effort in the course of many fruitful discussions. Special thanks to Karl Werner Brand, Helmut Haberl, Fritz Kragler, Klaus Kubeczko, Jürgen Pelikan, Gene Rosa, Heinz Schandl, and Verena Winiwarter for helpful comments on earlier versions and to Antje Lewis, Barbara Smetschka, and Ekke Weis for technical support. Thanks also to Lee Freese, series editor, for patiently accompanying the whole process.

NOTES

1. Briefly summarized, the problem of Cartesian dualism originates from a mechanistic worldview (*Mechanistisches Weltbild*), which conceives of the universe as consisting of invisible small particles with merely quantitative features. The problem, then, is how qualitative phenomena-such as perceptions (e.g., of color or pain) and psychological phenomena can be explained. Descartes' suggestion of a solution for this dilemma has been influential. He claimed the existence of two mutually exclusive realms, one being the world of materials (*res extensa*) which functions according to the laws of mechanics and exists in space but is not conscious, and the other being the nonmaterial, symbolic

world of meanings (*res cognita*), which is concious but does not exist in space. However, this leads directly to the problem of Cartesian dualism: how can the material and the symbolic interact?

2. This is, of course, a continuation of the Cartesian dualism.

3. The term mode of subsistence originated with Adam Smith (1776), who distinguished four "stages:" hunting, breeding, agriculture, and commerce. While Smith's distinctions of stages may be somewhat outdated, as is his belief in universal progress, we welcome the fact that this refers to particular society-nature relations much more than does Marx's (1867) terminology of modes of production.

4. An earlier German version can be found in Fischer-Kowalski et al. (1997).

5. Here we would question the precision of the definition. Typically, human biometabolism is embedded into some technometabolism. Technical devices are used to extract food from nature and to prepare it; then it is eaten, digested, and excreted; and finally, human excrements are removed into the sphere of nature, usually again by way of some technical device. Thus, biometabolism and technometabolism should not be visualized as existing apart from one another (as with Boyden; see Figure 1), but as intersecting spheres. Equally, we do not quite understand why "technometabolism" is not mediated via "artifacts." Finally, this model does not help to classify the biological metabolism of the livestock kept by humans as a source of labor or food.

6. Cf. Levi-Strauss' theoretical masterpiece *Le pensée sauvage* (1966[1962]).

7. The weight that Godelier places upon mental structures makes him reject some other anthropological approaches, so that he condescendingly addresses Harris and Sahlins as "vulgar materialists" and reproaches them for "economistic" arguments (Godelier 1986, p. 59).

8. "The fact is this: Human beings, in contrast to other social animals, do not just live in society, they *produce society in order to live*. In the course of their existence, they invent new ways of thinking and of acting—both upon themselves and upon the nature which surrounds them. They therefore produce culture and create history" (Godelier 1986, p.1).

9. According to Schmidt (1971), Marx's notion of the appropriation of nature implies a higher degree of interwovenness, or interpenetration, of humans with nature than does the notion of using nature, which was common among his contemporaries. But Marx's notion still makes it very clear which part is in control of the process.

10. This conception becomes even more obvious when Godelier deals with the origin of class societies (Godelier 1986, p. 16).

11. Essentially, Sieferle's notion of culture is much the same as Luhmann's concept of society. In particuar, he follows Luhmann in applying the concept of biological autopietic systems (Maturana and Varela 1975) to social systems (see Luhmann 1984).

12. For a discussion of concepts of society-nature interaction in early sociology, see also Lutz (1998).

13. According to Schmidt (1971, p. 86), Marx drew much of his understanding of metabolism from this source and imported a notion of the trophic hierarchy, food chains, and nutrient cycling.

14. Most social scientists of those times tended to be highly interested in the advances of biology, particularly in evolutionary theory and its implications for universal progress (e.g., Spencer 1880[1862]; Morgan 1877).

15. This work provided one of the founders of sociology, Max Weber, with the opportunity for an extensive discussion. Weber reacted in quite a contradictory, even double-bind manner. On the one hand, he dismissed Ostwald's approach as "grotesque" (Weber 1909, p. 401) and as "mischief" (p. 381) and challenged its core thesis on natural science grounds. In no way would industrial production be more energy-efficient than manual production—it would only be more cost-efficient (p. 386). At the same time, Weber rejects natural science's packaging of value judgements and prejudices as "facts" and its arrogance toward the "historical" sciences (p. 401). On the other hand, he admits that energy may possibly be important to sociological concerns (p. 399; see also Weber 1958[1904]), but he never elaborated such considerations.

16. To explain very briefly: While both seek to describe and explain differences between prein-dustrial societies, the functionalist tradition (sometimes also termed materialist or ecological) focuses on problems of survival and economic reproduction, while the culturalist tradition focuses on cultural patterns, their development and coherence.

17. Martinez-Alier (1987, p. 13) claims that Leslie White recognized the above-mentioned Ost-wald as one of the forebears of evolutionary ecological anthropology.

18. This is, as Sieferle stressed, the formal precondition for an anthropogenic environmental cri-sis.

19. Which processes may and should be studied on hierarchical levels beyond the individual organism is a matter of debate in biology that dates back to Clements (1916) and is still ongoing. The concept of metabolism is widely applied at the interface of biochemistry and biology when referring to cells and organs. Whether this term can be applied to any higher level in the biological hierarchy seems to be a matter of dispute. Tansley (1935) established the ecosystem as a proper unit of analysis. He did so by opposing Clements' "creed" in an organismical theory of vegetation. He also opposed the term "community" by arguing that it did not seem legitimate to lump animals and plants together, since they are too different to be put on an equal footing (p. 296). Lindemann (1942) then proceeded to analyze ecosystems mathematically in terms of energy conversion, with plants being the producer organisms that convert and accumulate solar radiation into complex organical substances (chemical energy) serving as food for animals, the consumer organisms of ecosystems. Every deceased organism then becomes a potential source of energy for specialized decomposers (saprophagous bacteria and fungi), thereby closing the cycle in generating inorganic nutrients for plants. This is basically what E.P. Odum is referring to when he talks about the metabolism in an ecosystem. Odum, one of the lead-ing system ecologists, clearly favors the use of terms such as "growth" or "metabolism" on every bio-logical level from the cell to the ecosystem (see, e.g., Odum 1959). This is contested by authors such as Engelberg and Boyarsky (1979), who challenge Odum and Patton (1981) on the cybernetic nature of ecosystems. Engelberg and Boyarsky claim that the dominant interaction between different popula-tions of an ecosystem is the exchange of brute matter and energy in the absence of information-medi-ated feedback cycles. Odum and Patton also see the food web (as an interconnection of material and energetic rather than informational processes) as the most fundamental element of ecosystems, but claim that a secondary information network is superimposed on this network of material and energetic flows. A somewhat similar debate is carried on by Salt (1977) as contradicted by Edson and colleagues (1981), regarding the existence of emergent properties in ecosystems, that is, properties of the system that cannot be reduced to properties of the components and that must be distinguished from mere sum-mations or distributional characteristics of the properties. Basically, this is a debate about holism (or organicism) versus reductionism. Do populations (that is, the reproductively interconnected members of a species), communities (that is, the total of populations in a habitat), or ecosystems (that is, the total of populations and the effective inorganic factors in a habitat) have a degree of systemic integration comparable to individual organisms? Does evolution work upon them as units of natural selection? These questions are matters of contention in biology and, thus, the use of the term "metabolism" for a system constituted by a multitude of organisms does not pass unchallenged. Although energy conver-sion and nutrient cycling in ecosystems would be taken as an accepted fact, whether there exist any kind of controls, information-mediated feedback cycles, or evolutionary mechanisms working on the systems level as such—and not just by way of individual organisms—is a matter of debate. Notwith-standing the answers to these questions, it is widely accepted that, in effect, biotic communities and ecosystems have self-organizing properties that allow them to optimize the utilization of energy and nutrients. As early as 1925, Lotka proposed a "law of maximum energy in biological systems." Similar arguments are presented in theories of succession and climax in plant communities (Odum 1959, 1969).

20. A society need not define all humans within reach as "members of its population." It may well be that slaves are not considered to be members and are deliberately kept below the minimum required

to live and to reproduce, thereby "exporting" the ecological costs of the reproduction of (part of) the population to some other society from which the slaves are imported.

21.   Average body weight depends on size and nutritional state. If the population is overweight, it will have a higher metabolic rate (to sustain the excess of fat cells). The range of variation in terms of energy, according to Giampietro (1997, p. 120) is about 20% (averages of contemporary societies).

22.   The operational problem to be resolved here, as with domestic plants/animals above, concerns the timescale. For how long must the object be "maintained" in order to be considered a "compartment" and not just a material flow? This is not dissimilar to the debate in economics, where the line between capital and income has to be drawn somewhere.

23.   We confine ourselves here to a very schematic description for illustrative purposes. More closely scrutinized, the metabolic needs of an Inuit community (e.g., Kemp 1971) will be quite different to those of a savannah people like the !Kung (Lee 1979). On hunter and gatherer ecology, see Harris (1991, p. 75).

24.   According to Ponting (1991), the thrifty extinction of the glacial megafauna on all continents seems to have been the doing of skillful human paleolithic hunters.

25.   Typically, metals are used in very small quantities only. Thus, their concentration only occasionally exceeds natural concentration.

26.   As Crosby argues, these microbes were later useful as a "weapon" for the older urban civilizations from the Mediterranean region in their conquest of new territory—for example, in the New World.

27.   See, for example, the analysis of a contemporary rural village in India by Mehta et al. (1997) or that of a contemporary Thai village by Gruenbuehel et al. 1999.

28.   The numbers in this table refer only to what is called direct material input into the national economies, that is, the amounts extracted from the domestic environment (without "hidden flows") plus amounts imported (in weight at border), minus amounts exported. What is not shown in this table is the considerable scale of the renewable resources—air and freshwater—that accompany the utilization of fossil energy (air for combustion and water for cooling).

29.   Another connotation of colonies and colonialization exists, implying political and military domination. Although we do not deny a certain association in this direction, we prefer the plain analytic link to the Latin term *colonus*, or peasant.

30.   For biology, for example, this implies that it is not organisms that evolve, but populations (that is, all the individuals of a propagation community) and that all system levels (from genes, cells, and organisms to populations) channel evolution (cf. Riedl 1975).

31.   "The underwriters of the Biosphere-2 experiment did not actually pay this much in dollars because they had their own power plants and could produce energy at commercial rates" (Odum 1996, p. 18).

32.   Here is one of the fundamental difficulties in realizing sustainable development, which necessitates a radical change in the interactions between society and nature. Logically, this would result in the destabilization of society, since it is these society-nature interactions that stabilize society. At the same time, maintaining the given dynamics of these interactions would strain or even exceed the ability of natural systems to provide services for the society in question. In the long run, therefore, this would likewise be unsustainable.

33.   In this form, this is valid only for modern societies. For most societies in history, only certain parts of society (defining themselves by way of gender, seniority, social class/estate, or ethnic affiliations) were granted the privileged status of subjects.

34.   It is also possible to discuss this with reference to the concept of colonization. Colonization implies that a cultural system controls and regulates certain natural processes operatively (by means of work/labor). Colonization is a purely processual model of the interactions between society and nature and cannot be directly assigned to "objects" (in their spatial and temporal totality). Generally speaking, cultural self-understanding expresses itself preferably in objective distinctions rather than in processual distinctions, although there may be some who would consider that to be a historical

248 MARINA FISCHER-KOWALSKI AND HELGA WEISZ

simplification. Rights of disposal are usually awarded to things—to material elements characterized by a certain size, dimension, and particular properties. (Taking a closer look, this is also not altogether correct: although the owner of a dog may have the right to keep it on a long or a short lead, she certainly does not have the right to inflict pain on it; all culturally defined rights of disposal over things are likewise processually restrained). The concept of colonization permits distinctions according to the intensity of colonization, thus articulating the extent to which processes in a certain natural system are culturally regulated. Nevertheless, it is hardly possible to construct a dichotomous separation between what belongs to the system in question and what does not belong to it. Therefore, the concept of colonization itself provides few cues as to how one might define the sphere or zone in which natural and social/cultural systems overlap. It is possible, however, to demonstrate that many cultural systems maintain that there is a specific relation between colonizing efforts and rights of disposal. One may lose the right to own a field if one does not cultivate it, in the same way that one loses the right to any other good that is neglected and left to degrade without care and maintenance. One can best attribute to a cultural system those natural systems which are relatively intensively colonized (for example, objects of everyday use which are regularly taken care of and maintained in a certain desired state, or living systems like animals whose material and energetic metabolism is regulated by way of labor). From the perspective of colonization alone, however, it is impossible to provide a clear dichotomous distinction between what "belongs" to a social system and what does not.

35.   This is what the neoclassical economic model fails to do. Matter and energy are not categories in this model. They have no price per se. Price, and therefore value, emerges only within the circular economic process between production and consumption. Before and after entering this process, the material components have a value of zero (cf. Ayres and Kneese 1969).

REFERENCES

Adriaanse, A., S. Bringezu, A. Hammond, Y. Moriguchi, E. Rodenberg, D. Rogich, and H. Schütz. 1997. *Resource Flows: The Material Basis of Industrial Economies.* Washington, DC: World Resources Institute.

Anderson, J.N. 1973. "Ecological Anthropology and Anthropological Ecology." Pp. 179-239 in *Handbook of Social and Cultural Anthropology,* edited by J.J. Honigmann. Chicago, IL: Rand McNally.

Ayres, R.U., and A.V. Kneese. 1969. "Production, Consumption and Externalities." *American Economic Review* 59(3): 282-297.

Beck, U. 1995. *Ecological Politics in an Age of Risk.* Cambridge: Polity Press.

Berkhout, F. 1998. "Aggregate Resource Efficiency: A Review of Evidence." In *Managing a Material World: Perspectives in Industrial Ecology,* edited by P. Vellinga. Dordrecht, The Netherlands: Kluwer.

Boulding, K. 1966. "The Economics of the Coming Spaceship Earth." Pp. 3-14 in *Environmental Quality in a Growing Economy: Essays from the Sixth RFF Forum,* edited by H. Jarrett. Baltimore, MD: John Hopkins Press.

Bourdieu, P. 1985. *Distinction.* London: Routledge & Kegan Paul.

Boyden, S.V. 1992. "Biohistory: The Interplay Between Human Society and the Biosphere—Past and Present." *Man and the Biosphere Series. Vol. 8.* Paris: UNESCO—Parthenon Publishing Group: Casterton Hall, Park Ridge, New Jersey.

Buckley, W. 1968. *Modern Systems Research for the Behavioral Scientist.* Chicago, IL: Aldine Publishing.

Clements, F.E. 1916. *Plant Succession.* Carnegie Institute Washington Publications. Vol. 242. Washington DC: Carnegie Institute.

Cottrell, F. 1955. *Energy and Society.* New York: McGraw-Hill.

Crosby, A.W. 1986. *Ecological Imperialism: The Biological Expansion of Europe 900-1900*. Cambridge, UK: Cambridge University Press.

Daly, H.E. 1973. "The Steady-State Economy: Toward a Political Economy of Biophysical Equilibrium and Moral Growth." Pp. 149-174 in *Toward a Steady-State Economy*, edited by H.E. Daly. San Francisco, CA: W.H.Freeman.

De Bruyn, S.M., and J.B. Opschoor. 1997. "Developments in the Throughput-Income Relationship: Theoretical and Empirical Observations." *Ecological Economics* 20: 255-268.

Elias, N. 1994. *The Civilizing Process*. Oxford, UK: Blackwell.

Engelberg, J., and L.L. Boyarsky. 1979. "The Noncybernetic Nature of Ecosystems." *The American Naturalist* 114(3): 317-324.

Fischer-Kowalski, M., and H. Haberl. 1998. "Sustainability Problems and Historical Transitions. A Description in Terms of Changes in Metabolism and Colonization Strategies." Pp. 57-76 in *Sustainable Development and the Future of Cities*, edited by B. Hamm and P.K. Muttagi. New Delhi, India: Oxford Publishers.

Fischer-Kowalski, M., H. Haberl, W. Hüttler, H. Payer, H. Schandl, V. Winiwarter, and H. Zangerl-Weisz. 1997. *Gesellschaftlicher Stoffwechsel und Kolonisierung von Natur. Ein Versuch in Sozialer Ökologie* [Societal Metabolism and Colonization of Nature. An Approach to Social Ecology]. Amsterdam: Gordon & Breach Fakultas.

Fischer-Kowalski, M., and W. Hüttler. 1999. "Society's Metabolism: The State of the Art; The Intellectual History of Material Flow Analysis, Part II: 1970-1998". *Journal of Industrial Ecology* 2(4): 107-137.

Fischer-Kowalski, M., and R.P. Sieferle. 1998. "Der sozial-ökologische Wirkungszusammenhang." Pp. 45-58 in *Technologische Zivilisation und Kolonisierung von Natur* [The Socio-Ecological Sphere of Causation], edited by H. Haberl, E. Kotzmann, and H. Weisz. New York: Springer.

Foin, T.F., C.M. Knapp, and M.M. Edson. 1981. "'Emergent Properties' and Ecological Research." *The American Naturalist* 118: 593-596.

Foucault, M. 1977. *Discipline and Punish—the Birth of the Prison*. London: Allen Lane.

Geddes, P. 1997. *Civics as Applied Sociology*. Leicester, UK: Leicester University Press.

Georgescu-Roegen, N. 1971. *The Entropy Law and the Economic Process*. Cambridge, MA: Harvard University Press.

Giampietro, M. 1997. "Socioeconomic Pressure, Demographic Pressure, Environmental Loading and Technological Changes in Agriculture." *Agriculture, Ecosystems & Environment* 65: 201-229.

Godelier, M. 1986. *The Mental and the Material: Thought Economy and Society*. London: Blackwell Verso.

Gruenbuehel, C.M., H. Schandl, and V. Winiwarter. 1999. *Agrarische Produktion als Interaktion von Gesellschaft und Natur. Fallstudie SangSaen* [Agrarian Production as the Interaction of Nature and Society: The Case-Study of Sang Saeng]. IFF Social Ecology Series Vol. 55. Vienna: IFF.

Habermas, J. 1981. *Theorie des kommunikativen Handelns*. Frankfurt, Germany: Suhrkamp.

_____. 1984. *The Theory of Communicative Action*. Cambridge, UK: Polity.

Harner, M. 1977. "The Ecological Basis for Aztec Sacrifice." *American Ethnologist* 4(1): 117-135.

Harris, M. 1966. "The Cultural Ecology of India's Sacred Cattle." *Current Anthropology* 7: 51-59.

_____. 1977. *Cannibals and Kings: The Origins of Cultures*. New York: Random House.

_____. 1991. *Cultural Anthropology*. New York: Harper & Collins.

Kemp, W.B. 1971. "The Flow of Energy in a Hunting Society." *Scientific American* 224(3): 105-115.

Lee, R.B. 1979. *The !Kung San: Men, Women and Work in a Foraging Society*. Cambridge, UK: Cambridge University Press.

Levi-Strauss, C. 1966[1962]. *"The Savage Mind."* Nature of Human Society Series. London: Weidenfeld & Nicolson.

Lindemann, R.L. 1942. "The Trophic-Dynamic Aspect of Ecology." *Ecology* 23(4): 399-417.

Lotka, A.J. 1925. *Elements of Physical Biology*. Baltimore, MD: Williams & Wilkins.

Luhmann, N. 1984. *Soziale Systeme. Grundriß einer allgemeinen Theorie* [Social Systems. Outlines of a General Theory]. Frankfurt, Germany: Suhrkamp.

Luhmann, N. 1989. *Ecological Communication.* Cambridge, UK: Polity.

———. 1993. "Risiko und Gefahr." In *Reflexion und Regulation. Einführung in die sozialwissenschaftliche Risikoforschung* [Risk and Danger], edited by W. Krohn and G. Krücken. Frankfurt, Germany: Suhrkamp.

———. 1997. *Die Gesellschaft der Gesellschaft* [The Society of the Society]. Frankfurt, Germany: Suhrkamp.

Lutz, J. 1998. *Der Naturbegriff und das Gesellschaft-Natur-Verhältnis in der frühen Soziologie* [Nature and the Society-Nature Interrelation in Early Sociology]. Vol. 52. Vienna: IFF.

Martinez-Alier, J., and K. Schlüpmann. 1987. *Ecological Economics: Energy, Environment and Society.* Oxford, UK: Basil Blackwell.

Marx, K. 1990[1867]. *Capital*, Vol. 1. Harmondsworth, Middlesex, UK: Penguin Books.

Maturana, H.R., and F.G. Varela. 1975. *Autopoietic Systems. A Characterization of the Living Organization.* Report BCL Champaign, IL: University of Illinois Press.

Metha, L., V. Winiwarter, M. Fischer-Kowalski, and H. Schandl. 1997. *Stoffwechsel in einem indischen Dorf: Fallstudie Merkar*[Mebabolism of an Indian Village: Case Study Merkar]. Vol. 49. Vienna: IFF.

Morgan, L.H. 1963 [1877]. *Ancient Society.* Cleveland, OH: World.

Müller-Herold, U., and R.P. Sieferle. 1998. "Surplus and Survival: Risk, Ruin and Luxury in the Evolution of Early Forms of Subsistence." Pp. 201-220 in *Advances in Human Ecology*, Vol. 6, edited by L. Freese. Greenwich, CT: JAI Press.

Murphy, R., and J.H. Steward. 1955. "Tappers and Trappers: Parallel Process in Acculturation." *Economic Development and Cultural Change* 4: 335-355.

Netting, R.M. 1981. *Balancing on an Alp: Ecological Change and Continuity in a Swiss Mountain Community.* London: Cambridge University Press.

Norgaard, R.B. 1997. "A Coevolutionary Environmental Sociology." Pp. 158-168 in *The International Handbook of Environmental Sociology*, edited by M. Redclift and M. Woodgate. Cheltenham, UK: Edward Elgar.

Odum, E.P. 1959. *Fundamentals of Ecology.* Philadelphia, PA: Saunders.

———. 1969. "The Strategy of Ecosystem Development." *Science* 164: 262-270.

———. 1983. *Basic Ecology.* Philadelphia, PA: Saunders College.

———. 1996. "Cost of Living in Domed Cities." *Nature* 382: 18-18.

Odum, E.P., and B.C. Patton. 1981. "The Cybernetic Nature or Ecosystems." *The American Naturalist* 118: 886-895.

Odum, H.T. 1983. *Systems Ecology—An Introduction.* NY: Wiley.

Orlove, B.S. 1980. "Ecological Anthropology." *Annual Review of Ecology and Systematics* 9: 235-271.

Ostwald, W. 1909. *Energetische Grundlagen der Kulturwissenschaften* [Basing Cultural Sciences upon Energy]. Leipzig, Germany: Dr. Werner Klinkhardt Verlag.

Purves, W.K., G.H. Orians, and H.C. Heller. 1992. *Life: The Science of Biology.* Sunderland, MA: Sinauer.

Riedl, R. 1975. *Die Ordnung des Lebendigen. Systembedingungen der Evolution* [The Order of Life. Systemic Conditions of Evolution]. Hamburg/Munich/Berlin, Germany: Parey.

Rosa, E.A. 1998. "Metatheoretical Foundations for Post-normal Risk." *Journal of Risk Research* 1(1): 15-44.

Roy, W., R. Bechtel, T. MacCallum, D.E. Paglia, and L.J. Weber. 1996. "'Biospheric Medicine' as Viewed From the Two-Year First Closure of Biosphere 2." *Aviation, Space, and Environmental Medicine* 67(7): 609-617.

Sahlins, M.D. 1972. *Stone Age Economics.* New York: Aldine de Gruyter.

Salt, G.W. 1977. "A Comment on the Use of the Term Emergent Properties." *The American Naturalist* 113(1): 145-148.

Schandl, H. 1998. *Materialfluß Österreich–die materielle Basis der österreichischen Gesellschaft 1960-1995* [Material Flows Austria. The Material Background of the Austrian Society from 1960 to 1995]. Vol. 50. Vienna: IFF Eigenverlag.

Schmidt, A. 1971. *Der Begriff der Natur in der Lehre von Marx* [The Concept of Nature in the Writings of Marx]. Frankfurt, Germany: Europ.Verlagsanstalt.

Schmidt-Bleek, F. 1994. *Wieviel Umwelt braucht der Mensch? MIPS – das Maß für ökologisches Wirtschaften* [How Much Environment Does Man Need?]. Berlin: Birkhäuser.

Sieferle, R.P. 1997. *Rückblick auf die Natur: eine Geschichte des Menschen und seiner Umwelt,* [Looking Back at Nature. A History of Man and His Environment]. Munich, Germany: Luchterhand.

_____. 1997b. "Kulturelle Evolution des Gesellschaft-Natur-Verhältnisses." Pp. 37-56 in *Gesellschaftlicher Stoffwechsel und Kolonisierung von Natur. Ein Versuch in Sozialer Ökologie,* [Cultural Evolution of Society-Nature Relations], edited by M. Fischer-Kowalskiet al. Amsterdam: Gordon & Breach Verlag Fakultas.Smith, A. 1980 [1776]. *An Inquiry into the Nature and Causes of the Wealth of Nations. The Glasgow Edition of the Works and Correspondence of Adam Smith.* Glasgow.

Smith, A. 1776. *An Inquiry into the Nature and Causes of the Wealth of Nations.* Dublin: Whitestone.

Soddy, F. 1912. *Matter and Energy.* London: Oxford University Press.

_____. 1922. *Cartesian Economics: The Bearing of Physical Science Upon State Stewardship.* London: Hendersons.

_____. 1926. *Wealth, Virtual Wealth and Debt: The Solution to the Economic Paradox.* New York: Allen & Unwin.

Sombart, W. 1919[1902]. *Der moderne Kapitalismus.* 2. [Modern Capitalism, Vol. 2]. Band. München-Leipzig: Duncker & Humblot.

Spencer, H. 1880[1862]. *First Principles.* New York: A.L.Burt.

Steward, J.H. 1968. "The Concept and Method of Cultural Ecology." Pp. 337-344 in *International Encyclopedia of the Social Sciences,* edited by D.L. Sills. New York: Macmillan.

Swenson, R. 1997. "Autocatakinetics, Evolution, and the Law of Maximum Entropy Production: A Principled Foundation towards the Study of Human Ecology." Pp. 1-48 in *Advances in Human Ecology,* Vol. 6, edited by L. Freese. Greenwich, CT: JAI Press.

Tansley, A.G. 1935. "The Use and Abuse of Vegetational Concepts and Terms." *Ecology* 16(3): 284-307.

Vasey, D.E. 1992. *An Ecological History of Agriculture, 10 000 B.C.-10 000 A.D.* Ames, IA: Iowa State University Press.

Vayda, A.P., and R. Rappaport. 1968. "Ecology, Cultural and Non-cultural." Pp. 476-498 in *Introduction to Cultural Anthropology,* edited by J.A. Clifton. Boston, MA: Houghton Mifflin.

Weber, M. 1909. "'Energetische' Kulturtheorien." *Archiv für Sozialwissenschaft und Sozialpolitik* [Energetic Theories of Culture] 29: 375-398.

_____. 1958 [1904]. *The Protestant Ethic and the Spirit of Capitalism,* trans. by Talcott Parsons. New York: Scribners.

Weizsäcker, E.U. v., A.B. Lovins, and L.H. Lovins. 1997. Factor Four Doubling Wealth—Halving Resource Use. The New Report to the Club of Rome. London: Earthscan.

White, L. 1949. "Energy and the Evolution of Culture." Pp. 363-393 in *The Science of Culture: A Study of Man and Civilization.* New York: Grove Press.

Young, G.L. 1974. "Human Ecology as an Interdisciplinary Concept: A Critical Inquiry." Pp. 1-105 in *Advances in Ecological Research,* edited by A. Macfayden. New York: Academic Press.

[7]

CONSTRUCTING NATURE

Elements for a poststructural
political ecology

Arturo Escobar

INTRODUCTION: THE DISCOURSE OF NATURE
AND THE NATURE OF DISCOURSE

This chapter argues for a poststructural political ecology. The project reflects a growing belief that nature is socially constructed, something entirely different from saying "There is no real nature out there"; but it takes the further step of insisting that the constructs of political economy and ecology as specifically modern forms of knowledge, as well as their objects of study, must be analyzed discursively. It is necessary to reiterate the connections between the making and evolution of nature and the making and evolution of the discourses and practices through which nature is historically produced and known. The relationship between nature and capital has been articulated historically by different discursive regimes, including in recent times – as we shall see – the discourses of sustainable development and biodiversity conservation. The argument developed here is thus a reflection on the discourses of nature from the vantage point of recent theories of the nature of discourse.

From a certain poststructural perspective (Foucaultian and Deleuzian in particular) there cannot be a materialist analysis which is not, at the same time, a discursive analysis. The poststructural analysis of discourse is not only a linguistic theory; it is a social theory, a theory of the production of social reality which includes the analysis of representations as social facts inseparable from what is commonly thought of as "material reality." Poststructuralism focuses on the role of language in the construction of social reality; it treats language not as a reflection of "reality" but as constitutive of it. That was the whole point, for instance, of Said's (1979) *Orientalism*. For some, there is no materiality unmediated by discourse, as there is no discourse unrelated to materialities (Laclau and Mouffe 1985). Discourse, as used in this chapter, is the articulation of knowledge and power, of statements and visibilities, of the visible and the expressible. Discourse is the process through which social reality inevitably comes into being.

46

POSTSTRUCTURAL POLITICAL ECOLOGY

Anthropologists have recently incorporated these insights into analyses of systems of production and systems of signification, systems of meanings of nature, and systems of use of resources, as inextricably bound together (Comaroff and Comaroff 1991; Gudeman and Rivera 1990; Hvalkof 1989). Political ecologists are beginning to emulate this fruitful trend. Space, poverty, and nature are seen through the lens of a discursive materialism "where ideas, matter, discourse, and power are intertwined in ways that virtually defy dissection" (Yapa 1995: 1). Insisting that we look at the way local cultures process the conditions of global capital and modernity (Pred and Watts 1992) is another important step in this direction.

In this chapter, I also take as point of departure a recent claim in political economy: the suggestion that capital, undergoing a significant change in form, enters an "ecological phase." No longer is nature defined and treated as an external, exploitable domain. Through a new process of capitalization, effected primarily by a shift in representation, previously "uncapitalized" aspects of nature and society become internal to capital. "Correspondingly, the primary dynamic of capitalism changes form, from accumulation and growth feeding on an external domain, to ostensible self-management and conservation of the system of capitalized nature closed back upon itself" (M. O'Connor 1993: 8). This transformation is perhaps most visible in discussions of rainforest biodiversity: the key to the survival of the rainforest is seen as lying in the genes of the species, the usefulness of which could be released for profit through genetic engineering and biotechnology in the production of commercially valuable products, such as pharmaceuticals. Capital thus develops a conservationist tendency, significantly different from its usual reckless, destructive form.

This proposal significantly qualifies views of the dialectic of nature and capital. The argument has been that capitalist restructuring takes place at the expense of production conditions: nature, the body, space. Driven by competition and cost-shifting among individual capitals/capitalists, this restructuring signifies a deepening of the encroachment of capital on nature and labor, an aggravation of the ecological crisis, and an impairment of capital's conditions of production – what James O'Connor (1988, 1989) calls "the second contradiction" of capitalism. For M. O'Connor, the expansionist drive of capital onto external nature implied by the second contradiction is only one tendency. Another entails a more pervasive discursive incorporation of nature as capital. This calls not for exploitative accumulation – with the concomitant impairment of production conditions – but, on the contrary, the sustainable management of the system of capitalized nature. Although the two forms may coexist, the first is prelude to the second, which appears when brute appropriation is contested by social movements. To the extent that the second entails deeper cultural domination – even the genes of living species are seen in terms of production and profitability – we are led to conclude that it will continue to achieve dominance in the strategies of both capital and social movements.

The present chapter is a contribution to the understanding of the articulations

ESCOBAR

established by capital between natural and social systems. It argues that both forms of capital – exploitative and conservationist, modern and postmodern, let us say – are necessary given current conditions in the Third and First Worlds; both – not only the second form – require complex cultural and discursive articulations; both take on different but increasingly overlapping characteristics in the Third and First Worlds, and must be studied simultaneously; both can be studied by appealing to a poststructural political ecology; and that social movements and communities increasingly face the double task of building alternative productive rationalities and strategies, and culturally resisting the inroads of new forms of capital and technology into the fabric of nature and culture.

The first part of the chapter develops a nuanced reading of the discourse of sustainable development to bring out its mediation between nature and capital, particularly in the Third World. The second part elaborates the two forms of ecological capital; a brief example from the Pacific Coast region of Colombia is presented to show their respective rationalities and modes of operation. The third part analyzes the discourses of technoscience and biotechnology through which a veritable reinvention of nature is being effected, most clearly in the most industrialized countries, but increasingly in the Third World as well. The fourth part discusses the implications of the analysis for social practice; it focuses on the possibility of building alternative production rationalities by social movements faced with the two logics of ecological capital. The conclusion restates the case for the development of a poststructuralist political ecology as a means of ascertaining the types of knowledge that might be conducive to eco-socialist strategies.

"SUSTAINABLE DEVELOPMENT": DEATH OF NATURE, RISE OF ENVIRONMENT

By starting with the contemporary discourse that most forcefully seeks to articulate our relation to nature, we can "unpack" dominant assumptions about society and nature, and the political economy that makes such assumptions possible: the discourse of "sustainable development," launched globally in 1987 with the report of the World Commission on Environment and Development convened by the United Nations under the chair(wo)manship of Norway's former prime minister, Gro Harlem Brundtland. That report, published under the title *Our Common Future*, begins as follows:

> In the middle of the twentieth century, we saw our planet from space for the first time. Historians may eventually find that this vision had a greater impact on thought than did the Copernican revolution of the sixteenth century, which upset the human self-image by revealing that the earth is not the center of the universe. From space, we saw a small and fragile ball dominated not by human activity and edifice, but by a pattern of clouds, oceans, greenery, and soils. Humanity's inability to fit its doings into that pattern is changing planetary systems, fundamentally. Many such

POSTSTRUCTURAL POLITICAL ECOLOGY

changes are accompanied by life-threatening hazards. This new reality, from which there is no escape, must be recognized – and managed.
(World Commission on Environment and Development 1987: 1)

The category "global problems," to which *Our Common Future* belongs, is of recent invention. Its main impetus comes from the ecological fervor fostered by the Club of Rome reports of the 1970s, which provided a distinctive vision of the world as a global system where all parts are interrelated, thus demanding management on a planetary scale (Sachs 1988). The notion that nature and the Earth can be "managed" is an historically novel one. Like the earlier scientific management of labor, the management of nature entails its capitalization, its treatment as commodity. Moreover, the sustainable development discourse purports to reconcile two old enemies – economic growth and the preservation of the environment – without significant adjustments to the market system. This reconciliation is the result of complex discursive operations involving capital, representations of nature, management, and science. In the sustainable development discourse, nature is reinvented as environment so that capital, not nature and culture, may be sustained.

Seeing the Earth from space was not so great a revolution. This vision only re-enacted the scientific gaze established in clinical medicine at the end of the eighteenth century. The representation of the globe from space is but another chapter of the alliance which, two centuries ago, "was forged between words and things, enabling one *to see* and *to say*" (Foucault 1975: xii). Twentieth-century space exploration belongs to the paradigm defined by the spatialization and verbalization of the pathological, effected by the scientific gaze of the nineteenth-century clinician. As with the gaze of the clinician at an earlier time, environmental sciences today challenge the Earth to reveal its secrets to the positive gaze of scientists. This operation only ensures, however, that the degradation of the Earth be redistributed and dispersed, through the professional discourses of environmentalists, economists, geographers, and politicians. The globe and its "problems" have finally entered rational discourse. Disease is housed in nature in a new manner. As the medicine of the pathological led to a medicine of social space (the healthy biological space was also the social space dreamt of by the French Revolution), so will the "medicine of the Earth" result in new constructions of the social that allow some version of nature's health to be preserved.

In the Brundtland Report, we find a reinforcing effect between epistemology and the technologies of vision.

The instruments of visualization in multinationalist, postmodernist culture have compounded [the] meanings of disembodiment. The visualizing technologies are without apparent limit. ... Vision in this technological feast becomes unregulated gluttony; all seems not just mythical about the god trick of seeing everything from nowhere, but to have put the myth into ordinary practice.
(Haraway 1988: 581)

49

ESCOBAR

The Report thus inaugurated a period of unprecedented gluttony in the history of vision and knowledge with the concomitant rise of a global ecocracy.

This might sound too harsh a judgment. We should construct the argument step by step. To begin with, management is the sibling of gluttonous vision, particularly now when the world is theorized in terms of global systems. The narrative of management is linked to the visualization of the Earth as a "fragile ball." Carrying the baton from Brundtland, *Scientific American*'s September 1989 Special Issue on "Managing Planet Earth" reveals the essence of the managerial attitude. At stake for this group of scientists (all either male academics or businessmen) is the continuation of the existing models of growth and development through appropriate management strategies. "What kind of planet do we want? What kind of planet can we get?" asks the opening article (Clark 1989: 48). "We" have responsibility for managing the human use of planet earth. "We" "need to move peoples and nations towards sustainability" by effecting a change in values and institutions that parallel the agricultural or industrial revolutions of the past.

The question in this discourse is what new manipulations can we invent to make the most out of nature and "resources." But who is this "we" who knows what is best for the world as a whole? Once again, we find the familiar figure of the (white male) Western scientist-turned-manager. A full-page picture of a young Nepalese woman "planting a tree as part of a reforestation project" is exemplary of the mind-set of this "we." Portrayed are not the women of the Chipko movement in India, with their militancy, their radically different forms of knowledge and practice of forestry, defending their trees politically and not through carefully managed "reforestation" projects. Instead there is a picture of an ahistorical young dark woman, whose control by masculinist and colonialist sciences, as Shiva (1989) has shown, is assured in the very act of representation. This regime of representation assumes that the benevolent hand of the West should save the earth; the Fathers of the World Bank, mediated by Gro Harlem Brundtland, the matriarch-scientist, and the few cosmopolitan Third Worlders who made it to the World Commission, will reconcile "humankind" with "nature." It is still the Western scientist that speaks for the Earth.

But can reality be "managed"? The concepts of planning and management embody the belief that social change can be engineered and directed, produced at will. The idea that poor countries could more or less smoothly move along the path of progress through planning has always been held to be an indubitable truth by development experts. Perhaps no other concept has been so insidious, no other idea gone so unchallenged, as modern planning. The narratives of planning and management, always presented as "rational" and "objective," are essential to developers (Escobar 1992). A blindness to the role of planning in the normalization and control of the social world is present also in environmental managerialism. As they are incorporated into the world capitalist economy, even the most remote communities of the Third World are torn from their local context, redefined as "resources" to be planned for, managed.

50

POSTSTRUCTURAL POLITICAL ECOLOGY

The rise of sustainable development is related to complex historical processes, including modifications in various practices (of assessing the viability and impact of development projects, obtaining knowledge at the local level, development assistance by NGOs); new social situations (the failure of top–down development projects, new social and ecological problems associated with that failure, new forms of protest, deficiencies that have become accentuated); and international economic and technological factors (new international divisions of labor with the concomitant globalization of ecological degradation, coupled with novel technologies that measure such degradation). What needs to be explained, however, is precisely why the response to this set of conditions has taken the form of "sustainable development," and what important problems might be associated with it. Four aspects are involved in answering this question.

First, the emergence of the concept of "sustainable development" is part of a broader process of the problematization of global survival, a process which induces a re-working of the relationship between nature and society. This problematization appeared as a response to the destructive character of development, on the one hand, and the rise of environmental movements in both the North and the South, on the other, resulting in a complex process of internationalization of the environment (Buttel *et al.* 1990). What is problematized is not the sustainability of local cultures and realities, but rather that of the global ecosystem, "global" being defined according to a perception of the world shared by those who rule it. Ecosystems professionals tend to see ecological problems as the result of complex processes that transcend cultural and local contexts. The slogan "Think globally, act locally" assumes not only that problems can be defined at a global level, but also that they are equally compelling for all communities. The professionals believe that since all people are passengers of spaceship earth, all are responsible for environmental degradation. They do not always see, in short, that there are great differences and inequities in resource problems between countries, regions, communities, and classes.

Second, the sustainable development discourse is regulated by a peculiar economy of visibilities. Ecosystems analysts have discovered the "degrading" activities of the poor, but have seldom recognized that such problems were rooted in development processes that displaced indigenous communities, disrupted people's habitats and occupations, and forced many rural societies to increase their pressures on the environment. Now the poor are admonished not for their lack of industriousness but for their "irrationality" and lack of environmental consciousness. Popular and scholarly texts alike are filled with representations of dark and poor peasant masses destroying forests and mountainsides with axes and machetes, thus shifting visibility and blame away from the large industrial polluters in North and South, and the predatory way of life fostered by capitalism and development, to poor peasants and "backward" practices such as slash-and-burn agriculture.

Third, the ecodevelopmentalist vision expressed in mainstream versions of sustainable development reproduces central aspects of economism and

ESCOBAR

developmentalism. The sustainable development discourse redistributes in new fields many of the concerns of classical development: basic needs, population, resources, technology, institutional co-operation, food security and industrialism are found reconfigured and reshuffled in the sustainable development discourse. That discourse upholds ecological concerns, although with a slightly altered logic. By adopting the concept of "sustainable development," two old enemies, growth and the environment, are reconciled (Redclift 1987), unfolding a new field of social intervention and control. Given the present visibility of ecological degradation, this process necessitates an epistemological and political reconciliation of ecology and economy, intended to create the impression that only minor corrections to the market system are needed to launch an era of environmentally sound development, and hiding the fact that the economic framework itself cannot hope to accommodate environmental concerns without substantial reform (Marglin 1992; Norgaard 1991a, 1991b). The sustainable development strategy, after all, focuses not so much on the negative consequences of economic growth on the environment, as on the effects of environmental degradation on growth and the potential for growth. Growth (i.e. capitalist market expansion) and not the environment has to be sustained. Poverty is believed to be a cause, as well as an effect, of environmental problems; growth is needed to eliminate poverty and, in turn, protect the environment. Unlike the discourse of the 1970s, which focused on "the limits to growth," the discourse of the 1980s was fixated on "growth of the limits" (Sachs 1988).

Fourth, the reconciliation of growth and environment is facilitated exactly by the new concept of the "environment," the importance of which has grown steadily in the post-Second World War ecological discourse. The development of ecological consciousness accompanying the rapid growth of industrial civilization also effected the transformation of "nature" into "environment" (Sachs 1992). No longer does nature denote an entity with its own agency, a source of life and discourse, as was the case in many traditional societies, and with European Romantic literature and art of the nineteenth century. For those committed to the world as resource, the "environment" becomes an indispensable construct. As the term is used today, "environment" includes a view of nature from the perspective of the urban-industrial system. Everything that is relevant to the functioning of this system becomes part of the environment. The active principle of this conceptualization is the human agent and his/her creations, while nature is confined to an ever more passive role. What circulates are raw materials, industrial products, toxic wastes, "resources"; nature is reduced to stasis, a mere appendage to the environment. Along with the physical deterioration of nature, we are witnessing its symbolic death. That which moves, creates, inspires – that is, the organizing principle of life – now resides in the environment.

The danger of accepting uncritically the sustainable development discourse is highlighted by a group of environmental activists from Canada:

> A genuine belief that the Brundtland Report is a big step forward for the environmental/green movement . . . amounts to a selective reading, where

POSTSTRUCTURAL POLITICAL ECOLOGY

the data on environmental degradation and poverty are emphasized, and the growth economics and "resource" orientation of the Report are ignored or downplayed. This point of view says that given the Brundtland Report's endorsement of sustainable development, activists can now point out some particular environmental atrocity and say, "This is not sustainable development". However, environmentalists are thereby accepting a "development" framework for discussion.

(Green Web 1989: 6)

Becoming a new client of the development apparatus by adopting the sustainable development discourse means accepting the scarcity of natural resources as a given fact; this leads environmental managers into stressing the need to find the most efficient forms of using resources without threatening the survival of nature and people. As the Brundtland Report put it, the goal should be to "produce more with less" (World Commission on Environment and Development 1987: 15). The World Commission is not alone in this endeavor. Year after year, this dictum is reawakened by the World Watch Institute in its *State of the World* reports, a main source for ecodevelopers. In these reports, ecology is reduced to a higher form of efficiency, as Wolfgang Sachs (1988) perceptively says.

Although ecologists and ecodevelopmentalists recognize environmental limits to production, a large number do not perceive the cultural character of the commercialization of nature and life integral to the Western economy, nor do they seriously account for the cultural limits which many societies have set on unchecked production. It is not surprising that their policies are restricted to promoting the "rational" management of resources. Environmentalists who accept this presupposition also accept imperatives for capital accumulation, material growth, and the disciplining of labor and nature. In doing so they extrapolate the occidental economic culture to the entire universe. Even the call for a people-centered economy runs the risk of perpetuating the basic assumptions of scarcity and productivism which underlie the dominant economic vision. In sum, by rationalizing the defense of nature in economic terms, advocates of sustainable development contribute to extending the economization of life and history. This effect is most visible in the World Bank approach to sustainable development, an approach based on the belief that, as the President of the Bank put it shortly after the publication of the Brundtland Report, "sound ecology is good economics" (Conable 1987: 6). The establishment in 1987 of a top level Environment Department, and the "Global Environmental Facility" (read: the Earth as a giant market/utility company under Group of Seven and World Bank control) created in 1992, reinforce the managerial attitude towards nature: "Environmental Planning" – said Conable (1987: 3) in the same address – "can make the most of nature's resources so that human resourcefulness can make the most of the future."

Again this involves the further capitalization of nature, the propagation of certain views of nature and society in terms of production and efficiency, not of respect and the common good. This is why Visvanathan (1991) calls the world of Brundtland and the World Bank "a disenchanted cosmos." The Brundtland

ESCOBAR

Report, and much of the sustainable development discourse, is a tale that a disenchanted (modern) world tells itself about its sad condition. As a renewal of the contract between the modern nation-state and modern science, sustainable development seeks not so much to caricature the past, as with early development theory, as to control a future whose vision is highly impoverished. Visvanathan is also concerned with the ascendancy of the sustainable development discourse among ecologists and activists. It is fitting to end this section with his call for resistance to co-option:

> Brundtland seeks a cooptation of the very groups that are creating a new dance of politics, where democracy is not merely order and discipline, where earth is a magic cosmos, where life is still a mystery to be celebrated. ... The experts of the global state would love to coopt them, turning them into a secondary, second-rate bunch of consultants, a lower order of nurses and paramedics still assisting the expert as surgeon and physician. It is this that we seek to resist by creating an explosion of imaginations that this club of experts seeks to destroy with its cries of lack and excess. The world of official science and the nation-state is not only destroying soils and silting up lakes, it is freezing the imagination. ... We have to see the Brundtland report as a form of published illiteracy and say a prayer for the energy depleted and the forests lost in publishing the report. And finally, a little prayer, an apology to the tree that supplied the paper for this document. Thank you, tree.
>
> (1991: 384)

CAPITALIZATION OF NATURE: MODERN AND POSTMODERN FORMS

The sustainable development strategy is the main way of bringing nature into discourse in what still is known as the Third World. The continuous reinvention of nature requires not only bringing nature into new domains of discourse but also bringing it into capital in novel ways. This process takes two general forms, both entailing discursive constructions of different kinds. Let us call these forms the modern and postmodern forms of capital in its ecological phase.

The modern form of capital

The first form capital takes in its ecological phase operates according to the logic of the modern capitalist culture and rationality; it is theorized in terms of what J. O'Connor (1988, 1989, 1991) calls "the second contradiction" of capitalism. Let it be recalled that the starting point of Marxist crisis theory is the contradiction between capitalist productive forces and production relations, or between the production and realization of value and surplus value. It is important to emphasize that from the perspective of traditional Marxist theory capitalism

POSTSTRUCTURAL POLITICAL ECOLOGY

restructures itself through realization crises. But there is a second contradiction of capitalism that has become pressing with the aggravation of the ecological crisis and the social forms of protest this crisis generates. This theorization shows that we need to refocus our attention on the role played by the *conditions of production* in capital accumulation and capitalist restructuring, insufficiently theorized by Marx, yet placed at the center of inquiry by Polanyi's (1957) critique of the self-regulating market. Why? Because capitalist restructuring increasingly takes place at the expense of these conditions. A "condition of production" is everything treated as if it were a commodity, even if it is not produced as a commodity – that is according to the laws of value and the market: labor power, land, nature, urban space, fit this definition. Recall that Polanyi called "land" (that is, nature) and "labor" (that is, human life), "fictitious commodities." The history of modernity and the history of capitalism must be seen as the progressive capitalization of production conditions. Trees produced capitalistically on plantations, privatized land and water rights, genetically altered species sold in the market, and the entire training and professionalization of labor – from its crudest form in slavery to today's Ph.D.s – are all examples of the "capitalization" of nature and human life.

This process is mediated by the state; indeed, the state must be seen as an interface between capital and nature, including human beings and space. As far as human beings are concerned, the disciplining and normalization of labor, the management of poverty, and rise of the social (Donzelot 1979, 1988; Foucault 1979, 1980; Procacci 1991) marked the beginning of the capitalization of life within the modern era, while urban planning normalized and accelerated the capitalization of space (Harvey 1985; Rabinow 1989). This type of capitalization has been central to capitalism since the beginning of the primitive accumulation process and enclosure of the commons. The instrumental tendency of science was crucial in this regard, as discussed by philosophers, feminists, and ecologists (Merchant 1980; Shiva 1989).

In fact, one of the defining features of modernity is the increasing appropriation of "traditional" or pre-modern cultural contents by scientific knowledges, and the subsequent subjection of vast areas of life to regulation by administrative apparatuses based on expert knowledge (Foucault 1979; Giddens 1990; Habermas 1975). The history of capital not only involves exploitation of production conditions; it is also the history of the advance of the scientific discourses of modernity in areas such as health, planning, families, education, economy, and the like, through what Habermas (1987) refers to as the colonization of the lifeworld and Foucault (1980) as the advance of bio-power. The accumulation of capital, in other words, required the accumulation of normalized individuals and the accumulation of knowledge about the processes of capital and populations. This is the primary lesson of the anthropology of modernity of Western societies since the end of the eighteenth century. With this observation we wish to emphasize that the modern form of capital is inevitably mediated by the expert discourses of modernity.

ESCOBAR

Capital's threatening of its own conditions of production elicits manifold and contradictory attempts at restructuring those conditions in order to reduce costs or defend profits. Conversely, social struggles generated around the defense of production conditions must seek two objectives: to defend life and production conditions against capital's excesses; and to seek control over policies to restructure production conditions, usually via further privatization. In other words, social movements have to face simultaneously the destruction of life, the body, nature, and space, and the crisis-induced restructuring of these conditions (O'Connor 1988, 1991). Often, these struggles pit the poor against the rich as both cultural and economic actors; there is an "environmentalism of the poor" (Guha 1994; Martinez-Alier 1992) which is a type of class struggle and, at the same time, a cultural struggle, to the extent that the poor try to defend their natural environments from material and cultural reconversion by the market. These struggles are often gender struggles, in that many aspects of the destruction of production conditions affect women particularly and contribute to the restructuring of class and gender relations (Mellor 1992; Rao 1989, 1991).

The postmodern form of ecological capital

In the Third World, the continued existence of conventional forms of capitalist exploitation of people and the environment is organized according to the rules of the dominant development discourse of the last forty years, for which nature exists as raw material for economic growth activities (Escobar 1995). While there are areas "sold" to the sustainable development discourse, others remain firmly in the grasp of that crude and reckless developmentalism characterizing the post-Second World War period. As we shall see in the Colombian case, both forms may coexist schizophrenically in the same geographical and cultural region.

M. O'Connor (1993) is right, however, in pointing at a qualitative change in the form capital tends to take today. If with modernity one can speak of a progressive semiotic conquest of social life by expert discourses and economistic conceptions, today this conquest is being extended to the very heart of nature and life. This new conquest takes for granted the normalization already achieved by the modern discourses of science and its administrative apparatuses; not only does it move on to new territories, it also develops new modes of operation, which O'Connor understands particularly in the Baudrillardian sense of the pre-eminence of the sign. Once modernity is consolidated, once "the economy" becomes a seemingly ineluctable reality (a true descriptor of reality for most), capital and the struggles around it must broach the question of the domestication of all remaining social and symbolic relations, in terms of the code of political economy, that of production. It is no longer capital and labor that are at stake *per se*, but the reproduction of the code. Social reality becomes, to borrow Baudrillard's (1975) phrase, "the mirror of production."

This second form of capital relies not only on the symbolic conquest of nature

POSTSTRUCTURAL POLITICAL ECOLOGY

(in terms of "biodiversity reserves") and local communities (as "stewards" of nature); it also requires the semiotic conquest of local knowledges, to the extent that "saving nature" demands the valuation of local knowledges of sustaining nature. Local, "indigenous" and "traditional" knowledge systems are found to be useful complements to modern biology. However, in these discourses, knowledge is seen as something existing in the "minds" of individual persons (shamans or elders) about external "objects" ("plants," "species"), the medical or economic "utility" of which their bearers are supposed to transmit to us. Local knowledge is seen not as a complex cultural construction, involving movements and events profoundly historical and relational. Moreover, these forms of knowledge usually have entirely different modes of operation and relations to social and cultural fields (Deleuze and Guattari 1987). As they are brought into its politics modern science recodifies them in utilitarian ways.

This triple cultural reconversion of nature, people, and knowledge represents a novel internalization of production conditions. Nature and local people themselves are seen as the source and creators of value – not merely as labor or raw material. The discourse of biodiversity in particular achieves this effect. Species of micro-organisms, flora, and fauna are valuable not so much as "resources" but as reservoirs of value – this value residing in their very genes – that scientific research, along with biotechnology, can release for capital and communities. This is a reason why communities – particularly ethnic and peasant communities in the tropical rainforest areas of the world – are finally recognized as the owners of their territories (or what is left of them), but only to the extent that they accept seeing and treating territory and themselves as reservoirs of capital. Communities in various parts of the world are then enticed by biodiversity projects to become "stewards of the social and natural 'capitals' whose sustainable management is, henceforth, both their responsibility and the business of the world economy" (M. O'Connor 1993: 5). Once the semiotic conquest of nature is completed, the sustainable and rational use of the environment becomes imperative. It is here that the fundamental logic of the discourses of sustainable development and biodiversity must be found.

"Biodiversity conservation" in Colombia

A brief example illustrates the differences between the two forms of capital. The Pacific Coast region of Colombia has one of the highest degrees of biological diversity in the world. Covering about 5.4 million hectares of tropical rainforest, it is populated by about 800,000 Afrocolombians and 40,000 indigenous people belonging to various ethnic groups, particularly Emberas and Waunanas. Since the early 1980s the national and regional governments have increased their development activities in the region, culminating in the elaboration of ambitious development plans (DNP 1983, 1992). The 1992 *Sustainable Development Plan* is a conventional strategy intended to foster the development of capitalism in the region. Since the early 1980s, capital has flowed to various

ESCOBAR

parts of the region, particularly in the form of investments in sectors such as African palm plantations, large-scale shrimp cultivation, gold mining, timber, and tourism. These investments operate, for the most part, in the mode of the first form of capital. All of the activities of this type of capital tend to contribute to ecological degradation and the displacement and proletarianization of local people, who can no longer subsist as farmers and must find precarious jobs in palm oil plantations and shrimp-packing plants.

Parallel to this, the government has launched a more modest, but symbolically ambitious, project for the protection of the region's almost legendary biodiversity, in peril of being destroyed by activities mediated by the development plan. The Biodiversity Project (GEF–PNUD 1993), conceived under the directives of the Global Biodiversity Strategy (WRI/WCU/UNEP 1992) and within the scope of the World Bank's Global Environmental Facility (GEF), purports to effect an alternative strategy for the sustainable and culturally appropriate development of the area. The project is organized along four different axes: "to know" (to gather and systematize modern and traditional knowledge of the region's biodiversity); "to valorize" (to design ecologically sound strategies to create economic value out of biodiversity); "to mobilize" (to foster the organization of the black and indigenous communities so they can take charge of the sustainable development of their environments); and "to formulate and implement" (to modify institutional structures so they can support community-oriented sustainable development strategies).

The Biodiversity Project obeys the global logic of the second form of ecological capital. The Project became possible not only because of international trends, but was formed also by pressure exerted on the state by black and indigenous communities in the context of territorial and cultural rights accorded by the reform of the National Constitution of 1991. The Project designers had to take into account the views of local communities, and had to accept as important interlocutors representatives of the black movement which was growing in the context of the developmentalist onslaught and the reform of the constitution. A few progressive professionals associated with the black movement have been able to insert themselves in the national and regional staff of the project. While these professionals seem aware of the risks involved in participating in a government project of this kind, they also believe that the Project presents a space of struggle they cannot afford to ignore.

Along with new forms of biotechnology, the discourse of biodiversity conservation produced mostly by Northern NGOs and international organizations in the 1990s achieves an important transformation in our consciousness of and practices towards nature. As far as the world rainforests are concerned, this discourse constructs an equation between "knowing" (classifying species), "saving" (protecting from total destruction), and "using" (through the development of commercial applications based on the genetic properties of species). Biodiversity prospectors would roam the rainforest in search of potential uses of rainforest species, and the biotechnological developments that would allegedly ensue from

POSTSTRUCTURAL POLITICAL ECOLOGY

this task would provide the key to rainforest preservation – if appropriately protected, of course, by intellectual property rights so that prospectors and investors have the incentive to invest in the epic enterprise of saving nature (WRI/ WCU/UNEP 1992; WRI 1993). Both capitalism and nature would not only survive but would thrive under the new scheme dreamed up by scientists, planners, multinational corporations, and genetic and molecular biology laboratories, among others. Social movements confront a greening of economics, knowledge, and communities more pervasive than ever before.

MAKING NATURE: FROM (MODERN) DEATH TO (POSTMODERN) REINVENTION

It should be clear by now that sustainable development and biodiversity strategies play a crucial role in the discursive production of production conditions. Production conditions are not just transformed by "capital": they have to be transformed in/through discourse. The Brundtland Report, indeed the entire sustainable development movement, is an attempt at resignifying nature, resources, the Earth, human life itself, on a scale perhaps not witnessed since the rise of empirical sciences and their reconstruction of nature – since nature's "death," to use Carolyn Merchant's expression (1980). Sustainable development is the last attempt at articulating nature, modernity, and capitalism before the advent of cyberculture.

The reconversion of nature effected by the discourses of biodiversity and sustainable development may be placed in the broader context of what Donna Haraway (1991) calls "the reinvention of nature." Reinvention is fostered by sciences such as molecular biology and genetics, research strategies such as the Human Genome Project, and biotechnology. For Haraway, however, reinvention began with the languages of systems analysis developed since the early post-Second World War period; it marks the final disappearance of our organic notions of nature. The logic and technologies of command-control have become more central in recent years, particularly with the development of immunological discourses (Martin 1994) and projects such as the mapping of the human genome. The language of this discourse is decidedly postmodern and is not inimical to the post-Fordist regime of accumulation (Harvey 1989), with its new cultural order of "flexible labor," which might also be read symbolically as an attempt to keep dark invaders at a distance or quickly phagocytize them if they come close enough or become numerous enough to threaten contagion and disorder.

Haraway reads in these developments the de-naturalization of the notions of "organism" and "individual," so dear to pre-Second World War science. She sees the emergence of a new entity, the cyborg, which arises to fill the vacuum (1985, 1989b, 1991). Cyborgs are hybrid creatures, composed of organism and machine, "special kinds of machines and special kinds of organisms appropriate to the late twentieth century" (1991: 1). Cyborgs are not organic wholes but

ESCOBAR

strategic assemblages of organic, textual, and technical components. In the language of sustainable development one would say that cyborgs do not belong in/to nature; they belong in/to environment, and the environment belongs in/to systems.

Haraway concludes that we need to develop a different way of thinking about nature, and ourselves in relation to nature. Taking Simone de Beauvoir's declaration that "one is not born a woman" into the postmodern domain of late twentieth-century biology, Haraway adds that "one is not born an organism. Organisms are made; they are constructs of a world-changing kind" (1989b: 10). To be more precise, organisms make themselves and are also made by history. This deeply historicized account of life is difficult to accept if one remains within the modern traditions of realism, rationalism, and organic nature. The historicized view assumes that what counts as nature and what counts as culture in the West ceaselessly changes according to complex historical factors. Since at least the end of the eighteenth century, "the themes of race, sexuality, gender, nation, family and class have been written into the body of nature in western life sciences," even if in every case nature "remains a crucially important and deeply contested myth and reality" (1989a: 1). Nature as such (unconstructed) has ceased to exist, if indeed it ever existed.

Nature, bodies, and organisms must thus be seen as "material-semiotic" actors, rather than mere objects of science pre-existing in purity. Nature and organisms emerge from discursive processes involving complex apparatuses of science, capital, and culture. This implies that the boundaries between the organic, the techno-economic, and the textual (or, broadly, cultural) are permeable. While nature, bodies, and organisms certainly have an organic basis, they are increasingly produced in conjunction with machines, and this production is always mediated by scientific and cultural narratives. Haraway emphasizes that nature is a co-construction among humans and non-humans. Nature has a certain agency, an "artifactuality" of sorts. We thus have the possibility of engaging in new conversations with/around nature, involving humans and unhumans together in the reconstruction of nature as public culture. Furthermore, "there are great riches for feminists [and others] in explicitly embracing the possibilities inherent in the breakdown of clean distinctions between organism and machine and similar distinctions structuring the Western self" (Haraway 1985: 92).

Haraway's work reflects, and seeks to engage with, the profound transformation brought about by new computer technologies and biotechnology advancing in the core countries of the capitalist system. The advent of the new era – which we can perhaps call cyberculture, as a truly post-industrial and postmodern society (Escobar 1994) – entails a certain cultural promise for more just social configurations. We should have no doubts by now that a fundamental social and cultural transformation is under way, which promises to reshape biological and social life, and which involves both dangers and possibilities. A new regime of bio-sociality is upon us, implying that "nature will be modeled on culture understood as practice. Nature will be known and remade through technique and

POSTSTRUCTURAL POLITICAL ECOLOGY

will finally become artificial, just as culture becomes natural" (Rabinow 1992: 241). This might bring the dissolution of modern society and of the nature/ culture split, marking also the end of the ideologies of naturalism – of an organic nature existing outside history – and even the possibility that the organic might be improved upon by artificial means.

What all this means for the Third World is yet to be examined. This examination has to start with inventing a new language to speak of such issues from Third World perspectives, a language of transformative self-affirmation that allows the Third World to reposition itself in the global conversations and processes that are reshaping the world, without submitting passively to the rules of the game created by them. Sustainable development will not do. Biodiversity, on the contrary, is becoming inextricably linked to other discourses, such as biotechnology, genetics, and intellectual property rights (Shiva 1992). But the implications for the Third World communities placed as "stewards" of organic nature are by no means well understood. The issues are crucial for communities, as the Afrocolombian activists of the Pacific Coast have discovered. Not for nothing are corporations developing aggressive policies of privatizing nature and life. Communities in various parts of the Third World will have to dialogue with each other to face the internationalization of ecological capital. Ecological solidarity (South–South and North–South) must travel this perilous terrain, and perhaps entertain the idea of strategic alliances between the organic and the artificial (in terms of biotechnology applications of rainforests' biodiversity, for instance) against the most destructive forms of capital.

SEMIOTIC RESISTANCE AND ALTERNATIVE PRODUCTIVE RATIONALITY

The role of discourse and culture in organizing and mediating "nature" and "production conditions" is still undeveloped in both the eco-socialist and eco-feminist conceptions. For the most part, the economistic culture of modernity is taken as the norm. Behind this lie the relationships between natural and historical processes. Haraway's work provides valuable elements for examining this relation particularly in the context of rising technoculture. The Mexican ecologist, Enrique Leff, has made a general case for theorizing the mutual inscription of nature, culture, and history in terms useful for thinking about Third World situations. As the ecological becomes part of the accumulation process, Leff argues, the natural is absorbed into history and can thus be studied by historical materialism. Yet he insists that culture remains an important mediating instance. The transformation of nature and ecosystems by capital depends upon the cultural practices of specific societies and the processes of cultural transformations that are taking place (Leff 1995; see also Godelier 1986).

Leff's (1986, 1992, 1993, 1995) conceptual effort is linked specifically to the articulation of an alternative, ecologically sustainable productive rationality from an integrated perspective of ecology, culture, and production. For Leff,

ESCOBAR

ecological, technological, and cultural productivity must be woven together to theorize a new view of rationality that generates equitable and sustainable processes. "The environment should be regarded as the articulation of cultural, ecological, technological and economic processes that come together to generate a complex, balanced, and sustained productive system open to a variety of options and development styles" (1993: 60).

At the cultural level, cultural practices should be seen as a principle of productivity for the sustainable use of natural resources. Most clearly in the case of indigenous and ethnic groups, every social group possesses an "ecological culture" that must be seen as forming part of the social relations and forces of production. At the level of production, Leff advocates the development of "a productive paradigm that is not economistic yet pertains to political economy" (1993: 50). The result would be an alternative production paradigm that relates technological innovation, cultural processes, and ecological productivity. Less clear in Leff's work is how concepts such as "production" and "rationality" can be theorized from the perspective of different cultural orders.

Based on this reformed view of the environment, Leff calls on ecology activists and theorists to think in terms of "ecological conditions of production" and a "positive theory of production," in which nature is not seen only as production condition, but actively incorporated into a new productive rationality along with labor and technology. This call parallels J. O'Connor's redefinition of production conditions from the standpoint of the second contradiction, particularly through the actions of social movements. Leff's formulation brings into sharper focus the real need that social movements and communities have for articulating their own views of alternative development and alternative productive schemes specifically from the perspective of ecology. The pressure mounts on social movements and community activists in many parts of the world to engage in this constructive task, as the case of the black and indigenous activists in the Colombian Pacific Coast shows. Leff's ongoing effort at conceptualizing an alternative productive rationality is helpful in this regard.

The creation of a new productive rationality would entail forms of environmental democracy, economic decentralization, and cultural and political pluralism. The creation of spaces in which to foster local alternative productive projects is one concrete way of advancing the strategy. In sum, Leff seeks to redefine and radicalize three basic constructs: production, away from economistic cultural constructions and pure market mechanisms; rationality, away from the dominant reductionistic and utilitarian views; and management, away from bureaucratized practice and towards a participatory approach. A strategy such as this, one might add, implies cultural resistance to the symbolic reconversion of nature; socioeconomic proposals with concrete alternative strategies; and political organizing to ensure a minimum of local control over the entire process. In the landscape of Latin American hybrid cultures (Garcia Canclini 1990), strategies seem to be required combining modern and non-modern, capitalist and non-capitalist forms and practices.

POSTSTRUCTURAL POLITICAL ECOLOGY

One thing is clear in this debate: social movements and communities in the Third World need to articulate alternative productive strategies that are ecologically sustainable, lest they be swept away by a new round of conventional development. The fact that these alternatives must also be culturally defined – from the perspectives of cultures which, although hybrid, nevertheless retain a socially significant difference *vis à vis* Western modernity – necessarily entails that a certain semiotic resistance takes place. The worst would be for communities to opt for conventional development styles. To accede to an era of post-development – in which the hegemonic effect of the constructs of modernity might be held in check (Escobar 1995) – communities will need simultaneously to experiment with alternative productive strategies and to culturally resist capital's and modernity's material and symbolic restructuring of nature. Communities will need to prevent conventional development, green redevelopment via sustainable development discourses, and the greening of communities and local knowledge via discourses of biodiversity.

Is it really possible to imagine an alternative ecological economy based on a different cultural (not only social) order? If one accepts that this has become an essential political task, how could analysts investigate the concrete cultural practices that might serve as a basis for it? What are the macro-economic conditions and political processes that could make its implementation and survival possible? How should this alternative social reality engage with dominant market-driven forces? The importance of such questions will grow as researchers come to realize the increasing complexity of the cultural politics of nature under way in the wake of new forms of capital, technoscience, and globalization.

CONCLUSION: TOWARDS A POSTSTRUCTURAL POLITICAL ECOLOGY

The two socially necessary forms of capital – modern and postmodern – maintain an uneasy articulation depending on local, regional, and transnational conditions. Both forms are mediated by discourse: conventional discourses of development, plus the scientific discourses of modernity, in the case of the first form of ecological capital; discourses of biodiversity and sustainable development (particularly in the Third World), and molecular biology, biotechnology, and cyberculture in the First (and increasingly Third) Worlds, in the case of the second form of ecological capital. The regime of sustainable development in the South, and of bio-sociality and cyberculture in the North show a certain degree of geographical unevenness; yet the connections between them are becoming clearer. While some regions in the Third World join the ranks of the cyberculture, poor communities in the First are affected by the logic of reckless capital and the paradoxes of sustainability. The division between First and Third Worlds is undergoing a fundamental mutation in the wake of post-Fordism, cyberculture, and the ecological phase of capital.

The discursive nature of capital is evident in the case of the production of

ESCOBAR

"production conditions." The resignification of nature as environment; the reinscription of the earth into capital via the gaze of science; the reinterpretation of poverty as an effect of destroyed environments; the destruction of vernacular gender and the concomitant proletarianization and re-articulation of women's subordination under modern principles; and the new interest in management and planning as arbiters between people and nature, all are effects of the discursive construction of sustainable development. As more and more professionals and activists adopt the grammar of sustainable development, the reinvention of production conditions produced by this discourse will be more effective. Institutions will continue to re/produce the world as seen by those who rule it.

Although many people seem to be aware that nature is "socially constructed," many also continue to give a relatively unproblematic rendition of nature. Central to this rendition is the assumption that "nature" exists beyond our constructions. Nature, however, is neither unconstructed nor unconnected. Nature's constructions are effected by history, economics, technology, science, and myths of all kinds as part of the "traffic between nature and culture" (Haraway 1989a). Leff (1986, 1995) emphasizes a similar point in his own way. Capital accumulation, he says, requires the articulation of the sciences to the production process, so that the truths they produce become productive forces. Thus the sustainable development discourse must be seen as part of the creation of knowledge linked to capital, to the extent that the concepts produced participate in reinscribing nature into the law of value. Although the process of transdisciplinarity involved in the sciences of ecology is hopeful, Leff (1986) believes, the lack of epistemological vigilance has resulted in a certain disciplining of environmental themes which has precluded the creation of concepts useful for the formulation of alternative ecological rationalities. The analysis of discourses can serve as a basis for elaborating practical concepts useful to reorient strategies concerning development and the environment.

If nature and other life forms must now be understood as articulations of organic, techno-economic, and cultural elements, does this not imply that we need to theorize this mixture as the appropriate object of biology and ecology, perhaps at the same time – and dialectically – that these sciences seek to theorize the "laws of nature" in and of themselves? As Leff (personal communication) rightly says, one must be cautious in this endeavor, and raise the question of "to what extent by manipulating nature as reality you manipulate the scientific object of biology. By manipulating evolution and genetics, to what extent do we also manipulate and reconstruct the object and the internal laws of biology and genetics?" Perhaps what is needed is a new epistemology of biology, such as that proposed by the phenomenological biology of Humberto Maturana and Francisco Varela (1980, 1987; Varela *et al.* 1991). Works of this kind, attempting to step outside the traditional space of science by taking seriously the continuity between cognizant self and world, between knowledge and the social practices that make that knowledge possible, might contribute important elements to a

POSTSTRUCTURAL POLITICAL ECOLOGY

new biology and ecology. The question of the epistemology of the natural sciences is being broached both from poststructuralist perspectives and reformed phenomenology in Maturana and Varela's case. Should not it be broached from that of political ecology as well?

The worldwide spread of value seems to privilege the new biotechnologies. These further capitalize nature by planting value into it through scientific research and development. Even human genes become conditions of production, an important arena for capitalist restructuring, and so for contestation. The reinvention of nature currently under way, effected by/within webs of meaning and production that link the discourses of science and capital, should be incorporated into a political ecology appropriate to that new age whose dawn we are witnessing. What will count as "organisms" and even "human" for biology, ecology, geography, and biological anthropology will be intimately mediated by these processes.

Nature is now modeled as culture; sooner or later, "nature" will be produced to order. If the production of trees in plantations constituted an important step in the capitalization of nature, for example, the production of genetically produced trees (or the "perfect" tomatoes produced at the University of California at Davis) takes this process to new levels; it takes the tree a step further away from "organic nature." The implications of this are unclear. This is why the rising regime of bio-sociality must find its place at the base of a political ecology and biology as forms of knowledge about material-semiotic objects – organisms and communities – that are historically constituted.

This is to say we need new narratives of life and culture. These narratives will likely be hybrids of sorts; they will arise from the mediations that local cultures are able to effect on the discourses and practices of nature, capital, and modernity. This is a collective task that perhaps only social movements are in a position to advance. The task entails the construction of collective identities, as well as struggles over the redefinition of the boundaries between nature and culture. These boundaries will be reimagined to the extent that the practice of social movements succeeds in reconnecting life and thought by fostering a plural political ecology of knowledge. As the analysis of concrete practices of thinking and doing, discursive approaches have much to contribute to this reimagining. Materialist approaches do not need to exclude this type of analysis.

NOTE

This chapter was originally prepared for the Wenner-Gren Symposium "Political-economic Perspectives in Biological Anthropology: Building a Biocultural Synthesis" 1992. I thank Alan Goodman and Thomas Leathermann, conference organizers, and Richard Peet, James O'Connor, Enrique Leff, and Richard Lichtman for thoughtful comments on previous versions of the manuscript.

ESCOBAR
REFERENCES

Baudrillard, Jean. 1975. *The Mirror of Production.* St. Louis: Telos Press.

Buttel, Frederick, A. Hawkins, and G. Power. 1990. "From limits to growth to global change: contrasts and contradictions in the evolution of environmental science and ideology," *Global Environmental Change* 1, 1: 57–66.

Clark, William. 1989. "Managing Planet Earth," *Scientific American* 261, 3: 46–57.

Comaroff, Jean and John Comaroff. 1991. *Of Revelation and Revolution.* Chicago: University of Chicago Press.

Conable, Barber. 1987. "Address to the World Resources Institute," Washington, DC: The World Bank.

Deleuze, Gilles and Félix Guattari. 1987. *A Thousand Plateaus.* Minneapolis: University of Minnesota Press.

DNP (Departamento Nacional de Planeación de Colombia). 1983. *Plan de Desarrollo Integral para la Costa Pacífica.* Cali: DNP/CVC.

—— 1992. *Plan Pacífico. Una Estrategia de Desarrollo Sostenible para la Costa Pacífica Colombiana.* Bogotá: DNP.

Donzelot, Jacques. 1979. *The Policing of Families.* New York: Pantheon Books.

—— 1988. "The promotion of the social," *Economy and Society* 17, 3: 217–34.

Escobar, Arturo. 1992. "Planning," in Wolfgang Sachs (ed.) *The Development Dictionary,* London: Zed Books, pp. 132–45.

—— 1994. "Welcome to Cyberia: notes on the anthropology of cyberculture," *Current Anthropology* 35, 3: 211–31.

—— 1995. *Encountering Development: The Making and Unmaking of the Third World.* Princeton, NJ: Princeton University Press.

Foucault, Michel. 1975. *The Birth of the Clinic.* New York: Vintage Books.

—— 1979. *Discipline and Punish.* New York: Vintage Books.

—— 1980. *The History of Sexuality. Volume I. An Introduction.* New York: Vintage Books.

García Canclini, Néstor. 1990. *Culturas Híbridas: Estrategias para Entrar y Salir de la Modernidad.* México, DF: Grijalbo.

GEF–PNUD (Global Environmental Facility–Programa de las Naciones Unidas para el Desarrollo). 1993. *Conservación de la Biodiversidad del Chocó Biogeográfico. Proyecto Biopacífico.* Bogotá: DNP/Biopacífico.

Giddens, Anthony. 1990. *The Consequences of Modernity.* Stanford, CA: Stanford University Press.

Godelier, Maurice. 1986. *The Mental and the Material.* London: Verso.

Green Web. 1989. "Sustainable development: expanded environmental destruction," *The Green Web Bulletin* 16.

Gudeman, Stephen and Alberto Rivera. 1990. *Conversations in Colombia.* Cambridge: Cambridge University Press.

Guha, Ramachandra. 1994. "The environmentalism of the poor," presented at the Conference, "Dissent and Direct Action in the Late Twentieth Century," Otavalo, Ecuador, June.

Habermas, Jürgen. 1975. *Legitimation Crisis.* Boston, MA: Beacon Press.

—— 1987. *The Philosophical Discourse of Modernity.* Cambridge, MA: MIT Press.

Haraway, Donna. 1985. "Manifesto for cyborgs: science, technology, and socialist feminisms in the 1980s," *Socialist Review* 80: 65–107.

—— 1988. "Situated knowledges: the science question in feminism and the privilege of partial perspective," *Feminist Studies* 14, 3: 575–99.

—— 1989a. *Primate Visions.* New York: Routledge.

—— 1989b. "The biopolitics of postmodern bodies: determinations of self in immune system discourse," *Differences* 1, 1: 3–43.

66

POSTSTRUCTURAL POLITICAL ECOLOGY

—— 1991. *Simians, Cyborgs and Women. The Reinvention of Nature.* New York: Routledge.

Harvey, David. 1985. *The Urbanization of Capital.* Baltimore, MD: Johns Hopkins University Press.

—— 1989. *The Condition of Postmodernity.* Oxford: Basil Blackwell.

Hvalkof, Søren. 1989. "The nature of development: native and settlers' views in Gran Pajonal, Peruvian Amazon," *Folk* 31: 125–50.

Laclau, Ernesto and Chantal Mouffe. 1985. *Hegemony and Socialist Strategy.* London: Verso.

Leff, Enrique. 1986. "Ambiente y articulación de Ciencias," in Enrique Leff (ed.) *Los Problemas del Conocimiento y la Perspectiva Ambiental del Desarrollo*, México, DF: Siglo XXI, pp. 72–125.

—— 1992. "La dimensión cultural y el manejo integrado, sustentable y sostenido de los recursos naturales," in Enrique Leff and J. Carabias (eds.) *Cultura y Manejo Sustentable de los Recursos Naturales.* Mexico, DF: CIIH/UNAM.

—— 1993. "Marxism and the environmental question: from the critical theory of production to an environmental rationality for sustainable development," *Capitalism, Nature, Socialism* 4, 1: 44–66.

—— 1995. *Green Production: Toward an Environmental Rationality.* New York: Guilford Press.

Marglin, Steve. 1992. "Alternatives to the greening of economics: a research proposal," unpublished proposal.

Martin, Emily. 1994. *Flexible Bodies.* Boston, MA: Beacon Press.

Martinez-Alier, Juan. 1992. *Ecología y Pobreza.* Barcelona: Centre Cultural Bancaixa.

Maturana, Humberto and Francisco Varela. 1980. *Autopoiesis and Cognition: The Realization of the Living.* Boston, MA: D. Reidel Publishing Company.

—— and —— 1987. *The Tree of Knowledge: The Biological Roots of Human Understanding.* Boston: New Science Library/Shambhala.

Mellor, Mary. 1992. *Breaking the Boundaries: Towards a Feminist Green Socialism.* London: Virago.

Merchant, Carolyn. 1980. *The Death of Nature.* New York: Harper & Row.

Norgaard, Richard. 1991a. "Sustainability as intergenerational equity," Internal Discussion Paper No. IDP 97. Washington, DC: World Bank.

—— 1991b. "Sustainability: the paradigmatic challenge to agricultural economics," presented at the 21st Conference of the International Association of Agricultural Economists, Tokyo, 22–9 August.

O'Connor, James. 1988. "Capitalism, nature, socialism: a theoretical introduction," *Capitalism, Nature, Socialism* 1, 1: 11–38.

—— 1989. "Political economy of ecology of socialism and capitalism," *Capitalism, Nature, Socialism* 1, 3: 93–108.

—— 1991. *Conference Papers*, CES/CNS Pamphlet 1, Santa Cruz.

O'Connor, Martin. 1993. "On the misadventures of capitalist nature," *Capitalism, Nature, Socialism* 4, 3: 7–40.

Polanyi, Karl. 1957. *The Great Transformation.* Boston, MA: Beacon Press.

Pred, Alan and Michael Watts. 1992. *Reworking Modernity.* New Brunswick: Rutgers University Press.

Procacci, Giovanna. 1991. "Social economy and the government of poverty," in Graham Burchell, Colin Gordon, and Peter Millers (eds.) *The Foucault Effect.* Chicago: University of Chicago Press, pp. 151–68.

Rabinow, Paul. 1989. *French Modern: Norms and Forms of the Social Environment.* Cambridge, MA: MIT Press.

—— 1992. "Artificiality and enlightenment: from sociobiology to biosociality," in

67

ESCOBAR

Jonathan Crary and Sanford Kwinter (eds.) *Incorporations.* New York: Zone Books, pp. 234–52.

Rao, Brinda. 1989. "Struggling for production conditions and producing conditions of emancipation: women and water in rural Maharashtra," *Capitalism, Nature, Socialism* 1, 2: 65–82.

—— 1991. *Dominant Constructions of Women and Nature in Social Science Literature,* CES/CNS Pamphlet 2, Santa Cruz.

Redclift, Michael. 1987. *Sustainable Development: Exploring the Contradictions.* London: Routledge.

Sachs, Wolfgang. 1988. "The gospel of global efficiency," IFDA Dossier No. 68: 33–9.

—— 1992. "Environment," in Wolfgang Sachs (ed.) *The Development Dictionary.* London: Zed Books, pp. 26–37.

Shiva, Vandana. 1989. *Staying Alive. Women, Ecology and Development.* London: Zed Books.

—— 1992. "The seed and the earth: women, ecology and biotechnology," *The Ecologist* 22, 1: 4–8.

Varela, Francisco, Evan Thompson and Eleanor Rosch. 1991. *The Embodied Mind: Cognitive Science and Human Experience.* Cambridge: MIT Press.

Visvanathan, Shiv. 1991. "Mrs. Brundtland's Disenchanted Cosmos," *Alternatives* 16, 3: 377–84.

World Commission on Environment and Development. 1987. *Our Common Future.* New York: Oxford University Press.

World Resources Institute. 1993. *Biodiversity Prospecting.* Washington: WRI.

World Resources Institute, World Conservation Union, and United Nations Environment Program. 1992. *Global Biodiversity Strategy.* Washington: WRI.

Yapa, Lakshman. 1995. "Can postmodern discourse theory help alleviate poverty? Yes!" paper presented at Meeting of the American Association of Geography, Chicago, 17 March.

[8]

Foucault and the Environment: An Introduction

Éric Darier

Grazing sheep can be beautiful, very different from 'sulphureous vapours' though actually . . . no more natural.

– Raymond Williams

The desire for knowledge has been transformed among us into a passion which fears no sacrifice, which fears nothing but its own extinction. It may be that mankind will eventually perish from this passion for knowledge. If not through passion, then through weakness, we must be prepared to state our desire or choice: do we wish humanity to end in fire and light or to end on the sand?

– Nietzsche

The law doth punish man or woman
That steels the goose from off the common,
But lets the greater felon loose,
That steals the common from the goose.

– author unknown; eighteenth-century protest against
the Enclosure Act in England, quoted by Parsons

[I]f it is extremely dangerous to say that Reason is the enemy that should be illiminated, it is just as dangerous to say that any critical questioning of this rationality risks sending us into irrationality.

– Foucault

Contexts

Despite – and because of – 30 years of environmental legislation, regulation, institution building at national and international level, and the emergence of a diverse and relatively powerful

2   Éric Darier

environmental movement, there is a general concern and anxiety
about the 'environment' in the North. As a result, there has been
a proliferation of discourses about the environment from most
quarters of society which has also coincided with a general increase
in scepticism about scientific knowledge and the meaning and
efficacy of political and social change. For example, at least since
Thomas Kuhn (1962), there has generally been less confidence
that scientific knowledge and technological innovations are the
necessary conditions for human betterment. This scepticism mani-
fests itself through discourses of scientific 'uncertainty' and 'complexity'. Jerome Ravetz accurately noted that 'while our knowledge
continues to increase exponentially, our relevant ignorance does
so even more rapidly. And this is ignorance generated by science'
(1987: 100). In this context of 'generated ignorance', there is
increased anxiety among the population of the North about the possible consequences of rapid scientific and technologically induced
changes on humans and the environment. Apart from business,
which has vested interests in always justifying changes in positive
terms like 'benefits' and 'improvements', very few experts would
volunteer a resolutely optimistic outlook for the environment in
the future (Simon and Kahn 1984; Easterbrook 1995). The absence
of obvious credible solutions and the knowledge to implement
them sustain concerns and anxiety for the environment. This is
reflected in the extreme diversity of assumptions and solutions
offered by many in the 'environmental movement' (Eckersley 1992:
33–47; Marshall 1992; Merchant 1992: 85–210; Murphy 1994:
x–xi). As Andrew Ross has noted, 'Except for the name of "ecology" itself, virtually nothing unites the bioregionalists, Gaians,
eco-feminists, eco-Marxists, biocentricists, eco-anarchists, deep
ecologists and social ecologists who pursue their ideas and actions
in its name' (1994: 5).

According to some of the environmentalists from the spectrum
identified above, one of the obstacles to addressing the environmental crisis has been the perceived extreme relativism and the
'anything goes' attitude of what they call 'postmodernism' (Bookchin 1990; Gare 1995; Sessions 1995a; Soulé and Lease 1995) or
'moral pluralism' (Callicott 1990). Their position seems to be
based on nostalgia for a presumed lost coherence. For example,
Callicott feels

> that we must maintain a coherent sense of self and world, a unified
> moral world view. Such unity enables us rationally to select among

Foucault and the Environment   3

or balance out the contradictory or inconsistent demands made upon us when the multiple social circles in which we operate overlap and come into conflict. More importantly, a unified world view gives our lives purpose, direction, coherency, and sanity. (Callicott 1990: 121)

Bookchin echoes Callicott in condemning postmodernism as 'a veritable campaign . . . to discard the past, to dilute our knowledge of history, to mystify the origins of our problems, to foster dememorisation and the loss of our most enlightened ideals' (Bookchin 1990: 73–4). Because of the vagueness and general confusion regarding what is understood by 'postmodernism',[1] it would probably be sterile and simplistic to embark on a prolonged debate pitting 'postmodernism' against 'environmentalism'. Recent works have recontextualized this debate (Andermatt Conley 1997; Bennett and Chaloupka 1993; Bird 1987; Darier 1995; Haraway 1991; Jagtenberg and McKie 1997; Macnaghten and Urry 1998; Oelschlaeger 1995: 1–20; Redclift and Woodgate 1997; Ross 1994; Soper 1995, 1996; Zimmerman 1994, 1996). One of the central issues in this debate is the tension between, on the one hand, the argument that for humans, 'nature' can only make sense through the various filters of 'social construction'[2] and, on the other hand, the argument that nature has an irreducible positivist reality outside human interpretations. Kate Soper calls these two views 'nature-skeptical' and 'nature-endorsing' respectively (Soper 1995; 1996: 23). In part, this debate reflects the two broad general perspectives and worldviews offered by the social sciences and the natural sciences. It also reflects the 'primacy of epistemology' in the natural sciences over the more interpretative practices in the social sciences (Connolly 1992; Taylor 1987). Even within the 'primacy of epistemology', this disciplinary divide reflects irreconcilable differences regarding the possibility of knowledge, ranging from 'value-free' positivism to absolute relativism (Feyerabend 1981a, 1981b, 1991; Taylor 1971, 1980). Nevertheless, there are examples of cross-over between the two broad categories of disciplines and epistemological premises, of natural scientists adopting a constructivist approach (Latour and Woolgar 1986; Latour 1987; Woolgar 1988) and of social scientists opting for a more positivist approach. Beyond this excessively Manichaean framing of the controversy, it is important to note that others have attempted to find an intermediate position which doesn't epistemologically deny – or affirm – the material existence of what is referred to as 'nature' or

4   Éric Darier

'environment', but stresses the diversity and changes in human interpretations of 'nature' through history, which might in turn explain the 'domination', the 'destruction', the 'protection' and/or the 'transformation' of 'nature' by human activities (Benton 1994; Ellen 1996; Hannigan 1995; Murphy 1994;[3] Simmons 1993).

It may be time to reframe the controversy in different ways. In a rare, probably unique insight into this topic, Michel Foucault perceived the heated debate in environmentalism in terms not of epistemological options from which one has to choose, but, on the contrary, of essential and necessary conditions for the emergence of an ecological/environmental movement itself.

> [T]here has been an ecological movement – which is furthermore very ancient and is not only a twentieth-century phenomenon – which has often been, in one sense, in hostile relationship with science or at least with a technology guaranteed in terms of truth ['*nature-endorsing*']. But in fact, ecology also spoke a language of truth. It was in the name of knowledge concerning nature, the equilibrium of the processes of living things, and so forth, that one could level the criticism ['*nature-sceptical*']. (Foucault 1988b: 15)

Ulrich Beck has restated Foucault's observation in a similar manner:

> The observable consequence is that critics [i.e. environmentalism] frequently argue more scientifically than the natural scientists they dispute against . . . [but] fall prey to a naïve realism about definitions of the dangers one consumes. On the one hand, this naïve realism of hazards is (apparently) necessary as an expression of outrage and a motor of protest; on the other it is its Achilles' heel. (Beck 1995: 60)

One of the main objectives of this book is to explore this essential, necessary tension between currents in environmentalism as noted by Foucault and Beck, and, more precisely, the controversy between the 'nature-endorsing' claim of a truth-discourse about nature and the 'nature-sceptical' radical critique about the inescapable power effects of all knowledge, of all truth-claims. Despite the fact that the work of Foucault seems to promise a challenging contribution to our understanding, there has been a tendency to omit Foucault from most critical studies in environmental theory (Andermatt Conley 1997; Eckersley 1992; Goldblatt 1996; Hayward 1994; Merchant 1994). Hopefully, this book will fill the obvious gap and explore the possible creative synergy between two large corpora of critical literature which surprisingly haven't yet met in a systematic fashion: (a) the works by, and about, French theorist Michel Foucault and (b) environmental criticism.

Foucault and the Environment: 'My Back is Turned to It'

Before embarking further on an exploration of the possible relevance of Foucault for environmentalism, it is important to state a few points.

Michel Foucault (1926–84) is probably one of the most influential thinkers of our time, at least in France, the English-speaking world and parts of Latin America. The evidence is the large number of books and articles about Foucault published since his death. However, this is only the tip of the Foucauldian iceberg. The real extent of his influence is far more extensive than books with the name 'Foucault' on their cover, in their chapter titles, in their index or in their bibliography. To get an idea of the extent of the influence of Foucault, one must also take into account the gigantic body of works which use some of the concepts developed by Foucault without making any explicit reference to him. Those concepts include 'discourse analysis', 'power/knowledge', 'disciplinary techniques', 'field of power', 'governmentality', 'normalization', 'resistance', 'non-strategical ethics' and 'aesthetic of existence'. What is also surprising is the breadth of the influence of Foucault across virtually every academic domain, ranging from legal studies, gender and queer studies, cultural studies, anthropology, sociology, political studies, to philosophy, history, literary criticism, media and communication studies, geography and so on. Foucault's influence can also be encountered in non-academic, openly activist contexts such as the gay, lesbian, bisexual movement, the women's movement, the anti-racist movement, the prisoners' rights movement and community activism generally. In North America, Foucault – alongside non-essentialist strands of feminism and queer theory (Bersani 1995; Halperin 1995; McNeil 1993; Terry 1991) and a 're-discovery' of aboriginal peoples in the context of an 'age of diversity' (Tully 1995) – is also having a profound impact on the reworking of pluralism, or rather in the 'ethos of pluralization' (Connolly 1995).

To my knowledge, there are no systematic studies aimed at exploring the possible connections and relevance of Foucault to environmental thinking, although the idea has been suggested (Gare 1995: 94). This is a puzzling lacuna when one examines Foucault's intellectual legacy in more detail: for example, his concept of 'biopolitics' is a strong, direct reflection of a 'politics of life' which is close to the concerns of environmentalism. It is true that Foucault

6   Éric Darier

never addressed the environmental issue directly, or the ecological crisis as such, except in the brief insightful quote already given. It is also true that Foucault 'detested nature', or rather, that he preferred 'visiting churches and museums'. Éribon's biography recounts a car trip through the Italian Alps that Foucault took with a colleague, Jacqueline Verdeaux, which revealed his attitude to nature. '[Verdeaux] remembers . . . well that Foucault detested nature. Whenever she showed him some magnificent landscape – a lake sparkling in the sunlight – he made a great show of walking off toward the road, saying, "My back is turned to it" ' (Éribon 1991: 46).[4]

If one shouldn't look in Foucault for an obvious aesthetic appreciation and/or some empathy with nature, it doesn't mean that Foucault's work is irrelevant or unimportant for environmental thinking. In fact, as this collection of essays illustrates, Foucault's concepts can be made highly relevant to environmental thinking, whatever attitude to 'nature' Foucault himself might have held. Therefore, bracketing Foucault's attitude toward 'nature' is not an attempt to side-step an embarrassing 'character' trait in Foucault! It is also a way to put into practice Foucault's own position regarding the highly historical contingency of the function of 'author' and 'text' in our societies. Foucault noted that the disappearance – or death – of the author was due to the fact that the 'author function is . . . characteristic of the mode of existence circulating, and functioning of certain discourses within society' (Foucault 1984g: 103, 108). This means that increasingly, in our current society, texts 'could be read for themselves' without the anchoring presence of an 'author' (ibid. 110). Consequently, Foucault was advocating the 'total effacement of the individual characteristics of the writer' (ibid.). He also systematically resisted the boxing of his work in the existing intellectual categories such as 'structuralism', 'poststructuralism', 'modernism' or 'postmodernism'. In order to achieve this, he employed several 'de-locations' in the focus of his research (the literal translation of the French word *déplacements* is more accurate than the too mild word 'shifts'). The rupture between 'author' and 'text' explains how concepts can have unintended, unpredictable effects in 'back of the author'. I would argue that despite his having 'turned his back to nature', Foucault's writings are having profound, albeit indirect, effects on environmental thinking. The virulent critique of Foucault by many environmental thinkers, via the postmodernist category, may also indicate that Foucault is having an effect 'in the back' of environmental thinkers themselves.

Mapping Foucault in Contexts

Mapping Foucault's work may help us to understand and appreciate the various possible Foucauldian contributions to critical environmental theory. But before embarking on this task, I wish to make the following general remarks.

First, it is generally recognized that there are not one or two but at least three Foucaults (archeological, genealogical and ethical). Foucault 're-located' his research agenda several times. However, this doesn't mean that each period in Foucault's intellectual life was totally divorced from the others or was part of an overall singular project. Because of the existence of multiple Foucaults, it is important to be as clear as possible about the periods in which concepts emerged before engaging in a critique of Foucault's work. For example, the early archeological period may indeed have been structuralist in tone. However, it is more difficult to make the structuralist label stick for the intermediate genealogical period, and it is quite irrelevant to use it for the final ethical period.

Second, Foucault's books and articles were written in typical scholarly style, which may make them difficult to read at times. This is why so many commentators use the numerous interviews he gave all through his life. The problem with the interviews is that Foucault, as a member of the French intellectual star system[5] (centred of course in Paris), was very aware of the audience he was addressing when interviewed. For example, if he was giving an interview to a Marxist journal, he would employ Marxist vocabulary. Therefore, one has to go beyond Foucault's textual answers to the context of the particular interview to gain an accurate appreciation of what he was trying to say. Unlike some, such as Habermas, who considered the activities of intellectuals as serious matters – such as shaping the communicative expression of the transparent and increasing manifestation of 'Reason' – Foucault saw his intellectual production as 'tactics', 'strategies', 'toolbox', 'laughter' (de Certeau 1994), 'irony' (Connolly 1992; Rorty 1989: 61), 'games' (Kroker 1987) or 'fiction'. 'I have never written anything but fictions. . . . It seems to me that the possibility exists for fiction in truth, for a fictional discourse to induce effects of truth, and for bringing about that true discourse engenders or "manufactures" something that does not as yet exist' (Foucault 1980c: 193).

Third, there are major differences in the interpretations of Foucault's work. For example, the English-speaking world (especially Americans) tends to see Foucault, in the best case, as some

8   Éric Darier

kind of closeted ironic liberal (Rorty 1989) or as 'normatively confused' but with 'empirical insights' (Fraser 1989); whereas in France (and in southern Europe more generally), he tends to be seen as closer to Nietzsche than to the liberal tradition. Foucault was able to get lots of attention because of the generally privileged position of intellectuals in France as cultural icons extensively involved in political and social life. Although Foucault has now become an intellectual icon, his academic career in France was not easy or straightforward. This was due to what I have called elsewhere his 'marginal belonging' (*appartenance marginale*) in the French university milieu (Darier 1993: 5–51). Despite being marginal in the sense that he didn't fit into any of the dominant intellectual schools or in any precise academic discipline, Foucault did manage to obtain a Chair at the prestigious Collège de France, a symbol of the intellectual establishment in France, but experienced the 'solitude of the acrobat' (Éribon 1991: 212–13). Elsewhere, especially in the Anglo-Saxon world, Foucault's influence – and the influence of intellectuals generally – is more limited, to pockets inside the walls of university campuses. At best, intellectuals are tolerated as long as they don't disrupt the dominant preoccupations of society, such as 'economic efficiency and competition', 'fiscal responsibility' and widespread 'commercialism'. The differences in intellectual contexts lead to different readings of Foucault (Dumm 1996: 9–15; Gordon 1996: 253–70). However, one should not underestimate the influence of Foucault, especially in the current reworking of liberalism (Connolly 1993b; Dumm 1996; Flathman 1992; Kateb 1992) into what William Connolly prefers to call 'an ethos of pluralization' (Connolly 1995).

The Three Foucaults

With others (Davidson 1986; Smart 1994), I believe that there are three broad periods in Foucault's intellectual *oeuvre* which involve different 'methodological'[6] approaches: (1) an archeological approach to scientific discourse and knowledge generally; (2) a genealogical approach analysing social practices; and (3) an ethical concern for the possible conditions for the creation of the self by itself. Furthermore, there are at least two ways of entering the Foucauldian constellation. First, one can survey the three periods one at a time; or one can choose a key concept from one of the three periods and show how (and if) it relates to the other two periods. For example, the concept of 'governmentality' developed in the genealogical period not only offers a way into a historical survey of the conditions for the emergence of the modern form of power called 'government'; it also incorporates an archeological understanding of knowledge (hence 'power/knowledge') and a tool with which to examine conditions for the emergence of the problematization of subjectivities, as the 'ethical', 'final' Foucauldian period suggests.[7] For the purpose of this book, I hope to show that not only are both ways of entering the Foucauldian constellation valid, but that both should be used simultaneously. By negotiating this dual entry into Foucault, one may be able to avoid transforming Foucauldian thought into either a discontinuous collage of three periods or a single coherent 'meta-theory'. To try to live up to this dual entry approach, I suggest the following: for mainly pedagogical reasons, I shall briefly review separately each of the three Foucauldian periods. However, in my subsequent general introduction to the contributions to this book, it should become obvious that most of them, although using concepts from one of the periods as a starting-point, end up making linkages to the other periods. Consequently the titles of the three parts of this volume don't 'follow' the periodization of Foucault's work.

The archeological approach

This first period is that of the early Foucault, and includes books published in the 1960s (Foucault 1961, 1963, 1966, 1969).[8] The most comprehensive and systematic critical examination of Foucault's archeological approach to date is that of Gary Gutting (1989). At least one theorist has explicitly adopted Foucault's archeological approach to his study of the environment (Berman 1981: 74).

The method, or more precisely the approach, is called 'archeological' because it attempts to undertake excavations of historical texts. The purpose of these intellectual archeological digs is to reveal the various historical layers of what constitutes, or constituted, knowledge. Foucault was interested in what he called *épistème*, which is a historically specific, coherent configuration of how knowledge is organized (around disciplines, concerns, themes, etc.) and what kind of justifications are deemed acceptable to support that knowledge. It is important to stress two points. First, 'archeology is not an isolated method reflecting Foucault's idiosyncratic approach to the history of thought. Rather, it is rooted

10   Éric Darier

in the French tradition of history and philosophy of science' (Gutting 1989: x–xi) represented by, among others, Jean Cavaillès,
Gaston Bachelard and Georges Canguilhem (Canguilhem 1988,
1989). However, this 'tradition' doesn't represent the established
intellectual mainstream even in France. It may be a 'tradition',
but it is a marginal one in the ocean of Marxisms, ranging from
Garaudy through Althusser to Bourdieu, and of the different
schools of the 'philosophy of experience' (J. Miller 1993: 59)
represented by Sartre, Merleau-Ponty and post-Freudian/Lacanian
psychoanalysis. This illustrates further what I described earlier
as Foucault's 'marginal belonging'. Secondly, archeology is not a
coherent theory or 'method' from which flow Foucault's studies
of madness (Foucault 1961, 1963) and the human sciences
(Foucault 1966). Rather, archeology is a *post facto* reconstruction/
justification of his earlier case studies. In fact, archeology is an
'ill-defined methodology' (Gutting 1989: 109) emerging from specific historical studies. Foucault only attempted to systematically
work through his archeological method in the last book of this
period – *The Archaeology of Knowledge* – which already pointed
to the subsequent *déplacement* toward 'genealogy' (Foucault 1969).

The main point that Foucault tried to make throughout this
period was that knowledge is relative to the historical context
from which it emerges. 'We are doomed historically to history, to
the patient construction of discourses about discourses, and to the
task of hearing what has already been said' (Foucault 1963: xvi).
For Foucault, there can be no adjudicating positivist external
'reality' by which to evaluate the 'truth', the validity of a discourse
about knowledge. However, this position doesn't make Foucault
a relativist in the sense that 'anything goes', that it is impossible
to know anything and so forth. On the contrary, Foucault's
archeology adopts 'truth-claims' in themselves as the factual
background on which he builds his detailed studies. The only
level of factual 'reality' that interests Foucault is statements about
a presumed objective reality. This makes Foucault a contextualist
of the statements of observers of 'objective reality', an observer of
'situated knowledge' (Haraway 1989), an observer of the 'manufacturing of knowledge' (Knorr-Cetina 1981, 1983).

Foucault's main focus during his archeological period was on
scientific discourses and how objects of legitimate scientific investigations emerge. His principle interest was the emergence of
discourses about human nature through the 'human sciences', and
how humans become the objects of their own scientific enquiries.

For example, one of the specific scientific discourses that Foucault studied was 'madness' and the creation of social medical institutions in the European context around the eighteenth century (Foucault 1961, 1963). In *Order of Things* (1966) Foucault offers a more global, or at least structural, view of the historical landscape of knowledge. According to him, there was a clear rupture, a clear break (sometime around the sixteenth century), between what he calls the 'Classical Age' and 'Modernity'. In *Order of Things*, he takes three areas of knowledge, which we now might call linguistics, economics and biology. Foucault found that around the end of the eighteenth century there was a rupture in the epistemological field, which led to the emergence of these disciplines. For example, in the Classical Age, there was a direct link between words and things. This was the point that the French title of *The Order of Things – Les Mots et les choses* ('words and things') – was trying to convey. Words directly represented the objects they named. The Classical Age was the age of 'representation'. After the Classical Age, a gap between 'reality' and language opened up, which meant that representation ('representationalism' to use Charles Taylor's term) was no longer credible (Taylor 1985). 'Representation no longer exists; there's only action – theoretical action and practical action which serve as relays and form networks' (Deleuze in Bouchard 1977: 206). The new focus became the meaning and significance of linguistic signs. The second example is the transition from an analysis of 'wealth' as static, which was prevalent during the Classical Age (Adam Smith), to an economic analysis based on the dynamic circulation of production and consumption (Ricardo and Marx).

The third example is more directly pertinent to the contemporary environmental debate. It is about the emergence of the biological sciences. During the Classical Age, knowledge about the natural world was based on the construction of categories built around 'resemblance'. Thus, Carolus Linnaeus the well-known Swedish naturalist (1707–78) established a comprehensive nomenclature of plants and animals based on their similarities. For flowers, this nomenclature was based on the number of flower parts. After the Classical Age, classification was based no longer on Linnaeus's visual similarities of flower parts, but on a radically new concept centred on hidden dynamic mechanisms of life called now 'biology' (Foucault 1970). It is the knowledge of this new discipline called 'biology' which created the conditions for an articulation of the contemporary environmental critique. For

Foucault the emergence of 'biology' as a new scientific discipline signals the 'entry of life into history', what Foucault later calls 'biopower'. This historical contextualization of biology makes some environmental theorists worried about the tactical use of non-epistemological grounded environmental knowledge in the current struggle against polluters who could argue that there is no 'objective' yardstick by which to measure 'pollution', that the 'environmental crisis' is relative, and therefore that there is no need to change existing practices (Soulé and Lease 1995). Because Foucault was not a relativist but a contextualist, this charge cannot be sustained. Furthermore, because validated environmental scientific knowledge often retains a certain degree of uncertainty, and is subject to challenge and change over time, there is little point in trying to anchor it in a static epistemological justification system. In my view, it is more productive to follow Foucault's path and highlight some of the historical contingencies in the construction of knowledge about the 'environment', including the justifications for what some might call 'environmental pollution' and others a minor price to be paid for 'progress'. A Foucauldian discursive approach might help us to understand 'science as an environmental claim-making activity' (Hannigan 1995: 76–91) or the process of 'constructing environmental risks' (ibid. 92–108). It might be more productive than investing effort in establishing a homogenized, fundamentalist environmentalist epistemology as desired by Callicott, for example (1990).

However, there are at least four problems with Foucault's archeological approach (Gutting 1989: 222–6). First, in Foucault's archeological method, 'there is nothing that goes beyond the methodology of Canguilhem's history of concepts' (ibid. 218) and, I might add, very little beyond the British school of science historians (Porter 1977; Rousseau and Porter 1980). Furthermore, Foucault's historical case studies present 'major gaps at crucial points in the argument' (Gutting 1989: 226). Second, Foucault's archeology remains, in the final analysis, a structuralist approach, in the sense that it tries to reveal the deep historico-epistemological structure of the conditions of knowledge that Gutting calls the 'structuralist temptation' (ibid. 266). There is indeed a tension between Foucault's truth-claim about revealing the structure of knowledge and the contextuality of all knowledge, including presumably Foucault's own archeology. Foucault's subsequent response to this critique was to say that he was never a structuralist, but instead offered a critique of structuralism. The irony is that this critique of structuralism happened to be structural in approach.[9] Foucault may have tried to 'turn his back' to structuralism, but structuralism remains stuck to his back! Third, the 'structuralist temptation' of Foucault's archeology creates what Charles Taylor would call a 'kind of distance from its own value commitments, which consists in the fact that it alone is lucid about their status as fruits of a constructed order, which lucidity sets it apart from other views and confers the advantage on itself on being free from delusions' (Taylor 1989: 100). Ultimately Taylor finds 'this view as deeply implausible as its empiricist cousins' (ibid. 99).[10] Fourth, the archeological approach was criticized mainly – but not exclusively – by Marxists for being too focused on ideal categories of knowledge and for ignoring social relations and power relations in the everyday life (Gutting 1989: 224–6). Reading the early Foucault, one might indeed get the impression that what makes history tick are the ruptures/discontinuities which occurred in the historico-epistemological structures of knowledge. In the next section, we'll see how Foucault responded to this criticism through his genealogical approach.

In conclusion, Foucault's archeological 'history is sufficiently responsible and challenging to be worth serious attention, but it is also often greatly oversimplified and lacking in evidential support' (Gutting 1989: 262).[11] His archeological approach has definitively challenged some environmentalists in either reassessing or coming to the defence of their epistemological justification – and the need for such epistemological justification – to articulate their own environmental critique. In this context, it is important to restate what Foucault said later about environmental knowledge (i.e. 'ecology'): '[I]n fact, ecology also spoke a language of truth. It was in the name of knowledge concerning nature, the equilibrium of the processes of living things, and so forth, that one could level the criticism' (Foucault 1988b: 15).

However, this 'language of truth' about nature can also lead to a form of environmental / green fundamentalism. As Andrew Dobson reminds us,

> [T]he foundation-stone of Green politics is the belief that our finite Earth places limits on our industrial growth. This finitude, and the scarcity it implies, is an *article of faith for Green ideologues*, and provides the fundamental framework within which any putative picture of a green society must be drawn. (Dobson 1990: 73, my emphasis)

14   Éric Darier

Even if Foucault's archeological methodology is shaky, one of
its political effects might be to help environmentalists resist the
'fundamentalist temptation' of unreflexively reducing the justification for environmental activism and actions to a presumed epistemologically solid ground of what is understood by 'nature' as
defined by the natural sciences. It is becoming more urgent to resist
this fundamentalist temptation, because, while the 'geopolitical
reach of environmental science has become more and more expansive, its intellectual temper has become more reductionist' (Wynne
1994: 171).

The genealogical approach

This second period – the 'middle' or 'genealogical' Foucault –
includes Foucault's writings published in the 1970s. It includes
not only his main books (Foucault 1969, 1975, 1976) but also
numerous articles, book reviews, interviews and course descriptions (Defert and Ewald 1994).

The genealogical approach is in part an attempt to respond to
critiques levied against archeology. By adopting genealogy, Foucault
tried to distance himself further from structuralism and detached
empiricism. This genealogical *déplacement* operates at two levels.
First, as a method, genealogy 'rejects the metahistorical deployment
of ideal significations and indefinite teleologies' (Foucault 1984c:
77). On the contrary, genealogy

> record[s] the singularity of events outside of any monotonous
> finality, it must seek them in the most unpromising places, in what
> we tend to feel is without history, in sentiments, love, conscious-
> ness, instincts, it must be sensitive to their recurrence, not in order
> to trace the gradual curve of their evolution, but to isolate the
> different scenes where they engaged in different roles. (Foucault
> 1984c: 76)

Foucault borrowed strongly from Nietzsche's analysis of 'descent',
which is 'not the erecting of foundations: on the contrary, it
disturbs what was previously considered immobile; it fragments
what was thought unified; it shows the heterogeneity of what was
imagined consistent with itself' (Foucault 1984c: 82).

Secondly, genealogy adds to the archeological and contextualizing understanding of knowledge within a scientific discursive

rationality, the broader context of social practices. This broader genealogical context refers to the vast heterogeneous webs of social practices criss-crossed by relations of power, which include the human 'body – and everything that touches it: diet, climate, and soil' (1984a: 83). Instead of searching for a grand structural narrative explaining the various layers of knowledge, his project became more specific in the scope of his studies, and more modest in his objectives. He wanted to offer a description of the conditions of emergence of the present ('a genealogy of the present') at the micro-level of 'forgotten' social practices.[12] For Foucault the genealogist, the structure and structuration of knowledge became less important than what he identified as a 'will to knowledge', which seems to be the main driving motivation behind modern sciences. Furthermore, Foucault is not only highly sceptical about the one universal truth sought by this 'will to knowledge'; he also pointed out some of the unintended effects, including environmental effects, of the 'will to truth' (Sheridan 1980).

> Even in the greatly expanded form it assumes today, the will to knowledge does not achieve a universal truth; man is not given an exact and serene mastery of nature. On the contrary, it ceaselessly multiplies the risks, creates dangers in every areas, it breaks down illusory defenses . . . ; it releases those elements of itself that are devoted to its subversion and destruction. (Foucault 1984c: 95–6)

Beyond the general ranting against 'postmodernism' by some environmental theorists (Sessions 1995a; Bookchin 1990: 73–4), it is interesting to note the similarities between the critique of environmental 'management' (i.e. instrumental knowledge) by the same environmental theorists and Foucault's concept of the 'will to knowledge'.

> [I]ncreasingly intensive management produces a host of unintended consequences which are perceived by the managers and the public, and specially by the environmental/ecology movement, as real and severe problems. The usual approach, however, is to seek more intensive management, which spawns even more problems. And each of these problems is seen as separate, with separate experts and interest groups speaking to each other across a chasm of different technical vocabularies. (Devall and Sessions 1985: 146)

These similarities between the environmental theorists' critique and Foucault's suggest that there may be common ground in their analyses of contemporary social practices despite differences in their epistemological premisses. However, nature sceptics like Foucault would remain deeply suspicious of the 'belief that society ought to conform to nature' because of the normalizing effects of this belief and the danger identified by Andrew Ross 'that the authority of nature, and hence of the status quo, will become a despotic vehicle for curtailing rights and liberties' (Ross 1994: 12).

Through genealogy, Foucault also responds to the Marxist critique of archeology by looking not only at discourses about knowledge ('discursive practices'), but also at the social practices through which people live (non-discursive practices').[13] This genealogical *déplacement* led him to consider power relations which occur in social practices, specially at the micro-level, and at the 'practice of everyday life' (de Certeau 1984). Foucault refrains from explicitly defining his concept of 'power'. In fact, he spends a lot of effort stating what power *is not*, rather than what power *is*. This radical 'negation' has to be situated in the context of Foucault's tactical writing.[14] By constantly defining power as what it *isn't* and refusing to say what it *is*, Foucault resists the temptation to adopt 'power' as an essentialist, empiricist category. Or at least, this enables Foucault to keep the concept of 'power' within the various contexts which led to its emergence, and removes the need to anchor it in any precise fixed location. Genealogy is the approach which enables Foucault to show that any anchoring point for the concept of 'power', for example, is historically contingent. Far from adopting a privileged objectivist/empiricist position, as Taylor seems to believe, Foucault's 'own value commitment' (Taylor 1989: 100) is explicitly Nietzschean in theory *and* in practice through his tactical writings.[15] Foucault's refusal to define concepts like 'power' is not a 'failure', as Taylor would argue, but, on the contrary, highlights the constraints imposed on us by the contingency of language and vocabulary in which we are embedded and by which we are constituted. Therefore, Foucault's 'own value commitment' is the systematic, constant transgression of the limits of the given language, as with the term 'power' (Lemert and Gillan, 1982) Foucault has no interest in defining/anchoring a theory of power 'outside' the limits of what power is currently understood to be. On the contrary, his only purpose is to constantly challenge the limits as defined by the various discourses and practices. Within these constraints, it is possible, nevertheless, to make the following points about the various concepts emerging from Foucault's genealogy.

First, 'power' is not something which the State or a dominant class *has* or *possesses* and which others don't have. Power is not a zero-sum game. Power is mostly relational; it rarely entails absolute domination. Even in the most unequal situations of relations of power, those subjected to power do exercise some choices, however limited. In Michel de Certeau's view, Foucault attempts

> to bring to light the springs of this opaque power that has no pos-
> sessor, no privileged place, no superiors or inferiors, no repressive
> activity or dogmatism, that is almost autonomously effective through
> its technological ability to distribute, classify, analyse and spatially
> individualize the objects dealt with. (de Certeau 1984: 46)

The Foucauldian idea of power can be conceptualized as a 'field of power' similar to the field of forces and vectors described by physics or the workings at the level of the 'microcellular' de-scribed by biology (Baudrillard 1987: 12). However, it is import-ant to stress that Foucault wasn't making a strong epistemological claim about a presumed superiority of physics and biology to explain social phenomena; he was using the imaginary of physics and biology as a tactical allegory to undermine prevalent dis-courses about 'power'.[16]

Second, 'power' for Foucault is more than simply preventing or forcing others to do something they would not do on their own. It is more than just 'naked' violence. In fact, under the specificity of European 'Modernity', the practice of power

> has been characterized on the one hand, by a legislation, a dis-
> course, an organisation based on public right, whose principle of
> articulation is the social body and the delegative status of each
> citizen; on the other hand, by a closely linked grid of disciplinary
> coercions whose purpose is in fact to assure the cohesion of this
> same social body. (Foucault 1980h: 106)

These two simultaneous, 'heterogeneous' aspects of modern power – 'a right of sovereignty' and a 'mechanism of discipline' – mean that, for Foucault, the exercise of power has *normalizing* effects on the population. Disciplinary mechanisms can indeed restrict the possibilities regarding what individual and collective identities can do, be or become. However, the existence of disciplinary mechanisms with a 'right of sovereignty' also enables individuals or groups to take on an identity which might be the condition for

18   Éric Darier

subsequent, unintended actions. It is because of this process of
constructing identities – through the 'heterogeneity between a public
right of sovereignty and a polymorphous disciplinary mechanism'
(ibid.) – that Foucault qualified power as being 'positive', in contrast to the more conventional view of power ('royal' form of
power) as solely repressive. For example, current 'gay', 'lesbian' or
'queer' identities are the unintended effects of, on the one hand,
legal and medical discourse creating and disciplining 'homosexuality' in late nineteenth-century Europe and, on the other hand, the
'delegative' urge of the discourse on public right.[17] For Foucault,
the 'strategies of normalization' (like constructing 'heterosexu-
ality' as the norm, by contrasting it with the 'abnormality' of
'homosexuality') constitute one effect of power which in many
cases is resisted by those who are supposed to be normalized as
'abnormal'. One of the central objectives of Foucault's genealogy
was to reveal these 'tactics of resistance' which may have been
forgotten and use them as 'counter-memories'. The distinction
between strategies of normalization and tactics of resistance[18] can
be appreciated only at the micro-analytical level, in the sense that
only detailed, localized studies of events can capture that distinction within the specificity of its own context. Because instances of normalization and resistance constantly interact in a
dynamic manner, reversals occur. Yesterday's resistance can become
today's normalization, which in turn can become the conditions
for tomorrow's resistance and/or normalization. The concept of
normalization / resistance cannot be understood as a fixed meta-
narrative describing 'power' in the abstract, but, on the contrary,
should be approached as a constant recontextualization of power
relations as lived and experienced by humans. For example, it is
important to understand how populations living in industrialized
countries had their daily conduct normalized to become throw-
away 'consumers' (de Certeau 1984: 30–4; Luke 1993b), and
how parts of the radical environmental movement can be seen as
tactics of resistance against it (e.g. Darier 1996b). Environmental
tactics of resistance can include the systematic use of irony against
an extremely 'serious' normalizing discourse like the one coming
from the pro-nuclear lobby (Chaloupka 1992; Seery 1990).

Third, the field of power is not a structuralist framework in
which humans are passive objects and mere products. Humans
have some degree of 'liberty' or 'freedom'. However, 'liberty' as
understood by Foucault is not an ontological quality of humans
or an ideal state of suspended power relations – as it is for Liberals,

Foucault and the Environment   19

Marxists and humanists generally – but an expression of individuals' very own existence in the specificity of power relations.[19]
For Foucault, there cannot be liberty in a space without power
relations. Total liberation from 'oppression', from power relations,
is a delusion, because power is not exclusively repressive, and
because power is 'capillary', diffused and everywhere. Those who
still want to believe in a grand teleological narrative of liberation
see Foucault as being pessimistic because of the impossibility of
escaping power relations. However, Foucault's view is simultaneously more accurate in terms of the conceptualization of power
('repressive' *and* 'positive'; constitutive *and* enabling) and ultimately
more optimistic for several reasons. First of all, Foucault's concept of power is less deterministic than that of those who believe
that humans are limited by their inherent nature or by the economic structure or by the iron law of historical materialism.
Foucault's focus on the 'conditions of emergence' and 'resistance'
suggests that power relations in the 'field of power' are not deterministic, but, on the contrary, a form of what I would call an 'open-
ended determinism'. The field of power imposes constraints about
the possible options open to individuals and groups, but it is those
individuals and groups which ultimately make choices to accept
these constraints or to challenge them. Foucault reminds us that

> [i]f one or the other were completely at the disposition of the other
> and became his thing, an object on which he can exercise an infi-
> nite and unlimited violence, there would not be relations of
> power. . . . In order to exercise a relation of power, there must be
> on both sides at least a certain form of liberty. (Foucault 1988b: 12)

Even in situations of extreme domination, there are possibilities
of freedom. Thomas Dumm's interpretation of the biography of
Nazi camp survivor Primo Levi is an illustration of Foucault's
point (Dumm 1996: 144–52). Secondly, this 'open-ended determinism' is very unnerving for believers in a grand narrative of
liberation or for some of those who are 'nature-endorsing'. Their
critique can be summarized in relation to the following question:
what is the clear direction / the teleological purpose which can
guide humans in their resistance and in the choices open to them?
Before even trying to answer this question, it is important to point
out that Foucault was highly suspicious of any grand narratives
of liberation such as humanism, liberalism or Marxism, because
they also turned into new disciplinary regimes. Humanism's

20   Éric Darier

anthropocentrism led to justification for the 'domination' of nature; Liberalism justified disciplining humans as workers and consumers; Marxism – or at least its Stalinist experimentation – resulted in fast industrialization; and all three created the conditions for ecological 'crises'. For Foucault, ignoring the possibilities of a 'dark side' of any liberation project is the sure recipe for the demobilization of social activists once the liberation project turns sour or becomes obviously unfulfillable. It is in this context that one can see how Foucault would be suspicious of the brand of environmentalism which desires a world free of pollution, in which life is simpler, and social and natural harmony are established upon presumed 'natural limits'.[20] Foucault's counter-suggestion is that humans should be constantly vigilant and critical of all actions, especially those undertaken in the name of liberation or in the name of 'saving the environment' or obeying 'natural limits'.[21] In brief, social change, revolution or environmental activism is a never-ending activity in which tactics and 'goals' are constantly re-evaluated and adapted to changing circumstances within the field of power. Foucault's position on this point is not far from Marx's refusal to give precise details about what Communism would be: Marx thought that it was presumptuous to define precisely the form of a future society which could only be imagined by individuals and groups located in radically different sets of power relations in a different historical context.

Foucault was attacked not only by 'modernists', but also by postmodernists like Jean Baudrillard. His critique of Foucault centres on Foucault's alleged (over-) preoccupation with 'power'. For Baudrillard, 'Foucault's discourse is a mirror of the powers it describes' (Baudrillard 1987: 10) in the sense that 'with Foucault, we always brush against political determination in its last instance' (ibid. 40). For Baudrillard, Foucault's 'theory of control by means of a gaze that objectifies, even when it is pulverized into micro-devices is passé. With the simulation device we are no doubt as far from the strategy of transparence as the latter is from the immediate, symbolic operation of punishment which Foucault himself describes' (ibid. 16).

Baudrillard complains that Foucault 'does not tell us anything *concerning the simulacrum of power itself*' (ibid. 40, emphasis original). For Baudrillard,

> [i]t is useless ... to run after power or to discourse about it *ad infinitum* since from now on it also partakes of the sacred horizon of appearances and is also there only to hide the fact that it no

longer exists, or rather to indicate that since the apogee of the political has been crossed, the other side of the cycle is now starting in which power reverts into its own simulacrum. (ibid. 51)

There are at least two ways of responding to Baudrillard's critique. First, Foucault's preoccupation was *not* about power *per se*. It is not by design that Foucault defined power by saying what it is not. For Foucault, 'power is not an institution, and not a structure; neither is it a certain strength we are endowed with' (Foucault quoted in ibid. 42). The systematic use by Foucault of 'negatives' to define – or rather to '*n*/efine' – a concept is evidently a tactical move to avoid having to redefine concepts that one might not want to employ in the first place. Foucault lifts the concept of power (its simulacrum?) from its context (by the use of the negative), and leaves it suspended in order to lose the conventional meaning of 'power'. Baudrillard would probably answer that 'it is a good thing that terms lose their meaning at the limits of the text', but would still complain that Foucault doesn't 'do it enough' (ibid. 38). Secondly, when Foucault doesn't use a negative to describe 'power', he gives an open definition which might not be too far from what Baudrillard might consider to be a definition of the 'simulacrum of power itself': 'it is the name that one attributes to a complex strategical situation in a particular society' (Foucault, cited in ibid. 93). Although Baudrillard would argue against the 'strategical' aspect of Foucault's definition, might it be possible to say that this 'complex strategical situation' is the *mise-en-scène* of the 'simulacrum of power itself'? After all, isn't a *mise-en-scène* a strategy even if it is without any strategist or strategical intentions?

Toward a genealogical critique of environmental practices: environmental governmentality, eco-politics and space

There are at least three concepts emerging from the genealogical period which can be particularly helpful for an environmental critique: 'governmentality', 'biopower' and 'space'.

'Governmentality' is the broadest term, and occurs in the context of Foucaults historical interpretation of the literature on 'reason of state' in Europe from around the sixteenth century. Foucault identifies and qualifies the emergence of modern deployment of power in the context of three axes: institutional centralization around governmental agencies, the emergence of new instrumental knowledge, and the capillary diffusion of power effects across the entire social body. For Foucault, 'governmentality' is:

22   Éric Darier

1   The ensemble formed by institutions, procedures, analyses and
     reflections, the calculations and tactics that allow the exercise
     of this very specific albeit complex form of power, which has as
     its target population, as its principle form of knowledge polit-
     ical economy, and as its essential technical means apparatuses
     of security.
2   The tendency which over a long period and throughout the
     West, has steadily lead towards the pre-eminence over all other
     forms (sovereignty, discipline, etc.) of this type of power which
     may be termed government, resulting, on the one hand, in the
     formation of a whole series of specific governmental appara-
     tuses, and, on the other, in the development of a whole com-
     plex of *savoirs*.
3   The process, or rather the result of the process, through which
     the state of justice of the Middle Ages, transformed into the
     administrative state during the fifteenth and sixteenth centur-
     ies, gradually becomes 'governmentalized'. (Foucault 1991a:
     102–3)

The concept of governmentality has potential for an environmental
critique, because it explicitly deals with issues of (state) 'security',
techniques of control of the population, and new forms of knowledge (*savoirs*). Contrary to more traditional analyses of 'public
policy', which focus narrowly on 'objectives', 'results' within an
instrumental framework of linear causalities and quantifiable data,
governmentality focuses on the deeper historical context and on
the broader power 'effects' of governmental policy (Dean 1994b;
Pal 1990). A certain number of studies explicitly using the concept of 'environmental governmentality' already exist (Rutherford
1994a, 1994b; Darier 1996a).

The more specific concepts of 'biopower' / 'biopolitics' emerged
initially from Foucault's archeological studies of the natural sciences and, more precisely, biology, but were recontextualized in
the framework of governmentality and power/knowledge. Biopolitics is the series of governmental strategies centred on this
new concept called 'life'. More precisely, for Foucault, biopolitics
is 'the manner by which it has been attempted, since the sixteenth
century, to rationalize the problems posed to government practices by phenomena concerning the totality of human beings constituted as a population: health, hygiene, natality, longevity, race'
(Foucault 1989d: 109, my trans.).

This concern for life ('biopolitics') identified by Foucault is largely
anthropocentric, in that the prime target is the control of all aspects

of human life, especially the conditions for human biological reproduction. Current environmental concerns could be seen as an
extension of 'biopolitics', broadened to all life-forms and called
'ecopolitics' (Rutherford 1993). On this scenario, the normalizing
strategy of ecopolitics is the most recent attempt to extend control
('management') to the entire planet (Sachs 1993). In this context,
the promotion of ecocentrism by deep ecology, for example, can
be seen as not only a critique of prevalent, increasing instrumental
control of the natural world, but as inserting itself very well into
the new normalizing strategy of an ecopolitics. My point here
should not be interpreted as a negative evaluation of deep ecology
per se. Instead, I want to illustrate the complexity of power relations and the constant dangers – but also opportunities – lurking
in the field of power. In this context, the adoption of a Manichaean
approach to environmental 'issues' by many environmental theorists fails to acknowledge that their tactic of environmental resistance is always what de Certeau calls 'maneuver "within the enemy's
field of vision",' and cannot be positioned as a referential 'externality' (de Certeau 1984: 37). This is why Foucault's genealogical
approach is so important for an environmental critique.

Foucault's approach to 'space' is the third concept which might
also be extremely relevant to an environmental critique. Foucault
explored the problematization of 'space' within a historical context
(Foucault 1984e; 1989d: 99–106). According to the framework of
governmentality, the 'security' of the state is guaranteed not so
much directly by the control of a territory (space), but rather
through the increasing control of the population living in that
territory. In fact, Foucault suggested that at the beginning of the
seventeenth century the government of France started to 'think of
its territory on the model of the city'. According to Foucault,

> The city was no longer perceived as a place of privilege, as an
> exception in a territory of fields, forests and roads. . . . Instead, the
> cities, with the problems that they raised, and the particular forms
> that they took, served as the models for the governmental rationality
> that was to apply to the whole of the territory. A state will be well
> organised when a system of policing as tight and efficient as that of
> the cities extends over the entire territory. (Foucault 1984b: 241)

Consequently, one historical rupture which became a condition for
the environmental 'crisis' was the attempt to extend the system
of social control in place in the cities to the countryside. This historical analysis of the increasing control of the non-urban space (the

more 'natural' environment) is similar to the critique of social ecologists who might agree with Foucault that the domestication of
nature was part of a system of (urban) power relations among
humans which had for its objective the maintenance of the given
social order (Bookchin 1982). As the environmental 'crisis' was
one of the results of specific power relations – such as social
inequalities and political hierarchy – it would presumably have to
be addressed before – or at least at the same time as – the environmental 'crisis'. Obviously, deep ecologists, like George Sessions,
would interpret this focus on human issues as the continuation of
anthropocentrism which created the environmental 'crisis' in the
first place (Sessions 1995b). Locating Foucault with social ecologists
against deep ecologists is not accurate either. Foucault's studies of
the emergence and rise of 'human sciences' in the context of
governmentality – as a specific 'reason of state' based on security
– could also be the basis for a critique of anthropocentrism. However, unlike deep ecologists, Foucault would not suggest replacing
anthropocentrism by ecocentricism, which also presents its own set
of traps. For example, Foucault would probably agree with Timothy
Luke's critique of ecocentrism (i.e. anti / non-anthropocentrism)
as being also, ultimately, a humanly constructed category which is
policed by all-too-human ecocentrists. Justifying human actions in
the name of 'nature' leaves the unresolved problem of whose
(human) voice can legitimately speak for 'nature' and the inherent
dangers of such an approach.

As Luke remarks admirably,

> deep ecology could function as a new strategy of power for nor-
> malising new ecological subjects – human and non-human – in
> disciplines of self-effacing moral consciousness. In endorsing self-
> expression as the inherent value of all ecospheric entities, deep
> ecology also could advance the modern logic of domination by
> retraining humans to surveil and steer themselves as well as other
> beings in accord with 'Nature's dictates'. As a new philosophy of
> nature, then, deep ecology provides the essential discursive grid for
> a few enthusiastic ecosophical mandarins to interpret nature and
> impose its deep ecology dictates on the unwilling many. (Luke
> 1988: 85)

This longing for 'nature', either through the self-effacement of
humans before 'wilderness' (deep ecology)[22] or through nostalgia
for a simpler social order in harmony with nature (social ecology)[23]
is possible only in the context of an 'intimate distance' brought

about by the 'dislocation of nature in modernity' (Phelan 1993). Consequently, the 'space' that Foucault is talking about is not the unproblematized physical and material environment of the environmentalists, but the various problematizations of 'space' raised, for example, by feminists (Lykke and Bryld 1994). In this sense, Foucault and the environmentalists are not located in quite the same space! However, the reconceptualization of space – for example, as 'heterotopias' (Foucault 1986) – enabled Foucault to create a break in our current 'physical' understanding(s) of space. We shall come back to the important concept of 'heterotopias' as two of the contributors to this volume, Thomas Heyd and Peter Quigley, apply it.

The final Foucault

After the publication of the first volume of his *History of Sexuality* (1976), Foucault remained silent until just before his death in 1984. Foucault's silence was relative in the sense that he carried on giving numerous interviews. In retrospect, however, one can see a shift occurring sometime in the 1977–84 interval. Just before dying of AIDS, Foucault published the second and third volumes of *The History of Sexuality* (Foucault 1984a, 1984f). The introduction to *The Use of Pleasure* constitutes another *déplacement* from the second Foucault and from the first volume (Foucault 1976). Until *The Use of Pleasure* was published, the assumption was that, for Foucault, the forms taken by our subjectivities were the contingent effects of power relations and nothing more. For this reason alone, Foucault was highly suspicious of any teleological project such as, for example, 'ethics', which he saw as a technique for the normalization of the population, a technique whose objective was to control daily human conduct.[24] In this sense one could argue that Foucault was strongly against ethics. What surprised many readers after the publication of the second and third volumes was the focus on Greek ethics or, more precisely, on conditions for the emergence of the self-construction, by some Greeks, of how humans related to themselves. Now the question for Foucault was: how can individuals or groups of individuals shape / construct their own self / their own subjectivity / their identity and consequently their conduct in the world / in relative distance / autonomy from the process of normalization? This exercise illustrates what Foucault called a 'practice of freedom'. Some readers

26   Éric Darier

saw in Foucault's final volumes the affirmation of an ontological subject which he spent all his life seeking to escape. I believe that this is a gross misreading of Foucault. In the first place, Foucault was not an 'anti-humanist' in the sense of rejecting humanity; he simply offered a critique of 'one style of being human' (Dumm 1996: 15). The only thing he was doing in the second and third volumes was debunking over-determinist readings of normaliza- tion, as outlined by the genealogical Foucault and more precisely in the first volume of *History of Sexuality*. Up to the end, for Foucault, there was no ontological subject, as humanists would have every- one believe. However, for him the subjectivities of individuals were not the sole effects of the normalization process. The various forms that the subject takes also emerge from the specificity of the field of power: this is to say, the occasional cracks in the *dispositif* between normalization and resistance.

According to the second and third volumes, the subject can also be self-constituted in 'a more autonomous way, through practices of liberation, of liberty'. This 'autonomous way' is not based on an ontological autonomy of the subject. 'I do indeed believe that there is no sovereign, founding subject, a universal form of subject to be found everywhere. I believe, on the contrary, that the subject is constituted through practices of subjection, or, in a more autonomous way, through practices of liberation, of liberty' (Foucault 1988a: 50).

What Foucault was *not* doing in the last two volumes of *The History of Sexuality* was giving a prescriptive ethical norm. He was not suggesting that the ethics of the Greeks should be our norms. On the contrary, the final volumes should be interpreted as containing examples of non-strategic ethics – that is, ethics which are not part of a strategy to normalize / control the popu- lation, but an ethics which emerges in relative autonomy from the normalization process. The central objective of Foucault was to tell his contemporaries that, in some cases, it is possible to remake ourselves, to remake our self-identity independently of the nor- malization process, and for us to 'understand the ways in which we are free' (Dumm 1996: 63). Thus the 'ethics' described in the second and third volumes are merely examples of radical alterity, of practices of freedom, from other spaces and from other times, not a universal, ahistorical ethical prescription to be followed to the letter. Foucault's ultimate position / ethical stand is well summarized by Lawrence Kritzman, for whom 'the quintessential challenge in the post-Sartrean age is to invent new forms of life based on an ethical stance endlessly disengaging itself from all forms of discourse based on the familiar and accepted' (Kritzman 1988: xxiv–xxv).

Foucault's non-ethics has important consequences for environmental ethics in that the focus shifts away from the presumed discovery or 'rediscovery' of a true permanent 'ecological self'[25] to the active constitution of subjectivities which constantly rework humans' relations with themselves, with other life-forms, and with the world generally. The ethical constitution of what might be called 'green' subjectivities might be the endless process of 'ethicization' of being human in the world.

Where Do We Go from Here?

In summary, we have seen a degree of overlap between Foucault and environmentalism. In general, there is an irreconcilable conflict between the contextualizing premises of Foucault's archeology and the frequent recourse by many environmental theorists to a naturalistic position in the last instance. However, Foucault and the environmental activists have potentially more in common when it comes to practical political tactics of resistance and to understanding the construction / deconstruction of subjectivities. Foucault wasn't interested in defining what is 'good' or 'bad' in the abstract, because these terms make sense only within the specificity of their contexts. Rather, Foucault's ethico-political project is to 'determine which is the main danger'. For him, 'not everything is bad, but everything is dangerous'. And if this is the case, then 'we always have something to do', which 'leads not to apathy but to a hyper- and pessimistic activism' (Foucault 1984d: 343). Surely this is the way that most environmentalists approach their political practices, asking 'What are the main dangers we are facing – including the normalizing dangers of environmental discourses themselves?' Even if there is deep pessimism in the environmental movement about the chances for the ecological survival of humans and many other life-forms on this planet, it hasn't lead to quietism. On the contrary, it has stimulated both a 'hyper-activism' of environmental resistance and a constant refashioning of one's own subjectivities. Despite 'turning his back to nature', Foucault's provocative and creative thinking may help us to face up to the environmental challenge.

Because of the stimulating diversity and richness of Foucault's approaches, themes and concepts, it is only possible to touch on some of them. This collection of essays intends to illustrate only the diversity of unintended Foucauldian effects on environmental critique. The first part of this volume approaches discourses of the 'environment' from a Foucauldian historical angle – that is, a genealogy of the present with several 'histories'.

In his chapter ' "The Entry of Life into History" ', Paul Rutherford focuses on 'biopolitics', which is probably the closest Foucault ever came to addressing the environmental issue from the perspective of how the mechanisms of biological life themselves became an object of 'reason of state' calculations and strategy. In this sense, 'life' as an object of scientific knowledge, as a state preoccupation, and as an ethical / normalizing guiding principle for individual conduct enters 'history', because it becomes an articulated, explicit strategy. Building on the Foucauldian concept of 'biopolitics', but pushing it beyond its central concern for human life, Rutherford shows that the current interest in ecology can be characterized as an 'ecological governmentality' in which all life-forms become objects of scientific enquiry, a series of state calculations based on 'security' and on the disciplining / normalization of the population. He illustrates this 'ecological governmentality' by reviewing in detail the procedures for *environmental impact assessment* as an emergence of discourse about eco-risks.

Using a Foucauldian-inspired 'archeo-genealogical' approach, Isabelle Lanthier and Lawrence Olivier also address the theme of 'biopolitics', and identify a recent rupture in the discourse of medicine and human health which introduces the concept of 'life-style', linking issues of human life to the quality of air, water, urban space and working environment. It is the technique of normalization of individual conduct through 'life-style' practices which created the conditions for the emergence of an environmental 'awareness'. Lanthier and Olivier show that the current environmental 'awareness' is not simply an extension or a deepening of biopolitics, but also an unexpected effect.

For her part, Catriona Sandilands's 'Sex at the Limits' critically explores the theme of ecological 'limits' and, more precisely, 'population control' in the recent history of environmental discourses. For Sandilands, 'calls for limits' have disciplinary and normative consequences which environmentalism rarely acknowledges. For example, the problematization of population control translates 'natural limits' into 'sexual limits', which have racialized, gendered and heterosexualized power relations. Sandilands concludes by advocating 'the reassertion of an overt sense of "polymorphous" pleasure into environmental discourses' as a tactic of resistance to the normative constraints of the discourses about 'population control'.

In 'Ecological Modernization and Environmental Risk', Paul Rutherford reviews part of the debate between German social theory and Foucault and its possible consequences for an understanding of the current problematization around the issue of 'environment'. It seems that the concerns for 'security' which emerge out of the 'reason of state' result in taking more environmental risks in order to guarantee more 'security'!

The second part of this collection is devoted more specifically to the effects of various techniques of enviro-normalization on the construction of subjectivities and conceptions of space. To reflect the plurality and heterogeneity of these techniques, this second part is entitled 'Environmentalities'.

The article by Timothy W. Luke on 'Environmentality as Green Governmentality' is a practical case study of 'ecological / green governmentality' in the current American environmental political context, which includes among others the Wise Use / Property Rights movement, the pro-business agenda of the Republican Congress, and President Clinton and Vice-President Gore's 'environmental musings'. Luke illustrates very well how 'environmentality' is one central characteristic of the new political economy of 'globalization' which includes 'eco-knowledge' and 'enviro-discipline'.

In his article, 'Art and Foucauldian Heterotopias', Thomas Heyd explores the concept of space in Foucault, especially heterotopias as an example of resistance against the homogenization and normalization of space. Heyd suggests that 'medicine wheels' located on the plains of North America and their occasional use as a source of inspiration in contemporary arts are an illustration of the importance of 'other places' in imagining other possibilities for the present and the future.

Sylvia Bowerbank's article 'Nature Writing as Self-Technology', warns us about the dangers in techniques of nurturing a 'green self' by a growing number of environmentalists. Bowerbank reminds us that 'self-technologies' such as nature retreats and 'eco-pastoral' exercises used by contemporary environmentalists are not new, but are part of a broader history of disciplinary strategies.

The third and final part of the volume deals with the intense debate between the 'nature-endorsing' and 'nature-sceptical' sides of environmental theory and the deployment of many strategies of resistance.

30   Éric Darier

In 'Nature as Dangerous Space', Peter Quigley offers a fierce critique of the 'grounded responsibility' suggested in recent publications, most notably by Aaron Gare, Charlene Spretnak, Neil Evernden and George Sessions. To get away from problematic 'grounded responsibility' and/or 'nature-endorsing', Quigley proposes using Foucault's concept of resistance. As an example of resistance, Quigley mentions Foucault's 'heterotopias' as 'places where sites of opposition are created'.

For his part, Neil Levy resists the discourses associated with poststructuralism and Foucault because they tend to be 'profoundly anti-naturalistic', 'dangerously relativistic' and 'abstract'. If Levy identifies overlaps between the anti-humanist critique of poststructuralism and the anti-anthropocentrism of some of the environmental discourses, he also identifies profound differences. For Levy, 'if there is nature in Foucault's work, we can have no knowledge about it'. Nevertheless, he acknowledges the importance of the Foucauldian concept of resistance as one which works 'without committing us to a belief in an ontological referent'.

In the final chapter I build on Quigley's critique and also try to resist environmental ethics, which I see as moralistic and justified ultimately on the 'naturalistic fallacy'. I suggest instead a contextualized concept of resistance *à la* Foucault and use the example of non-essentialist gay/queer political tactics to outline what a Green aesthetic of existence might look like.

Notes

1   Madan Sarup identifies four features of poststructuralism, which he equates with postmodernism: (1) dissolution of the subject and subversion of the notion of structure; (2) critique of historicism; (3) critique of meaning; (4) critique of philosophy (1989: 2–3, 118). For a general introduction, see also Smart 1993. For a critique of postmodernism, see Norris 1990.

2   The 'filters' can also be considered as the only reality. The metaphor of the filter as filtering an objective reality for humans might be part of the illusion. Paraphrasing Derrida, one could say, 'il n'y a pas d'hors filtres'! For a stimulating discussion of textuality in Foucault and Derrida, see Said 1978b.

3   For an illustration of an acrobatic statement on the topic, see Murphy 1994: ix: 'The sociological construction of the relationship between the social and the natural must be done in a way that maintains the importance of social constructions without reducing reality to a social construction.'

4   There are three important biographies of Foucault (Éribon 1991;
     Macey 1993; J. Miller 1993) and a more recent rebuttal of critiques
     by Éribon (1994).

5   This is probably why Thomas Dumm see Foucault as a performer, as
     'a sort of intellectual Elvis'. '[Foucault's] referentiality is not a sign
     of his lack of originality but is instead, an artifact of the unusually
     meticulous preparation of the archival retrieval' (Dumm 1996: 72).

6   I agree with Olivier (1995: 20) that Foucault's intentions were more
     philosophical than methodological.

7   For a similar 'bothends' way of approaching Foucault, see Mahon
     1992, which, starting from a Nietzschean genealogical perspective,
     explores the foci of research of the three Foucaults: viz. 'truth',
     'power' and the 'subject'.

8   For the purpose of chronological coherence and clarity, I give the
     date of the first publication in French, but in the Bibliography, I
     also give (in square brackets) the date of the first publication of the
     English translation, followed by the title in English.

9   Gutting shows that Foucault removed the word 'structural' from
     the later reprinting of *The Birth of the Clinic*. With archeology, it
     may be 'possible to make a *structural* analysis of discourses that
     would evade the fate of commentary by supposing no remainder,
     nothing in excess of what has been said, but only the fact of its
     historical appearance' (Foucault 1963: xvii; quoted in Gutting 1989:
     134, my emphasis).

10   It is important to note that the target of Taylor's critique in this pass-
     age (1989: 99–100) is 'neo-Nietzscheans', which explicitly includes
     Foucault. Taylor's critique was directed not against the archeological
     approach, but against the Nietzschean position taken by Foucault
     in response to the limitations of the archeological approach. I took
     Taylor's critique out of its context on purpose, because, although I
     may disagree with Taylor's view of the Nietzschean Foucault, I believe
     that Taylor's critique is perfectly pertinent to the archeological period.

11   For an example of a subsequent archeological study of scientific
     knowledge which incorporates a genealogical 'power' dimension (i.e.
     'power/knowledge'), see Rouse 1987.

12   For an example of genealogical re-memorization of forgotten prac-
     tices, see Kubrin 1981, which shows that the founding father of
     'modern' physics, Isaac Newton, was also an adept of magic.

13   It is interesting to note that the most supportive 'Marxian' (not Marx-
     ist?) evaluation of Foucault focuses exclusively on the genealogy,
     not the archeology (Smart 1983). For another stimulating Marxian
     reworking of Marxism through Foucault, see Poster 1985. Foucault
     also offered his own genealogical critique of Marxism: 'What strikes
     me in the Marxist analyses is that they always contain the question
     of "class struggle" but they pay little attention to one word in the
     phrase, namely "struggle" . . . But when they speak of the "class

32   Éric Darier

struggle" as the mainspring of history, they focus mainly on defining
class, its boundaries, its membership, but never concretely on the
nature of the struggle. One exception comes to mind: Marx's own
non-theoretical, historical texts, which are better and different in
this regard' (Foucault 1988d: 123).

14   Another technique of tactical writing employed by Foucault is the
     use of quotation marks to create a rupture between the accepted
     meaning of a word and the object it is suppose to signify. For a
     discussion of the use of quotation mark by Foucault, see Visker
     1995: 74–135.

15   For an account of Foucault as a 'self-professed' Nietzschean, see
     Olivier 1995.

16   For a similar likening of 'chaos theory of contemporary physics and
     postmodern critique of modernity's search for a univocal, stable
     structure that organizes all phenomena', see Zimmerman 1994: 13,
     318–77.

17   Among many 'gay' historical studies, see Halperin 1990; Weeks
     1985. From a historico-legal perspective, see Moran 1996; Stychin
     1995.

18   I borrow this useful distinction from de Certeau. 'I call a *strategy*
     the calculation (or manipulation) of power relationships that becomes
     possible as soon as a subject with will and power (a business, an
     army, a city, a scientific institution) can be isolated. It postulates a
     place that can be delimited as its *own* and serve as the base from
     which relations with an *exteriority* composed of targets or threats
     (consumers or competitors, enemies, the country surrounding the
     city, objectives and objects of research, etc.) can be managed' (de
     Certeau 1984: 35–6). '[A] *tactic* is a calculated action determined
     by the absence of a proper locus. No delimitation of an exteriority,
     then, provides it with the condition necessary for autonomy . . . it is
     maneuver "within the enemy's field of vision". . . . It does not, there-
     fore, have the options of planning general strategy and viewing the
     adversary as a whole within a district, visible, and objectifiable
     space' (ibid. 36–7).

19   I am not using the word 'individual' to affirm an individualist onto-
     logy and/or epistemology. On the contrary, one should see the
     'individualization' of self-identity as one of the effects of modern
     power relations. Again, we are trapped in the boundaries of lan-
     guage, for we don't have vocabulary for describing what is not!

20   '[E]nvironmental consciousness has . . . helped to reinforce the cur-
     rent recessionary messages about self-sacrifice and deprivation in
     our daily lives' (Ross 1994: 266). 'While it may be necessary to
     rebut the calls for limits – sounding across a whole spectrum from
     the economics of corporate environmentalism to the cultural pol-
     itics of traditional values – it would be historically naive to suggest
     that cultural freedoms can be uncoupled from the social conditions

in which they were won and are maintained today. On the one hand, popular consciousness tenaciously insists that people are less free when they have less to consume even though many consumers recognise that higher levels of consumption involve them in socially constraining networks of dependency and debt that are not always visible or economically quantifiable. But it is rank First World arrogance to suggest that people in non-consumer societies are somehow more free in their less commodified ways, or more healthy in their freedom from diseases associated with life in high-consumption societies' (ibid. 267). For a study of the social construction of human 'needs', see Leiss 1976.

21 Baudrillard makes a direct link between 'consumption' and the 'desire for totality' which implies that, for example, the longing for a coherent ecological totality in fact sustains 'consumption'. For Baudrillard, '[t]he desire to "moderate" consumption or establish a normalising network of needs is naive and absurd moralism. At the heart of the project from which emerges the systematic and indefinite process of consumption is a frustrated desire for totality' (Baudrillard 1982: 25). It is because we cannot achieve a totalizing objective world-view that we are consuming the world.

22 The discourse of 'wilderness' by deep ecologists is indeed the 'litmus test of whether someone has firmly adopted a non-anthropocentric ecological ethic that transcends mere environmental pragmatism and enlightened human self-interest' (Chase 1991: 18).

23 'The fourteenth and fifteenth centuries may well have marked a unique watershed for Western humanity. History seemed to be poised at a juncture: society could still choose to follow a course that yielded a modest satisfaction of needs based on complementarity and the equality of unequals. Or it could catapult into capitalism with its rules of equivalence and the inequality of equals, both reinforced by commodity exchange and a canon of "unlimited needs" that confront "scarce resources"' (Bookchin 1982: 214–15).

24 For a superb application of the conceptual framework of the normalization of 'conduct' to the seventeenth century, see (Tully 1993a). See also Rose 1990.

25 For an example of this position, see Mathews 1991. For Mathews the issue is to 'find a metaphysical and ethical expression for the intuition of "oneness" and interconnectedness' (p. 3). Despite the obviously fundamentalist character and non-Foucauldian approach of Mathews's search for the 'ecological self', it is possible to read Mathews as a strategic counter-example to current non-ecological modern selves. However, it is quite clear that Mathews does literally 'believe' in her metaphysical ethics. Again, this illustrates the tension that Foucault identified in the environmental movement between a critique of existing truth-claims and a political practice justified by similar truth-claims (Foucault 1988b: 15).

References

Baudrillard, Jean (1982): 'The Systems of Objects', in *Selected Writings*, Stanford, Calif.: Stanford University Press.

Baudrillard, Jean (1987): *Forget Foucault*. New York: Semiotext(e).

Beck, Ulrich (1995): *Ecological Politics in an Age of Risk*. Cambridge: Polity

Bennett, Jane and Chaloupka, William (eds) (1993): *In the Nature of Things: Language, Politics and the Environment*. Minneapolis: University of Minnesota Press.

Benton, Ted (1994): 'Biology and Social Theory in the Environmental Debate', in Michael R. Redclift and Ted Benton (eds), *Social Theory and the Global Environment*, London: Routledge, 28–50.

Berman, Morris (1981): *The Reenchantment of the World*. Ithaca, NY: Cornell University Press.

Bersani, Leo (1995): *Homos*. Cambridge, Mass.: Harvard University Press.

Bird, Elizabeth Ann R. (1987): 'The Social Construction of Nature: Theoretical Approaches to the History of Environmental Problems', *Environmental Review*, 11, 255–64.

Bookchin, Murray (1982): *The Ecology of Freedom*. Polo Alto, Calif.: Cheshire Books.

Bookchin, Murray (1990): *Remaking Society*. Boston: South End Press.

Bouchard, Donald E. (ed.) (1977): *Language, Counter-Memory, Practice: Selected Essays and Interviews by Michael Foucault*. Ithaca, NY: Cornell University Press.

Callicott, J. Baird (1990): 'The Case against Moral Pluralism', *Environmental Ethics*, 12(2), 99–124.

Canguilhem, Georges (1988): *Ideology and Rationality in the History of the Life Sciences*. Cambridge, Mass.: MIT Press.

Canguilhem, Georges (1989): *The Normal and the Pathological*. New York: Zone Books.

Chaloupka, William (1992): *Knowing Nukes: The Politics and Culture of the Atom*. Minneapolis: University of Minnesota Press.

Chase, Steve (1991): 'Whither the Radical Ecology Movement?', in Murray Bookchin and Dave Foreman, *Defending the Earth – A Debate between Murray Bookchin and Dave Foreman*, Montreal: Black Rose Books, 7–24.

Conley, Verana Andermatt (1997): *Ecopolitics – The Environment in Poststructural Thought*. London: Routledge.

Connolly, William E. (1992): 'The Irony of Interpretation', in Daniel W. Conway and John E. Seery (eds), *The Politics of Irony – Essays in Self-Betrayal*, New York: St Martin's Press, 119–50.

Connolly, William E. (1993b): 'Beyond Good and Evil – The Ethical Sensibility of Michel Foucault', *Political Theory*, 21(3), 365–89.

Connolly, William E. (1995): *The Ethos of Pluralization*. Minneapolis: University of Minnesota Press.

Darier, Éric (1993): 'L'Environnement au Canada: une approche foucaltienne'. (Ph.D. Thesis, McGill University, Montreal).

Darier, Éric (1995): 'Environmental Studies in Context: Knowledge, Language, History and the Self', in Michael D. Mehta and Eric Ouellet (eds), *Environmental Sociology: Theory and Practice*, Toronto: Captus Press, 153–69.

Darier, Éric (1996a): 'Environmental Governmentality: The Case of Canada's Green Plan', *Environmental Politics*, 5(4), 585–606.

Darier, Éric (1996b): 'The Politics and Power Effects of Garbage Recycling in Halifax, Canada', *Local Environment*, 1(1), 63–86.

Davidson, Arnold I. (1986): 'Archeology, Genealogy, Ethics', in David Couzens Hoy (ed.), *Foucault: A Critical Reader*, Oxford: Blackwell, 221–33.

Dean, Mitchell (1994b): ' "A Social Structure of Many Souls": Moral Regulation, Government, and Self-Formation', *Canadian Journal of Sociology*, 19(2), 145–68.

de Certeau, Michel (1984); *The Practice of Everyday Life*. Berkeley: University of California Press.

Defert, Daniel and Ewald, François (eds) (1994): *Dits et écrits*, 4 vols. Paris: Gallimard.

Devall, Bill and Sessions, George (1985): *Deep Ecology: Living as if Nature Mattered*. Salt Lake City: Perigrine Smith.

Dobson, Andrew (1990); *Green Political Thought*. London: Unwin Hyman.

Dumm, Thomas L. (1996): *Michel Foucault and the Politics of Freedom*. Thousand Oaks, Calif.: Sage.

Easterbrook, Gregg (1995): *Moment on the Earth – The Coming Age of Environmental Optimism*. New York: Viking.

Eckersley, Robin (1992): *Environmentalism and Political Theory*. London: UCL Press.

Ellen, Roy (1996): 'Introduction', in Roy Ellen and Katsuyoshi Fukui (eds), *Redefining Nature – Ecology, Culture and Domestication*, Oxford: Berg, 1–36.

Éribon, Didier (1991): *Michel Foucault*. Cambridge, Mass.: Harvard University Press.

Feyerabend, Paul (1981a): *Problems of Empiricism*. Cambridge: Cambridge University Press.

Feyerabend, Paul (1981b): *Realism, Rationalism, and Scientific Method*. Cambridge: Cambridge University Press.

Feyerabend, Paul (1991): *Three Dialogues on Knowledge*. Oxford: Blackwell.

Flathman, Richard (1992): *Willful Liberalism: Voluntarism and Individuality in Political Theory and Practice*. Ithaca, NY: Cornell University Press.

Foucault, Michel (1961) [1965]: *Madness and Civilization*. New York: Pantheon Books; London: Tavistock Publications, 1971.

Foucault, Michel (1963) [1973]: *The Birth of the Clinic: An Archaeology of Medical Perception*. New York: Pantheon Books.

Foucault, Michel (1966) [1971]: *A The Order of Things: An Archaeology of the Human Sciences*. New York: Pantheon Books; London: Tavistock Publications, 1970.

Foucault, Michel (1969) [1972]: *The Archaeology of Knowledge*. New York: Harper Colophon; London: Tavistock Publications, 1972.

Foucault, Michel (1975) [1977]: *Discipline and Punish: The Birth of the Prison*. New York: Pantheon Books; London: Allen Lane.

Foucault, Michel (1976) [1978]: *The History of Sexuality*, Vol. 1: *Introduction*. New York: Pantheon Books.

Foucault, Michel (1980h): 'Two Lectures', in Colin Gordon (ed.), *Power/Knowledge: Selected Interviews and Other Writings, 1972–1977*, New York: Pantheon Books; Brighton: Harvester Wheatsheaf, 1980, 78–108.

Foucault, Michel (1984a) [1986]: *The Care of the Self*. New York: Pantheon Books.

Foucault, Michel (1984b): *The Foucault Reader*, ed. Paul Rabinow. New York: Pantheon Books.

Foucault, Michel (1984c): 'Nietzsche, Genealogy, History', In Paul Rabinow (ed.), *The Foucault Reader*, New York: Pantheon Books, 76–100.

Foucault, Michel (1984d): 'On the Genealogy of Ethics: An Overview of Work in Progress', in Paul Rabinow (ed.), *The Foucault Reader*, New York: Pantheon Books, 340–72.

Foucault, Michel (1984e): 'Space, Knowledge, and Power', in Paul Rabinow (ed.), *The Foucault Reader*, New York: Pantheon Books, 239–56.

Foucault, Michel (1984f): [1985]: *The Use of Pleasure*. New York: Pantheon Books; London: Viking, 1986.

Foucault, Michel (1988b): 'The Ethic of Care for the Self as a Practice of Freedom – An Interview with Michel Foucault Conducted by Paul Fronet-Betancourt, Helmut Becker and Alfredo Gomez-Muller on January 20, 1984', in James Bernauer and David Rasmussen (eds), *The Final Foucault*, Cambridge, Mass.: MIT Press, 11–20.

Foucault, Michel (1988d): 'Power and Sex', in Lawrence Kritzman (ed.), *Michel Foucault – Politics, Philosophy, Culture – –Interviews and Other Writings 1977–1984*, London and New York: Routledge, 110–24.

Foucault, Michel (1989d): *Michel Foucault – Résumé des cours 1970–1982*. Paris: Collège de France / Julliard.

Foucault, Michel (1991a): 'Governmentality', in Burchell, et al. (eds), *The Foucault Effect*, Hemel Hempstead: Harvester Wheatsheaf, 87–104.

Fraser, Nancy (1989): 'Foucault on Modern Power: Empirical Insights and Normative Confusions', in *Unruly Practices – Power, Discourse and Gender in Contemporary Social Theory*, Minnesota: University of Minnesota Press, 17–34.

Gare, Arrane E. (1995): *Postmodernism and the Environmental Crisis*. London: Routledge.

Goldblatt, David (1996): *Social Theory and the Environment*. Cambridge: Polity.

Gordon, Colin (1996): 'Foucault in Britain', in Andrew Barry, Thomas Osborne and Nikolas Rose (eds), *Foucault and Political Reason – Liberalism, Neo-Liberalism and Rationalities of Government*, Chicago: University of Chicago Press, 253–70.

Halperin, David (1990): *One Hundred Years of Homosexuality and Other Essays of Greek Love*. New York: Routledge.

Halperin, David (1995): 'The Queer Politics of Michel Foucault', in David Halperin, *Saint Foucault – Towards a Gay Hagiography*, New York: Oxford University Press, 15–125.

Hannigan, John A. (1995): *Environmental Sociology: A Social Constructionist Perspective*. London: Routledge.

Haraway, Donna (1989): 'Situated Knowledges: The Science Question in Feminism and the Privilege of Partial Perspective', *Feminist Studies*, 14(3), 575–99.

Haraway, Donna (1991): *Symians, Cyborgs, and Women: The Reinvention of Nature*. London: Free Association Books.

Hayward, Tim (1994): *Ecological Thought: An Introduction*. Cambridge: Polity.

Jagtenberg, Tom and McKie, David (1997): *Eco-Impact and the Greening of Postmodernity*. London: Sage.

Kateb, George (1992): *The Inner Ocean: Individualism and Democratic Culture*. Ithaca, NY: Cornell University Press.

Knorr-Cetina, K. D. (1981): *The Manufacture of Knowledge: An Essay on the Constructivist and Contextual Nature of Science*. Oxford: Pergamon Press.

Knorr-Cetina, K. D. (1983): The Ethnographic Study of Scientific Work: Towards a Constructivist Interpretation of Science', in K. D. Knorr-Cetina and M. Mulkay (eds), *Science Observed: Perspectives on the Social Study of Science*, London: Sage, 115–40.

Kroker, Arthur (1987): 'The Games of Foucault', *Canadian Journal of Political and Social Theory*, 11(3), 1–10.

Kubrin, David (1981): 'Newton's Inside Out!' Magic, Class Struggle and the Rise of Mechanism in the West', in Harry Woolf (ed.), *The Analytic Spirit – Essays in the History of Science*, Ithaca, NY: Cornell University Press, 96–121.

Kuhn, Thomas (1962): *The Structure of Scientific Revolutions*. Chicago: University of Chicago Press.

Latour, Bruno (1987): *Science in Action: How to Follow Scientists and Engineers through Society*. Milton Keynes: Open University Press.

Latour, Bruno and Woolgar, Steve (1986): *Laboratory Life: The [Social] Construction of Scientific Facts*. Princeton: Princeton University Press.

Leiss, William (1976): *The Limits of Satisfaction – An Essay on the Problem of Needs and Commodities.* Toronto: University of Toronto Press.

Luke, Timothy W. (1988): 'The Dreams of Deep Ecology', *Telos*, 76, 65–92.

Luke, Timothy W. (1993b): 'Green Consumerism: Ecology and the Ruse of Recycling', in Bennett and Chaloupka (eds), *In the Nature of Things*, Minneapolis: University of Minnesota Press, 154–72.

Lykke, Nina and Bryld, Mette (1994): 'Between Terraforming and Fortune-Telling – Space Flight and Astrology: Ambivalences of a Post-modern World', in Wendy Harcourt (ed.), *Feminist Perspectives on Sustainable Development*, London: Routledge, 109–27.

Macey, David (1993): *Lives of Michel Foucault*. London: Hutchinson.

Macnaghten, Phil and Urry, John (1998): *Contested Natures*. London; Sage.

Mahon, Michael (1992): *Foucault's Nietzschean Genealogy – Truth, Power, and the Subject*. Albany, NY: SUNY Press.

Marshall, Peter (1992): *Nature's Web – An Exploration of Ecological Thinking*. London: Simon and Schuster.

Mathews, Freya (1991): *The Ecological Self*. London: Routledge.

McNeil, Maureen (1993): 'Dancing with Foucault: Feminism and Power-Knowledge', in Ramazanoğlu (ed.), *Up against Foucault*, London: Routledge, 147–75.

Merchant, Carolyn (1994): *Key Concepts in Critical Theory – Ecology*. Atlantic Heights, NJ: Humanities Press.

Miller, James (1993): *The Passion of Michel Foucault*. New York: Simon and Schuster.

Moran, Leslie (1996): *The Homosexual(ity) of Law*. London: Routledge.

Murphy, Raymond (1994): *Rationality and Nature – A Sociological Inquiry into a Changing Relationship*. Boulder, Colo.: Westview Press.

Noris, Christopher (1990): *What's Wrong with Postmodernism*. Baltimore: Johns Hopkins University Press.

Oelschlaeger, Max (1995): 'Introduction', in Max Oelschlaeger (ed.), *Postmodern Environmental Ethics*, Albany, NY: SUNY Press, 1–20.

Olivier, Lawrence (1995): *Michel Foucault – Penser au temps du nihilsme*. Montréal: Liber.

Pal, Leslie A. (1990): 'Knowledge, Power and Policy: Reflections on

Foucault', in Stephen Brooks and Alain-G. Gagnon (eds), *Social Scientists, Policy, and the State*, New York: Praeger, 139–58.

Phelan, Shane (1993); 'Intimate Distance: The Dislocation of Nature in Modernity', in Bennett and Chaloupka (eds), *In the Nature of Things*, Minneapolis: University of Minnesota Press, 44–62.

Porter, Roy (1977): *The Making of Geology – Earth Science in Britain 1660–1815*. Cambridge: Cambridge University Press.

Poster, Mark (1985): *Foucault, Marxism and History*. Cambridge: Polity.

Ravetz, Jerome R. (1987): 'Usable Knowledge, Usable Ignorance', *Knowledge*, 9, 87–116.

Redclift, Michael R. and Woodgate, Graham (1997): 'Sustainability and Social Construction', in Michael Redclift and Graham Woodgate (eds), *The International Handbook of Environmental Sociology*, Cheltenham: Edward Elgar, 55–70.

Rorty, Richard (1989): *Contingency, Irony and Solidarity*. Cambridge: Cambridge University Press.

Rose, Nikolas (1990): *Governing the Soul —The Shaping of the Private Self*. London: Routledge.

Ross, Andrew (1994): *The Chicago Gangster Theory of Life: Ecology, Culture, and Society*. New York: Verso.

Rouse, Joseph (1987): *Knowledge and Power: Towards a Political Philosophy of Science*. Ithaca, NY: Cornell University Press.

Rousseau, G. S. and Porter, Roy (eds) (1980): *The Ferment of Knowledge – Studies in the Historiography of 18th Century Science*. Cambridge: Cambridge University Press.

Rutherford, Paul (1993): 'Foucault's Concept of Biopower: Implications for Environmental Politics', in I. Thomas (ed.), *Ecopolitics VI: Interactions and Actions*, Melbourne: Royal Melbourne Institute of Technology.

Rutherford, Paul (1994a): 'The Administration of Life: Ecological Discourse as "Intellectual Machinery of Government"', *Australian Journal of Communication*, 21(3), 40–55.

Rutherford, Paul (1994b): 'Foucault and Ecological Governmentality', paper read at Foucault, Politics and Freedom Conference, April 1994, at the University of Melbourne.

Sachs, Wolfgang (ed.) (1993): *Global Ecology – A New Arena of Political Conflict*. London: Zed Books.

Said, Edward W. (1978b): 'The Problem of Textuality: Two Exemplary Positions', *Critical Inquiry*, 4, 673–714. Reprinted in Smart (ed.), *Michel Foucault – Critical Assessments*, London: Routledge, 1994, vol. 2, 88–123.

Sarup, Madan (1989): *An Introductory Guide to Post-Structuralism and Postmodernism*. Athens, Ga.; University of Georgia Press.

Seery, John Evan (1990): *Political Returns – Irony in Politics and*

Theory from Plato to the Antinuclear Movement. Boulder, Colo.: Westview Press.

Sessions, George (1995a): 'Postmodernism, Environmental Justice, and the Demise of the Ecology Movement?', *The Wild Duck: Literature and Letters of Northern California*, June/July.

Sessions, George (1995b): 'Reinventing Nature: The End of Wilderness?', *The Wild Duck: Literature and Letters of Northern California*, Nov.

Sheridan, Alan (1980): *Michel Foucault: The Will to Truth.* London: Tavistock.

Simmons, Ian G. (1993): *Interpreting Nature – Cultural Constructions of the Environment.* London: Routledge.

Simon, Julian L. and Kahn, Herman (1984): *The Resourceful Earth.* Oxford: Blackwell.

Smart, Barry (1983): *Foucault, Marxism and Critique.* London: Routledge and Kegan Paul.

Smart, Barry (1993): *Postmodernity.* London: Routledge.

Smart, Barry (ed.) (1994): *Michel Foucault – Critical Assessments*, 3 vols. London: Routledge.

Soper, Kate (1995): *What is Nature? Culture, Politics and the non-Human.* Oxford: Blackwell.

Soper, Kate (1996): 'Nature/"Nature", in George Robertson et al. (eds), *Future Natural – Nature/Science/Culture*, London: Routledge, 22–34.

Soulé, Michael E. and Lease, Gary (eds) (1995): *Reinventing Nature? Responses to Postmodern Deconstruction.* Washington, DC: Island Press.

Stychin, Carl F. (1995): *Law's Desire – Sexuality and the Limits of Justice.* London: Routledge.

Taylor, Charles (1971): 'Interpretation and the Social Sciences of Man', *Review of Metaphysics*, 24, 3–51.

Taylor, Charles (1980): 'Understanding in the Human Sciences', *Review of Metaphysics*, 33, 25–8.

Taylor, Charles (1985): *Human Agency and Language: Philosophical Papers I.* Cambridge: Cambridge University Press.

Taylor, Charles (1987): 'Overcoming Epistemology', in Kenneth Baynes, James Boham and Thomas McCarthy (eds), *After Philosophy*, Cambridge, Mass.: MIT Press, 464–88.

Taylor, Charles (1989): *Sources of the Self – The Making of Modern Identity.* Cambridge, Mass.: Harvard University Press.

Terry, Jennifer (1991): 'Theorizing Deviant Historiography', *Differences: A Journal of Feminist Cultural Studies*, 3(2), 55–74.

Tully, James (1993a): 'Governing Conduct: Locke on the Reform of Thought and Behaviour', in James Tully, *An Approach to Political*

Philosophy: Locke in Contexts, Cambridge: Cambridge University Press, 179–241.

Visker, Rudi (1995): *Michel Foucault – Genealogy as Critique*. London: Verso.

Weeks, Jeffrey (1985): *Sexuality and its Discontents: Meanings, Myths, and Modern Sexualities*. London: Routledge and Kegan Paul.

Woolgar, Steve (1988): *Science: The Very Idea*. London: Tavistock.

Wynne, Brian (1994): 'Scientific Knowledge and the Global Environment', in Michael Redclift and Ted Benton (eds), *Social Theory and the Global Environment*, London: Routledge, 169–89.

Zimmerman, Michael E. (1994): *Contesting Earth's Future – Radical Ecology and Postmodernity*. Berkeley: University of California Press.

Zimmerman, Michael E. (1996): 'The Postmodern Challenge to Environmentalism', *Terra Nova – Nature and Culture*, 1(2), 131–40.

[9]
Society, Nature, Knowledge: Co-constructing the Social and the Natural

We must find another relationship to nature beside reification, possession, appropriation and nostalgia. No longer able to sustain the fictions of being either subjects or objects, all the partners in the potent conversations that constitute nature must find a new ground for making meanings together.

> Haraway 1995, p. 70

Real *things* are independent of us, but what it *means* to be real depends on us ... in order to understand what it means to be real, we have to look at how things present themselves as real *in the context of human life*.

> Polt 1999, p. 82[1]

We now consider the implications of the previous chapters for the sociological analysis of the environment and for environmental practice. Beginning with a review of the realist–constructivist debate within environmental sociology and a clarification of the constructivist perspective in particular, we look to the future through the concept of co-construction. As I suggest, such a perspective encourages us not only to frame environmental matters differently but also to take a critical look at the construction of the 'social' within the discipline (even if the 'social construction of the social' sounds an improbable catch phrase). We then move on to consider the practical significance of sociological inquiry for environmental policy-making and action.

162   *Society, Nature, Knowledge*

> Sociology and the Environment *concludes with a plea for theoretical pluralism and open-mindedness. Rather than imposing a single intellectual framework, we should stay alert to the new sociological possibilities in this emerging area of scholarship, research and practice.*

This book began with the general argument that sociology can no longer afford to disregard the natural environment. In making such an uncontroversial point, it was also stressed that this sociological disregard is not a mere oversight (if such were possible) but has been built upon a particular dualism between science and social science. According to the conventional viewpoint, science deals with nature and sociology with society. As we have suggested, an acceptance of this division of intellectual labour either leads to a weak and subordinated position for the discipline (dealing with the 'soft' side of environmental problems) or a sociological dismissal of the natural (as if only 'social' issues deserved attention). Either way, the crude social/natural separation is analytically flawed and practically unhelpful.

However, and as we saw in the Introduction, the increasing acceptance by sociologists of the need to engage with environmental issues has led to the incorporation of this same dualism within the discipline itself – and hence the entrenched battle between realists and constructivists. Simply put, whilst one group maintains the ultimately real (or natural) character of environmental problems and concerns, another emphasizes the centrality of human constructions and social interpretations. Whilst realists trade on the objectivity of environmental problems, constructivists are accused of social reductionism (i.e. of eliminating anything other than social causes from their analyses). Either way, the same social–natural duality remains in operation but is now embedded within the discipline itself.

From a realist perspective, it is essential to recognize that the natural ultimately exists apart from social constructions and cultural projections. For constructivists, there are broadly two kinds of response to this reassertion of a social–natural distinction. The majority form of 'mild' constructivism acknowledges that there is indeed a distinct realm of the natural but argues that this is not necessarily relevant to the social selection and treatment of environmental problems. Meanwhile, a smaller number of radical or 'strong' constructivists argue that, since truth is the outcome of (rather than input to) social negotiations and processes, there is little to be gained (and a lot to be lost) by assuming that nature is a predetermined category. The realist response to strong constructivist claims is to suggest that such an approach has overwhelming analytical flaws (since it cannot distinguish between the social and the natural) and offers no basis for practical action.

In this final chapter, I want to review the realist–constructivist debate briefly before clarifying the perspective advocated in this book: a perspective that has aimed to move beyond the social/natural dichotomy (*either* environmental problems are real *or* they're constructed). Rather than getting bogged down in a philosophically unresolvable and sociologically distracting debate, we have attempted instead to address the more complex, dynamic and hybrid character of environmental issues and concerns. Equally, and rather than attempting to reduce the issues and processes at work to a crude two-dimensional model, the previous chapters have tried to enrich the sociological understanding of social–environmental relations. Within such an approach, it is especially important to explore the non-discrete character of environmental problems and issues. The environment does not sit apart from everyday reality but is encountered, constructed and shaped by a range of social and institutional processes.

In presenting this concluding review, I will focus on two key questions:

1. How should we conceptualize the relationship between sociology and the environment (and, more specifically, between the social and the natural)?
2. What does this mean for the relationship between sociology and environmental practice?

Basic background to this debate was presented in the Introduction and it might be helpful to re-read the relevant section ('Elements of an Environmental Sociology') before continuing here.

Constructive Realists and Real Constructivists: The Social–Natural Debate in Environmental Sociology

...the by now rather dull debate between 'realists' and 'constructivists'. (Macnaghten and Urry 1998, p. 2)

It would be misleading to conclude on the constructivist–realist debate without placing it in a wider intellectual context – although how this context is defined depends very much on the particular stance one adopts. Right now, so-called 'relativism' is under attack from a number of directions and especially for what is presented as its intellectual pretensions and practical irrelevance. Furthermore, whilst many of the constructivist perspectives presented in this book would characteristically distance themselves from (or at least treat very cautiously) the language of postmodernism, this has not prevented various critics of constructivism from making that connection in a decidedly negative fashion.

In one illustration of these contested connections, Hannigan (1995) deals very circumspectly with the possible linkage between his version of constructionism and arguments over the postmodern. He notes that there may be various 'echoes' of postmodernism in his analysis of environmental problems. Thus, constructivism typically suggests a deconstruction of fixed analytical categories (such as science and truth) and a suspicion of 'grand narrative'. Certainly, a congruity can be identified between the constructivist perspectives offered in previous chapters of this book and Zygmunt Bauman's (1992) account of a postmodern world where old certainties have faded and unsettling uncertainties have taken their place.

However, Hannigan rightly observes that 'most environmental researchers who have considered the matter have shied away from adopting a postmodernist perspective' (1995, p. 181). Thus, the SSK perspective indicates that scientific knowledge still retains substantial significance within contemporary social life. At the same time, the examples in previous chapters of the public reconstruction of environmental knowledges are not suggestive of a widespread loss of social identity. Furthermore, Beck's influential account of the risk society is explicitly designed to draw on certain elements of postmodern discourse whilst offering a criticism of what he regards as its broad and ill-focused perspective.[2] Latour (1992) too has objected to talk of postmodernity on the grounds that 'we have never been modern' in the first place. At a methodological level, SSK's commitment to 'following the actors' is very different from the more sweeping and less empirical style of postmodern philosophy.

Despite these important points of contrast, for realist critics constructivism has been seen to suffer from many of the same faults as have been attributed to postmodernism. John Barry (1999, pp. 171–5) presents the social constructionist approach of Hannigan as closely linked to the 'postmodern engagement with

Society, Nature, Knowledge   165

the environment'. In line with my argument in previous chapters, Barry notes:

> While most social constructionist approaches, such as postmod-
> ernism, would not go so far as to deny the reality of environmental
> problems, the important point they raise is that in analysing environ-
> mental issues one must be aware of the different actors, claims, types
> of knowledge, communication and cultural contexts in which these
> problems are articulated, contested, presented and re-presented. (ibid.,
> p. 171)

However, Barry also argues that such 'postmodern analysis' is incapable of dealing with the 'political economy' of environmental
destruction. Equally, it can engage neither with environmental politics nor with the material dimensions of environmental problems.
Such charges are characteristic of a realist critique of social
constructivism.

A better known (or perhaps more infamous) attack on the
claimed 'cognitive' or 'epistemic' relativism of constructivists
such as Bruno Latour has been presented by Alan Sokal and his
collaborator Jean Bricmont. Sokal, a professor of physics, set
out to undermine postmodernism[3] in very direct fashion. Sokal
submitted to a leading US cultural studies journal a paper entitled
'Transgressing boundaries: towards a transformative hermeneutics
of quantum gravity'. He wrote the paper as a parody of the postmodern treatment of science: full of intentional absurdities and
non sequiturs, deliberately asserting an extreme form of cognitive
relativism, proclaiming that 'physical "reality", no less than social
"reality" is at bottom a social and linguistic construct' (Sokal
and Bricmont 1998, p. 2). Sokal's moment of triumph came
when the paper was published in 1996 by editors who were
unaware of its subversive and satirical intent. Sokal then announced his successful hoax: 'For the editors of *Social Text*, it was
hard to imagine a more radical way of shooting themselves in the
foot' (ibid.).

The 'Sokal affair' attracted substantial attention and was further
fuelled by the publication in the late 1990s of a book by Sokal and
Bricmont, which extended the line of attack so as to include writers
such as Jean Baudrillard, Jacques Lacan, Julia Kristeva and Bruno
Latour. 'Postmodern' authors were accused of abusing scientific concepts and terminology (either by using scientific ideas totally outside
their proper context or 'throwing around scientific jargon') and/or

of espousing 'epistemic relativism' (the idea that modern science is 'nothing more' than a myth, a narration or a social construction). Tarred with the same brush as a diverse body of Sokal-branded postmodernists, social constructivism was put very much on the defensive.

In the scholarly setting of sociological arguments over the environment, realist critics of social constructivism have been rather more specific in their targeting. Realists have acknowledged an inevitable element of social construction in all knowledge claims since, as Dickens suggests, 'No knowledge has fallen out of the sky with a label attached pronouncing "absolute truth"' (1996, p. 71). However, it has been axiomatic for realists to maintain that 'the fact that knowledge is socially constituted does not entail that knowledge is *only* socially constituted' (ibid., p. 72). Whilst acknowledging an unavoidable element of overlap, the fundamental argument is that the social and natural worlds are ultimately distinct from one another. It follows that, whilst 'mild' constructivism is of some (albeit limited) value, more radical claims (of the kind deemed 'postmodern' in character) should be dismissed as no more than sociological reductionism.

In a useful review of this debate, Burningham and Cooper observe that the critique 'is not simply that social constructionism is incorrect in denying independent agency to the natural world, but also that the position is dangerous and morally or ethically wrong' (1999, p. 300). Certainly, one prevalent criticism of constructivism has been that it represents a disengagement from pressing environmental problems: an indulgence in sociological pyrotechnics whilst the rainforest burns.[4] In response to these charges, Burningham and Cooper suggest that most forms of constructivism acknowledge the existence of the natural world, and argue, very importantly, that even strong constructivism can engage usefully with environmental and ethical problems.

The starting-point for this defence of a constructivist perspective is a closer consideration of the more specific arguments being made by constructivist sociologists. Just as sophisticated realists such as Dickens acknowledge the relevance of some element of social construction in our interpretation of nature, most environmental constructivists do not correspond to the demonizing presented by Sokal or the sterility and over-abstraction alleged by realist critics such as Martell and Dunlap.

Instead, and as we have argued here, an SSK perspective specifically draws attention to the more detailed and nuanced treatment of risk and environmental issues within specific contexts. In the attacks on constructivists for their alleged sociological reductionism and lack of environmental concern, this more specific and context-sensitive analysis is usually overlooked. Instead, the realist onslaught tends to be played out at an abstract and categorical level and in terms of headlines rather than empirical studies. One immediate defence of the constructivist position is therefore that it brings *more* rather than less 'reality' to the issues (and especially in terms of social and cultural processes). Jasanoff puts this point as follows in a wider discussion of the constructivist perspective within science and technology studies (STS);

> It is, of course, profoundly misleading to identify the idea of decon-struction that has developed in STS scholarship with relativism or a denial of reality. On the contrary, the constructivist strain in STS represents, quite possibly, the most dedicated attempt to grasp the nature of reality that is currently underway in any of the social sciences. (1999, p. 66)

As Burningham and Cooper observe, most constructivist accounts in this area deliberately distance themselves from epistemic relativism and environmental quietism. Thus, it is actually rather hard to find constructivist accounts that fail to acknowledge the importance of natural and material factors. To take two quotations from authors in the constructivist and discursive tradition:

> [T]o show that a social problem has been socially constructed is not to undermine or debunk it; both valid and invalid social problem claims have to be constructed. The detachment required for social science should not become an excuse for cynical inaction. (Yearley 1991, p. 186)

> [J]ust because something is socially interpreted does not mean it is unreal. Pollution does cause illness, species do become extinct. . . . But people can make very different things of these phenomena. (Dryzek 1997, p. 10)

Although, as we have seen, Barry may have no hesitation in placing Hannigan within the 'postmodern' category, Hannigan's own position is self-consciously distanced from relativism: 'I am not by any means attracted to an extreme constructionist position which insists that the global ensemble of problems is purely a creation of the media (or science or ecological activists) with little basis in objective conditions' (Hannigan 1995, p. 3). Closer consideration therefore suggests that the attack on what we might term 'unrestrained and unprincipled' constructivism is largely wide of the mark within environmental sociology. Perhaps because of the general intellectual climate as demonstrated by the Sokal affair, but also a genuine desire to engage with environmental problems, there appears instead to be considerable caution about even appearing to deny the importance of natural causes.

The apparent animosity directed towards constructivism appears something of an over-reaction given the moderate claims generally put forward.[5] At the same time, and very importantly, the realist–constructivist divide seems more bridgeable than it is often presented – especially when we move beyond the cruder definition of both realism and constructivism.

As we can see from the above quotations, the argument being made by constructivists is *not* that the natural environment is a mirage or fantasy but rather that our only way of interpreting (or 'knowing') this environment is through human and social processes. Rather than making an ontological judgement (about how the world is), constructivism is characteristically stressing the unavoidable problems of epistemology (in coming to know about the world). Presented in this way, it may be that this entrenched battle over 'realism versus constructivism' has become rather pointless and, indeed, dull. The challenge instead, as I will argue, is to draw creatively on a broad range of sociological insights – whatever their theoretical provenance. Rather than seeking to reach a non-attainable level of theoretical purity, our objective should be to enhance understanding of the relationship between environmental issues and sociology. In this, the seminar room sniping may have become a distraction rather than a stimulus.

However, and building again upon Burningham and Cooper, this is not to concede that the minority form of 'radical constructivism' is necessarily deficient in analytical terms or incapable of environmental engagement. As Burningham and Cooper observe, even 'strong' arguments about the social construction of environmental reality may be based less on a denial of the natural world than on analytical scepticism and the methodological imperative to maintain an agnosticism in the face of competing knowledge claims. Rather than denying the existence of 'nature' (or indeed of reality[6]), they argue that 'radical' constructivists such as Woolgar can be considered as once again drawing our attention to the fundamental difficulties of 'knowing' the world in which we live (a point that has been central in earlier chapters): 'The strict constructionist position, then, can be summarised as a radical scepticism about ontological claims, and not as an ontological claim about the non-existence of (in this case envi-

Society, Nature, Knowledge   169

ronmental) reality' (1999, p. 309). Thus, and to take a vivid example from outside the environmental field, Grint and Woolgar have asked the stark question: what's social about being shot (1997, pp. 140–68)? Taking up the challenge to present a constructivist account of Russian roulette, they rather bluntly characterize the realist stance as 'a bullet is a bullet and no amount of wishful thinking will wish it away' (ibid., p. 153). It is not too hard to imagine a similarly direct assertion being made about global warming or pesticide-related cancers.

In response to the realist challenge, Grint and Woolgar energetically pursue the social constructions and epistemological assumptions involved in reaching the conclusion that someone has been shot by a particular firearm. From the social shaping of the revolver in question to the logical complexities of linking cause and effect, the argument is that social factors are fundamental. However, the point of this provocative treatment is not to deny the existence of a particular reality (in other words to reach an ontological judgement) but rather to argue that we cannot escape social reconstructions. As the previous chapters have repeatedly argued with regard to environmental problems, consequences do not simply present themselves to us in an unproblematic and 'objective' fashion. Or, as Grint and Woolgar put it: 'The sceptical perspective on technology ... does not argue that technology (the bullet) is irrelevant, but it does argue that the process by which we come to know about its relevance is irredeemably social' (ibid., p. 164).

One immediate response to this reinterpretation of the realist–constructivist debate might be to acknowledge the sociological merits of such a position but to insist that such sophistication at the level of epistemology only leads to environmental quietism. Thus, it may be intellectually stimulating and entertaining to unravel the epistemological problems of 'knowing' the environment (or indeed that one has been shot), but it leaves us without any tools (or weapons) when dealing with environmental problems. Are we not at risk of turning pressing environmental problems into a language game and of building sociological careers on a wilful obfuscation of the world in which we live? Put differently, can we afford such analysis when the problems are so pressing?

There are a number of possible responses to this question of environmental engagement. One plausible argument is that it is not a necessary responsibility on the sociologist to get involved in this fashion. After all, we don't expect all botanists to campaign for the protection of meadows or every physicist to take a public stand on

170   *Society, Nature, Knowledge*

nuclear power. There is nothing ignoble about sociologists bringing their best analytical skills to bear and then handing over to other parties. Equally, an unwillingness to take sides in environmental controversies should not detract from the quality of analysis – and could indeed enhance this. It may also be that sociology is weakened by an over-enthusiasm to prove its value within the objective frameworks provided by scientific institutions rather than adopting a more critical perspective on the framing of environmental issues and problems. As a variant on this, it could be argued that the epistemological radicalism espoused by constructivism is in itself every bit as important as the more familiar political radicalism demanded by certain realists.

However, and assuming the importance of sociological engagement with the environment (as I have generally argued in the previous chapters), it is not necessarily the case that an acknowledgement of the social constructions at the heart of knowledge claims leads to environmental quietism or inactivity. Whilst certain forms of realism argue that the 'reality' of environmental problems is a precondition for action, the approach advocated in this book emphasizes the judgemental and institutional dimension to environmental engagement. Certainly, a constructivist perspective does not necessarily lead to a dismissal of environmental problems as mere symbols, representations and forms of talk (as is presumably implied by the pejorative usage of the 'postmodern' tag). Instead, to employ the phrase used by Burningham and Cooper, constructivists argue that social scientists should avoid playing the 'ontological trump card' (1999, p. 311):

> There is therefore no reason why a constructionist should not engage in political debate, or make political interventions: however, such an intervention will not justify itself in objectivist terms by making reference to, by suggesting non-mediated access to, or by claiming knowledge of an assumed incontestable reality. In other words ... his or her epistemological privileges have been withdrawn. (ibid., p. 310)

Building on this point, it can be argued that, by avoiding inevitably contestable claims to 'know better' than one's opponents, constructivism opens up the ethical and political choices at the core of environmental engagement. *Rather than presenting sociology as bringing 'truth' to environmental disputes, the constructivist responsibility is to highlight value choices, challenge epistemological assumptions and avoid recourse to unjustifiable certainties.*

Accordingly, there is no reason why constructivism should be incapable of dealing with the political economy of environmental destruction, with environmental politics or with the material dimensions of environmental problems. On the contrary, and whilst constructivism is suspicious of rigidly attributed terms such as 'social interest', 'power' and 'materiality' – preferring again to see these as relationships and social processes rather than fixed categories – there is every reason why constructivism is well placed to explore such matters.

By refusing to accord 'truth' to any party to environmental disputes (including, of course, sociologists), we can be open and imaginative in our exploration of the social reconstructions and alliances at work within environmental politics. Crucially also, constructivist approaches encourage the challenging of existing political and cognitive framings of the environment rather than simply taking them at face value. This suggests that the critical analysis of what is presented as 'environmental reality' (for example, within debates over the best direction for sustainable development) is not a distraction but a practical necessity.

It is also reasonable to argue that there is no absolute requirement on constructivist sociology to maintain a neutral stance within environmental disputes. As the research discussed in chapter 4 implied, it can be entirely proper to take the position of the underdog (in that case, disenfranchised local publics) rather than claiming to analyse objective social conditions or, put more bluntly, adopting a 'God's eye view'. Whilst constructivism suggests the need to be explicit about the researcher's normative commitments, it certainly does not suggest non-engagement or non-commitment.

Co-constructing the Social and the Natural

The previous section was intended to defend constructivist claims against charges of intellectual inadequacy and practical irrelevance. I have argued that, in the wider intellectual climate of attacks on relativism, the more cautious constructivism presented by sociologists and discourse analysts such as Hannigan, Yearley and Dryzek is being inappropriately criticized.

I have also suggested that realist critics have generally neglected the detailed contextual treatments offered by constructivist sociologists – presumably since the critics interpret such research as illustrative of wider theory rather than (as in the SSK tradition) the very core of sociological analysis. To these points it might be added that certain forms of realist sociology may be inclined to take scientific arguments on trust rather than delving more intimately into the social construction of scientific knowledge. Meanwhile, radical constructivists' emphasis on analytical scepticism (on methodological agnosticism in the face of knowledge claims rather than predetermining what is a valid or truthful explanation) is often represented as ontological relativism and a dismissal of the material world.

Going further, I argued that constructivism could indeed be compatible with environmental engagement whilst characteristically emphasizing the conditional nature of knowledge claims. Such an approach has already been identified in chapter 5 with particular regard to the work of Brian Wynne and his argument that social scientists can play an important role in opening up implicit institutional assumptions about environmental decision-making to larger critical scrutiny.

Certainly, the constructivist tradition has been an important inspiration to the previous chapters. Whether exploring the local interpretation of environmental threats, institutional judgements over pesticide safety or the relationship between technology and environmental consequences, the intention has been to identify the cultural assessments and human choices at the heart of environmental action. In this way also, the aim has been to challenge the cruder realist assumptions within 'sustainability talk' and their suggestion that social concerns are secondary to the scientifically framed policy agenda. Instead, social and political matters now appear central to environmental action.

In building upon the emerging constructivist tradition, however, I have also drawn attention to some of the difficulties inherent in this realist–constructivist debate (or, more accurately, *non*-debate) and especially the fundamental constraint of continuing within a dualistic framework. Drawing upon previous chapters, I want to reinforce the point that the analytical challenge is to move *beyond* the natural–social dichotomy. As Demeritt has noted, both conventional realist and conventional constructivist approaches can suffer from the same fundamental limitation: 'Oddly, objectivists and relativists agree about one thing: representations must be explained either by nature or by society but the two transcendences can never be mixed together' (1996, p. 497). Very importantly, it has to be acknowledged that the previously identified tendency for constructivism to be caricatured as denying external reality and as 'quietist' is frequently matched by the constructivist portrayal of realism as simple-mindedly essentialist and scientistic. As we observed in the Introduction, more critical forms of realism are also committed to transcending the nature–society dualism – and, indeed, were pioneers of this argument within environmental sociology (as in the work of Riley E. Dunlap). Far from being unaware of the contested character of scientific understanding, writers such as Dunlap, Dickens and Benton have explicitly attempted to theorize the relationship between society, nature and knowledge – and in a manner that moves beyond this outdated dualism. Realism and constructivism, therefore, face the same sociological challenge – even if the consequent strategies to deal with this have varied substantially.

It may also be that constructivists have failed to distinguish consistently between epistemological anti-realism and ontological relativism. Instead, the tendency has been to push social causation to its logical extreme and then acknowledge that material factors may also be significant.[7] Meanwhile, realists have tended to play the 'ontological trump card' at a decidedly abstract level rather than engaging with the messier world of the laboratory, the advisory group or the field trial. Rather than emphasizing the significance of the natural world and then bringing in the social or vice versa, the apparent need – as suggested in the opening quotation of this chapter from Haraway – is to 'find another relationship to nature'. It is at this point that the notion of 'co-construction' may be of particular value.

Rather than maintaining that the social and the natural are separate entities, I have suggested in this book that these might be better seen as *actively generated co-constructions*. Co-construction as employed here captures the dual process of the social and the natural being varyingly constructed within environmentally related practices and particular contexts. To quote Demeritt again, 'nature and society are feats and co-constructions, not pre-existing tendencies that, in the final instance, can explain it all' (1996, p. 498). The concept of co-construction owes a major debt to social constructivism. However, it also avoids some of the perils of social reductionism inherent in constructivist analysis and takes us away from the sterility of dualistic logic. At the same time, the notion of co-construction forces us to re-evaluate not only the usage of natural arguments within environmental debates but also the shifting definition of the social.

Conducted at a broad theoretical level, the argument over whether a particular phenomenon (for example, the environmental con-

174   *Society, Nature, Knowledge*

sequences of genetically modified foods) is 'real' or 'constructed' appears unresolvable (and ultimately rather futile). Such a stark dichotomy misses the dynamism, richness and significance of this important case. Faced with competing knowledge claims, shifting political alliances, ethical ambiguities, divisions within the biotechnology industry, arguments between nations and ferocious disputes among environmentalists, the insistence that we must distinguish between social and natural factors takes on a sterile and almost theological character. Rather than engaging with the complex processes involved, over-emphasis on the social–natural duality represents a form of disengagement and retreat to the more comfortable world of established social theory and unchallenged natural science.

Accordingly, insistence on the division between the social and the natural becomes a barrier to adequate understanding: a fundamental division, which the realist–constructivist debate is simply reproducing. It can plausibly be argued, based on the evidence of the previous chapters, that the social and the natural can no longer be defined apart from one another. Instead, environmental and social problems draw upon the same nature–culture nexus and, as such, are co-constructed within environmental and sociological discussion.

As Latour (1992) has developed this analysis, rather than finding distinct entities (so that the world in which we live can be categorized into the social and the natural), we have encountered *hybrids*, which cross domains and interlink a diversity of phenomena. Hybrids do not fall into either of the competing categories of social or natural but instead weave together elements of both. No longer separable, humans and non-humans form networks within which it becomes impossible to tell where one ends and the other begins. Was the Chernobyl disaster caused by human or technological failure? Is GM food a social or an environmental problem? Is the destruction of the rainforests a social or natural disaster? In such contexts, the division of the human from the non-human and the social from the natural is a characteristic of contemporary thought that is falling apart under the weight of its own contradictions. Whilst we might attempt to tidy the world into discrete boxes, the current awareness of environmental problems and the difficulties of neatly classifying them remind us that reductionist thinking has severe limitations.

Rather than concerning ourselves with where to draw the line between the social and the natural (a task that is ultimately futile since the line is not fixed but shifting even within specific

Society, Nature, Knowledge   175

social and environmental contexts), we have viewed this very
process of 'line-drawing' (including, for example, various groups
claiming to 'speak for nature') as an important focus for sociological analysis. At the same time, rather than prejudging what
is natural and what is social within environmental debate, the
methodological challenge is to maintain (or at least attempt,
since every analyst brings her own preferences, prejudices
and blindspots) a sceptical perspective on environmental claims-
making.

In chapter 3, we suggested that the mad cows at the centre of the
BSE debate can be varyingly construed as social or natural, just as
the BSE debate itself can be presented as a matter of science or of
politics. Equally, various parties to the controversy have shifted categories within the cut and thrust of debate. The British government
has frequently represented the mad cow issue as essentially scientific
in character (the experts know best), but has at times represented it
as a political battle between the UK and its European partners (the
politicians and civil servants know best). On various occasions also,
government sources have represented the issues as fundamentally economic in character (whatever we know, British farmers must be saved
from extinction).

Sociology needs to be attentive to these multiple, changing and
competing definitions rather than seeking to constrain a highly
dynamic set of discussions within a set of predetermined boxes.
Simply shouting 'it's really social' in the face of those who proclaim
'it's really natural' seems a less than productive basis for environmental sociology.

In chapter 4's discussion of the local construction of environmental threats, we witnessed shifting definitions of environmental issues
and problems. It is quite clear in such cases that the environment does
not simply impact upon social life, but instead that environmental
constructions can serve as projections of wider socially generated
concerns and problems. For example, in the Jarrow case, issues of
cultural identity and social powerlessness provide a wider framework
for a range of local issues.

Environmental problems do not sit apart from everyday life (as if
they were discrete from other issues and concerns) but instead are
accommodated within (and help shape) the social construction of
local reality. Within such situations also, attempts to tell local people
what is 'really' going on (whether from the viewpoints of science,
sociology or official institutions) are likely to be viewed in a critical
(or even dismissive) fashion – again in line with the local construction of everyday meaning.

176   *Society, Nature, Knowledge*

The key point about such environmental constructions is that they should be seen *as fluid rather than fixed*. We should not replace the conventional notion of a 'given' environment with the view that social responses are likewise fixed or static. Instead, the discussion in chapter 4 suggests that environmental attitudes are not simply free-floating (as if waiting for the sociological researcher to come along and 'collect' them) but are *discursively formed within particular social settings and contexts*. The point is not to privilege the social over the natural (as if the former was somehow more real than the latter). Instead, a more open-minded approach is required to both of these categories and their mutually constituted character.

As has been suggested here, environmental *knowledge* is central to these hybrid negotiations. In particular, we have seen that scientific accounts do not possess an unmediated access to the environment but must themselves depend upon, often unacknowledged, assumptions and cultural interpretations. In chapter 5's discussion of pesticides, we considered the tension between attempts to impose a standardized scientific framework for evaluation (especially in the context of European harmonization) and the varying local and national contexts for regulatory science. We have been especially alert to the significance of *social and institutional practices* and the embedded (and embodied) character of environmental assumptions and beliefs. As in the 2,4,5-T and aldrin/dieldrin case-studies, institutions may claim to operate on the basis of objective and universal principles (especially for reasons of social legitimation) but inevitably depend upon cultural understandings and (to use Wynne's term once more) 'naïve sociology'. Thus, negotiations within regulatory science bring together the scientific and the political (how do we convince Brussels that this test failure is insignificant?) alongside the ecological and the economic (how commercially successful is this product likely to be?). In the modern conditions of scientific practice, and especially within fields of such social and technical uncertainty, social assumptions cannot be kept outside the laboratory door but instead form an integral part of scientific assessment.

In more policy-oriented terms, it was suggested that, rather than criticizing the contemporary character of regulatory science – as if with a little more effort a fully standardized and objective system can be reached – the point is to acknowledge the inevitability of contextual assessments but also consider, for example, how greater transparency might be introduced into institutional processes.

Thus, whilst a conventional scientific account might imply that contextual mediation and local negotiation represent unfortunate weaknesses in the system, which can be overcome with 'better science' or greater efforts at standardization, it becomes important to recognize the inevitability of environmental hybrids. Rather than seeking to iron out local and cultural differences within environmental policy-making, the challenge for both sociologists and policy-makers is to build creatively upon an awareness of difference as well as similarity.

The treatment of technology added a new dimension to the discussion of these local, institutional and technical practices. The adverse impact of modern technology is one of the recurrent themes of environmental discussion. I suggested that 'impacts' are not fixed or given but are instead the outcome of social negotiations. Does biotechnology represent a threat to nature or a means of enhancing nature's productivity? In chapter 6, we noted both the differential construction of technologies (as in Zonabend's study of a nuclear community) and, in opposition to technological determinism, the manner in which technology can serve as a 'commonplace' for competing views of our social futures. Both 'technology' and 'nature' were presented as malleable rather than fixed categories.

Our general approach – especially in chapter 4 – has also stressed that there is little point in attempting to calculate whether social and institutional understandings are 'real' or 'imagined'. A more appropriate sociological task is to consider the multiple experiences and constructions of environmental hazard – including, very importantly, the manner in which risk constructions interact with self-identities and wider social understandings. At this point, the relationship between social identity – including local cultural understandings, a sense of institutional and personal trust, the experience of power and powerlessness – and environmental concerns becomes central. However, what I want to emphasize here is that this encourages a fresh look at *social* as well as natural relations. Socially generated knowledges and understandings are not relegated – by comparison with the knowledges and understandings of science – to the level of (mere) perceptions, but represent an important means of interpreting (or making sense of) the world in which we live. Public fears and anxieties are not measured against 'natural' indicators but are seen as valid in themselves. Concepts such as social class and social power are not simply reified (or 'black-boxed') but are seen to be actively constituted and experienced within particular settings. Public

178   *Society, Nature, Knowledge*

fears over the environmental and social consequences of new technologies are not viewed as 'irrational' but instead are granted legitimate status.

These points are further reinforced by the differential and flexible manner in which, for example, the people of Jarrow can portray their own social setting. Whilst Jarrow residents will at times present themselves as culturally separate from even their immediate regional neighbours, they are also capable of constructing a common identity with socially disadvantaged groups elsewhere. The lines of self-identity and social construction are not set in stone but are continually redrawn within different contexts – and, inevitably, reflect the desire to present oneself in particular fashions (as oppressed or empowered, as the same or different, as anxious or playful, as secure or at risk). In these ways, the construction of the social can be as contextual, negotiated and dynamic as that of the natural.

In reconsidering and reconceptualizing the social, an argument is also being made for an empirically grounded sociology that does not simply trade in sweeping generalizations but also considers the complexities (and contextual specificities) of environmental understanding. In this we are indeed seeking to avoid, in Mills's (1973) famous terms, both 'abstracted empiricism' and 'grand theory'. Put more broadly, a changed understanding of the social–natural relationship challenges the conventional boundaries of sociological practice. The social can be considered as no more self-contained, fixed or given than the natural. Sociology enters a more exciting – and risky – territory, where existing categorizations – the social, the natural, the scientific, the technological, the human, the non-human – are seen to be fluid and contextually constituted rather than predetermined. On the one hand, this represents a threat to existing sociological categorizations. On the other, such a reconceptualization allows us to explore the diverse ways in which self-identities and risk experiences interact with and shape one another.

In final illustration of this, the Jarrow case-study raises questions of the relationship between environmental understanding and social powerlessness – especially in a community characterized by high levels of unemployment and relative social deprivation. It would be possible to apply an environmental realist approach to this case: do people worry about real or perceived risks? Equally, a social realist perspective could be adopted: how does environmental awareness relate to socio-economic status? The approach adopted here was instead to consider how residents' own sense of social exclusion related to risk awareness. How, for example, does a sense of one's lack of agency (the ability to change the conditions of one's life) affect response to everyday hazards? Does the construction of environmental problems stand apart from – or interlink with – the experience of other expressed concerns (such as crime, education or employment)? In approaching the issues in this manner, we can identify the discursive formation of categories and the close relationship between these formations and local experience.

Rather than representing a weakness, an acknowledgement of the constructedness of knowledge claims (including those of sociologists) leads to a reconsideration of sociological analysis at a profound level. My argument here is indeed an argument – and one that is open to challenge, criticism and disagreement from a variety of perspectives. The task of sociology is not to produce undying truths but rather to engage, provoke and reconstruct. In that way also, sociology should be seen as dynamic rather than static – as a changing formation rather than as a body of social facts. As Bauman has expressed a similar concept: 'I am rather inclined to see sociology today as an eddy on a fast-moving river, an eddy which retains its shape but changes its content all the time, an eddy which can retain its shape only in so far as there is a constant through-flow of water' (1992, p. 213). As the environmental arena in all its dynamism and speed of movement serves to emphasize, this realization should not lead to frustration or despair but rather to an acknowledgement of the constructed (and constructing) character of sociological investigation. This may well be one of the more valuable points that environmental sociology can draw from the 'postmodern' tradition. To quote Bauman again: '[S]ociology is a transient activity, confined to its time and place. It is part and parcel of the stage in the development of culture and it is no worse for this reason. I think that is precisely where it derives its value from' (ibid., p. 216).

Rather than undermining sociological analysis, an awareness of the co-construction of the social and the natural raises fresh possibilities for sociological analysis. At the same time, the call for an environmental sociology is also a challenge to sociologists to be alert to research emerging from different intellectual traditions. No longer is it possible for sociologists simply to hive off the social bits of the environmental discussion. Instead, a much broader and more challenging role is being created.

As demonstrated in previous chapters, this has taken us to the possibly carcinogenic effects of pesticides, the environmental impact of biotechnology and the operation of a nuclear power plant – areas that may look intimidatingly technical for many sociologists. One major implication of the analysis offered in this book is that a greater openness is required across disciplinary boundaries. This is not to deny the value of disciplinary concerns, but it does suggest the wider intellectual seas across which sociologists will need to navigate if they are serious in their wish to engage with environmental problems and concerns.

The environmental challenge to sociology is also a challenge for sociology to emerge from its self-imposed disciplinary exile and, especially, the social–natural duality that underpins this. In that sense, it is not a problem that environmental concerns and social experiences overlap and intertwine so extensively. Instead, this represents a major challenge for the discipline in advancing from the defensive academic posture it has assumed since its formative years.

Towards an Environmental(ist) Sociology

It follows from the discussion in this chapter that environmental sociology cannot simply ring-fence the social aspects of any environmental problem and then stay safely within recognized home territory. Instead, the challenge is for sociological analysis to explore matters of problem construction, underlying assumptions and the relationship between science, institutions and the policy process. In all this, the sociologist may appear a troubled (and troublesome) figure – more prepared to challenge existing social models and expectations than to state what should be done (how can sociologists claim moral or scientific authority?). Equally, sociology can seem marginal to environmental discussion: able to criticize but not to act, eager to deconstruct existing categories but not to engage or persuade, unhappy with the role of 'underlabourer' (Hannigan 1995, p. 13) but unwilling to adopt a position of intellectual leadership.

In opposition to this characterization, I want to suggest that the sociological approach outlined here can play an important role within environmental discussion. Furthermore, an awareness of the constructed nature of environmental claims opens up new possibilities for environmental action and policy-making. As part of this argument, I would like to emphasize that engagement with practical environmental concerns can be a vital learning experience for sociologists who generally have as much to learn as to offer. Sociologists certainly need to be alert to analyses that emerge from outside the institutional parameters of sociology, but which may nevertheless contain significant sociological insights. Over-concern with the social–natural duality represents a turning-away from such debates rather than a wholehearted and enthusiastic engagement.

Going further, a co-constructivist approach to environmental matters suggests a number of possibilities for practical intervention and contribution. One of the most important of these is the argument that the environment is not a self-contained and discrete entity but a topic and theme that overlap broadly with – and depend upon – social and institutional practices. Whilst 'environmental policy' is often represented as a special subject removed from other areas of governance and social activity, this book has suggested that environmental matters are embedded in a variety of processes and practices: from innovation strategy to local community action, from expert advisory committees to industrial manufacture.

The whole thrust of the co-construction concept is towards the recognition that environmental matters overlap and interconnect with a diversity of social practices. In that way also, it is possible to surmise that environmental change will be a product of a whole range of social practices and not simply of intentional environmental engagement. The international agenda of sustainability may not in the end be as important as smaller changes in social practice that cumulatively and undramatically change our world. Whilst it is relatively easy to focus on high-profile environmental decisions, the incremental shifts of industry, institutional politics and the wider publics may ultimately have greater socio-environmental impact.

To this basic point can be added a number of practical implications from the above discussion. First of all, and as Wynne argued in chapter 5, sociological accounts can be especially useful in opening up the (generally unacknowledged) social assumptions upon which environmental constructions often depend (including, of course, the constructions of scientists). In so doing, a more transparent basis for institutional actions can be established. Equally, sociological analysis is well placed to bring out underlying themes of uncertainty, indeterminacy and ambivalence within environmental assessment. Characteristically, policy processes tend to play down or deny such elements of decision-making.

Sociological accounts are also able to offer a symmetrical treatment of different environmental constructions and, in that sense, can provide a meeting point between competing definitions of environmental problems. For example, effective communication between oppositional groups and government institutions may be impossible so long as environmental issues are framed only in modernistic and scientific terms. In addition, and whilst policy-makers, as in the two case-studies discussed in chapter 4, tend to frame environmental issues within a technical discourse that constructs public responses and concerns as secondary to the facts, sociological explanation is able to explore the deeper-rooted questions of self-identity and local experience, which are linked to environmental concern. More generally, sociological analysis can serve a useful purpose in exploring and expressing the knowledges and expertises of lay groups. Whilst not advocating a form of sociological ventriloquism, a full awareness of competing forms of knowledge (including those generated by lay people as a consequence of living and working in hazardous environments) can make an important contribution to environmental debate.

Meanwhile, and although environmental debates frequently present 'technology' either as an alien presence or as an environmental saviour, the analysis in chapter 6 indicates the social constructedness of technological impacts. In so doing, sociological treatments can suggest (and lend significance to) possibilities for social debate that do not simply lead to a 'pro' or 'anti' dichotomy over technological change.

As Jasanoff has emphasized, not only sociology but also policy analysis has a tendency to take the boundaries between the 'scientific, the social and the technological worlds' as rigid and unalterable. This intellectual and institutional perspective can then lead to a 'premature narrowing in both the framing and solution of perceived problems' (1999, p. 67). Thus, technological fixes and institutional initiatives are imposed on complex socio-technical problems and cultural factors are disregarded in the search for rational solutions. Genetically modified foods are put forward as a sustainable response to pesticide risks and food shortages. European regulatory regimes claim to supersede national systems. International agreements offer new sustainable pathways. In each case, the neglect of the more complex and co-constructed character of the challenges at hand can generate unsatisfactory forms of practical response – as many current initiatives in sustainable development may unfortunately illustrate. Put negatively, inadequate sociological analysis leads directly to inadequate policy response. Put more positively, there is a substantial challenge here for sociologists to demonstrate their social value and make a real contribution to public policy.

There are ample possibilities for new forms of sociological engagement in environmental matters. As I write, new approaches to

Society, Nature, Knowledge   183

deliberative decision-making and inclusive democracy are being increasingly recognized as an important means of testing out the cultural assumptions embedded in policy-making and bringing the fullest range of knowledges and assessments to bear. The precautionary principle is being reassessed as both a technical and social judgement. Narrowly defined 'sound science' is no longer seen as a sufficient basis for decision-making but is under review in terms of the best relationship between science, the wider publics and policy-making. Civil servants and policy-makers are becoming ever more aware of the significance of public trust and credibility. In all of this, sociology has an important role to play in unravelling the connections between society, nature and knowledge and in creating critical and informed deliberation over alternative socio-technical paths.[8]

In the end, the practical role for sociology is not that of environmental arbitrator or judge. The challenge is to open up new possibilities for reflexive and democratic engagement and debate that do not reduce environmental concerns to narrow technical disputes or simple social–natural polarizations. At the same time, a sociological discussion of these issues reveals the intellectual paucity of most environmental discussions – and especially their dependence upon a narrow definition of environmental problems (generally as set by scientific institutions).

Returning to the sustainability agenda, which has proved so significant for environmental discussion since the late 1980s, sociological analysis seems uniquely placed to draw out the value choices, implicit assumptions and epistemological judgements upon which environmental debate seems to depend – but without suggesting that either values or knowledges can exist outside of social relationships and human experiences. Equally, these need to be seen as dynamic rather than static and as contextually generated rather than predetermined. In proposing a more satisfactory understanding of human and non-human relationships, sociology can also draw attention to the social and institutional questions that can be hidden behind scientific and policy constructions. Above all, sociology can recognize that lurking behind 'environmental' problems are a series of very human challenges and questions.

Once we step outside the conventional assumption that the social and the natural can exist independently of one another, fresh possibilities emerge for constructing new relations and more productive forms of dialogue and interaction. For the sociologist, this will mean engagement with a variety of human and non-human agents. In terms of the policy process, the need is for institutional forms that

184   *Society, Nature, Knowledge*

recognize the constructedness of environmental meaning and, in so doing, avoid the conventional pretence that the environment can simply speak for itself.

At this point, a variety of possible initiatives take on new significance: from local attempts to improve the quality of everyday life to discussions of how to draw into practical engagement those who see themselves as socially powerless. The diversity of environmental meanings suggests that there cannot be a single way forward from here. Instead, the sociological study of environmental problems indicates that environmental response is inseparable from larger questions of self-identity, sense of agency, reflexive awareness and trust in institutions. Put in that fashion, our study of environmental concerns has taken us from contemplation of a natural world 'out there' to the consideration of a set of human issues that exist very much within our existing institutions and everyday practices. In addressing environmental matters, we are unavoidably addressing the very constitution of society.

Conclusion

> [T]ruth from a pluralistic vantage point is not a search for the indisputable. Rather, it is more like a tolerance for difference that opens up possibilities and keeps them open. Its focus is not on whether a particular stance is true or false, but whether or not its particular terminology or vocabulary works to intelligibly frame the particular interests of the investigator. Stripped of its claims to universality, truth becomes a 'tool which helps us cope or make sense of the world'. (Kroll-Smith et al., 2000, p. 58)

At an early stage in this book's development, I discussed its structure with a very experienced colleague. The problem, as I explained it, was that there were so many interesting theoretical frameworks and empirical examples available that I couldn't impose any *order* on the material. Her nonchalant reply was 'why not do the usual thing?'. On being met with what was obviously a very blank look, she patiently explained that the 'usual thing' was to establish several competing frameworks, advocate one in particular, and then spend the rest of the book justifying that selection and ignoring (or dismissing) the others.

Pondering this well-intentioned (if rather cynical) advice afterwards, I guiltily realized that the 'usual' response to this academic manoeuvre was for reviewers to perform the same trick in reverse: observe the author's selection of a particular framework, and then either support this or (more likely) bemoan the failure to adopt an alternative/better-informed/richer approach of the sort generally favoured by the reviewer.

Now, just because something is 'usual' doesn't mean that it is wrong. Certainly, academic arguments need structure. Furthermore, it is only proper for competing perspectives to be respectfully reviewed and one's own preferences clearly argued. This at least stimulates engagement and debate – and so fuels the discipline's development. Indeed, such a structure can be discerned in *Sociology and the Environment*. In the latter half of this book, I have specifically advocated a theoretical and empirical perspective that draws on the sociology of scientific knowledge (SSK), science and technology studies (STS) and a broadly constructivist perspective. All of this represents a serious effort at responding to the question first asked in the Preface: what should be the relationship between the discipline of sociology and the study of environmental issues, problems and concerns? However, what I want to emphasize at this stage is that I do *not* want to conclude with the usual justification for 'my' choice.

Rather than pretending that only one sociological perspective still stands and that all the other theoretical bodies can now be dragged lifeless from the stage, I want to emphasize the importance of a pluralistic and open-minded approach to these questions. I recognize that I risk confusing those readers who might prefer at this stage to be given the 'solution' to social–natural relations. However, I would rather encourage further discussion and inquiry than attempt premature closure. At one level, this final plea for pluralism stems from my awareness that there are other sociological approaches and sociological topics than those presented here. Equally, there are alternative ways of dividing the field than the categorizations I have offered.[9] I take great heart from this, since it re-emphasizes the dynamism and diversity of environmental sociology.

This book is very much an invitation to go further than I have been able to do in one text. On that basis also, I do not find it all hard to identify future research sites and theoretical concerns. In fact, the possibilities stretch readily in front of me. In clear illustration of this, the book has said too little about gender, the developing world and concepts of environmental citizenship, environmental politics and environmental justice.

186   Society, Nature, Knowledge

At a more profound level, however, I want to avoid the conclusion that sociological investigation is primarily about vanquishing the opposition or triumphantly brandishing the latest 'truth'. As I have already suggested, for example, whilst the rhetorical clash between realism and constructivism may have usefully served to highlight certain key issues, there is also an important sense in which it has represented a turning away from environmental engagement and sociological research (which I would define as both theoretical and empirical in character).

As I have argued, it may be that the issue of whether the environment is real or constructed is both unresolvable and ultimately irrelevant. Rather than seeking to establish the right line and then relax back into our sociological armchairs, we should critically scrutinize the merits of different approaches but then be prepared to move on in both theoretical and empirical terms. In making this point, I am also arguing that the merits of any framework cannot be judged solely in the abstract but instead stem largely from the new light they shed on the *doing* of sociological research. My case is for theories not simply to be assessed on the basis of their philosophical strengths but also, and very importantly, in terms of how they help us interpret, unravel and contextualize social and environmental problems. In that sense too, there may be more in common between critical realism and social constructivism than is keeping them apart. Equally, philosophical disagreement does not necessarily get in the way of stimulating and insightful research. Furthermore, no theoretical perspective can generate *all* the best ideas.

In adding my modest weight to a particular SSK and constructivist perspective, I am seeking to emphasize a set of sociological concepts and approaches that I believe has been neglected (and at times distorted) within environmental sociology. This is not to deny the importance of other approaches or to downplay the historical and current significance of critical and sophisticated discussions within the 'realist' tradition. From my viewpoint, there is no special merit in tying our conceptual hands behind our back when tackling such challenging and dynamic problems. To quote another sociologist whose work I would rather (critically) celebrate than sweep aside:

I consider realism and constructivism to be neither an either–or option nor a mere matter of belief. We should not have to swear allegiance to any particular view or theoretical perspective. The decision whether to take a realist or a constructivist approach is for me a rather *pragmatic* one, a matter of choosing the appropriate means for a desired goal. (Beck 1999, p. 134; emphasis in orginal)

It is therefore entirely healthy for the discipline that it should be open to alternative perspectives – and that these perspectives should in turn be open to mutual criticism and debate. However, the prime challenge is to find imaginative and creative ways of transcending the social–natural dualism and considering the implications for the discipline and for practical engagement. Rather than narrowing the theoretical and empirical possibilities or backing one approach entirely, it seems more helpful to retain an open-minded and inclusive dialogue over such matters. This of course extends to developments emanating both within and outside the disciplinary boundaries of sociology.

In advocating a particular approach and demonstrating its capacities, it is vital that we also maintain an awareness of the theoretical and empirical opportunities within this exciting field. As I stated in the Preface, my aim has been to stimulate and provoke rather than to place this challenging subject in one tidy corner of the sociological edifice.

Far from standing at the end of a sociological journey, it seems instead that we are only at the beginning.

Chapter 7 Society, Nature, Knowledge

1. Emphasis in original. With thanks to Christina Durkin.
2. Beck argues that 'the philosophies and theories . . . of so-called "post-modernity" . . . cannot answer very basic questions about how and in what ways everyday lives and professional fields are being transformed' (1999, p. 133).
3. Defined by Sokal and Bricmont as 'an intellectual current characterized by the more-or-less explicit rejection of the rationalist tradition of the Enlightenment, by theoretical discourses disconnected from any empirical test, and by a cognitive and cultural relativism that regards science as nothing more than a "narration", a "myth" or a social construction among many others' (1998, p. 1).
4. As it was put to me informally at a North American conference: 'Surely you can only be a constructivist if you don't care about the environment?'
5. 'The constructivist approach has had a pernicious effect on the sociology of environmental issues' (Murphy 1994a, p. 197).
6. For one science-studies based response to the question 'Do you believe in reality?', see Latour 1999.
7. See Collins and Yearley 1992.
8. As an illustration of this positive relationship between social science and environmental policy, see the output from the environmental programme of the UK ESRC: Economic and Social Research Council 2000.
9. See, for example, Kroll-Smith et al. 2000.

References

Barry, J. 1999. *Environment and Social Theory*. London and New York: Routledge.

Bauman, Z. 1992. *Intimations of Postmodernity*. London and New York: Routledge.

Beck, U. 1999; *World Risk Society*. Cambridge: Polity.

Burningham, K. and Cooper, G. 1999: Being constructive: social constructionism and the environment. *Sociology* 33 (2), pp. 297–316.

Collins, H. M. And Yearley, S. 1992: Epistemological chicken. In Pickering, A. (ed.), *Science as Culture and Practice*. Cambridge: Cambridge University Press, pp. 301–26.

Demeritt, D. 1996: Social theory and the reconstruction of science and geography. *Transactions of the Institute of British Geographers* 21, pp. 484–503.

Dickens, P. 1996: *Reconstructing Nature: alienation, emancipation and the division of labour*. London: Routledge.

Dryzek, J. 1997: *The Politics of the Earth: environmental discourses*. Oxford: Oxford University Press.

Economic and Social Research Council (ESRC) Global Environmental Change programme 2000: *Risky Choices, Soft Disasters: environmental decision-making under uncertainty*. University of Sussex, Brighton. *www.gecko.ac.uk*

Grint, K. and Woolgar, S. 1997: *The Machine at Work: technology, work and organization*. Cambridge: Polity.

Hannigan, J. A. 1995: *Environmental Sociology: a social constructionist perspective*. London and New York: Routledge.

Haraway, D. 1995: Otherworldly conversations, terran topics, local terms. In Shiva, V. and Moser, I. (eds), *Biopolitics, a feminist and ecological reader on biotechnology*. London and New Jersey: Zed Books, pp. 69–92.

Jasanoff, S. 1999: STS and public policy: getting beyond deconstruction. *Science, Technology and Society* 4 (1), pp. 59–72.

Kroll-Smith, J. S., Gunter, V. and Laska, S. Spring 2000: Theoretical stances and environmental debates: reconciling the physical and the symbolic. *The American Sociologist*, pp. 44–61.

Latour, B. 1992: *We Have Never Been Modern*. London: Harvester Wheatsheaf.

Macnaghten, P. and Urry, J. 1998: *Contested Natures*. London, Thousand Oaks, New Delhi: Sage.

Mills, C. W. 1973: *The Sociological Imagination*. Harmondsworth: Penguin.

Murphy, R. 1994a: *Rationality and Nature: a sociological inquiry into a changing relationship*. Boulder, San Francisco, Oxford: Westview Press.

Polt, R. 1999: *Heidegger; an introduction*. London: UCL Press.

Sokal, A. and Bricmont, J. 1998: *Intellectual Impostures: postmodern philosophers' abuse of science*. London: Profile Books.

Yearley, S. 1991: *The Green Case: a sociology of environmental issues, arguments and politics*. London: HarperCollins.

Zonabend, F. 1993: *The Nuclear Peninsula*. Cambridge: Cambridge University Press.

Part II
Ecological Modernisation

[10]

PERGAMON

Geoforum 31 (2000) 1–8

GEOFORUM

www.elsevier.com/locate/geoforum

Editorial

Ecological modernisation

1. Introduction

During the 1980s and early 1990s ecological modernisation was discussed and developed by a relatively small group of environmental social scientists, particularly within politics and sociology. From here interest spread to other disciplines, such as geography, whilst the sphere of influence expanded away from Germany to the Netherlands, the UK and the USA. The growth of academic interest in ecological modernisation is such that it is now becoming part of mainstream debate in the environmental social sciences. Indeed most of those working on the relationship between environment and society and focussing on the state, production and consumption are likely to be aware of it. If evidence is needed to support this claim then it is found in the discussion of ecological modernisation by social theorists such as David Harvey (1996, pp. 377–383) in *Justice, Nature and the Geography of Difference* and Anthony Giddens (1998, pp. 57–58) in *The Third Way*.

Outside academia programmes of environmental action which are informed by ideas of ecological modernisation and which can usefully be interpreted from an ecological modernisation perspective have also become more widespread. This is particularly the case with respect to strategic environmental planning by governments and the restructuring of production by some major manufacturers. The most often used example of a country putting ecological modernisation into practice is the Netherlands. The series of National Environmental Policy Plans and associated instruments developed and implemented by the Dutch government throughout the 1990s has had a major impact on the ecological modernisation debate. With respect to production the chemicals industry in the Netherlands has also been used as a case example (see for example, Weale, 1992; Hajer, 1995; Mol, 1995; Gouldson and Murphy, 1998).

This growing interest in ecological modernisation, within academia and without, makes a special issue of *Geoforum* timely. In putting this collection together I have attempted, with the help of the other authors, to achieve a number of things. Most importantly the aim of the collection is to develop the ecological modernisation debate theoretically and empirically. Beyond this I have tried to put together a collection of papers that reflects the international scope of the ecological modernisation

debate. The intention also has been to produce a volume that is firmly grounded with respect to all the existing literature. This latter point is important because there has been a tendency recently in ecological modernisation discussions to focus almost exclusively on specific contributions, particularly that of Hajer (1995), without acknowledging the other work in the area. Although Hajer's work is very important the exclusive attention it has received by some writers has skewed the debate considerably, at the expense of work which is arguably more significant, particularly that of Mol (1995).

Finally, in this collection, and again with the help of the other authors, I have attempted to clear up some misunderstandings and to address some of the poorly conceived criticisms that surround the ecological modernisation debate. One common error, for example, involves the failure to clearly distinguish between the analytical and prescriptive dimensions of ecological modernisation. A second one involves the prescriptive dimension of ecological modernisation. That is to view it as a free market approach to solving environmental problems. A third is to assume that those writing about ecological modernisation are uncritically offering it as a way of solving contemporary environmental problems. I hope that this collection goes some way to addressing these misconceptions.

As part of the introduction to this collection I will set the scene by reviewing the important literature in the area. This should help to familiarise readers with the theory if they have not encountered it before. Because each of the following papers draws on this literature it will also provide background detail for the papers themselves. The review is structured in a way that follows the development of ecological modernisation theory over time, whilst also identifying important commentators. Five dimensions of the ecological modernisation literature are discussed and following that some of the main weaknesses of the literature are identified.

2. Technology, entrepreneurs and the transformation of society

Following Mol (1995, pp. 34–40) it is useful first of all to introduce ecological modernisation theory as a

2 Editorial / Geoforum 31 (2000) 1–8

theory of unplanned social change. This will allow the work of Joseph Huber to be considered whilst at the same time establishing the nature of ecological modernisation more concretely. Mol argues that Joseph Huber should be acknowledged as the father of ecological modernisation theory due to his theoretical contributions to the environment and society debate from the 1980s onwards. In this work, Huber (1982, 1984, 1985) began to promote the idea that environmental problems could be addressed through superindustrialisation.

For Huber superindustrialisation involves addressing environmental problems primarily through the transformation of production via the development and application of more sophisticated technologies. In the third of his trilogy written in the 1980s Huber established the spirit of ecological modernisation as a solution to environmental problems when he said that:

> ... the dirty and ugly industrial caterpillar will transform into a[n] ecological butterfly. (Huber, 1985, p. 20 as quoted by Mol, 1995, p. 37)

Concerning the role of government in this process, Huber believed that a limited amount of intervention was desirable. Consistent with a lot of free market economic theory at the time he felt that government involvement was as likely to confound the process of innovation as it was to produce useful outcomes. He also argued that new social movements, such as the environmental movement, had a limited role to play in bringing about a shift to a more environmentally benign form of industrial society. Economic actors and entrepreneurs were identified as most important in achieving the transformation associated with ecological modernisation.

Huber also proposed that ecological modernisation was an inevitable phase in the development of industrial society. He argued that ecological modernisation is a phase that follows industrial breakthrough (1789–1848) and the construction of industrial society (1848–1980). Throughout all three stages the driving forces are the economy and technology but the third stage of development is driven by the need to reconcile the impacts of human activity with the environment. Huber was convinced that this would be done through ecological modernisation because the associated programme of action fits conveniently with existing social structures.

3. Macroeconomic restructuring: the gratis effect

Subsequent work has selectively built on Huber's ideas. His emphasis on technology has been supplemented, for example, by interest in the role of macroeconomic structural change as a result of Martin Jänicke

and Udo Simonis's work (Jänicke, 1985; Jänicke et al., 1988, 1989; Simmonis, 1989a,b). These authors emphasise that a central element of ecological modernisation is the restructuring of national economies involving both their technological and sectoral composition. As described by Gouldson and Murphy (1997, p. 75):

> ... ecological modernisation seeks structural change at the macro-economic level. It looks for industrial sectors which combine higher levels of economic development with lower levels of environmental impact. In particular, it seeks to shift the emphasis of the macro-economy away from energy and resource intensive industries towards service and knowledge intensive industries.

This represents partial de-industrialisation and may involve the phasing out of ecologically 'maladjusted' technical systems and economic sectors that cannot be reconciled with environmental goals.

In a series of papers Jänicke and Simonis established the potential for structural change to solve some environmental problems at the national level by examining the growth trajectories of a range of national economies in association with their consumption of basic resources. In this work the authors recorded the growth of gross domestic product (GDP) in a range of countries including, for example, the Federal Republic of Germany, Japan, and Czechoslovakia. They then examined changes in a number of variables in each of these countries that had associated environmental impacts, e.g. crude steel consumption, weight of freight transport (road and rail), energy consumption and cement consumption. These variables therefore acted as proxy variables for environmental impact.

The results of this kind of analysis indicated that the evolution of these economies had significant implications for environmental impacts. In the case of the Federal Republic of Germany, for example, it was shown that from at least 1960 there had been an almost continuous increase in GDP year on year. However, from 1973 onwards the consumption of cement and steel began to decrease slightly and from 1979 onwards the same happened with energy consumption and the weight of freight transport. Essentially, the authors' argued, the growth of GDP had de-linked itself from these variables and this had positive implications for the environment.

As a result of this kind of analysis Jänicke and Simonis have described an environmental gratis effect – environmental benefit which results seemingly unintentionally from macro-economic structural changes that take place as advanced industrial economies evolve. They have also argued that such macro-economic restructuring is an important dimension of ecological modernisation.

Editorial / Geoforum 31 (2000) 1–8 3

4. The new politics of pollution

A third strand to the ecological modernisation debate is the assessment of the environmental policy choices of governments against what would be consistent with actual ecological modernisation. This type of work generally accepts the prescriptions that can be derived from the theory of ecological modernisation as being at the forefront of policy-making, whilst not saying that they will necessarily solve environmental problems. A list of such policy prescriptions can be inferred from the arguments associated with the theory. In particular it focuses on the changing nature of environmental policy, regulation and decision making. Examples of work in this group is that of Weale (1992), Gouldson and Murphy (1996, 1998) and to some extent Boehmer-Christiansen and Weidner (1995).

In this literature the theory of ecological modernisation is understood as suggesting a government-led programme of action with various key elements. First, to be consistent with ecological modernisation it is argued that policy must be based on its central tenet – that there is no necessary conflict between environmental protection and economic growth and that they may in fact be mutually supportive. To investigate this further the nature of national environmental policies has been examined. For example, Weale (1992) examined the Dutch National Environmental Policy Plan and concluded that its interventionist approach, and the way that it attempted to stimulate innovation through the setting of strict environmental targets, established it as an example of policy consistent with the theory of ecological modernisation.

Second, the integration of environmental policy goals into all policy areas of government is considered as central to a programme of ecological modernisation. Thus ecological modernisation recognises that effective environmental protection can only be achieved through a realignment of broader policy goals relating to areas such as economics, energy, transport and trade. Ecological modernisation requires strong integration with the strategic and operational characteristics of government departments modified to the extent that their original character may be lost altogether.

Third, there is a theme of exploring alternative and innovative approaches to environmental policy within ecological modernisation theory. For example, Mol (1995) identifies the "economization of ecology" as central to ecological modernisation, meaning the introduction of economic concepts, mechanisms and principles into environmental policy. This may involve placing an economic value on nature with the general aim of encouraging economic actors to take the environment into consideration. However, also attracting a considerable amount of attention has been the role for voluntary agreements, such as the Dutch covenanting system, where firms sign up voluntarily to reduce polluting emissions (see Gouldson and Murphy, 1998). The overall argument here is that new ways of thinking about the relationship between the state and industry should be explored with the broad aim of reregulating (but not deregulating) the environment.

Fourth, because ecological modernisation is based on the invention, innovation and diffusion of new technologies and techniques of operating industrial processes government action in these areas is a focus of ecological modernisation theory. As stated by Weale (1992, p. 78):

> Public intervention... is an essential part of ensuring a progressive relationship between industry and environment... implicit is a positive role for public authority in raising the standards of environmental regulation, as a means of providing a spur to industrial innovation.

Therefore, by deriving a set of policy principles and approaches from the theory of ecological modernisation it is possible to assess individual governments against these to determine the extent to which they have adopted the ideas of ecological modernisation, or, to use Weale's phrase, "the new politics of pollution". Using this kind of approach the Netherlands, Germany and Japan, for example, have been identified as countries that have broadly adopted an ecological modernisation position.

5. Cultural politics and discourse

The fourth dimension of ecological modernisation is to view it as an example of cultural politics and discourse. This strand of work has been developed mainly by Hajer (1995, 1996), particularly in the book *The Politics of Environmental Discourse: Ecological Modernization and the Policy Process*, but more recently Dryzek (1997) has followed a similar line in *The Politics of the Earth: Environmental Discourses*.

The cultural politics perspective on ecological modernisation, according to Hajer (1996, p. 256), asks:

> ... why certain aspects of reality are now singled out as 'our common problems' and wonders what sort of society is being created in the name of protecting 'nature'.

In other words it analyses the social construction of environmental issues.

From this perspective a very critical view of problem claims and solution claims can be adopted. It is suggested that crucial political issues are hidden behind discursive constructs and the aim is to reveal the "feeble basis" upon which one particular choice of development path,

4   Editorial / Geoforum 31 (2000) 1–8

such as ecological modernisation, is made. For Hajer this is done by examining discourse, principally through the concepts of story-lines and discourse-coalitions. From Hajer's (1995, p. 64) perspective ecological modernisation can be usefully interpreted this way:

> Ecological modernization is based on some credible and attractive story-lines: the regulation of the environmental problem appears as a positive-sum game; pollution is a matter of inefficiency, nature has a balance that should be respected; anticipation is better than cure... Each story-line replaces complex disciplinary debates.

Consequently Hajer develops a specific view of environmental politics which he views as constituted by discourse. From this standpoint environmental conflicts do not appear to be primarily conflicts over what sort of action should be taken, or whether action should be taken at all, but over the interpretation of physical and social phenomena.

To illustrate this approach empirically Hajer (1995) has described the discourse coalitions that were present in acid rain politics in the UK and the Netherlands during the 1980s and early 1990s. Broadly he argues that in the UK the traditional approach to policy rebuffed the discourse of ecological modernisation although the Netherlands did adopt it to some extent. However, in the latter case, this was because of existing social and institutional affinities for the discourse, and because of the need for arguments that could move beyond the presumed conflict between environment and economy. It was not adopted as a result of any objective quality or truth that could be associated with the arguments.

6. Restructuring and institutional reflexivity

The final strand in the development of ecological modernisation theory has been to view it as an example of institutional reflexivity and the transformation of society. This approach is particularly associated with Mol (1995) and his book *The Refinement of Production: Ecological Modernization Theory and the Chemical Industry* along with the work of Spaargaren (cf. Spaargaren and Mol, 1992; Mol, 1992, 1994, 1996; Spaargaren, 1997). It is essentially an optimistic interpretation of ecological modernisation building on the work of Beck and Giddens who have attempted to understand the nature of risk in modern society, particularly environmental risk, and the reflexivity of individuals or groups in the face of such risks.

For Mol ecological modernisation is an empirical phenomena. It is detectable in the transformation of the institutions of modernity (public and private) and he interprets this as representing their reflexivity in the face of environmental problems. In other words ecological modernisation is manifest in institutional transformations in government and industry and one of the goals of these transformations is to overcome the environmental crisis. However, this attempt to overcome the environmental crisis does involve making use of these institutions.

Mol's (1995) principle work on ecological modernisation examines the way the Dutch chemicals industry is restructuring in the face of environmental pressures. He examines the response of three branches of the chemicals industry (paints, plastics, pesticides) and concludes that overall the environment has moved from the periphery to the centre of decision making. On a theoretical note Mol concludes that:

> Economic institutions such as the commodity and labour markets, regulating institutions such as the state and even science and technology are redirected in the sense that they take on characteristics that cause them to diverge from their productivity-oriented predecessors... Ecological modernization can thus be interpreted as the reflexive (institutional) reorganization of industrial society in its attempt to overcome the ecological crisis. (Mol, 1995, p. 394)

7. The value of the ecological modernisation debate

From the brief review provided above it is clear that the ecological modernisation debate includes a diverse range of literature. This literature crosses academic disciplines and includes fairly pragmatic policy analysis as well as more abstract and theoretical work. In order to begin to assess the value of ecological modernisation it is useful to distinguish between its prescriptive/normative and analytical/descriptive dimensions.

The prescriptive and normative dimension to the theory suggests that the state should explicitly intervene in the market in order to achieve economic growth *and* environmental protection. To do this it should establish demanding environmental standards with the aim of communicating priorities for industrial innovation. It should also pursue macro-economic restructuring in favour of less resource intensive industries. Beyond traditional command and control instruments government's should make use of a range of more innovative policy measures including, for instance, environmental taxes, strategic environmental assessment and voluntary agreements. At the same time industry should seek out

Editorial / Geoforum 31 (2000) 1–8 5

solutions to production problems through the exploration of cleaner technologies and production techniques. It is argued that if this kind of programme is pursued environmental protection will improve economic competitiveness at the micro and macro-economic levels.

However, the agenda has a number of potential problems and some of these are worth highlighting at this stage. For example, as recently argued by Giddens (1998, p. 58):

> The somewhat comfortable assumptions of ecological modernization deflect attention from two fundamental questions raised by ecological considerations: our relationship to scientific advance, and our response to risk.

Here Giddens focuses on the scientific and technological optimism of prescriptive ecological modernization and highlights the fact that it does not appear to be informed by the contemporary concern about risk (see Cohen, 1997).

Beyond the risk debate ecological modernisation's focus at the national level is problematic. So-called solutions to environmental problems may actually only represent the resolution of the immediate problems facing advanced industrial countries with issues such as "regulation flight" to "pollution havens" not addressed (Yearly, 1991). In addition to these concerns Christoff (1996) points out the Eurocentric nature of ecological modernisation which is heavily influenced by regional debates concerning problems like acid rain, he also notes that:

> ... [In ecological modernisation] the environment is reduced to a series of concerns about resource inputs, waste and pollutant emissions. As cultural needs and non-anthropocentric values (such as are reflected in the Western interest in the preservation of wilderness) cannot be reduced to monetary terms, they tend to be marginalised or excluded from consideration (Christoff, 1996, p. 485).

With respect to the descriptive and analytical dimension of the theory, as mentioned above, the literature is diverse. The problems associated with particular approaches have often been acknowledged and highlighted by the authors themselves. In the case of Huber's work the almost exclusive emphasis on technology and entrepreneurs as determinants of social change, along with the teleological nature of his argument, is problematic. Concerning Hajer's work on discourse Dryzek (1995) has highlighted the fact that he does not acknowledge that the environment may be real and may

exist independently of social construction. Also, Hajer does not convincingly argue the relative impact of discourse on policy outcomes in comparison to more traditional policy literature variables like the nature of chosen instruments, institutional structures, staffing and resources.

Finally, with respect to Mol's interpretation of ecological modernisation as institutional reflexivity, Hajer (1995) raises the possibility that the interpretation is flawed. He doubts whether the phenomena described by Mol necessarily represents reflexivity in practice and to make his point he draws a broad distinction between techno-administrative ecological modernisation and truly reflexive ecological modernisation. Where reflexive ecological modernisation would be a democratic process involving deliberate social choice between alternative development (or non-development) paths techno-administrative ecological modernisation involves experts determining problems and solutions in a less democratic way. It would rely on experts making decisions in relative isolation about superindustrial responses to environmental problems. Techno-administrative ecological modernisation is, Hajer argues, what Mol describes.

Consequently, like all social theory, the ecological modernisation literature may have a number of weaknesses. This is the case in both its prescriptive and descriptive forms. However, this body of work does offer valuable ways of thinking about environmental policy in the short to medium term, even if these will not necessarily solve environmental problems. Most important of all it provides a way of thinking about how to move beyond the conflictual relationship that is often assumed to exist between the economy and the environment. In its descriptive form the literature is valuable for those attempting to interpret and understand the interaction between environment and society. Perhaps most interesting of all is the fact that it provides a way of dealing with the evidence that suggests advanced industrial countries have made progress in dealing with some environmental problems although there may be a long way to go. This is an almost unique contribution given that most work in environmental social science starts by assuming the inability of industry and the state to do anything other than create such problems.

References

Boehmer-Christiansen, S., Weidner, H., 1995. The Politics of Reducing Vehicle Emissions in Britain and Germany. Pinter, London.

Christoff, P., 1996. Ecological modernisation, ecological modernities. Environmental Politics 5 (3), 476–500.

Cohen, M., 1997. Risk society and ecological modernization: alternative visions for postindustrial nations. Futures 29 (3), 105–119.

Dryzek, J., 1995. Towards an ecological modernity: a book review essay. Policy Sciences 28, 231–242.

Dryzek, J., 1997. The Politics of the Earth: Environmental Discourse. Cambridge University Press, Cambridge.

Evans, P., 1995. Embedded Autonomy. Princeton University Press, Princeton.

Evans, P., 1996. Government action, social capital, and development: reviewing the evidence on synergy. World Development 24, 1119–1132.

Evans, P. (Ed.), 1997. State-Society Synergy. Institute for International Studies, University of California Press, Berkeley, CA.

Giddens, A., 1998. The Third Way. Polity Press, Cambridge.

Gouldson, A., Murphy, J., 1996. Ecological modernization and the European union. Geoforum 27 (1), 11–27.

Gouldson, A., Murphy, J., 1997. Ecological modernisation: economic restructuring and the environment. The Political Quarterly 68 (5), 74–86.

Gouldson, A., Murphy, J., 1998. Regulatory Realities: the Implementation and Impact of Industrial Environmental Regulation. Earthscan, London.

Hajer, M., 1995. The Politics of Environmental Discourse: Ecological Modernisation and the Policy Process. Oxford University Press, Oxford.

Hajer, M., 1996. Ecological modernisation as cultural politics. In: Lash, S., Szerszynski, B., Wynne, B. (Eds.), Risk, Environment and Modernity: Towards a New Ecology. Sage, London.

Harvey, D., 1996. Justice, Nature and the Geography of Difference. Blackwell, Oxford.

Huber, J., 1982. Die Verlorene Unschuld der Ökologie: Neue Technologien und Superindustrielle Entwicklung (The Lost Innocence of Ecology: New Technologies and Superindustrialized Development). Fisher Verlag, Frankfurt am Main.

Huber, J., 1984. Die Zwei Gesichter der Arbeit: Ungenutzte Möglichkeiten der Dualwirtschaft (The Two Faces of Labour: Unused Possibilities of the Dual Economy). Fisher Verlag, Frankfurt am Main.

Huber, J., 1985. Die Regenbogengesellschaft: Ökologie und Sozialpolitik (The Rainbow Society: Ecology and Social Politics). Fisher Verlag, Frankfurt am Main.

Jänicke, M., 1985. Preventive environmental policy as ecological modernisation and structural policy, Discussion Paper IIUG dp 85-2. Internationales Institut Für Umwelt und Gesellschaft, Wissenschaftszentrum Berlin Für Sozialforschung (WZB).

Jänicke, M., Mönch, H., Ranneberg, T., Simnois, U., 1988. Economic structure and environmental impact: empirical evidence on thirty-one countries in east and west, Working Paper FS II 88-402. Internationales Institut Für Umwelt und Gesellschaft, Wissenschaftszentrum Berlin Für Sozialforschung (WZB).

Jänicke, M., Mönch, H., Ranneburg, T., Simonis, U., 1989. Economic structure and environmental impacts: east west comparisons. The Environmentalist 9 (3).

Mol, A., 1992. Sociology, environment, and modernity: ecological modernization as a theory of social change. Society and Natural Resources 5 (4), 323–344.

Mol, A., 1994. Ecological modernization and institutional reflexivity: sociology and environmental reform in the late modern age. Paper presented at the XIIIth International Sociological Association Congress at Bielefeld, Germany, July 1994.

Mol, A., 1995. The Refinement of Production: Ecological Modernization Theory and the Chemical Industry. CIP-DATA KONINKLIJKE BIBLIOTHEEK, The Haag.

Mol, A., 1996. Ecological modernization and institutional reflexivity: environmental reform in the late modern age. Environmental Politics 5 (2), 302–323.

Simmonis, U., 1989a. Industrial restructuring for sustainable development: three points of departure. Working Paper FS II 89-401, Internationales Institut Für Umwelt und Gesellschaft, Wissenschaftszentrum Berlin Für Sozialforschung (WZB).

Simmonis, U., 1989b. Ecological modernization of industrial society: three strategic elements. International Social Science Journal 121, 347–361.

Spaargaren, G., 1997. The ecological modernization of production and consumption: essays in environmental sociology. Dissertation, Department of Environmental Sociology WAU, Wageningen.

Spaargaren, G., Mol, A., 1992. Sociology, environment and modernity: ecological modernization as a theory of social change. Society and Natural Resources 5 (4), 323–344.

Weale, A., 1992. The New Politics of Pollution. Manchester University Press, Manchester.

Yearly, S., 1991. The Green Case: A Sociology of Environmental Issues, Arguments and Politics. Routledge, London.

Joseph Murphy

Oxford Centre for the Environment, Ethics and Society,
Mansfield College,
Oxford OX1 3TF, UK

E-mail address: joseph.murphy@mansfield.oxford.ac.uk

[11]

Journal of Environmental Policy & Planning
J. Environ. Policy Plann. 2: 269–285 (2000)

Towards Industrial Ecology: Sustainable Development as a Concept of Ecological Modernization

JOSEPH HUBER*

Institut für Soziologie, Martin-Luther-Universität, Halle, Germany

ABSTRACT   This paper deals with the key role of ecological modernization in bringing about sustainable development. So far, two strategies of sustainable development have been discussed: sufficiency and efficiency. Sufficiency is preferred by the organized ecology movement (non-governmental organizations (NGOs)), meaning self-limitation of material needs, withdrawal from the free world-market economy and an egalitarian distribution of the remaining scarce resources.
    Contrary to that, industry and business have adopted the 'efficiency revolution' as a strategy to allow further economic growth and ecological adaptation of industrial production by improving the environmental performance, i.e. improving the efficient use of material and energy, thus increasing resource productivity in addition to labour and capital productivity.
    There are good reasons for both sufficiency and efficiency. Nevertheless, they do have important shortcomings. An additional, third kind of transformational strategy needs to be pursued. In the present name-giving context, one could call it the strategy of 'consistency'. A term with a similar meaning in the current discussion is 'industrial ecology'. Industrial ecology aims at an industrial metabolism that is consistent with nature's metabolism. The transformation of traditional industrial structures, which are often environmentally unadapted to an ecologically modernized consistent industrial metabolism, implies major or basic technological innovations, as being different from incremental efficiency increasing change. Copyright © 2000 John Wiley & Sons, Ltd.

Key words: ecological modernization; industrial ecology; sufficiency; efficiency; consistency

Introduction and summary

This paper deals with core aspects of ecological modernization, and how these have been received in the debate on sustainable development during the Rio de Janeiro process, particularly by two social milieus: one being industry and business; the other representing the red–green current of the ecology movement, which, at the Rio conference in 1992, was part of the group of non-governmental organizations (NGOs).

The NGOs' understanding of sustainable development has been formulated by themselves as an anti-industrial and anti-modernist strategy of 'sufficiency', meaning self-limitation of material needs, combined with 'industrial disarmament', withdrawal from the free world-market economy, and an egalitarian distribution of the remaining scarce resources. Contrary to that, the industry's understanding of sustainable de-

velopment is the 'efficiency revolution'. Industry and business are looking for a strategy that would allow for further economic growth *and* ecological adaptation of industrial production at the same time. The means for achieving this goal is seen in the introduction of environmental management systems aimed at improving the environmental performance, i.e. improving the efficient use of material and energy, thus increasing resource productivity in addition to labour and capital productivity.

There are good reasons for both sufficiency and efficiency. Nevertheless, I will argue that both strategies do have important shortcomings, so that, even if combined, they will not yet represent a sustainable answer to the ecological challenge. In order to open up a truly sustainable development path, an additional, third kind of transformational strategy needs to be pursued. In the present name-giving context, one can call it the strategy of 'consistency'. A term with a similar meaning in the current discussion is 'industrial ecology' (Socolow *et al.*, 1994; Ayres & Ayres, 1996). Industrial ecology aims at

* Correspondence to: Institut für Soziologie, Martin-Luther-Universität, D-06099 Halle (Saale), Germany. Tel: + 49 345 55 24 241; fax: + 49 345 55 27 149; e-mail: huber@soziologie.uni-halle.de

Received 2 February 2000
Accepted 5 June 2000

an industrial metabolism that is consistent with nature's metabolism. The transformation of traditional industrial structures, which are often environmentally unadapted, to an ecologically modernized, consistent industrial metabolism implies major or basic technological innovations, not just incremental efficiency-increasing change and minor modifications of existing product chains.

The content of this contribution can be seen as a piece of policy design. It is of a conceptual nature, i.e. it is not mere theoretical analysis, nor is it a report on empirical research work. It should be stressed, however, that the issues discussed here were not worked out by voluntaristic 'scenario writing', but closely correspond to empirical, practical and historical knowledge.

The concept of sustainable development in the Rio process

The meaning of sustainable development

When using the term sustainable development, reference is made to the meaning this term has taken on in the Rio process and its written documents. The Rio process refers to the ongoing international interaction between new social movements, academia, politics and business that has led to the formulation of environmental policy strategies in the context of the United Nations Conference on the Environment and Development (UNCED) in Rio de Janeiro in 1992. The Brundtland report (WCED, 1987) belongs to the most important written documents of the Rio process, as does *Agenda 21* (UNCED, 1992), or specific environment-related contributions such as *Sustainable Netherlands* (Buitenkamp *et al.*, 1992) by the Dutch *Vereniging Mileudefensie* (Friends of the Earth Netherlands), or *Changing Course* by the World Business Council for Sustainable Development (Schmidheiny, 1992a).

However controversial these contributions may be in detail, they basically agree upon the threefold mission any politics of sustainability has to fulfil:

1. to promote further *economic development*, while

2. ensuring *ecological sustainability*, by not exceeding the earth's carrying capacities, and
3. bringing about *social equity*, by creating a better balanced distribution of opportunities to use natural resources and sinks, and giving access to a fair share of the wealth produced.

Sustainable development not only deals with the interdependencies between economy and ecology, but also combines the ecological question with the social question on a global scale. A complete formulation would thus have to read 'sustainable and equitable development'. But the participants in the Rio process tend to differ with regard to their main focus of concern, and economic and ecological goals seem to be more objectively measurable than the goal of equitable distribution. Thus, it is not by chance that the shorter term 'sustainable development' is likely to prevail, and that speakers of less-developed countries have cause for complaint, particularly about a widespread attitude among Europeans who tend to see sustainable development as an exercise in the conservation of nature and in environmental management, while forgetting about equitable distribution and economic growth in less-developed countries.

Polanyi (1944) described 'the great transformation' from traditional to industrial society as a process of disembedding the growing industrial system from its social and natural context. Following this perspective, one can conceive of sustainable development as a concept aimed at re-embedding industrial activities into their social and natural context. There are two re-embedding relationships: one concerning the ecological links of the industrial economy, and one concerning its social links. Accordingly, two types of rules have been postulated in the Rio process: the so-called management rules, concerning the ecologically proper use of resources and sinks, and a set of distributional rules.

Economy's ecological link, and categorical imperatives of use ('management rules')

A number of important principles of modernization, the supposed failure of which had only recently been declared, were reborn in the Rio process. This was especially true of world trade and development, which are now being revitalized in an expanded context of globalizing markets and production structures. One of the most important concerns in the concept of sustainable development is to overcome poverty in less-developed countries by enabling them to catch up through a renewed process of modernization designed to permit environmentally sound growth. Accordingly, Rio's *Agenda 21* (UNCED, 1992) deals not only with the global protection of certain transnationally significant ecosystems, but also with such directly related issues as increasing global prosperity and transferring capital, science and technology.

To define the ecological sustainability of economic development, the Brundtland report set up a number of rules for the use of resources. These 'management rules' have since been accepted as a basis for further work (WCED, 1987, pp. 44–60). The following five rules are among the most important.

- Population development must be in keeping with the carrying capacity and productive forces of the ecosystem.
- Ambient concentrations of pollutants in environmental media and living creatures must not exceed their absorption and regeneration capacity.
- The consumption rate of renewable matter and energy (e.g. water, biomass and, to some extent, soil) must not exceed their given rate of reproduction.
- The consumption rate of exhaustible resources (ecologically sensitive resources such as land or oil, coal and natural gas, but not commonplace materials such as sand and stones) is to be minimized by
  (a) substituting renewable resources for exhaustible ones;
  (b) increasing material and energy efficiency; and
  (c) recycling to the extent that is ecologically reasonable and economically justifiable.
- The development and introduction of ecologically benign, clean resources, technologies and new products is to be intensified.

In the interest of establishing a consistent industrial ecology, the last rule would seem to be the most important as an imperative for innovation and substitution. However, it is given relatively little attention in the Brundtland report, the Rio documents, in contributions by NGOs, and even by business. One of the reasons may well be that substituting ecologically problematic material flows and innovating cleaner products and processes involves a considerable degree of science and research, know-how, capital, legal regulation, effective administration and political stability (Wallace, 1995). Given the economic and technological disparities between north and south, the topic of innovation and substitution is unlikely to receive priority in the north–south dialogue any time soon.

By contrast, the first rule—appropriate population development—is given a great deal of space in the documents. But it is apt to be suppressed in the current discussion in most of the European countries, presumably because the question of whether people are allowed as many offspring as they wish collides with religious traditions and modern ideals of individual liberty and self-actualization. But with the issue of an equitable global distribution of resources, one cannot help but be aware of the challenge the question of population control poses.

The rules listed above are helpful orientations. It should be noticed, however, that they are empirically empty categorical imperatives. One of the great problems of contemporary research on ecosystems is that it is hardly ever able to determine clear, critical, maximal and minimal limits for population sizes and the carrying capacity and regenerative capacity of ecosystems. Attempts to empirically define and measure sustainability have not been successful so far, even if they produce ever more valuable insights into the complexities of ecosystems (Munasinghe & Shearer, 1995). In addition, limits to growth, which no doubt always do exist, are incessantly being extended or restricted, and qualitatively changed by both geogenic and anthropogenic processes.

Economy's social link and categorical imperatives of distribution

The sustainability rules for getting access to and using resources and sinks in a just way are oriented to the principles of equity and the common interest. The rule of distribution says that the equity of resource use is to be guaranteed under both the current world population, primarily by overcoming poverty, and future generations. The distributional equity it proposes is thus intergenerational and intragenerational: 'social equity between generations and within each generation . . . Sustainable development is development that meets the needs of the present without compromising the ability of future generations to meet their own needs' (WCED, 1987, pp. 32, 43). It gives overriding priority to 'the essential needs of the world's poor' (WCED, 1987, p. 43).

This noble rule, too, is blemished by being a mere categorical imperative. As such, it is understandable as a normative construct, but it is not tied to empirical premises, not yet linked to specific historical conditions. As far as the economics of welfare and distribution go, and from a philosophical viewpoint of equity, one immediately recognizes the endless conflicts over values and measurements that will inevitably ensue from the application of such a rule. This is not to argue against the rule but to point out that it does not apply to just anything, and that the different and even contradictory notions of justice linked to it need to be clarified (Bryant, 1995; Huber, 1995).

The role of social democrats in the Brundtland commission and the role of NGOs in authoring the concept of sustainable development stands out when it comes to the question of the equitable distribution of benefits. When in doubt, they tend to understand equity as equality, and the call is raised for 'equal access to the resource base' and 'equal distribution' (WCED, 1987, pp. 29, 32). It goes without saying that this quasi-socialist definition of sustainable development will remain controversial.

A clearer notion of the controversy over distribution emerges in a study called *Sustainable Netherlands* by Friends of the Earth Netherlands (Brakel & Buitenkamp, 1992; Buitenkamp *et al.*, 1992). The study became a model for similar approaches in other European countries, e.g. the report on *Zukunftsfähiges Deutschland* (Futurity for Germany) by the Institute for Climate, Environ-

ment and Energy in Wuppertal (Loske & Bleischwitz, 1995), commissioned by the NGOs B.U.N.D., a large conservationist organization, and MISEREOR, a development aid charity of the Catholic Church.

Without wishing to oversimplify these studies, one may say that their approach consists essentially in adding up the resources and sinks (environmental media) available in the foreseeable future and dividing them by the number of living human beings. One thus arrives at per capita quotas or, in other words, contingents of resources and emissions. Accordingly, the Dutch, for example, would be entitled to 80% less aluminum, 45% less agricultural land, 40% less water and 60% less CO_2 emission than they have today.

But for whom is this calculation equitable? First, the volumes to be distributed do not usually represent constants, which is always a consideration in distributional conflicts. Resources are scarcer at some points in time than at others. Very few resources, then, can be distributed homogeneously and purposefully over space and time. Dutch agricultural land cannot be transferred to Bangladesh. Besides, the Bangladeshi could not pay for it, and the agricultural capital accumulated by the Dutch would have to be expropriated. Alternatively, ought the Dutch to give away 45% of their agricultural yield to the Bangladeshi or take 45% of the Netherlands' agricultural land out of production? Or should perhaps the 16 million inhabitants of the Netherlands have their country take in 7 million Bangladeshi? Obviously, the programme of *Sustainable Netherlands* does not give due consideration to certain ecological and geogenic facts of life. Presumably, an attempt to put it into practice would itself not be very sustainable.

A radically egalitarian version of need equity is underlying the programme, whereas principles of achievement-based equity and legal and legitimate possession are completely negated. An absolutely equal per capita quota of resource intensity is used as the index for need equity. But certain circumstances are tabooed. In various respects, for example, it is both equitable and inequitable to bring few or many children—hence, resource-intensive needs—into the world. However, given the development of the welfare state and the international discussion on basic needs, one would expect a different, more appropriate approach to prevail. Need equity would not then be tainted by crude resource communism. Instead, it would be satisfied by the fact that all people on earth would be given a certain minimum share of resources that would have to be large enough to guarantee an existence worthy of human beings, but not more, so as to avoid violating achievement-based equity and the social policy principle of less eligibility.

In this context, achievement-based equity is to be taken into consideration primarily in terms of resource and sink efficiency. The one who understands how to exploit resources more efficiently and reduce the specific environmental burdens of using them should be entitled to take in the full benefits. Indices for this are the consumption of resources and the demands made on environmental media per product unit or unit of service (as in the material intensity per unit of service (MIPS) proposed by Schmidt-Bleek, 1994). In each case, the *absolute* resource *intensity* is to be measured against the *relative* resource *intensity* (per capita), as these are to be measured against the resource *efficiency* (per economic unit).

However controversial it may be, achievement-based equity also exists as acquired purchasing power. Acknowledging it as a fact, if not accepting it outright, brings up the issue of the equity of possession. Whoever entertains a concept of resource distribution that requires the expropriation of existing property is playing with the fire of renewed cold or hot wars. A non-belligerent policy, even one that has good reason to aim for changing ownership structures, cannot help but begin with the status quo.

Solow calculated that about 88% of the advance in industrial productivity (and, hence, growth in prosperity) stem from the productive forces of science and technology—i.e. from the modernization of technology, skills and organization (in short, from the development of productive capacities)—and that only 12% stem from capital growth, which in certain nations in certain periods may include gains from colonial-

ist exploitation (Solow, 1957, pp. 316–320). Capital growth has thus always been of little significance in this regard. The lead enjoyed by the advanced industrialized countries is explained primarily by the cumulative build-up of productive *capacity* created by many generations in the course of great sacrifice, and times of social conflict and class struggle. Recognition of productive capacities that have been built up over many generations is as much part of inter-generational equity as the opportunity for future generations to achieve something similar.

The distribution of resources *is* unequal in favour of the rich. But neither a unilateral renunciation by the rich nor a gratuitous transfer from the rich to the poor can improve the structural predicament of the poor. Improvement comes about only by structural change and capacity-building, because only productive capacities can mobilize capital, labour, and natural resources in effective and efficient ways.

Earth policy and global politics

The discussion on sustainable development has helped to identify fields of 'earth policy' (Weizsäcker, 1989); that is, areas of environmental policy with transnational economic and thus political impacts. By virtue of their resulting significance in world politics and global economic policy, certain environmental policies require internationally agreed procedures for the scientific study of problems, as well as for the formulation of problem-solving policy and its technical, organizational, and economic implementation.

These fields of earth policy issues and action include

- climate and air-quality control;
- forests in general and tropical rain forests in specific;
- oceans and thermal cycles;
- soil erosion and desertification;
- biodiversity of earth's flora and fauna; and
- the genetic patrimony of the human race.

Treating these problems and fields of action resurrects old questions of national sovereignty and colonialism. Only occasionally do political borders coincide with the boundaries of natural ecosystems. Air-mass currents, rivers and oceans, forests and deserts, radiation, and weather and climate follow their own laws, the context of which extends, in principle, from the regional to the global. Superimposing political maps onto ecological ones, one finds complicated import–export flows of environmental freight and complex vectors of interference.

Protecting the environment in one country necessitates comparable and complementary efforts in others. It makes little sense, for example, to stop coal burning in Europe with its 500 million inhabitants, if China with its 1.7 billion people will increase coal consumption tenfold in the years to come. Ascertaining the marginal utility of environmental protection costs is meaningful only on the basis of international comparison. Countries and regions of the world today are interdependent ecologically, much as they are economically, technologically, etc. Clearly, the ecological interdependencies contradict the purported independence postulated by the principle of national sovereignty. At this point, the principle of non-interference or non-intervention becomes partially absurd, and yet remains indispensable in the interest of orderly procedures (Litfin, 1998).

Because countries differ in relative weight and in their degree of dependency on others, charges of neo-colonialism were revived in the Rio process. The suspicion is that rich countries, hoping to perpetuate their advantages and prosperity, will seek to misuse the ecological issue to saddle poorer countries with exorbitant environmental protection measures, while erecting protectionist barriers against new industrial countries' products that they claim represent 'ecodumping.' Sustainable development is playing an ever more important role in the World Trade Organization (WTO), known previously as the General Agreement on Tariffs and Trade (GATT).

Yet, as a matter of fact, self-inflicted economic harm has ensued from lack of environmental protection. The costs of environmental damage always come to several times the costs of environmental protection. As shown by the problems associated with the export of hazardous waste, the affront represented by inferior or completely non-existent environmental and health protection represents also a kind of neo-colonialism. Moreover, every long-term environmental impact, whether it is passed from the wealthier to the poorer, as can occur between any two parties, is a *de facto* physical intervention of a colonialist nature when it involves uncompensated externalization of environmental damages (as is the case with the policy of high smokestacks).

A neo-colonialist reproach of a different sort is levelled at the factual access of the prosperous and monied to the resources and land of the less wealthy. Producing the cotton consumed in Germany today, for example, requires tracts of land about twice the area of the Federal Republic (Griesshammer, 1993, p. 50). Our 'ecological footprints' are reaching far beyond our immediate surroundings (Rees & Wackernagel, 1994). Of course, the same is true for what used to be called colonial goods and southern commodities such as rubber, cane sugar, coffee, cocoa, peanuts, bananas, lemons, oranges and, today, soybeans, all of which are all but impossible to raise in middle and north-western European countries. These export goods, as any others, are interpreted by some radicals as naked confiscation of resources or outright occupation of land.

Such charges of neo-colonialism usually spring either from Marxist theories of exploitation (unequal exchange) or from the purist nationalist ideology of self-sufficiency. But there is nothing to be said against 'ecological footprints', international division of labour and world trade, as long as the sum of all 'footprints' does not exceed the earth's carrying capacity, and as long as the price paid for the products covers all costs, including the prices of primary materials, the work force and 'rent' for the land used, at levels that allow for the reproduction of these factors. Nothing is seen to be wrong, for example, if agricultural products are imported in Europe from the United States, for then it is regarded as an example of a beneficial mutual division of labour in the framework of a free world order.

The real problem is that, for example—for reasons of ruinous price competition owing to oversupply in an attempt to earn hard foreign currency in order to pay back foreign debt or import foreign goods—prices paid for Third World goods at the world-markets do not always fully contain these reproductive costs; that is, the costs of the land, the work force and the environment remain to a certain extent externalized instead of being fully internalized. But it is hard to say to what extent this is a home-made problem of the exporters, or irresponsible negligence on the part of the importers.

Transformational strategies for a sustainable development

The recommendations in UN documents and other literature on sustainable development (Barbier, 1987; Harborth, 1991; Lélé, 1991; Amelung, 1992; Dietz *et al.*, 1992; Kommission der Europäische Gemeinschaften, 1992; Jansson *et al.*, 1994; McKenzie-Mohr & Marien, 1994) can be grouped into three different strategies for achieving sustainability:

- *sufficiency* with regard to population growth, as well as the level of affluence, life-style and consumption patterns;
- *efficiency* with regard to production processes and the use of products; and
- ecological *consistency* of production processes and products in order to achieve compatibility between the industrial and natural metabolism.

The main strategy of NGOs: sufficiency

The NGOs—associations for the conservation of nature, grass-roots citizen's initiatives, human rights associations, Third World action groups, religious charities and church organizations—continue to play an influential role in the Rio process. Among the active and important NGOs are the International Union for the Conservation of Nature and Natural Resources (IUCN), with its 1980 World Conservation Strategy, the World Wide Fund for Nature (WWF), the Global Tomorrow Coalition (GTC), Greenpeace, Robin Wood, Friends of

the Earth, or *Brot für die Welt* (Bread for the World).

Their criticism of the industrial society traditionally includes a broad range of issues, from the utilitarian world-view over capitalist free-market economy to science and technology. But they tend to focus on the evils of a life too good for being pure and sane. High levels of affluence are seen by them as worshipping the golden calf. Instead, they are out for being worshippers of a simple life pleasing to God and nature. For reasons of sustainability, as well as solidarity, one shall stop running the endless race for positional goods, and turn to becoming caring and sharing instead.

The concept of sufficiency again raises the question with which two Swedish futurologists shaped the debate about growth in the early 1970s: how much is enough? The answer was, and still is, that one cannot know exactly the limits of carrying capacities, but that moderation, thus applying the precautionary principle, definitely seems called for because things cannot continue the way they are now in the long run. The word at that time was not 'sufficiency' but 'self-limitation', be it as voluntary simplicity ('living poor with style'), or be it as authoritarian management in an ecodictatorship. Whether voluntarily or by force, establishing sufficiency means doing without.

Sufficiency as a strategy of self-limitation within the boundaries of low-level production and consumption is open to the same criticism today as the one aimed at concepts of zero growth or a shrinking of the economy a quarter of a century ago. It is unrealistic because of the inexorable worldwide advance of utilitarian thinking and the pursuit of happiness as the greatest possible material benefit for the greatest possible number of people. It is undesired in that imposing it by force would destroy due process and civil rights and liberties. And it is both ineffective and defective because freezing current or even lower rates of consumption under present, ecologically inappropriate conditions of industrialization and a world population of 6 billion—before long, 10–12 billion—would sooner or later result in ecological catastrophe. If one earnestly wanted to pursue a strategy based purely on sufficiency, it would imply scaling world population back to pre-industrial proportions. How should that happen? Could friends of nature become enemies of humans? Arguing for lower levels of consumption in the name of social equity, while neglecting the problem of high levels of population, remains ambivalent.

The call for sufficiency, however, can claim the irrefutable truth that there really is no such thing as insatiability and that every real system is still finite within its niche in space and time. Of course, the limits of satiation have their own dynamics. It remains to be seen whether there actually are 'new models of wealth' (Loske & Bleischwitz, 1995). But abiding social debate over the issue of ecologically appropriate lifestyles is essential—primarily, however, for creating a sustainable value base and cultural conditions of environmental action, and to a much lesser degree, for directly controlling environmental impacts.

Environmental management

Industry and business found themselves accused of being the main polluters since the 1960s. Therefore, they took a defensive attitude for a long time. The situation began to change in the mid-1980s, when the phase of 'resistant adaptation 1970–1985' (Fischer & Schot, 1993) came to an end in favour of a more active and even proactive attitude of business towards environmental protection. Within a short period of 5–10 years environmental management systems (EMS) were developed, and green business networks began to form and grow in size and numbers.

Among these green business networks are, for example, in Germany, the *Bundesdeutscher Arbeitskreis für Umweltbewußtes Management* (BAUM, Federal Working Group on Environmental Management; the acronym BAUM stands for 'tree'), established in 1984, and *Förderkreis Umweltfuture* (which could be translated as 'Futurity Support Group for Environmental Management'). The conceptualization and implementation of environmental management tools through business, academia and politics was flourishing (Steger, 1988; Dyllick, 1989, 1990;

Kirchgeorg, 1991; Meffert & Kirchgeorg, 1992; Wicke *et al.*, 1992).

Soon after the green entrepreneurial pioneers, who came from rather medium-sized firms, big multinational corporations took the lead (Smart, 1992). This can be seen in the formation of green business networks since the beginning of the 1990s, such as the World Business Council for Sustainable Development, founded in 1992 by Stefan Schmidheiny, a Swiss businessman, at the initiative of Maurice Strong, who was then secretary general of the UNCED (Schmidheiny, 1992b). Other examples are the international Responsible Care initiative of the chemical industry, the European Partners for the Environment, the Social Venture Network, the International Network for Environmental Management (INEM), or the Global Environmental Management Initiative (GEMI). There are also bridging networks with a mixed membership from business, academia, NGOs and government, for example, the European Round Table on Clean Technologies, and the Greening of Industry Network.

EMS are being developed in all of the industrially advanced countries, and increasingly in new industrial countries too. Despite national differences in law and culture, the environmental management activities in Europe and America had a stimulating influence upon each other, and have developed similarly during the same time. Compared with this, it looks as if Japan and other Asian countries were following routes of their own. Japanese corporations, for example, tend to be reluctant with regard to environmental disclosures. There seems to be little environmental reporting and stakeholder communication (IISD, 1993). Japan seems to be more of a 'corporation-centered society' or 'company-centered society' (Shinoda, 1993; Matsuba, 1996) than American or European countries are. Thus, industry in Japan may be confronted less with political and civil society counterpowers. Even if a number of environmental policy tools and environmental management measures from the Japanese industry are known, it is not easy for a foreigner to obtain a comprehensive impression of current EMS practices in Japanese firms.

Today's leading companies in environmental management are multinational corporations or medium-sized companies with worldwide activities. In the course of the 1990s, it has turned out that they tend to adopt the highest environmental standards and the best available technology wherever possible, rather than to choose the lowest possible standards. There was evidence for the orientation towards higher-level environmental performance for some years already, for example, from the international pulp and paper industry (Lundan, 1995).

The original fear was that companies would seek to avoid tough environmental regulations by relocating production to locales with lower standards. The low-level expectation became known as the 'pollution haven' hypothesis. But a certain need for internal corporation-wide harmonization of rules and procedures, a certain necessity to avoid image-damaging and costly environmental risks, and to harmonize because of internationally integrated vertical and horizontal production chains represent incentives for the higher-level orientation. High-performing companies are likely to display high levels of ecological performance at the same time, and pioneers and early adopters of EMS are likely to be found among the market leaders and high performers in general (Azzone & Manzini, 1994; Elkington, 1994; Porter & Van der Linde, 1995). In addition to these complex but apparently existing competitive advantages (Bertolini, 1995), there is a negative incentive to avoid certain incalculabilities on the part of national and local environmental bureaucracies by 'outperforming' them proactively, even if principles of negotiated regulation and co-evolution of industry and regulators are nowadays being taken into consideration more than before. It is still government, not industry, who is setting the standards, but internationally active industries tend to disseminate the highest of the differing national standards (Angel & Huber, 1996).

The factors and motives driving companies to adopt environmental management practices are well investigated (FUUF, 1991; Jänicke & Weidner, 1995):

- laws, ordinances, targets set by local authorities, in 74% of cases;
- image, external stakeholder pressure, in 43% of cases;
- direct costs, cost control, alternative cost avoidance, in 40% of cases;
- securing market shares, strategic market position, in 13% of cases;
- general prevention of risks, in 10% of cases;
- doing what others do, in 10% of cases.

Generalizing these findings, one can distinguish three types of reasons for a firm to become greener.

1. *Legal reasons.* Compliance with the law and administrative regulations, on the basis of loyalty to the rule of law.
2. *Economic reasons.* Preventive cost reduction, cost competitiveness, and—becoming more important—the context of finance (Schmidheiny & Zorraquin, 1996). Bankers and insurers, for example, are demanding risk and pollution prevention for fear of liability assumptions.
3. *Social reasons.* Image, stakeholder demand, work force, consumers, etc.—in short, the necessities to be a fully integrated member of society and the international community. This reason should not be misconstrued as an idealistic need, but understood as an absolute necessity. A company's widespread acceptance and good reputation are decisive factors in areas such as attracting good personnel, getting on with authorities, banks and insurers, obtaining swift service from suppliers, and winning as many customers as possible to attain the greatest turnover possible.

The voluntary approach to environmental management continues to have an involuntary background of public pressure and national, as well as international, regulation. The need to comply with the laws still forms the backbone of any EMS. But as things evolve, more and more EMS go far beyond compliance. Even if this is not the place for a full discussion, the main elements of today's EMS shall be listed here. They can be grouped into three categories (see Table 1).

Table 1. Main elements of environmental management systems

A. Environmental information (monitoring, analysis, reporting, communication)	B. Environmental organization and personnel development	C. Environmental strategic and operational management
Environmental statistics, performance measurement, benchmarking Environmental accountability Environmental auditing and risk assessment Life-cycle assessment and eco-balances Environmental issues management, reporting and communication (shareholders, stakeholders, personnel, suppliers, customers)	Environmental officers, environmental committees Green responsibilities from the board to the shop floor, top-down along the command line Environmental concern being an integrated part of every activity Environmental training and education Special campaigning (e.g. energy saving at the office) Green awarding schemes	Vision statement, mission statement (corporate identity, corporate culture) Green agenda setting, action planning, green targeting Compliance with legal regulations (auditing etc.) Implementing best available technology, Continual Improvement Process, Total Quality Management (ISO 14.000 ff, BS 7750/EU-EMAS) Green purchasing policy, supply-chain management Green sales policy, approaching the green-appreciative customer Product stewardship In-site and inter-site recycling, industrial symbiosis projects, closed-loop procedures Product design for environment Introduction of cleaner products and processes Substitution of environmentally benign materials for harmful substances and material flows

It can be seen from this list how things start by creating a knowledge base and finding general goal orientations, and, via organization and personnel development, finally lead into specialized fields of technology. This is interpreted by some deep-green critics, misleadingly so, as a technocratic tendency. Ecology is the science of the metabolism of populations within their living space. Today's 'ecological question' concerns the metabolism of industrial civilization within Earth's geo- and biosphere: the industrial metabolism (Ayres, 1993; Ayres & Simonis, 1994), which is realized through work and technology. That is why the metabolic relations need to be analysed in terms of science and engineering. The social and human sciences come in as soon as the question is about how and why metabolism is caused and controlled by economic, legal, institutional, political and cultural factors. These factors necessarily play an important and decisive role in any strategy of change, but the final change of the industrial metabolism is always put into practice through changes in work and technology. Even a pure sufficiency approach to sustainability has un-

avoidably final implications for work and technology, be it the simple result of making do with less of everything by decreasing, reducing and slowing down any productive and consumptive activities.

So it is basically not wrong to characterize even general sustainability strategies that include important economic, institutional, political and cultural elements by their technical implications. For example, it has become common knowledge that so-called end-of-pipe measures or downstream approaches to environmental protection are of limited value, and come with unintended side-effects. There is a preference now to look for process-integrated solutions wherever possible (Hirschhorn *et al.*, 1993). Accordingly, the environmental policy discussion aimed at prevention revolves around approaches with explicit technological features, such as clean technology (Kemp & Soete, 1992; Jackson, 1993; Kemp, 1993), eco-efficiency (Schmidheiny, 1992a,b; Weizsäcker *et al.*, 1995), material flow and chain management (Enquete-Kommission, 1994), economics of reproduction (Hofmeister, 1998), management of industrial metabolism (Ayres, 1993, 1996; Ayres & Simonis, 1994; Ayres & Ayres, 1996), as well as design for environment (Kreibich *et al.*, 1991; Stahel, 1991, 1992; Paton, 1994), bionics (Rechenberg, 1973; Gleich, 1998), eco-effectiveness (Braungart & McDonough, 1999), constructive technology assessment (Rip *et al.*, 1995), ecological modernization (Huber, 1995; Mol, 1995; Spaargaren, 1997), and industrial ecology (Graedel, 1994; Socolow *et al.*, 1994; Ayres & Ayres, 1996; a *Journal of Industrial Ecology* is published by MIT Press since 1997), whereby all of the approaches listed in the second group of the list have a focus on ecological consistency of industrial metabolism rather than 'dematerializing'.

Concepts such as these cannot be prescribed by government in the same way as emission standards, and certain end-of-pipe measures can be forced upon the actors. Therefore, the role of government and administration is shifting from interventionist command-and-control approaches to frame-setting, communicating and negotiating, and applying economic instead of bureaucratic instruments (Opschoor & Vos 1989; Prittwitz, 1993; Georg, 1994; OECD, 1994). Correspondingly, attention and expectations in environmental action are shifting from government to industrial corporate actors and their potential for product and process innovation based on capital- and knowledge-mobilizing capacities.

The current strategy of business: the efficiency revolution

For the time being, industry does not seem to be fully aware yet of the ecological transformation process it is an active and ever more important part of. The innovative capacities and tools of the EMS tend to be understood and used in a rather narrow sense, for example, in the sense of improving the input–output relations of *existing* production processes and product chains. Industry still displays a more or less disregarding attitude to new processes and products such as renewable resources and renewable energy. There is certainly some research and development work on alternatives that can be shown at

press conferences, but there is no big investment in fundamentally new development paths.

This is understandable in so far as vested interests are touched—be it the interests of the managers, the shareholders, or the work force. For example, companies in the German energy sector have learned how to make a living by mining and burning brown coal. They have not learnt how to develop and utilize hydro-solar energy. Thus, the management, the researchers and technical staff, and the work force of these companies in general perceive the ecologically better alternative as a threat to their own existence—and in an attempt to find ways out of the ecologically untenable position, they become protagonists of the efficiency 'revolution' by heavily investing in still more efficient brown-coal-fuelled power plants.

The strategy of efficiency is aimed at applying principles of input–output rationalization even more systematically than has hitherto been the case. Desired production output is expected to be achieved with the least possible use of material and energy. This means improving the input–output ratio—that is, increasing the efficiency of material and energy use—thereby boosting *specific* resource productivity. The rise in the productivity of labour and capital is complemented by the rise in resource productivity.

In the context of the sustainability concept, the purpose of increasing efficiency is to achieve a relative, and perhaps even an absolute minimization of resource consumption and burden on the sinks (the environmental media air, water and soil). The means to do so lie in advances in operative technology (e.g. more efficient engines and other combustion equipment), recycling and cascade reprocessing of material in an economy of recycling. Materials are supposed to be used over and over again for as long as possible before they are lost for human purposes as waste in the natural cycle. Concepts relating to the durability of certain utility goods, such as clothes, furniture, electrical appliances and cars head in the same direction. (To the extent that the influence of fashions and rhythms of technological innovation are excluded from the equation, the concept of durability belongs more to the strategy of sufficiency.)

The efficiency strategy is the most applicable and appealing in the prevailing economic system. That is why newly converted industrialists are apt to go so far as to confound sustainability and efficiency. In reality, efficiency can only be intermediate between sufficiency and consistency. Ecologically inappropriate or incompatible material flows ultimately subject efficiency to the same limitations as the strategy of sufficiency. But a high level of material and energy efficiency is, of course, suited to expanding the latitude of sufficiency.

In the end, however, a substantial increase in efficiency may still be pretty insubstantial. For example, if both the fuel efficiency of cars and the mileage travelled by the vehicle pool are doubled, the ecological effect of economizing is nil. More generally speaking, halving the consumption rate of exhaustible resources means doubling the amount of those resources. That is a great deal, but in effect, too little. Things look better for renewable resources, where it is possible to approximate the ongoing recreation of production volume according to the economic logic of living on the yield, not on the capital.

A joint strategy for government, business and research: consistent metabolism in an industrial ecology

If, on the one hand, in following the sufficiency strategy, it was possible to reduce consumption by half—just to give a model calculation—the available environmental space would double. Translated into a time perspective, the breakdown limits to growth (in the sense of the Meadows modellings) would perhaps be reached in 100 years instead of 50 years. If, on the other hand, in following the efficiency strategy, resource productivity was increased by a factor of four, the time perspective would be 200 years.

One can certainly combine both strategies. Many NGO activists openly advocate such a combination, which is even seen by some as the 'yin and yang of sustainability' (Schmidt-Bleek, 1994). Contrarily, industrial worshippers of the efficiency revolution do not want to relate to sufficiency ideas aimed at limiting needs and

consumption. In both cases, however, results are not satisfying. Even in combination, both cases would add up to 300–400 years—which is certainly six to eight times better than the 50 years for a business-as-usual scenario, but still not enough for being sustainable in a true long-term historical perspective. Bolder assumptions, for example, shrinking the affluence to a mere fourth of its present level, and increasing efficiency tenfold within the next 100 years, do not fundamentally change the message of the model calculation.

A basic and simple truth of ecology is that populations cause environmental impact, large populations major impact, and large industrial populations major industrial impact. An earth population of billions of people cannot prevent itself from operating on giga and tera levels of volumes. That is why a further transformational strategy for sustainable development going beyond sufficiency and efficiency needs to be adopted, a strategy of *qualitative* change of the industrial metabolism by modernizing the basic structures of technology and products, allowing for a permanent turnover of material flows on a large scale and in large volumes. This is what I previously referred to as the strategy of *consistency* (Huber, 1995).

Consistency refers to the nature of matter. Figuratively speaking, consistency means compatibility, coherence among things, correspondence among related aspects. Applied to the ecological issue, it means the environmentally compatible nature of industrial material flows and energy use. It means that anthropogenic and geogenic material flows symbiotically and synergistically reinforce each other, or that they do not interfere with each other. Consistent material flows are, therefore, ones that are either carried on with little interference in their own closed technological cycle, or ones that are so consonant with the metabolic processes of their natural setting that they fit in with relatively little problem, even when large volumes are involved.

There is a temptation to ask for practical examples of ecological consistency (not natural ones such as the anabolism of biomasses through photosynthesis and their catabolism through bacteria). In principle, one should not succumb to trying to give such illustrations, because technological forecasting for longer periods than 5–10 years has always been difficult and risky, if not impossible. Who around the year 1900 could really have predicted what technology around 1950 would look like and what it has evolved into since then?

Nevertheless, one could hint, for example, at the principles of ecologically appropriate farming. Every percentage point of growth of traditional industrial agriculture with its intensive use of heavy machinery, agrochemicals and irrigation, goes hand in hand with a corresponding increase in environmental damage. Ecologically appropriate farming, instead, maintains and improves the soil and water, thereby perpetually reproducing, and perhaps even increasing, the yield of biomass. So every percentage point of economic growth is welcome, because it means maintenance and growth of biodiversity and ecological stability at the same time. Under conditions of consistency, anthropogenic environmental impacts do not inevitably lead to environmental degradation, but make a lasting contribution to maintaining or enlarging ecosystems instead. In principle, the task of producing consistent new material flows is much greater and far more profound than that of minimizing traditional industrial material flows.

Another hint one could give, for example, are fuel cells and/or hydro-solar energy. The biggest ecological problems of today stem from the use of fossil fuels in 'hot' burning processes. Relatively 'cold' burning processes, such as in fuel cells, have much less environmental impact, and burning hydrogen instead of fossil fuels would practically lead to 'zero bad emissions'. If, in addition, the hydrogen came from solar sources, the total environmental impact would be very low, and thus—though it is certainly not a perpetuum mobile—would allow for permanent production activities on a very large scale, for example material recycling, because hydro-solar energy is material intensive. If the energy base is clean, and if the materials used are pure and of high quality (stoneware, concrete, metals, glass), a 'circular economy' would not be much of a problem. With regard to fibres and long-chain molecules (plastics, textiles, paper, wood), a similar statement with certain

restrictions owing to the downgrading of the fibres and chains can be made. Limits to closed-loop procedures on a large scale are imposed by economics rather than physics (Ayres, 1996).

Further examples would certainly include biotechnological production processes instead of traditional physico-mechanical processes in the chemical industry (OECD, 1998). The latter operate at high pressures and temperatures that are dangerous and often toxic, and resource productivity is rather low. Biotechnological production tends to be 'soft' on a high level of both effectiveness and efficiency. This is all the more true if the micro-organismic helpers are genetically modified (GM). GM enzymes, bacteria and similar 'bio-work force' often do 10–100 times better than natural ones. Genetic engineering, as much as everything in evolution, may open up new risk potentials. Thus, it must certainly be considered in a critical and selective way. An important task, seen from today's viewpoint, will be to maintain diversity in seeds and semen. The manyfold environmental advantages of GM biotechnology, however, are so obvious that it will undoubtedly have an important role in the process of ecological modernization. Today, the followers of organic farming are fierce fighters against GM biotechnology. But in a generation's time or so, both sides may possibly have merged into an environmentally benign synthesis.

The strategy of consistency is fully in keeping with the objectives and principles of *integrated* environmental problem solutions (as opposed to end-of-pipe, or downstream, measures) and with all of the preventive EMS strategies of technological innovation listed above. Whereas the sufficiency version of sustainable development is a programme for the *conservation* of nature, and the efficiency version is a programme for the *improvement* of *existing* technologies and infrastructures in order to economize on natural resources and sinks, the consistency version of sustainable development is a programme for *innovation* of *new* technologies, products, and material flows in order to change the *qualities* of the industrial metabolism, thus rendering possible a true industrial ecology.

The notion of industrial ecology is close to the concept of consistency. Unfortunately, industrial ecology is often understood in a rather narrow sense as 'redesigning industrial processes so they mimic natural ecologies where there is no waste because all outputs become inputs for something else' (*Business and the Environment*, 1996, pp. 2–5). Hence, projects such as the 'Zero Emissions Research Initiative' of the United Nations University aimed at 100% recovery of the carbon dioxide emitted during the brewing of beer. The idea is that of an inter-site industrial symbiosis where waste streams from brewing, aquaculture, fish processing, greenhouses and algae production will feed on each other.

Industrial symbiosis projects like this one can certainly be useful and contribute to a better adapted industrial ecology. But the idea is not as new as the word is. Known long before as 'combined production' (in German *Verbundproduktion*), it has a certain tradition in centrally planned economy in general, and in the chemical industry in particular. There were certainly economic and ecological benefits to be experienced, but also evidence for undesired inflexibilities or lock-ins (e.g. difficulties to do away with the chlorine chemistry), because once such a structure has been installed, it is difficult to change one element without severe repercussions upon the others.

If it is possible, in special cases, to mimic nature, this may represent a valuable contribution. But usually we are dealing with technical artifacts non-existent in the non-civilized realms of nature. One should let oneself be inspired by nature's metabolism (e.g. in the sense of bio-evolutionism, or industrial symbiosis of hitherto separate material flows, as in the Kalundborg case),[1] but humankind will probably not be able to literally mimic nature. A similar comment could be made on the idea of zero emissions. Even if we agree upon keeping emission levels as low as necessary so as not to violate the earth's carrying capacity, the substantial question remains that of *what kind* of emissions we are dealing with. The environmental space for emissions of oxygen and hydrogen is of a much higher order of magnitude than that of gaseous carbons and nitrogen.

That is also to say that there still *are* limits to growth, and a strategy of consistency should not lead one to expect a boundless land of milk and honey any more than the other strategies do. The point is to avoid setting arbitrary and, hence, probably both tyrannical and incorrect ecological limits, and let them instead emerge from a process of innovation and development that takes full advantage of modern society's creative and productive capacities.

Introducing ecologically better adapted new technology means to develop 'basic innovations', in the sense of Schumpeter, which is nowadays sometimes called 'system innovations'. Bringing them about represents a complex enterprise, going far beyond the task of special process improvements, or single product innovations. Even very large multinational corporations do not have the size and the capacities to meet the challenges of basic system innovations by themselves alone. What is needed, and what has always been the case in the history of complex technological innovations, is a systematic, broad and long-term cooperation between government, research, industry and finance. This cooperation must be promoted on an international level as much as possible.

Complex innovations of the 'basic' or 'system' type come with both pleasant and unpleasant implications. They represent major structural change, and this means processes of 'creative destruction' (Schumpeter). There are winners and losers, and, therefore, social and political conflicts. New generation knowledge, know-how and skills imply a devaluation of older generation knowledge, know-how and skills. New capital stocks have to be built up, as old ones will have to diminish and dissolve. New sites and regions may see chances, while old ones face the dwindling of theirs. Thus, a programme of ecological consistency of the industrial metabolism is not only a call for the innovative productive capacities of industry and the means-mobilizing capacities of finance, or for the inventiveness of research, construction and design, but is concurrently as much a call for social support and political leadership.

The strategies of sufficiency, efficiency and consistency can be combined, although the degrees of combinatorial freedom are less arbitrary than one might think. The best overall strategy will be the one that places priority on long-term

J. Environ. Policy Plann. 2: 269–285 (2000)

consistency and utilizes mid-term efficiency as much as possible, while fully acknowledging that certain limitations, thus sufficiency, must finally be respected.

Notes

1. In Kalundborg, Denmark, four big companies and a number of small businesses utilize each other's residual products in a network on the basis of bilateral contracts with freely negotiated prices— the Asnaes power station, Gyproc, a plasterboard producer, Statoil refinery, Novo Nordisk, a pharmaceutical and biotechnological group, and greenhouses and fish farms. The residual products exchanged are waste water and cooling water, steam, heat, gas, sulphur, gypsum and others.

References

Amelung T. 1992. Sustainable development: a challenge for the world economy. *Zeitschrift für Umweltpolitik* 4: 415–431.

Angel D, Huber J. 1996. Building sustainable industries for sustainable societies. *Business Strategy and the Environment* 5: 127–136.

Ayres RU. 1993. Industrial metabolism: closing the materials cycle. In *Clean Production Strategies: Developing Preventive Environmental Management in the Industrial Economy*, Jackson T (ed.). Lewis Publishers: Boca Raton, FL; 165–188.

Ayres RU. 1996. Industrial ecology. Paper presented at the Greening of Industry Network workshop on 'Regional Sustainability: from Pilot Projects to an Environmental Culture', Milan, 9 May.

Ayres RU, Ayres LW. 1996. *Industrial Ecology: Towards Closing the Materials Cycle*. Edward Elgar: Cheltenham.

Ayres R, Simonis UE (eds). 1994. *Industrial Metabolism: Restructuring for Sustainable Development*. United Nations University Press: Tokyo.

Azzone G, Manzini R. 1994. Measuring strategic environmental performance. *Business Strategy and the Environment* 3: 1–15.

Barbier EB. 1987. The concept of sustainable economic development. *Environmental Conservation* 14: 101–110.

Bertolini F. 1995. Green management—una strategia orientata al network. *Economia & Management* 8(2): 15–28.

Brakel M van, Buitenkamp M. 1992. *Action Plan Sustainable Netherlands: A Perspective for Changing Northern Lifestyles*. Vereniging Milieudefensie: Amsterdam.

Braungart M, McDonough WA. 1999. Von der Öko-Effizienz zur Öko-Effektivität. Die nächste industrielle Revolution. *Politische Ökologie* 62: 18–22.

Bryant B (ed.). 1995. *Environmental Justice: Issues, Policies, and Solutions*. Island Press: Washington, DC.

Buitenkamp M, Venner H, Wams T. 1992. *Sustainable Netherlands: Action Plan for a Sustainable Development of the Netherlands*. Vereniging Milieudefensie: Amsterdam.

Business and the Environment. 1996. Implementing industrial ecology: a progress report. *Business and the Environment* 7(2): 2–5.

Dietz FJ, Simonis UE, Straaten J van der (eds). 1992. *Sustainability and Environmental Policy: Restraints and Advances*. Edition Sigma: Berlin.

Dyllick T. 1989. *Management der Umweltbeziehungen: Öffentliche Auseinandersetzung als Herausforderung*. Gabler: Wiesbaden.

Dyllick T (ed.). 1990. *Ökologische Lernprozesse in Unternehmungen*. Lang: Bern.

Elkington J. 1994. Towards the sustainable corporation: win–win–win business strategies for sustainable development. *California Management Review* 36(2): 90–100.

Enquete-Kommission 'Schutz des Menschen und der Umwelt' des Deutschen Bundestages. 1994. *Die Industriegesellschaft gestalten.Perspektiven für einen nachhaltigen Umgang mit Stoff- und Materialströmen*. Economica Verlag: Bonn.

Fischer K, Schot J. 1993. The greening of the industrial firm. In *Environmental Strategies for Industry: International Perspectives on Research Needs and Policy Implications*, Fischer K, Schot J (eds). Island Press: Washington, DC; 3–33.

Forschungsgruppe Umweltorientierte Unternehmensführung (FUUF). 1991. *Umweltorientierte Unternehmungsführung*, Studie im Auftrag des Umweltbundesamtes. E. Schmidt: Berlin.

Georg S. 1994. Regulating the environment: changing from constraint to gentle coercion. *Business Strategy and the Environment* 3(2): 11–20.

Gleich A von (ed.). 1998. *Bionik: Ökologische Technik nach dem Vorbild der Natur?*. Teubner: Stuttgart.

Graedel T. 1994. Industrial ecology: definition and implementation. In *Industrial Ecology and Global Change*, Socolow R, Andrews C, Berkhout F, Thomas V (eds). Cambridge University Press: Cambridge; 23–42.

J. Environ. Policy Plann. 2: 269–285 (2000)

Griesshammer R. 1993. *Chemie und Umwelt.* C.H. Beck Verlag: München.

Harborth H-J. 1991. *Dauerhafte Entwicklung statt globaler Selbstzerstörung. Eine Einführung in das Konzept des Sustainable Development.* Edition Sigma: Berlin.

Hirschhorn J, Jackson T, Baas L. 1993. Towards prevention—the emerging environmental management paradigm. In *Clean Production Strategies: Developing Preventive Environmental Management in the Industrial Economy,* Jackson T (ed.). Lewis Publishers: Boca Raton, FL; 125–142.

Hofmeister S. 1998. *Von der Abfallwirtschaft zur ökologischen Stoffwirtschaft. Wege zu einer Ökonomie der Reproduktion.* Westdeutscher Verlag: Opladen.

Huber J. 1995. *Nachhaltige Entwicklung.* Edition Sigma: Berlin.

International Institute for Sustainable Development (IISD), Deloitte Touche Tohmatsu International, SustainAbility. 1993. *Coming Clean: Corporate Environmental Reporting.* Deloitte Touche Tohmatsu International: London.

Jackson T (ed.). 1993. *Clean Production Strategies: Developing Preventive Environmental Management in the Industrial Economy.* Lewis Publishers: Boca Raton, FL.

Jänicke M, Weidner H (eds). 1995. *Successful Environmental Policy: A Critical Evaluation of 24 Cases.* Edition Sigma: Berlin.

Jansson A, Hammer M, Folke C, Costanza R (eds). 1994. *Investing in Natural Capital: The Ecological Economics Approach to Sustainability.* Island Press: Washington, DC.

Kemp R. 1993. An economic analysis of cleaner technology: theory and evidence. In *Environmental Strategies for Industry: International Perspectives on Research Needs and Policy Implications,* Fischer K, Schot J (eds). Island Press: Washington, DC; 79–116.

Kemp R, Soete L. 1992. The greening of technological progress: an evolutionary. *Futures* 24(5): 437–457.

Kirchgeorg M. 1991. *Ökologieorientiertes Unternehmensverhalten.* Gabler Verlag: Wiesbaden.

Kommission der Europäische Gemeinschaften. 1992. *Für eine dauerhafte und umweltgerechte Entwicklung,* Kom (92) 23/Vol. II. Amt für amtliche Veröffentlichungen der Europäische Gemeinschaften, Luxemburg.

Kreibich R, Rogall H, Boes H (eds). 1991. *Ökologisch produzieren.* Verlagsgruppe Beltz: Weinheim.

Lélé SM. 1991. Sustainable development: a critical review. *World Development* 19: 607–621.

Litfin KT (ed.). 1998. *The Greening of Sovereignty in World Politics.* MIT Press: Cambridge, MA.

Loske R, Bleischwitz R. 1995. *Zukunftsfähiges Deutschland: Ein Beitrag zu einer global nachhaltigen Entwicklung.* Birkhäuser Verlag: Basel.

Lundan SM. 1995. Internationalization and Environmental Strategy in the Pulp and Paper Industry. Paper presented at the Greening of Industry Network Annual Conference, Toronto, 12–14 November.

Matsuba M. 1996. An introduction to the analysis of contemporary Japanese economy. *Ritsumeikan Business Review* 34(5): 77–92.

McKenzie-Mohr D, Marien M (eds). 1994. Special Issue on 'Visions of Sustainability'. *Futures* 26(2): 115–256.

Meffert H, Kirchgeorg M. 1992. *Marktorientiertes Umweltmanagement: Konzeption, Strategie, Implementierung, mit Praxisfällen.* C.E. Poeschel Verlag: Stuttgart.

Mol APJ. 1995. *The Refinement of Production: Ecological Modernization Theory and the Chemical Industry.* Van Arkel: Utrecht.

Munasinghe M, Shearer W (eds). 1995. *Defining and Measuring Sustainability: The Biogeophysical Foundations.* World Bank Publications: Washington, DC.

OECD (Organisation for Economic Co-operation and Development). 1994. *The Economics of Climate Change.* OECD: Paris.

OECD (Organisation for Economic Co-operation and Development). 1998. *Biotechnology for Clean Industrial Products and Processes: Towards Industrial Sustainability.* OECD: Paris.

Opschoor JB, Vos HB. 1989. *Economic Instruments for Environmental Protection.* OECD: Paris.

Paton B. 1994. Design for environment. A management perspective. In *Industrial Ecology and Global Change,* Socolow R, Andrews C, Berkhout F, Thomas V (eds). Cambridge University Press: Cambridge; 349–358.

Polanyi K. 1944. *The Great Transformation.* New York: Beacon Press.

Prittwitz V von (ed.). 1993. *Umweltpolitik als Modernisierungsprozeß.* Leske & Budrich: Opladen.

Porter ME, Van der Linde C. 1995. Green and competitive: ending the stalemate. *Harvard Business Review* 73(5): 120–134.

Rechenberg I. 1973. *Evolutionsstrategie. Optimierung technischer Systeme nach Prinzipien der biologischen Evolution.* Friedrich Frommann Verlag: Stuttgart.

Rees WE, Wackernagel M. 1994. Ecological footprints and appropriated carrying capacity: measuring the natural capital requirements of the human economy. In *Investing in Natural Capital: The Ecological Economics Approach to Sustainability,* Jansson A, Hammer M, Folke C, Costanza R (eds). Island Press: Washington, DC; 362–391.

Rip A, Misa TJ, Schot J (eds). 1995. *Managing Technology in Society: The Approach of Constructive Technology Assessment.* Pinter: London.

Schmidheiny S. 1992a. *Changing Course: A Global Business Perspective an Development and the Environment.* MIT Press: Cambridge, MA.

Schmidheiny S. 1992b. The business logic of sustainable development. *The Columbia Journal of World Business* 27(314): 18–24.

Schmidheiny S, Zorraquin F. 1996. *Financing Change: The Financial Community, Eco-Efficiency, and Sustainable Development.* MIT Press: Cambridge, MA.

Schmidt-Bleek F. 1994. *Wieviel Umwelt braucht der Mensch? MIPS, das Maß für ökologisches Wirtschaften.* Birkhäuser Verlag: Basel.

Shinoda T. 1993. Japanese capitalism and 'Toyotism'. *Ritsumeikan Business Review* 29(3): 1–55.

Smart B (ed.). 1992. *Beyond Compliance: A New Industry View of the Environment.* The World Resources Institute: Washington, DC.

Socolow R, Andrews C, Berkhout F, Thomas V (eds). 1994. *Industrial Ecology and Global Change.* Cambridge University Press: Cambridge.

Solow RM. 1957. Technical change and the aggregate production function. *Review of Economics and Statistics* 39: 312–320.

Spaargaren G. 1997. The ecological modernization of production and consumption: essays in environmental sociology. PhD thesis, Wageningen Agricultural University.

Stahel W. 1991. *Langlebigkeit und Materialrecycling.* Vulkan Verlag: Essen.

Stahel W. 1992. Gemeinsam nutzen statt einzeln verbrauchen. In *Vernetztes Arbeiten: Design und Umwelt.* Rat für Formgebung: Frankfurt am Main.

Steger U. 1988. *Umweltmanagement.* Gabler: Wiesbaden.

United Nations Conference on Environment and Development (UNCED). 1992. *Documents of the Rio-Conference on Environment and Development [including Agenda 21, Rio Declaration on Environment and Development, Forest Principles, Climate Convention and others].* United Nations Press: New York.

Wallace D. 1995. *Environmental Policy and Industrial Innovation: Strategies in Europe, the US and Japan.* Earthscan Publications: London.

World Commission on Environment and Development (WCED). 1987. *Our Common Future.* Oxford University Press: Oxford.

Weizsäcker EU von. 1989. *Erdpolitik.* Wissenschaftliche Buchgesellschaft: Darmstadt.

Weizsäcker EU von, Lovins AB, Lovins LH. 1995. *Faktor Vier: Doppelter Wohlstand, halbierter Naturverbrauch.* Droemer Knaur: München.

Wicke L, Haasis H-D, Schafhausen F, Schulz W. 1992. *Betriebliche Umweltökonomie.* Verlag Franz Vahlen: München.

                       J. Environ. Policy Plann. **2**: 269–285 (2000)

[12]

Urban Studies, Vol. 34, Nos 5–6, 845–871, 1997

Environmental Policy: Ecological Modernisation or the Risk Society?

Andrew Blowers

1. The Environment and Society: A Defining Moment of Change

The concern with the environmental risks created by modern society has emerged against a background of a major geopolitical change. With the ending of the Cold War an era of bipolar confrontation has ended. Apart from a few beleaguered enclaves the majority of the world's nation-states have been penetrated by global processes of trade, competition and production that reflect Western values and economic and political dominance. Instead of a fundamental conflict between two opposing world economic and political systems, arguably there has been only one model on offer since the end of the 1980s—that is, the international capitalist economic system. Yet, the continuing tension of the previous era has been replaced, not by greater stability but by increasing uncertainty and insecurity. Already the economic and political problems of the countries in the former Soviet empire are giving rise to new anxieties; regional conflicts in former Yugoslavia and the Middle East have exposed inherent ethnic and national tensions; and civil war is an endemic condition which threatens wider instability in several countries, for instance in sub-Saharan Africa (Somalia, the Sudan, Zaire, Rwanda and Burundi), Latin America (Colombia) and,

latterly, in the Russian Federation (Chechenya) and Afghanistan. The disappearance of East–West conflict has revealed more starkly the underlying global instability in relations between North and South which hinges on the problem of systemic uneven development, poverty and inequality (see, for example, Independent Commission, 1980; WCED, 1987; Adams, 1990; Sage, 1996).

Against this background of global economic and political instability is the problem of global environmental insecurity. Over the past decade or more there has been a perceptible shift in the issues, scale and nature of concern about the environment, at least as they are expressed in international political concern. There has been a diminution of concern about nuclear risks as the threat of nuclear war appears to have receded—though the problem of horizontal proliferation persists, particularly with the break-up of the Soviet Union. Meanwhile, the focus of anxiety has turned from predominantly national and regional concerns to longer-term global threats emanating from ozone depletion, the enhanced greenhouse effect, desertification and the loss of biodiversity (Goodin, 1992). These issues have focused attention on the global scale of modern pro-

Andrew Blowers is in the Faculty of Social Sciences, Open University, Walton Hall, Milton Keynes MK7 6AA, UK. Fax: 01908-654488. E-mail: a.t.blowers@open.ac.uk. The support of the Economic and Social Research Council is gratefully acknowledged. This review is part of the research conducted under the Global Environmental Change Programme at the OU (GECOU) on 'Setting Environmental Agendas: NGOs, democracy and global politics'. The author is also greatly indebted to Pieter Leroy whose ideas and criticism helped in the development of this review and to David Humphreys for his careful criticism of an earlier draft.

duction impacts and have emphasised the relationships between local and global processes. Consonant with this changing focus on global issues and global scale has been an emphasis on resource depletion from overexploitation and on the burden on the sustenance base created by pollution which together threaten the survival of ecosystems.

It is conceivable that the challenge posed by the process of global environmental change heralds a defining moment of social change. Sustainable development has emerged as an all-encompassing idea suggesting as it does a process of social transformation (development) brought about by irresistible physical constraints (sustainability). It is at once a scientific principle, a political goal, a social practice and a moral guideline. Definition of the meaning of the term (see Blowers, 1993) remains elusive and continues to be explored (for example, Owens, 1994) despite the scepticism of those who consider conceptual exploration indulgent (Beckerman, 1994). But there is now a widespread recognition that global environmental change has crossed the threshold of passing concern. The relationship between the environment and society poses a challenge both at the level of thought and of action. Intellectually, the social implications of environmental change are being taken increasingly seriously by social scientists (Jacobs, 1991; Lipschutz and Conca, 1993; Redclift and Benton, 1994; Leroy, 1995; Hannigan, 1995; Yearley, 1996; Lash et al., 1996, Vogler and Imber, 1996). At a political level, policy-making routinely genuflects to the constraints of sustainable development at all levels from the United Nations (Commission on Sustainable Development), to the nation-state (HMSO, 1994) to the sub-state level.

This review reflects on both the intellectual and policy implications of global environmental change. It explores opposing perspectives on the relationship between environmental and social change. These perspectives represent an enduring debate in social scientific discourse between, on the one hand, a liberal, pluralist and reformist explanation of social change and, on other, a radical perspective which stresses conflict, inequality of power and revolutionary change. These perspectives possess an ideological component, sometimes differentiated as environmentalism, essentially recognising environmental constraints on development; and ecologism, which is an altogether more radical perspective envisaging fundamental changes in social institutions and lifestyles (Dobson, 1990; Humphreys, 1996). Environmentalism has an established provenance concerned predominantly with national issues of conservation and remedial action. Ecologism, by contrast, has emerged more recently coinciding with disenchantment with modernism and concern for broader, global issues and more radical means of dealing with them (Christoff, 1997).

These perspectives also relate to a theoretical discourse about the nature of modern society and the sources of change. One approach, now widely termed ecological modernisation, holds that while environmental constraints must be taken fully into account, they can be accommodated by changes in production processes and institutional adaptation. It is consistent with environmentalism and may be seen as an extension of the process of modernisation. Conversely, opposing theories offer a critique of modernisation contending that the environmental crisis is of such proportions that nothing less than fundamental social and economic changes will be able to cope with it. There has been a consistent thread of socialist and neo-Marxist writings taking a demodernisation perspective (see for example, Stretton, 1976; Schnaiberg, 1980; Gorz, 1980; Pepper, 1993). In terms of a social critique, probably the most influential exponent of the radical ecologist perspective is Ulrich Beck whose 'theoretical soliloquy' on the risk society may be regarded as "a seminal work which could lift environmental sociology into the mainstream of debate in the broader field of sociology" (Hannigan, 1995, p. 12).

At the level of political action and policy shift, again two contrasting approaches may be discerned each reflecting specific ideological and theoretical predilections. By far the most common, one might say universal, approach reflects ecological modernisation. It is, at once, a technical theory, a policy discourse and, for some, a belief system as well (Christoff, 1996). Ecological modernisation regards the environmental challenge not as a crisis but as an opportunity. The assumption here (and the assumptions are usually unquestioned) is that a process of industrial innovation encouraged by a market economy and facilitated by an enabling state will ensure environmental conservation. The process is one of gradual change and institutional adaptation achieved through consensus. A typical illustration of this view is provided by Frances Cairncross

> But merely to oppose growth will achieve little. Instead a wiser strategy for environmentalists is to look for ways in which growth and environmental improvement support each other, and to study ways to protect the environment at minimal economic cost. (Cairncross, 1995, p. 4)

By contrast, those commentators expounding opposing positions, regard environmental changes, if unheeded, as leading to catastrophe threatening survival. Tampering with the system will not do—only a thoroughgoing overhaul at all levels (production, consumption, distribution of wealth and power) will suffice to avert the impending crisis. This is not so much a policy prescription as an analysis, a critique of modernisation. It is characterised by its

> emphasis on cultural renewal, the emphasis on developing an ecological consciousness, and the critique of industrialism. (Eckersley, 1992, p. 27)

In terms of the notion of a 'defining moment' of social change introduced at the outset, the two approaches suggest very different conclusions. From the perspective of environmental modernisation and its political programme of technological innovation and institutional adaptation, it can be seen as a *moment of transition* as society continues to pursue the project of modernisation while

taking due care and attention of environmental constraints. For opponents of this view who advocate revolutionary, if unspecified changes, the present historical juncture appears as potentially a *moment of transformation*.

This review sets out to examine how far environmental change has become a central issue both in social scientific discourse and in political strategy. In particular, it seeks to answer the question as to whether environmental change is capable of being absorbed through adaptation or whether it provokes entirely new or different ways of organising, managing and living in society. There are four stages to the argument. The paper will first set out the nature of the contemporary environmental issue in terms of its defining characteristics. This will provide a context for then examining the contributions of contrasting theoretical approaches to understanding the relationship between society and environment. The third stage will consider changes occurring at the political level that are relevant to the process of environmental change. Particular attention will be paid to the changing role of the state and the rise of environmental social movements as agents of change. The final part of the paper will evaluate the strengths and weaknesses of alternative approaches and speculate on the prospects for change.

Before commencing, two notes of caution are in order. First, although global environmental change is widely recognised and sustainable development is commonly regarded as the necessary direction for change, the environment has, until recently, been a marginal and insignificant issue both in academic discourse and in policy-making. Within the social sciences, it is only just emerging as a central topic of concern in debates about modernism and post-modernism (Gandy, 1996). Claims that environmentalism is a "new ideological tradition" (Eder, 1996, p. 204) or ecologism an "ideology in its own right" (Dobson, 1990, p. 3) may yet be premature. The most that can be said is that, having occupied a fringe position in the social sciences focusing on attitudes and solutions to specific problems, the environmental dimension is now increasingly considered to inform and challenge central theoretical debates.

Secondly, at the political level, sustainable development is more rhetoric than reality. As a statement of faith it may be appropriated by interests with very different views of how the environment should be managed and what institutional changes are necessary. As a political priority, it still remains well below the politician's quotidian preoccupations with the economy, law and order, defence, health or education. 'Sustainable development' is not exactly a term on the lips of the person in the street. Nevertheless, there are good grounds for arguing that the environment as a subject of academic discourse and as a focus for political action is more firmly based now than at any time in recent history.

2. Global Environmental Change: A New Paradigm?

The contemporary environmental problem is distinctive in a number of dimensions (Blowers and Leroy, 1996). The first of these characteristics is its *interdisciplinary context*. Concern about environmental change is, of course, nothing new. Indeed, it might be argued that contemporary concern about the environment has diminished somewhat since its apogee in the period leading up to Rio in 1992. This could be true at the somewhat superficial level of public opinion about the importance of issues but there are grounds for concluding that the contemporary concern for the environment is different, distinctive and unlikely to wither away as did the anxieties provoked by *The Limits to Growth* thesis in 1972 (Meadows *et al.* 1972). The limits-to-growth thesis failed to hold the public imagination; the flaws in its methodology were exposed; its authoritarian solutions were discredited; and the OPEC oil crisis, paradoxically focusing on resource limits, at the same time diverted attention towards the needs of the economy rather than the environment. Interestingly, the limits-of-growth argument has been revived (Mead-

ows *et al.*, 1992) though, on this occasion, it is part of the broader debate about global environmental change and its implications.

By contrast, global environmental change and its associated strategy of sustainable development is "a consensus concept which forms a focal point for social and political mobilisation" (Leroy, 1995, p. 42). It has achieved influence and impact at a theoretical, ideological and political level. Ozone depletion, global warming, loss of biodiversity, desertification and nuclear proliferation are evident risks, even if their scale, timing and precise impacts are unforeseeable. And it is increasingly recognised that they are problems with both physical and social dimensions. Their solution requires analysis from both the natural and the social sciences. The social sciences are belatedly joining the natural sciences in the attempt to understand the implications of environmental change. According to Leroy,

> interdisciplinarity or, better still, multidisciplinarity in environmental science should be nothing more and also nothing less than a pragmatic and critical interplay of various scientific fields and disciplines. (Leroy, 1995, p. 31)

At the political level, too, global environmental change requires a degree of co-operation which has major implications for state sovereignty, North–South relationships and the role of transnational organisations and movements.

A second characteristic is that contemporary environmental problems are almost always *anthropogenic in origin*. It is the intervention—indeed, the imposition—of human activities on the natural environment that results in the depletion of resources or pollution of ecosystems. Of course there are some environmental problems which appear to be the result of natural disasters such as volcanoes or floods, but their causes or their consequences are associated with human activities such as deforestation, overexploitation of soil, settlements located in vulnerable areas and so on. It is also true that some of these problems are not new but, like deforestation, have occurred on a wide scale from time to time and from place to place throughout civilisation. But the difference is that contemporary problems, for the first time, threaten the capacity of natural systems at a global level to cope with the burden placed upon them.

The linkage of the physical and the social leads to a third, related, characteristic—namely that contemporary problems are *socially constructed* (Liberatore, 1995). This does not imply that they only exist as social constructs, for the physical impacts of these problems are (or will be) real enough. It is simply that

> environmental problems do not materialise by themselves; rather, they must be 'constructed' by individuals or organisations who define pollution or some other objective condition as worrisome and seek to do something about it. (Hannigan, 1995, p. 2)

It does mean that certain problems will command attention while others may be neglected. Hence global warming has achieved a prominence as an issue which some would argue it may not have merited based purely on scientific evidence alone (Buttel *et al.*, 1990). Furthermore, it is quite possible that some problems are simply ignored through lack of attention or political priority or because they are suppressed. Power relationships may succeed in preventing certain issues from reaching the decision-making agenda—for example, high-rise housing (Dunleavy, 1981); air pollution (Crenson, 1971; Blowers, 1984); water pollution (Bartlett, 1980). It is certainly true that the advanced industrial countries of the North are sufficiently powerful to establish the agenda of global environmental change. For this reason, ozone depletion, global warming and loss of biodiversity have received more attention than issues affecting the developing countries such as desertification (Carr and Mpande, 1996).

What is clear is that contemporary society is in the act of creating risks from which none can escape. Therefore, a fourth characteristic is the *concern for survival* which

accompanies contemporary global environmental risk. In the past, especially when environmental risks were evidently more localised, it was issues such as public health (de Swaan, 1988) or amenity and environmental quality that were predominating concerns. They stimulated élites to seek better environments and to introduce policies of environmental protection. Thus, much social scientific work on the environment was concerned with issues of countryside and landscape, urban settlement and land-use policy and industrial pollution. It was also concerned with issues of class and power in the articulation of environmental conflicts. Contemporary concern has centred on resource depletion and on long-term survival (Goodin, 1976) and is reflected in a focus on global environmental issues. In the South, of course, day-to-day survival may be both a more pressing and a more immediate concern.

This global focus constitutes the fifth characteristic, namely, that many contemporary environmental problems are now *global in reach*. This is a result, either of the diffusion of sources—for example, the transfer of polluting industries or the export of hazardous substances across the world—or, of the diffusion of impacts as environmental media absorb and transfer pollution on a global basis causing such problems as ozone depletion, radioactive fall-out, acid rain or global warming. It is self-evident that while some environmental problems (for example, pollution of water sources and soil degradation) are confined within defined territories, environmental processes do not respect political boundaries. Consequently, they are addressed by transnational organisations, inter-governmental and non-governmental; indeed, Yearley (1994) considers a key defining characteristic to be the transnational character of environmental movements.

Environmental change is sometimes seen as a key component of a more general process commonly described as 'globalisation'. This includes such phenomena as the international (or 'global') economy and finance, media and culture, political organisations both inter-governmental and non-governmental, as well as networks of scientists, social movements and so on, all of which transcend national boundaries. The globalisation of communications has led to

> the world ... being compressed through the electronic overcoming of distance and through the cultural similarities advanced by the global entertainment industry. (Yearley, 1996, p. 9)

It is through electronic communication, in particular with the instantaneous spread of information, that global communities of interest can be established, developing networks, promoting ideas that can be shared by those near and far. When distance is no barrier, some would argue, place and space relinquish their grip on the imagination. The potential for influence, for action and for the flow of ideas is limitless.

Yet, the enthusiasm which has greeted globalisation in some quarters needs to be tempered with caution. In the economic sphere, Hirst and Thompson (1996) point out that the world economy is still dominated by the triad of Europe, Japan and North America and they argue that the notion of a global economy is a myth. Other commentators have pointed out that the decline of the nation-state, a concomitant process of globalisation, has been much exaggerated. Furthermore, in some respects, the idea of globalisation provides a comforting idea of unity, homogeneity and common purpose which is easily contradicted by the reality of vast differences (in culture, wealth, power and environment) that survive. Diversity and inequality remain persistent features of the world today.

Consequently, a sixth characteristic related to global environmental change is the *unevenness of impact*. The benefits and burdens of modern industrial and agricultural processes are inequitably distributed. There may be temporal displacement as the risks created by the present generation are passed down to succeeding generations (for instance, radioactive waste or global warming). There also may be spatial displacement (in the form of industrial pollution and risk in

the form of 'pollution havens' or 'nuclear oases' or widespread environmental degradation through resource depletion) as externalities are imposed by one area on another, especially between North and South. The process of uneven impact, at the local level, has been described theoretically and empirically as a process of 'peripheralisation' (Blowers and Leroy, 1994).

This pattern of spatial inequality is both created and reinforced by a seventh characteristic, *conflicts between interests*, with those able to deploy power gaining at the expense of those who are weak. At the global level, these interests include business corporations who exploit resources and create pollution (especially multinationals operating on a global basis) with an interest primarily in profit. Another set of interests are the nation-states, with an interest in sustaining economic growth and protecting their sovereignty. Intergovernmental organisations with an interest in trade (WTO, EU, NAFTA), aid (World Bank) or financial stability (IMF) also influence the environmental agenda while international conventions, regimes and treaties on environmental protection explicitly do so. The scientific community is also an interest-group. While scientists may appeal to rationality, disinterested research and the pursuit of understanding, they are also part of society and therefore concerned with such necessities as funding, status and power. Environmental movements form another interest-grouping. While they are dedicated to a variety of causes, they also have an interest in maintaining their influence (and power) over the environmental agenda and decision-making. Indeed, Sklair (1994) has detected what he calls a transnational environmentalist élite composed of major (Northern) environmental NGOs, green bureaucrats, politicians and professionals and the green media and merchants.

There is conflict between and within all these interest-groupings over the relative priorities to be accorded to economic and environmental goals and over which specific issues should be given priority and there is conflict over policies, instruments and time-scales for implementation. At a global level, the conflict between North and South has begun to transcend all other levels of conflict over global environmental change. At any rate, the emergence of these various transnational interest-groupings is a major distinguishing feature of the contemporary environmental problem.

In order to achieve influence, interest-groups must deploy expertise and the *dominance of experts and expert systems* in both identifying and providing solutions for environmental problems is the eighth characteristic. Debate on environmental issues is conducted via scientific evidence and counter-evidence in a culture of expertise. Haas (1990) has coined the term 'epistemic communities' for those

> transnational networks of knowledge based communities that are politically empowered through their claims to exercise authoritative knowledge and motivated by shared principles and causal beliefs. (Haas, 1990, p. 349)

Science has acquired, or rather appropriated, the role of identifying environmental problems, setting priorities for the environmental agenda and, consequently, society looks to science for solutions (Boehmer-Christiansen and Skea, 1991; Boehmer-Christiansen, 1994; Wynne, 1994). Yet, scientific knowledge—both theoretical and empirical—though apparently so authoritative, is uncertain, contestable and, consequently, refutable (Yearley, 1992). The power of science is such that scientists

> have entered the policy arena in an unprecedented way and are now willing to stand behind data that are not entirely conclusive, but which have awesome potential implications for humankind. (Buttel *et al.*, 1990, p. 65)

Global warming is, perhaps, the defining example of the supremacy of a scientific consensus in defining environmental risks. Such risks, which threaten annihilation of life as we know it, cannot be contradicted (unless and until scientific knowledge points strongly in another direction) and lead to the conclusion that evasive, precautionary action must be taken. But, such action needs more than scientific justification; it requires a policy process capable of implementation.

Environmental groups have necessarily been drawn into this culture. They increasingly use scientists to provide the evidence for their cause, often leading to conflict between experts supporting opposing sides. Moreover, environmental groups and, increasingly, international regimes recognise the expertise residing in the knowledge of indigenous peoples. The Intergovernmental Panel on Forests has considered the role of traditional forest-related knowledge (Humphreys, 1996) and the importance of using local skill, experience and knowledge has been stressed in the International Convention on Desertification.

In the development of expertise, social science has a part to play. Many scientists and politicians—and some social scientists—regard that role as quite specific and limited to problem-solving, devising appropriate policy frameworks and models, and identifying instruments and mechanisms for implementation. But such an instrumental approach is responsive and passive and takes for granted the priorities and preferences of decision-makers. Social science plays a subordinate, indeed subservient, role to powerful interests. Therefore, it is also necessary for social scientists to provide a sceptical, critical analysis of the provenance of policy, the interests it serves and the consequences that may arise both now and in the future (Leroy, 1995). As Wynne observes,

> sociological deconstruction of global environmental science is necessary to expose the hidden interests of the rich countries in concealing the more demanding political challenges of exploitation, domination and inequity underlying global environmental change. (Wynne, 1994, p. 185)

The social response to environmental change will hinge on a ninth and final characteristic, which for want of a better phrase, may be called the *ethical dimension*. This is taken in its broadest sense to cover the values that shape attitudes (and ultimately behaviour) towards the environment and the ideologies that influence interests and, at the political level, the policies to deal with environmental problems. There is a whole range of concepts involved here ranging from the concern for the intrinsic value of nature, through the rights of individuals and future generations, to the nature of participation in decision-making, the value and costs of environmental assets and the problem of social inequality. The implications for policy of the ethical dimension have been the subject of a number of texts in environmental economics (for example, Jacobs, 1991, 1995; Daly and Cobb, 1990), environmental sociology (for example, Redclift and Benton, 1994; Hannigen, 1995; Liberatore, 1995), environmental politics (Dobson, 1990, 1991; Eckersley, 1992) and environmental ethics (CEC, 1989; Pepper, 1996). It has stimulated the production of new journals such as *Environmental Values* and *Ethics and the Environment*.

Policies for sustainable development are ideologically determined and influenced by different ethical values. There are, on the one hand, those definitions which reflect a 'weak' sustainability emphasising the substitutability of resources and the reduction of polluting processes. They are basically congruent with the environmentalist approach to conservation achievable through ecological modernisation referred to earlier. In contrast, is 'strong' sustainability, reflecting an ecological approach, which focuses on the significance of all forms of life and the need for environmental protection (Naess, 1991). This version of sustainability advocates decentralisation, changing life-styles and greater social equality, and consequently presents a challenge to the belief that global environmental change can be managed through the adaptation of the modern economy and related institutions.

These nine defining characteristics of the contemporary environmental problem form the context for theoretical and practical debate about how global environmental

change is to be confronted and managed. They are given different interpretations and significance by the two contrasting views identified earlier. One, ecological modernisation, holds that change can be managed through continuity and consensus; the other believes that fundamental change in modern ways of organisation, production and living is essential if environmental crisis is to be averted. These viewpoints are 'ideal types'; and as such they are mutually incompatible. In practice, there is a continuum of possibilities between extremes and the way forward may very well be a combination of aspects of both positions. This possibility will be returned to later; first, let us examine the propositions of each perspective.

3. Alternative Perspectives on Environmental Change

Ecological Modernisation: The Case for Reform

Ecological modernisation theory (EMT) originated in the 1980s through the work of the German sociologist Joseph Huber but it has been adopted elsewhere, notably in the Netherlands and latterly in other countries including the UK. EMT is both a normative and a prescriptive theory and, as such, its theoretical premises are descriptive. It is essentially a conservative theory espousing a weak version of sustainability achievable through a greater emphasis on environmental conservation. It breaks with the idea that environmental needs are in conflict with economic demands; it argues instead that "economic growth and the resolution of ecological problems can, in principle, be reconciled" (Hajer, 1996, p. 248). Thus, EMT presumes that "the way out of the ecological crisis seems only possible by going further into the process of industrialization" (Spaargaren and Mol, 1990, p. 14).

Ecologisation of production. EMT has the following features (Mol, 1995, 1996). First, and perhaps most important, is the emphasis on introducing ecological criteria into the production and consumption processes. Consequently EMT assigns a pivotal role to science and technology in the production process. This the 'refinement of production' through technology. Its particular features are

> clean technology, economic valuation of environmental resources, changing consumption and production styles, prevention and monitoring of compounds through production–consumption cycles. (Spaargaren and Mol, 1990, p. 16)

Weale is positively enthusiastic about the possibilities:

> Instead of seeing environmental protection as a burden upon the economy the ecological modernist sees it as a potential source for future growth. Since environmental amenity is a superior good, the demand for pollution control is likely to increase and there is therefore a considerable advantage to an economy to have the technical and production capacity to produce low polluting goods or pollution control technology. (Weale, 1992, p. 76)

The market economy and the enabling state. EMT regards the market economy as the most effective way of securing the flexibility, innovation and responsiveness needed to promote the ecological adaptation of industry. The role of the state is enabling, establishing a regulatory framework which assists the efficiency of the market and ensures environmental protection. It is remarkable how the language of EMT corresponds so neatly to the contemporary political dispensation. The Brundtland Report exudes ecological modernisation (WCED, 1987). The UN Commission on Sustainable Development has imbibed the doctrine. And the UK's strategy on sustainable development pronounces,

> Sustainable development does not mean having less economic development: on the contrary, a healthy economy is better able to generate the resources to meet people's needs, and new investment and environ-

mental improvement often go hand in hand. (HMSO, 1994, p. 7)

The role of industry and environmental movements. EMT also considers the supporting role of major actors. Transnational companies (TNCs) are the progenitors of the global economy and are regarded as the initiators of change. Furthermore, environmental movements may also be supportive in so far as they can be incorporated into the modernisation project. Indeed, collaboration is increasingly common between TNCs and some transnational environmental organisations (TEOs). Those environmental movements which maintain their oppositional stance are dismissed as irrelevant, lacking either political or ideological support (Mol, 1995, p. 58). Sklair sums up the situation thus,

> There is evidence that at least some TEOs are already collaborating with, if they have not actually been co-opted by, the TNCs. I predict that those who refuse to be co-opted will be marginalized. (Sklair, 1994, p. 210)

Reservations. EMT, is a moderate and conservative theory confirming business as usual.

> It assumes that the existing political institutions can internalise ecological concerns or can at least give birth to new supranational forms of management... (Hajer, 1996, p. 253)

It is optimistic,

> All that is needed ... is to fast forward from the polluting industrial society of the past to the new superindustrialised era of the future. (Hannigan, 1994, p. 184)

Moreover, it has wide appeal as a 'modern' concept since it goes with the grain of political and personal aspirations. In the UK context, it speaks at once both to the New Right with its focus on the market economy and to the notion of a 'stakeholder society' promoted by New Labour. EMT is a celebration of contemporary capitalism with a greener face. Mol presents EMT as "a radical reform programme as regards the way modern society deals with the environment" (Mol, 1996, p. 309) and states that it "brings the environment back into the centre of social theory" (p. 310).

The very strengths of EMT—focus on technological adaptation, celebration of the market economy, belief in collaboration and consensus—are also the source of its weaknesses and limitations. In the first place, it is a theory based entirely on Western industrial experience. While aspects of modernisation may equally apply in developing countries (especially through the export of technology), it may also prove unsustainable. Subsistence economies which are prevalent over much of the South may actually be more sustainable than modern agricultural systems based on the intensification of production (Sage, 1996).

Secondly, EMT focuses on the economic and technological dimensions; it is largely innocent of the social context of change and the ethical issues that are raised. It does not go beyond the assumption that

> the existing political institutions can internalise ecological concerns or can at least give birth to new supranational forms of management that can deal with the relevant issues. (Hajer, 1996, p. 253)

Further, it seems that ecological modernisation combines happily with a consensus on economic growth and a comfortable collaboration in institutional learning and adaptation between various interests. What it neglects to note is that modern society is composed of very divergent interests and that inequalities of wealth and power are endemic—indeed, a natural outcome of the process of the market economy. EMT appears to be indifferent to the processes by which its project is brought about. It may be thought that an authoritarian regime is equally as able to enforce modernisation as a liberal, pluralist one—and both are unlikely to address questions of social inequality.

Thirdly, EMT regards the free market and

the enabling state as compatible and complementary. While the state, by removing barriers to trade and competition, may support the market, there comes a point when state interference or intervention may be in conflict with market forces. As Christoff points out, the state must both support the market through bearing infrastructure costs and taking the burden of welfare and education provision while, at the same time, responding to the appeal of business to alleviate the tax burden (Christoff, 1997). This can lead to crises of both accumulation (O'Connor, 1973) and legitimation (Habermas, 1976)— problems identified in the 1970s but no less real today with environmental protection as an added burden on both state and business.

Finally, while EMT can minimise risk, it cannot eliminate it. EMT tends to focus on the national rather than the international level. It cannot ultimately deal with those high-risk/low-probability technologies where the risk of catastrophe, no matter how remote, nevertheless exists and is potentially global. The nuclear industry is obviously one of these and no amount of refinement can rid us of the awful potentiality of annihilation. Mol acknowledges the point:

> the main frame of reference of ecological modernisation includes "normal" environmental problems such as water pollution, chemical waste and acidification...In dealing with high-consequence risks such as the greenhouse effect and the Chernobyl disaster, an analysis based on the Risk Society theory may yield significant additional insights... (Mol, 1995, pp. 395–396)

It is to the risk society thesis that we now turn.

Risk Society: The Case for Fundamental Change

Reflexive modernisation. It was the growing importance of global risks of high consequence that led Ulrich Beck to formulate his thesis of the risk society. The risk society theory (RST) is the most developed critique of the social consequences of environmental change (or, as Beck prefers it, 'ecological crisis'). His initial ideas, first published in German in 1986 (and translated as *Risk Society* in 1992), were formulated in the context of the nuclear age and appeared at the time of the Chernobyl disaster. The nuclear issue hangs ominously, though not always explicitly, over his writings and is clearly in his mind when he defines risk societies as those

> that are confronted by the challenges of the self-created possibility, hidden at first, then increasingly apparent, of the self-destruction of all life on this earth. (Beck, 1995, p. 67)

His thesis has been further elaborated in subsequent essays (1995, 1996; and Beck *et al.*, 1994) in which he describes the present condition of society as one of 'reflexive modernisation'. By this he means that Western modernisation has led to a transition from an industrial society to a risk society and with it there comes the confrontation with the self-destructive consequences which cannot be overcome by the system of industrial society.

> Risk society is *not an option* which could be chosen or rejected in the course of political debate. It arises through the automatic operation of autonomous processes which are blind and deaf to consequences and dangers. In total, and latently, these produce hazards which call into question— indeed abolish—the basis of industrial society. (Beck, 1996, p. 28)

Ecological risk from high technology. The risks he refers to are those arising from nuclear, chemical, ecological and genetic engineering which are limited in neither time nor space; cannot be accounted for in terms of causality, blame and liability; and which cannot be compensated for or insured against. They are anthropogenic, global and threaten survival.

> The world has become a testing ground for risky technologies, and thus also a potential refutation of the safety guarantees of state, economic and technical authority. (Beck, 1995, p. 8)

More and more, the centre comes to be occupied by threats that are neither visible nor tangible to the lay public, threats that will not even take their toll in the life-span of the affected individuals. (Beck, 1992, p. 162)

The benefits from such technologies are also dispersed and can be enjoyed by individuals who "can do something and continue doing it without having to take personal responsibility for it" (Beck, 1992, p. 33). It is rather like the case of the 'tragedy of the commons' (Hardin, 1968) where there is an incentive for production to continue for individual benefit while risks to the society as a whole continue to multiply. The only certain 'solution' is to cease the activity altogether.

Nuclear risk is a test case. It is a product of high technology; it is a high-consequence risk; it is an unfamiliar, involuntary and unavoidable risk; once in train it is irreversible and substantially uncontrollable and safety and security cannot be guaranteed. But, it also has a number of features which make it unique. It is a 'dread risk' (Slovic *et al.*, 1980; Royal Society, 1992) which engenders greater and more widespread fear than any other form of socially induced risk (Blowers *et al.*, 1991). It is invisible and it is feared— whatever the source and whatever the level of radioactivity (Bertell, 1985). Furthermore, it is a risk associated with both civil and military nuclear activities. It emanates from routine emissions, from the possibility of accidents and from deliberate military action. Its impacts can be gradual and long-lasting, resulting from fall-out scattered widely (Milliken, 1986) but also devastating and immediate as in the case of such traumatic events as Hiroshima, Nagasaki and Chernobyl. In the case of nuclear war,

> the effect only exists when it occurs, and when it occurs, it no longer exists, because nothing exists any more. (Beck, 1992, p. 38)

The 'worst-case scenario' is, ultimately, possible.

856   ANDREW BLOWERS

Dependence on experts. The second element of the thesis arises as a consequence of high technology, an increasing dependency on experts and expert systems (one of the defining characteristics of contemporary environmental problems as we saw earlier). Unlike ecological modernisation where science and technology are seen as the solution to the problem, in the risk society analysis scientific expertise is portrayed as exercising control over technologies that cannot ultimately be controlled. Consequently efforts are bent to minimise risks, to persuade society that the possibility of a major hazard is infinitesimally small. There has developed a lexicon of 'objective' risk assessment measuring probabilities of risk of death in terms such as one in a million per year over periods of up to 10 000 years.

It is clear that zero risk is an unattainable concept and the notion of 'acceptable' risk is elusive in that it is rooted in feelings about justice, fairness and democracy (O'Riordan *et al.*, 1988). Since it is not possible to assess what is acceptable, the notion of tolerability has been introduced. In the nuclear industry, the tolerability of risk (TOR) concept is now widely used in radiological protection criteria (RWMAC/ACSNI, 1995). Risk is presented in terms of three zones a zone where it is unacceptable; one where risks need to be considered carefully; and one where it is broadly acceptable (see Figure 1). It is a flexible concept and levels of risk (measured in terms of possibility of fatal cancers in a year to the general public) must be monitored and reduced when feasible. Tolerability is thus based on a subjective evaluation of possibilities of exposure and prevention; it is not an unambiguous scientific criterion.

The TOR illuminates the core of the risk society thesis. Since risk, no matter how catastrophic its consequences, cannot be entirely eliminated, it becomes necessary to formulate a probabilistic level of risk that is justified by the supposed benefits enjoyed as a result of the risky activity. There is the further problem that risks to future generations which derive no benefit from the activity may be greater than those to the

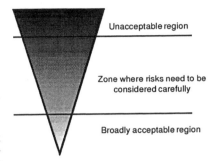

Figure 1. The "tolerability of risk" concept. *Source:* Report of a Study Group drawn from members of the Radioactive Waste Management Advisory Committee and the Advisory Committee on the Safety of Nuclear Installations (RWMAC/ACSNI, March 1995).

present generation which does enjoy the benefits. For example, in the case of a nuclear waste repository, it is acknowledged that "Quantitative assessments of risk can be considered meaningful for up to about ten thousand years" (RWMAC/ACSNI, 1995, p. 57); in other words, any 'objective' assessment of risk disappears eons before the risks inherent in some of the most dangerous radionuclides (such as plutonium with a half-life of 24 000 years) are likely to begin to reduce.

The purpose of such concepts as TOR is to provide a rationale for the maintenance of activities which present low-probability/high-consequence risk. It supports what Beck calls a condition of 'industrial fatalism' based on a system of 'organised irresponsibility'. Despite the occasional—and eventually inevitable—break-downs (of which Chernobyl has so far been the most dramatic), a combination of cover-up, public relations and inquiry serves to bolster the industry and reinforce the confidence of (and confidence in) experts.

> The plausibility of experts is only superficially undermined by accidents, and essentially serves to expand the power of industrial-technocratic elites. (Beck, 1992, p. 66)

By definition, risk involves uncertainty. There are two aspects of this. One is the uncertainty of the event predicted by the risk assessment occurring. It might never happen but it could happen at any time. In Beck's doleful words,

> In an age of world wide growth of large-scale technological systems, the least likely event will occur in the long run. (Beck, 1995, p. 1)

The other uncertainty is the disagreement among the experts themselves. Expert advice is contestable; it is frequently countered by counter-expertise. But, experts are not disinterested. They are frequently employed by the industries whose safety they pronounce upon. Governments decide which experts to use. Therefore, even 'independent' advice provided to governments is predicated on certain underlying assumptions about the necessity of industrial development. Nevertheless, decision-makers must place themselves in the hands of experts, trust to their judgement and make choices. And their choice will lean heavily on the expertise they employ, however uncertain that advice may be. Thus experts hold enormous power in society.

Beck's analysis of environmental risk encapsulates the condition of late modernity with its dependence on industrial systems that conceivably threaten the whole world and its reliance on expert systems whose judgement on the risks that may be tolerated is supreme. Against this backdrop we turn now to the third component of the risk society thesis, individual risk.

Individualisation. Beck's thesis is also concerned with the social consequences of ecological risk. Risk societies are societies experiencing within themselves a process which he describes as 'individualisation', a condition of increasing personal insecurity in which the individual is increasingly exposed to personal risks which are, partly, a consequence of wider (sometimes global) economic and social risks. Thus, a risk society is one where global ecological risk combines with increasing risk at the individual level to create a condition of continuing uncertainty.

This condition of individualisation comprises three basic elements. One is the economic insecurity felt in unemployment, threat of redundancy and loss of rights experienced as a result of economic restructuring and liberalisation with its attendant privatisation and deregulation. Connected to this is a second element, the withdrawal of state welfare, safety nets and security systems. And, a third element (which is arguably connected to the first two), is an increasing dislocation in personal life and threats to individual physical security. This includes: insecurity in personal relationships (as evidenced in an increasing divorce rate, approaching 40 per cent of first-time marriages in the UK); the fear of crime (though not necessarily matched by crime statistics); fear of such diseases as AIDS (for which there is no cure); increasing mobility (which increases social polarisation); and the lack of opportunity especially as perceived by the young of all classes.

The concomitant of this condition of individualisation has been a weakening of those institutions and organisations which have been hitherto the means of social integration in modern society. These include both more 'traditional' integrating institutions such as family, kinship, neighbourhood, community and religion, as well as the 'modern' institutions associated with work (trade unions and professional associations) and politics (political parties). With the loss of support, identity and sense of continuity that is bestowed by such institutions, the individual has become more rootless, more vulnerable. Lacking the props of these erstwhile integrating institutions, the individual is increasingly responsible for his or her destiny in an increasingly uncertain world. In Beck's words,

> Individualization ... means that each person's biography is removed from given determinations and placed in his or her own hands, open and dependent on decisions. (Beck, 1992, p. 135)

Negative fatalism or new enlightenment? Beck's thesis is deeply pessimistic, as he is at pains to admit.

> Certainly, hopelessness is ennobling and the advantages of wallowing in superiority, while at the same time being relieved of all responsibility for action, are not to be underestimated. (Beck, 1996, p. 38)

A condition of imponderable ecological risk, a destiny in the hands of experts, combined with personal insecurity may well lead to a 'negative fatalism'. Individuals blunder blindly onwards, dimly aware of the dangers that lie ahead but incapable of forestalling them. There is a pervasive air of, 'If we can't change it, let's welcome it'. But, insists Beck, "it is precisely the power of fatalism which makes fatalism wrong" (Beck, 1996, p. 39).

In this well of despair, Beck spies a glimmer of hope in the condition of reflexive modernisation. It is conceivable that the loss of direction, certainty and security once offered by integrating (often conservative and confining) institutions acts not to constrain but to liberate individuals opening up new possibilities for thought and action. Acceptance becomes replaced by self-criticism, by society as well as individuals.

> It is therefore the combination of reflex and reflections, which, as long as the catastrophe fails to materialise, can set industrial modernity on the path to self-criticism and self-transformation. (Beck, 1996, p. 34)

The opportunity opens up for major shifts in attitudes and values. It must be said that Beck remains unclear about the outcomes of such a process beyond an expression of hope that an age of 'New Enlightenment' will dawn "counteracting the disempowerment and expropriation of everyday life in hazard civilisation" (Beck, 1995, p. 184). This ringing appeal following a portrayal of general hopelessness has all the substance, as Beck concedes, of "a sigh to the end of the world" (Beck, 1996, p. 38). But the possibility

exists, even though Beck is unclear about the process and outcomes of the transformation.

Reservations. Like ecological modernisation, the risk society thesis appears to apply only to advanced Western (possibly only western European) societies. Experience of risk takes on quite different connotations elsewhere—especially in the South, where risk of war, famine and disease provide immediate dangers. The risks in Western countries appear to be almost luxurious by comparison. Beck tends to treat Western society as if it were relatively homogeneous and to underplay the uneven impacts of contemporary environmental problems. The process of individualisation is neither all-pervasive, nor complete. While aspects of the condition obviously affect everyone directly or indirectly, the impact will vary widely and, given the social inequality which appears to have grown in some countries, the disadvantaged will suffer most from a combination of personal risks. It may be only the relatively privileged who are able to take stock of their situation and to apply the self-critical awareness that is the essence of reflexive modernisation. For the disadvantaged, comprising a growing underclass in many Western societies, an abject and uncomprehending fatalism is the more likely condition.

Furthermore, many of the personal risks experienced by people in Western societies are nothing new. For example, unemployment and poverty were much more prevalent during the inter-war years and were not mitigated by the state to the same extent as occurs even today; contagious diseases were much more threatening a generation ago; and the support provided by integrating institutions was not available to everyone and, for those who were embraced by them, such institutions could be stifling. For many people, the integration provided by institutions remains and traditional and modern institutions have been joined by some (post) modern ones, too, such as social movements focused around major issues such as the environment, women's rights, the rights of minorities and indigenous peoples.

There is, then, the possibility that Beck's ideas on social change are of limited application. His argument about ecological risk is founded upon those technologies which contain awesome destructive power. By implication we must desist from such activities if risk is to be eliminated. Yet, such a strategy is not feasible politically. Beck's argument is, in the end, a polemic—albeit a compelling one. Its analysis is persuasive but its solutions—in terms of institutional and social change—are vague.

4. Constraint and Opportunity for Social Change

The two approaches reviewed here provide very different theoretical expositions of environmental change and they point in very different directions. On the one hand, ecological modernisation essentially advocates a continuation of the changes which it perceives as already occurring in industrial society. It makes a virtue of the seemingly inevitable and aligns itself with contemporary trends in the economy, society and politics. It appears to be politically realistic and therefore achievable, at least within Western economies. It abstains from a broader diagnosis of the conflicts within capitalist societies, the problem of inequality (especially between North and South) and the trends associated with those industrial processes which, if not arrested, may eventually threaten survival. It is these very points which risk society addresses. It is a more embracing theory concerned with the relationships between industrial growth, institutional and social change. It offers a different form of realism, peering into the abyss that awaits the hubristic progress of modern society. It is a vision of dystopia, a warning from which escape is only possible through society confronting the awesome prospect of its own destruction. The problem with the risk society thesis is that it is ultimately tendentious, leading inexorably onward to its predetermined conclusion. Moreover, it neglects some of the significant changes in environmental protection now occurring in

industrial societies which are emphasised by ecological modernisation theorists.

These perspectives are ideal-types, each representative of opposing viewpoints and values. They indicate the gulf between conservative and radical views of social change; between consensus and conflict; between the market economy and intervention; between continuity and change; and between transition and transformation. But this gulf may be spanned as opposing tendencies overlap and are influenced by each other and as new ways forward develop. This part of the review will examine certain institutional changes identified by commentators which suggest how the gap may be bridged and which point the way forward, if only hesitantly. It will focus on two areas of change that appear to be potentially significant. One is changes in political structures which open up the space for change; the other the rise of environmental social movements. Together, they suggest a way forward which combines elements of both ecological modernisation and the risk society.

4.1 The Creation of Political Space

World civil society. Change at the level of political institutions is occurring at all levels in response to global environmental change. At the international level, there has been the rapid development of a number of regimes, principles, conventions, treaties and protocols to deal with such problems as global warming, desertification, ozone depletion, the pollution of the oceans, endangered species and hazardous substances. The post-Rio period has seen the establishment of the UN Commission for Sustainable Development which is entrusted with the development of the 40 chapters of Agenda 21 based on national programmes and leading up to a major review in 1997. These have been supported by regional agreements, notably by the European Union, which have added a range of other issues.

This development of international activity has led to some surrender of state power and, according to some observers, to a loss of

860   ANDREW BLOWERS

sovereignty. But, as Potter (1995) comments, this is nothing new.

> The theory of sovereignty—that states have 'supreme authority' within their boundaries—is both a legal fiction and a powerful idea. (Potter, 1995, p. 107)

Sovereignty and the state are quite separate ideas. While states have surrendered sovereignty to international organisations, they still remain powerful in that the agreement and co-operation of states is essential both for the development and implementation of policy. For example, it remains difficult, though not impossible, to apply sanctions on states unwilling to co-operate and states are free (or unable to resist) the degradation of their own environments or to impose environmental damage on others via shared pathways or the global commons.

The development of formal inter-state arrangements to protect the environment has been parallelled by another process, the networks of interaction of non-state international organisations (business and environmental) seeking to exert influence on the process of environmental policy-making. These organisations have been able to occupy the political space that has opened up. According to some observers, this interaction has both created and occupied political space; it has, as it were, resulted in a kind of world 'civil society' enabling a process of 'social learning' to take place through the exchange of ideas and experience (Wapner, 1995a, 1995b; Lipschutz, 1993; List, 1996)). In principle, this process is co-operative and collaborative, providing a political context for the elaboration of ecological modernisation. But, it may equally well open up the opportunity for alternative values and strategies to be explored.

Changes within the state. Within Western states, and notably within Britain, the past two decades have witnessed parallel processes of centralisation and decentralisation together with a decline of formal politics. The local level of government has been stripped of power and strapped for cash

while the executive has become more dominant. At the same time, power has become dispersed through a proliferation of quangos. There has been a "hollowing out of the state" (Rhodes, 1994) as the ascendancy of the market has led to deregulation and privatisation and the withdrawal of the state's frontiers from many areas of public provision. Political parties, searching for the middle ground, have converged on many policy areas and loyalty to particular parties among the electorate has diminished.

This diminution of participation and power at the more formal level has been offset by a remarkable growth of influence and participation in the non-state sector. Business people have occupied roles in health trusts, in schools, in a range of quangos including environmental quangos, as well as in the privatised utilities and other industries. And, non-governmental organisations in various fields, including the environment, have attracted membership, have become involved in policy-making and have exerted increasing influence. Civil society is flourishing and vigorous.

It is this arena which Beck calls the 'zone of sub-politics' that offers a vehicle for political change. Unconstrained by the necessity for electoral support and unconfined by territorial limitations, actors within this zone are relatively free to develop ideas and seek to influence the society at large as well as to mobilise support for particular issues and policies. Within the zone of sub-politics, environmental movements have been particularly active and successful.

4.2 The Rise of Environmental Movements.

Environmental movements are often identified as one group of several 'new' social movement organisations (SMOs) which have emerged as prominent political forces over the past two decades or so. They are called 'new' to distinguish them from older social movements, such as the labour movement, and from earlier expressions of environmental concern such as the nature conservation movement. They are social movements in the sense that they mobilise support in order to effect social change and examples include the women's, peace, civil rights and animal welfare movements as well as the environmental movement. They are 'organisations' in that they are not simply latent or passive forces, like public opinion;

> they are instances of social behaviour which are more organised than protesting crowds or mobs, less formalised than political parties and more concerned than simple social trends. (Yearley, 1994, pp. 152–153)

Nevertheless these new SMOs comprise a motley collection of values, strategies, policies and organisational types. They include locality action groups or citizen-based organisations (CBOs) of the kind which arise spontaneously around an issue and wither once the conflict is resolved. Non-governmental organisations (NGOs) represent a higher level and more permanent form of organisation, operating at national and sometimes international level. The essential features of NGOs are that they are, as the name suggests, non-governmental; they are organisations with an administration and budget; and they are non-profit-making, and hence are sometimes known, especially in the UK, as voluntary organisations (Potter and Taylor, 1996; Potter, 1996). Although they vary widely in size, issue focus, type of organisation and strategy, as a group environmental NGOs appear to have grown in support and influence over recent decades (Lowe and Goyder, 1983; Princen and Finger, 1994; Arts, 1996). In addition there are those political parties, usually called 'green' parties, with an ecologically based ideology and which seek not merely to influence policy-making but also to gain access to the policy process through the formal political system (Dobson, 1990; Goodin, 1992). Strictly speaking, therefore, green parties are not non-governmental but they are clearly part of the environmental movement.

It is difficult to know whether or how far environmental movements are influential in policy-making (Potter and Taylor, 1996). There are many interests competing for influence and it is impossible to unravel the full complexity of all the factors which shape policy during its various stages of gestation, formulation and implementation. The influence of environmental movements on global policy-making, in so far as it exists, derives from their capacity to link the local to the global, their ability to deploy a range of strategies and their access to knowledge and expertise. Although some movements operate at the local level while others are concerned with national or trans-boundary issues, it is the ability to develop networks, coalitions and alliances relating local issues to a broader context transcending political frontiers which provides considerable leverage (Eccleston, 1996).

They are increasingly able to back their campaigns with scientific expertise. This is true at the local level where scientific expertise is recruited to support a cause right up to global level where scientists have played such a prominent role both as interest groups themselves and in support of environmental groups. They use a variety of strategies. Thomas (1996) categorises these as the four 'Cs':

(1) collaboration (including reform and entryism);
(2) confrontation (or opposition);
(3) complementary activities; and
(4) consciousness-raising (indirect, generalised campaigning).

The first three relate primarily to strategies for influencing policy-making, while consciousness-raising operates more at the level of values.

Influence over values. The efforts of environmental movements in influencing values have sometimes been "ignored or devalued because they are not considered to be genuinely political in character" (Wapner, 1995a, p. 312). Indeed, this may be their most important contribution to social change in the long run. But, here too, there is an evident tension between the two perspectives manifested in different organisations. Among NGOs, there are those, often long-established, which focus on issues of conservation at the national—for example, in the UK, the CPRE, the RSPB, the Civic Trust—or international level—for example in the WWF, the IUCN, the WRI—whose policies are moderate and which seek influence through conventional political structures. They fit neatly into an ecological modernisation perspective. By contrast, there are those more radical organisations which advocate alternative policies and engage in direct action sometimes including civil disobedience. In their efforts to prevent activities such as nuclear power, they appear to align more closely to a risk society perspective.

But, even the more radical environmental movements do not explicitly challenge the system. Mol argues that they increasingly conform to an ecological modernisation approach in that they

> change their ideology, and expand their traditional strategy of keeping the environment on the public and political agendas towards participation in direct negotiation with economic agents and state representatives close to the centre of the decision-making process ... (Mol, 1995, p. 58)

Greenpeace is an example, although it has become increasingly schizophrenic maintaining its direct actions on the one hand while negotiating within established political frameworks on the other. It is a classic instance of the tension as well as the complementarity of opposing perspectives.

Influence over policy making. This tension may also be observed in efforts of environmental movements to influence specific policies at the local level. By looking at this local context, certain possibilities may be revealed for social changes which have wider ramifications. Some limited, but nevertheless suggestive evidence may be gleaned from conflicts over locally unwanted land uses (LULUs) (Lake, 1987). These include activities which are often locally dangerous

(nuclear, chemical and toxic waste facilities), polluting (fossil-fuel power stations, heavy industrial plant) or intrusive in their impact on amenity (major roads, railways, airports). Conflicts over LULUs present the following four characteristics.

1. They generate alliances which cut across conventional social structures. During environmental conflicts over LULUs, alliances are constructed between interests which, in modern society, either have little else in common or which are in conflict. This characteristic has been identified in empirical studies of environmental conflicts over, for example, nuclear facilities or chemical works (notably, Blowers, 1984; Loeb, 1986; Zonabend, 1993; Blowers and Leroy, 1994). These alliances transcend the boundaries of class, community and politics thus presenting a powerful coalition which is often able to defeat specific projects. Local protest movements are sometimes able to mobilise widespread support by combining with similarly threatened communities elsewhere.

2. They link local issues to broader concerns. The local movements generated by these conflicts are often linked to broader environmental movements which operate at national, regional and even global scale. The relationships are mutually exploitative. Thus, environmental NGOs, like Greenpeace, offer support to local movements opposing a specific LULU such as a nuclear waste facility as part of their broader campaigns. Friends of the Earth acted with local protesters in the conflict over the Newbury by-pass in the UK. Local campaigners often welcome the scientific expertise, publicity and lobbying skills that can be mobilised by the big NGOs to support their specific cause.

3. They combine conservative and radical ideologies. The cross-cutting nature of these locally based coalitions and their linkage with broader movements enable them to embrace both conservative and radical ideologies. At the coalface of protest there will be those acting together to defeat a project who may have quite opposite beliefs about the broader policy. For example, in nuclear protests there will typically be unholy alliances between those who oppose nuclear power and who wish to prevent nuclear projects anywhere, the 'not in any body's backyard' (NIABY) or 'not over there either' (NOTE) syndrome; and those who are quite content for the project to be sited elsewhere, the 'not in my backyard' (NIMBY) tendency.

4. *They revive traditional integrating institutions.* These movements are conservative in two senses. In the ecological sense, they are 'conservationist' in varying degrees devoted to the protection and preservation of the environment. In a social sense, they are conservative in that they rediscover or re-emphasise those integrating institutions which, as was noted earlier, have been weakened and fragmented by the progress of modernisation. Thus, environmental protests revivify the appeal to a latent sense of place and of local community which has been apparently dormant or (some would say) overwhelmed by the allegiances based on class and social status which accompany modernisation (Blowers and Leroy, 1994).

The symbiotic relationship between place, environment and community gains expression through protest movements. It is, in its way, an evocation of the desire for continuity in a sustainable relationship between environment and society. Indeed, Eder (1996) goes so far as to claim that the impact of environmentalism

> consists in the emergence and stabilisation of an ideological current beyond liberalism and socialism; it favours an ideological position that represents the first really modern version of conservatism. (Eder, 1996, p. 208)

A new environmental politics? In these various ways, environmental movements engaging in local conflicts over LULUs reflect the different perspectives analysed earlier. On the one hand, they mobilise those who support environmental conservation provided that it is consistent with economic growth and industrial progress; theoretically their position is aligned to ecological modernis-

ation. On the other hand, the movements also embrace those who wish to prevent the continuing development and growth of certain high-risk activities on the grounds that they will result in ecological disaster. In theoretical terms, their analysis confirms the risk society thesis.

Although these conflicts offer some theoretical insights, as a basis for any broad generalisations about social and environmental change they have obvious limitations. Such conflicts tend often to be ephemeral, highly active during the process of the issue, but disintegrating quickly once the conflict is over and the *status quo* is reasserted. They are conflicts which occur in localised communities facing localised projects. Nevertheless, they illustrate the tendency for different perspectives to become intertwined, for different interests to be combined and for latent institutions to be revitalised. They demonstrate the possibilities for opening up the policy process, for engaging in wider participation and for challenging the prevailing values of modern society.

Whether this adds up to a new form of politics, a politics emanating from environmental concerns must be doubted. Environmental movements play an increasingly significant role in policy-making. They act alongside, in opposition to but increasingly in collaboration with, other major actors, nation-states and TNCs. Compared to their powerful rivals for influence, environmental movements appear puny—still operating on the margins rather than at the centre of affairs. They lack the political muscle of nation-states or the vast resources commanded by business.

They have other weaknesses, too. Governments, by whatever means they hold power, represent national interests in policy-making; businesses represent the interests of shareholders. Environmental movements are just that; movements, claiming to represent particular values, constituencies of interest or membership but not, ultimately, accountable to an electorate or to investors. Furthermore, environmental movements are dispersed, diverse and fragmented, a collection of organisations which does not constitute a coherent or united force. There is a noticeable cleavage between the North and the South in terms of NGOs (Eccleston, 1996). Northern NGOs are often well funded, focus on global environmental questions and may be heavily involved in the policy-making process. By contrast, many Southern NGOs are weak, sometimes face political oppression and, in the absence of state institutions, are often involved in environmental management at local level. Environmental policy is often integrated with the endemic problems of poverty and development.

> This linkage between poverty and environmental degradation provides perhaps the clearest demonstration of the centrality of social, political and economic issues in questions of environment and development. (Adams, 1990, p. 87)

5. The Way Forward

Opposing Perspectives

The phenomenon of environmental change has begun to occupy a central role in social science discourse and analysis at the level of both theory and policy. In charting the possible way forward for society in its relationship with the environment, alternative theoretical perspectives offer different and, at first encounter, apparently irreconcilable insights. On the one hand, exponents of ecological modernisation offer what appears to be a celebration of modernity and its ability to adjust to the ecological problems created by industrial society. The environmental problem provides a challenge for further innovation and the transition to an industrial society in which ecological protection and economic development are complementary rather than in conflict (Mol, 1996). On the other hand, critics of the whole project of modernisation hold that the extension and continuation of industrial progress inevitably spells disaster for the environment and, with it, for humanity itself. The hope here lies in the process of 'reflexive modernisation' whereby society confronts the crisis it has

created and a transformation ensues at the levels of production, institutions and, consequently, in values and life-styles.

These are idealised models, combining various strains of thought and posing a dichotomy which offers analytical clarity at the expense of empirical validity. They are partial models. Ecological modernisation focuses largely on the technical and economic aspects of change and, even here, ignores the implications of a continuation of high-consequence risky technologies. The alternative approach, exemplified by its most developed ideal type, risk society, exaggerates the importance of such technologies whilst underestimating the significant changes in the direction of environmental protection already occurring and potentially available. Each perspective projects an inevitability in the trends it identifies, although the directions of change they foresee are entirely divergent. Both theories are conceived in a Western context but their focus on the aggregate society and economy ignores the fundamental issue of social inequality which is likely to act as a barrier to progress in either direction. Furthermore, in a sense they are devoid of politics. Whereas ecological modernisation presumes a continuation of the politics of liberal democratic societies, the risk society regards such politics as irrelevant to deal with the coming crisis. Thus, neither theory has very much to say about the nature of the political institutions necessary to deliver a society that is able to develop sustainably. The theoretical debate is clearly at an early stage and further elaboration of the links between the economy, society and the environment and a detailed analysis of social institutional change may be expected as the debate proceeds.

Meanwhile, other social scientists, political scientists in particular, have detected two broad trends that potentially provide the political context for responding to environmental change. The first of these is at the level of the state where the transboundary nature of environmental processes has been paralleled by the creation of transboundary political institutions. At the same time, the localised nature of environmental issues requires a response at the sub-state level. Quite aside from the environmental pressures, the state is undergoing change as an integral part of the globalisation of economic forces and the dominance of the market economy. All this, according to some scholars, has led to some surrender of sovereignty upwards and the withdrawal of the state's boundaries internally opening up political space which is occupied by various interests and actors.

Environmental movements are one set of interests in civil society which have begun to thrive in this emerging space. The rise of such movements, their influence on policy and their impact at the level of consciousness-raising and value-shift has been a feature of political change. In particular their contribution (with other actors) to a process of social and institutional learning (List, 1996; Breyman, 1993; Hajer, 1996) is arguably a major factor in the incorporation of the environmental dimension into all levels of policy-making.

The Urban Dimension

The theoretical debates about global environmental change and its political and social consequences have implications at the urban level. There are, perhaps, four areas where the urban dimension provides illustration for the debates and reveals the limitations of the analysis.

1. The local/global. Neither ecological modernisation nor risk society theories address the urban dimension and it may be thought that political concern with global environmental issues diverts attention away from the immediate problems of development, deprivation, environmental degradation, transport and energy which are currently faced by cities world-wide (Christoff, 1996). On the other hand, there is ample evidence that concern for the urban dimension remains vigorous at the policy level. The post-Rio process has placed emphasis on the development of local Agenda 21 and has stimulated wide-spread participation in developing ideas and plans at the urban level. Sustainable development has been at the heart of several significant national policy statements on transport and retail development. At a more local level, structure and local plans have taken sustainability as their theme and have included detailed policies for transport (reducing car travel and emphasising public transport, cycling and walking), urban development (concentrating development in urban areas or major transport corridors), energy (conservation, use of renewable energy and combined heat and power and reduction of CO_2 levels), resource depletion (recycling and re-use and conservation of land and heritage) and waste management (minimisation and reduction). Although the focus of attention for all these policies is local, the connections are readily made to the global implications of action taken (or not taken) at the local level.

2. The social question. Ecological modernisation focuses entirely on the economic sphere and, while Beck draws attention to the problem of insecurity and social fragmentation engendered by modernised societies, he concentrates on the psychological rather than the political consequences of the phenomenon. Yet, the need to address issues of social inequality (and especially the problems of the South), in order to encourage social cohesion becomes especially evident when viewed in the urban context. Problems of poverty, alienation and environmental deprivation which are especially evident among the underclass of major cities (and especially rife in the burgeoning cities in the developing world) constitute a significant social and political issue and threat, if only because of their sheer spatial concentration. In terms of sustainability, it must be recognised that the disadvantaged are hardly likely to co-operate in programmes for environmental protection so long as they see the rich and powerful enjoying and consuming a disproportionate share of resources and producing a burden of pollution which degrades already-impoverished environments.

3. *Institutional implications*. Neither ecological modernisation nor the risk society theory have much to say about the form of institutional adaptation or change required to inaugurate sustainable development. Ecological modernisation sublimates the 'enabling state' as the institutional response that will secure the efficient functioning of the market economy within a framework of state regulation. However, the role of the state as an enabling institution for individuals through the provision of welfare, housing, social services, good education and an accessible health service tends to be diminished in this model. By contrast, Beck turns his attention to the demise of integrating social institutions which the process of modernisation has undermined or swept away. At the urban level, it is the very decline of support structures, the absence of opportunity and the weakening of integrating institutions that contributes, among other impacts, to the deteriorating environmental conditions.

4. *Political participation and governance.* Ecological modernisation is based on the presumption of corporatist relationships primarily between government and industry but also incorporating environmental movements where mutually acceptable. Questions of political participation are absent from the analysis. Beck's observations on questions of political participation go little beyond identifying the 'zone of sub-politics' as a fertile arena for political participation. Indeed, both theories, as was observed earlier, are, in a sense, apolitical. Looked at in terms of urban governance, the idea that environmental or urban social movements are given space to operate in a vigorous civil society does not adequately deal with the problem of legitimating and implementing decisions. Environmental movements are not representative, nor are they accountable and, consequently, their influence must be secured ultimately through the formal political process.

One of the worrying features of modern political institutions is the tendency to depoliticise large areas, including the environment. In the UK, recent reforms have largely completed a process whereby environmental regulation and control is in the hands of regulatory bodies appointed by central government. Local government reform has had a mixed impact. While the creation of unitary authorities can be seen as a positive move towards providing greater integration and authority at the urban level, elsewhere many county councils have been severely weakened through the loss of financial resources and the surrender of their function in co-ordinating urban and rural development.

The Role of Planning.

Appropriate institutional frameworks and representative political structures are both necessary but not sufficient conditions for securing sustainable development. The long time-spans and detailed co-ordination across policy areas that are necessary for environmental policies to be made effective require a form of decision-making that transcends the prevailing short-term, sectoral structures. Under ecological modernisation, the state engages in 'partnership' with business, the voluntary sector and other interests while retaining a residual coordinating and regulatory role. The notion of risk society certainly implies the need for more imperative co-ordination, but does not spell it out. In a word, the missing dimension is the need for planning.

The case for planning goes well beyond the current limited role of urban and land-use planning. First, there is the need for an holistic approach which combines both land-use and environmental aspects. This necessary integration is emphasised in many planning statements but, at the institutional level, powers remain diffused and fragmented. Secondly, the local/global relationship between environmental problems must be recognised in the articulation of integrated plans at different levels (local, regional, national and international). These plans would establish indicators, set targets and identify measures of implementation. Thirdly, planning needs to revivify its *social* purpose interpreting the relationships between social inequality and environmental sustainability. In the past planning has engaged in a social vision which has been physically manifest in such ideas as new towns, neighbourhood units, green belts, national parks and urban regeneration and, in a contemporary context, there is a need for concepts which combine social purpose with sustainable living (Blowers, 1997).

All this would require greater intervention and public investment but also commitment to a participatory framework of decision-making which provides people with effective power. The dangers are obvious. More intervention and subsidy will revive the spectre of the overpowering state; more participatory democracy will introduce lengthy, untidy and contradictory decision-making leading to outcomes that endanger rather than protect the environment. There is the possibility that it will merely reinforce patterns of power and inequality. On the other hand, it is very difficult to see how change in the direction of sustainability can be achieved without changes at the institutional, political and social level as well, in which people are given both freedom and responsibility. Unless this is achieved at the local level, there is little chance that sustainability at the global level can ever be secured.

Prospects for Change

Fundamental social changes and the introduction of long-term planning would appear hopelessly unrealistic and idealistic. It must be doubted whether the environmental challenge yet has the potential to bring about fundamental changes in the relationship between economy and society. The state and the market economy remain the twin pillars of power, mutually dependent and mutually reinforcing (Lindblom, 1977). Although states vary in size, competence and degree of legitimacy, all, to a greater or lesser degree, possess territorial monopoly, bureaucratic administration and coercive power (Conca, 1993; Giddens, 1985). The capitalist econ-

omy, in its turn, provides production, wealth and employment. Its leading actors, the TNCs, "are nationally based and trade multinationally on the strength of a major national location of production and sales" (Hirst and Thompson, 1996, p. 2).

Given the remarkable adaptability and persistence of state and market power, a gradual transition in the direction of ecological modernisation appears to be the most likely direction of change, at least for the foreseeable future. With the apotheosis of the capitalist market economy on an almost global basis, environmental protection will emphasise the sustenance of the resource base necessary for economic development. It will be achieved by a combination of market-based economic incentives and state regulation and standard setting. The environment will be a more significant constraint on the market, the more so in advanced industrial societies where the environment is increasingly valued as a component of well-being than in developing or impoverished countries where environmental resources are ravaged for economic growth or to maintain a subsistence economy. The problem with ecological modernisation is that it may become the victim of its own propaganda, promising more than it can conceivably perform.

The risk society portends catastrophe if present trends continue, either sooner (through nuclear proliferation or accident), or later (through global warming or ozone depletion). But its dire pronouncements also have a rhetorical, almost biblical, ring, warning us of the tyranny of technology, the concentration of power among élites, the fragmentation of society and the inevitability of disaster. Risk society is a contemporary version of the radical critiques that are an enduring element of theoretical and political debate. The problem with the approach (as with its forbears) is that the appeal to the notion of reflexive modernisation, the social self-criticism and perception that can arrest the trend and pave the way to a new Enlightenment is vague and offers no practical prescription or notion of how a transformation will proceed.

868 ANDREW BLOWERS

There is, perhaps, the possibility that the response to environmental change can be managed without the high risks attached to strategies of ecological modernisation or the dire consequences of the risk society. The task for social scientists is to engage in the analysis of change and speculation about outcomes. This will involve the elaboration of perspectives which take account both of political feasibility and the avoidance of risk. Such perspectives will also focus on the claims of political participation, the problem of social inequality and the development of forms of planning that ensure a sustainable environment. To do this, it will be necessary to imagine what a sustainable society will look like in terms of production, consumption, institutions and living patterns.

It is conceivable that, as the problems of environmental change become more evident, a common interest in the need to protect resources and avoid the overloading of ecosystems will prevail. In such an analysis, a countervailing power must develop, perhaps motivated by environmental movements, but spreading its influence beyond into government, business and the society at large; a power sufficient to bring about the abandonment of those technologies that are not, ultimately, capable of ecological modernisation.

This suggests a conception of sustainable development far different from the present dispensation, one that integrates environment and economy. In the political realm, it is likely to require a revival of concern about social equality and a commitment to long-term planning as a method of environmental management. Such an analysis has scarcely begun, but the debate about environmental change and its social implications has, in the past few years, entered the centre stage of social scientific concern. The outcome of the debate in terms of policy is as yet unclear; but thought is the prelude to action.

References

ADAMS, W. M. (1990) *Green Development: Environment and Sustainability in the Third World*. London: Routledge.

ARTS, B. (1996) *The politics of the global environmental movement: an assessment of the framework convention on climate change (FCCC)*. Paper presented to the *28th International Geographical Congress*, symposium S6, The Hague, 8 August.

BARTLETT, R. V. (1980) *The Reserve Mining Controversy: Science, Technology and Environmental Quality*. Bloomington: Indiana University Press.

BECK, U. (1992) *Risk Society: Towards a New Modernity*. London: Sage.

BECK, U. (1995) *Ecological Politics in an Age of Risk*. Cambridge: Polity Press.

BECK, U. (1996) Risk society and the provident state, in: S. LASH *ET AL. Risk, Environment and Modernity: Towards a New Ecology*, pp. 27–43. London: Sage.

BECK, U., GIDDENS, A. and LASH, S. (1994) *Reflexive Modernization: Politics, Tradition and Aesthetics in the Modern Social Order*. Cambridge: Polity Press.

BECKERMAN, W. (1994) Sustainable development, *Environmental Values*, 3(3), pp. 191–210.

BERTELL, R. (1985) *No Immediate Danger*. London: The Women's Press.

BLOWERS, A. (1984) *Something in the Air: Corporate Power and the Environment*. London: Harper and Row.

BLOWERS, A. (1993) Environmental policy: the quest for sustainable development, *Urban Studies*, 30, pp. 775–796.

BLOWERS, A. (1997) Society and sustainability: the context of change for planning, in: A. BLOWERS and B. EVANS (Eds) *Town Planning into the 21st Century*. London: Routledge. (forthcoming).

BLOWERS, A. and LEROY, P. (1994) Power, politics and environmental inequality: a theoretical and empirical analysis of the process of 'peripheralisation', *Environmental Politics*, 3, pp. 197–228.

BLOWERS, A. and LEROY, P. (1996) Environment and society: shaping the future, in: A. BLOWERS and P. GLASBERGEN (Eds) *Environmental Policy in an International Context, 3 Prospects*, pp. 255–283. London: Arnold.

BLOWERS, A., LOWRY, D. and SOLOMON, B. (1991) *The International Politics of Nuclear Waste*. London: Macmillan.

BOEHMER-CHRISTIANSEN, S. (1994) Politics and environmental management, *Journal of Environmental Planning and Management*, 37, pp. 69–85.

BOEHMER-CHRISTIANSEN S. and SKEA, J. (1991) *Acid Rain: Energy and Environmental Policies in Britain and Germany*. London: Belhaven Press.

BREYMAN, S. (1993) Knowledge as power: ecology movements and global environmental problems, in: R. LIPSCHUTZ and K. CONCA (Eds) *The State and Social Power in Global Environmental Politics*, pp. 124–157. New York: Columbia University Press.

BUTTEL, F., HAWKINS, A. and POWER, A. (1990) From limits to growth to global change: constraints and contradictions in the evolution of science and ideology, *Global Environmental Change*, 1, pp. 57–66.

CAIRNCROSS, F. (1995) *Green Inc.: A Guide to Business and the Environment*. London: Earthscan.

CARR, S. and MPANDE, R. (1996) Does the definition of the issue matter? NGO influence and the international convention to combat desertification, in: D. POTTER (Ed.) *NGOs and Environmental Policies: Asia and Africa*, pp. 143–166. London: Frank Cass.

CHRISTOFF, P. (1996) Ecological modernisation, ecological modernities, *Environmental Politics*, 5(3), pp. 476–500.

CHRISTOFF, P. (1997) Environmental challenges for public policy: the search for ecological governance, in: T. BONYHADY (Ed.) *Ecological Discourses*. (forthcoming).

COMMISSION OF THE EUROPEAN COMMUNITIES (CEC) (1989) *Environmental Ethics: Man's Relationship with Nature: Interactions with Science*. Brussels: CEC.

CONCA, K. (1993) Environmental change and the deep structure of world politics, in: R. LIPSCHUTZ and K. CONCA (Eds) *The State and Social Power in Global Environmental Politics*, pp. 306–326. New York: Columbia University Press.

CRENSON, M. (1971) *The Un-politics of Air Pollution: A Study of Non-decisionmaking in the Cities*. Baltimore: The Johns Hopkins Press.

DALY, H. and COBB, J. (1990) *For the Common Good*. London: Green Print.

DOBSON, A. (1990) *Green Political Thought*. London: Unwin Hyman.

DOBSON, A. (Ed.) (1991) *The Green Reader*. London: Andre Deutsch.

DUNLEAVY, P. (1981) *The Politics of Mass Housing in Britain: A Study of Corporate Power, and Professional Influence in the Welfare State*. Oxford: Clarendon Press.

ECCLESTON, B. (1996) Does North–South collaboration enhance NGO influence on deforestation policies in Malaysia and Indonesia?, in: D. POTTER (Ed.) *NGOs and Environmental Policies: Asia and Africa*, pp. 66–89. London: Arnold.

ECKERSLEY, R. (1992) *Environmentalism and Political Theory: Toward an Ecocentric Approach*. London: UCL Press.

EDER, K. (1996) The institutionalisation of environmentalism: ecological discourse and the second transformation of the public sector, in: S. LASH ET AL. (Eds) *Risk, Environment and Modernity: Towards a New Ecology*, pp. 204–223. London: Sage.

GANDY, M. (1996) Crumbling land: the postmodernity debate and the analysis of environmental problems, *Progress in Human Geography*, 20, pp. 23–40.

GIDDENS, A. (1985) *The Nation-state and Violence*. Cambridge: Polity Press.

GOODIN, R. (1976) *The Politics of Rational Man*. London: Wiley.

GOODIN, R. (1992) *Green Political Theory*. Cambridge: Polity Press.

GORZ, A. (1980) *Ecology as Politics*. Boston: South End Press.

HAAS, P. (1990) Obtaining international environmental protection through epistemic consensus, *Millennium: Journal of International Studies*, 19(3), pp. 347–363.

HABERMAS, J. (1976) *Legitimation Crisis*. London: Heinemann.

HAJER, M. (1996) Ecological modernisation as cultural politics, in: S. LASH ET AL. (Eds) *Risk, Environment and Modernity: Towards a New Ecology*, pp. 246–268. London: Sage.

HANNIGAN, J. (1995) *Environmental Sociology: A Social Constructionist Perspective*. London: Routledge.

HARDIN, G. ((1968) The tragedy of the commons, *Science*, 162, pp. 1234–1248.

HIRST, P. and THOMPSON, G. (1996) *Globalization in Question*. Cambridge: Polity Press.

HMSO (1994) *Sustainable Development: The UK Strategy*. CM 2426. London.

HUMPHREYS, D. (1996) The global politics of forest conservation since the UNCED, *Environmental Politics*, 5, pp. 231–257.

INDEPENDENT COMMISSION ON INTERNATIONAL DEVELOPMENT ISSUES (1980) *North–South: A Programme for Survival*. London: Pan Books.

JACOBS, M. (1991) *The Green Economy*. London: Pluto Press.

JACOBS, M. (1995) *Sustainability and Socialism*. Socialist Environment and Resources Association.

LAKE, R. (Ed.) (1987) *Resolving Locational Conflict*. New Brunswick: Rutgers University Press.

LASH, S., SZERSZYNSKI, B. and WYNNE, B. (Eds) (1996) *Risk, Environment and Modernity: Towards a New Ecology*. London: Sage.

LEROY, P. (1995) *Environmental science as a vocation*. Inaugural lecture, Catholic University of Nijmegen, 9 June.

LIBERATORE, A. (1995) The social construction of environmental problems, in: P. GLASBERGEN and A. BLOWERS (Eds) *Environmental Policy in an International Context, 1 Perspectives*, pp. 59–84. London: Arnold.

LINDBLOM, C. (1977) *Politics and Markets: The*

World's Political-Economic Systems. New York: Basic Books.

LIPSCHUTZ, R. (1993) *Learn of the green world: global civil society, global environmental change and social learning*. Paper for *Annual Meeting of the International Studies Association*, Acapulco, Mexico, March.

LIPSCHUTZ, R. (1994) *Who are we? Why are we here? Political identity, ecological politics, and global change*. Paper for *Annual Meeting of the International Studies Organisation*, Washington DC, March/April.

LIPSCHUTZ, R. and CONCA, K. (Eds) (1993) *The State and Social Power in Global Environmental Politics*. New York: Columbia University Press.

LIST. M. (1996) Sovereign states and international regimes, in: A. BLOWERS and P. GLASBERGEN (Eds) *Environmental Policy in an International Context, 3 Prospects*, pp. 7–24. London: Arnold.

LOEB, P. (1986) *Nuclear Culture: Living and Working in the World's Largest Atomic Complex*. Philadelphia: New Society Publishers.

LOWE, P. and GOYDER, J. (1983) *Environmental Groups in Politics*. London: George Allen and Unwin.

MEADOWS, D. H., MEADOWS, D. L. and RANDERS, J. (1992) *Beyond the Limits*. London: Earthscan.

MEADOWS, D. H., MEADOWS, D. L., RANDERS, J. and BEHRENS, W. (1972) *The Limits to Growth*. London: Earth Island.

MILLIKEN, R. (1986) *No Conceivable Injury*. London: Penguin Books.

MOL, A. (1995) *The Refinement of Production: Ecological Modernization Theory and the Chemical Industry*. Utrecht: van Arkel.

MOL, A. (1996) Ecological modernisation and institutional reflexivity: environmental reform in the late modern age, *Environmental Politics*, 5(2), pp. 302–323.

NAESS, A. (1991) Deep ecology, in: A. DOBSON (Ed.) *The Green Reader*, pp. 242–247. London: Andre Deutsch.

O'CONNOR, J. (1973) *The Fiscal Crisis of the State*. New York: St Martin's Press.

O'RIORDAN, T., KEMP, R. and PURDUE, M. (1988) *Sizewell B: An Anatomy of the Inquiry*. London: Macmillan.

OWENS, S. (1994) Land, limits and sustainability: a conceptual framework and some dilemmas for the planning system, *Transactions of the Institute of British Geographers*, 19, pp. 439–456.

PEPPER, D. (1993) *Eco-socialism: From Deep Ecology to Social Justice*. London: Routledge.

PEPPER, D. (1996) *Modern Environmentalism: An Introduction*. London: Routledge.

POTTER, D. (1995) Environmental problems in their political context, in: P. GLASBERGEN and A. BLOWERS (Eds) *Environmental Policy in an International Context, 1 Perspectives*, pp. 84–110. London: Arnold.

POTTER, D. (1996) Non-governmental organisations and environmental policies, in: A. BLOWERS and P. GLASBERGEN (Eds) *Environmental Policy in an International Context, 3 Prospects*, pp. 22–50. London: Arnold.

POTTER, D. and TAYLOR, A. (1996) Introduction, in: D. POTTER (Ed.) *NGOs and Environmental Policies: Asia and Africa*, pp. 1–8. London: Frank Cass.

PRINCEN, T. and FINGER, M. (1994) *Environmental NGOs in World Politics*. London: Routledge.

REDCLIFT, M. and BENTON, T. (Eds) (1994) *Social Theory and the Global Environment*. London: Routledge.

RHODES, R. (1994) The hollowing out of the state: the changing nature of the public service in Britain, *The Political Quarterly*, 62, pp. 138–151.

ROYAL SOCIETY, THE (1992) *Risk: Analysis, Perception, Management*. London: The Royal Society.

RWMAC/ACSNI (1995) *Site selection for radioactive waste disposal facilities and the protection of human health*. Report of a Study Group drawn from members of the Radioactive Waste Management Advisory Committee and the Advisory Committee on the Safety of Nuclear Installations, March.

SAGE, C. (1996) Population, poverty and land in the South, in: P. SLOEP and A. BLOWERS (Eds) *Environmental Policy in an International Context, 2 Conflicts*, pp. 97–126. London: Arnold.

SCHNAIBERG, A. (1980) *The Environment: From Surplus to Scarcity*. Oxford: Oxford University Press.

SKLAIR, L. (1994) Global sociology and global environmental change, in: M. REDCLIFT and T. BENTON (Eds) *Social Theory and the Global Environment*, pp. 205–227. London: Routledge.

SLOVIC, P., FISCHOFF, B. and LICHTENSTEIN, S. (1980) Facts and fears: understanding perceived risk, in: R. SCHWING and W. ALBERS (Eds) *Societal Risk Assessment: How Safe is Safe Enough?*, pp. 181–214. New York: Plenum Press.

SPAARGAREN, G. and MOL, A. (1990) *Sociology, environment and modernity*. Paper presented to the *International Sociological Association Conference*, Madrid, July.

STRETTON, H. (1976) *Capitalism, Socialism and the Environment*. Cambridge: Cambridge University Press.

DE SWAAN, A. (1988) *In Care of the State*. Cambridge: Polity Press.

THOMAS, A. (1996) NGO advocacy, democracy and policy development: some examples relating to environmental policies in Zimbabwe and Botswana, in: D. POTTER (Ed.) *NGOs and Environmental Policies: Asia and Africa*, pp. 38–65. London: Frank Cass.

VOGLER, J. and IMBER, M. (1996) *The Environment and International Relations*. London: Routledge.

WAPNER, P. (1995a) Environmental activism and world civic politics, *World Politics*, 47(April), pp. 311–340.

WAPNER, P. (1995b) The state and environmental challenges: a critical exploration of alternatives to the state-system, *Environmental Politics*, 4(1), pp. 44–69.

WEALE, A. (1992) *The New Politics of Pollution*. Manchester: Manchester University Press.

WORLD COMMISSION ON ENVIRONMENT AND DEVEL-

OPMENT (WCED) (1987) *Our Common Future*. Oxford: Oxford University Press.

WYNNE, B. (1994) Scientific knowledge and the global environment, in: M. REDCLIFT and T. BENTON (Eds) *Social Theory and the Global Environment*, pp. 169–189. London: Routledge.

YEARLEY, S. (1992) *The Green Case*. London: Routledge.

YEARLEY, S. (1994) Social movements and environmental change, in: M. REDCLIFT and T. BENTON (Eds) *Social Theory and the Global Environment*, pp. 150–168. London: Routledge.

YEARLEY, S. (1996) *Sociology, Environmentalism, Globalization*. London: Sage.

ZONABEND, F. (1993) *The Nuclear Peninsula*. Cambridge: Cambridge University Press.

[13]

PERGAMON

Geoforum 31 (2000) 45–56

GEOFORUM

www.elsevier.com/locate/geoforum

The environmental movement in an era of ecological modernisation

Arthur P.J. Mol

Wageningen University, Wageningen, NL-6706 KN, The Netherlands

Received 5 November 1998; in revised form 12 August 1999

Abstract

Ecological modernisation theory has become one of the dominant sociological theories that try to understand and interpret how modern industrial societies are dealing with the environmental crisis. To do this it focuses on changing social practices and institutional developments associated with environmental deterioration and reform. This article both profits from and contributes to this theoretical framework by analysing the transformations of the environmental movement, in particular non-governmental organisations (NGOs). Although the spectrum of environmental NGOs remains broad and different form country to country, some general transformations can be identified. In contrast to the environmental NGOs of the 1970s and early 1980s, contemporary NGOs differ in their dominant ideologies, in their position vis-à-vis other actors engaged with environmental deterioration and reform, and in their strategic operations between (and beyond) state and markets. These differences can be interpreted as an answer to wider developments in environmental discourses and reform, but at the same time result in new challenges for NGOs. This paper shows that although ecological modernisation theory offers no simple answers, and does not suggest logical trajectories that environmental NGOs can or will follow in their future development, it proves able to frame their windows of opportunity. At the same time the transformations in NGOs are seen to be an important part of the wider process of ecological modernisation. © 2000 Elsevier Science Ltd. All rights reserved.

Keywords: Environmental movement; Ecological modernisation; Europe; USA

1. Introduction: the emergence of ecological modernisation

In the 1980s increasing numbers of environmental sociologists, and other social scientists who had environmental deterioration and reform as their central object of study, started to observe that some significant changes were taking place in both the environmental discourse and the social practices and institutions that actually dealt with environmental problems. Out of the sometimes vigorous debates concerning the interpretation of these transformations, their structural or incidental character, their geographical reach and their normative valuation, the theory of ecological modernisation emerged. For example, some empirical studies showed that from the mid to late 1980s onwards, in countries such as Germany, Japan, the Netherlands, the USA, Sweden and Denmark, a discontinuity could be identified in the tendency of enhanced economic growth to be paralleled by increased environmental disruption –

a process referred to as the decoupling or delinking of material flows from economic flows. In a number of cases (countries and/or specific industrial sectors and/or specific environmental issues) it was actually claimed that environmental reform resulted in an absolute decline of emissions and use of natural resources, regardless of growth in financial or material terms (cf. recently for the Netherlands RIVM, 1998). However, although these – sometimes controversial – empirical studies lie behind the idea of ecological modernisation, they do not form the core. Central stage in ecological modernisation is given to the associated social practices and institutional transformations, which are often believed to be at the foundations of these physical changes. In the debate on the changing character of the social practices and institutions since the 1980s, adherents to the theory of ecological modernisation positioned themselves by claiming that these transformations in institutions and social practices could not be explained away as mere window-dressing or rhetoric, but should indeed be seen as structural transformations in industrial society's institutional order, as far as these concerned the preservation of its sustenance base.

E-mail address: tuuR.mol@alg.swg.wau.nl (A.P.J. Mol).

0016-7185/00/$ - see front matter © 2000 Elsevier Science Ltd. All rights reserved.
PII: S 0 0 1 6 - 7 1 8 5 (9 9) 0 0 0 4 3 - 3

46   *A.P.J. Mol / Geoforum 31 (2000) 45–56*

Starting in the beginning of the 1980s the ecological modernisation theory was developed initially – and still primarily[1] – in a small group of West-European countries, most notably Germany, the Netherlands and the UK. Ecological modernisation theory can be understood as a sociological interpretation of how contemporary industrialised countries (try to) deal with the environmental crisis. However, among the various contributions to ecological modernisation theory – from the initial ideas as developed by the German sociologist Joseph Huber and the German political scientist Martin Jänicke, up to the more recent interpretations and contributions from American scholars such as Fred Buttel and David Sonnenfeld – there exists considerable diversity, not only by national background and theoretical foundations, but also throughout the relatively short period ecological modernisation theory has flourished. Without giving an extensive analysis and overview of the ecological modernisation literature,[2] I believe that three stages in its development can be distinguished. The first contributions, especially those by Joseph Huber and to a lesser extent Martin Jänicke, were characterised by a heavy emphasis on the role of technological innovation, especially in the sphere of industrial production, a rather critical attitude towards the (bureaucratic) state and a relatively favourable one towards the market, a system-theoretical perspective with a relatively underdeveloped notion of human agency, and an orientation at the nation-state level. The second period, from the late 1980s onward, showed a less strong emphasis on technological innovation as the motor behind ecological restructuring, a more balanced view of state and market dynamics in ecological transformation processes, more attention was given to the institutional and cultural dynamics of ecological modernisation, and studies on industrial production were complemented with attention paid to consumption processes. The emphasis was still very much on national studies regarding West-European countries. Recently, from the mid 1990s onward, increasing attention has been paid on the one hand to the global dynamics of ecological modernisation, and on the other to national studies in non-West European countries (developing countries, Central and East European nation-states but also for instance the USA).

Notwithstanding the geographical, temporal and theoretical differences in the variety of contributions, one can still find common denominators that justify reference to one school of thought: (i) environmental

deterioration is conceived of as a challenge requiring and 'forcing' socio-technical and economic reforms rather than as an inevitable consequence of current institutional structures, (ii) a major emphasis is placed on modern institutions for environmental reform, such as science and technology, the nation-state and global politics, and the (world) market, and (iii) a position is adopted in the academic field which distinguishes it from more or less strict neo-Marxists, as well as from counterproductivity and post-modernist analyses. To be more specific, most studies focus on and contribute to the understanding of one or more of the following institutional transformations:

1. the changing role of science and technology in environmental deterioration and reform; first, science and technology are not only judged to be involved in the emergence of environmental problems but they are also valued for their actual and potential role in curing and preventing them; second, traditional curative and repair options are replaced by more preventive socio-technological approaches that incorporate environmental considerations at the design stage of technological and organisational innovations; finally, the growing uncertainty of scientific and expert knowledge on definitions, causes and solutions with respect to environmental problems does not result in a marginalisation of science and technology in environmental reform;

2. the increasing importance of economic and market dynamics and economic agents (such as producers, customers, consumers, credit institutions, insurance companies, etc.) as social carriers of ecological restructuring and reform (in addition to state agencies and the new social movement) (cf. Mol, 1995);

3. the changes regarding the traditionally central role of the government and the nation-state in environmental reform; first, more decentralised, flexible and consensual styles of national governance with less top-down hierarchic command-and-control regulation emerge (often referred to as political modernisation; cf. Jänicke, 1993); second, more opportunities for non-state actors to take over traditional tasks of the nation-state (privatisation, but also conflict-resolution without state interference, often referred to as subpolitics; cf. Beck, 1994); finally, an emerging role for supra-national institutions that undermine to some extent the traditional role of the nation-state in environmental reform (cf. Group of Lisbon, 1995; Beck, 1997);

4. changing discursive practices and emerging new ideologies in political and societal arenas (cf. Hajer, 1995), where both the fundamental counterpositioning of economic and environmental interests as well as a complete neglect of the importance of environmental considerations, are no longer accepted as legitimate positions. Intergenerational solidarity in

---

[1] Although this is changing more recently if we look at the publications of, for instance, Harris (1996), Christoff (1996), Jokinen and Koskinen (1998), Rinkevicius (1998) and Sonnenfeld (forthcoming).

[2] See for a more detailed overview of the ecological modernisation literature and the debates with some of its critics, Mol and Spaargaren (1998).

A.P.J. Mol / Geoforum 31 (2000) 45–56 47

dealing with the sustenance base seems to have emerged as the undisputed core principle;

5. a modification of the position, role and ideology of social movements (vis-à-vis the 1970s and 1980s) in the process of ecological transformation.

While a large number of contributions have elaborated upon and contributed to the first four transformations, it is especially the latter transformation that I want to focus upon in this article. In order to do so I will start by elaborating on the kind of transformations environmental NGOs are engaged in and which can be understood from an ecological modernisation perspective. In three subsequent sections I analyse in more detail the consequences of these changes for the environmental organisations themselves, as well as the new challenges this movement faces in the near future.

In making such an analysis we have to be aware that ecological modernisation ideas have been developed against the socio-cultural and political–institutional background of west European countries. While starting my analysis on the developments of the environmental movement in this geographical (and thus socio-cultural and political–institutional) area, I gradually move more to the USA context and confront developments in the American environmental movement with westeuropean ecological modernisation ideas and developments.[3] The epilogue will have a summarising look at the challenges the environmental movement faces in this new era.

2. Changing environmental movement

In most of the writings on ecological modernisation the environmental movement, and the central modifications it has and is undergoing, are dealt with only marginally. Nevertheless, I think three central and returning themes can be distilled from on the one side the limited literature on the environmental movement under conditions of ecological modernisation, and on the other the (self-interpreted) transformations that representatives of major parts of the environmental movement have identified, proclaimed or actively stimulated. These three themes centre around:

- the changing ideologies that prevail in the movement;
- the modifications in the position of environmental organisations vis-à-vis other actors;
- and transformations in the strategic operations of NGOs between state and market.

Before elaborating on these three core features of change, however, three introductory remarks need to be made. First, within the 30 years of history of the (new) environmental movement numerous developments have taken place and a rich literature exists on the resources that are mobilised in environmental struggles, the contributions to culture and identity formation, the changing profile of its members and professional activists, and core themes that are 'in' or 'out' in the issue-attention cycle of environmental NGOs. This contribution does not aim to review this rich tradition of (new) social movement studies, but rather concentrates on those developments that seem essential to me within the framework of ecological modernisation. Or to put it differently: I want to focus on what ecological modernisation perspectives have to offer to the study of environmental NGOs. That means that, for instance, major developments in concrete action strategies, in the professionalisation of marketing and image building, in the number of organisations and their members, as well as in the members' social backgrounds, will remain untouched. Second, I will focus my analysis of the environmental movement on changes, but it goes without saying that most groups also show remarkable continuities. For instance, although several new groups have been established in the late 1980s and early 1990s, most of today's major organisations have a tradition of at least 25 years. Third, as I indicated above and as I will stress several times below, the analysed and observed tendencies are general and overall developments which do not necessarily have the same value or 'truth' for every single environmental NGO, nor for every country to the same extent. As ecological modernisation was originally developed in – and against the background of – a restricted number of – West-European countries, the observations made in this contribution might have similar limitations.

In comparing the ideologies of the major environmental organisations in the 1970s with those in the 1990s one can hardly miss the differences in the central assumptions concerning the causes of and the solutions to environmental problems, as put forward by both representatives of environmental NGOs and the social scientists studying the environmental movement. The ideas that stood central in, for instance, the *Blueprint for Survival* (1972) and the writing of Schumacher (1973), and that inspired the practices of local producer–consumer cooperatives of which Mondragon in Spain is among the best known, formed the ideological luggage of most of the environmental organisations that were established during the early 1970s (the heyday of the first

---

[3] Discussions at the 93rd American Sociological Association's round table on ecological modernisation (of which the contributions will be published in *Environmental Politics*, Sping 2000; volume 9, no. 1) as well as contributions from other scholars (cf. Blowers, 1997; Buttel, 1999; Mol, 1995) have pointed out the geographical restrictions of the still rather Eurocentric contributions to ecological modernisation theory. I will deliberately not engage with environmental movements in other – that is outside Europe and North America – geographical areas that are even more distinct from the European and American situation (e.g. the national and sub-national environmental movements and organisations of new industrialising and developing countries; see e.g. Sonnenfeld, forthcoming).

48   *A.P.J. Mol / Geoforum 31 (2000) 45–56*

wave of environmental concern). A group of social theorists – often labelled as counter-productivity or de-industrialisation theorists – further developed these often rather practical ideas by either grounding them in existing social theories or by distinguishing them from these mainstream schools-of-thought by emphasising that this new and original ideology could not be reduced to any of the existing ideological frameworks. In Germany, for instance, it was Otto Ulrich, Rudolf Bahro, Strasser and Traube and more recently Wolfgang Sachs who gave these ideologies of the emerging environmental movement their place in social theory, often by confronting them with neo-Marxist frameworks. In the USA it was especially the work of Barry Commoner that theorised about the new environmental NGOs of the 1970s. And, of course, in elaborating on these ideas they fortified and stimulated the development of this emerging environmental movement.

In a more or less similar way ecological modernisation theory tries to capture the changing ideologies that spread among environmental NGOs, and other environment-oriented segments of society, from the mid 1980s onward, particularly in the industrialised countries of Western Europe. The deindustrialisation, counter-productivity and neo-Marxist undertones of the ideologies of the early environmental movement started to fade during the eighties,[4] making room for ideas that still opted for radical environmental reforms, but no longer connected them to overall and massive social transformations that would alter industrial society beyond recognition. Although fierce opposition against the capitalist economic system, against industrialisation and large or complex technosystems, and against any form of large bureaucracy can still be found in the diverse ideological spectrum of the environmental movement, these ideas have definitely moved from a core position to the periphery between the 1970s and the 1990s.

Among other things (which I will discuss below), this shift resulted from the belief that capitalist production, complex technologies, industrialisation and state bureaucracies do not have to be environmentally harmful, nor are their suggested alternatives always environmentally beneficial. Boris Frankel Post-Industrial Utopians (1987) can be seen as exemplary in criticising from an environmental perspective some of these 'traditional' ideological positions of the environmental movement, although he was not yet able or willing to formulate a new perspective. Huber (1982, 1985), the founding father of ecological modernisation, was able to identify and formulate an alternative. But the departure from his

former ideological position, being strongly linked to the *Berlin SelbstHilfe Netzwerke*,[5] included such a radical shift in perspective that he lost communication lines with major parts of the environmental movement. His almost unconditional support of high-technological and super-industrial developments, his rather fierce criticism of the bureaucratic state, and his emphasis on market relations and dynamics in managing environmental problems was one bridge too far for the environmental movement, certainly at that time in Germany.

Today, over 15 years after Huber's initial pathbreaking and (still) controversial writings, a significant part of the ecological modernisation ideas can be found back in the environmental movement's contemporary ideology. The dominant positions within the current environmental movement are rather oriented towards reforming and fine tuning the institutions of modernity in order to let them fulfil environmental goals. A radical goodbye to these institutions is no longer considered necessary nor desirable from an environmental perspective. This in fact means the decoupling of environmental from other – social and political – perspectives or ideologies (such as socialism, conservatism and liberalism), as Cotgrove (1982) and Paehlke (1989) have stressed in an early stage and Giddens (1994) more recently. Or, to put it in terms of ecological modernisation theorists: this shows the emergence of an independent environmental rationality that is no longer automatically linked to, nor can be reduced to, more traditional political, economic, social or other rationalities.

Partly related to this changing ideology, the position of environmental NGOs in environmental and broader social struggles has changed considerably. While in the 1970s and early 1980s the environmental movement could be seen as part of a broader movement for social change regarding many developments in western societies – with for instance close connections to the peace movement, anti-nuclear organisations, the squatter movement, animal liberation groups, the Third World movement, and some parts of the female emancipation movement – they can increasingly be interpreted as an one-issue movement. Its prime focus is environmental quality, and automatic solidarity and common agendas with other progressive social movements is declining. The growing acceptance of its environmental criticism and ideological views by both lay actors and experts within those institutions that 'make a difference', is paralleled both by a changing ideology and a stricter environmental focus of environmental NGOs.

---

[4] In the early 1980s the Dutch environmental sociologist Tellegen (1983) could still claim that the common denominator of environmental NGOs in Western industrial societies was their struggle against modernity and their anti-modern ideology.

[5] The Berlin Selbsthilfe Netzwerke was a network of small scale production–consumption communities in West Berlin, much in the tradition of the writings of the *Blueprint for Survival* and *Small is Beautiful*. The main criticism of Joseph Huber against this network was that its productive units were neither economically viable nor environmentally sound.

A.P.J. Mol / Geoforum 31 (2000) 45–56   49

However, whilst they have become more reformist and more focussed on environmental quality environmental organisations have at the same time lost their monopoly on agenda setting and the representation of environmental interests. In the 1970s they were – together with concerned scientists – widely seen as the prime agenda setting agents and the only ones that could protect the 'interests' of the environment. Today the environmental movement has been joined by, and in some cases has 'lost' tasks to, the growing environmental state bureaucracy, the environmental consultants, the utility sector, scientific institutions, environmental industries and others (although the impact of these agents vary from country to country and issue to issue). This does not of course mean that they have completely lost their position in environmental debates, struggles and politics, but it does mean that 'competition' has increased and their automatic monopoly on representing environmental interests has vanished.

This brings me to the final point which concerns developments in the strategies of environmental organisations. But rather than focusing on the often quoted de-radicalisation of action strategies of the environmental movement, usually joined with some kind of criticism of the incorporation of environmental organisations in the establishments of power, I would like to emphasise the shift in their overall confrontation with state and market actors. In general, the state is no longer seen as the evident coalition partner of the environmental movement, if it ever was. In fact, in numerous cases the state is the enemy, as in the instances of major infrastructure projects (highways, airports, location of industrial areas). But also in those cases and circumstances where internal state conflicts or international configurations result in stagnation or weakening of environmental policies and reforms. At the same time, market actors that were so vehemently criticised for their capitalist, profit-making orientation in the 1970s, are no longer by definition interpreted as the movement's main opponent. Alternatively they can be often considered as companions in environmental struggles, as the increasing literature on coalitions and cooperation between environmental NGOs and business and the theoretical ideas of subpolitics illustrate (cf. below).

This means that environmental struggles and debates have gained in complexity and simple universal schemes for social change and environmental problem resolution are no longer adequate. Farmers' will be environmental victims on one issue one day (cf. highway construction or air pollution), while the next day they are polluters themselves (pesticides or (ground)water pollution). Environmental organisations are engaged in constant dynamic processes of coalition building with rapidly changing opponents and partners, with the aim of maximising and safeguarding environmental gains.

The time frames and the extent to which the three shifts in environmental reform practices discussed above have already taken place differ between European countries. The origins and backgrounds in ideology, strategy and position show of course strong domestic influences. However, in general, the more a country has been able to redesign and modernise its environmental policy, and the more it has made advances in actual environmental reforms to economic practices and institutions, the more large numbers of environmental NGOs have transformed themselves in the above mentioned directions. If I understand Albert Weale's (1992) analysis of differences in ecological modernisation penetration in the UK versus the Netherlands and Germany correctly, it should not come as a surprise to find transformations in environmental NGOs along the lines identified above occurring at an earlier occasion and stronger in the latter two countries than in the UK.[6]

Notwithstanding these differences and desynchronisation, some commonalties can be identified when analysing the cause and background of these transformations. First, progressive developments in – at least – the design of environmental policy, and to a lesser extent its implementation, appear to have made both very pessimistic scenarios and de-modernisation ideologies increasingly inadequate and less relevant. Second, increasingly some segments of society have proved receptive to environmental arguments and to some extent willing to take these arguments into consideration when designing the institutions, practices and actions they are engaged in (e.g. water boards, utility sectors, insurance companies, environmental industries, certain niches of industrial sectors). As a result a change in ideology and strategy seemed to provide environmental NGOs with better access to both the general public and the core of policy communities in the environmental field. The self-perception of significant parts of the environmental movement from the early 1980s onwards was that their confrontational ideologies and strategies had resulted in only limited successes and were increasingly counter-productive in reaching their goals: widespread support in society; a major influence in policy-making; and significant impacts on market developments. Third, changes in the wider socio-economic and cultural context of industrialised societies did not leave the environmental movement untouched. The no-nonsense and deregulation politics of the Thatcher and Reagan era did not have a similarly strong impact in

---

[6] A recent analysis of the contemporary transitions in the British environmental pressure groups (Rawcliffe, 1998), however, shows remarkable parallels with my 'ecological modernisation' analysis. Rawcliffe also uses, be it in a rather loose way, the concept of ecological modernisation as the common denominator for the environmental transformations that have taken and still take place in British social practices and institutions.

50   *A.P.J. Mol / Geoforum 31 (2000) 45–56*

every country, but it certainly meant a change of climate compared to the 1970s, affecting the position of the environmental movement and contributing to the reformulation of ideologies and strategies.

These transformations might look evident now to some in Western Europe, but what we analyse and observe today should not be interpreted as historical necessities. Rather they are the outcomes of social developments and struggles, actively promoted and developed by capable agents. Such transformations do not proceed without discussion and controversies (internal and external) and the actual outcomes cannot easily be predicted. Nevertheless, the general direction, trajectory and momentum of transformation are historic in the sense that they can no longer be interpreted as a short term deviation which will soon be corrected. Rather in this case it is a new phase in the development of the environmental movement, which is at the same time the medium and outcome of the new phase of ecological modernisation which we are moving into. Again, this is not to say that this new situation is clear, undisputed and without internal contradictions and controversies, or that simple models can predict the further development of the environmental movement in industrialised societies. The mere fact that some significant discrepancies exist between contemporary environmental NGOs in western Europe (as briefly analysed above) and the environmental movement in the USA (see below) makes us aware of the contextual factors that contribute to variations within and to some extent beyond the ecological modernisation ideas as quoted above. In elaborating upon the new positions and strategies of environmental NGOs in Sections 3–5, I also want to stress the ambivalences, the uncertainties and the new challenges for environmental NGOs, which are to some extent related to this new phase in environmental reform, which others and I have labelled ecological modernisation.

3. Between and beyond state and market

The changing relationship between state and market, not only (but certainly also) in the field of the environment, and the emergence of new social and political arrangements in-between state and market, have forced environmental organisations to reconsider their attitude and strategy towards both domains and to invent new ways of making use of these transformations in pushing for environmental reform. The state, and more precisely its environmental authorities and institutions, is no longer considered a 'natural ally' of, nor the principal focus for, the environmental movement. With the traditional role of the state as a welfare state 'on the move', and with the fading of hierarchical, centralised and directive state operations accompanied by the emergence

of in-between private–public arrangements as well as full private or market institutions that take over some of the state's traditional tasks, environmental organisations have been forced to reconsider their traditional preoccupation with the national Ministry for the Environment. In the past this 'natural ally' of the environmental movement has of course been criticised for not moving fast and far enough in environmental reforms, but in the end it was always seen as being supportive of at least some move towards environmental reform (as that was the final raison d'être of the Ministry).[7] In the era of ecological modernisation, the declining formal power of environmental authorities, the complexity and fast changing coalitions of environmental allies and opponents on a diversity of environmental issues, and the increasing role of private and market organisations and market dynamics in environmental reform processes have initiated developments within the environmental movement that indeed deserve the label innovative.

Environmental organisations are increasingly trying to develop into an independent 'third' force with their own resources, their own interest rationality, making alternating strategic alliances with state and market parties whilst allowing themselves more freedom to move through the spectrum of political parties and ideologies. Environmental organisations are no longer only engaged in their 'traditional tasks': agenda-setting and legitimation processes. Agreements with major polluters without any interference from the state,[8] the taking over of specific tasks formerly run by state agencies (such as education, extension, information dissemination), interest representation for their members via for instance privileged access to nature reserves, commissioners at major firms or (public) utility organ-

---

[7] This also differs from country to country. For instance, in Germany, the Netherlands and Denmark the relations between environmental NGOs and the Ministry for the Environment were closer and more supportive, than in the United Kingdom or the USA.

[8] In 1997 the influential Dutch environmental NGO SNM negotiated with Shell to reduce greenhouse gas emission beyond the level required by the government. Because of dissatisfaction with governmental pesticide policy, in 1994 Friends of the Earth Netherlands negotiated agreements with the potato sector to reduce pesticide use. Similar examples can be found in, for instance, the USA where – in reaction to the stagnation of pesticide policy – in 1986 a coalition of environmental and consumer organisations and agropesticide producers almost succeeded in getting a bill on pesticide reduction and innovation accepted by Congress (Bosso, 1998; Nownes, 1991). In his recent analysis of innovations in the strategies of British NGOs Rawcliffe (1998) mentions similar developments and lists numerous examples. A rich literature of experiences in solutions of environmental controversies beyond the state, with examples from several countries is recently emerging (cf. Stafford and Hartman, 1998; Murphy and Bendell, 1997; Hogenboom et al., 1999; special issue no. 24 of *Greener Management International*, 1999; Duyvendak et al., 1999), although the first significant experiments with this kind of sub-politics dates from at least the early 1990s in countries such as the Netherlands.

A.P.J. Mol / Geoforum 31 (2000) 45–56   51

isations (such as 'commissioners' of the water boards in the Netherlands that are officially backed by the environmental movement), engagements in product design and (supporting) marketing[9] are some of the more recent strategies that have been considered and implemented by environmental organisations in industrialised countries. Their new position and strategy is to some extent 'borrowed' from successful experiences of labour unions in contesting the power of state and markets, taking into account the differences in organisational structures, interest representation and resources that can be mobilised in putting pressure on state and market parties. At the same time the closer collaboration from the 1980s onward between more traditional nature conservation organisations (such as WWF, bird protection organisations, and those that acquire and preserve nature reserves) and the new environmental movement has accelerated this process, as nature protection organisations have a longer tradition in interest representation and the running of traditional state tasks. Some nature conservation organisations, such as the WWF, have transformed partly into environmental pressure groups themselves, negotiating directly with producers and retailers on environmental reforms (sometimes rewarding the latter by allowing them to use the Panda logo on products). If at all, environmental authorities then only appear on the stage to declare negotiated results 'generally binding' to prevent free riding.

To some extent these transformations are reflected in Ulrich Beck's (1994) notion of emerging subpolitics, the increasing importance of politics outside and beyond the formal political institutions of parliament, political parties and bureaucracy. Although it goes too far to identify at this moment an overall, massive and sudden transformation towards subpolitical alternatives, these major new innovations go in that direction. In another article (Hogenboom et al., 1999) we have argued that state involvement is increasingly criticised and bypassed by environmental subpolitics outside traditional institutions in those cases where governmental environmental policy: (i) remains restricted to natural science definitions of environmental problems and risks, leaving questions of public perceptions, norms and values unaddressed; (ii) is immobilised by internal conflicts of interest and legitimation or by stagnating international engagements; (iii) remains restricted to facilitating or coordinating conflicting societal interests without attempting to solve them; and/or (iv) proves to be too bureaucratic, rigid and universal to meet the complex diversity and local connotations of environmental problems. In addition, environmental subpolitics is advancing, because it is no longer sufficient for industries to follow only governmental standards and policies; they increasingly have to take non-state environmental requirements from civil society into account.[10] For the environmental movement these innovative subpolitical developments go along with – internal and external – debates, controversies and struggles. With respect to subpolitical arrangements social-democrats in the Netherlands have, among others, criticised environmental organisations (and remarkably enough not business representatives) on the lack of democratic legitimacy of arrangements where private partners, e.g. environmental organisations and major economic forces, bypass conventional democratic institutions when dealing with environmental problems and anxieties.

But I especially want to focus on the internal debates and controversies. These innovative developments clearly include some amount of compromise, as final decisions on solutions or measures to be taken are no longer left entirely to the state but are to some extent brought within the movement itself, although they will never be completely determined by the movement's priorities. At the same time, those parts of the environmental movement which do not (want to) follow this 'radical path of innovation' are in constant debate with the 'frontrunning entrepreneurs' on radical or reformist goals, strategies and ideologies, resulting – as I will claim in Section 4 – in marginalisation as well as a sharpening of the more 'fundamentalist' positions vis-à-vis 'realist' positions within the movement.

4. Radicals, reformists and counter-activists

Do these – partly actual and partly expected – transformations in the ideology, strategy and position of environmental organisations imply a final goodbye to those 'fundamentalist' or 'radical' parts of the movement that insist on deconstructing the institutions of modernity? A marginalisation of those parts that develop radical adversarial strategies to fight environmentally destructive practices and refuse to compromise whilst adhering to ideologies that were dominant in the 1970s and early 1980s. Or will the – wide spreading perception of – failure of environmental reforms reverse the 'realist' or 'reformist' position of major environmental organi-

---

[9] The involvement of Greenpeace in the development of the energy-efficient Smile car, the contribution of Greenpeace to the introduction and marketing of stand alone solar energy systems produced by Shell Renewables, and the activities of WWF in allowing producers to use the Panda logo for marketing purposes in reward for significant environmental improvements of production processes and/or products, are some recent examples.

[10] Genetically modified food seems to be an interesting case study as in some countries (e.g. the UK) official state policies and civil society – or lay-actor – perceptions and requirements are strongly diverging.

52   *A.P.J. Mol / Geoforum 31 (2000) 45–56*

sations and force them into more radical and 'fundamentalist' paths?

Within parts of the environmental movement an often heard expectation, hope, or even threat, focussed on those in power is that failure to make progress on environmental reform through these new arrangements will result in a reradicalising of the environmental movement. In pointing at the emergence of organisations such as Earth First! Sea Shepherd and animal liberation groups, or to fierce protests against UK highway construction programs, radical action strategies are put forward as a logical and unavoidable consequence of the failure of those environmental reform programmes that have increasingly committed environmental organisations to, or incorporated them into, more reformist trajectories of change. From an ecological modernisation point of view the increasing institutionalisation of environmental interests in the political and economic arenas, however, makes it very unlikely that such a reradicalisation in strategies or in ideologies will actual take place among major parts of the environmental movement in industrialised societies. The support for transformations that diametrically oppose the dominant institutions of modernity will be limited and will be perceived among large segments of sympathisers as a bridge too far, or may be rather as a bridge back, in the constant struggle for environmental reform.

It can also be questioned whether the majority of environmental organisations are prepared to pay the price that goes along with such radicalisation: marginalisation from members, from the central institutions in power, and from resources. Particularly because of the last point the professional environmentalists at the headquarters of mainstream NGOs are likely to feel highly uncomfortable with such reradicalisation. This interpretation should however be understood correctly. First, radical ideologies and strategies will remain part of the diversity of the environmental movement, although not to the extent that their adherents would like to believe or hope. This means that contradicting positions within the environmental movement might get sharpened, as the perception of the successes of reformist strategies, on problem definition and on final goals, diverge. The German Green Political Party, although not part of the environmental movement in the strict sense, has shown this sharpening of positions between *fundi's* and *realo's* since the late 1980s, the latter wing increasingly dominating as confirmed by the party's participation in the national red-green coalition government since 1998. The Belgium Greens seem to follow the German path of government participation in 1999. Second, dominant or mainstream environmental NGOs will constantly back negotiation, cooperation and compromise with more adversarial actions and campaigns. But these latter activities (i) are no longer their main focus although they are often instrumental in

improving their position at negotiations, (ii) have media attention rather than fundamental alternatives as their main goal, and (iii) are increasingly carried out by small groups of 'professionals' rather than large masses, Greenpeace being a main representative of the latter. The contributions to Duyvendak et al. (1999) on the participation of the Dutch environmental movement in what is called the Green Polder Model[11] show similar debates on the relation between negotiation, cooperation and compromise – now in a more institutionalised form – on the one hand and adversarial positions, actions and struggles on the other. The conflicts between the main American environmental NGOs in the negotiating process towards the NAFTA environmental side agreement (where the more critical ones such as Friends of the Earth and the Sierra Club stood against the more moderate NGOs like NRDC, the Audubon Society and WWF), have similar dimensions (cf. Esty, 1994; Vogel, 1997; Hogenboom, 1998).

What is likely is that radical/fundamentalist activists will be – and in fact are in most countries – surpassed in number and influence by counter-activists: increasingly well-organised groups, coalitions and movements of anti-environmentalists. This is the case because the institutionalisation of environmental interests, the successes of mainstream environmental organisations against vested interests and the high visibility of radical environmental activists have resulted in a number of countries – to different degrees – in a so-called *green backlash* (Rowell, 1996). This green backlash should be understood as the organised resistance against the environmental movement and their influence on vested interests. The United States is probably 'leading the way' with the Wise Use movement, a well-organised and intelligent coalition of ultraconservative politicians, economic interest groups, right-wing scientific institutions and citizen-consumers that feel threatened by environmentalists for various reasons. Opposition against environmental interests and their representatives is of course not new; in fact, it has paralleled environmental concerns from the early days onward. What is new, however, is the organisation of this opposition, as well as major segments of the population, into one movement that uses similar kinds of strategies as the environmental movement.

---

[11] The Green Polder Model should become the environmental equivalent of the successful – according to most national and international commentators – economic Polder Model, in which Dutch labour unions and peak associations of business negotiate and compromise on the main economic issues (employment, wages increases, etc.), in avoiding major strikes, high unemployment rates and large wage increases. In the Green Polder Model environmental NGOs should enter into comparable – more or less institutionalised – negotiations and package deals with business, governed by roughly similar rules of the game.

A.P.J. Mol / Geoforum 31 (2000) 45–56   53

In the heyday of the Wise Use movement several political commentators and social scientists (as quoted in Rowell, 1996) claimed that its political influence exceeded that of the environmental movement. European countries – for various reasons – have not witnessed a similar degree of anti-environmentalism up till now, although they have not stayed free of such developments (cf. Rawcliffe, 1998). The Heidelberg Appeal, made up of conservative politicians, economic interest groups, and natural scientists and economists, constantly challenge the environmental movement's knowledge claims, their legitimacy, their representing powers, their democratic outlook and their financial state support in countries such as Germany, the Netherlands, the UK and Austria. In the Netherlands, for example, the Heidelberg Appeal (HAN) contributed with scientific reports, media strategies and regional meetings to the protection of agrarian interest in both pesticide policy and acid rain policy. And in line with HAN, the not insignificant economic institute NYFER (1998) tries to dismantle the positions the environmental movement and their 'natural allies' in science and the state have reached after three decades. In analysing the success of these anti-environment coalitions in the USA Rowell (1996) points out, among others things, the failures of the environmental movement itself, including: its incorporation into the domains of power; its evolution into an one-issue movement without concern for the social consequences of environmental reforms; and the fact that the 'top' of the movement has lost sight of its grassroot organisations and their support.

It thus comes as no surprise that he and many other social scientists and political commentators see the environmental justice movement in the USA[12] as an example of not only a successful answer by environmentalists to the green backlash involving going back to the grassroots of environmental protest, but also of a renovation and reradicalising of the environmental movement (cf. Szasz and Meuser, 1997; Ringquist, 1997). Radicalisation not in terms of fundamental ideologies or strategies, but in terms of a politicisation of the environmental debate by focussing on environmental victims. However, the environmental justice movement in the USA is not the first to notice that the poor and minorities are disproportionately confronted with environmental risks. As Ringquist (1997) argues, this has been pointed out in the USA since at least 1971, and many scholars in the neo-Marxist tradition have argued along similar lines since then, also in Europe (cf. from Enzensberger, 1973 up to O'Connors, 1998). But what makes the environmental justice movement so special is

that it has succeeded in organising a movement around this subject and managed to get it high on the agenda of local and national US environmental authorities, which usually aim to depoliticise rather than repoliticise issues.

Environmental problems and risks have been passed on to the poor and/or racial minorities for many years. At the same time more environmentally sound houses, cars, food and services are to a major extent still the privilege of the rich (and are used to some extent as new means of distinction), while the poor are most strongly confronted with rising environmental taxes on water, energy and food. The neglect of these distributional effects by environmental authorities and environmental NGOs, among others, can severely affect public support – especially amongst the lower and middle income strata – for both movement and reform programme, ultimately supporting counter-tendencies such as the Wise Use movement. While examples of the detrimental effects of environmental reforms on the less well-off and disadvantaged minorities are numerous, environmental policies can also support the material and non-material improvements of the poor and those minorities, especially in those cases where they have been unequally victimised by environmental risks. The fact that both can – and do – take place has consequences for both social theory on the environment and the environmental movement.

To some extent neo-Marxist categories seem to return in these strongly American-based environmental ideologies, analyses and practices of environmental (in)justice, which seem to oppose sharply the more European-based Risk Society ideas that stress the democratisation of environmental risks. In elaborating on these differences, and their relevance for environmental movements, I will first focus on two explanations for this opposition (USA vs. Europe, local vs. global) and then formulate a more general conclusion on the issue of distributional consequences of environmental problems. The first explanation for the emergence of the environmental justice movement in the USA and the stronger prevalence of neo-Marxist categories in analysing distributional consequences can be related to the specific characteristics of the USA vis-à-vis Europe. Without going into large detail, the sheer size of the country (with major distances between local groups and national headquarters in Washington DC), the strong geographical segregation of race and class, the more adversarial policy style, and a distinct 'style' of capitalism, can be mentioned to at least partly explain both the stronger prevalence of a *green backlash* and the emergence of an environmental justice movement in the USA vis-à-vis Europe. Second, environmental justice arguments as put forward by this movement seem to have been used particularly for 'localised' environmental problems: chemical and nuclear waste disposal, local air pollution, and the like. In turning their attention and

---

[12] Fritz (1998) shows that also in other countries similar movements are emerging, although she – and others – expand the definition of environmental justice considerably.

54 *A.P.J. Mol / Geoforum 31 (2000) 45–56*

involvement increasingly to national and global environmental issues (biodiversity, global warming, ozone layer depletion, the oceans, etc.), national environmental organisations have initially been less receptive to these new ideas, as they initially seem to make less sense for such problems on a national basis. Together, this explains the strong bottom-up emergence of environmental justice ideas, especially in a country where the 'distance' between local groups and (inter) national lobbyists is so large. In addition, the development towards a one-issue movement has made mainstream environmental organisations less receptive to related social and economic issues (although with the notion of sustainable development one would expect this to change).

At the same time – and this is the concluding point I want to make – the relation between environmental victims and economic classes is far from one-sided and this should give us a cautious attitude towards generalising environmental justice ideas (both in an American and a European context). Arguing in a similar line ecological modernisation theory claims that, in contrast to earlier neo-Marxist analyses, environmental conflicts can no longer be interpreted as following predictable paths with static opposing parties and interests, and class or race biased distributional effects. Environmental struggles cross traditional (economic and other) interest lines and divisions in society and should be analysed increasingly as an independent – that is non-reducible – category. In that sense the neo-Marxist schemes claiming rather fixed parallels between conventional class inequalities and struggles and more recent environmental inequalities and struggles, might prove fruitful in individual empirical cases (such as the environmental justice movement shows us), but have increasingly lost their overall theoretical and analytical value. This is in fact the outcome of a growing number of empirical studies on environmental inequality: although on the average the poor and minorities are confronted with disproportionately high levels of local environmental risks (and even more so in the USA where segregation of class and race is more far reaching and thus the spreading of local environmental problems potentially more 'unjust'), there exists no one-to-one relation between high environmental risks and economic categories.

5. Beyond the level of the nation-state

In analysing environmental inequalities and agenda-setting by the environmental movement and social scientists in the USA, Szasz and Meuser (1997) rightly observe their complete separation from studies and traditions that focus on international dimensions of the unequal access to environmental resources and the unequal distribution of environmental risks. Thus opportunities are missed both for theoretical cross fertilisation and for strategic alliances between local and national environmental groups and the Third World movement. This marked separation reflects the fact that although environmental organisations and environmental ideologies were far from laggards in processes of globalisation – and in fact to some extent contributed to it – moving beyond the level of the nation-state is still a major problem for significant parts of the environmental movement.

The environmental movement has always expressed an ambivalent position vis-à-vis processes of globalisation. On the one side, with their phrases 'from one earth to one world' and 'think globally, act locally', they have showed a constant awareness of global ecological interdependencies and of the need to control the disturbance of these interdependencies at least to some extent at the global level. The subsequent establishment of international NGO coordination centres (cf. Friends of the Earth International), or even global organisations more or less run from one central office (cf. Greenpeace), provoked some analysts to draw parallels with transnational corporations. And regarding recent global environmental problems these international environmental organisations have indeed in a number of cases intervened effectively in world wide negotiations.

On the other side, however, the ideological basis of parts of the environmental movement is strongly rooted in local initiatives and local solutions, resulting in a suspicious attitude towards supra-national processes of production, consumption or governance. The stretching of production–consumption chains and cycles across the globe, the extension of corporations beyond the level of the nation-state, and the world wide movement of natural resources and wastes are in principle still criticised. Arguing in this line, even supra-national political structures, if they are not completely dedicated to environmental protection as in the case of UNEP or specific environmental treaties, contribute to the detachment of decisions from the localities where the origins and consequences of environmental problems are in the end rooted.

As a consequence of the growing inadequacy of national environmental policies and their partial replacement by sub- and supra-national political arrangements, as theorised by, among others, ecological modernisation adherents, the environmental movement cannot but concentrate increasingly also on regional (e.g. EU, NAFTA) and global economic and political processes. While developments within the environmental movement are indeed rather moving towards increasing attention to and awareness of global interdependencies in environmental controversies, there seems to be a growing tension between those cosmopolitan parts of the movement engaged in regional and global negotiations, and

A.P.J. Mol / Geoforum 31 (2000) 45–56   55

major parts of the movement that are basically oriented to local environmental quality. Although NIMBY motivations for joining the environmental movement cannot be considered as 'inferior' or less legitimate than some definition of 'common good' (as environmental authorities and opponents of environmental organisations often try to press), they do provide complications for professionals in environmental organisations that have to match local interest and local support with supra-national and global interdependencies and decision making structures. Struggles around limitations on the growth of air traffic often have this complex mix of local nuisance and local environmental groups with strong community support on the one side, and global climate change and supra-national political and economic decision-making structures on the other. The two might get along well together for some time but are in confrontation when alternative modes of medium to long distance transport (such as bullet trains) are under consideration. While in the 1970s the two sides of environmental protest could be connected by the prevalence of local action from a global analysis, today such simple connections seem no longer adequate. In an age of globalisation environmental organisations cannot stick to local actions alone. On the other hand, the danger for the global environmentalists of becoming detached from local grassroots, which was seen as one of the important causes behind the American green backlash, is real. The European environmentalists in Brussels hardly succeed in linking their priorities with the local and often not even with the national environmental organisations. A further specialisation, division of labour and fragmentation within the environmental movement can be a logical – but perhaps not favourable – consequence.

Challenges regarding global reform are particularly strong where environmental organisations from developing countries, which have developed less into one-issue organisations, meet the cosmopolitan environmentalists from the North. Global environmental organisations such as Greenpeace and WWF who have been constituted under ecological modernisation conditions are in conflict with environmental organisations from developing countries in the global arena of nongovernmental environmental politics. Equally, international umbrella organisations such as Friends of the Earth bring together organisations from distinct parts of the world, where transformations that we have labelled as ecological modernisation are not always dominant or present. Negotiation and cooperation between environmental NGOs and transnational corporations might increasingly seem 'business as usual' in countries such as the Netherlands and Germany, whilst among Southern NGOs it is still widely considered 'not done' – to put it mildly. And FOEI faces such (internal) discussions, debates and controversies. Strangely enough, via the backdoor of the practices of transnational corporations

in developing countries, ecological modernisation innovations seem to diffuse incidentally into the environmental NGOs in the South (cf. Shell's involvement in the Camisea project, Peru; Jones, 1997). However, overall the effect of these – and other – differences is often a paralysing of international umbrella organisations, or a less effective global coordination of national and international NGOs. The more these NGOs get access to and influence over the international powers that be, the less these differences between NGOs can be hidden or ignored.

6. Epilogue

Under conditions of what we have labelled ecological modernisation the modern European environmental movement that was founded in the early 1970s has transformed itself both relatively smoothly and radically. Although there still – and always will – exist varieties in environmental organisations within and between countries, the overall dominant ideologies, strategies and positions of the environmental movement's first decade have changed dramatically, due to internal pressures but especially following, and in active anticipation and reaction to, external developments. Although some activists in and radical commentators outside the environmental movement incidentally question these dominant or mainstream developments within the environmental movement, these debates should rather be interpreted as a rearguard action. Both the institutionalisation of the environment in the political, economic and socio-cultural domains of industrialised societies, as well as the fundamental transformations that are usually taken together under the notion of globalisation, mean that the analysed changes of the environmental movement will prove rather difficult to reverse. Although, due to some basic differences in among others styles of policy-making and capitalism, developments in for instance the American environmental movement will continue to show some dissimilarities with its European counterpart,[13] I would claim that the general direction of transformation is similar, as are the dilemmas and challenges both face.

These dilemmas and challenges which contemporary environmental organisations face relate to among others counter movements, fragmentation, global coordination, the widening of their one-issue focus and fading grassroot links. Some dilemmas are more strongly felt in America, others dominate in Europe. There will be no

---

[13] At another occasion paper (cf. Mol and Spaargaren, 1998) we have suggested that it might perhaps be interesting to develop American or other versions of ecological modernisation theory, partly diverging from the original Eurocentric interpretation.

56   *A.P.J. Mol / Geoforum 31 (2000) 45–56*

simple answers for these dilemmas, nor logical trajectories that follow from my ecological modernisation analysis. But the degrees of freedom and the range of possible outcomes and 'solutions' are to some extent restricted, and in analysing these framed windows of opportunities ecological modernisation theory might prove its value.

Acknowledgements

The comments and suggestions of two anonymous referees of Geoforum and of Joseph Murphy were very helpful in improving an earlier draft of this paper.

References

Beck, U., 1994. The reinvention of politics: towards a theory of reflexive modernization. In: Beck, U., Giddens, A., Lash, S. (Eds.), Reflexive Modernization. Politics, Tradition and Aesthetics in the Modern Social Order, Polity Press, Cambridge, pp. 1–55.

Beck, U., 1997. Was ist Globalisierung? Irrtümer des Globalismus-Antworten auf Globalisierung, Suhrkamp, Frankfurt am Main.

Blowers, A., 1997. Environmental policy: ecological modernisation and the risk society? Urban Studies 34 (5/6), 845–871.

Bosso, C.J., 1988. Transforming adversaries into collaborators. Interest groups and the regulation of chemical pesticides. Policy Sciences 21, 3–22.

Buttel, F., 1999. Classical theory and contemporary environmental sociology. Some reflections on the antecedents and prospects for reflexive modernization theories in the study of environment and society. In: Spaargaren, G., Mol, A.P.J., Buttel, F.H. (Eds.), Environment and Global Modernity, Sage, London, forthcoming.

Christoff, P., 1996. Ecological modernization, ecological modernities. Environmental Politics 5 (3), 476–500.

Cotgrove, S., 1982. Catastrophe or Cornucopia. The Environment Politics, and the Future. Wiley, Chichester.

Duyvendak, W., Horstik I., Zagema, B. (Eds.), 1999. Het Groene Poldermodel. Consensus en conflict in de milieupolitiek, Instituut voor Publiek en Politiek/Vereniging Milieudefensie, Amsterdam.

Enzensberger, H.M., 1973. A critique of political ecology. New Left Review 84, 3–32.

Esty, D.C., 1994. Greening the GATT. Trade, Environment, and the Future. Institute for International Economics, Washington DC.

Frankel, B., 1987. The Post-Industrial Utopians. Polity Press, Cambridge.

Fritz, J.M., 1998. Searching for environmental justice: national stories, global possibilities, paper presented at the 14th World Congress of the International Sociological Association, Montreal, July 1998.

Giddens, A., 1994. Beyond Left and Right. The Future of Radical Politics. Polity Press, Cambridge.

Group of Lisbon, 1995. Limits to Competition, MIT, Cambridge (Mass)/London.

Hajer, M., 1995. The Politics of Environmental Discourse. Ecological Modernisation and the Policy Process. Oxford University Press, New York/London.

Harris, S., 1996. The Search for a Landfill Site in an Age of Risk: The Role of Trust, Risk and the Environment, dissertation. McMaster University, Hamilton, Ontario.

Hogenboom, B.B., 1998. Mexico and the NAFTA Environment Debate. The Transnational Politics of Economic Integration, dissertation. University of Amsterdam, Amsterdam.

Hogenboom, J., Mol, A.P.J., Spaargaren, G., 1999. Forthcoming dealing with environmental risks in reflexive modernity. In: Cohen, M. (Ed.), Risk in the Modern Age: Social Theory, Science and Environmental Decision Making, MacMillan, Basingstoke.

Huber, J., 1982. Die verlorene Unschuld der Ökologie. Neue Technologien und superindustrielle Entwicklung. Frankfurt am Main, Fisher Verlag.

Huber, J., 1985. Die Regenbogengesellschaft. Ökologie und Sozialpolitik. Frankfurt am Main, Fisher Verlag.

Jänicke, M., 1993. Über ökologische und politische Modernisierungen. Zeitschrift für Umweltpolitik und Umweltrecht 2, 159–175.

Jokinen, P., Koskinen, K., 1998. Unity in environmental discourse? The role of decision-makers, experts and citizens in developing Finnish environmental policy. Policy and Politics 26 (1), 55–70.

Jones, M., 1997. The role of stakeholder participation: linkages to stakeholder impact assessment and social capital in camisea, Peru. Greener Management International 19, 87–97.

Mol, A.P.J., 1995. The Refinement of Production. Ecological Modernization Theory and the Chemical Industry. International Books, Utrecht.

Mol, A.P.J., Spaargaren, G., 1998. Ecological modernization in debate: a review, paper presented at the 14th World Congress of the International Sociological Association, Montreal, July 1998 (forthcoming in Environmental Politics, 9, 1).

Murphy, D.F., Bendell, J., 1997. In: The Company of Partners. Business, Environmental Groups and Sustainable Development Post-Rio. The Policy Press, Bristol.

Nownes, A.J., 1991. Interest groups and the regulation of pesticides: Congress, Coalitions, and Closure. Policy Sciences 24, 1–18.

O'Connor, J., 1998. Natural Causes. Essays in Ecological Marxism. Guilford, New York and London.

Paehlke, R.C., 1989. Environmentalism and the Future of Progressive Politics. Yale University Press, New Haven/London.

Rawcliffe, P., 1998. Environmental Pressure Groups in Transition. Manchester University Press, Manchester.

Ringquist, E.J., 1997. Environmental justice: normative concerns and empirical evidence. In: Vig, N.J., Kraft, M.E. (Eds.), Environmental Policy in the 1990s, Congressional Quarterly, Washington, pp. 231–254.

Rinckevicius, L., 1998. Ecological Modernization and its perspectives in Lithuania: attitudes, expectations, actions, dissertation. Kaunas University of Technology, Kaunas.

RIVM, 1998. (Rijksinstituut voor Volksgezondheid en Milieubeheer) Derde Milieuverkenning, RIVM, Bilthoven.

Rowell, A., 1996. Green Backlash: Global Subversion of the Environmental Movement. Routledge, London and New York.

Schumacher, F.E., 1973. Small is Beautiful. Blond and Briggs, London.

Sonnenfeld, D.A., forthcoming, Contradictions of ecological modernisation. Pulp and paper manufacturing in South-East Asia, Environmental Politics 9 (10), xx–xx.

Stafford, E.R., Hartman, C.L., 1998. Toward an understanding of the antecedents of environmentalist-business cooperative relations. In: Goodstein, R.C., MacKenzie, S.B. (Eds.), American Marketing Association's Summer Educators Conference Proceedings, American Marketing Association, Chicago, pp. 56–63.

Szasz, A., Meuser, M., 1997. Environmental inequalities: literature review and proposals for new directions in research and theory. Current Sociology 45 (3), 99–120.

Tellegen, E., 1983. Milieubeweging. Het Spectrum, Uttrecht/Antwerpen.

Vogel, D., 1997. International trade and environmental regulation. In: Vig, N.J. Kraft, M.E. (Eds.), Environmental Policy in the 1990s Reform or Reaction? CQ Press, Washington DC.

Weale, A., 1992. The New Politics of Pollution. MUP, Manchester.

Part III
Society, Nature and Knowledge, and the Formulation and Implementation of Public Policy

[14]

THE CONSTRUCTION OF NATURE AND THE NATURE OF CONSTRUCTION

Analytical and political tools for building survivable futures

Noel Castree and Bruce Braun

NATURE AT THE MILLENIUM

Nature, it seems, is on the agenda as never before. At a time of political-economic transformations global in reach and of unrivaled dynamism, technological changes of astonishing power and unfathomable extent, and apocalyptic pronouncements of ecological catastrophe and cultural crisis, the matter of nature has become a pressing issue, yet one bewildering in its complexity. From biotechnology to "wilderness" preservation, from the exciting medical promises and dark eugenic possibilities of the Human Genome Project to the moral imperatives and neo-imperialist rhetorics mixed together in discourses of "biodiversity," and from the complex politics of deforestation in India to the equally important struggles over models of global warming in Washington, nature is something imagined and real, external yet made, outside history but fiercely contested at every turn. It is at once everywhere and nowhere, the foundation for all "life" and the elusive subject of theoretical and political debate. As we face the twenty-first century, the matter of nature is no less difficult than Raymond Williams (1976) found it more than twenty years ago, and perhaps far more consequential.

That it should be both at once has everything to do with changes occurring at various levels in *fin-de-siècle* societies. The intense global economic restructuring of the last two decades has drastically reorganized networks of production and consumption at a variety of scales and sites, with the result that old industry–environment articulations have been intensified and new ones generated. Previously non-industrialized territories are today industrialized, while elsewhere formerly productive landscapes languish or become remade both materially and semiotically through the practices of "ecological restoration." With the fall of

3

NOEL CASTREE AND BRUCE BRAUN

actually existing socialisms and in a neo-liberal climate of "market triumphalism" (Peet and Watts 1996), local and global natures in both the developed and less developed worlds increasingly reflect strategies of accumulation. In turn these strategies have brought with them myriad environmental problems, problems today contested by the baffling array of environmental non-governmental organizations (NGOs), new social movements (NSMs) and political parties which are such a part of the contemporary political landscape.

In short, global nature is increasingly remade in the image of the commodity – whether it be logging in Madagascar or the new spatial and environmental logics of eco-travel – such that increasingly the nature–society distinction appears obsolete. At the turn of the twenty-first century, nature everywhere is "enterprised up" (Strathern 1992) or "operationalized" (Rabinow 1992). Where the juggernaut of capitalist development has not yet made this complete, technological innovations – increasingly in the form of "technoscience" – stand poised to finish the task. The controversial Human Genome Project may be the most recognizable, and anxiety-producing, example – promising to reconfigure our own bodily natures – but more prosaic interventions already exist, like those surrounding the genetic manipulation of food within modern agro-food complexes (Goodman *et al.* 1987). Elsewhere, technological innovations of a no less material kind – in information technology and the media – increasingly mediate and shape our access to the world. Indeed, in our emerging "network societies" (Castells 1996) there is now the promise of what Wark (1994) calls "third nature" – that is, the simulated natures of everyday TV and magazines, games like SimEarth, or the extraordinary optics of the geographical information system (GIS) all of which provide new, powerful means of manipulating nature as "information."

More than ever before, then, nature is something made. For some, this represents the "end" of nature (McKibben 1989), a response rooted firmly in a modern dualism in which nature is seen as external to society: its other. From this perspective nature must be defended against its "destruction" by humans, and battle lines are drawn to preserve its "pristine" character. For others, humanity's relationship with nature, in all its permutations, is ineluctable and inherently subversive of the nature–society dualism. From this perspective, human intervention in nature is thus neither "unnatural" nor something to fear or decry. This does not rule out limiting human actions in specific situations, but from this perspective what is at stake is not preserving the last vestiges of the pristine, or protecting the sanctity of the "natural" body, but building critical perspectives that focus attention on how social natures are transformed, by which actors, for whose benefit, and with what social and ecological consequences.

Over the past fifteen years an exciting, diverse, interdisciplinary field of critical theory has emerged which takes the second tack, and thus seeks to explain and illustrate the many ways in which nature is constructed and reconstructed within modern and late modern societies. From anthropology to geography, environmental history to cultural studies and political economy to science

CONSTRUCTION OF NATURE AND NATURE OF CONSTRUCTION

studies, critical theorists like Piers Blaikie, William Cronon, Klaus Eder, Evelyn Fox Keller, Donna Haraway, Richard Lewontin, Thomas Laqueur, Michael Redclift, Sharon Traweek, Alexander Wilson and Steve Woolgar, along with many of the contributors to this volume, have made significant theoretical and empirical contributions to our collective understanding of how the environments and bodies we inhabit are fabricated at different levels, through multiple relations, by various actors and as the effects of different forms of social power.

In this ferment of political-economic, technological and intellectual change, *Remaking Reality* brings together contributors from a variety of fields who critically explore, through theoretical debate and case studies, the making and remaking of nature at the millenium. Our book title deliberately speaks to two important points which our contributors seek, in different ways, to make axiomatic. The first point is that nature, in Haraway's (1992: 296) words, "cannot pre-exist its construction": it is figure, construction, artifact, displacement. It is something made – materially and semiotically, and both simultaneously. Those, like "deep greens," who would still appeal to "nature" as a source of moral and political guidance will, of course, find this argument scandalous. Yet, along with the contributors to this volume, we argue that Haraway's insight has profound implications and embodies a liberatory potential, radically opening the field of debate and action surrounding what kinds of natures we seek. But it is an insight that must be viewed with caution. Taken too far, it risks treating nature as a tabula rasa, or suggests that there are no limits – either physical or moral – to how human interventions in nature should proceed. If this is our first point – nature is always something made – then our second is that its making is always about much more than just nature. As our contributors show, it is increasingly impossible to separate nature off into its own ontological space. Thus, the remaking of nature(s) has wider implications – it becomes, quite simply, a focal point for a nexus of political-economic relations, social identities, cultural orderings, and political aspirations of all kinds.

These two general themes are woven into all the chapters collected here. But the volume also has three more specific aims. First, given the speed and intensity of contemporary political-economic and technological change, there is a need to identify and detail new and emerging sites at which social productions of nature occur or are contested, while attending to the social, ecological and political consequences of each. Many contributors do just that, conveying a sense of the complexity and variety of nature's construction in the 1990s. Second, after nearly two decades of writing about the social constitution of nature, it seems apposite to elaborate, put to work and explore the tensions between the various existing theoretical perspectives on social nature. Rather than quest after a meta-theory that can somehow explain nature's remaking across all sites, contributors draw on a variety of theoretical tools, including political economy, post-structuralism and science studies. Which approaches are enrolled depends in part on the conversations engaged, the sites studied and the constructions of nature that seem most in need of interrogation. What emerges is a sense that social

NOEL CASTREE AND BRUCE BRAUN

natures are made according to no one single, overarching logic. Accordingly, no one theory can or should be put forward to explain their fabrication. This is not a charter for an undisciplined theoretical pluralism; rather it is a recognition that different theoretical positions must be engaged if nature and environment at the millenium are to be properly understood. This has practical implications, of course, because, as our contributors show, the social construction of nature is above all consequential – for both humans and non-humans – and thus the question of politics flows logically from analysis and critique. The third aim, therefore, is to contribute to part of a larger project of building "survivable futures" (Katz 1995) for people and other organisms, predicated on social and environmental justice. As the contributors show, if struggles over nature and environment take on a wider resonance then they necessarily help us expand and redefine what a "politics of nature" is all about.

This introductory chapter explores in some detail three theoretical traditions which provide valuable analytical tools for understanding the mechanisms of nature's construction(s) at the end of the millenium. We begin with a critical appreciation of Marx's contribution to the questions of nature and environment as represented in recent work on the production of nature by several contemporary writers in the Marxist tradition. We regard work in political economy as vital to understanding social nature in our times, but suggest that its primary focus on nature's material transformation in capitalist production underplays other aspects of nature's making. Recently, post-structuralist interventions have drawn attention to questions of representation and what we call – following Heidegger – "enframing nature", and we argue that an appreciation of the materiality of representation allows for the recognition that nature's construction involves more than just capital and commodities conventionally understood. Post-structuralist accounts, however, risk locating agency only at the level of "culture" or "discourse," erasing the role that organisms and physical systems play in nature's remaking. The emerging field of "science studies" provides a third theoretical resource and a possible corrective to this erasure. With their focus on science-as-practice, science studies scholars like Donna Haraway and Bruno Latour have shown that what counts as nature, and nature's remaking, occur within networks that include social, technical, discursive and organic elements simultaneously. As is evident in the chapters that follow, all three traditions provide rich analytical resources, as well as important political resources, for the pressing task of building the future natures that we wish to inhabit.

THE PRODUCTION OF NATURE

Once we begin to speak of people mixing their labour with the earth, we are in a whole world of new relations between people and nature and to separate natural history from social history becomes extremely problematic.

(Williams 1980: 76)

6

CONSTRUCTION OF NATURE AND NATURE OF CONSTRUCTION

If nature at the millenium is, more than ever, a distinctively capitalist nature – one made and remade as a commodity form within the specific logics of capitalist production, and competition accumulation – then Marxian political economy offers indispensable critical resources for making sense of and contesting those logics. Despite Marx's well-known failure to offer a systematic account of nature and environment under capitalism, the last decade or so has seen a remarkable flowering of Marxist and neo-Marxist scholarship investigating what Neil Smith (1984), in a paradigmatic formulation, called the social "production of nature" within capitalist (and semi-capitalist) social formations.[1] This Marxian work, which has made an enormous contribution to our collective understanding of social nature under capitalism, has consisted of several overlapping streams, some overtly theoretical and some more empirically grounded.

Marx and nature

Marx's scattered reflections on nature and environment under capitalism meant that it was left to later commentators – notaby Alfred Schmidt – to comb his work for insights. Schmidt's (1971) *The Concept of Nature in Marx* showed that Marx's account of capitalist nature had two sides: on the one hand, a critique of representations of "nature" within bourgeois societies, what Smith (1984: 1) called "the ideology of nature"; and on the other, a fragmented theory of nature's creative destruction under capitalism. Schmidt realized that for Marx the various bourgeois meanings of nature made it resolutely external to society ("first nature") and, at the same time and in contradiction, universal – human beings, as biological entities, were seen as "natural" too. Smith (1984) has identified the cognitive and political implications of this dual representation of nature – a representation which underpins both the "save nature" rhetorics of contemporary ecocentrics and the "manage nature" discourses of technocentrics in government, business and the like. Rendering it external, Smith argued, is doubly ideological: first, it renders non-human objects and processes intractable barriers to which humans must at some point submit, and second it denies any social relation to environment, thus ruling out humanity's creative capacities to transform it. At the same time, Smith continued, the assumption of universality is also counter-revolutionary because it implies that social relations are as immutable as natural processes. Against this, Schmidt showed that Marx insisted on the relations between environment and society, thus avoiding the schism between them without collapsing the latter into the former as in the monistic doctrine of universal nature. As Smith (1984: 18) observed, "nature separate from society has no meaning . . . The relation with nature is an historical product, and even to posit nature as external . . . is absurd since the very act of positing nature requires entering a certain relation *with* nature." More specifically, Schmidt saw in Marx a dialectic between the two: "nature is mediated through society and society through nature" (Smith 1984: 19), a complex metabolic process which Marx centers on the labour process, the point at which

7

NOEL CASTREE AND BRUCE BRAUN

society systematically engages with nature. More particularly still, Schmidt identified in Marx a specifically capitalist appropriation of environment as labour value is placed on environmental goods as part of a system predicated on class relations, competition and accumulation.

Schmidt's argument, while timely, has since been charged with two major limitations. First, Smith (1984: 23–4) has provocatively argued that "incredible as it sounds, Schmidt ends up providing us with one of the most elaborate accounts of the *bourgeois* concept of nature. In Schmidt too there is an external conception of nature . . . and a universal conception." Following Adorno and Horkheimer (1972), Schmidt ends his treatise with the complaint that, despite himself, Marx's vision of a socialist transformation of environment is guilty of the "domination of nature." But for Smith this concept of domination connotes, in its very language, the externality and universality that are the hallmark of the bourgeois conceptions. In short, in his attempt to re-emphasize the realm of nature in Marx's oeuvre, Schmidt ironically underplayed the role of social relations in constituting nature and society. In the second place, Schmidt's account of the Marxist conception of nature is extremely abstract, and even his comments on use values and exchange values do not approach the kind of concrete analytics that Marx sought in *Capital.*

This is why Neil Smith's *Uneven Development* was such an important state-ment, pushing debate forward with his thesis about the production of nature under capitalism. As Smith (1984: xiii–xiv) readily conceded, this thesis "sounds . . . quixotic and . . . jars our traditional acceptance of what had hitherto seemed self-evident . . . it defies the conventional, even sacrosanct separation of nature and society, and it does so with such abandon and without shame." Nonetheless, it is of the utmost importance. First, it gets beyond the external and universal conceptions of nature, registering the redundancy of conceiving of nature as a pristine entity, untouched by human hand – conventionally known as "first nature." Second, it rightly points to the internal relations between society and nature: social projects are invariably ecological projects and vice versa (Harvey 1996). Third, accordingly it alerts us to how capitalism constructs and reconstructs whole landscapes as exchange values under the profit imperative, to how it determines particular constellations of "natural" products in particular places. This is exemplified well by recent work on the production of agrarian regions (Fitzsimmons 1986; Marsden *et al.* 1986a, b; Watts 1989, 1991), but most forcefully, perhaps, in William Cronon's marvellous *Nature's Metropolis* (see *Antipode* 1994). Fourth, it powerfully historicizes human relations with nature and thus opens up the politics and possibility of the transformation of both nature and society (see also Smith 1996). On the basis of this general proposition, Smith (1984: ch. 2) then went on to present one of the most sophisticated Marxist theorizations of nature's production under capitalism, moving with increasing historical–geographical specificity from "production in general," to "production for exchange," to, finally "capitalist production," with its specific social (class) relations and specific (profit-driven) "value relation"

CONSTRUCTION OF NATURE AND NATURE OF CONSTRUCTION

to environment, systematically generating patterns of geographically "uneven development." The effect was to define a powerful overarching critical research programme in which "the major [political-economic] issue . . . becomes the question of how nature is (re)produced, and who controls this process of (re)production in particular times and places" (Whatmore and Boucher 1993: 167).

Neither Smith, nor the other authors cited, were suggesting that capitalism "produces" nature in the sense of, to take an extreme example, determining how trees grow. The portmanteau term "production" seems to imply that capitalism determines every aspect of the natural world as it transforms it: right down to each particle of natural stuff. However, this is not what Smith was arguing. Rather, what the thesis of the production of nature does capture is the way in which "first nature" is replaced by an entirely different produced "natural" landscape. The competitive and accumulative imperatives of capitalism bring all manner of natural environments and concrete labour processes upon them together in an abstract framework of market exchange which, literally, produces nature(s) anew.

However, its insights notwithstanding, Smith's reconstruction of Marx arguably underplays the "materiality of produced nature" (Castree 1995) at a time when capitalism is wreaking more environmental havoc than ever. This, along with Marx's supposed "Prometheanism," is why over the last few years others have returned to Marx to enrich in more ecofriendly ways our understanding of nature's production. Notable here is O'Connor's (1988) well-known work on the "second contradiction of capitalism"; Altvater's (1993) dual thesis that discounting the future routinely leads to resource over-exploitation, while the removal and abstraction of individual commodities from their ecosystemic context frequently entails a hidden, because "unvalued," cost to those wider ecosystems; Benton's (1989) argument about the "naturally mediated unintended consequences of production"; and Harvey's (1996) contention that the distinctive spatio-temporal imperatives of capitalist valuation are anti-ecological. In addition, a number of other authors – notably, many contributors to the journal *Capitalism, Nature, Socialism* – have tried to develop specific political-economic concepts to concretise nature–society relations, while still others have begun to periodize "regimes of environmental accumulation." In this regard, Escobar's (1996) recent distinction between "modern" and "postmodern" ecological capital is a useful heuristic, marking the transition from an expansionary, anti-environmental regime of accumulation bent on "capitalising nature" to a "postmodern" one obliged to sustainably manage its own ecological future in the interests of profitability and survival.

The upshot of these various contributions towards an "ecoMarxism" has been twofold. First, they have tempered the unabashed anthropocentricism of Marx's political economy, but without evacuating it altogether. This is important, for any liberatory remaking of nature must acknowledge that it is only through socially specific structured human action and interpretation that "nature" can be known and transformed at all. Second, ecoMarxist writing has widened both

9

NOEL CASTREE AND BRUCE BRAUN

Marxian notions of political action and challenged the political separatisms of "green politics." Today, traditional concepts of class struggle simply must be linked to ecological struggles of which they are a part (Harvey 1996; Peet and Watts 1996), while the subject of "environmental politics" can no longer be simply "nature" alone.

First World agrarian political economy

If some have remained at the level of abstract theorisation, others have preferred the messier terrain of the empirical where the real complexities of nature's remaking become insistently apparent. Inspired by Kautsky's (1976) *The Agrarian Question*, the last decade or so has seen the rapid rise of an agrarian political economy, largely focussed on the First World and particularly associated with rural sociology and agricultural geography (Buttel and Newby 1980; Marsden *et al.* 1986a). Contesting the notion that agriculture is an "insulated" and "exceptional" industrial sector and pointing to the enormous importance of food production and consumption in advanced capitalist societies, a number of authors has tried to make sense of the dramatic post-war rise of "productivist agriculture" (Peterson 1990). A complex and heterogenous field of research – involving authors like Margaret Fitzsimmons, David Goodman, Terry Marsden and Sarah Whatmore – this agrarian political economy has several important dimensions, each speaking to the consequential remaking of agricultural nature in the 1990s.

The first concerns the understanding of "political economy" itself. Inspired initially by Marxism, agrarian researchers showed that its twin focus on production and distribution within distinctively capitalist economies undermined modern agriculture's supposed exceptionalism and made questions of competition, restructuring and class relations as relevant to agriculture as to manufacturing. However, pointing to the "structuralist" tendencies of classical Marxism, many researchers soon turned to more supple neo- and post-Marxist political-economic concepts in order to grasp the complexity of agricultural transformation. As Marsden *et al.* (1996) suggest, this has had four valuable features – a focus on patterns of uneven development, a focus on local specificity within broader social structures, a focus on family farms within capitalism, and a focus on the state at all levels – each contributing to a more sophisticated understanding of agricultural nature. A second dimension of concern is technological transformation. The biological foundations of agriculture make it a distinctive form of nature's production, but postwar agrarian capitalism has exhibited remarkable technological dynamism (in pesticides, herbicides, genetically manipulated seeds and the like) in order actively to reduce its biological dependency (Goodman *et al.* 1987). This dependency reduction has, significantly, entailed remarkably increased powers to "refashion nature" (Goodman and Redclift 1991) according to the requirements of socially created demand. A third aspect of agrarian political-economy is a focus on "agri-food

10

CONSTRUCTION OF NATURE AND NATURE OF CONSTRUCTION

complexes" (Friedmann 1982). Farming is clearly no longer a land-based activity alone, ending at the farm gates. As farms have been drawn unevenly into wider circuits of capital a significant development has been the rise of an agri-food industry, involving ramified connections between manufacturers of agricultural inputs, farmers, corporate food retailers, food processors and consumers. Farming thus becomes a "conferred" activity, increasingly reliant on distant markets, institutions and regulators within global food networks which are constitutive of and constituted by the local (Le Heron and Roche 1996). A fourth related concern is multinational corporations. While family farms are still important, the power to control agri-food complexes rests increasingly with multinational companies (MNCs), that largely control agricultural inputs, farming (e.g. through "contract farming"), food processing, and food retail. Finally, in an attempt to categorize and periodize these various forms of change, several authors have sought to theorize "international food regimes" (McMichael 1994) at the *fin de siècle*, paralleling efforts in studies of manufacturing to specify post-Fordist "regimes of accumulation."

This is only a summary account, but agrarian political-economy has pushed forward our understanding of late capitalist agricultural nature by putting abstract theory to the test of empirical specificities and, in the process, has generated more sensitive meso-level political-economic concepts. Capitalist agriculture emerges as a highly dynamic flashpoint of ecological transformation, technological innovation, global–local connections, and social relations of power. There remains much to be done – not least a further specification of local–global dialectics (Le Heron and Roche 1996), of individual agency within broader structures (Pile 1990), of nature's agency (Fitzsimmons and Goodman, this volume), of the discursive construction of food and agro-production (Arce and Marsden 1993), and of regimes of late capitalist agro-accumulation – but the enormous consequentiality of remaking agricultural natures is increasingly clear.

Third World political ecology

If agrarian political economy has dynamized the study of agricultural nature, "Third World political ecology" (Bryant 1992) lends that study greater ecological sensitivity and a sharper political edge in quite different geographical settings. Emerging as a concept in the mid-1970s, political ecology is perhaps most closely associated with the pioneering work of Blaikie (1985) and Blaikie and Brookfield (1987). For them, political ecology combines the concerns of ecology with "a broadly defined political-economy" (1987: 17). Consequently, rather than seeing Third World environmental problems as those of resource scarcity, overpopulation or ignorance, they focussed instead on the articulation of wider political and economic constraints with specific environmental uses. At the centre of this conjunction was the "land manager" whose relationship to environment must, Blaikie and Brookfield (1987: 239) insist, "be understood in a historical, political and economic context."

11

NOEL CASTREE AND BRUCE BRAUN

Since these beginnings political ecology has blossomed into a large but by no means coherent field (its leading practitioners today including diverse scholars like Nancy Peluso, Ramachandra Guha, Susanna Hecht, Michael Redclift and Michael Watts), lent integrity less by any theoretical confluences than by the sharing of common themes of inquiry (see, for instance, the essays in Peet and Watts 1996). Nonetheless, these themes encompass important and distinctive aspects of social nature in Third World settings, of which three stand out. First, given the preponderance of rural and agricultural workers in less developed countries (LDCs) the question of land use and management is particularly vital to many Third World livelihoods. Second, with economic globalization, many pre-modern agricultural production systems have been uneasily incorporated into global circuits of capital so that the question of the articulation of different social formations is especially germane. Third, it follows that when land degradation does occur it frequently becomes a highly politicized issue that, literally, can have life or death consequences.

Focussing on these and other features has generated important conceptual insights, many of which were already apparent in Blaikie and Brookfield's *Land Degradation and Society* (1987). First, by focussing on political-economic and ecological "marginality" – rather than ecological "limits" – they showed that marginality is both cause and effect of land degradation. Second, by inserting local land use into its social relational context they showed how the land manager is compelled to "transmit" excessive production pressures onto the land – pressures often issuing from distant sources and from the global level. Finally, hinting at later concerns about nature's discursive construction (see the third section below), Blaikie and Brookfield pointed to how perceptions of land degradation vary depending on the structured positionality of the viewer. Together, these insights radically undermined the idea that even in Third World settings nature was somehow an external and absolute limit to population growth by focussing instead on the political ecology of resource use. In particular they have affirmed poverty as the major cause of environmental deterioration, an argument which has lain at the heart of subsequent political-ecological research in all its forms (e.g. Hecht and Cockburn 1989; Redclift 1987; Stonich 1989; Peluso 1993). That these forms are varied is in many respects an advantage, for what is lost in theoretical integrity is made up for in developing specific areas of concern, such as an appreciation of regional ecological specificity (e.g. Bunker 1985), of different modalities of economic relations (e.g. Watts 1983), and of "development" itself as part of the land degradation problem (e.g. Collins 1987). Yet, as we approach 2000, political ecology also needs to build on these foundations to refine concepts – particularly regarding chains of causality in land degradation and the more careful theorization of production (Peet and Watts 1996: 7–8) – to look beyond the rural, to look at other environmental issues, and to draw out the political implications of its analyses if the Third World is to build socially and ecologically just "futurenatures" (Bryant and Bailey 1997).

CONSTRUCTION OF NATURE AND NATURE OF CONSTRUCTION

New directions

These debates on Marx and nature, agrarian political economy and political ecology are clearly not of a piece but do amount to a significant, if loosely structured, research programme on nature's production within capitalist and semi-capitalist societies. However, as capitalist nature has continued to change during the 1990s a number of important new avenues await much-needed exploration – involving both new sites of nature's production and new mechanisms of nature's production hitherto ignored or marginalized by Marxian work.

The first is ecology. With the possible exception of political ecology, work on the production of nature – even in its ecoMarxist incarnations – has offered only relatively weak understandings of the nature and materiality of transformed environments. However, two related areas of scholarship now offer the prospect of a more thoroughgoing appreciation of nature's materiality, without reverting to modernist dualisms. One is "environmental history," a now flourishing subdiscipline prioritizing nature's agency in history (Worster 1988), the other the "new ecological science" (Zimmerer 1994) which has overturned outdated notions of ecosystem stability to focus on chaos, disequilibrium and instability (Botkin 1990).

Second, with the realization that capitalist economies are "embedded" (Granovetter 1994) has come the insight that political-economy and ecology of nature is as much a question of gender and ethnicity as it is of class (see the essays in Rocheleau *et al.* 1996). Agrarian political economy and Third World political ecology have already made significant contributions to mapping these three axes of social identity and power as they coalesce (Whatmore 1991; Carney 1996), a conjunction that demands a "messy Marxism" where "production" and "labour" are both gendered and ethnicized.

Third, there is the question of discourse and representation. Theoreticians like Smith, by focussing on representation as negative (the "ideology of nature") have underplayed the proactive nature of representation, for the production of nature is both material and discursive (Castree 1997). As Gramsci (1971) argued a long time ago, struggles over meaning are every bit as "material" and important as practical struggles. Some of the newer work in political ecology has begun to demonstrate this very well (e.g. Moore 1996), but as "environmental discourse" proliferates, new efforts must be made to map discursive constructions and their power geometries (see e.g. Buttel and Taylor 1994). In addition, efforts must also be made to understand the specific mechanisms of this construction and, as we show in the next section, post-structuralism offers valuable theoretical resources here.

Fourth, despite its concern with political economy, Marxian work on nature's production has, ironically, said relatively little about the question of "politics." Politics does not just reside either in class action or state action, but has to be redefined in light of the "nature politics" of the *fin de siècle*. As recent work on political ecology shows well, the classical Marxian notions of socialist struggle are complicated by new political forms like NSMs, NGOs, local coalitions and special interest groups within civil society (Laclau and Mouffe 1985), and by quotidian "hidden" political activites like those "weapons of the weak" charted by Scott (1985) and others.

Finally, the literatures reviewed above tend to focus on human–environment relations. But, important as this focus is, it risks overlooking two of the most distinctive and dramatic arenas in which late capitalist nature is produced: "big science" and hi-technology and the media. Both have distinctive political economies and both, as we noted earlier, are increasingly important aspects of the social production of nature, semiotically and materially. Yet the modalities of these hi-tech natures, along with their consequences for specific ecologies and bodies, have not yet received the sustained attention they deserve from Marxist theorists. Perhaps the site where the need for such inquiry is most pressing is one that, on the face of it, seems too "natural" to be artifactual: the body. Yet today, from biomedicine, to fashion, to media "bodyscapes," the body is, of course, firmly situated within the complex technical, discursive and productive landscapes of late capitalism. Harvey (1998) has suggested one direction that such inquiry might take. For him the body must now be seen as an "accumulation strategy": the site, that is, of an astonishing array of commodification practices which connect specific bodies to wider relations of capitalism. As an "unfinished" project, the body is seen here as remade in historically and geographically specific modalities. And these are modalities every bit as semiotic as they are material: for changing images of the body are inextricably entwined with interventions in the body in corporeal accumulation regimes.

The possibilities here are legion. The former topic has, for example, been explored by Emily Martin (1987, 1994, this volume) who has mapped changing perceptions of the body in medical discourse and popular culture, from bodies "suited for and conceived in terms of the era of Fordist mass production to bodies suited for and conceived in the terms of the era of flexible accumulation" (1992: 121). The latter topic has been addressed in recent work on reproductive processes by Adele Clarke (1995). She distinguishes "modern" (or Fordist) means of regulating and capitalizing bodies and bodily practices which focussed on the "industrialization" of reproductive processes (as well as the mass produc- tion and consumption of contraceptives, commercial menstrual products and so on), from "postmodern" (or post-Fordist) means that are characterized by individualization and deep intervention along the lines of fetal surveillance, surgical interventions in utero, genetic testing, and so on, signaling a shift from Fordist mass production and distribution to "niche" body markets. In each the body becomes an accumulation regime, but the differences are important. In one, the regulation of the body and bodily practices becomes commodified; in the other, the body itself is capitalized and remade.

14

CONSTRUCTION OF NATURE AND NATURE OF CONSTRUCTION

ENFRAMING NATURE: CULTURAL INTELLIGIBILITY AND ECONOMIC AND POLITICAL CALCULATION

> It is necessary to reiterate the connections between the making and evolution of nature and the making and evolution of the discourses and practices through which nature is historically produced and known.
>
> (Escobar 1996: 46)

If today, then, the human body is an "accumulation strategy" it has become so not only because of important shifts at the level of production and consumption, but also in part because the body is now being made culturally intelligible – and thus available to forms of economic and political calculation – in new and often befuddling ways. Whether it be ultrasound imaging or mapping the human genome, new reproductive technologies or cybernetic systems which reconfigure the body as "information," the body is increasingly a "material-semiotic" object known in such ways that it can be changed (Haraway 1991, 1997; Rabinow 1992; Clarke 1995).

Perhaps more than at any other site, the artifactual body demonstrates the intertwined relations between capital, discourse and technology in the reinvention of nature at the beginning of the twenty-first century. This represents a significant challenge to understanding nature's social production and, accordingly, over the past fifteen years other critical approaches have emerged that owe less to Marx and political economy, and more to post-structuralism and to the sociology of scientific knowledge (SSK) and science studies. While they overlap, we choose to treat them as separate strands that provide their own unique insights into nature at the millenium.

Historicizing appearances: nature and representation in late modernity

> Nature is itself an entity which shows up within the world and which can be discovered in various ways and at various stages.
>
> (Heidegger 1962: 92)

The relatively slight attention paid to the constitutive role of discursive practices in Marxian theories of nature's social production should come as little surprise. Marxist theory – dialectics notwithstanding – has for the most part relied upon realist epistemologies where "nature" and "culture," and "scientific knowledge" and "politics," are kept separate or "regionalized" (Latour 1993; Castree 1995). Nature is assumed to be something that is unproblematically "ready-at-hand" to human actors; while its social transformation may be seen as historical, its "materiality" is not. Equally as important, Marx grounded human interaction with "nature" in biology. As Marx explained, humanity's relation with nature

15

NOEL CASTREE AND BRUCE BRAUN

was, in the first instance, practical rather than theoretical; it was related to, and determined by, quasi-transcendental "needs" rather than constituted and mediated through language:

> Men do not in any way begin by "finding themselves in a theoretical relationship to the things of the external world." Like every animal, they begin by eating, drinking, etc. That is, not by "finding themselves" in a relationship but by behaving actively, gaining possession of certain things in the external world by their actions, thus satisfying their needs. (They thus begin by production.)
>
> (Marx 1975: 190)

At one level the argument appears self-evident. The body has certain conditions for survival; we know that people risk death without sufficient food, a supply of oxygen, or protection from exposure. Thus, nature is continuously appropriated – and remade – as part of the "species existence" of humans. But this tells us little about how "needs" become defined, or, for that matter, what objects are taken up to meet "needs," or even how this is organized socially. As Baudrillard (1975) has shown, such questions are not so easily resolved, since both "needs" and the "use value" of things (or nature) are in part constituted culturally. For Baudrillard, it is not only capitalist modernity – with its logic of exchange value – that infuses a level of culture (or ideology) into what was previously an unmediated biological relation with nature.[2] Our relation with things is always already a sign relation; discursive relations and representational practices are constitutive of the very ways that nature is made available to forms of economic and political calculation and the ways in which our interventions in nature are socially organized.

The insights of post-structuralism have in recent years allowed us better to attend to these discursive mediations. They occur at a variety of levels, some more apparent than others. Arturo Escobar (1996), for instance, has shown how forms of capitalist development are always inflected in and through discursive formations, evident today in such discourses as "sustainable development" and "biological conservation" which authorize new processes of capitalizing nature. Far from being merely ideology, these discourses contribute to the very "production of production conditions." In other words, they mediate and organize human interventions in nature, including along which lines capital flows. This has important consequences, not only for which ecologies are transformed and how, but also, as Escobar intimates in his discussion of biodiversity conservation in Columbia, for whose relations to nature become foregrounded or displaced.

Interventions like Escobar's have challenged political ecologists to attend to how discursive relations – and not just market relations – organize social and ecological change and represent promising avenues of inquiry that bridge political economy and post-structuralism. Yet, we wish to extend Escobar's point

16

CONSTRUCTION OF NATURE AND NATURE OF CONSTRUCTION

further. The social production of nature is not just "mediated" by moral and political discourses like "sustainability"; rather, discursive relations infuse our relation with nature at every turn, including even at the micro level of knowledge and practice. This is different from saying that discourse is all there is, or that the world has no objective existence (cf. Haraway 1997; Demeritt, this volume). Rather, it is to insist that what counts as "nature," and our experience of nature (including our bodies), is always historical, related to a configuration of historically specific social and representational practices which form the nuts and bolts of our interactions with, and investments in, the world. Discourses like "sustainability" are important to the extent that they organize our attitudes towards, and actions on, nature. But, as a number of writers now insist, nature's materialization – its very visibility and availability – also requires careful attention, and is equally as important for how nature is known and remade with particular social and ecological consequences.

For many this "deep discursivity" is a challenging insight and it therefore merits further attention. Arguments which stress the constitutive role of discursive practices in the social production of nature can be traced to a crucial distinction between language as "instrumental" and as "expressive constitutive" (Taylor 1992; see also White 1991). The former – taking its initial form with Descartes – understands language as arising subsequent to, and as a means of organizing, our experience of an external reality. By this view, language serves to coordinate our actions in a world whose framework precedes or is independent of language, but to which language can be made to correspond. The latter – traced through Herder, Nietzsche, and Heidegger – understands language as disclosing a world of objects and involvements, thereby constructing a discursive field shared by both subjects and objects. Here, language is seen as the level at which social identities, and forms of subjectivity and intentionality are constituted. So, while in the former view language comes to reflect a pre-given reality; in the latter, language renders visible a "world" into which humans are "thrown."

Martin Heidegger is perhaps most closely associated with the view that in modernity we have forgotten the second – "enframing" – function of language,[3] and he is also largely responsible for drawing attention to the consequences of modern or subject-centered representational epistemologies. By placing a transcendental human consciousness at the centre, as does the instrumental view, human temporality becomes erased. In short – Heidegger warned (1962) – human knowing becomes dehistoricized, and the "order" of the world is seen as something "discovered" rather than something that itself requires explanation. This carries with it significant costs; indeed, Heidegger (1977) considered the lack of attention paid to the temporality of "being" (or the throwness of the subject) to be one of the most dangerous features of modernity, since it allowed moderns to mistake their "ordering" of the world with the world itself, and therefore rendered them unable to think the limits of representation – its closures and absences.[4] This is not merely an arcane philosophical debate but one with important moral and political dimensions. By stressing the temporal dimensions

NOEL CASTREE AND BRUCE BRAUN

of enframing, Heidegger showed knowledge about the world to be situated in specific historical contexts, and perhaps more important, to be always partial. In Heidegger's words, representation involved both "unconcealment" (bringing things into presence) and "concealment" (excluding other possible appearances). Or, as Foucault would later show, what was "visible" at any specific conjuncture was related to the production of ":spaces of visibility," which necessarily also involved producing "spaces of *in*visibility" (see Foucault 1977; Deleuze 1988; Rajchmann 1988).[5]

In short, nature – like all objects – is an entity which "shows up" within the world, but only in certain ways and not others. Forgetting this, Heidegger argued, gave to modern representation the character of *gestell* – a "stamping" – whereby representation took on a normalizing function, fixing identities as immutable, something captured especially well in Gayatri Spivak's (1985) notion of "epistemic violence." For this reason Heidegger (like Nietzsche and later Foucault, Derrida and Spivak, among others) sought to disrupt the familiar story of the Enlightenment. Far from a progressive movement from tradition and metaphysics into the "clear light" of Reason (unencumbered by history) Heidegger characterized modernity as carrying with it its own unexamined theology (cf. Mitchell 1988) which obscured the ways in which things were given to subjects and the relations of power that necessarily infused all identities.

Several consequences follow from historicizing nature's appearances. First, it allows us to recognize the irreducible presence of the discursive at all levels of human relations with nature – nature is constructed "all the way down." This does not mean that only through language and ideas do things have objective existence, only that, in Derrida's later – and oft-misunderstood – formulation, there is no "outside" a general textuality, no "getting beyond" the epistemo-logical clearings in which we stand from which to obtain certain knowledge. Here we find a crucial difference between Marx and Heidegger that remains a point of contention in debates over nature's social production. Whereas Marx argued that humans did not first encounter the external world through a "theoretical relationship" but a "practical" one, Heidegger suggested otherwise:

> That which is does not come into being at all through the fact that man first looks upon it, in the sense of a representing that has the character of subjective perception. Rather, man is the one who is looked upon by that which is; he is the one who is – in company with itself – gathered together toward presencing, by that which opens itself.
>
> (Heidegger 1977: 131)

Humans may have a practical interest in nature, but, following Heidegger, our interventions presuppose nature's intelligiblity within specific discursive regimes and orders of knowledge.

Second, just as there is no "getting beyond" discourse, so also, discursive

CONSTRUCTION OF NATURE AND NATURE OF CONSTRUCTION

relations are everywhere intricately involved in the material transformation of nature. Indeed, it is precisely because nature exists as *trópos* (Haraway 1992), that it can be remade as commodity, just as the tropes of Orientalism underwrote European imperialism and channeled its development along various lines. The social production of nature occurs within wider discursive fields in and through which "things" are rendered visible and available to forms of calculation. In other words – to follow Haraway's (1997) reworking of Ian Hacking's (1983) phrase – representation is intervening.

Third, post-structuralist accounts of nature's construction place attention firmly on the operation of power and widen what is taken to be the domain of politics. Power – as Foucault (1977) so brilliantly showed – is not only, or even primarily, something "held," as in models of sovereign power. Rather, power is diffuse – it operates unannounced in myriad social practices, including those we take as "merely" discursive. Indeed, it is precisely because we mistake our ordering of appearances for the world itself, unaware of how our knowledges reflect their social context, that power relations become naturalized in our representations of nature. The significance of representational practices there-fore lies not only in that they disclose a "world," but that representation is a worldly practice. Representational practices are material at the same time as they materialize; they are deeply embedded in social – and ecological – relations at the same time as they render "society" and "nature" intelligible. Thus, when Heidegger defines "thinking" as attending to the clearing in which things come into presence, he gestures towards an analytical space that is also a space of politics – although not a politics recognizable by familiar road signs. In this light, Donna Haraway's (1992) contentious claim that "nature" cannot pre-exist its construction is not an idealist position that denies the reality of a physical world, but rather an epistemological intervention that is deeply infused with political intent. For feminists like Haraway and Judith Butler – in dialogue with anti-racist and queer activism – politics involves disrupting the "self-evidence" of identities like "nature" and the "body." In Butler's words, "to call a presupposition into question . . . is to free it from its metaphysical lodging in order to understand what political interests were secured in and by [its] metaphysical placing, and thereby to permit the term to occupy and to serve very different political aims" (1993: 30).

Finally, prefiguring what has become a common theme in post-structuralist writing, Heidegger's anti-foundationalism provides an alternative to those modern subject-centered epistemologies in which the truthfulness and certainty of knowledge claims involved setting aside presuppositions (getting clear of our historical "situatedness"). Knowledge – including our knowledge of nature – is always social and historical and this has implications for the claims we make about nature. Indeed, configurations of specific social, institutional and technological practices are precisely what enable us to build our accounts of the world. As Haraway (1991) has persuasively argued, responsibility thus lies in taking seriously these enabling conditions, attending to how the ways in which our

NOEL CASTREE AND BRUCE BRAUN

constructions of nature occur within, and are suffused with, relations of class, gender, race and sexuality.

Effects of power and the domain of politics: constructing and contesting nature's materialization

Queering what counts as nature is my categorical imperative.
(Haraway 1994: 60)

Post-structuralist accounts of nature's construction are important, but they are not without their own problems. If we turn to a prominent example their strengths and weaknesses can be made apparent. Judith Butler's *Bodies that Matter* (1993) is arguably one of the most controversial post-structuralist accounts of how "nature" – in this case the "body" – comes to "matter" (a word whose double meaning neatly captures Butler's constructivist approach). It is worth exploring at some length.

In the book, Butler elaborates a theory of the "performativity" of sexual identity, part of a wider debate within feminist and queer theory over how gendered and sexed identities are constituted and lived. Performativity here should not be confused with free choice, as if one simply decided on sexual identity as one decides on what clothes to wear in the morning. Rather, performativity refers to how sexual identities are constituted (or "stabilized") in and through regulatory apparatuses, what Butler calls "citationality" (ritualized repetition or the iteration of cultural norms). As we shall see, it is precisely in performativity (seen as incomplete or imperfect iteration) that Butler also locates the disruption of what qualifies as a "viable" body within heterosexual cultural formations. For our purposes, the value of Butler's account lies in the crucial questions she raises about the body and its materiality or, more precisely, how the body is "materialized" along culturally and historically specific lines.

Like many other feminist scholars, Butler begins by placing in question the assumption that gender stands to sex, as culture does to nature or, in somewhat different terms, that gender is a discursive construct (culture) imposed upon pre-discursive sexual difference (biology). Rather, in what is by now the signal maneuver of post-structuralism, Butler places in question the self-evidence of the body-as-received and explores instead the conditions of possibility for speaking about and experiencing the sexed body, resulting in an account that turns on how a domain of "intelligible bodies" is constructed as well as "unthinkable, abject, unliveable bodies" which are excluded from, but haunt the former (see also Grosz 1994). It is important to highlight the political stakes involved. As Cheah (1996: 110) explains, writing the body as "constructed" disrupts post-Cartesian mechanistic accounts which understand the body as an immutable "natural entity," governed by natural laws of causality, or, in other cases, disrupts teleological accounts where intelligibility and matter are united in a body which strives toward an internally prescribed final goal. Such accounts are harmful,

20

CONSTRUCTION OF NATURE AND NATURE OF CONSTRUCTION

especially for women. As Cheah notes, they reduce the body to a passive object rather than a locus of power and resistance. But equally as important, they mistake biological discourse for the world itself (Haraway 1992), which, in the midst of a deeply phallocentric and heterosexist culture, is to remain inattentive to the deeply problematic closures and relations of power enacted in the body's intelligibility.

For Butler, writing that the body – or sexual difference – is "indissociable from discursive demarcations" (p. 2) is not the same as claiming that discourse causes sexual difference, or that bodies are not material. Rather it is to claim that how this materiality is understood, and how it becomes part of the ways that bodies are regulated and experienced, pivots on the sedimentation of historically specific modalities of how the body is "framed":

> The category of "sex" is, from the start, normative; it is what Foucault has called a "regulatory ideal". In this sense, then, "sex" not only functions as a norm, but is part of a regulatory practice that produces the bodies it governs, that is, whose regulatory force is made clear as a kind of productive power, the power to produce – demarcate, circulate, differentiate – the bodies it controls. Thus, "sex" is a regula-tory ideal whose materialization is compelled, and this materialization takes place (or fails to take place) through certain highly regulated practices . . . In this sense, what constitutes the fixity of the body, its contours, its movements, will be fully material, but materiality will be rethought as the effect of power, as power's most productive effect . . . [Bodies emerge from] a process of materialization that stabilizes over time to produce the effect of boundary, fixity, and surface we call matter.
>
> (Butler 1993: 1–2, 9)

The "matter" of the body is never pre-given, but instead takes form in and through a variety of discursive practices that regulate normative understandings of the sexed body, and are forcibly reiterated through time. It is important to follow Butler's Foucaultian emphasis on the productivity of power in order to grasp the full significance of her argument. Butler is not simply locating the misrepresentation of the "real" body in ideology or its repression by forms of sovereign power. For Butler, power does not repress, it produces; and what it produces are particular effects of truth, forms of subjectivity, and modes of materializing and experiencing bodies. In short, the very possibility of the "lived" body – or of any "lived" body – rests in the iteration of certain ways in which the intelligibility of the body has been circumscribed and "given to" subjects, simply on account that without these "we would not be able to think, to live, to make sense at all" (Butler 1993: xi). In a sense, the sexed body is one of those things that we cannot do without.

21

NOEL CASTREE AND BRUCE BRAUN

For Butler, understanding the "body" as performative suggests the possibility of its resignification, a topic to which we will turn later. But for Butler's critics – and there are many – her argument is problematic because she appears to claim that the "body" is merely an effect rather than the cause of its representation. Butler insists that hers is not an idealist position. "Construction" in her account points not to the willful "inventing" of bodies, but to deeply sedimented regulatory modes of conferring materiality upon bodies, an approach that highlights relations of power and one that, according to Butler, retains an essential link between the body's "appearance" (or form) and its "matter." Butler's preferred description is thus not "construction," but "constitutive constraint":

> If certain constructions appear constitutive, that is, have the character of being that "without which" we could not think at all, we might suggest that bodies only appear, only endure, only live within the productive constraints of certain highly gendered regulatory schemas . . . The discourse of "construction" . . . is perhaps not quite adequate to the task at hand. It is not enough to argue that there is no prediscursive "sex" that acts as the stable point of reference on which, or in relation to which, the cultural construction of gender proceeds. To claim that sex is already gendered, already constructed, is not yet to explain in which way the "materiality" of sex is forcibly produced. What are the constraints by which bodies are materialized as "sexed," and how are we to understand the "matter" of sex, and of bodies more generally, as the repeated and violent circumscription of cultural intelligibility? Which bodies come to matter – and why?
>
> (Butler 1993: xi–xii)

Butler's approach has attractive analytical and political advantages. By recasting the body as an effect of power, her account highlights the ways that power, knowledge and social practice are intricately interwoven in how bodies come to "matter." Further, it retains, or at least appears to retain, the centrality of the physical body, even as it historicizes its appearances. "Matter" remains central to "materialization" to the extent that Butler's account takes the cultural intelligibility of the "sexed" body to be a delimiting and constraining that occurs in and through discourses of what counts as the body and sex. In other words, the "body" is produced by repeated and violent circumscription: by exclusion, erasure, foreclosure, or abjection. Butler argues that there is therefore always a material "outside" to the body's social intelligibility, an "outside" that defines negatively what counts as the body. If this sounds remarkably similar to Heidegger's account of "enframing" it is not only coincidental, for Butler operates with many of the same distinctions between presence/absence, visiblity/invisibility, unconcealment/concealment, light/shadow, that organize Heidegger's account of the intelligibility and availability of the "object."

22

CONSTRUCTION OF NATURE AND NATURE OF CONSTRUCTION

Butler continuously draws attention to foreclosure, to how the "natural" body is constituted by excluding other "natures," and the way that the ontologizing of what is rendered "present" simultaneously hides the relations of power that draw these limits. Indeed, it is precisely when the body is taken for granted – when it appears outside discourse and power (or history) – that relations of power are most "insidiously effective" (1993: 35). Disrupting this ontologizing move thus becomes central to any refiguring of the body.

Yet, accounts like Butler's also have serious limitations. At first glance, it appears to avoid a strict linguistic constructivism; after all, "bodies that matter" are still bodies; it is only how they matter that is an "effect" of closure (power) and thus the "constructed" body is not, as some critics charge, an imaginary construct unrelated to the physical world.[6] The "real" continues to exist, only it lies "beyond" the imaginary/symbolic nexus, never immediately accessible as a "thing-in-itself." But one might question whether such accounts provide as adequate – and politically useful – an approach to the physicality of bodies as writers like Butler contend. If the "matter" of bodies is something that is made culturally intelligible only through exclusion, for instance, how are we to imagine a more complete, less constrained, physicality except as an inaccessible "shadow" that lies "outside" discourse? How are alternate "materializations" enabled?

This remains one of the most trenchant problems haunting post-structuralist approaches. Butler responds to this problem in two ways. First, she explains that the "materialization" of the body occurs through a "forcible reiteration" of regulatory norms, but that this materialization is never complete since bodies "never quite comply with the norms by which their materialization is impelled" (1993: 2). But again this begs the question, if there is no "outside" to citationality how does this "never quite" compliance become manifest? Does this not require acknowledging, at least at some level, that matter precedes form? Butler answers by locating counter-hegemonic articulations in the gaps and fissures within discursive formations. In short, by invoking notions of multiplicity and unfixity, Butler claims that it is the "instabilities" within materializations of the body that "spawn rearticulations that call into question the hegemonic force of that very regulatory law" (p. 2).[7] Yet, this too can be seen simply to remain fully internal to the "cultural," a point Butler acknowledges without apology: "To posit by way of language a materiality outside of language is still to *posit* that materiality, and the materiality so posited will retain that positing as its constitutive condition" (p. 30).

It is this "internalist" account that Cheah (1996) suggests results in a formulation that is essentially neo-Kantian, where cultural intelligibility occurs on a plane distinct from things. Drawing on Foucault, for instance, Butler writes that "ontological weight is not presumed but always conferred" (1993: 34), a statement that accords dynamism only to form and not matter. This differs from Kantian form/matter distinctions, Cheah suggests, only in that form is now seen as an instrument of power.[8] Indeed, Butler equivocates on this point. She writes, for instance, that "discursive possibilities opened up by the *constitutive outside of*

NOEL CASTREE AND BRUCE BRAUN

hegemonic positions . . . constitute the disruptive return of the excluded [nature] within . . . the symbolic" (p. 12, emphasis added) and states that her purpose is "to understand how what has been foreclosed or banished from the proper domain of "sex" [nature] . . . might at once be *produced as a troubling return*, not only as an imaginary contestation that effects a failure in the workings of the inevitable law, but as an enabling disruption, the occasion for a radical rearticulation of the symbolic horizon in which bodies come to matter at all" (p. 23, emphasis added). And yet, in the final analysis, in Butler's account the "constitutive outside" disrupts only through the instabilities of reiteration (only through more culture).[9]

Like other post-structuralist writers, Butler draws attention to the relations of power involved in the appearance of order. There can be no "nature" apart from its presencing. The implications for a "cultural politics" of nature should be readily apparent. "This unsettling of 'matter'," Butler writes (1993: 30) "can be understood as initiating new possibilities, new ways for bodies to matter." Yet, with post-structuralist accounts arise other difficult questions. As seductive as Butler's call for rearticulating the body may be, it is difficult to understand how she imagines this project proceeding. Caught between a political desire to open the body to counter-hegemonic materializations and a theoretical account that refuses to privilege a prediscursive realm (thereby figuring the materialized body as something defined only negatively through exclusion), Butler's account falters precisely at the moment of trying to imagine a site from which the body can be made to matter differently.[10] What is lacking, as Cheah suggests, is a recognition of a causal and dynamic relation between intelligibility and materiality.[11]

The limitations of post-structuralist accounts of "nature's" social construction notwithstanding, such approaches have placed considerable attention on the relation between discourse and materiality. Writing nature's "positivity" as something achieved through modes of delimiting and normalization rather than something found in journeys of discovery, has become increasingly central to critical studies of "nature," evident in the work of Haraway (1989, 1991, 1997), Martin (1994), Ross (1994), Cronon (1995) and Keller (1995) among others. This has occurred across numerous sites. A number of writers have shown the ways in which "forests" – especially "tropical rain forests" – are imbued with cultural meanings: as sites of fantasy and terror; as seen through edenic narratives of origins and purity; as layered with the rhetorics of nationalism; or even as understood through contesting paradigms in ecosystem ecology (see Botkin 1990; Harrison 1992; Schama 1995; Slater 1995; Willems-Braun 1997). Each is a way of valuing; none leave the forest untouched, and often these narratives contain social as well as ecological consequences (see, for instance, Hecht and Cockburn 1989). Cronon's (1995) eloquent critique of one of North American's most deeply held and emotional investments – the idea of "wilderness" – provides a striking example of the analytical and political stakes involved in disrupting the "self-evidence" of nature. Cronon shows "wilderness" – an identity iterated often in American culture – to be both the projection and inscription onto nature of

CONSTRUCTION OF NATURE AND NATURE OF CONSTRUCTION

forms of Romanticism together with frontier ideology, with the result that today "nature" – especially in the western half of the continent – is being remade in the image of these narratives. As Cronon also shows, this fascination with "wilderness" is not without consequences elsewhere, and these are both social and ecological in character. With such attention paid to "defending" the "last vestiges" of wilderness, already modified landscapes – and especially urban natures – receive far less attention, even though these now comprise the vast majority of the earth's lands, and are most closely related to issues of human health. Indeed, this quickly draws in questions of class and race, a point made by members of the far less exotic "environmental justice" movement (Alston 1990; Bullard 1990; Di Chiro 1995) who refuse to separate "nature" and "culture," but seek to build survivable futures characterized by environmental and social equity.

Finally – and perhaps most prolifically – feminist scholarship has drawn attention to the many ways that patriarchal culture is inscribed on the female body. Nellie Oudshoorn (1994), for example, has discussed the cultural assumptions that have underwritten the "medicalization" of women's bodies, and charted some of the consequences. The ways in which women's bodies – rather than men's – were mapped in medical and scientific discourse as "hormonal" bodies allowed for subsequent forms of social and sexual regulation (through contraceptive technologies), and also made the female body an "accumulation strategy" (through marketing products regulating the "hormonal" body). Likewise, Martin (1987) has shown the implicit (and often explicit) gendering of reproductive narratives in biology (see also Hartouni 1994). More recently, Martin has mapped parallels between economic and medical discourses on "flexible" bodies (Martin 1994), and has suggested (Martin, this volume) that different ways of "framing" the body (as machine, or as flexible) may authorize different normalizations and regulations of the body. Indeed, in these interventions Oudshoorn's phrase "beyond the natural body" takes on two distinct but related meanings: the body that we equate with nature is already deeply cultural (it is given form and meaning through particular discursive practices); and, the body is increasingly artifactual (it is remade materially in new and unique ways through an array of social practices that seize upon, and are enabled by, the body's cultural intelligibility).

Post-structuralist arguments about the "construction" of nature have drawn much-needed attention to the "cultural politics" of nature. They have also elicited angry charges that "reality" is taken to be merely a matter of desire, opinion, speculation or fantasy (see Gross and Levitt 1994). Yet, with Haraway, we argue that stressing the contingency of what counts as "reality" is not a denial of nature's materiality, but rather, a recognition that nature "is collectively, materially, and semiotically constructed – that is, put together, made to cohere, worked up for and by us in some ways and not others" (Haraway 1997: 301 n.12). On how this occurs, Haraway suggests, much turns – even the earth itself.

NOEL CASTREE AND BRUCE BRAUN

NETWORKS, ACTANTS AND TECHNOSCIENCE: BUILDING HYBRIDS

Post-structuralist accounts of nature's construction provide provocative arguments for the centrality of discursive practices for both nature's intelligibility and its availability to forms of instrumental power. Yet – as evident in the work of Butler – such accounts risk privileging active form over passive matter. A potential path beyond post-structuralism's "Leibnizian conceit" (Harvey 1996) may be found in the field of the sociology of scientific knowledge (SSK), or simply, "science studies." Already this is a vast terrain that draws on a variety of theoretical and philosophical traditions. Most practitioners share with post-structuralism the notion of nature's "constructedness," but they cast their net far wider than post-structuralism's narrow focus on discourse, or the "rules" that govern which statements can be made about things at any given moment. Instead, attention is paid to the intersection and simultaneity of multiple material and discursive practices: from the social, economic and institutional relations organizing scientific inquiry to the inscription devices and visual technologies that increasingly generate new possibilities for envisioning and intervening in the world; from the metaphors and narratives that help determine what are interesting questions to the "objects" of inquiry themselves, which – as Callon (1986) and Haraway (1992) argue – do not hold still, but provide surprises of their own. Thus, as Haraway notes, what counts as "nature" always has multiple dimensions – mythic, textual, technical, political, organic, and economic – which "collapse into each other in a knot of extraordinary density" (Haraway 1994: 63).

Such knots are difficult to disentangle. Yet, it is precisely exploring these threads and interconnections that makes SSK such a rich resource. As is evident in many of the chapters in this volume, SSK has begun to reshape how we talk about the social constitution of nature. There are many advantages to SSK approaches, but here we want to highlight four. First, with its emphasis on knowledge production as "worldly," SSK scholars trace nature's "emergence" in specific, historical practices (fieldwork, the laboratory, writing), not in order to dismiss or minimize science, but in order show how these world-changing knowledges are made in social and institutional contexts saturated with relations of power. Second, although the practice of science is fully social (and deeply technical), it still revolves around interactions with a physical world, and thus the knowledges produced cannot be reduced fully to the social. While science studies shares with post-structuralism a concern over how nature is rendered intelligible in certain ways and not others, it has the potential to provide more subtle and complex empirical accounts of how specific knowledges come to be held without compromising the sense that the materiality of nature is itself central to our knowledge of it (Callon 1986; see also Hayles 1991). Third, many SSK scholars attend not only to the myriad ways in which technoscience renders nature intelligible, but also to how our world – and nature – is increasingly an artifact of technoscience. Nature is today becoming a hybrid of machines and organisms,

CONSTRUCTION OF NATURE AND NATURE OF CONSTRUCTION

a hybridity entailing new social and political relations. Indeed, to rephrase Baudrillard (1983), today science precedes reality; things appear in technoscientific networks – as models or as information – before they appear as objects in the world. Although it is important not to conflate epistemology and ontology (the notion that our ideas generate the world), in technoscientific networks epistemology and ontology increasingly implode – the world "outside" the laboratory comes to mirror the world "inside" (Latour 1988). Finally, science studies scholars like Bruno Latour have also placed in question the autonomy of the "social," which is progressively stitched together through things (including not only technical objects, but also our productions of nature). This has received less attention. Where earlier sociologists talked about social relations as those between people (or classes), Latour speaks of collectivities that encompass people, things and machines. It follows, then, that politics is not solely something that occurs between people, but that the "quasi-objects" produced in modernity carry with them their own political rationality (see also Mumford 1964; Winner 1986) and thus that both analysis and politics must take seriously the complex mediations and networks that weave natural and social worlds into a "seamless fabric" (Latour 1993). In what follows we explore some of these themes in greater detail.

The social construction of scientific knowledge

Science is shadowed, at a constant distance, by its own anthropology.
(Serres 1987: 41, quoted in Latour 1990: 145)

If any one position characterizes science studies, it is that scientific knowledges are made in historically specific, socially situated practices, rather than "found." According to this view, science can therefore be studied using the tools of anthropology, sociology and so on. Indeed, one of Bruno Latour's most important interventions has been to show the relevance of ethnographic studies of "science in action," in a sense bringing anthropology home from the tropics. As Latour (1993) explains, in the past anthropology and Western science shared a central assumption: that a "great divide" separated "modern" from "primitive" cultures, and that this divide was essentially that between "reason" and "myth." Systems of belief about the external world found in "pre-modern" cultures ("ethnoscience") could be explained by reference to culture, religion or politics. Our beliefs ("Science"), on the other hand, were assumed to exist independent from culture, religion or politics, and thus could be explained by reference to Nature alone.

In a consequential early study of neuroendocrinologists at the Salk Institute in California, Latour and Woolgar (1979) showed that the air-conditioned, sterile laboratories of modern science were equally susceptible to anthropological inquiry, since necessarily they embodied social, technical, economic and institutional relations. There are now numerous ethnographies of science (for surveys

NOEL CASTREE AND BRUCE BRAUN

see Rouse 1992; Haraway 1994) as well as historical accounts of the social construction of scientific knowledges (e.g. Shapin and Schaffer, 1985; Haraway 1989) in which historians and social scientists have sought to produce finely textured accounts of the generation of "truths" about nature. Traweek's *Beamtimes and Lifetimes* (1988) provides one example: In a study of high energy physics laboratories in the USA and Japan, she showed that cultural and political considerations made a great difference in what knowledges were produced, in part because the detectors used by scientists took different forms depending on the funding and research contexts in each country. Likewise, Haraway (1991) has shown – as has Treichler (1987) – the various ways in which culture has infused HIV – research. In each instance, attention has been paid to the practices through which certain knowledges, rather than others, attain the status of "facts," following the principle set forward by members of the "Edinburgh School" who made symmetry in explanation a central principle in science studies. According to this principle, both "valid" and "false" knowledges must be explained in the same terms: one cannot be explained through reference to nature and the other through reference to culture (or ideology). Rather, both must be seen as a result of historically specific social and scientific practices.

Essentially, science studies remains agnostic on the question of "truth," although as Haraway (1997: 137, 301 n.12) explains, this should not be confused with a relativism that views all knowledges as somehow "equal." Reality, Haraway argues, is not a "subjective" construction, but rather a "congealing of ways of interacting" and these require a dense array of bodies, artifacts, minds, collectives, etc. Thus, "reality is eminently material and solid, but the effects sedimented out of technologies of observation/representation are radically contingent in the sense that other semiotic-material-technical processes of observation would (and do) produce quite different lived worlds" (302 n.12). Far from devaluing scientific inquiry, Haraway and other SSK scholars seek to rework the stories we tell about science – often for explicitly political reasons. By holding to a philosophy of science that maintains that science occurs in a sphere hermetically sealed from the "polluting" influence of society, we fail to see how science necessarily and always builds its knowledges through social means. The issue is to see how this matters.

Part of the project of science studies thus involves reworking our under-standings of "objectivity." Objectivity figured as disembodiment, Haraway (1991) argues, is an escape from the materiality of knowledge–production (as if our observations could somehow be independent of the observer!), and thus erases history from representation (precisely the move Heidegger describes as our forgetfulness of Being). In contrast, "strong objectivity" – borrowing from Harding (1986) – has everything to do with taking responsibility for the ways that our knowledge–production practices are "situated" in particular historical moments and social–spatial contexts, acknowledging rather than abdicating our responsibility for the ways that knowledge reflects its enabling conditions.

28

CONSTRUCTION OF NATURE AND NATURE OF CONSTRUCTION

Nature, science and the construction of "society"

Issues surrounding the social construction of scientific knowledges are of significance not only in terms of epistemology. They relate also to how nature and society are today reconfigured. This can be shown in two ways. First, if as Rabinow (1992: 236) suggests, "representing and intervening, knowledge and power, understanding and reform, are built in, from the start, as simultaneous goals and means," then how future natures are produced will respond in part to what Bachelard referred to as the "temporality" of science (which, he claimed was not reducible – but also not unrelated – to the temporal rhythms of other "levels" of social life). Indeed, the "world-changing" character of technoscience is progressively evident as we face the twenty-first century (although, contra Bachelard, the relays between science, economy, culture and state are arguably more intense and more frequent since World War II: see Heims 1980; Haraway 1982). Second, how technoscience makes possible our interventions in nature increasingly has social implications. This is plainly evident in such fields as genetics, but the point can be applied more broadly. As Latour (1993) notes, while sociologists of scientific knowledge (SSK) scholars have insisted on symmetry in explanation for "truth" and "falsity," they have remained largely asymmetrical at another level. In their accounts science is shown to be explained by reference to society, but society itself remains "solid," impervious to all but "internal" explanation. Yet, it is abundantly clear that technoscience and its artifacts are central to remaking society and nature simultaneously. Indeed, arguments surrounding the embeddedness of science and technology would matter little if it were not also that society is built, in part, through science and technology. But it is precisely the ways in which society is constructed through, or in relation to, things (microbes, door closers, machines, and so on) along with the various ways that science is the cause rather than medium of nature's representation that, as moderns, we are unable to see, since we live within a modern "constitution" that assigns "nature" and "culture" to two distinct realms, and similarly situates "knowledge" in one (nature) and "politics" in another (culture). This modern constitution, Latour argues, allows technoscience to build both nature and society simultaneously, but in ways that remain relatively unexamined.

For this argument Latour relies extensively on Shapin and Schaffer's (1985) *Leviathan and the Air Pump*. In this important study, Shapin and Schaffer located the separation of science and politics in the seventeenth-century dispute between Hobbes and Boyle over where political and epistemological authority was located. As they show, Boyle sought to locate authority in nature which could be known through scientific observation. In his experiments with the air pump, Boyle constructed the "laboratory" as a separate, regulated arena (with its own rules for witnessing and deciding on matters of fact). What was problematic, as Shapin and Schaffer explain, was that this rendered invisible the social and political relations involved in producing representations of nature. Hobbes, on

NOEL CASTREE AND BRUCE BRAUN

the other hand, rejected Boyle's theatre of proof, which he thought simply led to the political fragmentation that occurred when people could petition entities other than civil authority – like "Nature" or "God." For Hobbes, there could exist only one Knowledge and one State, both residing in the Sovereign designated by consent through the social contract. As Latour explains, SSK scholars have shown the "political" erasures that occurred in Boyle's laboratories, but have failed to recognize that Hobbes also constructed his own hermetically sealed sphere: "society." By constructing society as consisting only of humans (with its own science of representation – politics), Hobbes erased the multiple mediations of facts, things and machines! As Latour summarizes:

> It is not that Boyle invents scientific discourse and Hobbes political discourse, it is that Boyle invents a political discourse where politics should not count and that Hobbes devises a scientific politics where experimental science should not count. In other words, they are inventing our modern world, a world in which the representation of things through the medium of the laboratory is forever severed from the representation of citizens through the medium of social contract . . . From now on every one should "see double" and make no direct connection between the representation of non-humans and the representation of humans, between the artificiality of the facts and the artificiality of the Body Politic.
>
> (Latour 1990: 155–6)

The first half of this formulation – that concerning Boyle – is now commonplace. The second, we wish to argue, has received less attention, but is in part what renders the first crucial. Society is not simply the association of "naked individuals" – as Hobbes implied; rather, social actions always mobilize things (like nature) which are "actants" in their own right.

Latour makes this argument explicitly in his *Pasteurization of France* (1988). In late nineteenth-century France, Latour explains, a world "with" microbes resulted in very different forms of governmentality and social regulation, and different orders of behaviour, than did a society "without" microbes. In a social context where discourses on hygiene had already become dominant, Pasteur's "discovery" of the microbe was not socially innocent, but reconfigured a wider network of forces:

> The Pasteurians provided neither the level nor the weight nor even the worker who did the work, but they provided the hygienist with a fulcrum. To use another metaphor, they were like the first observation balloons. They made the enemy visible.
>
> (Latour 1988: 34)

In short, after Pasteur, microbes became social actors in their own right. On the one hand they strengthened the social and rhetorical positions of the hygienists

30

CONSTRUCTION OF NATURE AND NATURE OF CONSTRUCTION

for whom microbes provided an ally, and they also elevated the position of Pasteur, who became a central figure in French society. But Latour's point goes beyond this: by seeing the health of populations through the lens of microbes, many other elements of social (and material) life became rearranged. As one commentator from the period noted, "Ignoring the danger of the microbe awaiting us, *we have hitherto arranged our way of life without taking any account of this unknown enemy*" (Leduc: 1892: 234, quoted in Latour 1988: 35, emphasis added). Representation begets intervention; microbes become actants, they reconfigure both a semiotic terrain (environments suddenly were framed within different economies of signification) and, ultimately, a physical terrain. Put baldly, in nineteenth-century France, nature and society were both remade in the "image" of microbal theories of disease.

Importantly, Latour shows not only how actants like microbes become entangled in social life, but that the very possibility of social life proceeds through and is enabled by such actants:

> There are not only "social" relations, relations between man and man . . . for everywhere microbes intervene and act . . . We cannot form society with the social alone. We have to add the action of microbes. We cannot understand anything about Pasteurism if we do not realize that it has reorganized society in a different way. It is not that there is a science done in the laboratory, on the one hand, and a society made up of groups, classes, interests, and laws, on the other. The issue is at once much more simple and much more difficult.
>
> (Latour 1988: 35)

Elsewhere, Latour has drawn out the consequences more explicitly, arguing that without the many objects that gave to "society" its durability as well as its solidity, what we have commonly taken to be the traditional domain of social theory – empire, classes, professions, organizations, States – become "so many mysteries" (Latour 1993: 120). In short, the solidity of "society," even the constitution of the "subject" cannot be thought apart from things, whether these be "nature" or "machines."

Amodernity and the analytics and politics of quasi-objects

One of the distinct advantages of Latour's "symmetrical" approach to science and society is that it highlights the analytical and political stakes involved in how boundaries are drawn between science and society, nature and culture. Blurring how these boundaries are drawn serves a wider project of showing the relations of power involved in how social natures are built at the close of the twentieth century. Until now, these relations have remained invisible as a result of our adherence to what Latour (1993) calls the three "guarantees" of modernity. As

31

NOEL CASTREE AND BRUCE BRAUN

we noted earlier, Boyle assumed that scientists were merely modest witnesses to Nature (cf. Haraway 1997), and this provides the first guarantee: "*it is not men who make Nature; Nature has always existed and has always already been there; we are only discovering its secrets*" (Latour 1993: 30). Hobbes assumed that citizens alone spoke with one voice through their representative (or sovereign). This provides the second: "*human beings, and only human beings, are the ones who construct society and freely determine their own destiny*" (Latour 1993: 30). These are underwritten by a third guarantee: the absolute separation of nature and society. Here Latour makes the analytical and political stakes clear:

> The overall structure is now easy to grasp: the . . . guarantees taken together will allow the moderns a change in scale. *They are going to be able to make Nature intervene at every point in the fabrication of their societies while they go right on attributing to Nature its radical transcendence; they are going to be able to become the only actors in their own political destiny, while they go right on making their society hold together by mobilizing Nature* . . . The essential point about this modern Constitution is that it renders the work of mediation that assembles hybrids invisible, unthinkable, unrepresentable . . . Everything happens in the middle, everything passes between the two, everything happens by way of mediation, translation and networks, but this space does not exist, it has no place. It is the unthinkable, the unconscious of the moderns.
>
> (Latour 1993: 32, 34, 37, emphasis added)

Latour argues that we need to be "amodern," or, in other words, we need to retie rather than endlessly attempt to untangle, the Gordian knot between nature and society so as to recognize this "middle kingdom" of quasi-objects. As Goodman and Fitzsimmons (this volume) show in their discussion of agro-food systems, this allows entirely new actors and relations to be brought into view and new political interventions imagined. Although until now Latour has been wary of programmatic statements about what a politics of mediation, translation and networks entails (although see Latour, this volume), his intervention in our self-understanding as "moderns" (as believing in the absolute separation of nature and culture, science and society), is rich with analytical and political possibilities, and many contributors to this volume take these up explicitly (see the chapters by Demeritt, Watts, and Goodman and Fitzsimmons).

According to Latour, Haraway and other SSK scholars, tracing networks is where political hope lies. Recognizing the complex intertwinings of nature, culture, science and technology allows us to see the various ways that it is impossible to change the social order without at the same time modifying the natural order, and vice versa. Haraway and Latour refer to these hybrid nature-cultures as "illegitimate couplings," "monsters" or "quasi-objects" – entities that until now have had no standing in modernity's accounts of itself, yet all the while

32

CONSTRUCTION OF NATURE AND NATURE OF CONSTRUCTION

have silently worked to organize social and ecological life. By rendering these mixtures "unthinkable," Latour (1993: 42) explains, the moderns allowed for their proliferation but were unable to trace their consequences. Being amodern thus requires re-skilling, fashioning new political lenses with the hope of "seeing" differently. For amoderns, no longer held in thrall by modern stories of the absolute separation of nature and society, monsters become "visible and thinkable" and explicitly pose serious dilemmas for the social order. This all makes for a politics with which we are unfamiliar: neither technophilic nor technophobic, interested neither in preserving Eden nor rendering everything as resource, but attentive simply to the social and ecological consequences that everywhere are intertwined in everyday practices. For SSK scholars, tracing the Ariadne threads that lead through the linked worlds of science, culture, nature and politics allows us to see where responsibility lies, what stories need to be told, and what differences these make.

CONCLUSION: TOWARD A POLITICAL
THEORY OF SOCIAL NATURE

The intertwinings of social and ecological projects in daily practices as well as in the realms of ideology, representations, esthetics, and the like are such as to make every social (including literary or artistic) project a project about nature, environment, and ecosystem, and vice versa.

(Harvey 1996: 189)

In the preceding pages we have outlined some analytical and political tools available for interrogating nature at the millenium. Yet, if nature at the dawn of the twenty-first century is resolutely social this does not mean that the modern dualism between "nature" and "society" no longer retains a hold on our imagination. Indeed, the opposite may be the case: today we hear regularly of the "death of nature" or the "end of nature," and now as often as ever before "nature" is seen as a refuge – a "pure" place to which one travels in order to escape from society. Along similar lines, deep green environmentalism shuttles between apocalyptics and melancholy, mourning the loss, or desperately seeking to preserve (or at least witness!), the last remnants of a "pristine" nature. And yet, as Neil Smith (1996: 41) has recently reiterated, this desire to "save nature" is deeply problematic, since it reaffirms the "externality" of a nature "with and within which human societies are inextricably intermeshed." There are, to be sure, reasons to limit or regulate human interventions in specific environments which can be justified on both ecological and social grounds. But to focus on preserving a nature that "excludes" humans is today a self-defeating strategy – it is, as Smith argues, to save something that is no longer recognizable, if it ever was, while at the same time shifting attention from some of the most pressing and interlinked social and ecological problems that face late capitalist and

NOEL CASTREE AND BRUCE BRAUN

technoscientific cultures. Indeed, by rendering nature as something "external" to be saved "from" humans, we erase its social and discursive constitution, with the result that the nature to be preserved simply reflects our own social values and anxieties – it becomes a "fun-house reflection of ourselves" (Haraway 1992: 296).

The crucial issue therefore, is not that of policing boundaries between "nature" and "culture" but rather, of taking responsibility for how our inevitable interventions in nature proceed – along what lines, with what consequences and to whose benefit. As Smith (1996: 49) explains, we need a "political theory of nature": one which expresses the inevitability and creativity of our relationships with nature; which recognizes the destructive dynamics embodied in capitalist modes of production; which accounts for how relationships with nature are differentiated according to gender, class, race, and sexual preference; which accepts the implausibility of a nature "autonomous" from culture; and which, finally, helps us unlearn the "instinctive romanticism" which pervades treatments of nature in bourgeois and patriarchal society.

Our intention in this volume is to begin the task of developing an analytics and politics directed toward constructing survivable futures at the dawn of the twenty-first century. Contributors to this volume care deeply about the natures that are being built today and tomorrow in the midst of social, cultural and technological changes of unprecedented scope. Indeed, precisely for this reason, many find hope in social and political theories that eschew a nature–society split and instead insist on seeing the two as continuously constituted through the other – nature made artifactual, just as society is made natural. The costs of retaining the dualism have become too high; as Latour explains, too much is left unseen. Indeed, to claim that nature is everywhere becoming artifactual is not, as some suggest, to argue against nature or for its "destruction," for social natures are no less ecological than so-called "natural" systems from which humans have, at least in theory, been excluded. Indeed, as Harvey (1996: 186) provocatively notes, New York City is an "ecosystem"; and, if we truly are concerned about the natures that we are building, we need to get out of the habit of excluding urban historical geographies from our environmental histories. In short, we need to open the social fabrication of nature to interrogation at every level.

This is neither a simple, nor a singular, task. Nature is multiple; its social production proceeds according to no single temporality, occurs with no one underlying logic, follows no unified plan. Accordingly, struggles over the social production of nature are multifaceted; they occur at various levels, involve a large cast of actors (not all of which are human), and follow a plurality of social and ecological logics that cannot be reduced to a single story. This calls forth analytical and political responses that are multiple and often discontinuous: tracing circuits of capital, contesting the social and ecological logics of particular production processes and articulating relations between class, race, gender and ecology. Or it may take the form of showing how "nature" is mediated or constituted discursively, locating the consequences of this in terms of gender,

34

CONSTRUCTION OF NATURE AND NATURE OF CONSTRUCTION

race, or sexuality, and where necessary disrupting the "self-evidence" of nature-as-received in order to open space for different constructions less implicated in relations of domination. And elsewhere it may require tracing networks, attending to the "quasi-objects" so long excluded from political discourse but through which society and nature are churned up daily, and taking seriously the simultaneity of social, technical, discursive, political and organic elements in any and all productions of nature. These themes surface in various forms, and often conjoined, throughout the volume, and in large measure they cross-cut the two-part organization of the book. Broadly, however, chapters have been grouped according to one of two themes. Those in Part 2 – Capitalizing and Enframing Nature – explore the social, discursive and ideological practices that inform and organize nature's remaking in the wider context of late capitalism. Those in Part 3 – Actors, Networks and the Politics of Hybridity – trace the various networks (social, institutional, technical as well as discursive) and the many actors/actants (humans, machines, nature, etc.) that are mixed together in specific social productions of nature, with an eye to their social, economic and ecological consequences. This schematic division is, of course, somewhat arbitrary. What all contributors share is a commitment to rethinking environmental politics along lines aligned with social justice and in ways appropriate for the social natures of the twenty-first century. Revolutionary environmentalism, after all, cannot be about reinstating "nature." That time has passed, if indeed it was ever here. Rather, it must be about a continuous vigilance to the sorts of natures we are producing – to how reality is being remade. For this, we need to fashion new – or refashion old – analytical and political tools, tools for making the future natures that we wish to inhabit.

NOTES

1 It is no coincidence that the first stirrings of Marxist interest in social nature came in the wake of the neo-Malthusian debates of the early 1970s. Focussed particularly on the Third World, the frequently outspoken statements by Commoner, Ehrlich, Hardin and Meadows *et al.* pointed to "natural limits" to population growth and blamed peasant ignorance for Third World famine, soil erosion and the like. That such blame-the-victim thinking – with its baggage of population policies and "positive checks" – was so much a part of everyday "common sense" in the early years of environmental concern in the capitalist world made David Harvey's (1974) provocative inversion of Malthusian thinking that much more significant. Arguing for a paradigm shift in our conception of human–environment relations, Harvey unravelled the absolutisms of "population problem" thinking to argue that "resources" are always socially defined and that "scarcity" is always socially produced. By thus drawing attention to the political economy of resource use, Harvey rephrased the scarcity-of-resources view to argue instead that "There are too many people in the world because the particular ends we have in mind . . . and the materials available in nature, that we have the will and the way to use, are not sufficient to provide us with those things to which we are accustomed" (Harvey 1974: 274).

2 Production-for-exchange in modern, industrial capitalism is clearly organized in a

NOEL CASTREE AND BRUCE BRAUN

historically specific way, involving complex relations of production and consumption, and responding to very different spatial and temporal rhythms. This results in very *different* productions of nature than other historical modes, but such productions of nature, while different in form, are not different in type (i.e. are not *more* mediated) than what Neil Smith (1984) offers as an abstraction called "production-in-general." The result is that the critique of the production of nature in advanced capitalism cannot take as its starting point a "natural" relation to the environment from which capitalist modes of production depart, but rather, can only proceed relationally, as a comparison of the different socio-economic and cultural logics organizing nature's production, and with what social and ecological effects.

3 It is important to keep in mind that while for Heidegger language was the "house of Being," this does not mean that he understood the "appearance" of things through a simple linguistic constructivism. Rather, as Joseph Rouse (1987) explains, nature "shows up" or "emerges" in and through a configuration of practices, including Science (see also Demeritt, this volume).

4 In modernity, Heidegger argued, the historical specificity of how things are "given" to human subjects recedes and becomes the "invisible shadow that is cast around all things everywhere. By means of this shadow the modern world extends itself out into a space withdrawn from representation, and so lends to the incalculable the determinateness peculiar to it, as well as a historical uniqueness ... In truth, however, the shadow is a manifest, though impenetrable, testimony to the concealed emitting of light. In keeping with this concept of shadow, we experience the incalculable as that which, withdrawn from representation, is nevertheless manifest in whatever is, pointing to Being, which remains concealed" (1977: 135, 154).

5 Rajchman (1988) described Foucault's writings as the "art of seeing." Foucault, Rajchman claims, was not interested simply in what things looked like, but "how things were *made* visible, how things were *given* to be seen, how things were '*shown*' to knowledge or power ... [how] things became *seeable*" (p. 91, original emphasis).

6 Butler (1993: 5) is herself highly critical of strong constructivist arguments:

> When the sex/gender distinction is joined with a notion of radical linguistic constructivism, the problem becomes even worse, for the "sex" which is referred to as prior to gender will itself be a postulation, a construction, offered within language, as that which is prior to language, prior to construction. But this sex posited as prior to construction will, by virtue of being posited, become the effect of that very positing, the construction of construction. If gender is the social construction of sex, and if there is no access to this "sex" except by means of its construction, then it appears not only that sex is absorbed by gender, but that "sex" becomes something like a fiction, perhaps a fantasy, retroactively installed at a prelinguistic site to which there is no direct access.

7 In many ways this is the politics of the "catachresis" – that which disrupts by not speaking the proper (hegemonic) name.

8 Moreover, as Grosz (1994: 21) notes, this assumes a certain immutability to culture: "Culture [discourse] itself can only have meaning and value in terms of its own other(s): when its others are obliterated – as tends to occur within the problematic of social constructivism – culture in effect takes on all the immutable, fixed characteristics attributed to the natural order."

9 Cheah (1996: 120) reveals some of the ontological contradictions involved:

> By defining "constitution" as repeated identification, Butler confines the term within an ideational scenario. Consequently, she hesitates before the question of what sustains the causal power of intelligible form over matter,

36

CONSTRUCTION OF NATURE AND NATURE OF CONSTRUCTION

the question of what allows intelligible form to materialize as matter in general. Yet, this question seems unavoidable. For if, "'to be constituted' means 'to be compelled to cite, to repeat or to mime' the signifier itself," it must be asked: what are the ontological conditions under which the compulsion to identify can take place? . . . Does not the concept of morphology as a mediating term between psyche and matter presuppose this question of the causal power of ideas over matter and vice versa but cannot ask it? . . . if *nomos* or *tekne* can become *physis*, then must there not be another non-anthropologistic level of causality and naturalist teleology, of which the performativity of language would only be a case?

Cheah draws the following implications from his argument: "This would imply that political change can no longer be understood as a function of sociohistorical form qua the sole principle of dynamism. Instead, the category of the political itself needs to be rethought outside of the terms of history and culture, which are its time-honored cognates" (1996: 120).

10 Indeed, Butler (1993: 206) in many ways is caught in the same "prepolitical pathos" that she feels marks so many psychoanalytic accounts of the "subject":

> As resistance to symbolization, the "real" functions in an exterior relation to language, as the inverse of mimetic representationalism, that is, as the site where all efforts to represent must founder. The problem here is that there is no way within this framework to politicize the relation between language and the real. What counts as the "real," in a sense of the unsymbolizable, is always relative to a linguistic domain that authorizes and produces that foreclosure, and achieves that effect through producing and policing a set of constitutive exclusions. Even if every discursive formation is produced through exclusion, that is not to claim that all exclusions are equivalent: what is needed is a way to assess politically how the production of cultural unintelligibility is mobilized variably to regulate the political field . . . To freeze the real as the impossible "outside" to discourse is to institute a permanently unsatisfiable desire for an ever elusive referent: the sublime object of ideology. The fixity and universality of this relation between language and the real produces, however, a prepolitical pathos that precludes the kind of analysis that would take the real/reality distinction as the instrument and effect of contingent relations of power.

11 Cheah suggests that Derrida presents a way out of this dilemma by undoing the founding oppositions between nature and it others. Thus, he quotes affirmatively Derrida's statement that: "Culture [is to be thought] as nature different and deferred, differing-deferring; all the others of *physis* – *techne, nomos, thesis*, society, freedom, history, mind, etc. as *physis* different and deferred, or as *physis* differing and deferring. *Physis* in *differance*" (Derrida 1982: 17). Yet, it is not clear where this situates dynamism. In other words, even if one refuses to situate culture "outside" *physis*, culture becomes that part of *physis* that is dynamic, to the exclusion of "other" non-cultural elements.

REFERENCES

Adorno, T. and Horkheimer, M. (1972) *The Dialectic of Enlightenment*, trans. J. Cumming, New York: Herder and Herder.

NOEL CASTREE AND BRUCE BRAUN

Alston, D. (ed.) (1990) *We Speak for Ourselves: Social Justice, Race and Environment*, Washington: Panos Institute.

Altvater, E. (1993) *The Future of the Market*, London: Verso.

Antipode (1994) "Special Issue on *Nature's Metropolis*," 26.

Arce, A. and Marsden, T. (1993) "The social construction of international food," *Economic Geography* 69: 293–311.

Baudrillard, J. (1975) *The Mirror of Production*, trans. M. Poster, St. Louis: Telos Press.

—— (1983) *Simulacra and Simulations*, trans. P. Foss, P. Patton and P. Beitchman, New York: Sémiotexte.

Benton, T. (1989) "Marxism and natural limits," *New Left Review* 178: 51–86.

Blaikie, P. (1985) *The Political-Economy of Soil Erosion*, London: Methuen.

Blaikie, P. and Brookfield, H. (1987) *Land Degradation and Society*, London: Methuen.

Botkin, D. (1990) *Discordant Harmonies*, New York: Oxford University Press.

Bryant, R. (1992) "Political ecology," *Political Geography* 11: 12–36.

Bryant, R. and Bailey, S. (1997) *Third World Political Ecology*, London: Routledge.

Bullard, R. (1990) *Dumping in Dixie: Race, Class, and Environmental Quality*, Boulder: Westview Press.

Bunker, S. (1985) *Underdeveloping the Amazon*, Chicago: University of Illinois Press.

Butler, J. (1993) *Bodies that Matter: On the Discursive Limits of Sex*, New York: Routledge.

Buttel, F. and Newby, H. (1980) *The Rural Sociology of Advanced Societies*, Montclair: Allenheld Osmun.

Buttel, F. and Taylor, P. (1994) "Environmental sociology and global environmental change: a critical assessment," in M. Redclift and T. Benton (eds) *Social Theory and the Global Environment*, London: Routledge.

Callon, M. (1986) "Some elements of a sociology of translation: domestication of the scallops and the fishermen of St. Brieuc Bay," in J. Law (ed.) *Power, Action and Belief: A New Sociology of Knowledge?*, London: Routledge.

Carney, J. (1996) "Converting the wetlands, engendering the environment," in R. Peet and M. Watts (eds) *Liberation Ecology*, London: Routledge.

Castells, M. (1996) *The Rise of the Network Society*, Cambridge, MA: Harvard University Press.

Castree, N. (1995) "The nature of produced nature," *Antipode* 27: 12–48.

—— (1997) "Nature, economy and the cultural politics of theory: 'the war against the seals' in the Bering Sea, 1870–1911," *Geoforum* 28: 1–20.

Cheah, P. (1996) "Mattering," *Diacritics* 26: 108–39.

Clarke, A. (1995) "Modernity, postmodernity and reproductive processes, *c.*1890–1990," in C. Gray, H. Figueroa-Sarriera and S. Mentor (eds) *The Cyborg Handbook*, New York: Routledge.

Collins, J. (1987) *Unseasonal Migrations*, Princeton: Princeton University Press.

Cronon, W. (1995) "The trouble with wilderness; or, getting back to the wrong nature," in W. Cronon (ed.) *Uncommon Ground: Toward Reinventing Nature*, New York: W. W. Norton.

Deleuze, G. (1988) *Foucault*, Minneapolis: University of Minnesota Press.

Derrida, J. (1982) *Margins of Philosophy*, trans. Alan Bass, Chicago: University of Chicago Press.

Di Chiro, G. (1995) "Nature as commodity: the convergence of environment and social

CONSTRUCTION OF NATURE AND NATURE OF CONSTRUCTION

justice," in W. Cronon (ed.) *Uncommon Ground: Toward Reinventing Nature*, New York: W. W. Norton.

Escobar, A. (1996) "Constructing nature: elements for a post-structural political ecology," in R. Peet and M. Watts (eds) *Liberation Ecology*, London: Routledge.

Fitzsimmons, M. (1986) "The new industrial agriculture," *Economic Geography* 62: 334–53.

Foucault, M. (1977) *Discipline and Punish: Birth of the Prison*, London: Penguin.

Friedmann, H. (1982) "The political-economy of food: the rise and fall of the post-war international food order," *American Journal of Sociology* 88 (suppl.): 248–86.

Goodman, D. and Redclift, M. (1991) *Refashioning Nature*, London: Routledge.

Goodman, D., Sorj, B. and Wilkinson, J. (1987) *From Farming to Biotechnology*, Oxford: Blackwell.

Gramsci, A. (1971) *Selections from the Prison Notebooks*, New York: International Publishers.

Granovetter, M. (1994) "Economic action and social structure: the problem of embeddedness," *American Journal of Sociology* 91: 481–510.

Gross, P. and Levitt, N. (1994) *Higher Superstition: The Academic Left and its Quarrels with Science*, Baltimore: Johns Hopkins University Press.

Grosz, E. (1994) *Volatile Bodies: Toward a Corporeal Feminism*, Bloomington: Indiana University Press.

Hacking, I. (1983) *Representing and Intervening: Introductory Topics in the Philosophy of Natural Science*, Cambridge: Cambridge University Press.

Haraway, D. (1982) "The high cost of information in post-world war II evolutionary biology," *Philosophical Forum* 13: 244–78.

—— (1989) *Primate Visions: Gender, Race and Nature in the World of Modern Science*, New York: Routledge.

—— (1991) *Simians, Cyborgs and Women: The Reinvention of Nature*, New York: Routledge.

—— (1992) "The promises of monsters: a regenerative politics for inappropriate/d others," in L. Grossberg, C. Nelson and P. Treichler (eds) *Cultural Studies*, New York: Routledge.

—— (1994) "A game of cat's cradle: science studies, feminist theory, cultural studies," *Configurations* 1: 59–71.

—— (1997) *Modest Witness@Second Millennium*, New York: Routledge.

Harding, S. (1986) *The Science Question in Feminism*, Ithaca: Cornell University Press.

Harrison, R. (1992) *Forests: The Shadow of Civilization*, Chicago: University of Chicago Press.

Hartouni, V. (1994) "Breached birth: reflections on race, gender, and reproductive discourse in the 1980s," *Configurations* 2: 73–88.

Harvey, D. (1974) "Population, resources and the ideology of science," *Economic Geography* 50: 256–77.

—— (1996) *Justice, Nature and the Geography of Difference*, Oxford: Blackwell.

—— (1998) "The body as an accumulation strategy," *Society and Space*, forthcoming.

Hayles, N. K. (1991) "Constrained constructivism: locating scientific inquiry in the theatre of representation," *New Orleans Review* 18: 76–85.

—— (1995) "Searching for common ground," in M. Soulé and G. Lease (eds) *Reinventing Nature? Responses to Postmodern Deconstruction*, Washington: Island Press.

NOEL CASTREE AND BRUCE BRAUN

Hecht, S. and Cockburn, A. (1989) *The Fate of the Forest: Developers, Destroyers, and the Defenders of the Amazon*, London: Verso.

Heidegger, M. (1962) *Being and Time*, New York: Harper & Row.

—— (1977) *The Question Concerning Technology and Other Essays*, trans. W. Lovitt, New York: Harper and Row.

Heims, S. (1980) *John von Neumann and Norbert Wiener: From Mathematics to the Technologies of Life and Death*, Cambridge: MIT Press.

Katz, C. (1995) "Under the falling sky: apocalyptic environmentalism and the production of nature," in A. Callari, S. Cullenberg and C. Biewener (eds) *Marxism in the Postmodern Age*, New York: Guilford.

Kautsky, K. (1976) *The Agrarian Question*, selected parts, trans. J. Banaji, *Economy and Society* 5: 1–49.

Keller, E. (1995) *Refiguring Life: Metaphors of Twentieth-Century Biology*, New York: Columbia University Press.

Laclau, E. and Mouffe, C. (1985) *Hegemony and Socialist Strategy*, London: Verso.

Latour, B. (1988) *The Pasteurization of France*, Cambridge, MA: Harvard University Press.

—— (1990) "Postmodern? No, simply amodern! Steps towards an anthropology of science," *Studies in the History and Philosophy of Science* 21: 145–71.

—— (1993) *We Have Never Been Modern*, Cambridge, MA: Harvard University Press.

Latour, B. and Woolgar, S. (1979) *Laboratory Life: The Social Construction of Scientific Facts*, Beverley Hills: Sage Publications.

Le Heron, R. and Roche, M. (1996) "Globalisation, sustainability, and apple orcharding, Hawke's Bay, New Zealand," *Economic Geography* 72: 417–32.

Lowe, D. (1995) *The Body in Late-Capitalism*, Durham: Duke University Press.

McKibben, B. (1989) *The End of Nature*, New York: Random House.

McMichael, P. (1994) *The Global Restructuring of Agro-Food Systems*, Ithaca: Cornell University Press.

Marsden, T. *et al.* (1986a) "Towards a political-economy of capitalist agriculture: a British perspective," *International Journal of Urban and Regional Research* 10: 498–521.

—— (1986b) "The restructuring process and economic centrality in capitalist agriculture," *Journal of Rural Studies* 2: 271–80.

—— (1996) "Agricultural geography and the political-economy approach: a review," *Economic Geography* 72: 361–75.

Martin, E. (1987) *The Woman in the Body: A Cultural Analysis of Reproduction*, Boston: Beacon Press.

—— (1992) "The end of the body?" *American Ethnologist* 19: 121–138.

—— (1994) *Flexible Bodies: Tracking Immunity in American Culture from the Days of Polio to the Age of AIDS*, Boston: Beacon Press.

Marx, K. (1975) *Texts on Method*, T. Carver (ed.) Oxford: Blackwell.

Mitchell, T. (1988) *Colonizing Egypt*, Cambridge: Cambridge University Press.

Moore, D. (1996) "Marxism, culture and political-ecology," in R. Peet and M. Watts (eds) *Liberation Ecologies: Environment, Development, Social Movements*, New York: Routledge.

Mumford, L. (1964) "Authoritarian and democratic technics," *Technology and Culture* 5: 1–8.

O'Connor, J. (1988) "Capitalism, nature, socialism: a theoretical introduction," *Capitalism, Nature, Socialism* 1: 11–38.

CONSTRUCTION OF NATURE AND NATURE OF CONSTRUCTION

Oudshoorn, N. (1994) *Beyond the Natural Body*, London: Routledge.

Peet, R. and Watts, M. (1996) "Liberation ecology: development, sustainability, and environment in an age of market triumphalism," in R. Peet and M. Watts (eds) *Liberation Ecologies: Environment, Development, Social Movements*, New York: Routledge.

Peluso, N. (1993) *Rich Forests, Poor People*, Berkeley: University of California Press.

Peterson, M. (1990) "Paradigmatic shift in agriculture: global effects and the Swedish response," in T. Marsden *et al.* (eds) *Rural Enterprise*, London: David Fulton.

Pile, S. (1990) *The Private Farmer*, Aldershot: Avebury.

Rabinow, P. (1992) "Artificiality and enlightenment: from sociobiology to biosociality," in J. Crary and S. Kwinter (eds) *Incorporations*, New York: Zone Books.

Rajchman, J. (1988) "Foucault's art of seeing," *October* 44: 88–117.

Redclift, M. (1987) *Sustainable Development: Exploring the Contradictions*, London: Methuen.

Ross, A. (1994) *The Chicago Gangster Theory of Life: Nature's Debt to Society*, London: Verso.

Roucheleau, D., Thomas-Slayter, B. and Wangari, E. (eds) (1996) *Feminist Political Ecology*, London: Routledge.

Rouse, J. (1987) *Knowledge and Power: Toward a Political Philosophy of Science*, Ithaca: Cornell University Press.

Rouse, J. (1992) "What are the cultural studies of scientific knowledge?," *Configurations* 1: 1–22.

Schama, S. (1995) *Landscape and Memory*, New York: Alfred A. Knopf.

Schmidt, A. (1971) *The Concept of Nature in Marx*, London: New Left Books.

Scott, J. C. (1985) *Weapons of the Weak*, New Haven, CT: Yale University Press.

Serres, M. (1987) *Statues*, Paris: Francois Bourin.

Shapin, S. and Schaffer, S. (1985) *Leviathan and the Air-Pump: Hobbes, Boyle and the Experimental Life*, Princeton: Princeton University Press.

Slater, C. (1995) "Amazonia as edenic narrative," in W. Cronon (ed.) *Uncommon Ground: Toward Reinventing Nature*, New York: W. W. Norton.

Smith, N. (1984) *Uneven Development: Nature, Capital and the Production of Space*, Oxford: Blackwell.

—— (1996) "The production of nature," in G. Robertson, M. Mash, L. Tichner, J. Bird, B. Curtis and T. Putnam (eds) *Future Natural*, London: Routledge.

Spivak, G. (1985) "The Rani of Samur," in F. Barker *et al.* (eds) *Europe and Its Others*, Colchester: University of Sussex.

Stonich, S. (1989) "The dynamics of social processes and environmental destruction," *Population and Development Review* 15: 269–96.

Strathern, M. (1992) *Reproducing the Future: Anthropology, Kinship and the New Reproductive Technologies*, New York: Routledge.

Taylor, C. (1992) "Heidegger, language, and ecology," in H. Dreyfus and H. Hall (eds) *Heidegger: A Critical Reader*, Oxford: Blackwell.

Traweek, S. (1988) *Beamtimes and Lifetimes*, Cambridge, MA: Harvard University Press.

Treichler, P. (1987) "AIDS, homophobia and biomedical discourse: an epidemic of signification," *October* 43: 31–70.

Wark, M. (1994) "Third nature," *Cultural Studies* 8: 115–32.

Watts, M. (1983) *Silent Violence*, Berkeley: University of California Press.

—— (1989) "The agrarian question in Africa," *Progress in Human Geography*, 13: 1–41.

41

NOEL CASTREE AND BRUCE BRAUN

Watts, M. (1991) "Geography and struggles over nature," in F. Buttel and L-A. Thrupp (eds) *The Food Question*, London: Earthscan.

Whatmore, S. (1991) *Farming Women*, London: Macmillan.

Whatmore, S. and Boucher, S. (1993) "Bargaining with nature: the discourse and practice of "environmental planning gain," *Transactions of the Institute of British Geographers* 18: 166–78.

White, S. (1991) *Political Theory and Postmodernism*, Cambridge: Cambridge University Press.

Willems-Braun, B. (1997) "Buried epistemologies: the politics of nature in (post)colonial British Columbia," *Annals of the Association of American Geographers* 87: 3–31.

Williams, R. (1976) *Keywords: A Vocabulary of Culture and Society*, London: Fontana.

—— (1980) *Problems in Materialism and Culture*, London: Verso.

Winner, L. (1986) *The Whale and the Reactor: A Search for Limits in an Age of High Technology*, Chicago: University of Chicago Press.

Worster, D. (ed.) (1988) *The Ends of the Earth: Perspectives on Modern Environmental History*, New York: Cambridge University Press.

Zimmerer, K. (1994) "Human geography and the new ecology," *Annals of the Association of American Geographers* 84: 108–25.

[15]

SCIENCE, SOCIAL CONSTRUCTIVISM AND NATURE

David Demeritt

INTRODUCTION

Science, it seems, is in the news these days. Reports of further cancer risks, pollution problems, and environmental nightmares compete for space in the headlines with the technical triumphs of modern science: miracle medical cures, computer wizardry, and awe-inspiring discoveries about the origins of the human species and the universe itself. But science in this day and age is as commonplace as it is extraordinary. From the scientifically engineered food we eat to the space age materials like Goretex™ and Kevlar™ that clothe and shelter us, modern science and its technical creations have become ubiquitous, indeed indispensible, if also largely taken for granted, aspects of everyday life – at least in the industrialized world. Yet despite this success, because of it in fact, the sciences are met with increasing public unease and skepticism. Assurances from the grave men in white lab coats are no longer sufficient to ease public concern about toxic chemicals, nuclear contamination, and the other environmental "side effects" of industrial society.

This loss of public faith in the sciences is a characteristic of what Ulrich Beck (1992) calls the emergent "risk society." Whereas previously industrial society was organized around the application of scientific knowledge for the production and distribution of wealth, now, according to Beck (1992: 19–20), the defining feature of contemporary society is the distribution and management of hazards such as global warming that result "from techno-economic development itself." As the chief cause of these modern environmental problems as well as "the medium of [their] definition, and the source of solutions" (p. 155), the sciences occupy a controversial and contradictory position in the risk society. In the face of global environmental changes that seem to make them "more and more necessary," the sciences are "at the same time, less and less sufficient for the socially binding definition of truth" (p. 156).[1]

173

DAVID DEMERITT

Beck's notion of the "risk society" provides a useful starting point from which to begin making sense of the recent controversies about science, social constructivism, and nature. Against this backdrop of uncertainty about the risks associated with scientific and technological progress, the status of scientific knowledge has become the object of fierce, academic dispute. The controversy pits a variety of cultural critics who emphasize the socially contingent manner in which scientific knowledge is constructed against self-styled defenders of science, many of them practising scientists themselves, who uphold a conventional understanding of science as the progressively more accurate explanation of a real, independent, and pre-existing natural world. This commonsense explanation of science is epistemologically realist. It posits that scientific knowledge is true if it represents the world as it in fact really is. While a variety of philosophers have questioned the logical underpinnings for such a correspondence theory of truth (Rorty 1979; van Fraasen 1980; Rouse 1987), historians, sociologists, and anthropologists who study practising scientists have emphasized the ways in which the validation of scientific theories is determined socially rather than by correspondence to an independent reality.[2] These critiques of scientific and epistemological realism have become so widespread in the academy that the New York Academy of Sciences and the British Royal Society both sponsored high-profile symposia to defend science against social constructivism. The media, ever fixated by controversy, have given the debate considerable play, both as a news item and as grist for the op-ed page.

The academic debate over social constructivism is more complex than either the sensationalist coverage or the often glib dismissals would suggest. In its various forms, social constructivism poses fundamental questions about public trust and scientific credibility. What makes some knowledge scientific? How does science work? Why should we believe it? What accounts for its apparent success in explaining the world? Why are the sciences to be preferred over other ways of knowing and relating to nature? Who should decide?

There are a number of compelling, if not necessarily compatible, answers to these questions, but it is important to recognize that they concern more than just the foundations of scientific knowledge. The debate about social constructivism is also about social power and legitimacy, which is one reason why the furore has become so heated of late. My concern in this chapter is less to adjudicate the epistemological status of science (to my mind, largely a pointless exercise), than it is to use the debate to clarify what is at stake in the practice of science and the social construction of nature.

My discussion will be divided into three parts. First, I will review the controversy surrounding science and social constructivism. Although the debate is commonly staged in simplistic either/or terms such as science/anti-science and realist/constructivist, it is considerably more diverse and multi-faceted. A number of very different approaches to science, knowledge, and nature travel under the deceptively simple banner "social construction" (Sismondo 1993). Having described what it might mean to talk about the social construction of

SCIENCE, SOCIAL CONSTRUCTIVISM AND NATURE

science and nature, I shall discuss in turn the examples of forest conservation and global warming. Science has been crucial in constructing these environmental problems. In each case, the nature of the problem and the sort of techniques applied to address it have depended fundamentally upon the particular metaphors and scientific practices by which it has been constructed and represented. Indeed, it is difficult to imagine an environmental phenomenon less directly observable, more remote from everyday experience, and more dependent on the technical apparatus of science for constructing its apparent "reality" than the so-called greenhouse effect (Cronon 1994: 41). For climate change skeptics, the fact that atmospheric scientists must endlessly tune, correct, and parameterize their global circulation computer models (GCMs) in order to represent the facts of future climate change provides a reason to dismiss the entire problem as a phantasmic social construction, born of paranoid "hype" by "environmental pressure groups" and unproven by any "solid fact" or independently verifiable scientific observation of actual anthropogenic climate change (Singer 1992: 34). Such charges are vigorously denied by the scientists involved as well as by environmentalists, many of whom fear that social constructivism, by focusing on the human interests and agencies involved in constructing and promoting particular environmental problems, denies them any objective reality, thereby sapping political will for protecting the environment (cf. Dunlap and Catton 1994; Soule and Lease 1995). This analysis of social constructivism is incomplete and unhelpful. It rests on a problematic distinction between nature and society that confounds our understanding of the practice of science and the representation of nature. I try to address this difficulty in this chapter by outlining a theory of artifactual social constructivism that reconciles a recognition of the productive activity of scientists in constructing and representing the facts of science with an appreciation of the role of other, heterogeneous agencies in realizing the nature of the world.

SOCIAL CONSTRUCTIVISM

Social constructivism has become a popular, catch-all term to describe a variety of very different approaches to science, knowledge, and nature. Sergio Sismondo (1993) identifies four distinct uses of the construction metaphor, each describing a different object of construction (see Table 1).[3] First, there is what might be called social object constructivism. This refers to the construction, through the interplay of actors, institutions, habits, and other social practices, of subjective belief about reality that over time "congeals for the man on the street" into a "taken-for-granted 'reality'" (Berger and Luckman 1966: 3; see also Searle 1995).

Feminists have been among the most enthusiastic proponents of social object constructivism. Many, though by no means all, distinguish sharply between gender, the subjective and socially constructed beliefs about sexual difference that constitute a changeable, but no less real, "social reality," and sex itself, the

Table 1 A Typology of Social Constructivisms

	Common-sense realism	Social object constructivism	Social institutional constructivism	Artefactual constructivism	Neo-Kantian constructivism
Chief tenets	Observational statements refer directly to a pre-existing, independent, and, in this sense, objective reality	Taken-for-granted beliefs about reality, e.g. gender, constitute a social reality no less "real" in its causal effects than reality itself	Science is a social construction in the sense that its institutions and the social contexts of its discoveries are socially conditioned and constructed	The reality of the objects of scientific knowledge is the contingent outcome of social negotiation among heterogenous human and non-human actors	The objects of scientific thought are given their reality by human actors alone
Key proponents	Gross and Levitt (1994)	Berger and Luckman (1966); Searle 1995	Merton ([1938] 1970)	Latour (1987); Haraway (1992)	Woolgar (1988); Collins and Pinch (1993)
Ontology	Nature / society, subject/ object, mind/ matter are ontologically distinct realms	Socially constructed reality distinct from objective facts given by nature, e.g. sex	Objective reality distinct and independent from belief about it	No absolute ontological distinction between representation and reality, nature and society	Nature is whatever society makes of it
Epistemology	Truth value determined by correspondence between representation and reality	Scientific truth explained by nature; socially constructed belief is the cause of scientific falsehood	Ignorance and socially constructed bias explain belief in scientific falsehood	Ultimate truth is undecidable	Truth is what the powerful believe it to be

SCIENCE, SOCIAL CONSTRUCTIVISM AND NATURE

biologically given, immutable material reality of those differences. This distinction provides the basis for a well-established tradition of liberal feminism that Sandra Harding (1986; 1991) has dubbed feminist empiricism. Feminist empiricists criticize practising scientists for failing to live up to their own high standards of objectivity and allowing gendered and socially constructed beliefs to bias their representations of nature. Though under assault as part of the general right-wing counter-attack on social constructivism (Gross and Levitt 1994), this feminist use of the construction metaphor actually supports a conventional understanding of science and objectivity. Social object constructivism preserves the ontological distinction between a social reality of human making (gender) and an underlying material reality not of human construction (sex) that provides the epistemic basis for distinguishing true and objective scientific knowledge from subjective and socially constructed belief. In the hands of feminist critics, social object contructivism provides a way to expose sexist bias in science without giving up on the ideals of science as a means of exposing the objective reality of women's oppression.

A second variety of social constructivism is social institutional constructivism. This describes the development of the institutions of science and the social processes of theorizing, experimenting, and arguing by which scientists establish their knowledge of an objective reality. Much of the work of this type has been historical, tracing the social pressures influencing the conduct and direction of scientific research (cf. Merton [1938] 1970; Rudwick 1985). Even professed opponents of social constructivism acknowledge that these are legitimate subjects for social science research, for they speak to the ever-present problem of bias, which a rigorous scientific method is designed to weed out of science. Like social object constructivism, social institutional constructivism is what David Bloor (1976: 4–5) calls asymmetrical. It distinguishes sharply between, on the one hand, the properly sociological explanation of the social context for particular scientific discoveries or incorrect beliefs and, on the other hand, the explanation of scientifically valid knowledge, which is largely unquestioned. Indeed, in the classical tradition of sociology of knowledge, science was explicitly declared off-limits for sociological explanation (Mannheim [1929] 1954). As a result, social institutional constructivism, like social object constructivism, is not at all inconsistent with epistemological realism and the claim that scientific knowledge is true and objective because it describes the world as it in fact actually is, quite independent of any human volition or activity.

By contrast, a third variety of social constructivism, artifactual constructivism, poses more of a challenge to realism. Artifactual constructivism refers to the construction, through material interventions and interactions, of the artifacts and other phenomena of the laboratory. The purified samples and carefully calibrated apparatus, as well as the theories and technically mediated observations that scientists build up and work with, constitute a "highly preconstructed artificial reality" (Knorr-Cetina 1983: 119). As such, artifactual constructivists maintain that the objects of scientific knowledge are the outcome of carefully contrived

DAVID DEMERITT

practice, not pre-existing objects waiting to be discovered and correctly represented by science (Hacking 1983; Latour 1987; Haraway 1992). This poses several challenges to epistemological realism. In common with empiricist arguments against epistemological realism (van Fraasen 1980), artifactual constructivism deflates the sense of metaphysical truth on which realism depends. For artifactual constructivists, questions of abstract truth are undecidable, if not altogether meaningless. The criterion of success for scientific theory is empirical adequacy and pragmatic achievement, not ultimate truth or falsity.

By emphasizing the productivity of scientific knowledge and practice, artifactual constructivism also denies the sharp break postulated by realism between reality and scientific descriptions of it. Latour and Woolgar (1979: 64) articulate the criticism this way: "It is not simply that phenomena depend on certain material instrumentation; rather the phenomena are thoroughly constituted by the material setting of the laboratory. The artificial reality, which participants describe in terms of an objective [i.e. existing independent of human agency] entity has in fact been constructed . . . through material techniques." The so-called real world against which the truth of a particular scientific representation might be tested can only be grasped through other representations, because reality appears as such only as a condition and result of the specific, productive activities of its representation (Demeritt 1997). Such artifactual constructivism, it is important to emphasize, does not deny the ontological existence of the world, only that its apparent reality is never pre-given; it is an emergent property that "depends upon the configuration of practices within which [it] becomes manifest" (Rouse 1987: 160–1). This Heideggerian insight is a difficult one. It is easy to slip from artifactual constructivism that is ontologically realist about entities but epistemologically anti-realist about theories (the things we call electrons are real objects, but our ideas about them are constructed) into a much stronger use of the construction metaphor that is anti-realist about both theories and entities (electrons have no objective existence; our belief in them as social objects is what gives them their apparent "reality").

This much stronger, neo-Kantian sense of the metaphor is the fourth variety of social constructivism. Neo-Kantians like Steve Woolgar (1988) use social construction in the very strongest and most literal sense: the social construction of the objects of scientific thought and representation. They reverse "the presumed relationship between representation and object, [claiming] that representation gives rise to the object" (Woolgar 1988: 65). Other sociologists have been more circumscribed in their approach, adopting neo-Kantian constructivism as a methodological principle for explaining the production of scientific knowledge symmetrically: without reference to its ultimate "truth and falsity, rationality and irrationality, success or failure" (Bloor 1976: 7). From this perspective, the actual nature of reality plays no role in determining our beliefs about it. Methodological relativism allows the "apparent independence of the natural world" to be described as something "granted by human beings in social negotiation" (Collins and Yearley 1992: 320). It leads to the polemical

SCIENCE, SOCIAL CONSTRUCTIVISM AND NATURE

conclusion of Collins and Pinch (1993) (quoted in Mermin 1996: 11) that "the truth about the natural world [is] what the powerful believe to be the truth about the natural world."

This neo-Kantian variety of social constructivism, not surprisingly, has drawn fierce criticism. While the merits of this strong programme have been the subject of intense discussion within the field of science studies itself (Scott *et al.* 1990; Pickering 1992; Pels 1996; Wynne 1996), the loudest, or at least the best publicized protests have come from a number of self-appointed defenders of science, many of them practising scientists. They complain that social constructivism is relativist, irrational, and patently absurd. Its refusal to acknowledge any objective criteria for scientific verification makes it impossible to distinguish "reliable knowledge from superstition" (Gross and Levitt 1994: 45), thereby opening the door to our most "irrational tendencies" (Weinberg 1996). These realist defenders of science invite their constructivist critics to test the absurdity of the claim that "the laws of physics are mere social conventions . . . [by] transgressing those conventions from the windows of my [twenty-first floor] apartment" (Sokal 1996: 62). Gross and Levitt give a more elaborate homily on the foolishness of social constructivism:

> Imagine that a few of us are cooped up in a windowless office, wondering whether or not it's raining. Opinions vary. We decide to settle the issue by stepping outside, where we note the streets are beginning to fill up with puddles, that cars are kicking up rooster-tails of spray, that thunder and lightning fill the air, and, most significantly, that we are being pelted incessantly by drops of water falling from the sky. We retreat into the office and say to each other, "Wow, it's really coming down!" We all now agree it's raining. Insofar as we are disciples of Latour, we can never explain our agreement on this point by the simple fact that it is raining. Rain, remember is the outcome of our "settlement," not its cause! Badly put, this seems ridiculous. Nevertheless, if we accept the validity of Latour's putative insight, we are ineluctably obliged to accept this analysis of a rainy day.
>
> (Gross and Levitt 1994: 58)

This appeal to commonsense is compelling but ultimately deceptive. Common-sense would indicate that the sun revolves around the earth and that heavy objects fall more quickly than light ones, but the laws of physics say otherwise. Many objects of scientific knowledge do not lend themselves to verification as easily as rain, though the observation of even this everyday phenomena involves prior theoretical commitments about what constitutes "rain" (Hesse 1980: 65–83). The observation of molecular structures like DNA, if this is even the right word to describe the process of visualization involved in an electron microscope, is ever so much more complex a social and technical achievement. Other unobservable entities, like quarks and neutrinoes, can only be known

DAVID DEMERITT

indirectly, by observing the effects of their manipulation in multi-million dollar particle accelerators. It is difficult, therefore, to argue that the truth of our representations of these phenomena is in any way self-evident, as the most vocal opponents of social constructivism seem to be contending.

But the neo-Kantian account of scientific knowledge is no better. By denying the natural world any role in constraining scientific knowledge of it, neo-Kantian constructivism seems to suggest that nature is whatever science makes it out to be. This makes it difficult to understand how science could ever fail or a scientific theory be invalidated. The neo-Kantian case is much easier to sustain in the case of the unobservable entities of particle physics, a favored object of neo-Kantian explanation (cf. Collins and Pinch 1993), than it is for the more familiar objects of applied science, whose obdurate reality seems much harder to deny. The claim of Andrew Ross (1991: 217) that "the only difference" between modern atmospheric scientists and rain dancers "is that they appeal to differently organized systems of rationality" discounts the much great predictive success enjoyed by contemporary weather forecasters, with their satellite images and computer simulation models. Surely, weather forecasters know something about the weather; this is why we pay attention to them.

Realists take this practical and technical success as proof of the objective truth of scientific theory (Boyd 1984), but there are problems with this abductive argument for epistemological realism. The standards of empirical adequacy that define successful "working" and prediction are themselves socially determined norms and not given self-evidently as data by the nature of reality itself. Scientific standards of proof are prime examples of social object constructivism. No one would deny that airplanes and the other complex artifactual constructions of modern science do indeed work and that this success depends crucially (but not entirely) upon the successful predictions of scientific theory. The issue, for realists and anti-realists, is whether this explanatory and predictive success is in any way indicative of the truth of scientific representation. At one time, both phlogiston theory and Ptolemaic planetary models "worked": they provided reliable frameworks to predict and explain the available evidence, but both have now been discredited. While realists take this as evidence that scientific knowledge is converging on truth, it is not entirely clear what converging toward truth might mean when the historical development of scientific theory is taken as evidence of the very thing it is supposed to be explained by: convergence on truth (Laudan 1984).

Ultimately, the issue of scientific truth is not a very interesting one. It tells us nothing about whether a particular scientific theory works or why. And yet, the debate about science and social constructivism has been fixated by the objective truth of representation. Realists uphold truth as correspondence, and neo-Kantians deny it, by collapsing the realists' dualism into a single, socially constructed monism, thereby conflating anti-realism about scientific theories and the epistemological claim that the grounds for representations are arbitrary and socially constructed with anti-realism about scientific entities and the ontological

SCIENCE, SOCIAL CONSTRUCTIVISM AND NATURE

claim that reality itself is made up. Realists dismiss this out of hand as absurd, which it is, but their dualism is no less problematic. Focused exclusively on the correspondence of scientific representation to reality, they ignore the fact that this reality is only ever realized as an artifact of scientific representations.

Scientific knowledge depends crucially upon the human relationships described so insightfully by the work of social object and social institutional constructivists, but it also depends upon a variety of nonhuman actors. Scientists are, after all, struggling to understand the natural world. While their knowledges are figured in culturally specific (and materially significant) ways, they are "about" something more than just culture. The difficulty comes in acknowledging the active role played by the objects of scientific knowledge in shaping or constraining this knowledge without falling back into some kind of epistemological realism in which true knowledge is said to reflect the world as it is ontologically (pre-) given.

Artifactual constructivism provides a way out of this dead end. It refigures the actors in the construction of what is made for us as nature and society. The social in these social constructions is not just "us": it includes other humans, non-humans, and even machines and other, non-organic actors. Artifactual constructivism provides a way of acknowledging that these agencies "matter" without taking the particular configuration of their matter or the process by which it is realized for granted (Butler 1993). This makes it possible to talk about science, knowledge, and nature without recourse either to the objective and ontologically given Nature of epistemological realism or to the omnipotent and all-knowing Society of neo-Kantian constructivism. Instead, artifactual constructivism focuses on the powerful and productive practices of science by which the reality of nature and our socially constructed knowledge of it are produced and articulated, thereby dispelling the modern dualism on which the debate about science and social constructivism has turned.

Science appears rather differently once we abandon the illusion that it must either be a purely objective reflection of the world or an entirely subjective construction of it. Questions about scientific representation and correspondence to an external and ontologically given natural world give way to questions about scientific practice and the mediated relationships among humans and their ever-active, non-human partners in the social production of knowledge and nature. Artifactual constructivism makes these interactions visible. It makes it possible to interrogate the culturally specific knowledges and ways of being that scientific interventions in and reconfigurations of the natural world realize and produce. "Biology," as Donna Haraway (1992: 298) insists, "is a discourse, not the living world itself. But humans are not the only actors in the construction of the entities of any scientific discourse . . . So while the late twentieth century immune system, for example, is a construct of an elaborate system of bodily production, neither the immune system nor any other of biology's world-changing bodies – like a virus or an ecosystem – is a ghostly fantasy." These objects of scientific knowledge are co-constructions. This makes them no less real or materially

DAVID DEMERITT

significant. It simply highlights the complex and negotiated process of scientific practice and representation by which they are materialized and produced for us as natural–technical objects of human knowledge.

For too long we have been debilitated by the notion of disembodied, Olympian truth and the correspondence theory of knowledge. This has made it difficult to appreciate the diversity of the sciences and the differences in the ways they render the world. Silviculturalists, for example, represent the forest very differently than ecologists whose theoretical concern with ecological communities discloses interspecific aspects of the forest discounted by silviculture, for which the single-species age class was long the fundamental unit of analysis. These differences are consequential, but they cannot be explained in terms of the (un)truth of silvicultural representation of the forest. They are the products of practice, not representation. The issue is not whether one better reflects the underlying nature of the forest but how this nature is figured and realized and with what effects. In the next two sections, I explore these general issues around the artifactual construction of nature through a discussion of sciences of forest conservation and global warming.

SAVING THE FOREST

The science of forestry is founded on a series of metaphors representing the nature of the forest and dictating the practices that should be applied to conserve it. Concerned by the rapid depletion of the American forest, conservationists and professional foresters of a century ago, like US Forest Service Chief Gifford Pinchot (1905), argued that the only way to save the forest was to manage it scientifically: by which they meant treating the forest as a kind of natural capital to be conserved, rather than exploiting it shortsightedly, as had previously been the case, as if it were a mine and a non-renewable resource with no future beyond its immediate stumpage value. Since the turn of the century, this scientific construction of the forest as capital and the practice of sustained yield forestry that flowed from it have been the model, if perhaps not quite the norm, for forest management in North America. Recently, however, scientific forestry has come under fire from those who complain that the old conception of the forest as "working capital whose purpose is to produce successive crops" (Pinchot 1905: 41) is dangerously narrow. In place of the old ideal of sustained yield, proponents of so-called "new forestry," such as Jerry Franklin (1989), speak of sustaining forest ecosystems and forest health. The struggle between industrial advocates of sustained yield forestry and promoters of new forestry and ecosystem management turns as much on representing the nature of the forest as on the question of what should be done to it.

Very different programs of actions flow from these competing constructions of the forest as a quantity of capital to be conserved and an ecosystem whose health is to be protected. Turn-of-the-century conservationists seized on the

SCIENCE, SOCIAL CONSTRUCTIVISM AND NATURE

comparison of the forest to "a savings bank from which you could draw interest every year" as part of their campaign against the prevailing practice of cut-and-run logging (US Division of Forestry 1887: 9–10). The analogy provided a basis for protecting future forest supplies, but it was harder to justify the protection of non-market public goods derived from forests, such as flood abatement, in terms of natural capital. If flood abatement happens at all, it is only as an unanticipated byproduct of conservative timber harvesting. Strict profit-maximizers have no economic incentive to look after unpriced public goods, whose social value the market, and thus the notion of natural capital, does not account for. Mostly, the comparison of the forest to accumulating capital was didactic, made without much sense of the tensions inherent between the forest's value as a fixed source of socially necessary materials and as a fluid financial asset.

The idea of forest capital appealed to the interests of large forestland owners. It highlighted the difference between destructive so-called timber mining, which depleted the supply of natural capital, and conservative forestry in which "only the interest [was] taken . . . [and] the principal of the investment [was] retained" (Cary 1899: 161). In a very real sense, the forest was already being represented by the dollar sign; loggers sized it up in terms of its immediate monetary value. Turn-of-the-century conservationists simply took advantage of this fact to promote scientific, sustained yield forestry to a skeptical forest industry. In this way, then, the rise of scientific forestry might be understood as an example of social institutional constructivism in which the social power of the forest products industry explains the relatively rapid uptake and institutionalization of sustained yield forestry (cf. Hays 1959). But such an external influence explanation discounts the degree to which the new scientific understanding of the forest as an accumulation of natural capital affected the actual details of scientific practice.

Scientific representation of the forest as naturally accumulating capital illuminated a variety of forest properties and relationships that had long escaped notice. Since, as the forester C. A. Schenck (1911: 21) explained, "growth in conservative forestry is the making of revenue," foresters studied the growth rates of merchantable species as well as other physiological and ecological processes affecting their development and reproduction. Non-merchantable species, long ignored by loggers as little more than a nuisance, were suddenly reconstituted as competition. Foresters experimented with technical treatments, such as girdling, thinning, and herbicides, to favor the growth of merchantable species over their competitors. To this Darwinian view of the world, life in the forest is a zero-sum game, in which resources are limited and their use necessarily reduces the available supply. Scientific concern with competition dictated new harvesting practices. In the mountainous West, the US Forest Service mandated selective rather than the customary clear-cut logging to insure that sufficient trees were left to seed the next generation. While foresters tried to minimize inter-specific competition, intra-specific competition and dense thickets of young timber were ideal, because competition among seedlings was thought to insure that the hardiest and most vigorous individuals survived (Langston 1995: 31).

DAVID DEMERITT

The idea of conserving the forest as if it were capital and the confidence in science that it reflected has led foresters to treat the forest as an assemblage of individual objects that can be managed more or less in isolation from one another. Foresters sought to maximize the yield without much thought to how larger quantities of a merchantable species would interact with the rest of the forest. In the spruce fir forest of the Northeast, selective logging for spruce has transformed uneven aged stands dominated by mature red spruce into much simpler stands with two age classes: a canopy dominated by balsam fir and a sprinkling of immature, red spruce left as "seed trees" and a dense understory of suppressed firs, which reproduces more prolifically than spruce. As this fir-dominant understory matured, it became vulnerable to infestation by spruce budworm, an insect whose preferred food, in fact, is balsam fir. At periodic intervals, growing more devastating with each occurrence, spruce budworm outbreaks have devastated the forest, killing most mature fir and many spruce trees as well (Seymour 1992). This high mortality, combined with massive salvage efforts to harvest vulnerable stands before they are attacked, has created the ideal habitat for spruce budworm to thrive: large areas of dense, even-aged, fir-dominant forest stressed from fierce competition for canopy space and thus less able to fend off attack (Lansky 1992). Similar problems plague the Blue Mountain forests of eastern Oregon, where the suppression of fire, thought necessary to protect the second growth of ponderosa pine, actually led to its elimination by fire-intolerant and low-value grand fir that grew in dense, tangled stands which were vulnerable to insect infestation and subsequent fires that consumed millions of acres of forest. By the early 1990s, the diseased and fire-plagued forests of the Blue Mountain were widely condemned in the press as a "Man-made blight" brought on by well-meaning but misguided forest management focused narrowly on lumber production without regard to the wider ecological effects of this management strategy (*Seattle Post Intelligencer* 1991, quoted in Langston 1995: 6).

Within the forestry profession, problems such as these have led to recent calls for the development of a "new forestry," focused "on the maintenance of complex ecosystems and not just the regeneration of trees" (Franklin 1989: 38). Ecosystem management, designed to sustain the "health" of forest ecosystems, has recently been adopted as the official policy objective of the US Forest Service (1992). This new conception of forest conservation is undoubtedly a response by the Forest Service and by the forestry profession in general to outside pressure from environmentalists, but it is also a product of some of the different ways in which the forest is now being framed as an object of scientific knowledge. The aims and objects of so-called new forestry depend fundamentally upon scientific ideas and techniques, first developed by ecologists but now widespread in other scientific disciplines as well, that set up the forest as a coherent eco-system whose interrelated parts are connected by flows of matter and energy (Hagen 1992). These practices make it possible to imagine the forest as an ecosystem whose health might be monitored and managed, rather than, as in more traditional

SCIENCE, SOCIAL CONSTRUCTIVISM AND NATURE

silviculture, as a disparate collection of age classes (Costanza *et al.* 1992). For all its apparent simplicity, however, ecosystem "health" has proven frustratingly difficult to define and thus to manage for or sustain (Suter 1993; O'Laughlin *et al.* 1994).

In some sense the conceptual ambiguity of forest health and ecosystem management has proven to be its greatest appeal. Scientists, industry officials, and environmentalists can all heartily endorse these new constructions of the forest without necessarily agreeing about the specific technical details required to achieve them. There is fierce disagreement, for example, about whether clear-cutting mimics natural disturbance processes, and thus is consistent with new forestry principles of ecosystem management, or whether it is ecologically damaging. Nature and the naturalism of forest practices at issue here are certainly framed by science, but it is hardly the case, as advocates of neo-Kantian constructivism would contend, that scientists are the only actors of consequence when it comes to constructing the nature of the forest. Foresters struggling with insect infestations have learned from long experience that they are not free to make the forest in any way they choose. Other actors matter too. This realization was crucial in the recent development of new forestry and its concern, however instrumental, with forest characteristics and processes beyond the accumulation of merchantable fibre. It is important to acknowledge the ontological independence of this nature without losing sight of the ways in which its reality is only ever realized and produced for us as an artifact and object of scientific practice and representation.

GLOBAL WARMING

Global warming presents a rather different set of issues and actors, but like the struggle to conserve the forests, the nature of climate change is as much a politically charged production of science as it is a straightforward reflection of some independent biophysical reality. Although theories about anthropogenic climate change date as far back as ancient Greece (Glacken 1967), and scientific discussion of an enhanced greenhouse effect, caused by changes in the earth's radiation balance due to the accumulation in the atmosphere of carbon dioxide (CO_2) and other radiatively sensitive gases, began in the late nineteenth century (Rowlands 1995), global warming did not emerge as a serious environmental concern until the late 1980s, when, almost overnight, it burst onto the scene as "the most important problem facing mankind over the next fifty years" (Gribbin 1990, quoted in Buttel *et al.* 1990: 57).

This rapid take-off owed much to the ambitions of government bureaucracies and Western environmental lobby groups, who seized upon the issue as an organizing rationale for a wide range of environmental protection and pollution control policies, and to the promoters of so-called alternative energy sources such as nuclear and hydro-electricity that were struggling in the cheap energy markets

DAVID DEMERITT

of the 1980s (Boehmer-Christiansen 1994). Indeed, many of the participants in the Intergovernmental Panel on Climate Change (IPCC), the international organization of scientific experts created in 1988 to advise governments and parties to the UN Framework Convention on Climate Change, came to Working Group Three, which was devoted to policy responses to climate change, directly from energy modeling and the late 1970s debate about how best to respond to the imminent depletion of fossil fuels.[4] As important as these social institutional factors were to the acceptance of global warming as an environmental crisis caused by fossil fuel consumption, tropical deforestation, and other anthropogenic emissions of greenhouse gases (cf. Boehmer-Christiansen 1990; Rowlands 1995), I would like to focus here instead upon the internal scientific practices contributing to this construction and to the political implications of the representation of climate change as a global scale environmental problem demanding global environmental, rather than say local and regional or cultural and economic, solutions.

From the outset, global warming has been constructed in narrowly scientific terms as a problem of atmospheric emissions largely divorced from their social context. Whereas the Bruntland Commission of the United Nations and its notion of sustainable development addressed themselves to the whole range of cultural and economic imperatives contributing to environmental problems, atmospheric scientists leading the IPCC and other international scientific bodies have defined the problem of global warming in terms of flows of matter and energy, thereby excluding from the analysis the political economy responsible for producing greenhouse gas emissions in the first place. This reductionism makes climate change scientifically manageable, unlike sustainable development, which is an analytical abstraction difficult to define or work with in practice. By constructing global warming as a matter of simple physics, scientists are able to model it mathematically. Their computer visualizations represent the facts of future climate change in alarming hues of red and orange, making the problem "real" for policy-makers and the public at large. Indeed, global climate change is difficult to imagine apart from the massive general circulation models (GCMs), computer simulations of the global climate system so sophisticated and expensive to run that there are only a few worldwide. These models have provided the most authoritative evidence of future global warming (Shackley and Wynne 1995).

The reductionism of climate change science is aligned to both a moral–liberal and a rational–technocratic view of politics and science (Taylor and Buttel 1992). In either case, the reductionist conception of global warming as an exogenous environmental force affecting humanity as a whole appeals to the common and undifferentiated interests of a global citizenry. It bypasses the complex, locally specific problems of sustainable development, reducing them to the single question of controlling global greenhouse gas emissions. The only difference is how emission reductions are to be achieved. The moral–liberal formulation depends on communicating scientific knowledge of the objective risks of climate change to sway self-serving, naïve, or scientifically ignorant behavior contributing

SCIENCE, SOCIAL CONSTRUCTIVISM AND NATURE

to global warming, while the rational–technocratic relies on science to identify the optimal policy to which individuals must then submit. Both assume that the proper role for science is to provide certain knowledge on which to found political decisions and that therefore the first obstacle to addressing climate change is scientific uncertainty, which impedes the formation of democratic consensus (moral–liberal) and the optimization of policy (rational–technocratic).

This emphasis on objective scientific knowledge as the basis for rational political action serves well both scientists and policy-makers. The authority of science provides legitimacy for controversial public policy decisions, while the promise of still greater certainty secures funding for more research. To this end, researchers are developing a whole new generation of integrated assessment models in which global climate and physical impact models are linked to land use, energy, and general equilibrium economic models to evaluate the impacts of different policy and climate change scenarios (Parson 1995; *Climatic Change* 1996) Although these integrated assessment models incorporate many more socio-economic dimensions of climate change than the GCMs, for which society was black boxed as a source of emissions and a sink for climate impacts, the general approach remains resolutely reductionist. As such they are tied to the same alliance of moral–liberal and rational–technocratic politics in which the solution to global warming depends on the resolution of scientific uncertainty and the successful communication of this objective knowledge to policy-makers and the public (Shackley and Darier 1997).

Concentrating upon the political use of climate change science, such an interest-based analysis of the social construction of global warming leaves unquestioned the status of scientific knowledge. It discounts the degree to which social commitments are built into the technical details of scientific practice as well as their subsequent use in the public sphere. For example, Shackley and Wynne (1995) have shown how in global climate modeling the practice of flux-correction, which is necessary to keep the separate ocean and atmosphere components of coupled GCMs in synch over long time scales (Kattenberg *et al.* 1996), has been constructed as the technique of choice, despite concerns about the massive "fudge-factor" involved (Kerr 1994), on the basis of a political desire for long-term prediction, which, until recently, was only possible with flux correction, as much as on its technical merits alone. Thus, Wynne (1996: 372) concludes, "the *intellectual* order of climate scientific prediction, and the *political* order of global management and universal policy control, based as it is on the promise of deterministic processes, smooth changes, long-term prediction and scientific control, mutually construct and reinforce one another."

Similar political commitments are built into the scientific calibration of the global warming potential (GWP) of the various greenhouse gases, which each have different atmospheric residence times and radiative properties depending in turn upon their relative concentrations (Smith 1993). These processes are too complicated to be integrated into a GCM, so it is necessary to calculate the GWP for each individual greenhouse gas, converting its relative radiative forcing per

187

DAVID DEMERITT

unit to a standard measure (typically a CO_2 equivalent) that can be aggregated to produce an overall radiative forcing function to drive GCM predictions of future global warming. Activists from developing countries complain that the luxury emissions of CO_2 from fossil fuel consumption in industrial countries cannot justly be compared to the survival emission of methane from agricultural production in developing countries (Agarwal and Narain 1991; Bodansky 1993). Furthermore, because the decay rates of these gases differ so greatly, the choice of time horizon strongly influences the calibration of their relative GWP, and thus any calculation of national emission profiles or the cost benefits of CO_2 versus methane emissions. These are questions of considerable import for the ratification and enforcement of the international emission reduction convention recently negotiated at Kyoto, Japan, but climate change science is not set up to answer them. The GCMs, which construct global warming as a global environmental problem, depend upon reducing the differences between various atmospheric emissions to a universal system of equivalence. They are indifferent to the social meanings of the entities that have been artificially unified through the GWP index and the globalizing ambitions of climate change science (Wynne 1996: 376–7).

Such a social constructivist critique of the way in which science has set up and framed the threat of global warming does not imply that the problem is unreal or that our socially constructed and contingent knowledge of it is simply false. It does question the authority for that knowledge and the legitimacy of what has been done in its name. For this reason many critics of social constructivism, such as Scott *et al.* (1990), have concluded that it is inherently conservative in its political orientation because it provides entrenched interests with the intellectual tools to refute any scientific criticism of their actions. It is certainly true that the fossil fuel industry has founded its opposition to greenhouse emission reductions upon the uncertainties inherent to flux correction and other scientific practices (Singer 1992; Global Climate Coalition 1994), but they have not been alone in their resistance to the political solutions proffered by the moral–liberal and rational–technocratic formulation of global climate change. In the initial blush of excitement about global warming in the late 1980s, a coalition of Western environmentalists, government regulators, and atmospheric scientists called for global carbon taxes, tropical rainforest protection, and other measures to reduce greenhouse gas emissions and avert certain climate catastrophe. Their appeal to the universal interests of a global citizenry was founded on scientific certainty, rather than the more difficult work of making global warming meaningful to a differentiated international public. This has proven to be neither a very democratic nor an especially effective way of constructing a political response to global warming. Social activists complain that the narrow focus on greenhouse gas emissions, whose effects will not be felt for a generation or more, divorces them from their social context and displaces attention from far more pressing and immediate concerns, such as poverty and hunger. Developing countries are resisting pressure to reduce their greenhouse emissions as a new form of

SCIENCE, SOCIAL CONSTRUCTIVISM AND NATURE

environmental colonialism, designed to keep them poor and underdeveloped (Parikh 1992; Parikh and Painuly 1994). In industrialized countries, individuals hesitate to alter their lifestyles in response to climate change public education and outreach campaigns because they do not trust the corporations to do likewise or believe that individual action will make much of a difference (Hinchliffe 1996). What is worse, perhaps, is that continued scientific uncertainty has become the principal rationale for inaction in the face of climate change. To the extent that the narrowly scientific focus on global climate change addresses itself to an undifferentiated global "we" and relies exclusively on the authority of science to create this sense of global citizenship, "we" are likely to act more as spectators than participants in the shaping of our related, but different futures (Taylor and Buttel 1992: 406).

CONCLUSION

Through these brief discussions of forest conservation and global warming I have tried to articulate a theory of artifactual constructivism that is sensitive both to the cultural politics of scientific representations of nature and to the independent, if also ineluctably framed and socially mediated, reality of nature. If this makes the practice of science seem more problematic than it once did, it makes it no less essential for making our way in the world, as the example of global warming suggests. Here is an environmental problem that would be difficult even to imagine, let alone address, without the considerable technical abilities of atmospheric science and computer modeling. The image of a dangerously warmer global climate that comes out of the GCMs is unquestionably a social construction – after all, it would not exist, nor, arguably, would the present-day concern with global warming, without the intervention of scientists and their supercomputers. That its apparent reality is only ever realized as an artifact of scientific representation should not make the potential threat of climate change any less real for us. Such a reaction, born of age-old distinctions between nature and society, seems strangely misplaced in this day of artificial life and genetic engineering. It leaves us with an inflexible, take-it or leave-it understanding of scientific knowledge: either real, objective, and therefore true or artificial, subjective, and thus socially constructed. By dissolving these dualisms, artifactual constructivism tempers the tendency either to worship science for its God-like objectivity or to demonize it for failing to live up to our unrealistic expectations. It moves us away from the schoolboy philosophy squabbles of the social constructivism debate and its fixation with the truth of scientific representation. Instead, artifactual constructivism focuses upon the powerful and productive practices by which the truth of representation is realized and produced. This is long overdue. With science responsible for producing so many of our environmental problems and yet also indispensable to their solution, there can be no question of dispensing with science altogether. The challenge is how to live it

189

DAVID DEMERITT

better. This demands a more pragmatic and more critical understanding of
science and the politics of its constructions of nature.

NOTES

1 I have removed the emphasis from the original.
2 It should be said that van Fraasen (1980), though fiercely critical of the correspondence
  theory of truth underwriting the conventional understanding of scientific knowledge,
  is himself an empiricist and as such is not at all supportive of the stronger forms of
  social constructivism.
3 In his book, Sismondo (1996) breaks out several more varieties of social constructivism, but for my purposes here, I have consolidated his (1993) third kind of
  constructivism (the construction of artifacts and other phenomena in the laboratory)
  with his (1996) "heterogeneous construction."
4 I owe this observation to John Robinson, one of the lead authors for Working Group
  Three.

REFERENCES

Agarwal, A. and Narain, S. (1991) *Global Warming in an Unequal World*, New Dehli:
  Centre for Science and Environment.
Beck, U. (1992) *Risk Society: Towards a New Modernity*, trans. M. Ritter, London: Sage
  Publications.
Berger, P. L. and Luckman, T. (1966) *The Social Construction of Reality: A Treatise in
  the Sociology of Knowledge*, Garden City, NY: Doubleday.
Bloor, D. (1976) *Knowledge and Social Imagery*, London: Routledge and Kegan Paul.
Bodansky, D. (1993) "The UN Framework Convention on Climate Change: a
  commentary," *Yale Journal of International Law* 18: 451–558.
Boehmer-Christiansen, S. (1990) "Energy policy and public opinion: manipulation of
  environmental threats by vested interests in the UK and West Germany," *Energy Policy*
  18: 828–37.
—— (1994) "A scientific agenda for climate policy?," *Nature* 372: 400–2.
Boyd, R. (1984) "The current status of scientific realism," in J. Leplin (ed.) *Scientific
  Realism*, Berkeley: University of California Press.
Butler, J. (1993) *Bodies That Matter*, New York: Routledge.
Buttel, F. H., Hawkins, A. P. and Power, A. G. (1990) "From limits to growth to global
  change: constraints and contradictions in the evolution of environmental science and
  ideology," *Global Environmental Change* 1: 57–66.
Cary, A. (1899). "How to apply forestry to spruce lands," *Paper Trade Journal* 27
  (19 February): 157–62.
Climatic Change (1996) Special issue on integrated assessment, 34: 315–95.
Collins, H. M. and Pinch T. (1993) *The Golem: What Everybody Should Know About
  Science*, Cambridge: Cambridge University Press.
Collins, H. M. and Yearley S. (1992) "Epistemological chicken," in A. Pickering (ed.)
  Science as Culture and Practice, Chicago: University of Chicago Press.
Costanza, R., Norton, B. G., Haskell, B. D. (eds) (1992) *Ecosystem Health: New Goals for
  Environmental Management*, Washington, DC: Island Press.

SCIENCE, SOCIAL CONSTRUCTIVISM AND NATURE

Cronon, W. (1994) "Cutting loose or running aground?," *Journal of Historical Geography* 20: 38–43.

Demeritt, D. (1997) "Representing the 'true' St. Croix: knowledge and power in the partition of the Northeast," *William and Mary Quarterly* 54: 515–48.

Dunlap, R. E. and Catton, W. R. Jr (1994) "Struggling with human exemptionalism: the rise, decline, and revitalization of environmental sociology," *The American Sociologist* 25: 5–30.

Franklin, J. (1989) "Toward a new forestry," *American Forests* 95 (November–December): 37–44.

Glacken, C. J. (1967) *Traces on the Rhodian Shore: Nature and Culture in Western Thought from Ancient Times to the End of the Eighteenth Century*, Berkeley: University of California Press.

Global Climate Coalition (1994) *Potential Global Climate Change*, Washington, DC: Global Climate Coalition.

Gribben, J. R. (1990) *Hothouse Earth: The Greenhouse Effect and Gaia*, London: Bantam Press.

Gross, P. R. and Levitt, N. (1994) *Higher Superstition: The Academic Left and Its Quarrels with Science*, Baltimore: Johns Hopkins University Press.

Hacking, I. (1983) *Representing and Intervening: Introductory Topics in the Philosophy of Natural Science*, Cambridge: Cambridge University Press.

Hagen, J. B. (1992) *An Entangled Bank: The Origins of Ecosystem Ecology*, New Brunswick: Rutgers University Press.

Haraway, D. J. (1992) "The promises of monsters: a regenerative politics for inappropriate/d others," in L. Grossberg, C. Nelson and P. A. Treichler (eds) *Cultural Studies*, New York: Routledge.

Harding, S. (1986) *The Science Question in Feminism*, Ithaca: Cornell University Press.

—— (1991) *Whose Science? Whose Knowledge?*, Ithaca: Cornell University Press.

Hays, S. P. (1959) *Conservation and the Gospel of Efficiency: The Progressive Conservation Movement, 1890–1920*, Cambridge: Harvard University Press.

Hesse, M. (1980) *Revolutions and Reconstructions in the Philosophy of Science*, Bloomington: University of Indiana Press.

Hinchliffe, S. (1996) "Helping the earth begins at home: the social construction of socio-environmental responsibilities," *Global Environmental Change* 6: 53–62.

Kattenberg, A., Giorgi, F., Grassl, H., Meehl, G. A., Mitchell, J. F. B., Stouffer, R. J., Tokioka, T., Weaver, A. J. and Wigley, T. M. L. (1996) "Climate models: projections of future climate," in J. T. Houghton, L. G. Meira Filho, B. A. Callander, N. Harris, A. Kattenberg and K. Maskell (eds) *Climate Change 1995: The Science of Climate Change*, Cambridge: Cambridge University Press.

Kerr, R. (1994) "Climate modeling's fudge factor comes under fire," *Science* 265 (9 September): 1528.

Knorr-Cetina, K. (1983) "Towards a constructivist interpretation of science," in K. Knorr-Cetina and M. Mulkay (eds) *Science Observed: Perspectives on the Social Study of Science*, Beverly Hills: Sage Publications.

Langston, N. (1995) *Forest Dreams, Forest Nightmares: The Paradox of Old Growth in the Inland West*, Seattle: University of Washington Press.

Lansky, M. (1992) *Beyond the Beauty Strip: Saving What's Left of Our Forests*, Gardiner, ME: Tilbury Publishers.

DAVID DEMERITT

Latour, B. (1987) *Science in Action: How to Follow Scientists and Engineers through Society*, Cambridge: Harvard University Press.

Latour, B. and Woolgar, S. (1979) *Laboratory Life: The Social Construction of Scientific Facts*, London: Sage Publications.

Laudan, L. (1984) "A confutation of convergent realism," in J. Leplin (ed.) *Scientific Realism*, Berkeley: University of California Press.

Maine State Forest Commissioner (1891) *Annual Report*, Augusta, ME, Maine State Forest Commissioner.

Mannheim, K. ([1929] 1954) *Ideology and Utopia*, New York: Harcourt Brace.

Mermin, N. D. (1996) "What's wrong with sustaining this myth?," *Physics Today* 49 (April): 11–13.

Merton, R. K. ([1938] 1970) *Science, Technology, and Society in Seventeenth-Century England*, New York: Howard Fertig.

O'Laughlin, J., Livingston, R. L., Thier, R., Thornton, J., Toweill, D. E. and Morelan, L. (1994) "Defining and measuring forest health," *Journal of Sustainable Forestry* 2: 65–85.

Parikh, J. K. (1992) "IPCC strategies unfair to the South," *Nature* 360: 507–8.

Parikh, J. K. and Painuly, J. P. (1994) "Population, consumption patterns and climate change: a socioeconomic perspective from the South," *Ambio* 23: 434–7.

Parson, E. A. (1995) "Integrated assessment and environmental policy making: in pursuit of usefulness," *Energy Policy* 23: 463–75.

Pels, D. (1996) "The politics of symmetry," *Social Studies of Science* 26: 277–304.

Pickering, A. (ed.) (1992) *Science as Culture and Practice*, Chicago: University of Chicago Press.

Pinchot, G. (1905) *A Primer of Forestry: Practical Forestry*, Washington: US Department of Agriculture, Bureau of Forestry, Bulletin 24.

Rorty, R. (1979) *Philosophy and the Mirror of Nature*, Princeton: Princeton University Press.

Ross, A. (1991) *Strange Weather: Culture, Science and Technology in the Age of Limits*, New York: Verso.

Rouse, J. (1987) *Knowledge and Power: Toward a Political Philosophy of Science*, Ithaca: Cornell University Press.

Rowlands, I. H. (1995) *The Politics of Global Atmospheric Change*, Manchester: Manchester University Press.

Rudwick, M. J. S. (1985) *The Great Devonian Controversy: The Shaping of Scientific Knowledge Among Gentlemanly Specialists*, Chicago: University Chicago Press.

Schenck, C. A. (1911) *Forest Policy*, Darmstaadt: C. F. Winter.

Scott, P., Richards, E. and Martin, B. (1990) "Captives of controversy: the myth of the neutral social researcher in contemporary scientific controversies," *Science, Technology, & Human Values* 15: 474–94.

Searle, J. R. (1995) *The Construction of Social Reality*, London, Allen Lane.

Seymour, R. S. (1992) "The red spruce-balsam fir forest of Maine: evolution of silvicultural practice in response to stand development patterns and disturbances," in M. J. Kelty, B. C. Larson, and C. D. Oliver (eds) *The Ecology and Silviculture of Mixed-Species Forests*, Dordrecht: Kluwer.

Shackley, S. and Darier, E. (1997) "The seduction of 'Groping the Dark': a dialogue on global modelling," unpublished manuscript, Centre for the Study of Environmental Change, Lancaster University.

SCIENCE, SOCIAL CONSTRUCTIVISM AND NATURE

Shackley, S. and Wynne, B. (1995) "Global climate change: the mutual construction of an emergent science-policy domain," *Science and Public Policy* 22: 218–30.

Singer, F. (1992) "Warming theories need warning label," *Bulletin of the Atomic Scientists* (June): 34–9.

Sismondo, S. (1993) "Some social constructions," *Social Studies of Science* 23: 515–53.

—— (1996) *Science Without Myth: On Constructions, Reality, and Social Knowledge*, Albany: State University of New York Press.

Smith, K. (1993) "The basics of greenhouse gas indices," in P. Hayes and K. Smith (eds) *The Global Greenhouse Regime – Who Pays?: Science, Economics, and North–South Politics in the Climate Change Convention*, London: Earthscan.

Sokal, A. (1996) "A physicist experiments with cultural studies," *Lingua Franca* 6 (May/June): 62–4.

Soule, M. E. and Lease, G. (eds) (1995) *Reinventing Nature? Responses to Postmodern Deconstruction*, Washington, DC: Island Press.

Suter, G. W. II (1993) "A critique of ecosystem health concepts and indexes," *Environmental Toxicology and Chemistry* 12: 1533–9.

Taylor, P. J. and Buttel, F. H. (1992) "How do we know we have global environmental problems? Science and the globalization of environmental discourse," *Geoforum* 23: 405–16.

US Division of Forestry (1887) *Report*, Washington, DC: Government Printing Office.

US Forest Service (1992) *Ecosystem Management of the National Forests and Grasslands*, policy letter 1220–1, 4 June, Washington, DC: Government Printing Office.

Van Fraasen, B. (1980) *The Scientific Image*, New York: Oxford University Press.

Weinberg, S. (1996) "Sokal's hoax," *New York Review of Books* 48 (8 August): 11–15.

Whitford, H. N. and Craig, R. D. (1918) *Forests of British Columbia*, Ottawa: Commission of Conservation.

Woolgar, S. (1988) *Science, The Very Idea*, Chichester: Tavistock.

Wynne, B. (1996) "SSK's identity parade: signing-up, off-and-on" *Social Studies of Science* 26: 357–91.

[16]

Science and decisionmaking

Sheila Jasanoff & Brian Wynne

Contributors
Frederick H. Buttel, Florian Charvolin, Paul N. Edwards,
Aant Elzinga, Peter M. Haas, Chunglin Kwa,
W. Henry Lambright, Michael Lynch, Clark A. Miller

1

SCIENCE AND DECISIONMAKING

Climate change emerged in the 1980s as a public policy issue posing apparently intractable challenges to science and politics (Gore 1992). The possible dangers of inaction seemed compelling, and policymakers around the world agreed on the need for more reliable data and assessments from the natural and social sciences. The move to constitute the Intergovernmental Panel on Climate Change (IPCC) and to ask for periodic state-of-the-art assessments followed a familiar conceptual model for linking science to politics or knowledge to action. It presupposed that scientific research could be targeted, in linear fashion, to fill gaps in the existing knowledge base. Once the gaps were filled, and uncertainties either reduced or eliminated, policymakers could rationally apply the products of science to formulating policy responses.

Confidence in the power of strategic or mission-oriented research to influence policy led to the commitment of substantial public funds to new climate change programs. Scientists and policymakers generally accepted that planetary changes could best be understood, and mastered, by identifying a collection of causal forces, both natural and social; by objectively mapping, measuring, and analyzing them; by predicting their effects; by aggregating them through large-scale quantitative techniques of modeling and assessment; and, finally, by using the assessments as inputs to policy. US global change research programs reflected the orientation toward studying objectively accessible large-scale patterns, with inquiry centered in the natural sciences. Whereas natural scientists studied interactions among the Earth's biogeophysical systems, social science research focused primarily on the aggregate social forces thought to produce environmental impacts on a global scale. (Table 1.1 presents funding for research in the social sciences in the US Global Change Research Program, including support from 11 federal agencies.)

Table 1.1 US federal funding for global change research (in millions of US$).

Fiscal year	1989	1990	1991	1992	1993	1994
Total Global Change Program, all agencies	133.9	659.3	953.7	1109.8	1326.0	1475.1
Total human interactions, all agencies	22.7	4.8	28.3	16.8	22.2	23.6
Percentage of total program, all agencies	16.4	0.7	3.0	1.5	1.7	1.7

Source: Human Dimensions Quarterly 1(1), 12.

Almost immediately, however, it became clear that traditional policy-analytic approaches would not contain a problem of this dimension. The scale, complexity, and interconnectedness of the causes of climate change—and the fundamental links between climate change and other global processes—tested science's incremental and discipline-based approaches to investigating nature. Concurrently, the contested, open-ended, and geographically dispersed character of climate-linked phenomena strained the power of established policy

2

SCIENCE AND DECISIONMAKING

institutions, both national and international, to build scientific consensus or formulate adequate policy responses (Skolnikoff 1990, Mann 1991, Messner et al. 1992). Controversies about the IPCC's conclusions intensified, constituting a backlash not only against particular scientific findings and assessments but, more profoundly, against the politics of globalization (e.g., Seitz et al. 1989, Balling 1992, Michaels 1992, Bailey 1993).

This chapter draws on several decades of social science research on scientific knowledge and policymaking to show why initial assumptions about how to study and respond to climate change have proved inadequate and to present a richer accounting to guide future responses to this complex issue. The discussion draws upon and reinterprets several science–policy initiatives that have been extensively studied and that have instructive parallels to the science–policy relationship in climate change. These include the protection of stratospheric ozone, the Green Revolution, the International Biological Program, the International Geosphere–Biosphere Program, and environmental models such as general circulation models.

The relationship between natural and social science research on climate was initially conceived as a matter of mutual agenda setting: "Natural scientists help set the research agenda for social scientists by identifying human activities that are major, proximate causes of environmental change. . . . Social scientists help set the research agenda for natural scientists by highlighting environmental changes that would severely affect human welfare" (Young & Stern 1992: 2). This characterization validly represents one part of the social science research program, indeed the dominant part from the standpoint of state support.

However, social scientists also have complex stories to tell about the framing of problems for research, the production and validation of scientific knowledge, and its uptake into policy decisions. In addition, a considerable body of social science research has illuminated the origins of controversy and uncertainty in public policy. Given the prominence of backlash critiques of climate change, this line of work will grow in importance as policymakers confront the challenge of international cooperation on so indeterminate and potentially catastrophic a problem as climate change.

The early framing and funding of climate change research generally overlooked the contribution made by the qualitative social sciences to understanding the processes by which societies recognize new threats to their security or well-being, formulate responses, and collectively act upon them. Yet, knowledge about these issues has accumulated rapidly in the past two decades. A growing body of work—much of it located in social studies of science and technology (hereafter referred to as science and technology studies)—has challenged the notion that allegedly global problems such as climate change exist in a world that can be unproblematically accessed through direct observation

3

SCIENCE AND DECISIONMAKING

of nature. Contemporary science and technology studies suggest instead that environmental issues of global scale (or indeed of *any* scale) emerge from an interplay of scientific discovery and description with other political, economic, and social forces. Persuasive accounts of environmental phenomena are constructed, according to this view, by myriad social interactions, encompassing not only the diverse activities and practices of scientific communities, but also the work of nonscientific actors and institutions in defining problems and endorsing solutions.

Following Kuhn's (1962) seminal work on scientific revolutions, social scientists have questioned traditional assumptions about the relationship of knowledge accumulation to political, and even scientific, progress. This is evident in a challenging of themes commonly grouped together under the label of *modernity* and carrying significant implications for environmental policy: for example, that technological development is the prime marker of progress and enlightenment; that nonscientific belief systems are based on popular ignorance and superstition; that advances in scientific knowledge inevitably reduce uncertainty; and that increased absorption of science leads to convergence in social understanding and public policy. An account of climate change (or any other perceived environmental problem) grounded in contemporary social science research would reject as too linear and reductionist the modernist narrative in which science first finds evidence of new environmental phenomena, and further discoveries and inventions inevitably lead to informed social responses via avenues of prediction, rational choice, and control.

The more interpretive orientation of the social sciences, informed by the humanities, does not take issue with the enterprise of managerial policymaking but insists that the various contingencies inherent in such endeavors be recognized and taken seriously. Social science research has therefore attempted to illuminate the diversity of investigative, argumentative, institutional, and material resources that human beings bring to bear in creating the universal truths of science and applying them to technical problem solving. Work in this genre can be broadly characterized as *interpretive*, because it emphasizes the significance of meanings, texts, and local frames of reference in knowledge creation (Geertz 1973, 1983); *reflective*, because it focuses on the role of human reflection and ideas in building institutions (Keohane 1988, Beck et al. 1994); and *constructivist*, because it examines the practices by which accounts of the natural world are put together and achieve the status of reality (Fleck 1935, Bloor 1976, Latour & Woolgar 1979). For consistency, we use the term *constructivist* throughout the chapter to designate the array of qualitative social science approaches—grounded in such fields as cultural anthropology, sociology, comparative politics, policy studies, and international relations—that shed light on the social and cultural elements involved in producing environmental knowl-

4

SCIENCE AND DECISIONMAKING

edge. Our aim in this is not to understate the role of nature in shaping scientific knowledge but to foster a deeper understanding of how scientific knowledge assumes authority in the public domain.

The shift toward constructivist studies in the social sciences has encouraged a parallel shift in science policy studies toward an increased concern with the dynamics of problem framing and consensus building in the face of widespread uncertainty. This impetus arises from a recognition that problems and solutions in the policy realm are seldom clear-cut: in practice, there are no neat boundaries separating knowledge from ignorance, fact from value, scientific knowledge from other forms of knowledge about the world, and, indeed, policy questions from knowledge-based answers. To question how *science* acquires meaning and stability, by exploring its social commitments, is to question *policy* in the same way. Political institutions and structures, the issues they pose for solution, as well as their techniques of management and control, are all seen as more fluid, and more open to interpretation and manipulation by divergent actors, than was assumed in earlier approaches to policy analysis. At the same time, the institutionalization of social norms and practices into stable patterns of political culture is increasingly seen as influencing the direction of research strategies, the production of knowledge, and the application of knowledge to action.

Constructivist policy analysis recognizes not only that issue framings do not flow deterministically from problems fixed by nature, but also that particular framings of environmental problems build upon specific models of agency, causality, and responsibility. These frames in turn are intellectually constraining in that they delimit the universe of further scientific inquiry, political discourse, and possible policy options. Constructivist policy analysis, therefore, begins with the assumption that questions about how problems are defined and framed must be addressed to have a basis for evaluating the efficacy, merits or legitimacy of competing social policies. Why do some issues come to be expressed as matters of policy concern in particular ways, at particular times, in particular locations, and through the efforts of particular groups or cultures? What makes problem formulations change over time or, alternatively, cohere across different historical periods and political systems? How do issues come to be perceived as natural or technical rather than social, as public rather than private, or as global or universal rather than local? And what roles do science and scientists play in these processes of definition and change?

In the context of climate change, these new directions in policy research point to the centrality of several interlocking questions that remained unasked and virtually unacknowledged in earlier frameworks of analysis:

- *How do scientists and their societies identify and delimit distinct problems related to climate change that are considered amenable to scientific resolution?* What makes problems look mainly scientific or mainly social and political, and

5

SCIENCE AND DECISIONMAKING

in what ways do the institutions and processes of science and politics steer public perceptions on this issue? How are conflicts over alternative framings negotiated and resolved, both domestically and in international arenas?

- *How do scientists come to know particular facts and causal relationships regarding climate change and to persuade others that their knowledge is credible?* In particular, how does scientific knowledge generated in different disciplines, within specialized or localized research communities, and under varying conditions of epistemological and political uncertainty, come to be accepted as authoritative by wider scientific and social constellations? In what ways do scientific accounts of phenomena interact with competing or overlapping beliefs about the way the world works?
- *How do conflicts over risk arise, and how are responses to them handled in a world of conflicting and plural political interests?* With respect to the vigorous backlash on climate change, what procedures and mechanisms can best make room for open debate while also supporting closure around reasonable conclusions and commitments? On a global level, how can productive identification with such processes be secured from far-flung local actors and interests?
- *How do human societies and their designated policy actors draw upon scientific knowledge to justify collective action on a worldwide scale?* For example, how do environmental problems come to be construed as global and universal rather than private, particularistic, local, or national; and how, in turn, do they come to be defined as environmental—and therefore requiring a unique form of collaboration between scientists and policymakers— rather than economic, political, or cultural? How are conflicts about the scale or means of intervention understood, managed or resolved? To what extent is science itself counted upon to address these problems, and what distinctive issues of science policy and politics are raised by such characterizations?

This chapter reviews several bodies of social science literature that shed significant light on the foregoing questions. It begins with a critical examination of the place accorded to scientific knowledge in several current models of public policymaking, all of which view the production and validation of knowledge as largely independent of the use of knowledge in policy decisions. These approaches are contrasted with a theoretical framing of the science–policy linkage that appears more consistent with findings from constructivist studies of science, technology, and the environment. According to this latter view, scientific knowledge and political order are *co-produced* at multiple stages in their joint evolution, from the stabilization of specialized factual findings in laboratories and field studies to the national and international acceptance of

SCIENTIFIC KNOWLEDGE AND PUBLIC POLICY

causal explanations offered by science and their use in decisionmaking.

The central sections of the chapter review the evidence for the model of co-production, grouping it under the following specific topics:

- the production and validation of scientific knowledge and its integration across disciplines
- the standardization of science and technology, their movement outside their original locations of production, and the interplay of technical standardization with ideology and social belief systems
- the formation of closure or agreement around credible, public accounts of scientific phenomena or, alternatively, the deconstruction of such accounts in skeptical environments
- the management of uncertainty in policy processes and the uptake of science into both national and international decisionmaking.

Illustrative materials include, where possible, examples of environmental science, controversy, and policy closure, including the ongoing debates about the reality and implications of climate change (see Seitz et al. 1989, Lindzen 1990, Kellogg 1991, Balling 1992, Michaels 1992, Bailey 1993).

The final sections of the chapter discuss, in the light of theoretical issues raised earlier, the efforts of international science and science policymakers to model the human and physical determinants of climate change. Ambiguities in the design of models are associated with issues about their use in policymaking. The concluding section returns to the conflicts that have emerged in trying to build a policy-relevant consensus on climate change science and briefly outlines the institutional and political implications of bringing about substantial changes in the dynamics of international policymaking.

7

SCIENCE AND DECISIONMAKING

Conclusion

The production and dissemination of scientific knowledge have played a crucially important part in the elevation of climate change to a topic of worldwide interest and political concern. The social science literature on science and public policy helps us to paint a finely textured and critically informed picture of this process of globalization by tracing scientific knowledge from its places of production and validation to its ultimate incorporation into policy. Constructivist approaches in the social sciences illuminate the extent to which our knowledge of the global environment is made by human agency, and not simply given to us by nature. In particular, interpretive analyses of the framing of policy problems, the production of scientific claims, the standardization of science and technology, and the international diffusion of facts and artifacts all focus attention on the co-production of natural and social order. Constructivist accounts provide important resources for explicating the factors that lead to scientific controversy as well as to consensus, as in the case of the American backlash against climate change and ozone science. Thus, they also provide a more textured and useful account of how scientific knowledge becomes (or fails to become) robust in policy contexts.

Work in this genre pinpoints the many locations at which the cognitive and the political domains connect with, support, or (at times) conflict with one another. Accordingly, it has also been instrumental in revealing that technical knowledge deemed suitable for public action is not exclusively a production of the scientific community, with its vigorous, but publicly invisible, forms of self-criticism. Rather, it is a sociotechnical hybrid whose authority depends on active communication and collaboration among multiple cultures or forms of life—including the bureaucratic, scientific, economic and social—each of which possesses its own distinctive resources for producing and validating knowledge.

Research in the social sciences has been especially helpful in explaining two sets of transpositions that are important for understanding the relationship

· CONCLUSION

between scientific knowledge and decisionmaking for the global environment: these are the moves from the particular to the universal in the domain of knowledge, ideas, and beliefs; and from the local to the global in the domain of political action and policy choice. Each move involves an intertwining of cognitive and social elements in ways that are well-illuminated by fine-grained interpretive analysis that would elude the lenses of quantitative survey research or of grand social science theories. But although constructivist studies have tended to stress the local, contingent, and particular aspects of knowledge creation and its use in policy, the wealth of case studies accumulated by researchers performing science and technology studies also reveals certain broad patterns of globalization and internationalization. These approaches provide a basis for addressing as yet inadequately understood questions about the sources and limitations of political authority in a fragmented but globalizing world.

With regard to the transposition of knowledge from the particular to the universal, several themes emerge as particularly significant for policymaking. These include the black boxing of contingency and the constraining of local freedom of action through the development of standard procedures, techniques, and devices; the importance of practices, discourses, and institutions in sustaining standard measures or methods; and the capacity of standardized science and technology to draw together quite heterogeneous cultures of belief. With regard to the transposition from local to global action, themes of particular relevance to the management of climate change include, perhaps foremost, a new emphasis on the importance of ideas and abstractions in building transnational communities. Hardly less important is the observation that the globalization of knowledge requires the production of trust and participation on a hitherto unprecedented scale.

Two of the most salient contributions of this body of work to the policy domain have been to disclose how the social world becomes embedded in the technical at many levels, and vice versa, and to show how the concepts of *good science* or *scientific validity*, with all traces of the social washed out, continually resurface as important resources in the justification of policy. Governmental institutions, such as courts and advisory committees, are everywhere deeply involved in the acts of re-representation that erase the social from the scientific and technical. But social actors, too, display a commitment to the objectivity of science, especially in skeptical, participatory cultures. We have seen that this tendency has potentially deleterious consequences for the credibility of ruling institutions, because it sets up questionable models of public understanding in the minds of experts and, at the same time, separates the methods and goals of scientific inquiry from people's felt needs and from lay systems of acquiring, testing and acting upon knowledge. These kinds of disjunctions were clearly visible in controversies over nuclear power and toxic chemicals, and to a lesser

SCIENCE AND DECISIONMAKING

extent in the Green Revolution and the associated spread of a modern, internationalized agricultural science.

Constructivist social science research has also added depth and richness to the concept of uncertainty, both in science and in its ramifications within society. Uncertainty, like knowledge, is revealed as a deeply cultural product, reflecting such imperatives as the need to maintain particular models of human agency and causation, to safeguard valued social identities and relationships, to legitimate established political formations, and to assert moral sensibilities about the appropriate limits of controlling both human beings and nature. The ability (or inability) to acknowledge cognitive uncertainty—and its particular representation—surrounding issues in a given society is often a function of historical experiences with controlling social risks. The framing and control of environmental hazards, for example, reflects cultural features such as openness, diversity, civic participation, trust, and hierarchical control. Perhaps most significant in the context of climate change is the role played by various scientific institutions in appropriating domains of ignorance to study and control by scientific methods, thereby converting what was unknown into what is only uncertain, and hence in principle knowable. Scientific modeling is the increasingly encompassing vehicle through which the world's technical communities are seeking to bring what was formerly labeled trans-science—questions lying beyond the analytic reach of science—under rational and systematic control.

An overall observation of social science research on modeling is that judgments about what counts as an epistemically valid model incorporate judgments about prevailing institutional structures and policy assumptions. Implicit social commitments and assumptions are embedded within modeling practices and relationships—assumptions, for example, about the appropriate scale and distribution (global or local) of policy and institutions; about human rationality and agency; about appropriate degrees of control over human beings or nature; and about the purposes of knowledge making. These are shared across a hybrid culture of policy and science, and hence are often deployed and reproduced without explication or critical reflection, as if they were natural, that is, contained entirely within the realm of scientifically produced knowledge. Thus, particular forms of social order or culture, and particular forms of epistemic order mutually reinforce, construct, and validate one another at levels deeper than expressed scientific or policy choice.

A final, and in some ways paradoxical, conclusion relates to the potential vulnerability of policymaking institutions charged with responding to climate change. At one level of analysis, contemporary scientific research has been enormously successful in projecting the view that global risks can be deciphered, understood, and managed within the framework of existing institutions or institutional prototypes. In part, the standardizing and globalizing processes

76

of science have been instrumental in promulgating this belief. Thanks to the power of laboratory-generated, depersonalized, and universal science, informal knowledge systems—together with their supporting social and cultural institutions, and even their physical environments—have been reformed in many instances to fit into emerging global systems. The visibility and prestige of institutions such as UNEP and the IPCC testify to the successes of modern science. At another level, however, these very achievements may hold the seeds of their own undermining, as discussed by theorists of modernity (e.g., Habermas 1975, Beck 1992).

By mastering the problem of trans-science, and by casting its net of presumed cognitive and predictive control over ever more complex and dispersed phenomena, the scientific study of climate change threatens to generate expectations that cannot be met and promises that may begin to strike many as illusory. The political backlash against the ozone agreements and against the emerging scientific consensus on global warming in the United States offer a sobering foretaste of this possibility of implosion. Further, the very process of globalization cuts science loose from its moorings in all those localized, historically warranted, social and cultural spaces where trust and credibility have been for so long been produced hand in hand with natural knowledge.

Where will the universal, hegemonic, yet institutionally weakly grounded science of climate change turn for authentic, globally effective legitimation and public authority? The view from the social sciences suggests that the solution lies partly in the patient construction of communities of belief that provide legitimacy through inclusion rather than exclusion, through participation rather than mystification, and through transparency rather than black boxing. The gathering social and cultural challenges posed by these observations are likely to carry intellectual consequences that still remain to be defined. This chapter has offered some important resources for the task.

References

Bailey, R. 1993. *Eco-scam: the false prophets of ecological apocalypse*. New York: St Martin's Press.

Balling, R. 1992. *The heated debate: greenhouse predictions versus climate reality*. San Francisco: Pacific Research Institute for Public Policy.

Beck, U. 1992. *The risk society: towards a new modernity*. London: Sage.

Beck, U., A. Giddens, S. Lash 1994. *Reflexive modernity*. Cambridge: Polity.

Bloor, D. 1976. *Knowledge and social imagery*. Chicago: University of Chicago Press.

Fleck, L. 1935. *Entstehung und Entwicklung einer Wissenschaftlichen Tatsache*. Basel: Benno Schwabe. [Translated by F. Bradley as *Genesis and* development of a scientific fact. Chicago: University of Chicago Press, 1979.]

Geertz, C. 1973. The interpretation of cultures. New York: Basic Books.

—— 1983. Local knowledge. New York: Basic Books.

Gore, A. 1992. Earth in the balance: ecology and the human spirit. Boston: Houghton Mifflin.

Habermas, J. 1975. Legitimation crisis. Boston: Beacon Press.

Kellogg, W. 1991. Response to skeptics of global warming. Bulletin of the American Meteorological Society 74(4), 499–511.

Keohane, R. 1988. International institutions: two approaches. International Studies Quarterly 32, 379–97.

Kuhn, T. 1962. The structure of scientific revolutions. Chicago: University of Chicago Press.

Latour, B. & S. Woolgar 1979. Laboratory life: the construction of scientific facts. Princeton, New Jersey: Princeton University Press.

Lindzen 1990. Some coolness concerning global warming. Bulletin of the American Meteorological Society 71, 288–99.

Mann, D. 1991. Environmental learning in a decentralized world. Journal of International Affairs 44(2), 301–337.

Messner, W., D. Bray, C. C. Germain, N. Stehr 1992. Climate change and social order: knowledge for action? Knowledge and Policy 5(4), 82–100.

Michaels, P. 1992. Sound and fury. Washington DC: Cato Institute.

Seitz, F., R. Jashrow, W. Nierenberg 1989. Scientic perspectives on the greenhouse problem. Washington DC: George C. Marshall Institute.

Skolnikoff, E. 1990. The policy gridlock of global warming. Foreign Policy 79, 77–93.

Young, O. & P. Stern 1992. Human dimensions of global change. Environment 34(7), 2–3.

[17]

Consumption, Environment and Public Policy

Joseph Murphy and Maurie J. Cohen

1. Introduction

During the years since the 1992 Earth Summit in Río de Janeiro consumption has emerged as a significant environmental policy issue. Agenda 21, the conference's framework for sustainable development, devoted an entire chapter to consumption.[1] In it the satisfaction of a seemingly endless stream of consumer desires was identified as a major cause of global environmental problems. With hardly a pause, the newly minted United Nations Commission for Sustainable Development initiated a research programme to examine more rigorously the challenges associated with any attempt to achieve more sustainable consumption. Elsewhere within the networks of environmental high politics the Organisation for Economic Co-operation and Development, the Paris-based association that serves as a diplomatic club for the world's most affluent nations, quickly mustered some of its own resources for a parallel investigation (see for example OECD 1996; OECD 1997; OECD 1998).[2]

With bewildering speed a long list of learned societies, national governments and non-governmental organisations also rushed to articulate positions concerning the environmental effects of contemporary consumption practices. For instance, the Councils of the Royal Society of London and the United States National Academy of Sciences issued a joint statement in 1997 calling for a "better understanding of human consumption and related behaviours and technologies". This unusual collaboration went on to suggest that modifications in consumption practices were needed to assist in "the transition to a sustainable, desirable life for the world's people in the coming century." (IOCU 1993:xx) Some national governments, the most prominent perhaps being the Netherlands, have initiated multi-year research and policy programmes designed to reduce the environmental impacts of consumption in their countries and abroad (Aarts *et al.*, 1995; Noorman and

---

[1] A number of commentators have discussed the highly negotiated and contingent nature of Chapter 4 of Agenda 21, the section of the report explicitly concerned with consumption. Indeed, representatives at the pre-conference sessions encountered great difficulty coming to agreement on both substantive themes and technical details concerning the role of consumption as a contributing factor to global environmental deterioration. Numerous passages in the final document were 'bracketed' meaning that the intent was to revisit these issues in the period following the Earth Summit.

[2] The Copenhagen-based Nordic Council of Ministers is another secondary policymaking institution that has played an important role in advancing sustainable consumption as an agenda item in international deliberations.

Exploring Sustainable Consumption: Environmental Policy and the Social Sciences, Volume 1, pages 3–17.
Copyright © 2001 by Elsevier Science Ltd.
All rights of reproduction in any form reserved.
ISBN: 0-08-043920-9

4 Joseph Murphy and Maurie J. Cohen

Uiterkamp 1993; Spaargaren 1997). Traditionally concerned only with promoting consumer protection and increasing the range of choices available to consumers, advocates such as the International Organisation of Consumer Unions have also begun to press for less environmentally damaging forms of consumption.

Taken as a whole, these developments mark an unmistakable watershed in the understanding of environmental problems for purposes of public policymaking. For the past two centuries, and particularly during the last thirty years, solving environmental problems has been construed as a producer responsibility and consumers have been placed at a distance from the assignment of culpability. Such an allocation of blame has given rise to familiar forms of regulation in the world's wealthiest countries aimed at modifying production techniques and technologies. For instance, policymakers have typically viewed acid deposition in productionist terms, an interpretation that has resulted in legislation requiring operators of large combustion plants to install flue-gas desulphurisation equipment designed to cleanse emission streams. Also present, but much less prominent in this respect, have been proposals to shift electricity production away from coal toward less environmentally damaging fuel sources such as natural gas, wind and solar. Pollution problems generally have been targets for a variety of techno-fix solutions aimed at modifying the means of production. Even the design of more energy-efficient household appliances represents an obligation that has been placed squarely on the shoulders of producers. There has been little serious thought or effort devoted to regulating consumption itself in order to address environmental problems.[3]

Policymakers and consumers have therefore been quick to blame industry for environmental problems. Meanwhile, a growing array of global environmental problems, ranging from climate change to ozone depletion to declining biodiversity, has been blamed by some on high population growth rates in many of the world's poorest countries. Such an interpretation has suggested that if the world is serious about dealing with the environmental crisis, the first imperative is to address the demographic "disaster" in the Third World. Accordingly, international assistance programs, often disregarding the protests of target-country governments, have aggressively sought to disseminate modern forms of family planning to defuse the population "timebomb".

What this discussion suggests is that over the past four or five decades consumers in the richest nations have largely avoided being identified as responsible for the environmentally damaging effects of their consumption practices in part because other targets and explanations have been offered. This distancing has been encouraged by elected officials in the richest countries who have been reluctant to question consumer decision making, aspirations and sovereignty. This approach has been reinforced recently by the neo-liberal

---

[3]The main area where this needs to be qualified is energy. From the 1970s onward there have been some attempts to encourage consumers to use less energy. However, these have not been entirely successful. The US shifted responsibility for demand side management to producers partly because it became clear that government efforts to encourage frugality were the object of derision. Jimmy Carter's famous address to the nation in which he encouraged citizens to turn down the thermostat and put on an extra sweater is still widely remembered as the classic failure to launch a consumption debate, although the environment was not the primary concern. Nevertheless, most European governments have maintained programmes to encourage energy conservation in the home and private car use.

orthodoxy, which asserts that any political interference with consumer autonomy violates rights, and, more practically, is a recipe for economic and electoral disaster. One of the most notable effects of the 1992 Earth Summit has been to begin to call this interpretation into question and to initiate a process in which consumption is now coming to be viewed as a legitimate domain for environmental policymaking.

Despite this new interest in consumption, efforts to create a dialogue on how to link consumption with the environment have often been quite confused due to difficulties faced in pinning down core concepts and drawing boundaries around the discussion. Much of this difficulty stems from the fact that consumption is, on one hand, a very real material activity involving physical units of oil, wood, steel, and so forth. On the other hand, the acquisition of goods is undeniably tightly bound up with cultural practices aimed at achieving numerous social objectives including the production or reproduction of values, a cohesive society and individual identity. Consideration of the environmental impacts of consumption has traditionally privileged the material perspective and this has given rise to familiar moral appeals to consumers cautioning them, for example, to avoid artificial fibres in their clothing, to use public transportation, to purchase energy-efficient refrigerators and to adopt vegetarian diets. It is perhaps no surprise that these campaigns have been relatively unsuccessful in eliciting desired behavioural changes and, even in cases of apparently favourable adjustment people can find it difficult to act in a way that is consistent with what they believe.

To move the debate forward, this book folds into the customary materialistic view of consumption a series of more complex and nuanced perspectives on consumption and the environment drawn from the social sciences. During the past decade several branches of the social sciences — most prominently the disciplines of sociology, anthropology, history and cultural studies — have experienced an explosion of interest in the study of consumption as a set of social and cultural activities (key contributions include Miller 1995; Campbell 1987; Fine and Leopold 1993; Warde 1997). Consumption is seen by scholars working in these fields as a window of critical importance on modern/post-modern societies. Many contend that consumption has replaced production as the pivotal realm of social activity in an increasingly fragmented world. In this world, material objects as symbols serve as essential tools of communication. Curiously though they have been largely silent on matters of ecological impact. We hope that this volume will succeed in integrating the conventional view of consumption as the material throughput of resources (often with pronounced environmental consequences) with an understanding of the political, social and cultural significance of these practices. We believe it is only through such a synthesis that it will be possible to provide a theoretically sound and empirically rigorous basis for environmental policy that aims to move affluent nations toward more sustainable consumption patterns.

2. Boundaries and Definitions in Environment-Consumption Debates

Policy dialogue on sustainable consumption has to date been poorly focused and muddled, largely because of the ambiguous nature of core concepts and the problem of how to draw boundaries around the discussion. Political theorist Thomas Princen has considered the problem of defining consumption in a way that is useful for analysing

6 Joseph Murphy and Maurie J. Cohen

environmental problems and his work provides a useful starting point (Princen 1999). Princen argues that for a variety of reasons the clarity and value of efforts to conceptually link consumption and the environment are often limited. One common problem is defining consumption in a way that is too broad to be useful. Princen contends that a good example of this is the influential perspective advanced by biologist Norman Myers who defines consumption as "human transformations of material and energy" (Myers 1997; see also the accompanying rejoinder by J. Vincent and T. Panayotou). Arguably, such an expansive definition fails to establish consumption as a useful focus for public policy or the social sciences.[4] Associated discussions are condemned to remain hopelessly mired within the poorly defined realm of study that has come to be known as the human dimensions of global environmental change.

In many respects we encounter the opposite problem when we approach consumption from a narrowly disciplinary perspective, overly influenced by the assumptions and prejudices of a particular academic point of view. This dilemma is perhaps most concretely illustrated by the discussions that customarily take place among economists, although they are by no means the only offenders. Economists tend to define consumption simply as the exchange of goods in a market. The risks of adopting such an approach are considerable, mainly because there are plenty of consumption practices that do not involve financial exchange in markets. A gender bias, for example, becomes clear when we recognise that men are commonly the consumers of meals prepared by women. In a conventional domestic setting no money changes hands, though it would if the same service were to be provided in a restaurant. More generally substantial quantities of resources are used around the world outside the formal economy. Another problem is that by emphasising financial exchange economists are inevitably and prematurely drawn toward market-based public policy recommendations.

More generally, as Princen explains, there has been a tendency simply to conflate the emerging interest in consumption with a variety of existing debates. The most obvious ones are critiques of materialism, inequity between North and South, and population growth. Materialism, for example, has been roundly condemned for decades because of its supposedly alienating and ultimately dissatisfying nature (see various contributions in Crocker and Linden 1998.) Such critiques often have religious origins and stem from deep-seated misgivings about the social consequences of self-indulgent and immodest lifestyles. There has been a trend, with the rise of environmental problems, simply to graft the environmental critique of consumption onto critiques of this kind. In the area of the global distribution of wealth and opportunity a similar thing has happened. As Princen (1999, p. 352) says

> If the problem is one of inequity, no analytic advantage is gained by calling
> it consumption. Adding the environment and calling the problem consump-
> tion only muddles the long-standing debates of North and South, haves and

---

[4]Indeed, it is such thinking that has largely been responsible for relegating the study of consumption within the social sciences to a decidedly second class status, one best pursued by individuals with backgrounds in marketing and related disciplines. For a thorough discussion of the stigmatised position of consumption as a focus for serious intellectual inquiry refer to Douglas and Isherwood (1979).

have-nots, rich and poor, powerful and powerless, to include environmental inequities. These problems are real and serious, but, a priori, there is no reason why consumption per se should be identified as the problem.

In many ways the issue of population growth is similar. It is related, but analytically separate, from consumption and there is nothing gained by simply conflating them.

The task that Princen sets himself, therefore, is how to approach consumption in a way that acknowledges its complex character, establishes it as a discrete and useful conceptual category, and, at the same time, links it to the environment. His solution is to endorse a definition that emphasises material impacts. This acknowledges that consumption is a natural act, necessary for organisms to survive. Over-consumption occurs when consumption undermines the life-support system of a species. As he states:

> the human behaviour that intersects with the biophysical realm can be termed *material provisioning*, that is the appropriation of material and energy for survival and reproduction ... In sum, an ecologically grounded definition of consumption takes as a starting point human material provisioning and the draw on ecosystem services (Princen 1999 p. 355–356).

Such a 'using-up-of-resources' approach transcends the common production-consumption dichotomy.

Although this approach certainly satisfies what Princen sets out to achieve — namely the linking of consumption to environmental impacts — it does so at considerable cost, and a solely physical-systems approach offers an inadequate basis for discussions of sustainable consumption for several reasons. First, it has little or no relevance to consumption itself. People do not consider themselves to be 'materially provisioning.' In emphasising the physical dimensions of consumption, its social aspects are lost completely. This way of proceeding is narrowly disciplinary in much the same way as the economists' approach about which Princen is correctly quite critical. Second, Princen ignores the fact that consumption-environment interactions do not occur only at the material level. The environment is also very much a socially constructed aspect of consumption. Princen and others may argue that this aspect of consumption is not important because it does not involve *real* material impacts, but in practice it will. Also, the social construction of consumption-environment linkages is likely to be central to public policy and an exclusively material view of consumption and the environment risks missing an opportunity. Finally, and more serious still for prospects of developing a workable understanding of sustainable consumption, is the fact that a physical-systems approach to consumption does not allow issues of equity to enter easily into the discussion, within or between countries.

For these reasons, operationalising sustainable consumption within the conventional dichotomy of production and consumption seems appropriate. This allows direct engagement with prevailing approaches to public policy (which invariably continue to focus on production). It also enables easy interaction with academic social science where disciplines have historically tended to emphasise production and production-related explanations of society. However, endorsing a loose production-consumption approach is not the same as sanctioning a supply-demand framework that will tend to lead to discussions of exchange in markets and externalities. That said, because production-consumption is not radically removed it is still possible for those with a supply-demand mind-set to engage with such a discussion.

Against this background we can describe the boundaries around the sustainable consumption debate to which the discussion contained in this book will conform. In the context of the traditional production-consumption dichotomy consumption involves people acquiring (often but not necessarily in markets using money) and using objects, services, and places. This is not to deny that institutions are also consumers, however consumption by institutions does not provide the focus for the discussion that follows.[5] The environment enters in at different levels e.g., the physical and the socially constructed. It is the physical impacts of consumption that are of primary concern from a sustainability point of view, either because of their impacts on other people (often distant both geographically and temporally) or simply because of their implications for ecosystem integrity. However, the social construction of the environment is also very significant because, for example, the idea of 'nature' is often mobilised by producers to promote consumption of particular goods.[6] Also, public policy to achieve sustainable consumption may involve constructing environmental concern among consumers as a prerequisite for changes in their acquisition practices. The social dimensions of sustainable consumption involve primarily questions of distribution and equity. Such considerations may raise issues about the distribution of the negative impacts of consumption or the very distribution of opportunities to consume.

3. Consumption and Environment: A 'Levers, Knobs and Dials' View of Public Policy

We make an explicit attempt in this book to think about public policy and practical actions while making use of the informative capabilities of a broad range of the social sciences. To set the scene for the discussion that follows it is useful to describe, and possibly to caricature slightly for purposes of emphasis, existing approaches to consumption and environment problems. When policymakers engage with a problem it is inevitable that their proposals will be heavily influenced by the assumptions they make about what it is that is being manipulated. These assumptions are linked to the type of knowledge being applied. This is particularly the case with respect to consumption-related environmental problems where arguably it is the world-views of economists and technologists that dominate.

---

[5] It can be argued that consumption by institutions is substantially more important from the perspective of limiting environmental impacts than what takes place at the individual and household levels. We do not disagree with this claim, but choose in the current context to focus our attention on non-institutional consumers.

[6] Even so-called eco-friendly forms of consumption require the non-recoverable utilisation of resources and as such lead to some of the same forms of environmental deterioration as more conventional consumption. For an illuminating treatment of this consumerist mode refer to Price (1995).

Policymakers (public or private sector) typically make a variety of judgements about consumers and markets that have their origin in neo-classical economics. It is also common to hear members of the public voice similar opinions, even though their own actions often reveal them to be false. For example, consumers are generally thought to be autonomous and rational. They are autonomous in the sense that their consumption decisions are not influenced by other consumers and rational in the sense that they are egoistic beings interested only in maximising personal welfare. Another important dimension of the economist's perspective that infiltrates conventional thinking involves the market. The market is where consumers express their preferences by demanding goods. A standard assumption about markets is that to work efficiently prices must be correct and information must be readily available.

On the basis of this model a range of consumption-focused environmental policies immediately offer themselves. Many of them seem obvious. If, for example, a market is not functioning properly two explanations seem probable — either information is not conveniently accessible or the prices are not accurate.[7] Such apparent circumstances often produce a variety of proposals aimed at 'internalising the cost of environmental damage', 'removing perverse subsidies' and dealing with the 'information deficit.' We can refer to this as the eco-taxes and the eco-labelling approach to consumption and environment problems and it has attracted considerable support in recent years.[8]

The purpose of this volume is partly to undermine this atomistic and economistic mode of public policymaking in the area of consumption and the environment and to build a richer and more accurate view of consumption. The papers in this book clearly establish, for example, that consumers are in practice profoundly influenced by what other consumers buy. We also establish beyond doubt that consumers are not rational and egoistic welfare maximisers in the way economists customarily suggest. Consumers may be rational in the sense that they act purposefully to achieve particular goals, but their consumption practices are likely to be informed by a diverse range of ethical beliefs and value positions. In the face of these insights the eco-taxes and eco-labelling approach to policymaking is revealed as unhelpfully simplistic.

The second dominant form of knowledge influencing public policy at the nexus between consumption and the environment derives from the design and engineering professions.[9] The technologist's key assumption is that all consumption-related environmental problems

---

[7] There is also a substantial literature on "barriers" that refers to transaction costs, market entry barriers, imperfect competition and these lead to other policy proposals.

[8] Especially in northern Europe, ecological taxation in the form of carbon taxes and roadway charges has received a strong political embrace, although practical application has been less widespread, in part as a means of encouraging a shift away from taxes on labour toward taxes on environmentally harmful activities. A good review of the status of eco-taxation as a tool of environmental policymaking is offered by Tim O'Riordan (1997). Eco-labeling has become a common device and it is regularly used to identify the environmentally significant components and processes of products ranging from timber to tuna. The expectation is that consumers value such information and that it will aid them in purchasing goods that embody higher levels of environmental responsibility.

[9] Of course the design profession is very diverse. The argument here is built on one approach to design, which focuses on technology and materials. Design also has a "soft" side which is more focused on social relationships. Chapter 12 of this volume emerges from the design tradition and shows that not all approaches in that tradition can be criticised along the lines that follow.

10   Joseph Murphy and Maurie J. Cohen

can ultimately be solved through technical inventiveness. This assumption is grounded in a view that sees society as a machine whose purpose is to meet human needs. As such, the key constitutive social relationships involve resource and material flows, energy inputs and outputs. The ultimate goal is to make the system as efficient as possible in its use of resources and energy. Technological innovation is central to this project.[10] The economist simplifies the individual by assuming a limited number of universal characteristics; the technologist loses sight of the individual and society, except as the recipient of final goods and services or as a source of problems to be solved.

The policy proposals that emerge from the technologist's worldview commonly emphasise supply-side initiatives, not surprisingly because it is manufacturers and entrepreneurs who can mobilise the forces of innovation to solve society's problems. At its most limited scale this involves redesigning products to reduce their impact on the environment, particularly in the use phase. Such an approach has, for example, been regularly utilised to increase the fuel efficiency of automobiles. More recently, life-cycle assessment has become a frequently used tool to conduct these kinds of analyses and to aid in the ranking of various alternatives. Occasionally, the technologist may endorse more radical redesigns of products that have the potential to transform society and to ameliorate the environmental impacts of consumption. Tele-working to reduce commuting problems is an instance of this kind of 'outside the box' thinking. Take-back obligations requiring manufacturers to recover their products at the end of their useful lives and various product design and performance standards are policy options linked to this perspective.

While technological innovations, particularly those of a more visionary nature, no doubt have considerable potential to reduce the environmental impact of contemporary lifestyles, a technology-focused approach to sustainable consumption is extremely problematic for a number of reasons.[11] Firstly, underpinning the technological worldview is often an uncritical technological optimism. Arguably this is at least partly responsible for many of the environmental problems that we currently face. Second, in pushing society to the periphery technologists operate with little or no understanding of human agency and commonly fail to consider how people may change their behaviour to avoid realising the designed 'solution.' Finally, this perspective typically gives inadequate thought to the social costs of technology such as second order effects and impacts on marginalised groups.

In practice, therefore, despite their dominant positions in the policymaking process, the economist's and technologist's approaches to sustainable consumption are inadequate. But with these problems in mind it is worth reflecting on why, paradoxically, they are apparently so appealing to policymakers. We can identify a number of factors. First, the division of labour associated with the creation of discrete academic disciplines and perspectives is surely a necessary condition for the emergence of partial perspectives which come to dominate policy making. In the absence of somewhat arbitrary and reductionist boundaries

[10]A celebrated example of this perspective is Julian Simon (1986) *The Ultimate Resource 2*. For an excellent treatment of technocentrism within the history of ideas see Pepper (1996). The more general point being made here is that such thinking is central to essentially all forms of engineering education and practice.

[11]The new fields of industrial ecology and ecological design are largely organised around the reconceptualisation of manufacturing systems and the radical redesign of products (see, for example, von Weizäcker *et al.*, 1997; Zelov and Cousineau 1997).

such incomplete views of consumption (and social affairs more generally) would not be possible (Dickens 1996). Second, because these disciplines grossly understate the complexity of the world they promise relatively easy solutions and are therefore politically attractive if not effective. Third, the economic and technological approaches have much in common with each other and not surprisingly interventions deriving from them often operate in tandem and to some extent dovetail together. Both essentially offer a "levers, knobs and dials" view of the world. In academic circles this perspective might be called instrumentalist and mechanistic, and both are based on an atomistic ontology. Society itself is not really part of the picture at all. Finally, it is also the case that policymaking bodies often have cultures that promote similar perspectives. Bureaucratic organisations tend to employ people with either an economic or a technological worldview and contract research from institutions that are able to use the language and discourse. This does not just mean that alternatives get overlooked because they are outside the line of vision. Analyses of policy networks and discourses suggest that only people able to use the dominant approach will be seen as legitimate contributors to policy discussions (Hajer 1995).

Our aim here is not to disable the prevailing model guiding policymaking and to leave nothing in its place. Most of the contributors to this volume are sympathetic to the claim that contemporary consumption practices are woefully problematic from an environmental standpoint and are in need of modification and that achieving this will require new approaches to policymaking. Our objective in assembling this collection is to offer a more robust and comprehensive way of conceptualising the complex relationship between consumption and the environment and to forge recommendations that are consistent with this interpretation.

In many respects, therefore, this discussion helps to establish the task of this book. Somewhat ambitiously, we seek to draw on a diverse range of the social sciences that have evolved a sophisticated understanding of the relationship between consumption and the environment to outline new approaches to public policy in this area. It is necessary to show that an alternative is possible. At the same time, we should not casually discard the contributions made by economists and technologists. People *are* spurred on to behave in particular ways by concerns for personal welfare and prices do influence consumption practices. The point is that over-reliance on these perspectives leads to a heavily blinkered view. Furthermore, in our quest for acceptable solutions to some extraordinary problems it has become common to interpret this partial picture as constituting the full landscape. In a similar spirit, and to prevent misinterpretations of our intent, it is important to re-emphasise that technology may indeed have a major role to play in addressing a broad range of consumption and the environment problems. However, the role of technological innovation is surely less than is claimed by its most enthusiastic supporters and, if experience is any guide, such ingenuity is likely to throw up any number of unanticipated (and essentially unpredictable) surprises.

References

Aarts, W., Goudsblom, J., Schmidt, K., and Spier, F. (1995), *Toward a Morality of Moderation: A Report for the Dutch National Research Programme on Global Air Pollution and Climate Change*. Amsterdam: Amsterdam School for Social Science Research.

Campbell, C. (1987), *The Romantic Ethic and the Spirit of Modern Consumerism*. Oxford: Blackwell.

Crocker, D., & Linden, T. (eds) (1998), *Ethics of Consumption: The Good Life, Justice and Global Stewardship*. Lanham, MD: Rowman and Littlefield.

Douglas, M., & Isherwood, B. (1979), *The World of Goods: Towards an Anthropology of Consumption*. London: Routledge.

Dickens, P. (1996), *Reconstructing Nature: Alienation, Emancipation and the Division of Labour*. London: Routledge.

Fine, B., & Leopold, E. (1993), *The World of Consumption*. London: Routledge.

Hajer, M. (1995), *The Politics of Environmental Discourse*. Oxford: Oxford University Press.

IOCU (International Organisation of Consumers' Unions). (1993), *Beyond the Year 2000: The Transition to Sustainable Consumption: A Policy Document on Environmental Issues*. The Hague: IOCU.

Miller, D. (ed.). (1995), *Acknowledging Consumption: A Review of New Studies*. London: Routledge.

Myers, N. (1997), "Consumption: Challenge to sustainable development . . . or distraction?" *Science 276*, 53–57.

Noorman, K. J., & Uiterkamp, T. (ed.). (1998), *Green Households: Domestic Consumers, Environment and Sustainability*. London: Earthscan.

OECD (Organisation for Economic Cooperation and Development). (1996). *Sustainable Consumption and Production*. Paris: OECD.

OECD (Organisation for Economic Cooperation and Development). (1997). *Sustainable Consumption and Production: Clarifying the Concepts*. Paris: OECD.

OECD (Organisation for Economic Cooperation and Development). (1998). *Towards Sustainable Consumption Patterns: A Progress Report on Member Country Initiatives*. Paris: OECD.

O'Riordan, T. (ed.). (1997), *Eco-Taxation*. London: Earthscan.

Pepper, D. (1996), Modern Environmentalism. London: Routledge.

Price, J. (1995), " Looking for nature at the mall: A field guide to the nature company." In W. Cronan (ed.) *Uncommon Ground: Rethinking the Human Place in Nature* (pp. 186–203). New York: W. W. Norton.

Princen, P. (1999), "Consumption and Environment: Some conceptual issues." *Ecological Economics 31*, 347–363.

Simon, J. (1986), *The Ultimate Resource 2*. Princeton: Princeton University Press.

Spaargaren, G. (1997), *The Ecological Modernization of Production and Consumption: Essays in Environmental Sociology*. Wageningen: Thesis Landbouw.

von Weizäcker, E., Lovins, A., & Lovins, H. (1997), *Factor Four: Doubling Wealth, Halving Resourse Use*. London: Earthscan.

Warde, A. (1997), *Consumption, Food, and Taste*. London: Sage.

Zelov, C., & Cousineau, P. (1997), *Design Outlaws on the Ecological Frontier*. Brooklyn, NY: Knossus Publishing.

Part IV
Globalisation, the State and Environmental Governance

[18]

Globalization and Sustainability

Symbols are the more powerful the more meanings they are able to admit. They actually live on ambivalence. The Cross, for instance, counted both as a token of victory for conquerors and as a token of hope for the vanquished. That ambivalence raised it above the fray; a single clear message would have meant that it divided rather than united. The same may be said of the image of the blue planet, now a symbol unchallenged by either Left or Right, conservative or liberal. Whatever their differences, they are all fond of adorning themselves with this symbol of our epoch. To fall in with it is to announce that one is abreast of the times, in tune with the world, focused on the future, truly prepared to set off into the new century. In this picture are condensed the opposing ambitions of our age. It is hoisted like a flag by troops from enemy camps, and its prominence results from this plurality of meaning. The photograph of the globe contains the contradictions of globalization. That is why it could become an all-weather icon.

No sooner had it become available, in the late 1960s, than the international environmental movement recognized itself in it. For nothing stands out from the picture as clearly as the round margin that sets it off from the dark cosmos. Clouds, oceans and land masses gleam in the wan light; the earth appears to the observer as a cosy island in a universe unfriendly to life, holding all the continents, seas and living species. For the environmental movement the picture's message was plain: it revealed the earth in its finitude. That circular object made it obvious that the ecological costs of industrial progress could not be shifted forever to Noplace, that they were slowly building up into a threat to all within a closed system. In the end, the externalization of costs belonged to the realm of the impossible. In a finite world, where everyone was affected by everyone else, there was an urgent need for

129

130   *In the Image of the Planet*

mutual care and attention, for more thought about the consequences of one's actions. Such was the holistic message – and, certainly, it was not without some effect. Since the days when a few minorities launched their appeal so full of foreboding, the image of the planet as a closed system has steadily gained currency and even recognition in international law. The conventions on ozone, world climate and biodiversity prove that the perception of the earth's bio-physical limits has attained the supreme political consecration.

For some time, however, ecologists have no longer had a monopoly on the image. At various airports, in the endless passageways between check-in and exit, a well-lit publicity board has been visible in recent years that strikingly expresses a different view of globalization. It shows the blue planet pushing itself on the observer from its blue–black background, with a laconic text: 'MasterCard. The World in Your Hands.' The hurrying passengers are being told that, wherever they fly in this big wide world, they can count on the services of their cards and slot themselves into a global credit and debit network. The credit-card empire stretches out across all frontiers, with purchasing power in any location and accounting in real time, and its electronic money transfers ensure that the traveller is always provided for. In these and numerous other variations, the image of the planet has turned since the 1980s into an emblem of transnational business; hardly any company in telecommunications or tourism – not to speak of the news industry – seems able to manage without it.

This has been possible because the picture also contains quite a different message. In its detachment from the pitch-black cosmos, the terrestrial sphere stands out as a unified area whose continuous physical reality causes the frontiers between nations and polities to disappear – hence the visual message that what counts is the boundaries of the earth. Only oceans, continents and islands can be seen, with no trace of nations, cultures or states.

In the picture of the globe, distances are measured exclusively in geographical units of miles or kilometres, not in social units of closeness and foreignness. The satellite photographss generally look like renaturalized maps, seeming to confirm the old cartographical postulate that places are nothing more than intersections of two lines – the lines of longitude and latitude. In marked contrast to the globes of the nineteenth century, which sharply delineate political frontiers and often use different colours for different territories, any social reality is here dissipated into morphology. The earth is depicted as a homogeneous area offering no resistance to transit – or only resistance caused by geographical features, not to human communities and their laws, customs or purposes. Every point of the hemisphere turned towards the observer can be seen at the same moment, and this simultaneous access of the human gaze suggests the idea of unobstructed access on the ground too. The image of the planet offers the world up for unrestricted movement, promises access in every direction, and seems to present no obstacle to expansionism other than the limits of the globe itself. Open, continuous and controllable – there is an imperial message too in the photographs of the earth.

The image symbolizes limitation in the physical sense and expansion in the political sense. Little wonder, then, that it can serve as a banner for both environmental groups and transnational corporations. It has become the symbol of our times across all the rival world views, because it brings to life both sides of the basic conflict that runs through our epoch. On the one hand, the ecological limits of the earth stand out more clearly than ever before; on the other hand, the dynamic of economic globalization pushes for the removal of all boundaries associated with political and cultural space (Altvater and Mahnkopf 1996). The two narratives of globalization – limitation and expansion – have acquired a clearer form over the past three decades and fight it out in both the arena of theory and the arena of politics. The outcome of this struggle will decide the shape of the new century.

The Rise of the Transnational Economy

Since the mid-1970s, when the Bretton Woods system of fixed exchange rates gave way to floating parities determined by the market, the world economy has witnessed the collapse of boundaries in a process that started slowly but has gradually speeded up. Of course, the quest for raw materials and markets had for centuries been impelling capitalist companies beyond their national frontiers, but only in the last few decades has an international order been created that works pro-grammatically towards a transnational economy with open borders. Whereas all the first eight GATT rounds since the war dismantled more and more tariff obstacles to the exchange of goods, in line with the traditional ideal of free trade, the last of these, the Uruguay Round, and the newly constructed World Trade Organization have laid the legal foundations for politically unregulated movement of goods, services, money capital and investment right across the globe. The Uruguay Round, concluded in 1993, drew more widely the circle of freely tradeable commodities and also deregulated 'software products' such as planning contracts, copyrights, patents and insurance. Controls on the movement of capital, allowing easier inward and outward financial flows, have been progressively removed over the past 20 years, first in the USA and Germany, then in the mid-1980s in Japan, and finally in the countries of the South. In order to make foreign investors feel more at home everywhere, the WTO (and the OECD with its provisionally stalled multilateral investment agreement) have imposed on each state an obligation to accord at least the same rights to foreign as to domestic investors.

A Utopian energy is at work in all these initiatives. This can be seen in the ever more frequently declared intention to create a 'level playing field', a global arena for economic competition in which only efficiency counts, unfettered and undistorted by any special local traditions or structures. All economic players are supposed to have the right – at any place and any time – to offer, produce and acquire whatever they want. Up to now, this free play of the market has been hindered by the dizzying diversity of the world's social and legal orders, which have grown out of each country's history and social structure. The aim now, therefore, is to wrench economic activities from their embeddedness in local or national conditions and to bring them under the same rules (if any) everywhere in the world. There should be no blocking, weakening or interfering with market forces, because that leads to efficiency losses and suboptimal welfare.

This Utopian model of economic globalization also features the earth as a homogeneous area, to be crossed at will by circulating goods and capital. Only supply and demand, and in no case political priorities, are supposed to speed up or slow down these flows and to point them in the right direction. The world is conceived as a single huge marketplace, where factors of production are bought at their cheapest ('global sourcing') and commodities are sold at their highest obtainable price ('global marketing'). Just as in satellite pictures of the planet, no role is played by states and their particular laws; places where people live are foreshortened to mere locations of economic activity. And yet, to the continual annoyance of the neo-liberal heaven-stormers, societies everywhere prove sluggish and resistant. The globalizers thus have the onerous task of adapting base reality to ideal model; their mission is tirelessly to overcome obstacles to the free flow of commodities and thus to make the world comprehensively accessible. That is precisely the programme of the WTO's multilateral economic regime.

In the last few decades, of course, a material infrastructure has also been created for transnational integration. Without the global network of telephone lines, glass fibre cables, microwave channels, relay stations and communications satellites, there would be no open-border world – or at least not as a routine part of everyday life. For electronic data

Globalization and Sustainability   133

flows – which can be converted into commands and information, sounds and images – eat up kilometres at the press of a key or the click of a mouse. Geographical distance ceases to be of any significance, and since the costs of the transfer and processing of data have dramatically fallen, worldwide interaction has become the daily bread of globally oriented middle classes. Thus, electronic impulses translate what the external view of the planet already suggested: the unity of space and time for any action in the world. In principle, all events can now be brought into relation with one another in real time for all parts of the earth. Whereas the picture of the globe conveyed the absence of boundaries as a visual experience, electronic networking converts it into a communications (and air transport into a travel) experience. The constant high-volume, lightning-fast flow of bits of information around the globe achieves the abolition of distance as well as the compression of time; electronic space produces a spatio-temporally compact globe (Altvater and Mahnkopf 1996).

The information highways may be compared to the railways: the digital network is to the rise of a global economy what the railway network was in the nineteenth century to the rise of a national economy (Lash and Urry 1994). Just as the railway infrastructure became the backbone of the national economy (because falling transport costs enabled regional markets to fuse into a national market), so the digital infrastructure is the backbone of the global economy, because falling transmission costs enable national markets to fuse into a global market. Distance is not, of course, truncated in the same way everywhere in the world. This results in a new hierarchy of space: the 'global cities' stand at the top of the pyramid, closely bound together across frontiers by high-speed air and land links and by glass fibre cables, while at the bottom whole regions or even continents – Africa or Central Asia, for example – constitute 'black holes' in the informational universe (Castells 1998: 162), not connected to one another in any significant degree.

On closer examination, then, the networks of transnational interaction rarely assume configurations that stretch across the whole planet; they are not global but transnational, because they bind together only shifting segments of the earth. They are deterritorialized rather than globalized. Unlike earlier types of internationalization, this is particularly the case for the characteristic economic forms of the global age – geographically extended chains of value creation and global finance markets. Basing themselves upon an infrastructure of electronic and physical traffic, companies are now in a position to split up their value-creation process and locate individual parts in areas of the world with the most advantageous wage, skill or market environment. Thus, for a product taken at random, the early stages may take place in Russia, the further processing in Malaysia, the marketing in Hong Kong, the research in Switzerland, and the design in England. Instead of the traditional factory where products were largely manufactured from beginning to end, a network of partial locations makes it possible for previously unheard-of efficiency gains to be achieved. The textbook case of collapsing frontiers, however, is provided by the operations of finance markets. Shares, loans and currency stocks have long left 'paper' behind and become digitalized; their owners can be switched at the press of a key, quite regardless of borders or geographical distance. Nor is it an accident that the most extensively globalized market is the one that deals in the least physical of all commodities: money. Dependent only on an electronic impulse, it can move angel-like in real time anywhere within a homogeneous space. It seems as if the narrative of collapsing frontiers can best be translated into reality when it takes place within the incorporeality of cyberspace.

How Economic Globalization Reduces the Use of Resources

For the protagonists of economic globalization, there is no greater thorn in the side than closed economic areas. Import restrictions and export regulations, product standards and social legislation, investment guidance and laws on the sharing of profits – in short, political provisions of any kind that establish a difference between one country's economic system and those of others – are perceived by the globalizers as so many obstacles to the free movement of the factors of production. They therefore seek to undermine, and gradually to break up altogether, the state-defined 'containers' of national markets, and to replace them with a transnational arena where economic actors are no longer prevented by special rules and regulations from carrying through the dynamic of competition. The multinational economic regimes – whether geared continentally to ASEAN, NAFTA or the EU, or globally to GATT and the WTO – come down to the construction of homogeneous competitive areas stretching across nations.

The promise held out in these initiatives is one of a world that gets the utmost out of its limited means. A way has to be found of satisfying more and more people around the world, with more and more claims, and it is from this challenge that the friends of globalization derive their task – indeed, their mission – to subject the world's economic apparatuses to a course of efficiency-raising treatment. For the point of market liberalization is to ensure, through the selective power of competition, that capital, labour, intelligence and even natural resources are everywhere deployed in the most efficient manner. Only such treatment continually renewed, argue the globalizers, can lay the basis for the wealth of nations. True, companies do not act out of lofty motives but simply take advantage of opportunities for profits and competitive triumphs; nevertheless, the 'invisible hand' of the market is expected in the end to produce greater prosperity for all, even at a world level. A dynamic must therefore be set in train that exposes every protected zone of low productivity to the bracing wind of international competition.

The main targets for such a strategy are the state-run economic complexes in the former Soviet Union and in many countries of the South. In fact, external protectionism and internal sclerosis often go hand in hand, for parasitical structures arise most easily where power elites can use their possession of the state to appropriate a country's wealth. Insulated from competition, whether internal or external, the power elite can get away with deploying capital and other resources in short-term operations that produce a maximum surplus – a considerable part of which is then stashed away in foreign bank accounts. Along with the state monopoly of economic activity, the pressure on workers and the underprovision of consumers, it is especially the frenzied exploitation of natural resources that here rakes in a quick profit. Growth soon becomes synonymous with expanded extraction from nature: oil in the Soviet Union, Nigeria or Mexico, coal in India and China, wood in the Ivory Coast and Indonesia, minerals in Zaire. Of course, it was no accident that the use of resources in the former communist countries was much higher than in the West, for natural treasures were seen as a cost-free (because state-owned) means of fuelling industrial development – especially as growth pressures were directed to extensive rather than intensive ways of increasing production. The opening up of bureaucratically ossified economies to competition was thus to the benefit of resource efficiency. Almost as soon as the wall of restrictions and subsidies crumbled, new suppliers from outside appeared on the scene and placed the old wasteful economy in question. Globalization razes strongholds of mismanagement to the ground, and in such cases cuts down on the use of natural resources by enforcing at least economic rationality.

This efficiency effect does not operate only through expanded entry to the market. Trade and investment also increase access to technologies that, in comparison with domestic ones, often bring considerable gains in efficiency. This applies in particular to such sectors as mining, energy, transport and industry. Examples range from the export of more

economical cars from Japan to the United States, through the introduction of new power station technology in Pakistan, to the savings in
material and energy that came with new blast-furnaces in the Brazilian
steel industry. There is strong evidence that more open national economies deploy more resource-efficient technologies at an earlier date,
simply because they have better access to the most modern – which
usually means more efficient – technological investment. Moreover,
transnational corporations tend to standardize technologies between
countries at a more advanced level, rather than expose themselves to all
kinds of coordination costs. The connection is by no means necessary,
of course, but it is probable – and it may be said that more flexible
investment rules generally favour entry to a higher technological trajectory (Johnstone 1997). The efficiency effect of more open markets is
visible not only in supply-side technology transfers but also on the
demand side: commodity exports from the fast-developing countries to
the post-industrial regions of the North have to stand the test of
consumer preferences in the North, and since the market demand there
often displays greater environmental awareness, production structures
in the exporting country may have to adapt to those standards.

The justification for economic globalization, then, is supposed to be
that it establishes an empire of economic efficiency, and that this effect
often extends to the use of energy and raw materials (OECD 1998).
This is understood as a growth in micro-economic rationality, as a
striving to deploy the factors of production in an optimal manner
everywhere. Of course, the promoters of globalization have to play
down the fact that this can equally well go together with a decline in
macro-rationality as regards both political–social relations and the environment. For market rationalization may lower the use of particular
resources – that is, input per unit of output – but the total use of
resources will nevertheless grow if the volume of economic activity
expands. Growth effects may all too easily eat up efficiency effects. In
fact, so far in the history of industrial society, efficiency gains have quite
consistently been converted into new opportunities for expansion. This,
from an ecological point of view, is the Achilles' heel of globalization.

How Economic Globalization Expands and Accelerates the Use of Resources

In recent years globalization has been hailed, often with the full red-
carpet treatment, as opening a new era for humanity. Yet its goals are
surprisingly conventional: it serves on its own admission to spur world
economic growth, and it involves – under changed historical conditions

Globalization and Sustainability   137

– such long-standing strategies as intensive development and growth through expansion. On the one hand, there is the shifting distribution of the value-creation chain across far-flung regions of the world, which enables companies – in their choice of the best location for each stage of production – to enjoy to the full rationalization benefits that were simply not available before. The advancing digitalization of economic processes has also created new scope for productivity gains – for example, through flexible automation in manufacturing, simulation techniques in research, or perfectly timed logistics in networks of cooperation. With the restructuring of large parts of the world economy, it has thus become possible to wring further growth from long drawn-out productivity competition in OECD markets that were largely saturated at the end of the 1970s. On the other hand, growth has occurred through expansion – and, in particular, through the quest for new markets abroad. Many companies that might not have been able to make much further progress on local markets decided instead to tap demand in other OECD and fast-developing countries. The combined result of these two strategies may be seen in the fact that the world economy is well on its way to doubling between 1975 and the year 2000. Even if all GNP growth does not involve a parallel rise in the flow of resources, there can be no doubt that the biosphere is under ever greater pressure from the anthroposphere.

Direct foreign investment and the expansion effect   The Utopian horizon of globalization is a permeable borderless world in which goods and capital can move around freely. Whereas the various GATT agreements expanded the exchange of goods over a period of decades, the further elimination of national barriers has in the last 15 years mainly affected the mobility of private capital. Between 1980 and 1996 the cross-border exchange of goods increased by an annual average of 4.7 per cent, but foreign investment rose by 8.8 per cent per annum, international bank loans by 10 per cent, and the trade in currency and shares by 25 per cent (*Economist* 1997a). If one looks at the geographical distribution of these flows it becomes clear that, although the lion's share of the capital traffic remains as before within the USA–EU–Japan triad, transfers of private capital have sky-rocketed mainly in the ten 'emerging markets' of East Asia and South America. They rose from an annual $44 billion at the beginning of the 1990s to $244 billion in 1996, before settling down at some $170 billion after the 1997 financial crisis in Asia (French 1998: 7). An important sub-category – accounting for one-half in the case of manufacturing, more than one-third in services, and 20 per cent in the primary sector – has been foreign investment to buy up existing firms or to found new ones. For the investing company, the point of this has been to control the further extraction of natural resources, to erect a platform within a transnational chain of production, or to gain access to export markets. For the host state, on the other hand, the aim has been to draw in investment capital and know-how, as part of a fervent desire to take off economically and to catch up with the rich countries at some point in the future.

With the migration of investment capital from the OECD countries, the fossil model of development has spread to the newly industrializing countries and even well beyond them. Whether it is a question of factories in China, chemical plants in Mexico or industrial agriculture in the Philippines, the countries of the South are entering on a broad front the resource-intensive fossil stage of economic development. That fateful style of economics that consolidated itself in Europe in the late nineteenth century, resting to a large degree upon the transformation of unpaid natural values into commodity values, is now expanding to more parts of the world in the wake of foreign investment. Certainly, a good part of this development is also being driven by locally accumulated capital, but the gigantic influx of foreign investment has deepened and accelerated the spread of – environmentally speaking – robber economies. Everywhere prevails an industrial–social mimetism, a copying of modes of production and consumption that, in view of the crisis of nature, may already be regarded as obsolete. For in the conventional path of development, monetary growth always goes together with material growth; a certain uncoupling of the two appears only in the transition to a post-industrial economy. The favoured targets for investment are thus precisely raw materials extraction or energy and transport infrastructure, which all push the use of natural resources up and up. Even if input per unit of output is lower than at a corresponding stage in the development of the rich countries, the absolute volume of the flow of resources has been increasing prodigiously.

The removal of national obstacles to investment activity stands in an increasingly tense relationship with the earth's bio-physical limitations. Thus the fast-industrializing countries recorded a steep rise in their CO_2 emissions (varying between 20 and 40 per cent in the 1990–95 period), while the industrialized countries – at a higher level, of course – increased theirs only slightly (Brown et al. 1998: 58). All in all, fossil fuel use will double in China and East Asia between 1990 and 2005, to reach a volume almost comparable to that of the United States (WRI 1998: 121). The motor car may serve as a symbol in this respect. In South Korea (before the crisis broke), car ownership was expanding by 20 per cent a year (Carley and Spapens 1998: 35). On the

Globalization and Sustainability   139

streets of India, virtually the only car to be seen in 1980 was the venerable old Ambassador limousine – a real petrol-guzzler, of course, but limited in numbers and therefore discharging far less gas than the huge fleet of more efficient vehicles turned out by the nine automobile corporations now operating there. Thus, in countries where transport has until now been mainly a question of bicycles and public services, further development of their eco-friendly systems will be blocked and replaced by a structure dependent upon high fuel use. It is altogether consistent with the logic of fossil expansion that the World Bank, for all its lip-service to 'sustainable development', allocates two-thirds of its expenditure in the energy sector to the mobilization of fossil energy sources (Wysham 1997).

Another symbol of a lifestyle widely regarded as modern, the Big Mac, may serve to illustrate the mounting pressure on biological resources. In little more than five years between 1990 and 1996, the number of McDonald's restaurants in Asia and Latin America quadrupled (UNDP 1998: 56), against a background of tripled meat consumption over the past 25 years. Such trends mean more and more water, cereals and grazing land for cattle, so it is hardly surprising that, in the 1980s alone, the countries of South-East and South Asia lost between 10 per cent and 30 per cent of their forests (Brown et al. 1998). The forest fires in Indonesia, whose dense clouds of smoke covered half of South-East Asia in 1997–98, originated in massive slash-and-burn clearances and were widely interpreted as a warning of the destructive power of the Asian economic miracle.

Deregulation and the competitive effect The creation of a global competitive arena requires efforts not only a quantitative expansion but also a qualitative restructuring. Alongside the geographical extension of the transnational economy, its internal reordering has also appeared on the agenda of the day, for new rules of economic competition are indispensable if there is to be a homogeneous space no longer riven by national economic idiosyncrasies. There is no other way for would-be globalizers than to dismantle the national regulatory apparatuses that have previously encompassed economic activity. These apparatuses, which generally reflect a country's historical experiences, social sets of interests and political ideals, combine the logic of economics with other social priorities, in both fragile compromises and institutions built to last. At a later stage of the secular process that Karl Polanyi called 'disembedding', the dynamic of economic globalization is intended to release market relations from the web of national norms and standards and to bring them under the law of worldwide competition.

140 *In the Image of the Planet*

Whatever these norms cover – labour conditions, regional planning or environmental policy – they are neither wrong nor right but are seen as obstructing entry into the global competitive arena. In this view of things, norms might be acceptable at a global level – although the question does not really apply, of course, in the absence of a political authority. Deregulation is thus a catch-all term for attempts to further global competition by dissolving the links between economic actors and a particular place or a particular community.

Like any regulation of economic activity in the name of the public interest, protection of the environment is also coming under pressure in many countries. As the number of economic actors on the global market continues to grow, so too does the competition between them – which is why governments everywhere tend to attach a higher value to competitive strength than to protection of the environment or of natural resources. New ecological norms, often imposed by democratic public opinion after years of struggle and controversy, are perceived by companies as a hindrance to competition and in many cases fiercely resisted. As competitive interests gain the upper hand over protective interests, it becomes many times more difficult to halt deforestation in Canada or overmining in the Philippines, to stop the building of more motorways in Germany, to introduce eco-taxes in the European Union, or to maintain ecological product standards in Sweden. However, although governments are often enough determined to make their country a more attractive site for footloose capital, it is doubtless an exaggeration to speak of a 'race to the bottom' in matters concerning environmental standards (Esty and Gerardin 1998). Sometimes the protective interests are too strong, or it may be that environmental factors are not all that significant in a siting decision. It would be more accurate to say that environmental regulation has tended to get 'stuck in the mud' as a result of increased competition (Zarsky 1997). True, world market integration has brought a certain convergence among national regulatory systems, but this has been happening too slowly and at too low a level. In many countries, the process of economic global-ization has blocked any real progress in national environmental policy.

Not surprisingly, the ambition to standardize competitive conditions throughout the world – especially in the case of cross-border trade – clashes with the right of individual countries to shape economic pro-cesses. Now that tariff barriers for industrial goods have been largely dismantled through the successive GATT rounds, should environmental reasons be allowed to put certain categories of import at a disadvant-age? This question has been much disputed ever since the Uruguay Round, and it continues to give rise to controversy within the WTO and

Globalization and Sustainability   141

OECD over deregulation and protection interests. Under the trade rules currently in force, individual states are entitled to lay down environmental and health standards, so long as the same kinds of goods are subject to the same regulation regardless of whether they are imported or locally produced. Of course, this applies only to the composition of a product: a government might decide, for instance, to slap a special tax on all cars above a certain power threshold. Here, it seems, the principle of national sovereignty contradicts only the principle of the unregulated circulation of goods. What is forbidden in international trade, however, is to discriminate against goods whose production process does not conform to certain environmental standards. Which chemicals are used to produce an item of clothing, whether wooden products come from forest clearance areas, whether genetic engineering methods have been used to produce a plant – on none of these questions is a government allowed by WTO rules to express a collective preference. Thus, in the well-known tuna affair, the ban on dolphin fishing could not be maintained under NAFTA rules, and one of the present disputes between the USA and the EU is over whether governments have the right to keep hormone-intensive beef out of their markets. Moreover, since local production standards are also put under strain when importers are able to gain a competitive advantage by externalizing environmental costs, individual states lose the power to insist that production processes in their own country should be environmentally sustainable. The deregulation interest nullifies the protection interest. Through the competitive effect of free trade, even gentle course corrections towards a sustainable economy are soon brought to a standstill.

All the deregulation efforts are also meant to cleanse the economy of extraneous influences, thereby ensuring optimal deployment of the factors of production. Consumers are ostensibly the main ones to benefit, since deregulated operations encourage a more varied supply through easier market entry as well as lower prices through greater competition. Nevertheless, a regime of ruthless efficiency in environmentally significant sectors may lead to greater overall use of resources. If the price of heating oil, petrol, coal or water falls, then normally demand for them will rise and it will be even less worth introducing conservation technologies. Deregulation of the electricity market in the OECD countries, for example, certainly helped promoters of energy-efficient power stations to enter the market, but it also showed that lower prices may hinder a changeover to cleaner energy sources such as natural gas and, more important still, actually encourage higher electricity consumption (Jones and Youngman 1997). Anyway, it is fairly easy to see that falling prices within a price system that does not accurately reflect environmental costs will accelerate the quarrying of resources. So long as prices do not tell the ecological truth, de-regulation will only take the market further down the ecologically slippery slope – and it is not exactly rational to keep running more efficiently in the wrong direction. But the purer competition becomes as a result of deregulation, the less will ecological rationality be able to assert itself against economic rationality. Under the given price system, global competition will deepen the crisis of nature (Daly 1996).

Currency crises and the sell-out effect Nowhere has a global competitive space been raised so clear of national boundaries as in the case of the finance markets. Goods take time to be carried from one place to another, foreign investment requires factories to be built or dis-mantled, and even services such as insurance cannot be traded overseas without a network of branches and representatives. Only financial transfers in the form of shares, loans or currencies are scarcely subject any longer to restrictions of time and space. Every day, billions of dollars change hands online in virtual space through mere touches on VDU keyboards, irrespective of physical distance. Only on these electronic markets does capital finally attain its secret ideal of completely unfettered mobility. For the money markets have very largely shaken off the inertia not only of temporal duration and geographical distance, but also of material goods; less than 2 per cent of the currency trade is now covered by actual commodity flows (Zukunftskommission 1998: 73). This virtual economy has been made possible technologically by electronic networking, and politically by the deregulation of inter-national capital traffic in the industrialized countries in the 1970s and 1980s, as well as in major developing countries in the 1990s.

As we have seen, it was the collapse of the Bretton Woods system in 1971 that gave the impetus to this development. Currencies could become commodities, their price set by the laws of supply and demand on the capital markets. But the value of a currency is a matter of fateful significance for a country: it determines the purchasing power of the national economy in relation to other national economies around the world. In fact, the ups and downs of freely convertible currencies reflect the expectations of future growth and competitiveness that investors entertain about the respective economies. In a way, a country's whole economy thus becomes a commodity, whose relative value crystallizes through the return envisaged by investment fund managers. This gives the finance markets great power *vis-à-vis* economically weak countries, so great that fluctuations in the exchange rate can decide the fate of whole nations. Governments, whether democratic or authoritarian, often find themselves compelled to gear their economic, social and fiscal policies to the interests of investors, with the result that the interest of their own people in social and economic security all too easily goes by the board. It is as if investors cast a daily ballot by transferring huge sums of money from one country to another (Sassen 1996); the global electorate of investors lines up, as it were, against a country's local electorate, and not infrequently the government allies itself with the investors against its own electors. At the same time, however, the currency crashes in Mexico in late 1994, in several East Asian countries in 1997, and in Russian and Brazil in 1998 made it plain that investors are as jumpy as a herd of wild horses that stampedes off now in one direction, now in another as danger threatens. The collective optimism with which investors forget about risks during an upturn is matched by the collective panic with which they flee out of loans and currencies during a downturn. Investment-seeking capital storms into countries and back out again. On its way in, it gives rise to false dreams; on its way out, it leaves behind ruined human lives and ravaged ecosystems (Cavanagh 1998).

Currency crises are quite likely to threaten nature in the affected countries, for those that are rich in exportable natural resources come under intense pressure to exploit them more extensively and at a faster tempo. The falling value of the currency means that they have to throw larger quantities onto the world market in order to stop their export earnings falling through the floor. An exchange-rate crisis thus intensifies the already chronic hunger of indebted states for foreign currency, so that they will be able to repay loans and to import at least the minimum of food, goods and capital. But often the only option left is to use freely available nature as a currency-earner – as one can see from the current boom in the export of oil, gas, metals, wood, animal feed and agricultural produce from countries in the South hit by the financial crisis. Fishing rights are being sold by Senegal, for example, to fleets of vessels from Asia, Canada and Europe; tree-felling rights by Chile to US timber corporations; and exploration rights by Nigeria to the oil multinationals (French 1998: 23). In times of need, desperate countries have to flog off even their 'family silver'. So it is that valuable forest land is sold off stretch by stretch under the pressure of the debt burden. Mexico, for instance, after the peso collapse of 1994, rescinded its laws protecting national forests – and the people living in them – in order to promote a stronger export orientation. Brazil launched an action plan to make the export of wood, minerals and energy financially more attractive through massive infrastructural investment in Amazonia. Indonesia, after another currency crash, was compelled in talks with the International Monetary Fund to change its land ownership legislation so that foreign cellulose and paper corporations could move in on the forest (Menotti 1998b). One might even, as Menotti acerbically suggests, speak of a causal link between falling currencies and falling trees.

Measures to rectify the economy after a currency and debt crisis – measures imposed under the often blackmailing care of the IMF structural adjustment programmes – also usually lead to forced selling of natural assets on the world market, for the aim of the numerous structural adjustment programmes in both the South and the East is to bring the balance of payments back into equilibrium through an increase in exports, and thus to entice investors back into the country. A glance at the history of these programmes shows, however, that – alongside the weaker sections of society – the environment is supposed to make all the sacrifices for an export upturn. True, the removal of environmentally damaging subsidies and the liberalization of markets do generally promote a more efficient use of resources. But the rate of exploitation soon increases with the mobilization of raw materials and agricultural produce for export; land demand and pesticide use rise together with the switch over to cash crops; and tourism and transport also experience major growth (Reed 1996). Furthermore, the new exporters' rights to natural resources collide with the hereditary rights of less endowed sections of the population to use forests, water and land; the poor are pushed to the sidelines, and compelled by rising prices to plunder marginal ecosystems for their survival. In this connection, a number of studies have concluded that the negative environmental effects of structural adjustment programmes far outweigh the positive benefits (Kessler and Van Dorp 1998).

It is not uncommon, however, for the law of supply and demand to cancel out the fruits of the export drive. Prices often fall as demand increases on the commodity markets, and once more the lower earnings have to be offset by greater export volumes. Should the recipient countries also be hit by a financial crisis, both demand and commodity prices come under renewed pressure. This is precisely what happened after the Asian financial crisis of 1997. Commodity prices on the world market slid lower and lower – by more than 25 per cent within a year (*Die Zeit*, 24 September 1998). And since the crisis also depressed demand in countries such as Japan, South Korea and Malaysia, the price spiral kept moving downward and forcing dependent countries to intensify the exploitation of raw materials for export. Thus money flows overshadow commodity flows in quite a special way during periods of economic downturn.

Globalization and Sustainability   145

Vanishing distance and the transport effect The sudden awareness of living in a shrinking world may well be the fundamental human experience in the age of globalization. The satellite image of the blue planet visually presents what things are tending towards in reality: all places appear present at the same time. While distance between places becomes insignificant, the same time comes to prevail everywhere: space vanishes, time standardizes. For currency traders and news editors, company buyers and tourists, managers and scientists, less and less importance attaches to distance and, of course, more and more to time. It hardly matters any longer where on the globe something happens; what counts is when it happens – at the right time, too late, or not at all. Globalization, in all its facets, rests upon the rapid overcoming of space, rendering the present ubiquitous without delay. Computers, after all, count seconds, but not kilometres. How the earth is shrinking under the sway of time, how near everything is and how fast everything goes – it is in such experiences that the growing spatio-temporal compactness of the globe becomes discernible (Altvater and Mahnkopf 1996).

Spatial compression requires transport, whether along physical or electronic channels. Electronic networking is the first constitutive element in the process of globalization; without online data transfers there would not be the nervous system of signal communication that, in lightning-quick reactions, binds together events on the globe without consideration of space. If one thinks, however, that in 1995 there were 43.6 computers and 4.8 Internet users per thousand of the world's population (UNDP 1998: 167), four-fifths of whom lived in the industrialized countries, then it is all too clear that one can speak of globalization only in a geographical, and certainly not a social, sense. No more than 1 to 4 per cent of the world's population are electronically linked to one another, and no more than 5 per cent have even sat in an aeroplane. From an ecological point of view, electronic communication is assuredly less wasteful of resources than is physical transport. Yet one should not underestimate the additional strain that the construction and maintenance of a digital infrastructure place upon the earth's resources. High-quality materials used in hardware and peripherals are obtained through numerous refining processes that impose a large (and often toxic) extra burden on the environment, cables of all kinds use a lot of material, and satellites and relay stations also cannot be had without a drain on the environment. Finally, whatever the many prophets of the information age merrily predict, electronic networking will in the long term probably generate more physical travel than it replaces. Anyone who has established close contact with distant places via electronic media will sooner or later want to seal the contact face to face. In any event, the main effect is a positive feedback between electronic and physical transport systems: globalization itself means transport and still more transport.

All forms of economic globalization, outside the international finance markets, rely heavily upon physical transport. Everywhere distances are springing up – on both the consumption and factor markets, they are growing longer and more numerous. T-shirts come from China to Germany and tomatoes from Ecuador to the United States; machinery from Europe stands in Shanghai harbour; the global class of 'symbol analysts' (Castells 1996) keep bumping into one another in the airports of OECD countries. After all, the value of world trade has been rising by more than 6 per cent a year, roughly twice as fast as the world economy itself. Foreign products – from meat to precision machines – play a more prominent role in many countries, and even small firms seek their fortune on overseas markets. And yet the word 'international trade' has a number of false associations. It no longer means that nations exchange goods that they themselves do not produce – as in the classical exchange of raw materials for industrial goods – but that foreign suppliers appear alongside local ones in largely OECD-centred trade. They no longer make up for gaps in the local supply, but try to oust the local supply either through undercutting or through the use of different symbols (Pastowski 1997). Korean cars for Carland America, Mexican beer for Beerland Germany: roughly a half of world trade takes place *within* industrial branches; that is, the same commodities are being imported and exported at the same time (Daly 1996: 5). The main purpose of international goods transport is thus to ensure the competitive presence of many suppliers in as many places as possible.

Distance-chopping and rapid transport for high-quality goods and people are mainly provided by the international air system. Passenger transport, if it continues growing at its present annual rate of 5 per cent, will double every 15 years, and although by now roughly a half of air travel is for leisure purposes, the geography of economic globalization is reflected in the increased flow. Between 1985 and 1996, the income of airline companies grew sevenfold on routes within China and threefold within South-East Asia and between Europe or North America and North-East Asia, whereas on other routes there was at most a twofold increase or sometimes, as in the case of Africa, stagnation (Boeing 1998). Air freight has been rising still faster: after annual growth of 7 to 12 per cent in the mid-1990s (ibid.), the assumption is that it will now average 6.6 per cent and add up to a tripling of revenue by the year 2015 – figures naturally surpassed by the anticipated growth rate for international express services, where DHL and similar firms reckon on an annual increase of 18 per cent.

Without rapidly declining freight costs, the expansion of global markets would not have been possible. For such costs must not be a decisive factor, if the dynamic of supply and demand is to develop independently of geographical location. The more freight costs weigh in the balance, the less worthwhile it becomes to use price and innovation to gain an advantage over far-flung competitors; lower marginal costs in production would soon be eaten up by greater outlays on transport. Only if the costs of overcoming space tend towards insignificance can corporate strategies alone determine the choice of location. A number of reasons have been given for the relative cheapening of freight. First, it is precisely on global markets that transport volume is being constantly reduced in relation to a given value of trade. For a computer producer in Texas, for example, it matters little whether his hard disks come from Singapore or California, as transport costs become less significant, the more the economic value of a transported good is independent of its size or weight. In fact, those branches of the economy that go in most for 'global sourcing' – computers, motor vehicles, consumer electronics, textiles – are often not the largest-volume traders (Sprenger 1997: 344). Second, containerization and easier transfers between modes of transport have greatly increased efficiency (*Economist* 1997b). But the third and main reason why distance has been losing its resistance is that the price of fuel oil, used in nearly all forms of transport, has fallen dramatically since 1980. As a matter of fact, that price is far from reflecting the full ecological costs of the production and consumption of oil. For all the efficiency gains, transport in the OECD countries is the only sector in which CO_2 emissions have continued to increase in recent years. Transport also requires various facilities: vehicles, highways, harbours and airports, a whole infrastructure, which uses a considerable amount of materials and land. Yet most of these costs are passed on to society and do not show up in the freight bills. It becomes easy to overlook the extent to which the overcoming of geographical distance and temporal duration is paid for through the spoliation of nature.

How Economic Globalization Fosters a New Colonization of Nature

The results of the GATT Uruguay Round, which ended in 1993 with a package of trade agreements and the founding of the WTO, included

an accord on intellectual property rights. In contrast to the main
preoccupation, which had been to dismantle national controls on cross-
border trade, it was here a question of introducing a new level of
regulation. Yet both strategies – deregulation as well as re-regulation –
were pursued in the name of freedom of trade. The contradiction
disappears as soon as one realizes that the aim in both cases was to
create uniform legal foundations for a global economic space. While a
plethora of national obstacles to the circulation of goods and capital
had to be dismantled, it was also necessary to establish an international
legal framework that would give such circulation a powerful helping
hand. Factor mobility can be obstructed by a mass of laws, but it can
also be left hanging in mid-air if there are no laws at all. Especially
relevant in this respect was the case of property rights in goods based
on genetic engineering – a case in which legal security had been
defective in most countries around the world. This was the gap that
the agreement on 'trade-related intellectual property rights' (TRIPS)
was designed to close, for without it the exploitation of newly available
raw materials – the genetic material of forms of life – would not have
much of a commercial future.

Under the TRIPS agreement, all countries are required to provide
legal protection for patented inventions of both products and processes,
in all fields of technology. Industrial patents, of course, have long
assured their owners an exclusive income from inventions for a certain
length of time, but a similar system has only slowly come to apply to
biological products and processes. The protection of a patent is nevertheless indispensable for the commercialization of research-intensive
products, since only proprietary rights give them a commodity status
– otherwise they would just be useful objects freely available in the
public domain. For this reason, a guaranteed property system is the
legal–social corset of a market economy, just as the more or less forcible
enclosure and appropriation of common territory (fields, pasture, forest,
fishing grounds) was the historical prerequisite for the lift-off of
agrarian capitalism. If the research-intensive products are organisms
such as seeds or plants, this raises the additional marketing problem
that they easily reproduce themselves (Flitner 1998). Seeds, for example,
bring forth plants, which in turn bear the seeds for the next sowing.
The commodity character of a living organism does not last long,
therefore; the second generation no longer needs to be bought. But
this is bad news for any investor, since if commodities can reproduce
themselves, it means that the reproduction of capital is on shaky
ground. That leaves just two possibilities. Either their reproducibility is
curtailed (for example, through the insertion of 'terminator genes'), or

patents allow fees to be charged for the use of a technologically modified living process.

Patents to genetic innovations ensure the economic control of 'life industries' over modified organisms and their offspring. Only through the establishment of proprietary rights over cells, micro-organisms and organisms does the genetic material of the living world become available to be marketed. Patents empower firms to take ownership of parts of the natural realm, to turn it into an economic resource, and as far as possible to monopolize it so that no one can use it unless they pay for an approved purpose. Life patents thus play for 'life industries' the same role that land deeds played for emergent agrarian capitalism. They define ownership, keep other users away, and establish to whom the benefits of use should accrue. Activities such as planting, animal-raising or curative treatment, which used to be part of the public domain, thus come increasingly under the control of corporations. Whereas colonialists used to appropriate mineral or land resources by physically controlling a territory, the genetic engineering firms exploit genetic resources through world-recognized patents over DNA sequences.

The consequences for plant diversity, however, are likely to be similar. There is no need to consider the numerous dangers bound up with an uncontrollable spread of transgenic species; even the accident-free introduction of genetic technology into the agriculture of the South would cause a whole range of plants to disappear from the evolutionary picture. Whereas agrarian capitalism led in many places to monoculture of natural plant varieties, the life industries might force specialization in a few genetically optimized, and economically useful, plants (rather along the lines of the 'Green Revolution' of the 1960s and 1970s) (Lappé and Bailey 1998). In the fierce competition for markets that is likely to ensue, non-industrial and local strains would fall by the wayside – which would undermine food security, especially for poorer people without the means to purchase industrial produce. All plants other than a few strains capable of large-scale cultivation would be lost. A global system of legal patents for genetic inventions, which incorporated and irrevocably modified parts of the human biological heritage for commercial ends, would threaten to result in nothing less than a simplification of the biosphere.

How Economic Globalization Changes the Geography of Environmental Stress

In recent years, more and more salmon dishes – fresh, smoked or grilled – have been appearing on German menus, almost as if it were a fish from local waters. By now Germans consume nearly 70 million kilos a year of the favoured fish, which is brought from farms in Norway or Scotland to supermarket displays (Oppel 1999). But as in the mass farming of any other creature, large quantities of feed have to be supplied – to be precise, five kilos of wild deep-water fish have to be processed into one kilo of fishmeal, which is then used to feed salmon for consumption. This raw material is mostly caught off the Pacific coast of South America, where catches are declining because of overfishing, and it is then turned into meal in Peruvian harbour towns that are in danger of suffocating in the gaseous, liquid and solid waste matter that results from the process. While German consumers can feast themselves on fresh low-calorie (and rather expensive) fish, people in Peru are left with pillaged seas and filthy dirty towns.

This example shows how a lengthening of the supply chain can shift the ecological division of labour between countries of the South (and East) and those of the North. For economic globalization does not mean that the costs and benefits of economic activity are globalized. On the contrary, it is more likely that extension of the value-creation chain to different locations around the world will bring a new allocation of advantage and disadvantage. When a production process is divided up among different countries and regions, a tendency soon appears to separate costs and benefits by redistributing them up and down the chain. Anyway it would be wrong to imagine that the worldwide networking of offices, factories, farms and banks is accompanied by a decentralization of all functions from production and planning to finance, not to speak of the collection of profits (Sassen 1996). Despite many attempts to increase the autonomy of sub-units, the opposite is generally the case: that is, the diversification of economic activities leads to a concentration of control and profit at the nodal points of the network economy (Castells 1996). The flux of investment into distant countries is offset by a reflux of power and profits to the originating country, or, more precisely, to the 'global cities' of the North. As special export zones multiply in Bangladesh, Egypt or Mexico, where cheap labour, tax breaks and lax environmental norms considerably reduce production costs, the sky is the limit for the towers of banks and company offices in Hong Kong, Frankfurt or London.

The changed distribution of economic power goes together with a change in how the pressure on the environment is distributed across geographical space. If power, in an ecological sense, is defined as the capacity to internalize environmental advantages while externalizing environmental costs, then it may be supposed that the lengthening of economic chains will start a process that concentrates advantages at

Globalization and Sustainability   151

the upper end and disadvantages at the lower end. In other words, the environmental costs incurred within the transnational value-creation chains will become especially high in the countries of the South and East, while the post-industrial economies will become ever more environmentally friendly. Or to use an analogy (with the salmon example in mind), the rich countries will increasingly occupy the upper positions in the food chain (where larger volumes of low-value inputs have step-by-step been converted into smaller volumes of high-value food), while the developing or poorer countries will occupy the middle and lower positions. In fact, along with numerous individual examples, a series of highly aggregated data on international flows of materials lend credence to this interpretation. Thus, 35 per cent of total resource consumption is incurred abroad in the case of Germany, 50 per cent in Japan, 70 per cent in the Netherlands, and so on (Adriaanse et al. 1997: 13). The smaller the area of an industrialized country, the greater seems to be the geographical separation between the sites of pressure on the environment and the sites of consumption benefit. In all these countries, there has been a tendency over the past 15 years for a growing proportion of environmental consumption to take place abroad (involving not so much raw materials as semi-finished products).

In agriculture, Southern regions of the world no longer supply only agrarian mass produce as in the days of colonialism, but also supply goods with a high dollar value per unit of weight for affluent consumers in the North. Highly perishable items such as tomatoes, lettuce, fruit, vegetables and flowers come as air freight to Europe from Senegal or Morocco, to Japan from the Philippines, or to the United States from Colombia or Costa Rica (Thrupp 1995). As in the case of salmon, health-conscious shoppers with an average to high income are only too pleased to have a supply that does not depend on the season, while plantations and glasshouses in the areas of origin impose irrigation, pesticide use and the repression of local farmers. Nor are things much different with shrimp or meat production. The breeding of shrimps and prawns in Thailand or India for the Japanese and European markets means that people have to wade through toxic residue to catch them and that many a mangrove forest has to disappear from the scene. More refined consumption in the North at the price of the environment and subsistence economics in the South: this pattern has rooted itself deeply in the food-produce market since the 1970s. The raising of cattle and pigs in Europe draws in manioc or soya both from the United States and from countries such as Brazil, Paraguay, Argentina, Indonesia, Malaysia or Thailand. The old law that the market puts

purchasing power before human need asserts itself still more powerfully in a world economy beyond frontiers.

Of course, the expansion of the fossil development model into one
or two dozen aspiring economies in the South and East has done most
to change the geography of environmental stress. As the newly industrialized nations entered the age fuelled by fossil resources, the
possibility presented itself of stretching the industrial production chains
beyond the OECD countries. The South's share of world output has
thus been growing (and the OECD's slowly declining) in primary
industry, metalworking and chemicals (Sprenger 1997: 337; Mason
1997), rising in the last of these from 17 per cent in 1990 to 25 per cent
in 1996 (French 1998: 27). What is happening is not so much migration
for environmental reasons as a redistribution of functions within the
world economy. The stages of an international production chain that
put most pressure on the environment are usually in less-developed
regions, while the cleaner and less material stages tend to be in the G-
7 countries. In the aluminium industry, for instance, the quarrying of
bauxite takes place in Guyana, Brazil, Jamaica and Guinea (along with
Australia). The actual smelting of the aluminium, which is the next
stage along, moved more and more in the 1980s from the North to
countries such as Brazil, Venezuela, Indonesia or Bahrain, while the
research and development stage remained chiefly located in the OECD
area (Heerings and Zeldenrust 1995: 33). Despite higher use overall,
the production of aluminium grew strongly in Japan and weakly in
Europe; imports from the South filled the gap (Mason 1997).

A look at the computer branch further along shows just how much
high-tech industry lives off the new ecological division of labour. In
the case of 22 computer companies in the industrialized countries,
more than half of their (mostly toxic) microchip production is located
in developing countries (French 1998: 28). Does this not show in outline
the future restructuring of the world economy? The software economies of the North will pride themselves on their plans for a cleaner
environment, while the newly industrialized economies will do the
manufacturing and contend with classical forms of water, air and soil
pollution, and the poorer primary economies will do the extracting
and undermine the subsistence basis of the third of humanity that
lives directly from nature.

Which and Whose Globalization?

Globalization is not a monopoly of the neo-liberals: the most varied
actors, with the most varied philosophies, are also caught up in the

transnationalization of social relations; indeed the ecological movement is one of the most important agents of global thinking. Accordingly, the image of the blue planet – that symbol of globalization – conveys more than just one message. The imperial message of collapsing frontiers always found itself confronted with the holistic message of the planet's finite unity. A clear line can be drawn from Earth Day 1970 (often seen as the beginning of the American ecological movement) to the United Nations conference on world climate held in Kyoto in 1997. In the squares where people assembled on that first Earth Day, speakers and demonstrators underpinned their demands for comprehensive environmental protection with photographs of the earth taken less than a year before from the surface of the moon. And nearly thirty years later, the emblem of the planet was prominently displayed on the front of the conference hall where, for the first time, the world's governments entered into legally binding commitments to limit pollution levels. That picture shows the earth as a single natural body binding human beings and other forms of life to a common destiny; it globalizes our perception both of nature and of the human story. Only with that image did it become possible to speak of 'one earth' or 'one world' in the true sense of the term. For neither the name of Friends of the Earth, nor the title of the Brundtland Report, *Our Common Future* (WCED 1987), would have meant much without that photo of the planet.

But the 'blue planet effect' and its message of finitude go deeper still: they produce a way of seeing that places local action within a global framework. The picture shows the outer limits of the living space of everyone who looks at it. Does not everyone know that, if only the image were sufficiently enlarged, he or she would be able to find himself or herself on it? For the observing subject cannot be separated there from the observed object; in scarcely any other example is self-reference so inextricably woven into the image. This visual superimposition of global and individual existence has shifted the cognitive and moral coordinates of our perception of ourselves. The consequences of an action, it suggests, may extend to the edges of the earth – and everyone is responsible for them. All of a sudden, car drivers and meat buyers are linked to the greenhouse effect, and even a hairspray or an air ticket is seen as having overstepped the global boundaries. 'Think globally, act locally': this electoral slogan of the ecological movement has played its part in creating a 'global citizen' who internalizes the earth's limits within his or her own thinking and action. The narrative of limitation derives its moral force from this association of planet and subject in a common drama. The ecological experience is thus undoubtedly one dimension of the experience of globalization, because it overturns people's conventional notion that they live and act in national political and social spaces that are clearly demarcated and separated from one another (Beck 1997: 44).

Yet the ecological movement cannot escape the fact that, however provisionally, the imperial message has won through. One sign of this is the way in which multinational corporations have almost completely seized for themselves the image of the blue planet. The perception of the world as a homogeneous space, visible and accessible all the way across, has everywhere become hegemonic. This vision is imperial, because it claims the right to roam the world unhindered and to grab whatever it fancies – exactly as if there were no places, no communities, no nations. The mechanisms of GATT, NAFTA and the WTO were born in the spirit of frontier demolition. They codify the world as a freely accessible economic arena, in which economics enjoys the right of way. The newly established rules are designed to proclaim trans-national corporations as sovereign subjects within global space, exempt from any obligation to regions or national governments. State pro-tectionism is thereby abolished, only to be replaced by a new pro-tectionism that favours corporations. Transnational partnerships are entitled to claim all sorts of freedoms and rights, while territorial states – not to mention citizens or civic associations – have to take second place.

When people look back on the last century of this millennium, they will be forced to conclude that Rio de Janeiro was pretty good on rhetoric, but Marrakesh was taken in real earnest. Here the UN con-ference on the environment held in Rio in 1992 stands for a long series of international agreements – notably the conventions on climate and biodiversity – that were supposed to steer the world economy in less ecologically harmful directions. Marrakesh stands for the founding of the World Trade Organization after the end of the GATT Uruguay Round, and for the growing importance of the IMF as a shadow government in many countries. There the basis was laid for an economic regime in which the investment activity of transnational actors would be free of regulation anywhere on the globe. These transnational regimes – the environmental and the economic – are attempts to give a political–legal foundation to transnational economic society, but the two stand in marked contradiction to each other. The environmental regime is concerned with protection of the natural heritage, the economic regime with equal rights to exploit it; the environmental agreements are based on respect for natural limits, the economic agreements on the right to carry through economic ex-

Globalization and Sustainability 155

pansion successfully. Paradoxically, moreover, they wager on different systems of responsibility and accountability. On the one hand, the environmental agreements appeal to sovereign states as responsible entities that are supposed to uphold the public good in their territory. On the other hand, the economic agreements assume sovereign, transnationally active corporations that belong to no territory and are therefore responsible to no state. Already today the world's hundred largest economies comprise 49 countries and 51 corporations (Anderson and Cavanagh 1997: 37).

It is therefore not clear how the conflicting messages that appropriate the image of the blue planet can be reconciled with each other. Even transnational civil society has succeeded only on specific occasions in confronting corporations with their responsibility towards nature and the overwhelming majority of the world's citizens. If the holistic message stands for 'sustainability' and the imperial message for 'economic globalization', then it would seem necessary to suppose that, however great the synergies at a micro-level, the chasm between the two is continuing to widen. But that is the greatness of a symbol: it can hold together divergent truths within a single visual form.

References

Adriaanse, A. et al. (1977), *Resource Flows: The Material Basis of Industrial Economies*, Washington, DC: World Resources Institute.

Altvater, E. and B. Mahnkopf (1996), *Grenzen der Globalisierung*, Münster: Westfälisches Dampfboot.

Beck, U. (1997), *Was ist Globalisierung?* Frankfurt: Suhrkamp.

Boeing (The Boeing Company) (1998), www.boeing.com/commercial

Brown, L. et al. (1998), *Vital Signs 1998*, Washington, DC: Norton.

Carley, M. and Ph. Spapens (1998), *Sharing the World: Sustainable Living and Global Equity in the 21st Century*, London: Earthscan.

Castells, M. (1996), *The Rise of the Network Society. The Information Age: Economy, Society and Culture*, vol. 1, Oxford: Blackwell.

—— (1998), *End of the Millenium. The Information Age: Economy, Society and Culture*, vol. 3, Oxford: Blackwell.

Cavanagh, J. (1998), 'Background to the global financial crisis', paper presented at the San Francisco International Forum on Globalization, San Francisco.

Daly, H. (1996), 'Free trade, capital mobility and growth versus environment and community', public lecture given at The Hague Institute of Social Studies, The Hague, 26 September.

Economist (1977a), 'Schools brief: one world?', 18 October: 103–4.

Economist (1997b), 'Schools brief: delivering the goods', 15 November: 89–90.

Esty, D. C. and D. Gerardin (1998), 'Environmental protection and international competitiveness. A conceptual framework', *Journal of World Trade*, 32 (3): 5–46.

Flitner, M. (1998), 'Biodiversity: of local commons and global commodities', in M. Goldman (ed.), *Privatizing Nature: Political Struggles for the Global Commons*, London: Pluto, pp. 144–66.

French, H. (1998), *Investing in the Future: Harnessing Private Capital Flows for Environmentally Sustainable Development*, Worldwatch Paper no. 139, Washington: Worldwatch Institute.

Heerings, H. and I. Zeldenrust (1995), *Elusive Saviours. Transnational Corporations and Sustainable Development*, Utrecht: International Books.

Johnstone, N. (1997), 'Globalisation, technology, and environment', in *OECD Proceeedings, Globalisation and Environment*, Paris: OECD, pp. 227–67.

Jones, T. and R. Youngman (1997), 'Globalisation and environment: sectoral perspectives', in *OECD Proceedings, Globalisation and Environment*, Paris: OECD, pp. 199–221.

Kessler, J. J. and M. Van Dorp (1998), 'Structural adjustment and the environment: the need for an analytical methodology', *Ecological Economics* 27: 267–81.

Lappé, M. and B. Bailey (1998), *Against the Grain: The Genetic Transformation of Global Agriculture*, London: Earthscan.

Lash, S. and J. Urry (1994), *Economies of Signs and Space*, London: Sage.

Mason, M. (1997), 'A look behind trend data in industrialization. The role of transnational corporations and environmental impacts', *Global Environmental Change* 7: 113–27.

Menotti, V. (1998b), 'Globalization and the acceleration of forest destruction since Rio', *Ecologist* 28: 354–62.

OECD (1998), *Kein Wohlstand ohne offene Märkte, Vorteile der Liberalisierung von Handel und Investitionen*, Paris: OECD.

Oppel, N. V. (1999), 'Aus fünf Kilo Fisch wird ein Kilo Zuchtlachs', *Greenpeace Magazin* 1 (99): 40–1.

Pastowski, A. (1997), *Decoupling Economic Development and Freight for Reducing ist Negative Impacts*, Wuppertal Paper no. 79, Wuppertal: Wuppertal Institute for Climate, Environment and Energy.

Reed, D. (ed.) (1996), *Structural Adjustment, the Environment and Sustainable Development*, London: Earthscan.

Sassen, S. (1996), *Losing Control?*, New York: Columbia University Press.

Sprenger, R. U. (1997), 'Globalisation, employment, and environment', in *OECD Proceedings, Globalisation and Environment*, Paris: OECD, pp. 315–66.

Thrupp, L. A. (1995), *Bittersweat Harvests for Global Supermarkets: Challenges in Latin America's Agricultural Export Boom*, Washington, DC: World Resources Institute.

UNDP (United Nations Development Programme) (1998), *Human Development Report 1998*, Oxford and New York: Oxford University Press.

WCED (World Commission on Environment and Development) (1987), *Our Common Future* (the Brundtland Report), Oxford and New York: Oxford University Press.

WRI (World Resources Institute) (ed.) (n.d.), *World Resources*, pub. annually, New York: Oxford University Press.

Wysham, D. (1997), *The World Bank and the G-7: Changing the Earth's Climate for Business*, Washington, DC: Institute for Policy Studies.

Zarsky, L. (1997), 'Stuck in the mud? Nation-states, globalisation, and the environment', in *OECD Proceedings, Globalisation and Environment*, Paris: OECD, pp. 27–51.

Zukunftskommission der Friedrich-Ebert-Stiftung (1998), *Wirtschaftliche Leistungsfähigkeit, sozialer Zusammenhalt, ökologische Nachhaltigkeit. Drei Ziele – ein Weg*, Bonn: Dietz.

[19]

Rethinking the Global

The Sociology of Globalization and the Study of the Global Environment

There are several discrete issues to attend to in this concluding chapter. I will turn first to the question of the connection between sociological analyses of globalization and the study of global environmental problems. Though, as mentioned in Chapter 1, nearly all sociological authors dealing with globalization mention environmental issues or the Earth Summit, there has generally been little systematic attention to what environmental phenomena and environmentalism can tell us about globalization. In some cases, environmental issues appear to slip through the net of globalization analysis altogether. For example, while Appadurai offers five dimensions for analysing global cultural flows (1990: 296), environmentalism does not sit easily in any of them. At the same time – and reinforced by this lack of attention – there has been equally little consideration of the appropriate sociological approach to the analysis of the global environment (though see Redclift and Benton, 1994). Much writing on global environmental issues makes little room for sociology and finds no space at all for the sociology of globalization (as noted by Robertson, 1992: 187). Since these two approaches have often passed each other by, an initial – though rather obvious – conclusion from this study is that the rise of environmental problems and of environmental 'consciousness' constitute strong evidence in support of the significance of processes of globalization. As the preceding chapters have demonstrated, there are world-wide environmental problems, some of which are receiving transnational policy responses. There is growing awareness of 'the Earth' (or, as the yoghurt-pot example of the Preface reminded us, 'the planet') as a cultural reference point with widely accepted connotations. Furthermore, specialized discourses, such as that of sustainable development, are emerging in relation to the putative policy requirements of the globe.

But the present analysis of global environmental problems allows us to conclude more than merely that environmentalism is a globalized cultural phenomenon. The analyses presented in this book offer evidence relevant to the continuing debate over the nature of globalization. As described in Chapter 1, there are, loosely speaking, a group of approaches which ascribes globalization to one principal cause (for example, the logic of capitalist development or the cultural logic of modernity). These are opposed to accounts such as Robertson's which stress the multiplicity of causes and the heterogeneous nature of the influences on globalization (see 1992: 60, and McGrew, 1992: 66–7). Indeed, Robertson and Lechner had proposed:

> that cultural pluralism is itself a constitutive feature of the modern world system and that conceptions of the world system, symbolic responses to globalization, are themselves important factors in determining the trajectories of that very process. (1985: 103)

The arguments presented in this book lend weight to the latter position: there are multiple, interacting spurs to the globalization of environmental awareness and environmentalism. And this holds true, even though – as argued in Chapter 3 – we can see that economic factors are at the heart of the causation of many environmental problems.

The spurs to globalization are multiple in at least two senses. First, at the level of the *root of environmental problems*, it is evident that economic considerations are not the sole cause even though they do predominate. Some environmental problems are only loosely related to economic considerations. Thus, states' preference for nuclear power was often more attributable to political than to economic rationales, as the subsequent lack of commercial justification for nuclear power commonly showed (Yearley, 1992a: 43–4; for the case of France see Bunyard, 1988). As was seen in Chapter 2, the issue of population growth is even further from being directly economic. The problems surrounding population increase relate to cultural variables and, in particular, to women's educational opportunities, as well as to global income distribution and to families' prospects for economic development. Even the question of environmental accounting (about how 'natural capital' is to be priced and so on) depends as much on the professional practices of accountants and civil servants as on directly economic matters. Lastly, there are some widespread environmental problems which are barely economic at all, as with the genetic pollution caused by introduced species described in Chapter 2. In any case, the specific local impact of world-wide environmental problems can be affected by the details of geology and geography, as well as by cultural and by socio-economic factors.

But as well as the issue of how environmental problems are caused, there is the question of the *promotion of environmentalist concern for and awareness of the planet* as a cultural symbol. As Robertson expresses this, a crucial factor:

> is the scope and depth of consciousness of the world as a single place. . . . Globalization does not simply refer to the objectiveness of increasing inter-connectedness. It also refers to cultural and subjective matters. In very simple terms, we are thus talking about issues surrounding the idea of the world being 'for-itself'. (1992: 183)

The argument of this book is that 'global environmental problems' are *global problems* because people and organizations have worked at making

'the environment' a world-wide phenomenon. We have seen this operating
in very many ways. It has been shown in the names and images selected by
environmental groups, in their choice of campaigning targets and in their
developing cross-national organization. It is equally evident in the
operation of self-consciously international bodies such as UNEP, and in
the development of an interest in the global environment by the World
Bank. At first sight it might be tempting to suppose that environmental
issues are inherently global and that UNEP, NGOs, the World Bank and
all the rest are only pursuing the 'logic' of the globalization of environmental problems. In fact, however, this 'logic' has been cashed in very
differently by various actors. The Global Environmental Facility has
lighted on just four areas, while Greenpeace or Friends of the Earth or
CSE in Delhi have selected others. This conclusion mirrors closely the
outcome of Robertson's attempt to 'map' the global condition (1990: 27–
8). He calls for further empirical studies of the promotion of 'consciousness
of the world' and:

> In more theoretical vein, much more needs to be done so as to demonstrate the
> ways in which the selective responses of relevant collective actors – most
> particularly societies – to globalization play a crucial part in the making of the
> world-as-a-whole. (1990: 27)

Chapters 3 and 4 are offered as empirical and theoretical analyses which
advance our understanding of the making of the world-as-a-whole.

If the case of environmentalism shows globalization to be taking place,
and helps identify the nature and relative significance of the mechanisms by
which it is proceeding, there remains the separate question about how much
the sociological literature on globalization advances the understanding of
the world-wide environment and of global environmentalism. The answer
here is again two-fold. There are first of all insights which a sociological or
social-science perspective brings to the analysis of the global environment.
The question of how global environmental issues get their 'globality' or
questions about the practicalities of the operation of universalizing discourses are standardly sociological. Though they are important and have
been a central component of my argument, they do not specifically draw on
the globalization literature. From this literature itself comes the important
reminder that environmental issues are not alone in being globalized. Given
the way that environmentalists and the media have tended to align talk of
the globe with a concern for environmental protection – so that 'Earth
Day' is immediately recognized as a day supposedly committed to care for
the environment and so that the yoghurt-buying public knows what it
means to contribute a share of the company's profits to 'the planet' – it is
easy for greens to assume that only their concerns are global. As was noted
in Chapter 3, there is a utopian element in much green writing. Greens
cannot consider themselves deserving of exceptional support just on the
grounds that they are concerned with the 'global', since credible claims to
globality can be made in most socioeconomic and cultural spheres. The

globalization literature reminds those with environmental sensibilities that many other elements of present-day culture are globalized too, in the same ways as the environment and often for similar reasons.

Robertson emphasizes that the term globalization is itself contested (1992: 182). This should be no surprise as we have already noted Robertson and Lechner's observation that 'symbolic responses' – people's own conceptualizations – regarding globalization are constitutive of the phenomenon (1985: 103). Against the utopian assumptions of some greens and even some policy-makers, what we have seen in this book is the extent to which global 'common' interests, the identification of the globe's environmental problems, and the specification of facts about the global condition are themselves *all contested*. And this contestation is more significant than Robertson appears to recognize. The supposed capacity of global environmental discourses to speak on behalf of the world as a whole gives such discourses a heightened value. The pursuit of this value means that claims about 'global needs' and 'common interests' are prone to exceptional contestation and dispute.

A final conclusion about the globalizing of environmental issues appears contrary to one of the assumptions behind the last quote from Robertson. In that passage from his 'mapping' of globalization he implied that, among all possible 'collective actors', 'societies' have a particular role to play in processes of globalization. Though ultimately it is nations which strike agreements on many transnational environmental issues, a great many other collective actors play major roles. For example, in Chapter 3 I reviewed the contributory parts played by firms and financial organizations, by NGOs, by supranational bodies and even by local authorities and small-scale, local groups. As McGrew notes (1992: 74–5) in a globalized society one anticipates an increased diversity of actors in the shaping, negotiation and implementation of policy. This expectation is especially strong in the case of environmental issues since, as argued in Chapter 3, these issues themselves overlap with so many other aspects of economic and cultural life. There can be no policy towards CO_2 abatement which does not take energy generation into account, nor any transport campaign which does not impact on the interests of the motor-manufacturing industry and the 'great car economy'. A globalized world contains a complex and changing constellation of collective actors.

Globalization, Universal Discourses and the Sociology of Expert Knowledge

While Chapter 3 displayed the contests over the 'globality' of global issues and highlighted the diversity of collective actors involved in creating global identities and agreements about global environmental issues, Chapter 4 focused on discourses which purported to transcend the local and the global through their universal applicability (see also Ancarani, 1995). The

146   *Sociology, Environmentalism, Globalization*

first major point here concerns the potential for deconstructing the global/ universal authority of claims from science or microeconomics. While many authors, including otherwise sceptical ones, advocate acceptance of scientific authority in environmental matters (O'Neill, 1993: 144), the cases discussed in Chapter 4 indicated that scientific and other universalizing approaches to environmental problems have been routinely and successfully questioned. The central claim here was that it is always potentially possible to question a scientific viewpoint or finding. 'Facts' (whether about responsibilities for greenhouse-warming emissions, the value of blue whales or whatever) do not compel agreement, though they may facilitate it.

This is not an abstract point nor a 'merely' philosophical one. The history of attempts at environmental regulation in the USA indicates just how controversial the use of scientific expertise can be (see Jasanoff, 1990a; Yearley, 1995a: 465–7). Essentially there are two reasons why these issues came to particular prominence in the United States. First, major regulatory bodies such as the Environmental Protection Agency (EPA) were established relatively early and took steps which were seen as radical at the time, including pressing for the adoption of scrubbers in coal-fired power-station chimneys and for the fitting of catalytic converters to cars.

Second, the separation of political powers meant that there were various judicial remedies which could be used to challenge these bodies' rulings. Accordingly, when industrial interests and environmental groups wished to question the agencies' views they were able, on the one hand, to employ lobbying and various forms of political manoeuvre and, on the other, could pursue their regulatory interests through the courts, marshalling counter-expertise to combat the judgements and technical opinions of the EPA and other bodies.

Given the resources which industry could devote to challenging environmental regulations and the high stakes involved in these challenges – for example, a ruling that formaldehyde promotes cancer in humans would have affected a billion-dollar industry in the early 1980s (Jasanoff, 1990a: 195) – it is no surprise that disputes over scientific evidence were fought tenaciously and with great inventiveness. Since these challenges were channelled through the courts, technical disputes over safety and environmental hazards were all opened to judicial – and hence public – scrutiny.

From the point of view of the sociology of science (see Yearley, 1988: 16–43 and 1994b), these courtroom arguments ran a familiar course. As Yearley notes:

> Studies of controversy, both within academic science and in the public arena, have alerted analysts to ways in which scientific knowledge claims can face deconstruction. For example, if toxicity tests are repeated, leading to new and different results, we enter the domain of the 'experimenters' regress' (Collins, 1985: 2). The 'correct' results are, by definition, the ones produced by the better test, but there are no independent means of determining which test is better unless the 'correct' outcome is known in advance. There is no separate touchstone of credibility. This problem is bad enough in 'pure' science, where the reasons for distrusting others' results are disciplinary or occasionally personal. In

disputes over environmental safety, huge commercial and political motivations may also be involved, creating further incentives for discrediting the opposing side's claims to scientific knowledge. (1995a: 465–6)

There are of course some peculiar features to the scientific issues which the EPA and other environmental agencies often have to decide. They deal with quantities which are hard to measure, physical phenomena which are highly interactive, and diseases which occur over the course of a lifetime and for which there may be many plausible causes. The science involved in such issues lends itself to controversy (see Collingridge and Reeve, 1986). But the fundamental insight which science studies brings to the analysis of environmentalism and environmental policy concerns the disputability of scientific knowledge per se, not the special disputability of the science of cancer or of pesticide toxicity.

The intractability of these issues is further indicated by the subsequent experience of the EPA. Following setbacks and embarrassments, the EPA repeatedly had to take stock of its position. Internal reviews commonly proposed that the EPA improve its science and recommended that it separate issues of science from those of policy or political judgement (see Jasanoff, 1990a: 84; 1992: 15–23). However this was not possible in practice since key aspects of its scientific practice depended on methodological assumptions which could not be justified in exclusively scientific terms. For instance, evidence of environmental risk to humans comes – in part at least – from animal toxicity studies; yet the question whether evidence about deceased rats should be taken as relevant proof at all is both a policy matter and an issue of methodology.

In the case of the EPA Jasanoff concludes:

one of the bitter lessons of its first twenty years was that transparency alone is worth little in the public political arena unless it is accompanied by factual claims that can resist deconstruction. . . . In its earlier years the agency sought to defend its claims against skeptical assault primarily by asserting its specialized expertise, but although this approach won initial support from the courts, it failed to protect the agency from the more concerted opposition that it confronted after the 'Reagan revolution' of 1980. Rhetorical boundary drawing proved to be an inadequate instrument for certifying as 'science' decisions that fell on the murky boundary between science and policy. . . . The period of environmental decision making that began in the mid 1980s can rightly be seen as a return to fact making, but to fact making with a difference. . . . EPA recognized that it could no longer serve as the exclusive, or even the primary, forum for the construction (or reconstruction) of policy-relevant facts. The basis for making expert claims was renegotiated as the agency increasingly relied on satellite scientific bodies [special consultative bodies and ad hoc expert panels] . . . to originate or certify *claims that would stand up to political testing*. On the other hand, these institutions were themselves required to be sufficiently sensitive to the norms of politics to maintain scientific credibility. Their impartiality too, had to be secured through administrative and political controls. . . . *It is a final irony of environmental decision making that, in the effort to keep politics distinct from science, the processes of scientific fact making so freely accommodated themselves to the demands of politics.* (1992: 23; my italics)

148   *Sociology, Environmentalism, Globalization*

On this view, the EPA's relative success in winning credibility in the 1980s arose not from its ability to produce incontestable science but from its skill in devising ways of producing knowledge that already took account of likely opposition.

If universalizing discourses (and this includes legal principles as well as scientific ones – see the discussion of MacKinnon's work in Chapter 1) cannot take hold and direct policy within the relatively homogeneous culture of the USA, it is all the more unlikely that they will be able to do so internationally. The significance of these sociological studies for the analysis of relations between states has hardly been noticed (except by Jasanoff herself, 1996), which bears out the point Roberston makes about the distance between the various social science disciplines concerned with global phenomena. Where sociology 'came to deal often *comparatively* with societies . . . international relations (and portions of political science) dealt with them *interactively*, with relations between nations' (1992: 16; original italics). Sociologists of science and international relations scholars interested in science are relative strangers.

Writers from the international relations tradition – particularly those who talk of epistemic communities – tend to focus on the potential for scientific analysis to offer a common currency in which greenhouse-warming potential or the loss of biological riches in any part of the world can be assessed. As noted in Chapter 4 the universalizing discourse of science implies several things: that there is a common currency; that this common currency is not arbitrary but is founded in well established scientific theory; and that any properly trained scientist can use this common currency to make assessments which will be recognized as objectively valid by other scientists and policy-makers the world over. Though this remains the ideal of science, the case studies in Chapter 4 indicate that there is no practical reason to expect that epistemic communities will be able to end disagreements transnationally any more effectively than they did in the case of the US EPA – rather worse in fact given the greater diversity of interests on the global stage and the entrenched history of North–South distrust.

Without the benefit of detailed sociological work on the scientific community or on scientists as policy advisers, even those globalization writers who have recognized the problems with universalizing discourses have few ideas about their solution. Thus, Wallerstein ends his consideration of cultural universalism in the world system with the hope that:

> Beyond scientism, I suspect there lies a more broadly defined science, one which will be able to reconcile itself dramatically with the humanities. . . . This will make possible a new rendezvous of world civilizations. Will some 'universals' emerge out of this rendezvous? Who knows? Who even knows what a 'universal' is? . . . If we go back to metaphysical beginnings, and reopen the question of the nature of science, I believe that it is probable, or at least possible, that we can reconcile our understanding of the origins and legitimacies of group particularisms with our sense of the social, psychological, and biological meanings of

humanity and humaneness. I think that perhaps we can come up with a concept of culture that sublates [existing] usages. (1990b: 54)

This passage appears to me both unattractively vague and an exercise in wishful thinking. Instead of hoping for a new, transcendent culture (or railing against relativism as Archer (1990) does) we need instead institutions which face up to the practical shortcomings of universalizing discourses. We need to invent institutions which are flexible and self-aware, which are in that sense reflexive. They need, as Jasanoff says, to be 'sufficiently sensitive to the norms of politics to maintain scientific credibility' (1992: 23).

The issues of participation in technical decision-making and of scientification are clearly central ingredients of this need for reflexiveness. As we saw with the ozone negotiations, there is a danger that the conviction that science speaks objectively and disinterestedly means that one need have no qualms about excluding other people from decision-making since they would, in any event, have arrived at the same conclusions as oneself.]This beguiling line of reasoning may seem correct in principle. But, as is indicated by the experience of the US EPA, by the Corine database, by the WRI greenhouse figures, by Summers' economic logic and by the history of ozone diplomacy, such reasoning is practically inadequate. The difficulties encountered in the practical application of the universalizing discourse of science lead one to a sceptical view of any idea that the recognition of global 'oneness' prepares the way for authoritative 'master' discourses.

The Global Specificity of Environmentalism

This book has dealt with globalization in an area of social concern and social action which coincides with the interests of a leading social movement, environmentalism. The argument has been that, while many globalization authors have overlooked this topic in favour of the globalization of production, of media or of popular culture, the environment lends itself to analysis in these terms. Given the close links between the concerns of the environmentalist movement and globalization, the question of the implications of this study for the interpretation of other social movements naturally arises also.

As was noted in Chapter 3, proponents of many sorts of social movements and ideologies wish to claim that their view is somehow in everyone's or the world-wide interest. I have argued elsewhere that the environmental movement stands out from other movements in three ways: with regard to 'its intimate relationship to science, its practical claims to international solidarity and its ability to offer a concerted critique of, and alternative to, capitalist industrialism' (1994a: 167). In this final section I want to comment briefly on these differences in the light of globalization.

The relationship to science is the special feature most comprehensively considered in this book. The connection is complex. For one thing, as the

150   *Sociology, Environmentalism, Globalization*

experience of the 'progressive' EPA described above (see also Yearley, 1992c: 515–25) indicates, science has been no straightforward friend to the environmental movement, even though the urgency of environmental problems such as ozone depletion has often been attested to by scientific evidence. Scientific expertise and counter-expertise are crucial to the making of environmental arguments, even if epistemic communities are far less straightforward than the international relations literature tends to imply. Moreover, as the Brundtland Report acknowledged in a different context, questions about sustainability are anchored in physical, chemical and biological systems.

This physical basis is commonly also transboundary. As noted in Chapters 2 and 3, polluted rivers cross state boundaries, air pollution disperses internationally and marine pollution spreads from the rim of one continent to another. Though the environmental movement has an internationalist *ideology*, the issues to which it attends are also treated as transnational policy matters by states themselves and by other political agencies. Environmental pressure groups have become adept at international campaigning; on average, ecological groups cooperate across borders rather better than nations do, and supranational bodies such as UNEP and the EU have often facilitated environmental organizations' attempts to internationalize their cause. As noted in Chapter 3, some practical features militate against this internationalism. Environmental NGOs develop a deep familiarity with their own countries' laws, politicians, civil servants and media. The green movement has not, despite some advocates' claims, transcended national barriers. But in this book I have outlined sociological and political reasons for believing that it stands a better chance of doing so than other putatively universal social movements.

Lastly, let us turn to the idea that 'greens offer a critique of capitalism, an alternative value system and a view of the alternative society which they would wish to see ushered in' (Yearley, 1994a: 160). More than other contemporary social movements, environmentalists offer a comprehensive alternative. In terms of the useful phrase which came into brief currency on the disintegration of the Eastern bloc, only the environmental movement offers a distinctive challenge to the idea that we have arrived at the 'end to history'. Particularly through the concept of sustainable development they have a vocabulary for describing a coherent future which departs from 'business-as-usual' liberal capitalism. Greens have, as Dobson recently argued (1990), a coherent green political philosophy; they have distinctive views on the economy. They of all social movements have founded political parties in many countries, North and South, and experienced some electoral success. As asserted by Lowe and Rüdig, 'Only the ecological movement represents a totally new political cleavage' (1986: 537).

But it is all too easy to exaggerate the potential for international environmental solidarity. For one thing, however wrong Marxists were about the dynamics of capitalist societies, it was clear which social group was supposed to have the political interest and the potential for self-identification necessary to drive through fundamental social change. Environmentalists may feel they are on firmer ground than Marxists in identifying the problems with industrial capitalism, but environmentalism is much less clear about which social groups are supposed to be the agents for change (Dobson, 1990: 15). Moreover, though in principle there may be grounds for supposing that there is literally a global interest in environmental reforms, as we have seen in Chapters 3 and 4, the prospects for transnational unity on environmental matters are not favourable. Too often policies in the 'global interest' have been formulated without participation and consent. The special conditions shaping social movement formation in the Third World are still little researched as are relationships between Third-World environmentalists and development and environmental NGOs in the North.

Environmentalism surely counts as one of the best candidates we have for a global ideology and globalizing movement. Further study of its strengths and weaknesses can only advance the understanding of globalization and of the development of global awareness and planet-wide identities. A decisive element in improving our ability to deal with global environmental issues will be the shaking off of modernist assumptions about the ability of expertise to stand impartially for all. Such change will need to be accompanied by the transformation of major transnational institutions into far more reflexive bodies. Accordingly, a clear practical consequence of this book's argument is that environmentalists need to pay greater attention to the character of knowledge-making institutions and may in future need to grant demands for the re-design of such institutions a prominent place in their list of campaign objectives.

References

Ancarani, Vittorio (1995) 'Globalizing the world: science and technology in international relations', in Sheila Jasanoff, Gerald E. Markle, James C. Petersen and Trevor Pinch (eds), *Handbook of Science and Technology Studies*. London: Sage. pp. 652–70.

Appadurai, Arjun (1990) 'Disjuncture and difference in the global cultural economy', in Mike Featherstone (ed.), *Global Culture: Nationalism, Globalization and Modernity*. London: Sage. pp. 295–310.

Archer, Margaret S. (1990) 'Resisting the revival of relativism', in Martin Albrow and Elizabeth King (eds), *Globalization, Knowledge and Society*. London: Sage. pp. 19–33.

Bunyard, Peter (1988) 'The myth of France's cheap nuclear electricity', *The Ecologist*, 18 (1): 4–8.

Collingridge, David and Reeve, Colin (1986) *Science Speaks to Power: the Role of Experts in Policy Making*. New York: St Martin's Press.

Collins, H. M. (1985) *Changing Order: Replication and Induction in Scientific Practice*. London: Sage.

Dobson, Andrew (1990) *Green Political Thought: an Introduction*. London: Unwin Hyman.

Jasanoff, Sheila (1990a) *The Fifth Branch: Science Advisers as Policymakers*. London: Harvard University Press.

Jasanoff, Sheila (1992) 'Science, politics, and the renegotiation of expertise at EPA', *Osiris*, 7: 1–23.

Jasanoff, Sheila (1996) 'The normative structure of scientific agreements about the global environment', in Fen O. Hampson and Judith Reppy (eds), *Global Environmental Change and Social Justice*. Ithaca, NY: Cornell University Press. Forthcoming.

Lowe, Philip D. and Rüdig, Wolfgang (1986) 'Review article: political ecology and the social sciences – the state of the art', *British Journal of Political Science*, 16 (4): 513–50.

McGrew, Anthony (1992) 'A global society?', in Stuart Hall, David Held and Anthony McGrew (eds), *Modernity and Its Futures*. Cambridge: Polity Press. pp. 61–116.

O'Neill, John (1993) *Ecology, Policy and Politics: Human Well-Being and the Natural World*. London: Routledge.

Redclift, Michael and Benton, Ted (eds) (1994) *Social Theory and Global Environmental Change*. London: Routledge.

Robertson, Roland (1990) 'Mapping the global condition: globalization as the central concept', in Mike Featherstone (ed.), *Global Culture: Nationalism, Globalization and Modernity*. London: Sage. pp. 15–30.

Robertson, Roland (1992) *Globalization; Social Theory and Global Culture*. London: Sage.

Robertson, Roland and Lechner, Frank (1985) 'Modernization, globalization and the problem of culture in world-systems theory', *Theory, Culture and Society*, 2 (3): 103–17.

Wallerstein, Immanuel (1990b) 'Culture as the ideological battleground of the modern world-system', in Mike Featherstone (ed.), Global Culture: Nationalism, Globalization and Modernity. London: Sage. pp. 31–55.

Yearley, Steven (1988) *Science, Technology and Social Change*. London: Unwin Hyman.

Yearley, Steven (1992a) *The Green Case*. London: Routledge.

Yearley, Steven (1992c) 'Green ambivalence about science: legal-rational authority and the scientific legitimation of a social movement', *British Journal of Sociology*, 43 (4): 511–32.

Yearley, Steven (1994a) 'Social movements and environmental change', in Michael Redclift and Ted Benton (eds), *Social Theory and Global Environmental Change*. London: Routledge. pp. 150–68.

Yearley, Steven (1995a) 'The environmental challenge to science studies', in Sheila Jasanoff, Gerald E. Markle, James C. Petersen and Trevor Pinch (eds), *Handbook of Science and Technology Studies*. London: Sage. pp. 457–79.

[20]

THE NATION-STATE AND THE NATURAL ENVIRONMENT OVER THE TWENTIETH CENTURY*

David John Frank
Harvard University

Ann Hironaka
Stanford University

Evan Schofer
Stanford University

National activities to protect the natural environment are on the rise. Conventional explanations of the phenomenon emphasize domestic processes, set in motion by environmental degradation and economic affluence. We propose instead a top-down causal imagery that hinges on a global redefinition of the "nation-state" to include environmental protection as a basic state responsibility. We test our view using event-history analyses of five indicators of environmentalization: the proliferation of (1) national parks, (2) chapters of international environmental associations, (3) memberships in intergovernmental environmental organizations, (4) environmental impact assessment laws, and (5) environmental ministries in countries around the world over the twentieth century. For all five measures, the top-down global explanation proves stronger than the bottom-up domestic alternative: The global institutionalization of the principle that nation-states bear responsibility for environmental protection drives national activities to protect the environment. This is especially true in countries with dense ties to world society and prolific "receptor sites," even when controlling for domestic degradation and affluence. It appears that blueprints of nation-state environmentalization, which themselves become more universalistic over time, are drawn in world society before being diffused to and enacted by individual countries.

In the environmental realm, to a surprising extent, the blueprints for nation-state involvement are drawn in world society, from where they diffuse to individual countries. Such a top-down process may operate in other domains of national policy, but it is especially prominent in environmental protection, where laws and problems seem to flout national boundaries. We investigate the conditions under which nation-states have engaged in activities to protect the natural environment over the period 1900–1995. We expect that such activities have increased as the principle of national environmental protection has become institutionalized in world society, particularly among nation-states tightly linked to world society and among those with "receptor sites"[1] capable of receiving and transmitting global blueprints of national environmentalism to domestic actors. In contrast to much social scientific orthodoxy, we emphasize the global embeddedness of the nation-state form.

THE PROBLEM

The twentieth century has witnessed a spectacular rise in national activities to protect the natural environment.[2] On age-old prob-

* Direct all correspondence to David John Frank, Department of Sociology, William James Hall, Harvard University, Cambridge, MA 02138 (frankdj@wjh.harvard.edu). We thank John W. Meyer for advice and assistance throughout the development of this paper. We also thank Nancy Brandon Tuma for sponsorship, as well as Riley E. Dunlap and three anonymous *ASR* reviewers for helpful comments. Special thanks go to Mark Brogger.

[1] Receptor sites are social structures (e.g., scientific institutes) with the capacity to receive, decode, and transmit signals from world society to national actors.

[2] Indeed such activities began much earlier. Pollution control in England dates back to 1388

lems, such as drought and pestilence, and contemporary concerns, such as toxic waste and ozone depletion, countries around the world have mobilized. This is not to say that all environmental issues have been solved or have even been addressed; clearly, the accumulation of problems has outstripped the accumulation of solutions (Caldwell 1990). Nevertheless, nation-states have accepted a rapidly expanding portfolio of responsibilities vis-à-vis the natural environment, and some of the associated activities appear to have slowed rates of degradation (Dietz and Kalof 1992; Roberts 1996).

Figure 1 exhibits five indicators that we believe illustrate the embrace of responsibility for the natural environment by the nation-state: (1) cumulative numbers of national parks and protected areas (such as Yosemite), (2) chapters of international environmental nongovernmental associations (such as the World Wildlife Fund), (3) state memberships in intergovernmental environmental organizations (such as the International Whaling Commission), (4) environmental impact assessment laws, and (5) national environmental ministries (see Appendix A for data sources). At the same time, however, we do not mean to attribute to these indicators any exceptional significance. Faced with no established cross-national and historical data on environmental activity, we simply have collected data on every indicator available.

All five indicators in Figure 1 show exponential growth over the twentieth century: Notable increases in activity are apparent after the birth of the United Nations in 1945, and also after the creation of the United Nations Environment Programme at the Stockholm conference in 1972 (Meyer, Frank, et al. 1997). Taken together, the five indicators suggest an important reconstitution of the nation-state form: The nation-state has become environmentalized as a whole set of policies, once practically invisible in state organizations, now appears to be de rigueur.

In saying this, we do not assume the nation-state has become uniformly focused on environmental protection. This is clearly not the case, as examples around the world dramatically illustrate (e.g., the Three Gorges dam in China and ranchland policy in the United States). Rather our point is that a new dimension of state responsibility has emerged:

> Governments are now held accountable to new standards. . . . Not only has a stable set of expectations about reciprocal state practice been established, its form has evolved over time to become more comprehensive, reflecting growing scientific understanding about the behavior of ecosystems. Debates now are no longer about whether to protect the global environment but rather how it should be protected. (Haas 1995:333–34)

Of the five indicators of national environmentalism, national parks and protected areas, such as the United States' Yellowstone and South Africa's Cape Peninsula, show the earliest and steepest rise in numbers. Such parks preserve awesome landscapes and centers of biodiversity from human exploitation. Before 1900, there were fewer than 40 national parks worldwide that fit our definition,[3] and they were located mainly in the United Kingdom and its former colonies. By 1907, however, parks existed on every continent on Earth, and by 1990 the International Union for the Conservation of Nature listed nearly 7,000 national parks throughout the world. The number continues to multiply.

Also originating around the turn-of-the-last century, country chapters of international environmental nongovernmental associations, such as the International Friends of Nature (founded 1895) and International Council for Bird Preservation (founded 1922), also increased dramatically over the twentieth century. Such chapters represent citizen mobilization on environmental issues, embodying change in national polities more precisely than change in national states. Chapters undertake advocacy, education, and often direct action to protect the natural environment (Wapner 1996). According to the best available sources, country chapters of

---

(Lowenthal 1990), and game laws in the United States originated in 1769 (Andrews 1999). As early as 1942, an international observer wrote, "From 1850 on, the stream of national protective legislation rapidly widened, until by the present day all major and most minor nations have ample protective codes" (Hayden 1942:12).

---

[3] We define national parks and protected areas as areas legally dedicated to protecting and maintaining biodiversity or natural resources.

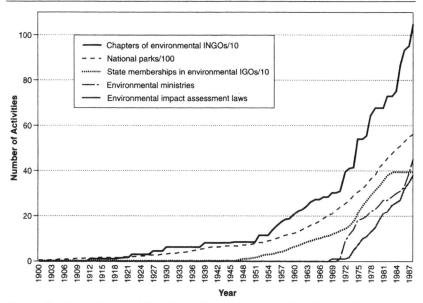

Figure 1. Cumulative Numbers of Five National Environmental Activities, 1900 to 1988

Note: INGOs are international nongovernmental organizations; IGOs are intergovernmental organizations.

international environmental nongovernmental associations were scant in 1900 (due partly to the paucity of the associations themselves), and those chapters that did exist were disproportionately in Western countries. As the century proceeded and the number of associations rose, however, country chapters diffused far and wide. By 1925, close to 25 percent of all chapters of international environmental nongovernmental associations were located outside Europe, and that proportion approximately tripled to 69 percent by 1990 (Frank et al. 1999).

The ascent of state memberships in intergovernmental environmental organizations was equally striking, but occurred later (e.g., the Asia and Pacific Plant Protection Commission was founded in 1955 and the Antarctic Mineral Resources Commission was founded in 1988). These organizations represent official state mobilization around environmental issues. They set parameters of action for the global commons (oceans, seas, rivers, the atmosphere) and increasingly establish standards of conduct within national borders (Haas and Sundgren 1993). Among

the earliest members of an intergovernmental environmental organization were the United States, Canada, Japan, and the USSR, all members of the North Pacific Fur Seal Commission, established in 1911. Now such memberships are much more broadly dispersed among nation-states. There are 58 countries on the Governing Council of the United Nations Environment Programme, the master intergovernmental environmental organization, whose broad mission it is "to provide environmental policy leadership within the world community" (UIA 1999:2177).

As Figure 1 shows, the numbers of environmental impact assessment laws grew from only 1 in 1969 to more than 50 by 1990 (Hironaka 1998). Such laws encourage decision-makers to take into account the possible effects of development investments on environmental quality and natural resource productivity (Horberry 1984). The United States, in 1969, was the first country to pass an environmental impact assessment law. Since then, the innovation has been widely adopted, becoming especially common in Europe, Asia, and the South Pacific.

Last, Figure 1 shows the proliferation of national environmental ministries. These organizations structure and routinize states' relationships to nature. At the highest level of government, environmental ministries provide official arenas for discourse and activity aimed at preserving nature. Environmental ministries are nearly always distinct from, and more recent than, natural resource ministries, as they seek to protect, rather than exploit, nature's bounty. From the time of the first ministries in 1971 to 1995, at least 109 nation-states formed national environmental ministries. Following the lead of the United Kingdom in 1971 were Japan and East Germany in 1972, Singapore and Poland in 1973, and Burkina Faso and Mauritius in 1974, among others. Nation-states embraced this new organizational form quickly and broadly, especially in the years around the two United Nations conferences on the environment —1972 and 1992.

Taken together, our five indicators illustrate a change in the "nation-state" over the twentieth century—the internalization of environmental concerns, which were once seen as outside the state's purview. All five indicators produce similar exponential curves in Figure 1: a period of introduction (longer for early innovations and shorter for later ones), followed by a period of explosive growth. The proliferation of national environmental policies by no means assures the arrest of environmental destruction. Nevertheless over the twentieth century a striking change has taken place, as the nation-state has become more and more accountable for the protection of nature (Haas 1995).

CURRENT EXPLANATIONS

By what process did virtually every country on Earth come to take some, and in many cases a great deal of, responsibility for environmental protection? Most social scientists find the answer in changing domestic factors, especially increasing degradation of the natural environment (Nanda 1983; Sprinz and Vaahtoranta 1994; Thomas 1992) and rising affluence (Inglehart 1990; Lowe and Goyder 1983).[4] In the former case, national

environmentalization is seen to be a direct, functional response to immediate problems: more despoliation (e.g., water and air pollution, overpopulation, declining biodiversity) spurs more action. In the latter case, countries undertake environmental activities because wealth is said to have satisfied basic human needs, such as food and shelter, thus shifting orientations toward quality-of-life issues, such as environmental protection and enhancement.

Neither of these standard accounts articulates well with the historical record. In centuries past, the most massively degraded areas were typically abandoned, regardless of the local society's affluence. Thus as early as 1864, Marsh wrote, "There are parts of Asia Minor, of Northern Africa, of Greece, and even of Alpine Europe, where the operation of causes set in action by man has brought the face of the earth to a desolation almost as complete as that of the moon" ([1864] 1965: 42). In that period, migration, not amelioration, was the normal response to environmental despoliation (McCormick 1989; Turner et al. 1990). More recently, neither the spectacular wealth of the oil-rich Middle East nor the pervasive natural degradation of Soviet-dominated Eastern Europe appears to have stimulated unusually high levels of environmental protection (e.g., Feshbach 1995).

Neither do the degradation and affluence explanations fit with the evidence presented in Figure 1. From the exponential rises in environmental activities, it appears that most countries have embraced environmental protection, not just the rich or despoiled (we test this proposition below).

Thus we propose an alternative explanation of environmentalization. Contrary to the view that nation-states are autonomous actors shaped by internal preferences and interests, the view so often portrayed by social scientists, we propose instead that nation-states are enactors of wider world cultural institutions. In making this argument, we build on earlier work showing the rise of global institutions for the environment (Frank 1997; Haas 1995; Meyer, Frank, et al. 1997). We investigate the impact of such global institutions on national environmental policies.

---

[4] An emerging literature challenges the relationship between affluence and environmental-

ism. See Brechin and Kempton (1994, 1997) and Dunlap and Mertig (1995, 1997).

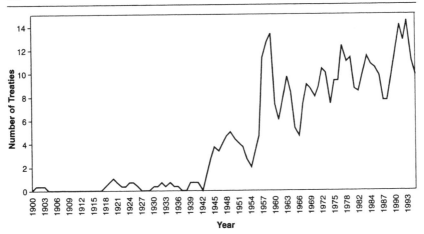

Figure 2. Annual Foundings of International Environmental Treaties, 1900 to 1995

Source: Burhenne (1997).

Note: Graph shows a three-year moving average.

THE ARGUMENT

Our argument begins from the premise that blueprints for the nation-state are drawn in world society (Meyer, Boli, et al. 1997). This means that rule-like definitions establishing what the nation-state is, what it can do, and how it can relate to other entities are organized and established globally. This has always been true to some extent, but it has become increasingly so with the proliferation of international organizations, treaties, and other forms of globalization (Anderson 1991; Robertson 1992; Ruggie 1993; Smith, Chatfield, and Pagnucco 1997).

Some global blueprints for the nation-state are more institutionalized than others. And both global blueprints and the extent to which they are institutionalized have changed over time. One such change is the elaboration and specification of environmental protection as a basic *purpose* of the nation-state. Driven first by a rising conception of nature as a life-sustaining global ecosystem and second by a general structuration of the world polity, global blueprints for national environmental protection have proliferated rapidly over the twentieth century (Frank 1997; Meyer, Frank, et al. 1997). These blueprints include the growing number of action plans produced by international environmental governmental

and nongovernmental organizations, the increasing variety of recommendations made by international policy experts, and the expanding set of guidelines issued by natural scientists (Caldwell 1990; McCormick 1989). The proliferation of protective blueprints by no means eradicates destructive ones, many of which are associated with global capitalism (O'Connor 1998; Schnaiberg and Gould 1994). Nevertheless, an elaborate and consequential global environmental regime has emerged (Levy, Keohane, and Haas 1993; Zürn 1998). To illustrate, Figure 2 shows that the average yearly number of international environmental treaties founded was less than one through 1945, but increased to around nine from 1960 onward. The rise is especially spectacular given the difficulties in coordinating nation-state interests (Young 1989). In many forms, in addition to international treaties, blueprints of nation-state environmentalism have multiplied in similar fashion.

One characteristic of nearly all global blueprints is their universalism (Boli and Thomas 1997). Produced by "unbiased experts" and "disinterested professionals"—individuals and/or organizations claiming to represent absolute truths and collective interests—world models of nation-state organization are constructed to apply universally, regardless of variations in domestic factors

(Meyer and Jepperson forthcoming).[5] This universalism is pronounced in the environmental realm, where depictions of nature in terms of the global ecosystem have expanded greatly over time. While the emphasis on universalism sometimes means blueprints of national environmental protection contain only lowest-common-denominator elements (Wapner 1996), Figure 2 attests that a great many common denominators are to be found, some of which lead to real action by nation-states (Haas and Sundgren 1993; Zürn 1998).

Sanctioned by universalism, blueprints for the nation-state diffuse throughout world society. The driving force behind diffusion is institutionalization itself: the growing agreement that the nation-state *is by definition* responsible for the continued vitality of the natural environment, and the growing agreement that specified activities (such as designating parks and participating in international environmental bodies) fulfill that responsibility. Yet beyond broad world sociocultural processes, many more grounded mechanisms of diffusion are produced by the distillation of new cultural understandings into organizational entities (Boli and Thomas 1997). We suggest several mechanisms below.

Mechanism of Diffusion: Some Examples

National parks and protected areas have long been encouraged by international environmental nongovernmental associations, whose promotional activities include evaluating and designating suitable land areas, lobbying government officials, purchasing land (sometimes with debt-for-nature swaps), and training park rangers (Lewis 1998).[6] Such activities are prominent at the International Union for the Conservation of Nature's World Parks Congresses, held each decade since 1962. At present, the World Wildlife

Fund is campaigning for the protection of 200 outstanding examples of the Earth's diverse habitats by the end of the year 2000. As such, international environmental non-governmental associations provide an interface between world society and individual countries.

Second, state memberships in intergovernmental environmental organizations have been advanced by natural scientists. The universalism of science and its cultural status as truth make it relatively easy for scientists to tie national interests to the activities of intergovernmental environmental organizations (Caldwell 1990; Strang and Meyer 1993; also see Schofer 1999; Schott 1993). Haas (1989) recounts the crucial role played by scientists in convincing Algeria to participate in the Mediterranean Action Plan. Initially resistant, Algeria was spurred toward membership only after the production of scientific data documenting the degraded state of Algeria's coastline. Scientists have been equally important in paving the way for state participation in the ozone and climate-change regimes (Benedick 1991). It is clear that scientists serve as conduits between global culture and nation-states.

As a third example, international organizations from the International Union for the Conservation of Nature to the World Bank have been active in spreading environmental impact assessment laws, occasionally using strong arm tactics to do so. In the 1950s and 1960s, the idea of environmental impact assessment laws began to appear in the discourse of international associations, both governmental and nongovernmental. Shortly thereafter, environmental impact assessments began to appear as features of international treaties, and recently they have been promoted by the World Bank and the United Nations Environment Programme, both of which provide advice and guidelines on assessment implementation. Standardized templates are available in such publications as the United Nations' *Environmental Impact Assessment: Training Resource Manual* (see Hironaka 1998). By the time the United States had adopted the first legislation in 1969, the concept of environmental impact assessment laws had been discussed thoroughly in the international realm (see Figure 3).

---

[5] Yearley (1996) claims that both scientists and some nation-states have significant sectarian interests in construing environmental problems as "global." While this is undoubtedly true, it is also true that the socially constructed universalism of science powerfully shapes international environmental discourse and activity.

[6] Lindborg (1992) and Wapner (1996) show other ways environmental associations promulgate global blueprints for nation-state environmentalism.

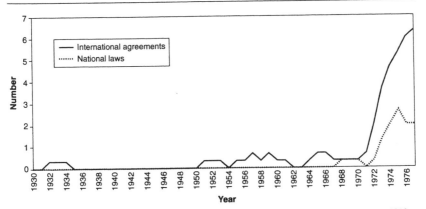

Figure 3. Environmental Impact Assessment: International Agreements and National Laws, 1930 to 1977

Sources: Ruster, Simma, and Bock (1983); Wood (1995).

Finally, it is also the case that states pressure other states to adopt forms of environmental protection. In many instances, the pressures emanate from the more powerful countries. For example, the colonizers established the first parks in Africa, sometimes against African interests (Hayden 1942). But often, alliances of the less powerful states pressure for environmental reform, as at the 1992 Rio conference on Environment and Development where the United States exhibited considerable foot-dragging in opposition to proposed reforms (McCoy and McCulley 1993). In the environmental realm, interstate pressures only rarely appear as exercises of raw power: More often views are promoted as education or enlightenment about universally agreed-upon principles and collective benefits (in which case power dynamics coalesce with the broader sociocultural processes emphasized throughout our article).

Thus, through mechanisms such as these (the workings of international environmental organizations, the advocacies of scientists, interstate pressures), global blueprints for national environmental activities diffuse to specific nation-states. The underlying forces of change are cultural, but the carriers are often organizational.

HYPOTHESES

Our main arguments are thus that blueprints for the nation-state are drawn in world soci-

ety, that such blueprints have, over time, increasingly specified environmental protection as a basic purpose of the nation-state, and that the provisions of such blueprints diffuse from world society to individual countries. These arguments stand in contrast to the prevailing orthodoxy, which emphasizes bottom-up causal processes hinging on environmental degradation and economic affluence. To test our ideas, we perform event-history analyses on the rates at which countries form national parks and protected areas, establish country chapters of international environmental nongovernmental associations, inaugurate state memberships in intergovernmental environmental organizations, pass environmental impact assessment laws, and create national environmental ministries. Our perspective generates three hypotheses.

The first hypothesis follows directly from our argument and operates at the world level, where it predicts increases in environmental protection by all kinds of countries—degraded or pristine, rich or poor. If nation-states arise from blueprints drawn in world society (e.g., those formed by resolution of the World Meteorological Organization or the United Nations Environment Programme), then increases in the extent to which those blueprints emphasize national environmental protection should generate actual increases in environmental activities in nation-states (Levy, Keohane, and Haas 1993).

Hypothesis 1: As the principle of national-level environmental protection becomes institutionalized in world society, global blueprints for nation-state environmentalism should diffuse at a faster rate.

The second hypothesis operates at the country level and predicts cross-national variation in environmental activities. If the definitions and forms of the "nation-state" originate in a world sociocultural system, then those nation-states most deeply embedded in this system should be most likely to embody its definitions and forms (Frank 1999; Meyer, Boli, et al. 1997).

Hypothesis 2: Global blueprints for nation-state environmentalism should diffuse at a faster rate to those nation-states most closely linked to world society.

The third hypothesis also operates at the country level and also predicts cross-national variation. If nation-states must learn the importance of global blueprints before enacting them, then nation-states with more prolific domestic "receptor sites" should be more likely to environmentalize than others (Finnemore 1996; Haas 1989, 1990).[7] We conceptualize receptor sites as social structures with the capacity to receive, decode, and transmit information from the outside (here, world society) to local actors (here, nation-states) (cf. Luhmann 1989). Without external stimuli, receptor sites remain inactive. Given scientists' role as arbiters of truth in the environmental realm, the most important domestic receptor sites are undoubtedly scientific ones (from private individuals such as E.O. Wilson to state organizations such as the Oak Ridge National Laboratory) (Buttel and Taylor 1992; Caldwell 1990; Frank 1997; Haas 1989, 1990; Taylor and Buttel 1992).

Hypothesis 3: To nation-states with more developed domestic receptor sites, global

---

[7] The idea of the "receptor site" is uncommon in the social sciences: Here, we mean it to correspond fairly directly to the common usage in biology, where it refers to an organ or structure that, upon receiving specific stimuli from its environment, generates nerve impulses conveying information about the environment.

blueprints of nation-state environmentalism should diffuse at a faster rate.

Because size may be a condition for many kinds of national activities, we include a population measure in our models. We also include iron and steel production, a measure of industrial development, to address the main competing explanations of nation-state environmentalization, which emphasize country-level degradation and affluence.

METHODS AND DATA

To test our hypotheses, we employ event history analysis. Event history analysis is a statistical tool used to model events occurring at particular points in time. We employ it to discern the causal processes that hasten (or slow) the rate of specific environmental events among nation-states. This focus on rates distinguishes event history analysis from OLS regression analysis, in which the dependent variables are amounts measured on a continuous scale. Analogous to regression, event history analysis yields coefficients (and standard errors) that reflect the impact of independent variables on the *rate* of the outcome of interest. Positive coefficients identify independent variables that increase the rate of events over time; negative coefficients identify variables that decrease the rate. Standard errors allow for hypothesis tests to determine if the observed effects are the product of random variation in the data (see Tuma and Hannan 1984).

As indicated above, the five events in question are the formation of national parks and protected areas, country chapters of international environmental nongovernmental associations, state memberships in intergovernmental environmental organizations, environmental impact assessment laws, and national environmental ministries. The first three events are recurrent, such that the dependent variable is the transition rate from a count of N to (N + 1). The last two events are absorbing, such that the dependent variable is the transition rate from 0 to 1. We use constant-rate models, which assume that transition rates are constant in the absence of time-varying independent variables.

Our basic aim is to show, corresponding to the hypotheses above, three main independent-variable effects on the five dependent variables: a positive effect from the institutionalization of environmental protection in global blueprints of the nation-state; a positive effect from nation-state linkages to world society; and a positive effect from nation-state domestic receptor sites. Furthermore, we aim to show that these effects remain, holding constant country-level measures of population, affluence, and environmental degradation.

Given that little quantitative work has been done in this area, these analyses take a strong first step toward explaining nation-state environmentalization. However, the analyses reported remain exploratory: It is difficult to find indicators, covering a long period of time, that can clearly capture the independent-variable effects we propose and show that the indicators form statistically distinct clusters. We also are limited by the availability of data for control variables for many countries over the whole century. Nevertheless, we believe our analyses can go a good distance toward explaining nation-state environmentalization.

Dependent Variables

The first dependent variable records the cumulative numbers of national parks or protected areas established by a nation-state. (See Appendices A, B, and C for sources, transformations, and the exact time period used for each event-history analysis.) We restrict the analysis to parks larger than 1,000 hectares. South Africa and New Zealand were the first countries to designate national parks in the twentieth century, both in the year 1900. By 1990, approximately 136 countries had at least one park that fit our definition, with the United States having more parks than any other country. A few small and/or peripheral nation-states had no parks larger than 1,000 hectares (e.g., Luxembourg and Qatar).

The second dependent variable measures the number of country chapters of international environmental nongovernmental associations established in a nation-state. We used 10 keywords from the *Yearbook of International Organizations* (UIA 1948–1998) (e.g., natural resources, environment) to construct an initial list of such associations; we

then pared the list to include only those having nature as a primary concern and having membership data for the whole century (or since founding). Before World War I, only a dozen countries had even one chapter of an international environmental nongovernmental association. By 1988, nearly every country in the world had at least one such organization (excepting a few peripheral countries, such as Cape Verde and Togo); Canada, the United Kingdom, and the Netherlands all had 19 association chapters, only one short of the maximum possible in our data set.

Third, we record the number of intergovernmental environmental organizations to which each nation-state belongs. Such organizations are established by intergovernmental agreement, have at least three countries as members, and have environmental concerns prominent on their agendas. Most intergovernmental environmental organizations were founded after the United Nations was established and their memberships were broadly dispersed from the start. By 1989, fewer than 20 nation-states, including Bhutan and Mongolia, had no memberships in intergovernmental environmental organizations. France had the most affiliations with 12, well short of the maximum possible 20 in our data set.

Fourth, we mark the year each country first adopts legislation requiring environmental impact assessments, which demand consideration of environmental implications in large construction projects. Although the first three nation-states to adopt environmental impact assessment laws were all developed Western countries (the United States, Canada, and Australia), the next three were Colombia, Malaysia, and Thailand. Already by 1990 the innovation had spread to more than 50 countries around the world (Hironaka 1998).

Finally our fifth dependent variable records the founding years of national environmental, conservation, and ecology ministries. From the first ministry in 1971 to 1995, the number of nation-states with such ministries grew to 109; 108 of these appeared in the wake of the United Nations Environment Programme (McCormick 1989; Meyer, Frank, et al. 1997). The roster of countries with environmental ministries continues to grow, although the United States itself is without a formal one (the director of the Environmental Protection Agency is not a Cabinet-level position).

We see these five dependent variables as *indicators* of an underlying process in which changes in the culture and organization of world society have rendered nation-states responsible for environmental protection. We expect our independent variables to have similar effects on all five indicators. Nevertheless, we keep the dependent variables separate to leave open the possibility that they are not as cohesive as we imagine.

Independent Variables

For each independent variable, we use multiple indicators to create latent-variable factors for the analysis. Given that no conventional measures of our independent variables exist, the factoring technique adds confidence that the key concepts have in fact been tapped. The indicators for the independent variables are culled from a wide variety of sources (see Appendix B for sources, transformations, and factor loadings).

Global institutionalization of national environmental protection. To capture the first independent variable, incorporation of environmental protection into the definition of the "nation-state" institutionalized in world society, we use three world-level indicators, with an average intercorrelation of .40: the staff size of the United Nations Environment Programme, founded in 1972; a dichotomous variable marking the years surrounding the two United Nations conferences on the environment, in 1972 and 1992; and the cumulative number of international environmental treaties over the century. We are trying, with these indicators, to gauge the global institutionalization of an environmentalized "nation-state." (See Appendix B for details.)

Nation-state ties to world society. To measure the extent to which countries have open conduits to world society, we employ two highly intercorrelated ($r = .73$), country-level indicators: national chapters of all kinds of international nongovernmental associations, except environmental ones; and national memberships in all kinds of intergovernmental organizations, except environmental ones. The intent is to capture a nation-state's general embeddedness in world society, in which new national environmental protection initiatives originate.

Nation-state receptor sites. As indicators of a country's domestic capacity to receive and interpret global blueprints for national environmental protection, we use two highly correlated ($r = .95$) measures: the number of domestic ecology associations, and the number of other domestic natural science associations. Scientists, and especially ecological scientists, are recognized as authorities in the environmental realm (Buttel and Taylor 1992; Frank 1997; Taylor and Buttel 1992). In measuring science organizations, we aim to assess each country's capacity to receive environmental "signals" from world society and transmit them to domestic actors.

Control Variables

Limited by the availability of data for many countries over the whole time period, we use population size as a control variable in the main analyses and add iron and steel production as a parallel control variable in the secondary analyses. National population counts are associated with a country's ability to pursue all kinds of activities, especially environmental ones, since large populations place more pressure on natural resources. Iron and steel production, as a gauge of industrial development, simultaneously measures both national wealth and environmental degradation. Because iron and steel production is highly correlated with other indicators of affluence and degradation (e.g., GDP and air pollution, themselves unavailable for many countries over the whole century), we use this variable to test the main competing arguments.

Each of the three independent-variable factors were created separately using SPSS (1988), and factor scores were computed based on these analyses.[8] Event-history anal-

---

[8] The indicators of the main independent variables loaded onto single factors with high weights (see Appendix B for factor loadings). We could not factor analyze the nation-state-level indicators into ties and receptor-sites variables owing to high multicollinearity, but we believe the substantive and theoretical grounds for the distinction are strong. Multicollinearity does not appear to be a problem in the event-history analyses re-

yses were conducted using the RATE program (Tuma 1992).

RESULTS

Table 1 summarizes the results. For each of the five dependent variables, we report the findings from two event-history analyses, the first without and the second with the control variable for industrial development (reported in columns a and b, respectively).

Across the top row of Table 1, we see that global institutionalization of the principle that "nation-states" protect the natural environment has positive and significant effects on all five dependent variables (both with and without the control for industrial development). The rates at which parks, chapters of international environmental nongovernmental associations, memberships in intergovernmental environmental organizations, environmental impact assessment laws and national environmental ministries appear in countries *all* increase significantly as national environmental protection becomes rule-like in the culture and organization of world society. The results provide strong support for our most basic argument—that blueprints for the nation-state are drawn in world society from which they diffuse to individual countries.

The effects of country ties to world society are also positive and significant across all five dependent variables, again regardless of the control for iron and steel production. More sociocultural ties to world society means greater likelihood of national implementation for every kind of environmental protection on which we have data. Unequivocally, the findings support the notion that deeply embedded countries are more likely to be constituted along the lines of globally institutionalized blueprints.

Finally, Table 1 shows that the presence of receptor sites has positive and significant effects across all five measures of nation-state environmentalization. Only in the second analysis of environmental ministries with industrial development controlled (column 5b) does the effect become nonsignificant, and even then it remains strongly positive. It appears that nation-states with prolific receptor

sites enact global blueprints for environmental protection at higher rates than do other countries.

Each of these effects remain even with population controlled. More populated countries do seem more likely to undertake some kinds of environmentally protective activities than less populated ones. Parks, environmental association chapters, and impact assessment laws are all significantly more likely to be founded in countries with large populations (for the other two dependent variables, the coefficient for population is nonsignificant and negative). The positive effect may show only that larger countries have higher organizational capacity for such activities as park formation than smaller countries, but it may reflect population pressures as well. Clearly, other things being equal, higher populations place a greater burden on natural resources, increasing a country's incentives to manage and protect its remaining resources effectively (Ehrlich 1968; Stern, Young, Druckman 1992).

Industrial development has positive and significant effects only on the formation of parks and the passage of environmental impact assessment legislation. Of the five dependent variables, these are the two that most obviously require financial resources for their implementation. The effects of this combined measure of degradation and affluence measure are otherwise limited.[9]

---

[9] To check these results, we tried more precise but time-limited indicators of affluence and degradation (results available on request). First we considered the effect of gross domestic product per capita on environmental ministries 1970–1995 (the first ministry appeared in 1971, after our GDP data begin). GDP has a nonsignificant negative effect, while our main variables have positive effects (significant effects for global institutionalization and nation-state ties). Analogously, Dunlap and Mertig (1995) find a generally negative relationship between national affluence and citizen concern for environmental quality. Although limited by the availability of data, we then log-regressed three measures of degradation (threatened bird species as a proportion of total bird species in 1990, proportion of forests lost 1990–1995, and industrial carbon dioxide emissions in 1990) on environmental ministry in 1995. None had a significant effect. Thus, the *social perception* of environmental degradation

---

ported in Table 1; standard errors show no signs of instability.

Table 1. Maximum Likelihood Estimates of the Hazard Rate at Which Five Indicators of Environmental Activity Occur in Nation-States, 1900 to 1995

Independent Variable	(1) National Parks[a]		(2) Chapters of Environmental INGOs		(3) State Memberships in Environmental IGOs		(4) Environmental Impact Assessment Legislation		(5) Environmental Ministry	
	A	B	A	B	A	B	A	B	A	B
Global institutionalization of national environmental protection	.35** (.02)	.38** (.02)	.71** (.05)	.71** (.05)	.88** (.08)	.88** (.08)	.91** (.30)	.94** (.30)	1.19** (.19)	1.20** (.19)
Nation-state ties to world society	.50** (.04)	.35** (.04)	.71** (.09)	.73** (.09)	.68** (.13)	.67** (.13)	1.11* (.55)	.88* (.54)	.51* (.28)	.45* (.27)
Nation-state receptor sites	.40** (.02)	.28** (.02)	.06* (.03)	.07* (.03)	.10* (.05)	.10* (.05)	.26* (.14)	.23* (.14)	.18* (.10)	.12 (.11)
Population size	.49** (.01)	.48** (.01)	.09** (.02)	.08** (.02)	-.03 (.04)	-.03 (.04)	.29** (.11)	.31** (.10)	-.11 (.07)	-.09 (.07)
Industrial development	—	.11** (.01)	—	-.16 (.15)	—	.05 (.18)	—	.91* (.46)	—	.76 (.60)
Constant	-9.02** (.16)	-9.08** (.16)	-3.93** (.36)	-3.86** (.36)	-2.83** (.57)	-2.87** (.58)	-10.8** (1.7)	-11.1** (1.74)	-3.55** (.99)	-3.77** (1.01)
Improvement over Model A	—	153.14**	—	1.29	—	.07	—	2.71*	—	1.43
Chi-squared	7,748.93**		910.89**		390.03**		63.65**		52.32**	
Number of events	4,330		1,027		395		47		101	

Note: Numbers in parentheses are standard errors. INGOs are international nongovernmental organizations; IGOs are intergovernmental organizations. See appendices B and C for variable definitions.

[a] In the parks analyses, we exclude countries smaller than 10,000 square kilometers.

*p < .05   **p < .01 (one-tailed tests)

For all three of our main independent variables, the effects are strikingly consistent. Without exception, the predicted relationships appear, and their magnitudes change little with the addition of iron and steel production as a control. Furthermore, buttressing our larger perspective, it is the world-level effect from global institutionalization that is the strongest predictor of national environmental activity across the board. Altogether, the results shown in Table 1 suggest that the seeds of national environmentalization are dispersed from a global warehouse. As the global seed supply rises, national activities also rise. The cross-national variation that remains is due to differences in links to the world supply source (embeddedness) and differences in domestic capacities to germinate the global seeds (receptor sites).

Overall, the evidence suggests the importance of conceiving of the "nation-state" as emanating from the world social system at large. Thus when it comes to the natural environment, important aspects of the nation-state form appear to be constituted externally, in the global society, and our results show the impact of the global environmental regime on internal national policies.

Questions of Interpretation

The evidence in Table 1 speaks clearly, but we thought it important to verify our findings along several dimensions. First we checked for change in the processes promoting nation-state environmentalization after 1972. In that watershed year the United Nations Conference on the Human Environment convened, the United Nations Environment Programme originated, and several important international environmental treaties were founded (Caldwell 1990; McCormick 1989). But in split analyses of the dependent variables that can be measured before 1972 (parks, environmental association chapters, and intergovernmental organization memberships), our three main independent variables show positive and significant effects both

---

may motivate environmental policies more than degradation itself (Luhmann 1989; Taylor and Buttel 1992).

before and after 1972. The global processes driving nation-state environmentalization may have intensified over time, but they do not change fundamentally.

Second we sought to verify our interpretation of the receptor sites effect. The same organizations we call domestic receptor sites (and place at the interface of world society and the nation-state), others conceive as social movement organizations (and place at the interface of mobilized citizens and governments). We question the latter interpretation's applicability in a cross-national context, since mass environmental movements exist in so few countries. Nevertheless, we investigated the effect of the number of receptor sites for a restricted set of countries—those with too few ecology and natural sciences associations to generate strong social movement pressures. Even among these select nation-states, the receptor-site variable retained significant effects on all five dependent variables. Thus, our original interpretation appears to hold. While ecology and natural science organizations undoubtedly function as social movements in some (mostly liberal Western) countries, the more general mechanism by which they influence national-level environmentalization is as receptor sites for global blueprints (for an example of the latter process, see Barbosa 1996).

Third, we tried some alternative indicators for the independent variables in Table 1:

As measures of *natural-resource pressures,* in place of iron and steel production we used the percentage of the population living in urban areas and logged population density (Banks 1990). In no case was the effect of urbanization significant. In only one case was the effect of population density significant, and then it was negative and thus contrary to orthodox expectations: high population densities slow the rate of park formation, as humans compete with nature for land. According to these indicators, degradation does not appear to drive environmentalization directly.

As a measure of *state openness to global innovation,* in place of receptor sites we tried democracy (Gurr 1990). According to the chi-square statistics, democracy's effect was stronger than that of receptor sites for two of the five dependent variables—environmental ministries and impact assessment laws, the most recent of the five innovations. In the other three cases, the receptor sites variable was stronger. Democracy proved to be a reasonable, but slightly less direct, measure of a country's openness to global environmental blueprints.

As a measure of *nation-state embeddedness,* instead of sociocultural ties to world society we used imports plus exports as a proportion of gross domestic product as a measure of economic ties to the world system (Summers and Heston 1991). In only one case was this economic linkages variable significant, and then negatively so (as ecological Marxists might predict; see O'Connor 1998): Dense trade linkages slowed the rate of park formation, suggesting economic pressures to retain unfettered access to natural resources (cf. Frank 1999).

Through all these alternative measures, our basic findings held. Nation-states are more likely to adopt environmentally protective policies as such activities become institutionalized in global blueprints for the nation-state, especially among countries deeply embedded in world society and among those with prolific domestic receptor sites.

THE CHANGING NATURE OF ENVIRONMENTAL PROTECTION

Thus far we have emphasized the relationship between the global institutionalization of the principle that nation-states should protect the natural environment and the rise of national activities to do so. We now call attention to a complementary effect. Global institutionalization involves not only a change in the "nation-state" but also a change in the meaning of "environmental protection." Increasingly, environmental protection has come to mean the preservation of the global ecosystem rather than the conservation of local natural resources (Dunlap and Mertig 1992; Frank 1997). Analytically, this shift involves rationalization, scientization, and globalization.

First off, models of environmental protection become more highly rationalized with institutionalization in world society (Meyer 1994; Weber [1968] 1978). In rationalization, entities and activities acquire practical, mundane purposes; their existential justification shifts from sacred fiat to means-ends chains. As it is becoming a standard feature of the "nation-state" over the century, "environmental protection" simultaneously gains a vastly expanded purpose: to sustain life on Earth (Pepper 1984). Every aspect of nature is reformed into an element vital for human survival.

Second, world models of environmental protection become more scientized with global institutionalization. In scientization, entities and activities come to be understood in terms of general, physical laws, under the authority of scientists and professionals (Schofer 1999; Schott 1993). At the level of culture, this entails the demystification of motive forces and the discovery of automatic control systems, which are stitched into the routine and regular workings of physical bodies and relationships. Organizationally, extensive machineries, both literal and figurative, arise to observe and expose the general laws. As national activities to protect the environment become increasingly rule-like, environmental protection is transformed from an enchanted and unpredictable process (e.g., one requiring sacrifice or heavenly supplication) to one requiring deference to biogeochemical rules (compare Hultkrantz 1961 and Thomas 1983 with Stern et al. 1992).

Third, models of environmental protection become more global with institutionalization in world society. In globalization, entities and activities are stripped of autonomy and lose their idiosyncratic connections to local settings. Organisms become embedded in cybernetic systems and become instances of abstract, universal categories (Haraway 1989).[10] Thus with the institutionalization of national environmental protection, protective activities are increasingly seen to affect a worldwide whole—the entire Earth and its atmosphere (Taylor and Buttel 1992).

Altogether, rationalization, scientization, and globalization reflect a new definition of "environmental protection" in world society—an environmental protection with vastly expanded universal value and importance. Concomitant with the institutionalization of environmental protection in global blueprints for the nation-state, nature becomes increas-

---

[10] It was Thoreau who first noted that the waters of the Ganges flow in Walden Pond.

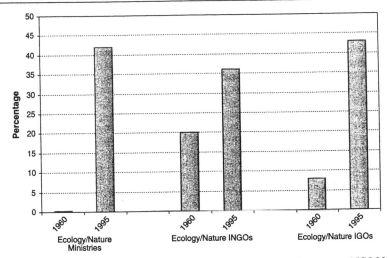

Figure 4. Changing "Nature": The Percentage of Nature Ministries, INGO Chapters, and IGO Memberships Addressing Ecosystem Preservation, at Two Points in Time

Note: INGOs are international nongovernmental organizations; IGOs are intergovernmental organizations.

ingly synonymous with the global ecosystem, without which *Homo sapiens* cannot survive.

A reflection of this overall process can be found in three of the dependent variables. In Figure 4, we show the percentages of all national nature activities that seek ecosystem preservation (as opposed to resource conservation) at two points in time: 1960 and around 1990. We show ecosystem-oriented nature ministries, ecosystem-oriented chapters of international nature associations, and ecosystem-oriented memberships in intergovernmental nature organizations.[11]

We see a marked change for all three variables over time. The percentage of ecosystem-oriented nature ministries rises from 0 to 42 percent, and the percentages of ecosys-

tem-oriented association chapters and intergovernmental organization memberships rise from 20 to 36 and from 8 to 43 percents, respectively. A shift is clearly in evidence: The activities of nation-states vis-à-vis nature have shifted toward the preservation of the global ecosystem.

These results, together with the preceding evidence, suggest twin aspects of the global institutionalization of national environmental protection: the environmentalization of the nation-state and a concomitant universalization of environmental protection, as "nature" becomes more rationalized, scientized, and globalized. The top-down processes that characterize change in the environmental realm may be less prominent in more particularistic realms (e.g., in military policy).

CONCLUSION

National activities to protect the natural environment have proliferated spectacularly over the twentieth century. Each of our five indicators of the process shows exponential growth. We show that such activities have increased not just in response to domestic degradation and affluence but also in response to a global redefinition of the respon-

---

[11] Ecosystem-oriented activities aim to integrate human society with the life-sustaining physical universe, such that natural processes proceed unhindered. Resource-oriented activities accept the intervention of human society in nature, but seek to regulate the exploitation of nature's bounty for long-term market interests. Conceptually, there is a continuum between the two models; in practice, the distinction is often sharp (e.g., tropical timber v. rainforests). Frank (1997) and Haas and Sundgren (1993) show related shifts in international environmental treaties.

sibilities of the nation-state. As the principle of national environmental protection has become institutionalized in world society, national activities to protect the environment have increased, particularly among those nation-states strongly tied to world society and those with receptor sites capable of transmitting emerging blueprints to domestic actors. In concrete terms, we see global social forces at work when national parks appear in Nepal, when a chapter of the International Council for Bird Preservation opens in The Gambia, when Mexico joins the International Whaling Commission, when environmental impact assessments begin in Kuwait, and when Romania founds an environmental ministry. With these activities, nation-states embody global institutional forms, which themselves have become more universalistic over time.

We intend our emphasis on world social and cultural processes to counter views of national environmental policies as arising mainly in response to domestic factors, and we believe the evidence supports our view. But we do not suppose that domestic factors—affluence, degradation (Walsh 1981), public opinion (Dunlap 1995; Kempton 1993), media coverage (Mazur 1998)—are unimportant to environmental policy formation in particular cases or in the short term; only that they recede from causal salience over many cases and over the whole century. We emphasize large-scale structural processes, in which "domestic factors" appear more as mechanisms of change rather than independent causal forces. Likewise we do not suppose that world sociocultural forces work in isolation from world economic and political forces, merely that the latter typically operate within parameters established by social reality, including definitions of the "nation-state" and "environmental protection."

If nation-states environmentalize in response to global institutionalization, then what forces drive the latter? The global institutionalization of the principle that nation-states bear responsibility for environmental protection follows the general structuration of the world polity and the rise of universalistic depictions of a global ecosystem. With their discoveries of the workings of a life-sustaining natural environment, scientists dramatically raise the stakes of environmen-

tal protection, and they do so in a world polity in which nation-states are the main legitimated actors. Thus emerges the principle that nation-states should protect the natural environment, setting in motion the processes on which we have focused here.

All this does not mean the environmental crisis is over. Problems still accumulate faster than solutions, and solutions still yield only partial successes. Nevertheless a positive change is strikingly evident. The lead actors on the global stage—nation-states—have come to bear greatly increased responsibility for environmental protection over the twentieth century. We see the transformation as resulting from global-institutional processes, which may be especially strong in the environmental realm due to its universalism.

In recent decades, social scientists typically have emphasized the ways nation-states are constructed from the bottom up, and there are many compelling examples of that occurring. Here we have illustrated a different kind of process, in which nation-states are constructed from the top down. We see blueprints for the nation-state being drawn in world society, and we see the institutionalization of these blueprints as establishing rule-like principles of what nation-states *are*, and what by definition they *do*.

David John Frank is Associate Professor of Sociology at Harvard University. In addition to ongoing work on changes in environmental sociology, with Bayliss Camp he is using penal-code data to investigate global transformations in the state regulation of sex; with Jay Gabler he is using shifting faculty compositions to evaluate worldwide revisions in university curricula; and with John W. Meyer he is examining changes in the cultural accounting schemes used by individuals.

Ann Hironaka recently completed her Ph.D. in sociology at Stanford University. Her dissertation examined historical changes in the nation-state and rates of warfare. She has also co-authored several papers on the global environmental regime.

Evan Schofer is a doctoral student in sociology at Stanford University. His dissertation research examines the expansion of scientific rationalization and scientific institutions in nations worldwide. His interests include comparative political sociology, globalization, sociology of science, organizations, and sociology of the environment.

Appendix A. Dependent Variables: Definitions, Data Sources, and Periods of Analysis

Dependent Variables	Definition	Data Source(s)	Period of Analysis
National parks and protected areas	Annual cumulative numbers of parks per nation-state	IUCN (1990)	1900–1990
Country chapters of international environmental nongovernmental associations	Annual numbers of chapters per nation-state	Fried (1905–1911); League of Nations (1921, 1938); UIA (1948–1990)	1900–1988
Nation-state memberships in intergovernmental environmental organizations	Annual numbers of memberships per nation-state	Fried (1905–1911); League of Nations (1921, 1938); UIA (1948–1990)	1900–1984
Environmental impact assessment laws	Year of founding	Wood (1995)	1966–1992
National environmental ministries	Year of founding	Europa Year Book (1970–1995)	1970–1995

Appendix B. Independent Variables: Definitions, Transformations, Data Sources, and Factor Loadings

Latent Independent Variable	Definition	Transformation	Data Source	Factor Loading
Global institutionalization of national environmental protection	UNEP staff size	Equals 0 before UNEP founding (1972); thereafter is logged	UNEP (1982–1993)	.87
	Years around 1972 and 1992 UN environment conferences	Equals 1 for the years 1970–1974 and 1990–1994; otherwise 0		.63
	Cumulative international environmental treaties	Excluded treaties that led to environmental intergovernmental organizations; logged	Burhenne (1997)	.90
Nation-state ties to world society	Memberships in all except environmental INGOs	1 added to all cases to eliminate zeros; logged and interpolated	UIA (1948–1990)	.97
	Memberships in all except environmental IGOs	1 added to all cases to eliminate zeros; logged and interpolated	UIA (1948–1990)	.97
Nation-state receptor sites	Annual numbers of domestic ecology organizations	1 added to all cases to eliminate zeros; logged	Zils (1998)	.91
	Annual numbers of domestic natural science organizations	1 added 1 to all cases to eliminate zeros; logged	Zils (1998)	.91

Note: INGOs are international nongovernmental organizations; IGOs are intergovernmental organizations.

Appendix C. Control Variables: Definitions, Transformations, and Data Sources

Control Variable	Definition	Transformation	Data Source
Population size	Annual population, in 1,000s	Logged	WRI (1998)
Iron and steel production	Annual production, in 1,000 metric tons	Logged and divided by the population size (in 1,000s)	Singer and Small (1990)
Gross domestic product per capita	Annual GDP per capita in current U.S. dollars	Logged	WRI (1998)
Population density	Annual persons per square kilometer	Logged; removed outlier (Maca) from the analysis	WRI (1998)
Threatened/known bird species	In 1990	Logged	WRI (1998)
Deforestation	Forest loss, percent change, 1990–1995	Removed outlier Cape Verde from the analysis	WRI (1998)
Industrial CO_2 emissions	1990, in 1,000 metric tons	Logged	WRI (1998)

REFERENCES

Anderson, Benedict. 1991. *Imagined Communities: Reflections on the Origins and Spread of Nationalism*. Rev. ed. London, England: Verso.

Andrews, Richard N. L. 1999. *Managing the Environment, Managing Ourselves: A History of American Environmental Policy*. New Haven, CT: Yale University Press.

Banks, Arthur. 1990. *Cross-National Time Series Data Archive*. Binghamton, NY: Center for Comparative Political Research.

Barbosa, Luis C. 1996. "The People of the Forest against International Capitalism: Systemic and Anti-Systemic Forces in the Battle for the Preservation of the Brazilian Amazon Rainforest." *Sociological Perspectives* 39:317–31.

Benedick, Richard Elliot. 1991. *Ozone Diplomacy: New Directions in Safeguarding the Planet*. Cambridge, MA: Harvard University Press.

Boli, John and George M. Thomas. 1997. "World Culture in the World Polity: A Century of International Non-Governmental Organization." *American Sociological Review* 62:171–90.

Brechin, Steven R. and Willett Kempton. 1994. "Global Environmentalism: A Challenge to the Postmaterialism Thesis?" *Social Science Quarterly* 75:245–69.

———. 1997. "Beyond Postmaterialist Values: National versus Individual Explanations of Global Environmentalism." *Social Science Quarterly* 78:16–20.

Burhenne, Wolfgang E., ed. 1997. *International Environmental Law*. London, England: Kluwer Law International.

Buttel, Frederick H. and Peter J. Taylor. 1992. "Environmental Sociology and Global Environmental Change: A Critical Assessment." *Society and Natural Resources* 5:211–30.

Caldwell, Lynton Keith. 1990. *International Environmental Policy*. 2d ed. Durham, NC: Duke University Press.

Dietz, Thomas and Linda Kalof. 1992. "Environmentalism among Nation-States." *Social Indicators Research* 26:353–66.

Dunlap, Riley E. 1995. "Public Opinion and Environmental Policy." Pp. 63–114 in *Environmental Politics and Policy*. 2d ed. Edited by J. P. Lester. Durham, NC: Duke University Press.

Dunlap, Riley E. and Angela G. Mertig. 1992. "The Evolution of the U.S. Environmental Movement from 1970 to 1990." Pp. 1–10 in *American Environmentalism: The U.S. Environmental Movement 1970–1990*, edited by R. E. Dunlap and A. G. Mertig. Philadelphia, PA: Taylor and Francis.

———. 1995. "Global Concern for the Environment: Is Affluence a Prerequisite?" *Journal of Social Issues* 51:121–37.

———. 1997. "Global Environmental Concern: An Anomaly for Postmaterialism." *Social Science Quarterly* 78:24–9.

Ehrlich, Paul R. 1968. *The Population Bomb*. New York: Ballantine Books.

Europa Year Book. 1971–1995. *The Europa World Year Book*. London, England: Europa Publications.

Feshbach, Murray. 1995. *Ecological Disaster: Cleaning Up the Hidden Legacy of the Soviet*

Regime. New York: Twentieth Century Fund.

Finnemore, Martha. 1996. *National Interests in International Society.* Ithaca, NY: Cornell University Press.

Frank, David John. 1997. "Science, Nature, and the Globalization of the Environment, 1870–1990." *Social Forces* 76:409–35.

——. 1999. "The Social Bases of Environmental Treaty Ratification, 1900–90." *Sociological Inquiry* 69:523–50.

Frank, David John, Ann Hironaka, John W. Meyer, Evan Schofer, and Nancy Brandon Tuma. 1999. "The Rationalization and Organization of Nature in World Culture." Pp. 81–99 in *Constructing World Culture: International Non-governmental Organizations since 1875,* edited by J. Boli and G. M. Thomas. Stanford, CA: Stanford University Press.

Fried, Alfred H. 1905–1911. *Annuaire de la Vie Internationale* (Yearbook of international life). Monaco: Institut International de la Paix.

Gurr, Ted Robert. 1990. *Polity II.* Ann Arbor, MI: Inter-university Consortium for Political and Social Research.

Haas, Peter M. 1989. "Do Regimes Matter? Epistemic Communities and Mediterranean Pollution Control." *International Organization* 43:377–403.

——. 1990. *Saving the Mediterranean: The Politics of Environmental Cooperation.* New York: Columbia University Press.

——. 1995. "Global Environmental Governance." Pp. 333–70 in *Issues in Global Governance,* edited by the Commission on Global Governance. London, England: Kluwer Law International.

Haas, Peter M. and Jan Sundgren. 1993. "Evolving International Environmental Law: Changing Practices of National Sovereignty." Pp. 401–29 in *Global Accord: Environmental Challenges and International Responses,* edited by N. Choucri. Cambridge, MA: MIT Press.

Haraway, Donna. 1989. *Primate Visions: Gender, Race, and Nature in the World of Modern Science.* New York: Routledge.

Hayden, Sherman Strong. 1942. *The International Protection of Wild Life.* New York: Columbia University Press.

Hironaka, Ann. 1998. "The Institutionalization and Organization of a Global Environmental Solution: The Case of Environmental Impact Assessment Legislation." Paper presented at the annual meeting of the American Sociological Association, August 24, San Francisco, CA.

Horberry, John. 1984. *Status and Application of Environmental Impact Assessment for Development.* Gland, Switzerland: International Union for the Conservation of Nature and Natural Resources.

Hultkrantz, Ake, ed. 1961. *The Supernatural Owners of Nature.* Stockholm, Sweden: Alqvist and Wiksell.

Inglehart, Ronald. 1990. *Culture Shift in Advanced Industrial Society.* Princeton, NJ: Princeton University Press.

International Union for the Conservation of Nature (IUCN). 1990. *1990 United Nations List of National Parks and Protected Areas.* Gland, Switzerland: IUCN.

Kempton, Willett. 1993. "Will Public Environmental Concern Lead to Action on Global Warming?" *Annual Review of Energy and Environment* 18:217–45.

League of Nations. 1921, 1938. *Handbook of International Organizations.* Geneva, Switzerland: League of Nations.

Levy, Marc A., Robert O. Keohane, and Peter M. Haas. 1993. "Improving the Effectiveness of International Environmental Institutions." Pp. 397–426 in *Institutions for the Earth,* edited by P. M. Haas, R. O. Keohane, and M. A. Levy. Cambridge, MA: MIT Press.

Lewis, Tammy. 1998. "Transnational Conservation Organizations: Shaping the Protected Area Systems of Less Developed Countries." Paper presented at the annual meeting of the American Sociological Association, August, San Francisco, CA.

Lindborg, Nancy. 1992. "Non-Governmental Organizations: Their Past, Present, and Future Role in International Environmental Negotiations." Pp. 1–25 in *International Environmental Treaty Making,* edited by L. E. Susskind, E. J. Dolin and J. W. Breslin. Cambridge, MA: Program on Negotiation Books at Harvard Law School.

Lowe, Philip and Jane Goyder. 1983. *Environmental Groups in Politics.* London, England: Allen and Unwin.

Lowenthal, David. 1990. "Awareness of Human Impacts: Changing Attitudes and Emphases." Pp. 121–35 in *The Earth as Transformed by Human Action,* edited by B. L. Turner II, W. C. Clark, R. W. Kates, J. F. Richards, J. T. Matthews, and W. B. Meyer. Cambridge, England: Cambridge University Press, with Clark University.

Luhmann, Niklas. 1989. *Ecological Communication.* Chicago, IL: University of Chicago Press.

Marsh, George Perkins. [1864] 1965. *Man and Nature.* Edited by D. Lowenthal. Reprint, Cambridge, MA: Belknap Press.

Mazur, Allan. 1998. "Global Environmental Change in the News: 1987–90 vs. 1992–6." *International Sociology* 13:457–72.

McCormick, John. 1989. *Reclaiming Paradise.* Bloomington, IN: Indiana University Press.

McCoy, Michael and Patrick McCully. 1993. *The Road from Rio: An NGO Action Guide to Envi-*

ronment and Development. Utrecht, Netherlands: International Books.

Meyer, John W. 1994. "Rationalized Environments." Pp. 28–54 in *Institutional Environments and Organizations,* by W. R. Scott and J. W. Meyer and Associates. Thousand Oaks, CA: Sage.

Meyer, John W., John Boli, George M. Thomas, and Francisco O. Ramirez. 1997. "World Society and the Nation-State." *American Journal of Sociology* 103:144–81.

Meyer, John W., David John Frank, Ann Hironaka, Evan Schofer, and Nancy Brandon Tuma. 1997. "The Structuring of a World Environmental Regime, 1870–1990." *International Organization* 51:623–51.

Meyer, John W. and Ronald Jepperson. Forthcoming. "The 'Actors' of Modern Society: Cultural Rationalization and the Ongoing Expansion of Social Agency." In *Bending the Bars of the Iron Cage: Institutional Processes and Dynamics,* edited by W. Powell and D. Jones. Chicago, IL: University of Chicago Press.

Nanda, Ved P. 1983. "Global Climate Change and International Law and Institutions." Pp. 227–39 in *World Climate Change: The Role of International Law and Institutions,* edited by V. P. Nanda. Boulder, CO: Westview.

O'Connor, James. 1998. *Natural Causes: Essays in Ecological Marxism.* New York: Guilford.

Pepper, David. 1984. *The Roots of Modern Environmentalism.* London, England: Croon Helm.

Roberts, J. Timmons. 1996. "Predicting Participation in Environmental Treaties: A World-System Analysis." *Sociological Inquiry* 66:38–57.

Robertson, Roland. 1992. *Globalization: Social Theory and Global Culture.* London, England: Sage.

Ruggie, John Gerard. 1993. "Territoriality and Beyond: Problematizing Modernity in International Relations." *International Organization* 47:139–74.

Ruster, Bernd, Bruno Simma, and Michael Bock, eds. 1983. *International Protection of the Environment: Treaties and Related Documents.* Dobbs Ferry, NY: Oceana Publications.

Schnaiberg, Allan and Kenneth Alan Gould. 1994. *Environment and Society: The Enduring Conflict.* New York: St. Martin's.

Schofer, Evan. 1999. "Science Association in the International Sphere, 1860–1994." Pp. 249–66 in *Constructing World Culture: International Non-governmental Organizations Since 1875,* edited by J. Boli and G. M. Thomas. Stanford, CA: Stanford University Press.

Schott, Thomas. 1993. "World Science." *Science, Technology, and Human Values* 18:196–208.

Singer, J. David and Melvin Small. 1990. *National Material Capabilities Data, 1816–1985.* Ann Arbor, MI: Inter-university Consortium for Political and Social Research.

Smith, Jackie, Charles Chatfield, and Ron Pagnucco, eds. 1997. *Transnational Social Movements and Global Politics: Solidarity Beyond the State.* Syracuse, NY: Syracuse University Press.

Sprinz, Detlef and Tapani Vaahtoranta. 1994. "The Interest-Based Explanation of International Environmental Policy." *International Organization* 48:77–105.

SPSS. 1988. *SPSS-X User's Guide.* 3d ed. Chicago, IL: SPSS.

Stern, Paul C., Oran R. Young, and Daniel Druckman, eds. 1992. *Global Environmental Change.* Washington, DC: National Academy.

Strang, David and John W. Meyer. 1993. "Institutional Conditions for Diffusion." *Theory and Society* 22:487–511.

Summers, Robert, and Alan Heston. 1991. "The Penn World Table (Mark 5): An Expanded Set of International Comparisons, 1950–1988." *Quarterly Journal of Economics* 106:327–68.

Taylor, Peter J. and Frederick H. Buttel. 1992. "How Do We Know We Have Environmental Problems? Science and the Globalization of Environmental Discourse." *Geoforum* 23:405–16.

Thomas, Caroline. 1992. *The Environment in International Relations.* London, England: Royal Institute of International Affairs.

Thomas, Keith Vivian. 1983. *Man and the Natural World.* New York: Pantheon.

Tuma, Nancy Brandon. 1992. *Invoking RATE.* Palo Alto, CA: DMA Corporation.

Tuma, Nancy Brandon and Michael T. Hannan. 1984. *Social Dynamics: Models and Methods.* Orlando, FL: Academic.

Turner, B. L., II, William C. Clark, Robert W. Kates, John F. Richards, Jessica T. Matthews and William B. Meyer, eds. 1990. *The Earth as Transformed by Human Action.* Cambridge, England: Cambridge University Press.

Union of International Associations (UIA). 1948–1999. *Yearbook of International Organizations.* Munich, Germany: K.G. Saur.

United Nations Environment Programme (UNEP). 1982–1993. *Annual Report of the Executive Director.* Nairobi, Kenya: United Nations Environment Programme.

Walsh, Edward J. 1981. "Resource Mobilization and Citizen Protest in Communities Around Three Mile Island." *Social Problems* 29:1–21.

Wapner, Paul. 1996. *Environmental Activism and World Civic Politics.* Albany, NY: State University of New York Press.

Weber, Max. [1968] 1978. *Economy and Society.* 2 vols. Edited by G. Roth and C. Wittich. Reprint, Berkeley, CA: University of California Press.

Wood, Christopher. 1995. *Environmental Impact*

Assessment: A Comparative Review. New York: John Wiley and Sons.

World Resources Institute (WRI). 1998. *World Resources 1998–99 Database.* Washington, DC: World Resources Institute.

Yearley, Steven. 1996. *Sociology, Environmentalism, Globalization.* London, England: Sage Publications.

Young, Oran. 1989. "The Politics of International Regime Formation: Managing Natural Resources and the Environment." *International Organization* 43:349–75.

Zils, Michael, ed. 1998. *World Guide to Scientific Associations and Learned Societies.* 7th ed. Munich, Germany: K. G. Saur.

Zürn, Michael. 1998. "The Rise of International Environmental Politics: A Review of Current Research." *World Politics* 50:617–49.

[21]

WORLD SOCIETY, THE NATION-STATE, AND ENVIRONMENTAL PROTECTION[*]
Comment on Frank, Hironaka, and Schofer

Frederick H. Buttel
University of Wisconsin–Madison

I t is useful for the discipline that the Frank, Hironaka, and Schofer paper (2000, henceforward FH&S)—a paper from the "world society"/"world polity"/"institutional structure" tradition[1]—finds a place in this special issue of *ASR*. While the world society approach has been represented in the sociological literature for over two decades (cf. Meyer 1980; Meyer and Rowan 1977; Meyer and Hannan 1979), its impact on the discipline (with the partial exception of the sociology of education) has been only modest.[2] This is unfortunate because the world society literature is based on two very intriguing insights: First, while the world's peoples have come from strikingly diverse sociocultural origins, there is a startling (and apparently growing) degree of global cultural homogenization. Second, there exists today a level of isomorphism of social structural and organizational forms across world societies that is far too great to be solely ex-

plicable in terms of functional necessity or task demands. In particular, the modern bureaucratic state has become the only legitimate form of political organization across the world, despite the fact that there are many dysfunctional aspects of such nation-state organization (see Finnemore 1996a: 332). Thus, for example, we can observe that states as diverse as those in Europe and Africa have roughly the same roster of ministries (defense, agriculture, finance, etc.), the same tripartite organization of the military (army, navy, air force), and quite similar educational systems (state-organized schooling with strikingly similar curricula).

How can one account for these patterns of cultural homogenization and organizational isomorphism? World society theory advances a bold, sweeping explanation. The basic argument is that over the past century or two there has emerged a "global society" of international organizations and related groupings that share the norm of the desirability of Western-style (i.e., essentially Weberian) rationality, and that as a result of the creation of this global culture there has been a steady global diffusion of particular organizational forms, such as bureaucratic states and bureaucratic organization generally, constitutions and citizenship, market institutions, and so on.

---

[*] Direct all correspondence to Frederick H. Buttel, Department of Rural Sociology, University of Wisconsin, 1450 Linden Dr., Madison, WI 53706 (fhbuttel@facstaff.wisc.edu).

[1] FH&S utilize the terminology "world society," but their perspective is essentially identical to the "world polity" (Meyer 1980) and "institutional structure" (Thomas et al. 1987) perspectives. Though the term world polity arguably does more justice to this theory than the expression world society, in this comment I utilize the terminology of FH&S.

[2] World society research is very closely associated with event history analysis and other sophisticated analytical methods. This arguably has helped research to achieve publication in major sociological research journals but may have limited world society theory's overall influence. Interestingly, world society theory has had more influence in political science, particularly in international relations and international political economy (see, e.g., Finnemore 1996a, 1996b; Katzenstein et al. 1998), than in sociology.

THE WORLD SOCIETY MODEL OF THE NATION-STATE AND ENVIRONMENTAL PROTECTION

FH&S's core argument is that the world society of international/intergovernmental environmental organizations has cultivated and helped diffuse the norm of nation-state responsibility for environmental protection, and that domestic factors and/or processes have played little part. FH&S examine the diffusion of the norm of nation-state responsibility for environmental protection by evaluating the emergence of five organizational forms of environmental regulation: proliferation of national parks, formation of national chapters of international environmental organizations, memberships in intergovernmental environmental organizations, passage of environmental impact assessment laws, and formation of state environmental ministries. FH&S note that their model of the "environmentalization" of the state is "top-down" and diffusionist. Their explanation of differential rates of diffusion among nation-states over time is largely twofold. First, FH&S posit that a high level of nation-state ties to world society increases the likelihood of state environmentalization. Second, they posit what might be called a "nation-state receptor-site effect," whereby societies with many national environmental organizations and natural science associations will be best able to "receive environmental 'signals' from world society and transmit them to domestic actors" (p. 105).

The event history, diffusion-type analysis of their five indicators of the institutionalization of state responsibility for environmental protection includes a three-item indicator of "global institutionalization of national environmental protection" plus indicators of nation-state ties and receptor site variables. In addition, FH&S incorporate several control variables to address competing hypotheses.

The results seem to bear out each of FH&S's hypotheses. The data reported in Figures 1 through 4 do show trends over time toward diffusion of the five indicators of environmentalization of the state. By the end of the 1990s there was a global isomorphism of environmentally related organizations and practices surpassing typical sociological expectations. FH&S thus demonstrate that the tendency toward homogenization and isomorphism observed in other realms (e.g., educational, citizenship, social welfare, and scientific institutions) is present in the environmental arena as well.

There are, however, some shortcomings in FH&S's conceptualization and data that require comment. First, the authors do not address whether their five measures of state responsibility for environmental protection have, or are likely to have, any definite connections with actual environmental protec-

tion outcomes. Addressing the degree to which the organizational forms documented by FH&S are correlated with actual societal outcomes would obviously be a difficult task. But this task is critical. An illustration: Those persons who have traveled extensively in developing countries, most of which have planning ministries, will attest that there is uneven, and often minimal, development planning or urban and regional planning.

This distinction between the existence of a given state-organizational form and its actual sociopolitical impacts or outcomes is a particularly important matter with regard to the authors' five dependent variables.[3] Environmental impact assessment legislation has been very uneven in its effectiveness across nation-states (Weale 1992:22–23). Many poor countries belong to intergovernmental environmental organizations but do not even have the resources to send delegates to meetings. Thus, while FH&S's data do show a long-term pattern of diffusion of organizational forms, there is no evidence that this diffusion is effecting actual outcomes.

Second, the authors ignore a great deal of literature on the domestic antecedents of national (and international) environmental policies. For example, there is scarcely a serious analysis of national (or comparative national) environmental policymaking that does not stress the role played by national environmental organizations in catalyzing state responsibility for environmental protection (e.g., see Andrews 1999; Hays 1987; Szasz 1994). Relatedly, in footnote 5 FH&S dismiss, prematurely I believe, Yearley's (1996) persuasive analysis, which discounts the notion that there is an intrinsic global character of modern environmentalism and environmental policy. In particular, Yearley notes that the globalization of environmental discourse during the 1980s and 1990s was, in part, a self-conscious strategy by scientists and certain environmental organizations to make environmentalism more persuasive.

Third, FH&S's attempt to dismiss empirically the role played by domestic factors has

---

[3] Note as well that the mean intercorrelation of the dependent measures is quite low ($r = .40$), given the authors' argument that state responsibility for environmental control is a singular or unidimensional construct.

serious shortcomings. They argue that a do-mestically-driven social movement logic of environmentalization of the state can be modeled by including population (a measure of "pressure" on natural resources) and iron and steel production (a measure of "national wealth and environmental degradation"; p. 105) as control variables. There is no refer-ence to existing literature illustrating or sub-stantiating that such variables are valid indi-cators of national environmental mobiliza-tion. I am not aware of any sociological lit-erature arguing that environmentalism tends to be a direct response to environmental deg-radation in objective terms; in fact, the lit-erature tends to endorse precisely the oppo-site—that the objective seriousness of envi-ronmental problems tends to have little ef-fect on mobilization (Hannigan 1995; Martell 1994). Moreover, they use no direct measure of the intensity of domestic environ-mental protest in their model. Thus, their dis-missal of the domestic social movement mo-bilization hypothesis is premature.

Fourth, problems with the overall world society perspective emerge as weaknesses in FH&S. One such concern is that the trans-mission of environmental rationality from global society to nation-state is portrayed by FH&S in essentially conflict-free terms. There is no mention of coercion or contesta-tion. The only reference made to interna-tional conflict is the claim that "in the envi-ronmental realm, interstate pressures only rarely appear as exercises of raw power" (p. 102). Perhaps so, but FH&S's account is in-consistent with the fact that there has been persistent conflict between the Group of 77 (G-77) developing countries and the Organi-zation for Economic Cooperation and De-velopment (OECD) countries (particularly the United States) over a range of environ-mental regulatory matters (e.g., see Paarlberg 1993; Porter and Brown 1996, chap. 4; Yearley 1996). In interpreting FH&S's results we also must recognize that many of the types of state environmental forms they measure have been imposed on developing countries against their will by the World Bank as a condition of receiving loans (Goldman 1999). Thus, a related weakness is that the world society perspec-tive tends to privilege statistical association over documentation of the actual process by which global cultural institutionalization occurs.

Finally, concern can be raised that the world society portrayal of Western rational-ity in general, and FH&S's portrayal of environmentalization of the nation-state in particular, overemphasizes the degree to which cultural consistency exists. The cul-ture of Western rationality has long involved deep contradictions—between capital accu-mulation and inequality, bureaucratization and democracy, and so on. Environmental-ism is no different. Contemporary environ-mentalism and cultures of environmental regulation exhibit important tensions. For example, should effective environmental management involve "command-and-con-trol" regulation or market- or incentive-based regulatory systems (Mol 1995; Weale 1992)? Should the burden of proof with re-gard to the safety of chemical products be placed on producer organizations (the "pre-cautionary principle" favored by many envi-ronmental groups) or on state regulatory or-ganizations (the predominant approach in most OECD countries)? Should environmen-tal regulation confine itself to the most per-nicious pollutants and the most serious waste problems in order to make the capital accu-mulation process "cleaner," or does effective environmental regulation ultimately presup-pose serious constraints on consumption and a shift to a no-growth society (Hajer 1995; Murphy 1994)? These contradictions are in-creasingly being played out in international environmental organizations and intergov-ernmental organizations (Yearley 1996). FH&S thus tend to ascribe to environmental culture and its "epistemic communities" (Haas 1992) a greater coherence than actu-ally exists and gloss over tensions within global environmentalism. In so doing, FH&S's world society approach removes the stuff of politics from the analysis of political institutions (also see Finnemore 1996a).

THE ENVIRONMENTAL INTERNATIONALIZATION DEBATE

One reason the FH&S's paper merits atten-tion, though, is that they may shed light on whether effective environmental control will be best accomplished through global/interna-tional dynamics versus through the nation-state (or some other level of politics and/or civil society). While this debate is multifaceted, much of it boils down to two issues: whether action at the global level (particularly that catalyzed by the environmental "epistemic community" [Haas 1992] and international environmental organizations) can ultimately be effective in overriding the more parochial regulatory patterns that tend to prevail within the nation-state; and whether structural inequalities in the world-economy and global politics will dictate that international environmental action will be conflictual, prone to stalemate, and successful only to the degree that the environmental concerns of the developed industrial countries are emphasized.

FH&S's approach and data are highly germane to what will be one of the most critical policy debates of the next millennium. Though they do not explicitly take sides in this debate, FH&S are clearly aligned with the "environmental internationalists," but they are not out on a limb in this regard. To a considerable degree the internationalization image of future environmental progress is assumed (Taylor 1997). Note, however, that the sociological literature contains some persuasive analyses and arguments to the contrary. Yearley (1996) makes the case that the globalization of environmentalism and environmental protection could ultimately be a discursive and political dead-end. In particular, global frameworks for promoting environmental protection are ultimately based on claims that all of humanity has a "common future" (WCED 1987) when, in fact, the more striking and enduring aspect of "world society" is that it is built on—and in many respects can be thought of as helping to sustain—a strikingly unequal and divided world order. The key shortcoming of the latest round of international environmental agreements (e.g., the 1997 Kyoto Protocol of the Climate Convention, the Biosafety Protocol to the Convention on Biological Diversity) has largely been that, in a highly unequal world order in which social exclusion is increasingly a core principle, a large share of the nation-states of the developing world have little to gain, and sometimes much to lose, from signing and adhering to international environmental agreements (Taylor 1997).

CONCLUSION

FH&S have made a noteworthy contribution to our understanding of states and environments. Sociologists from all areas of the discipline can benefit from confronting their observation that there is a good deal of social-structural isomorphism across the world's diverse nation-states. FH&S's results and the considerable literature written by sociologists who work within this perspective should signal the need to take more seriously international organizations, epistemic communities, and international regimes. FH&S have documented that the global organizational-homogenization process is relevant to environmental protection institutions, policies, and practices. Now that the organizational homogenization phenomenon is better understood in terms of extent, timing, and incidence, more work should be done to specify the social processes and the concrete societal impacts, outcomes, and implications of structural isomorphism—particularly of the political sort.

Fleshing out the world society research agenda will in all likelihood require moving beyond the "top-down" imagery employed by FH&S. The authors themselves acknowledge that there are arenas of environmental protection policy in which the impetus has come from the nation-states of the developing world, rather than being diffused from world society to the less modern nation-states (also see Martinez-Alier 1995). The world society research community may be best able to incorporate insights such as this into the core of its theory if it explores some of the parallels between their work and that of the world-systems community. Both world society and world-systems theories embrace a global level of analysis and posit that there is a tendency toward a singular world-scale dynamic that affects social life across the globe. World society and world-systems theory and research have both suffered from deterministic or reductionist tendencies. The world-systems community, however, has made some considerable theoretical and methodological strides in confronting this problem. For example, McMichael's (1990) work on comparative research in a world-systemic context advances the notion that the world-economy, the international state system, and individual nation-states must be seen as being mutually constitutive. Adapting McMichael's approach may provide a template for world society researchers to develop a more nuanced view of the antecedents and consequences of structural homogenization.

Frederick H. Buttel is Professor and Chair in the Department of Rural Sociology, and Professor of Environmental Studies at the University of Wisconsin, Madison. His interests are in environmental sociology, sociology of science and technology, and rural sociology, and he has published several books in these areas. Most recently, he is a co-editor of three anthologies: Hungry for Profit *(Monthly Review Press),* Environmental Sociology and Global Modernity *(Sage), and* Sociological Theory and the Environment *(Rowman and Littlefield), all of which are forthcoming in 2000. He is currently President of the Environment and Society Research Committee (RC 24) of the International Sociological Association.*

REFERENCES

Andrews, Richard N. L. 1999. *Managing the Environment, Managing Ourselves: A History of American Environmental Policy.* New Haven, CT: Yale University Press.

Finnemore, Martha. 1996a. "Norms, Culture, and World Politics: Insights from Sociology's Institutionalism." *International Organization* 50:325–47.

———. 1996b. *National Interests in International Society.* Ithaca, NY: Cornell University Press.

Frank, David John, Ann Hironaka, and Evan Schofer. 2000. "The Nation-State and the Natural Environment over the Twentieth Century." *American Sociological Review* 65:96–116

Goldman, Michael. 1999. "Green Hegemony." Department of Sociology, University of Illinois, Urbana-Champaign, IL. Unpublished manuscript.

Haas, Peter M. 1992. "Introduction: Epistemic Communities and International Policy Coordination." *International Organization* 46:1–35.

Hajer, Maarten A. 1995. *The Politics of Environmental Discourse.* New York: Oxford University Press.

Hannigan, John A. 1995. *Environmental Sociology.* London, England: Routledge.

Hays, Samuel P. 1987. *Beauty, Health, and Permanence: Environmental Politics in the United States, 1955–1985.* New York: Cambridge University Press.

Katzenstein, Peter J., Robert O. Keohane, and Stephen D. Krasner. 1998. "*International Organization* and the Study of World Politics." *International Organization* 52:645–85.

Martell, Luke. 1994. *Ecology and Society.* Cambridge, England: Polity.

Martinez-Alier, Juan. 1995. "Commentary: The Environment as Luxury Good or 'Too Poor to Be Green'." *Ecological Economics* 13:1–10.

McMichael, Philip. 1990. "Incorporating Comparison within a World-Historical Perspective: An Alternative Comparative Method." *American Sociological Review* 55:385–97.

Meyer, John W. 1980. "The World Polity and the Authority of the Nation-State." Pp. 109–37 in *Studies of the Modern World-System*, edited by A. Bergesen. New York: Academic.

Meyer, John W. and Michael T. Hannan, eds. 1979. *National Development and the World System.* Chicago, IL: University of Chicago Press.

Meyer, John W. and Brian Rowan. 1977. "Institutionalized Organizations: Formal Structure as Myth and Ceremony." *American Journal of Sociology* 83:340–63.

Mol, Arthur P. J. 1995. *The Refinement of Production.* Utrecht, Netherlands: Van Arkel.

Murphy, Raymond. 1994. *Rationality and Nature.* Boulder, CO: Westview Press.

Paarlberg, Robert L. 1993. "Managing Pesticide Use in Developing Countries." Pp. 309–50 in *Institutions for the Earth: Sources of Effective International Environmental Protection*, edited by P. M. Haas, R. O. Keohane, and M. A. Levy. Cambridge, MA: MIT Press.

Porter, Gareth and Janet Welsh Brown. 1996. *Global Environmental Politics.* 2d ed. Boulder, CO: Westview Press.

Szasz, Andrew. 1994. *Ecopopulism.* Minneapolis, MN: University of Minnesota Press.

Taylor, Peter J. 1997. "How Do We Know We Have Global Environmental Problems? Undifferentiated Science-Politics and its Potential Reconstruction." Pp. 149–74 in *Changing Life*, edited by P. J. Taylor, S. E. Halfon, and P. N. Edwards. Minneapolis, MN: University of Minnesota Press.

Thomas, George M., John W. Meyer, Francisco O. Ramirez, and John Boli, eds. 1987. *Institutional Structure.* Newbury Park, CA: Sage.

Weale, Albert 1992. *The New Politics of Pollution.* Manchester, England: Manchester University Press.

World Commission on Environment and Development (WCED). 1987. *Our Common Future.* New York: Oxford University Press.

Yearley, Steven. 1996. *Sociology, Environmentalism, Globalization.* London, England: Sage.

[22]

ENVIRONMENTALISM AS A GLOBAL INSTITUTION*
Reply to Buttel

David John Frank
Harvard University

Ann Hironaka
Stanford University

Evan Schofer
Stanford University

Environmentalism is global in two basic senses. It asserts the priority of a global entity—an ecosystem that operates according to universal laws in a tangled web of planetary interdependencies; and it refers to a worldwide social process—world-level discourse and activity that together have reconstituted nation-states and individuals.

Our work to date has focused on global environmentalism, describing and analyzing its rise and institutionalization (Frank 1997; Frank, Hironaka, Meyer, et al. 1999; Meyer, Frank, et al. 1997) and its impact on nation-states (Frank 1999; Frank, Hironaka, and Schofer 2000, henceforward FH&S; Hironaka 1998). In this reply, we explore the implications of our perspective for the important issues raised by Buttel (2000, henceforward B): improvements in environmental quality, the role domestic environmental social movements play in promoting national environmental activities, international conflict over environmental matters, and contradictions between environmentalism and other global institutions.

THE GLOBAL INSTITUTIONAL PERSPECTIVE

The global environmental regime began to appear in the late nineteenth century, spurred by a new social conception of nature and expanded world organization. Changes in the "facts" of nature first became more rapid in the middle-late 1800s. What, until then, had been conceived mainly as the outcome of "Creation," often separate from and even opposed to human society, became increasingly

rationalized as a means to human ends. Nature *versus* society, with attendant efforts at taming and eradicating nature, increasingly shifted to nature *for* society. At first this meant that nature could be harvested, used, and sold: whales for blubber, trees for timber, mountains for copper. Increasingly, however, thanks to the efforts of scientific authorities, nature became rationalized to mean life-sustenance. Outside an Earthly envelope, no human life was conceived to be possible. This important cognitive shift helped lay the foundations for the "global ecosystem."

The late 1800s also witnessed the increasing organization of the world polity, most strikingly in the expansion of the system of nation-states and colonies. Informal diplomatic networks gave rise to international conferences and treaties, and to later intergovernmental organizations. The process eventually led to the formation of the United Nations, an all-purpose forum for the discussion of world matters, which in turn sparked an even larger wave of world-level organization.

These two processes together, the social construction of a rationalized global nature and the institutionalization of a world polity, established the *motive* and *capacity* necessary for building a global environmental regime facilitated by environmental experts and authorities. International conferences, non-governmental associations, treaties, and intergovernmental organizations multiplied exponentially over the twentieth century, around issues as diverse as locust control, access to fisheries, acid rain, and climate change.

At the center of all such international activities lay the assumption that nation-states were the primary actors in the global arena (Meyer, Boli, et al. 1997). Thus the rise of the global environmental regime brought with it the notion that nation-states bore the

* Direct all correspondence to David John Frank, Department of Sociology, William James Hall, Harvard University, Cambridge, MA 02138 (frankdj@wjh.harvard.edu). We thank John W. Meyer for advice and comments.

responsibility for protecting nature: The regime reconfigured *what the nation-state is* in the institutions of world society (Boli and Thomas 1997). Nation-states that participated in world society were expected, encouraged, and sometimes even coerced into assuming responsibility for environmental protection. Countries formed parks, established hunting seasons, set water and air quality standards, founded ministries, passed impact assessment legislation, and so on. The catalysts for involvement emanated from the world social system, as did the rewards for proper implementation (e.g., Barrett and Tsui 1999).

Our story thus emphasizes a series of global institutional changes: first in the definition of nature, second in the organization of the world polity, and third in the constitutive bases of the nation-state. Environmentalism, we have argued, is fundamentally global, first in its conception of the natural entity and consequently in the social processes it conveys.

ENVIRONMENTAL QUALITY

A first question that follows from our perspective regards outcomes: Do the many changes in world and national policy actually improve environmental quality (B, p. 118)? Some studies suggest they do (Dietz and Kalof 1992; Roberts 1996). Populations of various endangered species (elephant, wolf, tiger) are strong, and even resurgent. Chlorofluorocarbon emissions, the culprits behind ozone depletion, have declined precipitously. Polluted rivers and bays throughout the industrialized world are returning to near pristine condition. Clearly some regulations, international and national, are working.

Holes in the system, however, are legend. One needs only to visit a few national parks in a few countries to witness surprising levels of resource extraction, poaching, or agriculture; or read the text of just a handful of international treaties (e.g., the Climate Change Convention) to find instances of flagrant violation; or scrutinize the conduct of only a few environmental impact assessments to see the obvious incursion of political and economic interests. The rules, it seems, are routinely flouted, and incur little in the way of consequences.

Are policies *effective enough* in restoring and maintaining environmental quality? The answer most certainly is no. Degradation is rampant and spreading. But are policies *effective at all?* The answer most likely is yes: Even a pockmarked system is better than no system at all.

Thus at the world level, we expect the proliferation of environmental policies to decrease rates of global environmental degradation, even while problems continue to accumulate. The nation-state-level effects should be much more variable than world-level effects, contingent mainly on a country's relationship to the wider system. Among nation-states more open to world society (and thus the fountainhead of environmental protection), we expect policies to be implemented relatively effectively, with attendant benefits for observed environmental quality. Among countries less open to world society, we expect more decoupling between policy and practice.

These ideas about environmental quality differ sharply from conventional emphases on nation-state-level outcomes and domestic capacities and commitments. In future work, we hope to test our views; the present evidence, however supportive, is merely anecdotal.

SOCIAL MOVEMENTS

A second question our perspective raises concerns the role of domestic social movements (B, pp. 118–19). Many theorists place environmental movements front and center in discussions of environmental policy change (e.g., Szasz 1994), and the secondary role social movements play in our analysis comes as a surprise to them.

As a practical matter, domestic environmental movements do not appear in our quantitative analysis for one reason only: No source to our knowledge provides information on the extent of environmental movement activity for many countries over the whole century. Even if the data were available, however, we would not expect social movements to play a strong *independent* role in global environmentalism. This is because most domestic environmental movements are generated exogenously—they are outcomes of the same global processes that produce national policy changes. The redefinitions that rendered nature as a global ecosystem and the reorganizations that rendered the world as a global interstate system catalyze environmental social movements just as they catalyze environmental ministries, national parks, and so on. Thus we expect social movements to have effects on national environmental policies that are mostly redundant with our measures of ties to world society and scientific receptor sites. (Note that in less scientific/universalistic sectors of policy, the independent effect of social movements may be greater.)

Strong support for the notion that environmental movements emanate from world society would require data over time, but some queries are possible using cross-sectional data. In particular, if environmental social movements are seeded by world society, then nation-states with strong ties to world society should have the most domestic environmental movement organizations.

Tests of this top-down hypothesis appear in Table 1. The dependent variable is a count of the number of environmental groups per nation-state "that influence policy or [were] major sources of information" in 1989 (Trzyna 1989:9). We show five pairs of regression models, without (Model A) and with (Model B) a lagged dependent variable measured in 1976 (Trzyna and Coan 1976). All models include logged population size in 1984 as a control.

In the first pair of models, the number of environmental social-movement organizations (logged) is regressed on ties to world society in 1984. In the four following pairs, we add the independent variables typically invoked to explain domestic environmental movements: a measure of resources (gross domestic product per capita in 1984), a measure of political openness (score on the Gurr index of mass democratic institutions in 1984 [Gurr 1990; also see FH&S, pp. 108–109]), and then two measures of environmental degradation (population density in 1984 and industrial degradation in 1980).

The results in Table 1 strongly support the notion that ties to world society promote environmental social movements. Across the board, the effect of links to world society is positive, and in 9 of the 10 models, the effect is significant: Strong ties to world soci-

ety predict a high number of environmental social-movement organizations five years later.

Undoubtedly, as the conventional literature predicts, environmental social movements grow best in fertile soil (i.e., in countries rich in resources and open in political opportunities). The results in Table 1 confirm as much. But environmental social movements also grow best where their seeds are prolific, and those seeds, we assert, filter downward from world society (cf. McAdam and Rucht 1993).

From our perspective, then, it is thus difficult to imagine environmental social movements as independent causal forces behind the environmental policies in most countries (the United States may be an exception). Rather, we see movements and policies as both flowing from the same source. Thus we expect reciprocal positive effects between the two, similar to those demonstrated for the lesbian and gay social movement and liberal state policies on homosexual sex (Frank and McEneaney 1999).

INTERNATIONAL CONFLICT

A third issue raised by our perspective pertains to international conflict (B, p. 119). The "global" label given to many environmental issues may be seen to obscure regional differences in responsibility for environmental problems and in the costs and benefits of their solution (Buttel and Taylor 1992; Yearley 1996). International conflicts may, and often do, follow, and examples are numerous. In the United States, for instance, the Amazonian rainforest is typically depicted in global-ecosystem terms—as a world "oxygen pump," as a planetary hub of species diversity, and so on. In Brazil, however, the same Amazon is seen as a local natural resource: in particular, as a store of timber for commodity markets (see Redclift and Sage 1998).

To some extent, such differences follow from disparities in national interests. The United States clearly benefits if the Amazon is treated as a global ecosystem more than if it is treated as a national resource, and the reverse is true for Brazil (at least in the short term). Our perspective leads us to add, and emphasize, that even "national interests" are constructed in the world social system

Table 1. Coefficients from the OLS Regression of Environmental Organizations in 1989 on Ties to
World Society, GDP per capita, Democracy, Population Density, Industrial Degradation,
and Population Size, without and with Control for Environmental Organizations in 1976

Variable	Model 1		Model 2		Model 3		Model 4		Model 5	
	A	B	A	B	A	B	A	B	A	B
Ties to world society, 1984	.326**	.111**	.213**	.068	.222**	.095*	.324**	.113**	.292**	.110**
	(.034)	(.040)	(.054)	(.052)	(.040)	(.041)	(.034)	(.040)	(.038)	(.040)
Lagged dependent variable, 1976	—	.452**	—	.429**	—	.409**	—	.445**	—	.457**
		(.056)		(.066)		(.063)		(.086)		(.060)
GDP per capita, 1984 (logged)	—	—	.143**	.043	—	—	—	—	—	—
			(.051)	(.047)						
Gurr democracy index, 1984	—	—	—	—	.062**	.021	—	—	—	—
					(.014)	(.014)				
Population density, 1984 (logged)	—	—	—	—	—	—	.066	.015	—	—
							(.034)	(.030)		
Industrial degradation, 1980	—	—	—	—	—	—	—	—	.054	−.015
									(.034)	(.030)
Population size, 1984 (logged)	.066*	.019	.166**	.079*	.095**	.034	.067*	.020	.095**	.027
	(.031)	(.027)	(.043)	(.040)	(.030)	(.028)	(.031)	(.027)	(.033)	(.030)
Constant	.159	.251	−2.371**	−.920	−.433	.037	−.160	.178	−.283	.130
	(.477)	(.404)	(.899)	(.815)	(.471)	(.425)	(.501)	(.431)	(.510)	(.439)
Number of organizations	162	162	134	134	162	162	162	162	157	157
R^2	.55	.68	.54	.66	.60	.68	.56	.68	.56	.68

Note: For data and variables, see Frank, Hironaka, and Schofer (2000:108–109 and app. C).
$^*p < .05$ $^{**}p < .01$ (two-tailed tests)

(Meyer, Boli, et al. 1997). The extent to which a nation-state views the Amazon or any other natural process or entity in global ecosystem terms versus natural resource terms is partly a function of that country's location in world society. Central nation-states are closer to the wellsprings of meaning in the world-system, and thus are more likely to embody newer (in this case global ecosystem) definitions of nature and nation-state responsibility.

All this implies (1) that conflicts over environmental issues will involve countries with different locations in the world social system (i.e., central versus peripheral); (2) that conflicts in substance will hinge on different definitions of the focal entity "nature," usually ecosystem versus natural resource; and (3) that conflicts will decline some over time, as nation-state responsibility for the global ecosystem becomes institutionalized more evenly throughout the system.

Some support for these views appears in the finding that nation-states densely tied to

world society are more likely to adopt environmental policies than are others: The global ecosystem view is more deeply institutionalized at the center. Narrower and more direct tests of these ideas, of course, would be preferable. Given the gap between our emphases on relations "external" to the nation-state and standard emphases on "internal" interests, further investigations are warranted.

GLOBAL INSTITUTIONAL CONTRADICTIONS

Finally, our perspective highlights the possibility of contradictions between environmentalism and other global institutions, particularly capitalism (B, p. 119). Many see the imperatives of national development and environmental protection as irreconcilable. As one sociologist puts it, "[I]f the Chinese try to eat as much meat and eggs and drive as many cars (per capita) as the Americans now do the biosphere will fry. This may be the

126   AMERICAN SOCIOLOGICAL REVIEW

most potent contradiction of global capitalism" (Chase-Dunn 1998:*xxi*).

Such contradictions arise with changes in
global institutional arrangements and are
driven by the advance of environmentalism.
But we see more evidence of institutional accommodation than of system demise. The
marriage (however convenient) of development and environmentalism appears in more
and more legal/organizational forms. The
Nature Conservancy, for example, collects
donations from corporate sponsors to purchase wilderness areas (see Hoffman and
Ventresca 1999). "Sustainable development"
was the hallmark of the 1992 United Nations
Conference on the Environment and Development (notice the title change from the
1972 UN Conference on the Human Environment). The Rio Declaration, produced at
the 1992 conference, simultaneously recognized "the integral and interdependent nature
of the Earth, our home" and also "the sovereign right [of nations] to exploit their own
resources" (McCoy and McCully 1993:24).
The contradiction between capitalism and
environmentalism hardly disappears under
the cover of such forms, but the tensions becomes less dramatic and more structurated
(Giddens 1979).

By virtually any measure, environmentalism is ascendant in the global institutional
scheme. Yet by no means does this suggest
that capitalism is thereby vanquished. Strategies for environmental protection could not
eliminate private property, for instance. But
mutual adaptation does occur: Pollution
credits are traded; debt is swapped for nature; and change, both in "capitalism" and
"environmentalism," both for good and ill,
proceeds accordingly.

CONCLUSION

At the root of our world society perspective
on environmentalism are the "facts" of nature: that a fragile net of global ecological
processes, highly interpenetrated and intertwined, supports life on planet Earth, and
that tears in the net threaten human survival.
That is the compelling cultural matter. Scientists author and broadcast these facts, and
they are disseminated throughout the world
in primary and secondary schools, and by the
media, social movements, and state policies.

The central "reality" of ecologized nature is
virtually uncontested. That it is also global
and urgent provides impetus to the many
changes in policy and practice we have outlined. The question of whether societal responses to environmental crises are deep
enough or fast enough seems to us a reasonable one. Whether they are or not, the question itself is alive in world society, and it is a
driving force behind much environmental
mobilization.

REFERENCES

Barrett, Deborah and Amy Ong Tsui. 1999.
"Policy as Symbolic Statement: International
Response to National Population Policies." *So-
cial Forces* 78:213–34.
Boli, John and George M. Thomas. 1997. "World
Culture in the World Polity: A Century of In-
ternational Non-Governmental Organization."
American Sociological Review 62:171–90.
Buttel, Frederick H. 2000. "World Society, the
Nation-State, and Environmental Protection:
Comment on Frank, Hironaka, and Schofer."
American Sociological Review 65:117–21.
Buttel, Frederick H. and Peter J. Taylor. 1992.
"Environmental Sociology and Global Envi-
ronmental Change: A Critical Assessment."
Society and Natural Resources 5:211–30.
Chase-Dunn, Christopher. 1998. *Global Forma-
tion: Structures of the World-Economy.* Up-
dated ed. Lanham, MD: Rowman and Little-
field.
Dietz, Thomas and Linda Kalof. 1992. "Environ-
mentalism among Nation-States." *Social Indi-
cators Research* 26:353–66.
Frank, David John. 1997. "Science, Nature, and
the Globalization of the Environment, 1870–
1990." *Social Forces* 76:409–35.
———. 1999. "The Social Bases of Environmental Treaty Ratification, 1900–90." *Sociological
Inquiry* 69:523–50.
Frank, David John, Ann Hironaka, John W.
Meyer, Evan Schofer, and Nancy Brandon
Tuma. 1999. "The Rationalization and Organi-
zation of Nature in World Culture." Pp. 81–99
in *Constructing World Culture: International
Non-governmental Organizations Since 1875,*
edited by J. Boli and G. M. Thomas. Stanford,
CA: Stanford University Press.
Frank, David John, Ann Hironaka, and Evan
Schofer. 2000. "The Nation-State and the Natu-
ral Environment over the Twentieth Century."
American Sociological Review 65:96–116.
Frank, David John and Elizabeth H. McEneaney.
1999. "The Individualization of Society and the
Liberalization of State Policies on Same-Sex

Sexual Relations, 1984–1995." *Social Forces* 77:911–44.

Giddens, Anthony. 1979. *Central Problems in Social Theory: Action, Structure, and Contradiction in Social Analyses.* Berkeley, CA: University of California Press.

Gurr, Ted Robert. 1990. *Polity II.* Ann Arbor, MI: Inter-university Consortium for Political and Social Research.

Hironaka, Ann. 1998. "The Institutionalization and Organization of a Global Environmental Solution: The Case of Environmental Impact Assessment Legislation." Presented at the annual meeting of the American Sociological Association, August 24, San Francisco, CA.

Hoffman, Andrew J. and Marc J. Ventresca. 1999. "The Institutional Framing of Policy Debates." *American Behavioral Scientist* 42: 1368–92.

McAdam, Doug and Dieter Rucht. 1993. "The Cross-National Diffusion of Movement Ideas." *Annals of the American Academy of Political and Social Science* 528:56–74.

McCoy, Michael and Patrick McCully. 1993. *The Road from Rio: An NGO Action Guide to Environment and Development.* Utrecht, Netherlands: International Books.

Meyer, John W., John Boli, George M. Thomas, and Francisco O. Ramirez. 1997. "World Society and the Nation-State." *American Journal of Sociology* 103:144–81.

Meyer, John W., David John Frank, Ann Hironaka, Evan Schofer, and Nancy Brandon Tuma. 1997. "The Structuring of a World Environmental Regime, 1870–1990." *International Organization* 51:623–51.

Redclift, Michael and Colin Sage. 1998. "Global Environmental Change and Global Inequality: North/South Perspectives." *International Sociology* 13:499–516.

Roberts, J. Timmons. 1996. "Predicting Participation in Environmental Treaties: A World-System Analysis." *Sociological Inquiry* 66:38–57.

Szasz, Andrew. 1994. *Ecopopulism.* Minneapolis, MN: University of Minnesota Press.

Trzyna, Thaddeus C., ed. 1989. *World Directory of Environmental Organizations.* 3d ed. Claremont, CA: California Institute for Public Affairs.

Trzyna, Thaddeus C. and Eugene V. Coan, eds. 1976. *World Directory of Environmental Organizations.* 2d ed. Claremont, CA: Public Affairs Clearinghouse.

Yearley, Steven. 1996. *Sociology, Environmentalism, Globalization.* London, England: Sage.

[23]

Environmental Security for People

The meaning of environmental security must be reconsidered if the concept is to make any meaningful contribution to the environment or human security. The principal failings of environmental security as presently conceived can be summarised as follows: it propagates the environmentally degrading security establishment; it talks in terms of, and prepares for, war; it defends the environmentally destructive modern way of life; and it ignores the needs and desires of most of the world's population. In short, at present, environmental security secures the processes that destroy the environment and create insecurity for the many for the benefit of the few. Ecological security has few such limitations, but fails to contest the meaning and practice of security because of the uncommon label 'ecological'.

What is required, then, is a reformulation of environmental security which does not prioritise national security and the issue of conflict above the needs of those who are most environmentally insecure. The approach that this book favours is to reformulate environmental security in terms of *human* security and peace, and drawing on the insights of ecological security. Taking the concept of security away from the state and towards people in this way 'points to a serious political project' (Walker 1987: 25). In this vein, the remainder of this book seeks to make some preliminary inroads into a new politics for a reformulated, human-centred concept of environmental security.

Reclaiming security

As a general rule, security is a function of power. The more power a person or group has to shape social life to suit their ends, the more secure they will tend to be. Those with less power tend to be more insecure: the landlord tends to be more economically secure than the tenant; the General is more secure from warfare than the foot soldier; and the food producer enjoys greater food security than the dependent food purchaser. Insecurity is therefore relative, and is a product of a broad milieu of social exchanges. This understanding of security and power is supported by Booth, for whom security defined as 'power over' occurs at the expense of others: 'true (stable) security can only be achieved by people and groups if they do not deprive others of it' (Booth 1991: 319). This suggests that any new approach to security must be based on the principles of equity and justice if it is to be sustained. In this respect socialism (however unfashionable it may now be in academic circles) is relevant to security.

From the advent of European colonisation through to contemporary globalisation, the concentration and centralisation of power has grown, and with it the geographic spread and degree of insecurity. Indeed, however nebulous, the phenomenon of globalisation (or at least enhanced economic integration) has heightened insecurity for the vast majority of people who are increasingly unable to control the economic environment which determines the provision of their most basic needs. This same economic system is also responsible for the degradation of the physical environment from which basic subsistence needs could formerly have been extracted with relative certainty. Certain insecurities are reasonably common, perhaps the first of these being the prospect of exposure to nuclear weapons. Yet many widespread insecurities, such as economic insecurity, are by no means universally experienced.

What is notable about this late-modern era is the relative impotence of the state to control the terms of security. The state is increasingly unable to act as regulator between global dynamics (such as speculative capital moving instantly through dense communication networks, or the illegal movement of drugs, weapons and people through the proliferation of cheap and rapid transport), and local places. In this respect initiatives to uniformly (de)regulate trade and investment, such as the WTO, can be read as proof that sovereignty no longer provides comprehensive security. Further, even the traditional concern for national security from external aggression is harder to control given the proliferation of weapons of mass destruction and the sophisticated nature of terrorism.

Security is the litmus test of sovereignty, and sovereignty is a corner-stone of modern politics. That there is less security for most people in most places suggests that this foundation of modern politics is being battered by globalisation. Another cornerstone is the common identity shared by all which is embodied in 'the nation', a construction whose necessary particularity is increasingly difficult to sustain in a world of cultural interpenetration facilitated by cheaper, faster and proliferating communication (and transport) technologies. While this may be construed as a crisis, the positive potential is that a different conception of politics and community might emerge (and some would say is emerging), which gives priority to difference, pluralism, conversation, and openness (Walker 1987).

This alternative politics is evident in critical social movements. The lesson learned from these movements is that insecurity takes many forms, and so approaches to security must be diverse, multi-dimensional, and located at many levels of society (Walker 1988). A single dominant security concept (such as national security) therefore does not satisfy the full range of security needs of people. Rethinking security therefore involves rethinking the relationship between security and political practice. A necessary first step is the democratisation of security issues: 'security is not something that can be left to someone else ... effective security must mean democratic security' (Walker 1988: 126). To this end the work of non-governmental organisations assists in building an alternative, action-based politics based on interconnected, globally aware communities (Boulding 1988).

Human security

In this context of late-modern politics, security has been liberated somewhat from the clutches of the state, so that now its meaning and practice can be contested more openly. This explains the genesis of environmental security, a sectoral categorisation (identifying a risk domain) which does not necessarily identify a referent to be secured (who is at risk). Another, not incompatible way of contesting and extending the concept of security involves prioritising the needs of people above the needs of the nation-state. Thus the notion of human security has been proposed. Human security says little about sectors (it does not explicitly classify sources of risk), but much about the referent to be secured (people). Human-centred conceptions of security begin by asking the question: *whose security?* This is a subversive question which casts into doubt the state's monopolisation of political legitimacy and violence (Walker 1987). Asking it opens up space to consider alternative meanings and referents of security, as well as alternative strategies.

The United Nations Development Programme (UNDP) uses the concept of human security to assist in the framing of development and justice issues. The UNDP adopts a comprehensive approach to human security, identifying seven sectors or domains: economic, food, health, environmental, personal, community, and political (1994). The 1994 *Human Development Report* says that:

> Human security is people-centred. It is concerned with how people live and breathe in a society, how freely they exercise their many choices, how much access they have to market and social opportunities – and whether they live in conflict or peace. (p. 23)

> In the final analysis, human security is a child who did not die, a disease that did not spread, a job that was not cut, an ethnic tension that did not explode in violence, a dissident who was not silenced. Human security is not a concern with weapons – it is a concern with human life and dignity. (p. 22)

The contribution of UNDP enhances the legitimacy of efforts to contest and reclaim the meaning and practice of security.

Human security requires the provision of basic material needs such as nutritious food, clean air and water, and shelter (as identified by the UNDP). There is a range of additional requirements, however, that are fundamental to an individual's existential well-being and security: an emotional support network for giving and receiving care; strong family ties; opportunities for extended community interaction; a diverse and stimulating environment; opportunities for creative expression and learning; opportunities for spontaneous behaviour; and a personal sense of involvement, purpose, belonging, excitement, challenge, satisfaction, love, enjoyment and confidence (Boyden 1987: 79). This view is explicitly linked to security by Tickner, who argues that the desire for close relationships and belonging are undervalued aspects of human nature, and should form the basis of a more humane approach to security (Tickner 1992).

Human security, as seen by this book at least, accepts Gandhi's radically challenging hypothesis (1951) that historically non-violence has been the normal state of affairs between humans. On this basis, then, the traditional practice of basing security strategy on the assumption that violence is the default condition does injustice to the processes which historically have ensured survival (Clements 1990). Thus good faith and trust become genuine factors in decision-making about human security. Because (most) people learn basic lessons about trust and security in close personal relationships, the principles that underlie these can be used to inform relationships between social groups, including states. Thus because the micro can influence the macro, the personal is inherently political, and 'issues of global security are interconnected with, and partly constituted by, local issues; therefore the achievement of comprehensive security depends on action by women and men at all levels of society' (Tickner 1992: 142).

Alternative approaches to security are 'dissident discourses' (Dalby 1996b). They are engaged in a conception of politics that transcends the state, understanding security not so much in the negative sense of protecting the status quo, but as the positive task of establishing and then maintaining basic human rights, justice and freedom. They are engaged in a contestation and reclamation of the concept of security to serve people and positive peace. These radical approaches are attuned to what Walker calls the 'dialectical interplay between security and insecurity' in human affairs, where vulnerability is not necessarily a negative phenomenon, but rather: 'to be vulnerable is to be open. To be open is to create the opportunity for communication and exchange, for learning and commitment' (Walker 1988: 126, 127). Security therefore entails balancing risks and fears with trust and dialogue.

At the 1997 people's Conference on Alternative Security Systems in the Asia–Pacific a declaration was passed which points to the future of a critically aware theory and practice of security. The Declaration was produced by concerned people in the industrialising world, and thus is more reflective of the concerns and needs of the most vulnerable of people. It stated that:

> Security must be fundamentally redefined, democratised and reclaimed by people. It must replace narrow state, military or market interests with comprehensive human security which includes the social, cultural, gender, economic and environmental aspects of security. It must also recognise the need for peace-building and the prevention of violent conflict. This requires both a transformation of existing structures and relationships and the creation of new structures and relationships which include groups previously marginalised.
>
> Real security is based on establishing democratic relations among men and

women, within societies, between people and the state and between states themselves, and within international institutions. Establishing substantive democracy is fundamental.
(*Democratising Security: Declaration of the Conference on Alternative Security Systems in the Asia Pacific*, 1997, http://www.nautilus.org).

Thinking in terms of human security shifts the scale of analysis away from nations to the local level. It focuses on the immediate vulnerability of most of the world's population, as opposed to hypothetical threats to nation-states. It provides a referent object which, when combined with environmental concerns, forms the basis for a new approach to environmental security.

Environmental security as human security

A human-centred environmental security concept places the welfare of people first and prioritises the welfare of the most disadvantaged above all else. This is consistent with the discussion of environmental insecurity presented in Chapter 2. A human-centred approach is justified on moral grounds and, in a more pragmatic way, because addressing the welfare of the most disadvantaged means addressing many of the future sources of environmental degradation; as Sachs says, 'protecting the rights of the most vulnerable members of our society ... is perhaps the best way we have of protecting the right of future generations to inherit a planet that is still worth inhabiting' (Sachs 1996: 151). This should not obscure the responsibility for poverty and environmental degradation that rests primarily with the well-off in industrialised countries.

This human-centred environmental security concept sees the enhancement of welfare, peace and justice as the fundamental purpose of politics. Peace and justice are the firmest pillars on which to build exactly the sort of authoritative yet genuinely legitimate institutions required for human and environmental security (Conca 1994c). Linking environmental security to peace in this way is supported by the recent linkage of environmental problems with human rights. For example, in 1990 the UN General Assembly agreed that 'all individuals are entitled to live in an environment adequate for their health and well-being'; and in 1995 the UN Commission on Human Rights passed a resolution that 'environmental damage has potentially negative effects on human rights and the enjoyment of life, health, and a satisfactory standard of living' (both cited in Cherry 1996: 3). As argued for here, environmental security is very much about the rights of all people to a healthy environment. Further, in so far as rights are meaningless without responsibilities, environmental security means all people have a responsibility to behave in such a way as to not impinge on the rights of others to a healthy environment.

This approach to environmental security argues that the primary purpose of the nation-state is to meet the basic needs of all people. This means that the interests of the state should be subordinate to the interests of people, and, as theoretically justified, that the state is not apart from, but is of the people. Thus environmental insecurity is seen not as a problem for the legitimacy and survival of modern institutions, but as a problem for which modern institutions are responsible. Those institutions that are most problematic, such as the military, are those that must be reformed first. This does not mean a naive hope that the military will see the error of its ways and atone; it means thinking seriously and acting carefully to achieve gradual and progressive reform.

This human-centred conceptualisation of environmental security does not concern itself with the possibility that environmental degradation may induce violent conflict. This is not seen as the most pressing problem: environmentally induced warfare is much less likely than most would suggest; is even less likely in a world where all people are environmentally secure; and the threat of it is often used to justify practices which are counterproductive to environmental balance and human security (see Chapter 5). Removing the warfare aspect from environmental security removes the basis upon which strategic rationality gains entry into the concept. Because rethinking security means rethinking politics, the continued saturation of contemporary politics with issues and metaphors of violence needs to be avoided.

In contrast to thinking about violent conflict, a human-centred conceptualisation of environmental security asserts the need for cooperation and inclusion to manage the environment for the equal benefit of all people and future generations. Support for this approach to environmental management is a key message of the 1992 Earth Summit (UNCED 1993). In Australia, cooperation, inclusion and conflict resolution are central to successful resource management institutions. This is demonstrated by high rates of community participation in Landcare and Total Catchment Management (Campbell 1994); it is proven in the effectiveness of intergovernmental institutional arrangements such as the

Great Barrier Reef Marine Park Authority and the Murray Darling Basin Commission; and it underlies the success of informal non-government agreements such as the Cape York cooperative management agreement between Aboriginal, industrial and Green groups. In the South Pacific, despite enormous environmental pressures, regional agreements and institutions such as the South Pacific Regional Environment Programme (SPREP) are successfully addressing environmental problems in cooperative and peaceful ways. Inclusion, mediation and cooperation are therefore key themes for environmental security.

Defining environmental security

All definitions are problematic (Tennberg 1995); in this book, nevertheless, environmental security is defined as 'the process of peacefully reducing human vulnerability to human-induced environmental degradation by addressing the root causes of environmental degradation and human insecurity'. Put another, more axiomatic way, environmental security is the process of minimising environmental insecurity.

There is a danger that this definition dichotomises humans and nature, a problem that also vexes ecological security. It is important to be clear, then, about the deeper implication of this definition. Humans are seen as nature rendered self-conscious (Bookchin 1982). This means, in Saurin's words, that humans are not counterposed to nature, but are 'constitutive of nature' (1996: 83). Accordingly, the definition's reference to 'human-induced environmental degradation' means not the degradation of an external or Other habitat, but of the habitat of humans themselves. Environmental degradation can thus be read as human degradation. In this way this book is not opposed to definitions of environmental (or ecological) security which seek to make the biosphere the referent of security, because securing the biosphere means securing the physical bases of human health and well-being. Nevertheless, the principal referent here is humans, as this is arguably a keener political incentive – which is to say that a concern for the environment *per se* is less likely to mobilise action (the problem with Deep Green ecophilosophy).

This definition seeks to treat the underlying *causes* that create environmental degradation. Environmental security as an absolute condition is arguably impossible, not least because security is a highly relative concept. Instead, like peace and sustainability, environmental security should be seen as a systemic goal. Defining environmental security as a process in this way overcomes the hitherto strong equation of security with stasis. Security as a process means ongoing monitoring and adaptation of programmes and policies. In this way security becomes an adaptive process which is sensitive to change and seeks to manage change peacefully (rather than defend against it).

The relationship between national security and human security warrants brief consideration. National security and human security are not necessarily mutually exclusive. At present, however, the issues of concern to (and the strategies to procure) national security are counterproductive to human security within and beyond any given nation-state. Although in theory the nation-state is obliged to provide human security, the continuing emphasis on conflict, threats and (scripted) malignant Others makes genuine security elusive. Environmental security demands that nation-states act domestically and in concert to curb global, regional and local processes that generate environmental degradation and human insecurity. This will necessitate stronger government on some issues, and conceding authority in others.

It was argued earlier that to be useful any approach to security must be able to answer a number of basic questions. In response to the question *whose security?* environmental security seeks the security of the individual and local groups, and more immediately the security of those people who are most vulnerable to the effects of environmental degradation. In response to the question *security from what?* environmental security addresses the impacts of environmental degradation on humans, including lack of clean water, malnutrition, inadequate access to energy for cooking and heating (most acute in the problem of fuelwood shortages), high infant mortality rates and maternal death rates, exposure to preventable debilitating or fatal illnesses, and greater exposure and vulnerability to risks such as floods, fires, earthquakes, tsunamis, cyclones, droughts and famines. This then leads to the question *insecurity how?* – the answer to which is the impoverishment of people and the degradation of nature largely through political-economic processes. Thus the problem is not humankind's struggle with nature, but humankind's struggle with the dynamics of its own cultures (de Wilde 1996).

This human-centred conceptualisation of environmental security is informed in part by ecology and hazards theory. These offer a new basis for thinking about security and politics, and central to this are the notions of risk, vulnerability and resilience.

Risk

Risk is a subjectively interpreted and therefore highly political phenomenon. For example, in the prevailing approach to national security those who identify the risks identify only those possibilities which may jeopardise their particular vested interests. Hence environmental security in US security policy discourse is concerned with those particular risks to the interests of the US policy community, and not the risks that others in distant places experience. Rayner (1992) analyses risk from a cultural theory perspective and finds that – like the response of the US to environmental security – 'of all the things people can be worried about, they will be inclined to select for particular attention those risks that help to reinforce the social solidarity of their institutions' (Rayner 1992: 91). Hewitt also talks of the prevailing approach to risk (from a hazards perspective) in a way that might well refer to the dominant approach to environmental security:

> its strength depends less upon its logic and internal sophistications than on its being a convenient productive 'world view' for certain dominant institutions and academic spokesmen. In other words it is, above all, a construct reflecting the shaping hand of a contemporary social order. (Hewitt 1983: 4)

There is therefore more than one discourse of risk, and it seems that common to all are exclusions and inclusions, emphases and biases which serve the interests of the already powerful. Talking about risks therefore requires democratically 'negotiating' risk (Handmer 1996a).

This raises the need for some reflection on the reasons why this book finds particular risks and effects of environmental degradation to be problematic. In a general sense what this book does is reassert the moral imperative of meeting the needs of those people who have not benefited from modernity. It is possible to construct a rough typology of needs: there are basic health needs, basic social needs, equal opportunity needs, and relative consumption needs. Basic health needs are such things as clean water, sufficient nutritious food and access to a level of health and hygiene. These enable people to be free from unnecessary debilitating sickness. They also make death a less likely prospect at any stage of a person's life (and more a factor of old age or remote chance) as is the case for most people in the industrialised world. That one fifth of the world's people do not have their basic health needs satisfied is the fundamental injustice with which this book is concerned. That these people are also extremely vulnerable to perturbations in weather or economics is also of great concern: these are risks proper.

Basic social needs are the requirements of a meaningful existence. They include diversity of experience, close family and personal relationships, and a sense of responsibility (Boyden 1987). Many of these have been denied by modern ways of living. Equal opportunity needs are those requirements necessary for an individual to participate as an equal member in her particular society: for example, in many industrialised societies having access to an automobile is necessary for an individual to gain employment and meet the demands of urban life. Relative consumption needs, then, are needs that in their absence will not result in unnecessary illness or death, nor unequal opportunity. This relates to the consumption of luxury items.

The risks of concern to environmental security are those which are immediate and necessary to health and well-being (basic health needs). There are exclusions in this approach, namely that the needs of the wealthy come last. But inverting the priorities of the industrialised world and countering the culture of consumption in this way is morally defensible, and is a useful strategy to reveal the contradictions of modernity and to begin to address a better future for all people.

Effective risk management requires a holistic approach which connects technical and political strategies, and which involves all people in ways that are cumulatively preventive. Decisions as to how to manage risk cannot be based solely on technical criteria or expert judgements; participatory decision-making procedures capable of accounting for moral and lifestyle choices are necessary (O'Riordan and Rayner 1991: 98). This points to social processes, empowerment and democracy as means to lessen vulnerability, and to strategies for preventing risk-generating activity (for example, the use of solar power to avoid burning fossil fuels which contribute to climatic instability). Environmental security is about risk, and risk needs to be democratically negotiated to determine the most urgent risks and the best ways of dealing with them.

Vulnerability

Vulnerability is a defining characteristic of insecurity. It is a product of poverty, exclusion, marginalisation and inequities in material consumption. People's vulnerability, then, is generated by social, economic and political processes. The cyclone that struck the coastal region of Bangladesh in April 1991 demonstrated clearly the interdependence between environmental degradation, insecurity and vulnerability to hazards. Bangladesh is a low-lying country and has in excess of 100 million people with a high population density. Given that the country is one of the world's poorest, this population density creates pressures which force the poorest people to live and work in the marginal and shifting coastal zone. This in turn places pressure on coastal ecosystems which are denuded of stabilising vegetation, and this magnifies the vulnerability of these people to environmental perturbations. The April 1991 cyclone battered the coastal zone for nine hours and with it came a storm surge that raised water levels along the coast by up to seven metres. The death toll reached 139,000 and up to three million people were exposed to severe health risks; 118,000 acres of crops were damaged; 190,000 homes, 9,300 schools and over 3,000 freshwater wells were destroyed (AODRO 1991). A lack of physical and service infrastructure meant that many died from diseases and malnutrition after the event. The victims of this cyclone were already extremely insecure by any standard. Their vulnerability was fundamentally a function of poverty. The painful lesson (learned repeatedly elsewhere), is that enhancing security means eliminating poverty, and vice versa.

Resilience

Resilience is the inverse of vulnerability, and is hence reasonably synonymous with security. It entails being less susceptible to damage from both short-term changes (such as cyclones and currency fluctuations) and long-term changes (such as rising sea levels and declining terms of trade). It also refers to the capacity to recover from short-term changes and adapt to long-term changes.

Resilience is a function of power, diversity and interdependence. The question of empowerment, fundamental to contemporary political theory and practice, is addressed in the following chapter. Diversity is desirable because it facilitates flexibility and choice. For example, after a cyclone a community with a wide range of food plants will be more likely to have some food reserves intact than a community relying solely on bananas, and a woman with a diversity of skills is more likely than her colleagues to find new employment in the event of retrenchment. Interdependence among diverse entities enhances resilience, at least in the social realm, as networks of reciprocity enable sharing of one group's burden among many related groups (which at the international scale is the essence of emergency relief). Enhancing resilience therefore involves making full use of diverse social resources such as cooperatives, churches and self-help groups. Resilience is about the ability of a group to draw on material and social resources for recovery from shocks, making traditional coping strategies just as relevant as institutional and technological strategies (Handmer 1996b).

Flexibility is also achieved through designing some 'slackness' into human systems (Handmer and Dovers 1996). Maintaining spare financial and material resources in social and ecological systems enables a surplus to be drawn on in times of difficulty. For example, a budget surplus hedges against welfare restrictions in times of economic downturn; vacant high land can be used as a safety zone in response to tsunami; food and water reserves kept aside ease recovery and minimise losses after cyclones; household savings ease the burden in the event of unemployment; and a healthy and well-nourished body is more likely to survive a season of drought than one already malnourished. In research conducted in West Africa, Mortimore (1989) found that resilience to drought was a function of flexibility in the use of labour, crop location in space and time, choice of crops to grow, and means of earning income. Flexible strategies demand vision and restraint from the dictum of optimum and maximal use of resources (Handmer and Dovers 1996).

Short-term strategies such as those discussed above are all important in enhancing the resilience of people to the day-to-day effects of environmental degradation as well as to disasters, but the long-term reduction of risk, vulnerability and insecurity requires fundamental changes in the institutions and beliefs of modernity. There will be no lasting environmental security unless these changes take place. Changes in power relations – a minimum requirement – can be achieved by extending democracy, enhancing political participation and improving governance. These issues are explored in the following chapter.

Environmental security and sustainability

The main concepts presently being used to address environmental problems are sustainable development and sustainability. Sustainable development involves a humanitarian element not unlike the value this book discovers in environmental security. It recognises that the problem lies in the disparities among people as well as the degradation of eco-systems (WCED 1987, UNCED 1993). The principal dilemma with sustainable development is the word 'development', which implies that development *per se* is not the problem; rather, it is the particular environ-mental effects of existing development practices that need to be addressed (see Redclift 1987, Sachs 1993). Of course, this depends on what one means by 'development', in the same way that the meaning of environ-mental security is contingent on the meaning of 'security'.

The concept of sustainability has evolved from sustainable develop-ment, and is now the preferred term of many because it avoids (at least semantically) the difficulty with the word development. Dovers defines sustainability as 'the ability of a natural, human, or mixed system to withstand or adapt to, over an indefinite time scale, endogenous or exogenous changes perceived as threatening' (Dovers 1997: 304). The difference between sustainable development and sustainability, then, is that sustainability is the system property and goal, whereas sustainable development is the policy activity aimed at achieving that goal (Dovers 1997: 304). Sustainability is concerned with a number of issues, including the structure of the economy, discounting (of the future), depletion of natural resources and environmental degradation, population growth, and sectoral sustainability (Pezzey 1992). Exploitation and equity are, by Pezzey's reckoning at least, secondary concerns. Sustainability is still therefore largely an economic paradigm, albeit one which is highly critical of conventional neo-classical economics (Common 1995). The meaning of sustainability is also somewhat ambiguous, yet paradoxically this enhances its popularity in that ambiguity makes it safe to use. Sustainable development, sustainability, and environmental security are thus all plagued by an ambiguity which makes them amenable to appro-priation by vested interests. This is the nature of concepts: they are contested, but such contests are one of the ways in which society negoti-ates its values and goals.

This book's reformulated concept of environmental security differs from, but complements, sustainability for a number of reasons. First, like sustainable development, issues of exploitation and equity are primary rather than secondary concerns. In this sense environmental security is compatible with the concept of environmental justice, which focuses on the discrimination inherent in the exposure of certain groups to environmental hazards. Second, environmental security explores the juncture of security/foreign policy and the environment. This is an area less explicitly covered in sustainability and sustainable development, and it is this (original) explicit international focus that is one of environmental security's distinguishing characteristics. In this respect environmental security serves a useful function in that it facilitates communication between a diverse range of interests (Brock 1997). Third, environmental security is concerned with the environmental impacts of military activities and explores the possibility of greening the military. Fourth, environmental security adds to the Rio Declaration's assertion that peace and environmental protection are interdependent and indivisible (UNCED 1993). It does this by understanding environmental degradation to be the product of violence both direct and structural.

Perhaps the most important contribution of environmental security is its political dimension. Whereas sustainable development and sustainability are still largely concerned with economics (of development and *ecological* economics respectively), environmental security is fundamentally concerned with politics. The issue is not just one of the politics of security as addressed in most of this book, but also one of what a reformulated notion of security holds for politics itself.

Concepts and the contestation of security revisited

A final and notable distinction of environmental security as opposed to sustainability is that environmental security seeks to securitise environmental problems, thereby making them more important than other politicised issues. Environmental security as presented here agrees that environmental degradation is a security issue, but security is seen as human security. If there is any truth in the original declared function of the state as provider of security to its citizens, then the state – so the argument runs – must respond to environmental insecurity with the same unrestrained vigour that it adopts to ensure military security. Environmental (human) security takes this security justification of the state seriously. It assumes that the primary purpose of government is to ensure that the basic needs of people are satisfied. This is the political intent of environmental security; it stems from the intuitive resonance and appeal of security, and it contests the meaning and practice of security because it is the favoured term of political discourse in this late modern era.

The question of whether it is valid to understand environmental problems as security problems recurs throughout any thoughtful discussion of environmental security. The dilemma should by now be apparent; securitising environmental issues runs the risk that the strategic/realist approach will coopt and colonise the environmental agenda rather than respond positively to environmental problems (as discussed in Chapter 6). For this reason critics of environmental security, such as Deudney (1991) and Brock (1991), suggest that it is dangerous to understand environmental problems as security issues. This book's position on the matter has been emerging in previous chapters. It contends that the problem turns not on the presentation of environmental problems as security issues, but on the meaning and practice of security in present times. Environmental security, wittingly or not, contests the legitimacy of the realist conception of security by pointing to the contradictions of security as the defence of territory and resistance to change. It seeks to work from within the prevailing conception of security, but to be successful it must do so with a strong sense of purpose and a solid theoretical base.

Understanding environmental problems as security problems is thus a form of conceptual speculation. It is one manifestation of the pressure the Green movement has exerted on states since the late 1960s. This pressure has pushed state legitimacy nearer to collapse, for if the state cannot control a problem as elemental as environmental degradation, then what is its purpose? This legitimacy problem suggests that environmental degradation cannot further intensify without fundamental change or the collapse of the state. This in turn implies that state-sanctioned environmentally degrading practices such as those undertaken in the name of national security cannot extend their power further if it means further exacerbation of environmental insecurity. While the system may resist environmental security's challenge for change, it must also resist changes for the worse. In terms of the conceptual venture, therefore, appropriation by the security apparatus of the concept of environmental security is unlikely to result in an increase in environmental insecurity (although the concept itself may continue to be corrupted). On the other hand, succeeding in the conceptual venture may mean a positive modification of the theory and practice of national security. It may also mean that national governments will take environmental problems more seriously, reduce defence budgets, and generally implement policies for a more peaceful and environmentally secure world. This dual goal of demilitarisation and upgrading policy may well be a case of wanting to have one's cake and eat it – but either the having or the eating is sufficient justification for the concept (Brock 1996).

The worst outcome would be if the state ceased to use the concept of environmental security, heralding the end of the contest and requiring that the interests of peace and the environment be advocated through alternative discourses. This is perhaps the only real failure that is likely to ensue from the project of environmental security.

The whole question of securitisation hinges, of course, on the meaning of security. The security component of environmental security as understood here is human-centred as opposed to nation-centred. Indeed, it directly contests the legitimacy of national security by challenging notions of threats and risks, and by questioning who is at risk. In this sense environmental security is as much about contesting a defining feature of modernity (national security) as it is about posing a new concept for dealing with environmental problems. Yet although this contest is a crucial function of environmental security, this book's reformulation of the concept also seeks to serve as a genuine alternative to understanding and addressing environmental problems.

A human-centred (as opposed to state-centred) concept of environmental security is consistent with the general direction of critical approaches to security. The consistency arises from the shared understanding that security is intuitively about the stable provision of basic needs – needs which states and the system of states have hitherto failed to provide. A strong, human-centred concept of environmental security can better contest the meaning of security in a way that, despite the concerns of critics, stands to gain much by highlighting the inherent contradictions of national security, yet stands to lose little from a failure to succeed in this venture. It may also serve as a valuable alternative concept to sustainable development and sustainability by highlighting the political aspects of environmental problems and their solutions, and by re-emphasising that environmental problems are very much problems of human vulnerability.

References

AODRO (Austrqalian Overseas Disaster Response Organisation) (1991) *Weekly Summary* (6 May, 12 May, 12 June), Australian Overseas Disaster Response Organisation, Surrey Hills (NSW).

Bookchin, M. (1982) *The Ecology of Freedom: The Emergence and Dissolution of Hierarchy*, Cheshire Books, Palo Alto.

Booth, K. (1991) 'Security and Emancipation', *Review of International Studies*, Vol. 17, No. 4, pp. 313–26.

Boulding, E. (1988) *Building a Global Civic Culture: Education for an Independent World*, Teachers College Press, New York.

Boyden, S. (1987) *Western Civilisation in Biological Perspective: Patterns in Biohistory*, Oxford University Press, New York.

Brock, L. (1991) 'Peace Through Parks: The Environment on the Research Agenda', *Journal of Peace Research*, Vol. 28, No. 4, pp. 407–23.

—— (1996) 'The Environment and Security – Conceptual and Theoretical Issues', paper read at the 16th General Conference of the International Peace Research Association, July, University of Queensland.

—— (1997) 'The Environment and Security: Conceptual and Theoretical Issues', in N. Gleditsch (ed.), *Conflict and the Environment*, Kluwer Academic Publishers, Dordrecht, pp. 17–34.

Campbell, A. (1994) *Landcare: Communities Shaping the Land and the Future*, Allen and Unwin, Sydney.

Cherry, W. (1996) 'Human Rights and Environmental Security: Forging the Links', paper read at the 16th General Conference of the International Peace Research Association, July, University of Queensland.

Clements, K. (1990) *Towards a Sociology of Security*, Working paper No. 90–4, Conflict Resolution Consortium, University of Colorado, Boulder.

Common, M. (1995) *Sustainability and Policy: Limits to Economics*, Cambridge University Press, Cambridge.

Conca, K. (1994c) 'Peace, Justice, and Sustainability', *Peace Review*, Vol. 6, No. 3, pp. 325–31.

Dalby, S. (1996b) 'Continent Adrift: Dissident Security Discourse and the Australian Geopolitical Imagination', *Australian Journal of International Affairs*, Vol. 50, No. 1, pp. 59–75.

Deudney, D. (1991) 'Environment and Security: Muddled Thinking', *The Bulletin of Atomic Scientists*, Vol. 47, No. 3, pp. 23–8.

de Wilde, J. (1996) 'Environmental Security Levelled Out: Tracing Referent Objects, Threats and Scales of Environmental Issues', paper read at the 16th General Conference of the International Peace Research Association, July, University of Queensland.

Dovers, S. (1997) 'Sustainability: Demands on Policy', *Journal of Public Policy*, Vol. 16, No. 3, pp. 303–18.

Gandhi, M. (1951) *Satyagraha (Non-Violent Resistance)*, Navajivan, Ahmedabad.

Handmer, J. (1996a) 'Communicating Uncertainty: Perspectives and Themes', in T. Norton, T. Beer and S. Dovers (eds), *Risk and Uncertainty in Environmental Management*, Centre for Resource and Environmental Studies, Canberra, pp. 86–97.

—— (1996b) 'Issues Emerging from Natural Hazard Research and Emergency Management', in T. Norton, T. Beer and S. Dovers (eds). *Risk and Uncertainty in Environmental Management*, Centre for Resource and Environmental Studies, Canberra, pp. 44–62.

Handmer, J. and Dovers, S. (1996) 'A Typology of Resilience: Rethinking Institutions for Sustainble Development', *Industrial and Environmental Crisis Quarterly*, Vol. 9, No. 4, pp. 482–511.

Hewitt, K. (1983) 'The Idea of Calamity in a Technocratic Age', in K. Hewitt (ed.), *Interpretations of Calamity*, Allen and Unwin, Boston, pp. 3–29.

Mortimore, M. (1989) *Adapting to Drought: Farmers, Famines and Desertification in West Africa*, Cambridge University Press, Cambridge.

O'Riordan, T. and Rayner, S. (1991) 'Risk Management for Global Environmental Change', *Global Environmental Change*, Vol. 1, No. 2, pp. 91–108.

Pezzey, J. (1992) 'Sustainability: An Interdisciplinary Guide', *Environmental Values*, Vol. 1, No. 4, pp. 321–62.

Rayner, S. (1992) 'Cultural Theory and Risk Analysis', in S. Krimsky and D. Golding, *Social Theories of Risk*, Praeger, Westport, pp. 83–155.

Redclift, M. (1987) *Sustainable Development: Exploring the Contradictions*, Methuen, London.

Sachs, A. (1996) 'Upholding Human Rights and Environmental Justice', in L. Brown (ed.), *State of the World 1996*, Earthscan, London, pp. 133–51.

Sachs, W. (ed.) (1993) *Global Ecology: A New Arena of Political Conflict*, Zed Books, London.

Saurin, J. (1996) 'International Relations, Social Ecology and the Globalisation of Environmental Change', in J. Vogler and M. Imber (eds), *The Environment in International Relations*, Routledge, London.

Tennberg, M. (1995) 'Risky Business: Defining the Concept of Environmental Security', *Co-operation and Conflict*, Vol. 30, No. 3, pp. 239–58.

Tickner, J. (1992) *Gender in International Relations: Feminist Perspectives on Achieveing Global Security*, Columbia University Press, New York.

UNCED (United Nations Conference on Environment and Development) (1993) *Report of the United Nations Conference on Environment and Development, Rio de Janeiro, 3–14 June 1992*, United Nations, New York.

UNDP (United Nations Development Programme) (1994) *Human Development Report 1994*, Oxford University Press, New York.

Walker, R. (1987) 'The Concept of Security and International Relations Theory', paper read at First Annual Conference on Discourse, Peace, Security and International Society, August, Ballyvaughan.

—— (1988) *One World, Many Worlds: Struggles for a Just World Peace*, Lynne Rienner, Boulder.

WCED (World Commission on Environment and Development) (1987) *Our Common Future*, Oxford University Press, Oxford.

[24]

Environmental Security and the Recombinant Human: Sustainability in the Twenty-first Century

MICHAEL REDCLIFT

Department of Geography
Kings College London
London WC2R 2LS, UK
Email: michael.r.redclift@kcl.ac.uk

ABSTRACT

Examining the concepts of 'security' and 'sustainability', as they are employed in contemporary environmental discourses, the paper argues that, although the importance of the environment has been increasingly acknowledged since the 1970s, there has been a failure to incorporate other discourses surrounding 'nature'. The implications of the 'new genetics', prompted by research into recombinant DNA, suggest that future approaches to sustainability need to be more cognisant of changes in 'our' nature, as well as those of 'external' nature, the environment. This broadening of the compass of 'security' and 'sustainability' discourses would help provide greater insight into *human* security, from an environmental perspective.

KEY WORDS

Nature, discourse, recombinant DNA, security, sustainability, carbon politics

SUSTAINABILITY IN THE TWENTIETH CENTURY

This paper examines the meaning of 'security' and 'sustainability' in the post-Cold War era, and the way in which the balance between the human individual and nature is changing. The discussion of 'sustainability' has largely been concerned with 'external' nature, with the physical environment and its implications for human societies (Goodman and Redclift 1991, Darier 1999). At the same time, the discourses surrounding 'nature' have also suggested ways in which the human subject itself is changing: through genetics and gender studies, for example (Jordanova 1986, Ginsburg and Rapp 1995). This paper argues that our concern with the sustainability of the environment has failed to establish

Environmental Values **10** (2001): 289–299

290

MICHAEL REDCLIFT

links with the parallel terrain of 'nature', which is located in genetic engineering and biotechnology.

The other strand in the argument concerns the multiple uses of 'security' within the burgeoning literature in environmental security (Barnett 2001). In 1987 the term 'security' was still defined solely in terms of military preparedness. That was the year the Brundtland Commission published its report, *Our Common Future*, which introduced the term 'sustainable development' into our vocabulary (WCED 1987). In 1987 there were still four years before the Cold War ended, unofficially, on 24 August 1991, in a message from President Gorbachev to the world, that the Soviet Union would be abolished.

ENVIRONMENTAL SECURITY

The roots of the twentieth century's 'environmental crisis' were laid in what I term the 'carbon politics' of the 1970s, a key decade for the emergence of hydrocarbons on the global stage, when oil prices rose dramatically in two bursts, and the power of OPEC was born. These difficulties led, in turn, to a public re-examination of the relationship between what came to be known as the 'North' and the 'South', in the form of the Brandt Report (Brandt Commission 1983). Eventually they were to lead to a shift towards incorporating 'environmental' concerns within the wider terrain of human security.

The Brandt Report charted a future for development that relied heavily on raising demand in the South for the goods and services provided in the North. In 1980 the development of the Asian 'Tiger' economies was not yet fully underway, and the so-called 'newly-industrialising countries' were still taking faltering steps towards development. Few people would have predicted, in 1980, that China would maintain a growth rate of between 7 and 10% throughout much of the 1990s, and that it would be expected to have a Gross Domestic Product by 2020 (at purchasing power parity) 20% larger than that of the United States.

In the early 1980s a number of reports were published that were to mark an important stage in the way environmental problems were perceived. First there was the World Conservation Strategy (1983). The evidence of serious environmental problems, many of them on a global scale, and linked to discernible 'global' systems, was becoming clearer, and the second World Conservation Strategy (1991) developed a stronger focus on their interaction with human systems.

The second significant report from the early 1980s was the Global 2000 Report (1982). This document, of over one thousand pages, barely mentioned climate, for example, but it did bring modelling to bear on global issues. Building upon the innovative science and breadth of the Man and the Biosphere programme (MAB) these reports, and the work of the United Nations Environment Program (UNEP) made loud warning noises to the international policy commu-

ENVIRONMENTAL SECURITY ...

nity. These assessments, like others at the time, were broadly influenced by the idea that *limitations in the resource base* would make it increasingly difficult to support economic and social development. This was the era, almost quaint from an historical perspective, of 'Limits to Growth' when it was assumed that the major impediment to 'development' was posed by the limited resources of the planet (Meadows 1972).

Two decades ago, then, the environment and development were still seen as parallel but distinct discourses and the 'problems' of development were seen as caused by the limits this placed on human ingenuity. The human individual was set apart from the environment and the effects of economic growth and global inequality on environmental sustainability (Redclift 1983, Redclift 1987). This was an era of modernist aspiration, in which 'development' was viewed as deeply problematic in only one sense – that it was not available to everybody, and that structural inequalities denied it to some. As yet there were few root and branch critiques of the whole 'development' project, as seen from Green or post-modern perspectives (Sachs 1993).

LATE TWENTIETH CENTURY ENVIRONMENTAL CONCERNS

The first environmental concern of the late twentieth century was prompted by the observations of British scientists working in Antarctica. They 'discovered' the ozone hole, an observation which was to drive political pressures for dramatic reductions in CFC gas emissions, culminating in the Montreal Protocol of 16 September 1987.

The Montreal Protocol was a 'second generation' environmental agreement. The first generation of multilateral environmental agreements date back to the early twentieth century, although most were signed in the 1970s and 1980s. They were largely single issue, sectoral agreements, primarily addressing the allocation and exploitation of natural resources, particularly wildlife, the atmosphere and marine environments, the so-called 'global Commons' (Vogler 2000) .

The second generation of multilateral environmental agreements have tended to bridge sectors, and to be based more on 'systems' than problems of resources and jurisprudence. They are more holistic in design. This second generation really commenced with the Earth Summit held in Rio de Janeiro in 1992. Unlike many earlier agreements, the two conventions to which Rio gave rise (the UN Convention on Climate Change and the Convention on Biological Diversity) were highly contested, and involved diplomatic battles and posturing throughout the negotiations. This was witnessed in the meeting of the Conference of the Parties (COP6) in the Netherlands in November 2000.

Both climate and biodiversity issues present major difficulties for a 'traditional' view of environment and development. After the early climate assessments of the Intergovernmental Panel on Climate Change (IPCC) it was more

292

MICHAEL REDCLIFT

difficult to view traditional economic activity as an unproblematic 'good'. In the year 2000, according to UNEP (*Global Environment Outlook* Report 1999), governments spent more than $700,000 million a year in subsidising environmentally unsound practices, in the use of water, energy, agriculture and road transport.

Many of these practices reflect 'underlying social commitments' – unquestioned social practices – with serious environmental consequences (Redclift 1996). They include the use that is made of domestic energy, waste disposal and motorised transport. In the wake of UNCED these everyday practices have attracted closer examination and a more concerted effort to identify sustainable alternatives. They have also led us back, inevitably, to the role of the human individual in helping to achieve sustainability.

Climate change was a 'problem' apparently caused not by scarcity but by 'plenty' – by high levels of personal and collective consumption, polluting the medium through which we dispose of our waste (water, air and land). Most obviously, carbon emissions contributed to Greenhouse gas concentrations in the atmosphere.

The 'discovery' that we lived in a 'global village', illustrated most vividly by the effects of human behaviour on global climate, was prefigured by the Chernobyl disaster in the Ukraine. Attention began to be given to the *systems* through which we breathe, eat and reproduce, as key elements in the failure to grapple adequately with sustainability. The reality of globalisation was revealed in the major food scares of the 1980s and 1990s, such as BSE/CJD, and the even larger and more complex issues prompted by the spread of HIV and AIDS. BSE and AIDS were examples of systemic problems which prompted unease with the links between humans and 'nature', as well as the reliability and risks of 'science'. Such problems were global in both senses: they occurred, and were transmitted globally, and they were part of *systems* which were difficult to access, or even fully understand without much more attention to individual human behaviour. They brought scientific uncertainty into the realms of intimacy, of our most intimate social experiences, our sexuality and our tastes in food.

The occurrence of these types of problem also served to undermine an earlier, more confident, view of 'mastering' nature through science.. The modernist impulse to conquer and consume seemed to have been arrested by doubts about the efficacy of science itself. The distinction between dangers that appeared 'out there', and those which concerned us as human individuals, was difficult to maintain. It was difficult to stand 'inside' or 'outside' global issues like climate change, BSE or AIDS, since they permeated territorial boundaries, space and, most significantly, our bodies.

The heightened environmental concern that led to the Earth Summit of 1992 also produced an important stimulus for civil society. This was the renewal of interest in 'grass-roots' environmental consciousness. It is easy to belittle the

ENVIRONMENTAL SECURITY ...

importance of Agenda 21, but it was probably this element of the Rio agenda that commanded greatest popular enthusiasm among 'non-experts', the many global publics which were concerned with environmental problems, often from personal experience. Without Local Agenda 21 campaigns fewer people might have listened to the victims of fuel explosions in Mexico, or damaged pipelines in Nigeria. After 1992 there was a 'global' template against which unsustainable practices, and corrupt governments, could be measured, and found wanting.

The raft of policy initiatives after the 1992 Earth Summit also introduced another important element into thinking about sustainable development at the global level. This was the new approach which was beginning to emerge around environmental security. A two-way process was distinguished, in which human societies posed problems for the physical environment (*ecological* security) while the threat of environmental degradation posed problems for national security (Barnett 2001).

Multilateral environmental agreements were increasingly based on '..a holistic approach under which all species should be exploited sustainably or not at all' in the words of UNEP's *Global Environmental Outlook* (1999). However, holistic, multi-sectoral agreements involve so many different and cross-cutting areas of law, policy and international politics that they invariably engender unprecedented conflict. Much more was at stake for contracting parties who sign up to the Framework Convention on Climate Change, than was the case with most agreements twenty years earlier. To paraphrase a recent important contribution to the discussion, understanding the absence of environmental security, means examining the effects of environmental degradation on *people*, on human populations, and their own cultural survival (Barnett 2001, Cocklin 2002).

Other policy research has taken us in important directions. The effort to establish the 'value' of nature has become an area of enormous controversy, in which even the charmed models of economists have been questioned. For those who take a 'radical' view of the imperfections of the market (often termed 'ecological economists') the challenge has been to find ways of internalising environmental costs, and the movement to do so even has a name, derived from the German, 'ecological modernisation' (Simonis 1988).

The other major conceptual, and policy, area that opened up to an unprecedented degree at the close of the old century, was that of 'managing' risks and uncertainties. The unbound copies of Ulrich Beck's *Risk Society* arrived in an unsuspecting academic world just as the British were beginning to recognise the realities, and perils, of CJD/BSE (Beck 1992). Beck's work, and that of others, laid bare the problems of 'high consequence' risks, which could not be contained by better 'reactive' environmental management, the name for most of the environmental policy that had marked the twentieth century. In future the management of risk took greater cognisance of the limitations of the 'expert witness'.

294

MICHAEL REDCLIFT

Valuation of nature, like much else, seemed trapped by patterns of thought which neglected things we could not count – largely because we had not developed ways of counting them. The neo-classical solution was to draw nature into the ambit of individual choice and markets. This, in turn, raised problems both in terms of public understanding and the usefulness of 'willingness to pay', when applied to very different publics.

In response to the injunction to quantify environmental damage, and express it in terms of 'external costs', a highly sceptical extreme constructionist 'backlash' set in among many in the humanities and social sciences.

In the view of some social scientists the existence of policy uncertainties, as well as scientific uncertainties, was a condition of modernity itself. We lived in a world of increasingly fragmented sites, which were the product of the way we understood problems, sometimes described as the 'new Medievalism'. In seeking the price of everything, in Wilde's epigram, we risked knowing the value of nothing.

CARBON POLITICS

Looked at differently – post Intergovernmental Panel on Climate Change (IPCC), post Earth Summit – many, if not most, of the twentieth century's concerns had environmental causes. The War in the Pacific is one example of a conflict in which the control over the supply of hydrocarbons played a bigger part in the 'security' of the globe than had hitherto been acknowledged. The collapse of the Soviet Union was another case, in which the weight of energy subsidies hindered the modernisation of the economy and the systems of allocation through central planning. A third example is the growing dispersion from within the so-called 'Third World' today, as significant numbers of people migrate, in the face of their inability to sustain a livelihood. The environment is rarely the only cause of human insecurity, but it is rarely absent from the bigger picture.

Security issues have been increasingly linked to a chain of 'natural' processes, and unanticipated consequences of human demand: bio-diversity losses, hydrocarbon supplies, water and likely climate change impacts. International agreements over Greenhouse gas emissions, and trade (World Trade Organisation), are frequently at variance with national sovereignty and national borders, or have led to borders being contested (the expansion of the European Union eastwards, and that of the United States within the North Atlantic Free Trade Area, in North America).

The other important dimension of the process through which we account for carbon use is that of carbon sinks. Many of the supposed carbon 'sinks' are in the developing world, and in areas such as tropical forests, which are under threat from a number of directions, including transnational corporations themselves. According to some recent models of sustainable development 'community

295

ENVIRONMENTAL SECURITY ...

mobilisation' can be undertaken through 'conservation-with-development'. Development is pursued more sustainably by tying it to the conservation of the environment. This approach emphasises the need to secure community access to valuable natural resources. However, the more we learn about the 'local' the more we realise that it is rarely *purely* local – it is created in part by extra-local influences and practices over time (Watts and Peet 1996, 79). Communities need to be situated within a broader institutional context (Agrawal 1999).

Defenders of the conservation of carbon sinks, as a future means of income-generation in poor, rural communities, argue that in future the valuation of carbon sequestration can enhance community development efforts. Future accords, they argue, will provide such communities with a much valued bargaining tool, in negotiations with governments and transnational companies. This will serve to transform theoretical 'willingness-to-pay' estimates into increased income opportunities.

As so often in the real world, however, these kinds of innovative mechanism could also have perverse effects. In Brazil, for example, the biggest interests in the conservation of carbon sinks are likely to be sugar-cane and paper-pulp industries, which are busily re-inventing themselves as 'Green' industries, positioning themselves for future carbon credits. Poor rural communities are still outside the policy 'loop' and unlikely to benefit in the short-term.

At the same time exciting changes should have taken place which will serve to *decarbonise* our societies. By 2050 the consumption of natural gas and hydrogen should surpass that of coal and oil. Natural gas would then represent a transition towards a *hydrogen-based* society, much of it sourced, admittedly, from hydrocarbons. Historically, the shift has been between dirty solid fuels, with a high carbon content, to liquid hydrocarbons, with a lower carbon content. From wood to coal to oil to gas and, ultimately, to hydrogen.

GENETICS: THE RECOMBINANT HUMAN

The materiality of the environment is evident from the way international politics, and security issues, have gradually incorporated carbon politics. Environmental security can, therefore, be understood in terms of the consequences of our consumption. The material effects of these changes (including climate change) are important, within a critical realist perspective, because they are transforming the 'external world', as well as the symbolic order in which the material world is understood. Changes in materiality have thus become associated with wider social and political changes: in 'self-hood', and governance, in what it means to participate politically, to have our ecological footprints measured, and our carbon contributions weighed. Neo-classical economics has also contributed to the disorder surrounding the human subject and the environment. Market individualism, although prompted by an instrumental logic which viewed

296

MICHAEL REDCLIFT

society as the sum of individual, rational calculations, might also be seen as part of a wider 'post-modern' reconfiguration. Under 'post-modernity' the market may even be seen, paradoxically, as bringing us closer to non-human 'nature', by leading us to question our links with nature, rather than setting us apart from it.

This paper began by posing the view that changes in human security have paralleled those in the sustainability of 'external' (non-human) nature. Changes in genetics, especially human genetics, have shifted towards a broader conception of 'nature', forcing us to reconsider what we mean by both 'sustainability' and 'society'. The 'recombination' of the human individual, through a variety of medical and genetic practices, is leading us to consider both social and environmental changes which might serve to eclipse even the carbon politics of the late twentieth century. In the fields of genetics, and particularly human genetics, both 'sustainability' and 'security' have been given additional meaning.

By the early 1980s the molecularisation of biology was already well under way. In a series of technical discoveries the landscape of possibility in molecular biology was fundamentally altered. What became practicable for the first time, was the controlled manipulation of pieces of genetic material. Researchers could snip out sections of DNA from one organism and transfer them to another. One could cut genes out of one cell and splice them into another. The technical term for this activity is 'recombinant DNA research', because what is involved is the controlled recombination of sections of DNA, the hereditary material.

In the wake of these changes in genetics, sustainability is no longer primarily a question of maintaining, and enhancing, existing environmental resources. It is also, increasingly, about engineering new environments. The publication of the first results from the Human Genome project marks a watershed in forcing us to challenge the largely 'taken-for-granted' biology that underpins most environmental politics. The world of individual rights, citizenship and governance is likely to be increasingly concerned with the new realities and thinking in genetics. Looking to the future, we might give more consideration to where this places environmental concerns, rights and governance in the future . Changes in genetics are likely to alter what it means to be socially connected, to participate in civil society. In an increasingly extra-territorial global system, and in which genetic materials can be moved without difficulty from one place (and one species) to another, questions of governance loom large. How do you *govern* a global system made up of genetically modified beings living in genetically modified environments?

In a recent book Kaya Finkler alerts us to the two processes through which the 'new genetics' is assuming authority (Finkler 2000). First, genetic modification has already reached the stage at which the individual is being recombined – beginning with the biological components of the body. By blurring the boundaries between animals and humans this is changing what it means to be 'human'. Concepts that we regard as inherently human, like *identity and*

297

ENVIRONMENTAL SECURITY ...

consciousness, which in turn underpin the acceptance of rights and responsibilities might appear, for the first time, to be infinitely malleable. The human being becomes, as it were, a genetically modified being.

The second noteworthy process, also captured in Finkler's book, concerns the way in which public discourse is being transformed by the new genetics. The communication of genetic knowledge, and the acknowledgement of genetic information, acquires a legitimacy, and a *primacy*, in political discourse, that was previously reserved for social rights and obligations. In a sense biology *becomes* social theory. The technological processes embodied in the new genetics serve to redefine the individual's relationship to society, by changing what it means to be an individual. In place of civil society as the ground of social negotiation, trust and rights, we have the 'alchemy' of the individual.

In *We Have Never Been Modern* Bruno Latour pointed to phenomena which were neither 'social facts' in the Durkheimian sense, nor natural objects – '... they emerge at the intersection of social practices and natural processes as socially constructed forms of mediation between society and nature' (Latour 1993, 11). In Latour's view phenomena like BSE or Global Warming are 'hybrids', incorporating elements of the material and the socially constructed. In the future human genetics, together with other systemic processes, may be poised to shift the ground even further in the direction of mediation between 'nature' and 'society', to the point where what we hybridise is not even perceived as *public* policy. The process of mediation will be complete when it is least recognisable within the public domain, or public discourse.

We already live in a global society where *selecting* a co-parent for genetic characteristics is a reality, and where *surrogate* motherhood is commonly practised. The research community has forced genetic cloning of animals on to the political agenda, and politicians, wary of something they have not begun to think seriously about, have reacted warily. Patenting nature *in vitro* has provoked mixed responses, as it appears to give transnational companies *carte blanche* to invade and remove genetic materials from 'other peoples'' environments.

Many of these moves follow directly from the impasse created by the efforts at global 'management' under the Biodiversity Convention (Luke 1999, McAfee 1999). In other quarters genetic manipulation is defended by medical researchers who are investigating ways of correcting human disability, and working under increasing public pressure. Smart cards, holding vital genetic 'prints' are foreseen as the future biological equivalent of today's passports and identity cards. Like the creatures in Aldous Huxley's imagination, we will soon have inhabited a 'brave new world' without ever really knowing it.

Where does this leave 'environmental security' and the political discourses which were outlined earlier? As the *human subject* itself is changing, then it is logical to assume that the notions of citizenship, democracy and entitlements with which it is linked, might also change. It might be suggested that, in the new world of the twenty-first century, materiality and consciousness bear an increas-

298

MICHAEL REDCLIFT

ingly complex relationship to each other. As species boundaries are eroded, and genetic choice dictates individual and public policy the very meaning of 'sustainability' changes. Human security is linked to 'environmental' problems not simply in terms of the physical environment, but also through the way in which the human subject is being transformed. The different rationalities being brought to bear on environmental problems will need to include those of genetic choice and management. The 'securities', and 'insecurities', that we identified as 'outside' ourselves, in external nature, have already been incorporated into our genetic being. After over a century of division between the environment and human 'nature', in which most social sciences forcefully denied a significant role for biology in the explanation of human behaviour, nature has returned to the human subject.

In the light of the much wider view of environmental security with which this paper has been concerned, together with an altered relationship between biological 'nature' and the environment, mapping the geopolitics of environmental security in the new century might begin with the human subject.

While we have been grappling with 'external' nature it is *we* who have been changing. It is not simply the transformation of the environment that is at stake, in the discourses of sustainability and security, but our transformation of ourselves. The divorce between 'our' nature and 'external' Nature has absorbed us in the way we view sustainability and security; in neither case has the radical changes in human and animal genetics been fully taken into account. In practice, of course, they are inter-linked.

This paper argues, then, that the future – for *human* security and the environment – is to recognise 'nature' as *both* internal and external to the human subject. The theoretical landscape of sustainability has changed, and is changing, almost beyond recognition. What happens 'inside' the city walls of post-modernity may be heavily influenced by what happens 'outside', and the city walls are no longer 'society' but the 'individual in society'. Perhaps this is a new Grand Narrative in the making, a product of the insecurity of the end of the Cold War, and designed for the twenty-first century?

NOTE

An earlier draft of this paper was given as an Inaugural Lecture, at King's College, London, in February 2001.

299
ENVIRONMENTAL SECURITY ...

REFERENCES

Agrawal, A. 1999. 'Community and Natural resource conservation', in Fred Gale and
   Michael McGonigle (eds) *Nature, Power and Production*. Cheltenham: Edward
   Elgar.
Barnett, J. 2001. *The Meaning of Environmental Security*. London: Zed Books.
Beck, U. 1992. *Risk Society: Towards a New Modernity*. London: Sage.
Brandt Commission 1983. *Common Crisis*. London: Pan Books.
Cocklin, C. 2002. In M. Redclift and E. Page (eds) *Environmental Security: International
   Comparisons*. Cheltenham: Edward Elgar (in press).
Darier, E. (ed.) 1999. *Discourses of the Environment*. Oxford: Blackwell.
Finkler, K. 2000. *Experiencing the New Genetics*. Philadelphia: University of Pennsyl-
   vania Press.
Ginsburg, F. and Rapp, R. 1995. *Conceiving the New World Order*. Berkeley: University
   of California Press.
Global 2000 Report 1982. *Report to the President*. Harmondsworth, London.
Global Environment Outlook 1999. International Union for Conservation of Nature
   (IUCN) and United Nations Environment Program (UNEP).
Goodman, D.E and Redclift, M.R. 1991. *Refashioning Nature: Food, Ecology, Culture*.
   London: Routledge.
Jordanova, L. (ed.) 1986. *Languages of Nature*. London: Free Association Books.
Latour, B. 1993. *We Have Never Been Modern*. Cambridge, MA: Harvard University
   Press.
Luke T.W. 1999. 'Environmentality as Green governmentability', in E. Darnier (ed.)
   Discourses of the Environment. Oxford: Blackwell.
McAfee, K. 1999. 'Selling nature to save it? Bioversity and green developmentalism',
   Environment and Planning D 17(2).
Meadows, D.C. Randers, D.H and Behrens, W.W. 1972. *The Limits to Growth*. London:
   Pan Books.
Redclift, M.R. 1983. *Development and the Environmental Crisis*. London: Methuen.
Redclift, M.R. 1987. *Sustainable Development: Exploring the Contradictions*. London:
   Methuen.
Redclift, M.R. 1996. *Wasted: Counting the Costs of Global Consumption*. London:
   Earthscan.
Sachs, W. (ed.) 1993. *Global Ecology: A New Arena of Political Conflict*. London: Zed
   Books.
Simonis, I. 1989. 'Ecological modernisation of industrial society: three strategic ele-
   ments', *International Social Science Journal* 121: 347–61.
Vogler, J. 2000. *The Global Commons: Environmental and Technological Governance*.
   Chichester: John Wiley.
Watts, M. and Peet, R. 1996. 'Towards a theory of Liberation Ecology', in R. Peet and
   M. Watts (eds) *Liberation Ecologies*. London: Routledge.
World Commission on Environment and Development (WCED) 1987. *Our Common
   Future*. Oxford University Press.
World Conservation Strategy 1983. *Living Resource Conservation for Sustainable
   Development*. . Gland, Switzerland: IUCN, UNEP.
World Conservation Strategy 1991. *Caring for Nature* (the Second World Conservation
   Strategy). Gland, Switzerland: IUCN, UNEP.

[25]
Leave it to the People: Democratic Pragmatism

Ours is a democratic age; it is decidedly unfashionable for anyone, anywhere in the world to proclaim themselves to be anything but a democrat. Francis Fukuyama (1989, 1992) recently declared that we have arrived at the "end of history," where there are no plausible global competitors to the basic ideology of liberal democracy in a capitalist economic context. Even military dictators take pains to argue that they are just stabilizing the situation so that democracy can be restored or attained in the fulness of time (of course, they also find ways of making that time a very long one). Thus it is increasingly easy to proclaim one's faith in democracy, just as it is increasingly hard to proclaim one's faith in bureaucracy and administrative rationalism. As I noted in the previous chapter, administration is not necessarily very popular as an ideal; rather, it is just what a lot of people, and a lot of institutions, actually end up doing. Even the people doing it rarely admit to liking it. Democracy is different; everyone wants to be a democrat. Whether they truly are democrats is a different question, made harder to answer by the sheer variety of meanings and models of democracy.

In this chapter I will treat democracy not as a set of institutions (elections, parliaments, parties, etc.), but rather as a way of apprehending problems. I will be concerned with democracy as a problem-solving discourse, which means it is reconciled to the basic status quo of liberal capitalism. Other discourses of democracy do exist, some of which challenge this status quo, advocating for example radical participatory alternatives to established institutions (see Dryzek, 1996a), and I shall return to some of these alternatives in later chapters. But for the moment it is appropriate to focus on what I call democratic pragmatism, which involves more or less democratic problem solving constrained by the structural status quo. For this is indeed the version of democracy which dominates today's world, especially after the revolutions of 1989 destroyed the credibility of some Marxist alternatives.

Democratic pragmatism may be characterized in terms of interactive problem solving within the basic institutional structure of liberal capitalist democracy. The word "pragmatism" can have two connotations here, both of which I intend. The first is the way the word is used in everyday language, as signifying a practical, realistic orientation to the world, the opposite of starry-eyed idealism.[1] The second refers to a school of thought in philosophy, associated with names such as William James, Charles Peirce, and John Dewey. To these pragmatist philosophers, life is mostly about solving problems in a world full of uncertainty. The most rational approach to problem solving, in life as in science, involves learning through experimentation. For problems of any degree of complexity, the relevant knowledge cannot be centralized in the hands of any individual or any administrative state structure. Thus problem solving should be a flexible process involving many voices, and cooperation across a plurality of perspectives. As long as this plurality is achieved, there is no need for more widespread public participation in problem solving. So the degree of democratic participation with which pragmatists are happy corresponds roughly to the limited amount found in existing liberal democracies, and this is why there is an essential congruence between the demands of rationality in social problem solving and democratic values, a happy coincidence indeed![2]

Pragmatist philosophy has recently received an explicit environmental twist with the arrival of "environmental pragmatism," which takes its bearings from philosophical debates in the field of environmental ethics. Environmental pragmatism does battle with all attempts to propose moral absolutes to guide environmental affairs, which are treated instead as ripe for tentative problem-solving efforts in which a plurality of moral perspectives is always relevant (see Light and Katz, 1996). In this chapter I will be concerned less with the finer points of environmental pragmatist philosophy, more with the way democratic and pragmatic discourse plays out in the real world of environmental affairs.

It should be emphasized that democratic pragmatism does not have to proceed within the formal institutional structure of liberal democracy; that is, it does not have to involve debate in legislatures. This style of problem solving can also be found within administrative structures, in negotiations between parties to a legal dispute, in international negotiations, in informal networks, and elsewhere.

---

[1] One connotation I do not intend is that pragmatism is anti-theoretical. Pragmatists still have to think!

[2] For a recent refinement of pragmatism as public philosophy, see Anderson (1990).

86 **Solving Environmental Problems**

Democratic Pragmatism in Action

Democratic pragmatism is often proposed in order to deal with manifestations of the crisis of administrative rationalism detailed at the end of the last chapter. If environmental administration involves adjustment within the basic structure of capitalist democracy in order to ameliorate ecological problems, then democratic pragmatism can involve readjustment of administration. On this account, there is nothing wrong with administration that a healthy dose of democracy cannot fix. This dose comes not in the form of taking problem solving away from administration and putting it in the hands of representative institutions such as legislatures; rather, it is a matter of making administration itself more democratic. This task can be accomplished in a variety of ways, many of which have in fact been pioneered in environmental policy (and are slowly diffusing to other policy areas).

In the previous chapter I noted that environmental administration is in crisis indicated by diminishing returns to administrative effort. Administration turns out not to be an effective problem-solving orientation in the context of complex problems: the relevant knowledge cannot be centralized in administrative hierarchy, and Weberian compartmentalization of bureaucratic structure tends to produce problem displacement rather than problem solution. Moreover, compliance with high-level administrative decisions proves problematical, leading to implementation deficit. Democratic pragmatism can speak directly to these aspects of administrative crisis, and later I will assess its performance in these terms. But in practice, the main reason for the democratization of environmental administration has been a felt need to secure legitimacy for decisions by involving a broader public. A number of devices are available for this task.

1. PUBLIC CONSULTATION

In the previous chapter I noted that an important item in the repertoire of administrative rationalism is environmental impact assessment, under which a statement is prepared detailing the anticipated impact of a project proposal (be it for a freeway, a pipeline, or a land-use plan) on the environment. At one level, impact assessment is simply designed to force administrators to consider environmental values and scientific evidence that they might otherwise have excluded or overlooked. But impact assessment is invariably accompanied by opportunities for public comment on the document produced. Sometimes this is mere symbolism, if there is nothing to force the department in question actually to take into account the substance of public comment in its subsequent decision on the proposal. Still, policy makers must both anticipate and respond to comment that is made. In the process set up in the United States, which pioneered environmental impact assessment with the passage of the National Environmental Policy Act in 1970, the responsible federal agency must produce a draft statement, release that document for comment, compile responses (from other government agencies, other levels of government, environmental and community groups, interested corporations, resource users, and ordinary citizens), and respond to these comments in the final version of the statement. Thus information from a variety of perspectives that might otherwise have been excluded from administrative decision making is systematically sought out. This information will rarely have direct, traceable impacts on agency decisions; but more subtly it may alter the context in which administrative decisions are made and implemented, by changing the discourse surrounding policy determination in a way that makes both environmental and democratic values more legitimate and more visible than before. The way Bartlett (1990) puts it, environmental impact assessment can constitute a "worm in the brain" of the administrative state, one that moves it in simultaneously more democratic and more environmentally sensitive directions.

Public consultation can also proceed without being tied to particular documents such as impact statements. For example, several European countries (Sweden, the Netherlands, and Austria) initiated extensive consultative efforts in the late 1970s concerning the future of nuclear power (see Nelkin and Pollack, 1981). These exercises did not involve anything much in the way of transfer of power from the state to the citizenry. But they did have real consequences: for example, in 1979 the Swedish government decided not to construct any more reactors, and to begin phasing out nuclear energy.

2. ALTERNATIVE DISPUTE RESOLUTION

Opportunities for public comment do not formalize any particular role for nongovernmental participants. One way of recognizing and involving particular interested parties is through the practice of alternative dispute resolution (ADR). ADR has arisen in legalistic systems—notably the United States—as an alternative to the expensive stalemate that prolonged legal actions entail. The idea is to bring the parties to a dispute together under the auspices of a neutral third party (often a professional mediator) such that they might reason through their differences and achieve a consensus sensitive to all their interests. Thus ADR is appropriate in any realm of life where conflict exists. It began to appear in the environmental realm in particular in

88   Solving Environmental Problems

the 1970s under the heading of environmental mediation, and since then disputes have been mediated on a wide variety of issues. These issues include construction of dams, irrigation schemes, mines, shopping malls, and roads; watershed management; siting of hazardous waste disposal operations; and anti-pollution measures. Mediation functions not just as an alternative to the courts. Government agencies can also use and sponsor it when encountering resistance to their proposals. The relevant participants might include community representatives, environmental groups, corporate developers, government departments, and local governments. Thus mediation can play a role in policy making rather than dispute resolution narrowly defined. Kai Lee (1993), in the context of a discussion of the Columbia River Basin in the United States, believes that this is a productive way of channelling political conflict into administrative decisions. In particular, he believes ADR has an essential role to play in effective ecosystem management, providing creative ways for conflicts to end in learning rather than in victory for one side and defeat of the other, as happens under the basically adversarial processes of environmental impact assessment. Other observers are more skeptical, seeing ADR mainly in terms of the co-option and neutralization of troublemakers by the administrative state (for example, Amy, 1987). It is perhaps best to note that ADR has an ambivalent potential. At a minimum, it demonstrates that administrative rationalists must legitimate their decisions through participatory procedures. These procedures can involve neutralization and co-option; but they can also involve democratic principles eating away at the administrative state, forcing it to open its ways. So it is up to democratic pragmatists and perhaps even proponents of more radical democracy to make the most of these cracks in the citadel of the administrative state (Torgerson, 1990: 141–5).

3. POLICY DIALOGUE

Environmental mediation and other forms of ADR often tend to be case-specific or site-specific. However, the same principles of reasoned discussion oriented to consensus can also be applied to more strategic policy issues, though the success rate (in terms of reaching an agreement and having it put into policy practice) is lower than for more circumscribed cases. An early example came with the National Coal Policy Project in the United States, which operated in the late 1970s to bring several national environmental groups and coal producers together to jointly devise a strategy for coal mining and coal burning (McFarland, 1984). The two sides achieved agreement on a number of issues: so, for example, the environmentalists agreed to a simplified one-stop permitting process for new coal-burning power plants, and in return the coal producers agreed to public funding of environmental objectors to such plants. However, the recommendations of the project were never put into policy practice, in part because public officials from government agencies with interests of their own were not included in the negotiations (nor were coal workers or their unions).

A clearer example of policy dialogue more explicitly connected to—indeed, sponsored and funded by—government may be found in Australia, with the Ecologically Sustainable Development (ESD) process initiated under Prime Minister Bob Hawke in 1990. ESD began with an invitation to the main national environmental groups and the relevant industry representatives to participate in a series of discussions oriented to the generation of strategic policy recommendations in a number of areas: agriculture, energy, fisheries, forests, manufacturing, mining, and tourism. In each area a working group was set up, and a report eventually produced. The four invited environmental groups were the Australian Conservation Foundation, World Wildlife Fund, Greenpeace, and the Wilderness Society. The Wilderness Society withdrew immediately due to its unhappiness with other government policies contrary to sustainability; later, Greenpeace withdrew. However, both groups remained in contact with the two groups that continued to participate. When it came time for the ESD groups to report, Hawke had been replaced by a Prime Minister committed to confrontation rather than consensus who placed a much lower priority on environmental issues, which had also faded from public prominence with the arrival of economic recession. Thus few of the recommendations found their way into public policy.

A more successful translation of policy dialogue into policy practice may be found in the Canadian province of Alberta, the only place in North America where a solution has been found to the NIMBY (Not In My Back Yard) problem for hazardous wastes. Nobody wants a hazardous waste treatment facility in their backyard. Given that everywhere is someone's backyard, and given the relative ease of access to veto power in the Canadian and US political systems (reinforced in the United States by the prominent role of the courts), the normal condition of policy on this issue is impasse. Recognizing this problem, the government of Alberta in the late 1980s initiated a process of dialogue with local community groups and industry, which eventually produced consensus on a site and principles for its development and operation. The process involved a referendum on the basic idea of siting, funding to communities to employ experts, regular seminars and public meetings. Once the site was selected and the treatment plant built, communities in the vicinity received further funding and access to

90 **Solving Environmental Problems**

monitoring reports and expert advice, so public participation did not end with site selection (for details on this case, see Fischer, 1993: 176–7; Rabe, 1991).

4. PUBLIC INQUIRIES

Public inquiries resemble impact assessment in that they are oriented by a specific project proposal. But rather than just producing a document and allowing public inspection and comment, a public inquiry involves a specific and visible forum in which proponents and objectors alike can make depositions and arguments. Obviously a great deal depends upon the terms of reference with which the inquiry begins, and the way these terms are interpreted by the individual presiding over the inquiry. The terms and their interpretation can be narrow and biased toward the project proponent. This is how inquiries into proposed nuclear installations in Britain typically proceed. So Kemp (1985) chronicles the case of a 1977 inquiry into a Thermal Oxide Reprocessing Plant (THORP) proposed for Windscale in Northwest England (then, as now, a notorious site of radioactive pollution). The project proponent, British Nuclear Fuels Ltd., was allowed to introduce evidence on the economic benefits of THORP, but objectors were not allowed to bring to bear economic evidence against it. The legalistic rules of the inquiry were congenial to the well-funded proponents, not to the resource-poor objectors; and the proponents could deploy the Official Secrets Act at key points. Not surprisingly, Mr Justice Parker presiding over the inquiry came down in favor of THORP. Contrast this with the contemporaneous inquiry into proposed oil and gas pipeline construction from the Arctic to Southern markets conducted in Canada by Mr Justice Thomas Berger. Berger took pains to make sure that resource-poor interests, especially indigenous peoples, were provided with funds, access to expertise, and an ability to testify in a forum under conditions with which they were familiar (the inquiry travelled to remote villages). He interpreted the terms of reference broadly, to encompass development strategies for the Canadian North, not just whether or not pipeline should be built. In this sense, the inquiry became more like a policy dialogue. Berger's report (Berger, 1977) proposes a reinvigorated renewable-resource based economy for the Canadian North, in which oil and gas development have little place. Berger pushed democratic pragmatism to its limits—and perhaps beyond, to the kind of participatory process favored by green radicalism.

5. Right-to-Know Legislation

Obviously if individuals from outside government are to be effective participants in more or less democratic processes they need access to the relevant
information. Sometimes this access will be facilitated by general freedom of
information laws under which governments must operate. These apply to
some governments more than others. For example, the British counterpart
to freedom of information is the Official Secrets Act, which essentially presumes that everything is secret if it has the remotest connection to national
security (this comes into play, for example, on anything relating to nuclear
power). More specific to environmental politics is right-to-know legislation
which specifies that corporations must disclose information relating to (say)
the risks to workers of particular chemicals, the routes and timetables of
shipments of noxious substances, and the toxicity of wastes being stored,
transported, and dumped. Such laws exist in a number of Canadian
provinces and US states.

These five developments all involve injections of democratic pragmatism
into the administrative state, with a concomitant displacement of administrative rationalism. In every case experience has been mixed, and a lot of
skepticism remains, especially from those committed to more radical
expression of both environmental and democratic values. But in some cases,
notably that of the Berger inquiry, we can glimpse the possibility of a more
radically participatory and discursive democracy that transcends the limits
imposed by the basic structure of capitalist democracy. If so, then political
change beyond problem solving is at issue. At any rate, taken together these
five developments indicate the degree to which the development of environmental policy has over the past thirty years been accompanied by greater
openness and participation in decision making. Indeed, the environmental
area has typically led all other policy areas in this respect. As Paehlke (1988)
notes, all this is a far cry from the gloomy prognostications of survivalists
who argued that environmental limits could only be confronted by centralized and authoritarian government. Of course, survivalists might still say
that all the policy effort of the last three decades has not really confronted the
issue of environmental limits head-on, and that we are still on course for
overshoot and collapse. Paehlke says nothing about the reality or otherwise
of limits.

Democratic Pragmatism as a Way of Governing

Democratic pragmatism describes an orientation to governing in its entirety, not just the inspiration for a variety of specific reforms and exercises of the kind described in the preceding section. This orientation stresses interactive problem solving involving participants from both within government and outside it. Such interaction can occur in the context of committee meetings, legislative debate, hearings, public addresses, legal disputes, rule-making, project development, media investigations, and policy implementation and enforcement; it can involve lobbying, arguing, advising, strategizing, bargaining, informing, publishing, exposing, deceiving, image-building, insulting, and questioning. In this light, the real stuff of liberal democratic government is not to be found in constitutions and formal divisions of responsibility. Rather, it is to be found in interactions that are only loosely constrained by formal rules. Quiet conversations in the bar may matter as much as speeches to parliament.

These interactions occur whether or not constitutions, laws, rules, and organization charts say they should. If we observe political interaction in liberal democracies, we find all kinds of complex paths of communication. To the administrative rationalist, this might sound like chaos and subversion. But arguably, this apparent chaos has its own rationality, what Charles Lindblom (1959) has called "the science of muddling through," or, later, "the intelligence of democracy" (Lindblom, 1965). This "science" is the exact opposite of administrative science, for it revels in unclear divisions of responsibility, political conflict, bending the formal rules so as to make things work, and substituting ordinary knowledge for analysis. Problems are solved piecemeal, usually through series of rough compromises among the different actors concerned with an issue. Interaction substitutes for analysis; different actors bring different perspectives and concerns, which are somehow agglomerated into policy decisions.[3]

I have already noted that pragmatists believe such processes are the best means for attacking public problems. A justification for the essential rationality of liberal democracy has also been advanced (quite famously) by Sir Karl Popper (1966).[4] Popper's model problem-solving community is found in successful sciences, where the rational attitude is to advance theories capable

---

[3] There are numerous case studies of this kind of process in the political science literature. Among the best may be found in the work of Aaron Wildavsky (Wildavsky, 1988; Pressman and Wildavsky, 1973).

[4] Popper differs somewhat from the pragmatists in believing that there can be general laws of nature and of society which natural scientists and social scientists alike can discover. Pragmatists believe only that there are particular problems to be solved, not laws to be discovered.

of being put to the test, then seek criticism of them through as many tests as possible, especially experimental tests. Popper believes that this attitude should apply in politics and policy making too. Public policies are like experiments. Nobody knows in advance if a particular policy (for example, a regulatory regime for pollution control) will succeed or fail. So it should be tried first on a limited scale, and reactions sought from as many different directions as possible about its positive and negative effects. Popper calls this kind of policy making "piecemeal social engineering." The only way to ensure feedback from as many different directions as possible is to have policy proceed in a liberal democratic setting, where different interests and actors (such as environmental and community groups, professional associations, different kinds of scientists, elected representatives, corporations and their officials, labor unions, and journalists) are all able to give their opinions without fear, and in the knowledge that will find an audience among policy makers. Real-world liberal democracies are only imperfect approximations to Popper's "open society" ideal, but no closer style of politics has yet been found.

Is this sort of policy making by interaction appropriate to an ecological context? To begin, the apparent chaos of piecemeal, interactive politics might belie a deeper organization, even if nobody in the system perceives it or really understands why and how this organization happens. Liberal democracies in one sense resemble ecosystems, for both are self-organizing systems (diZerega, 1993). That is, complex structures of order evolve without anyone designing them, as a result of the relatively simple and short-sighted choices and actions of the individual organisms within the system. In this light, the real order of liberal democracy is not to be found in constitutions, but in the informal, interactive processes at the heart of democratic pragmatism. Of course, the precise structure of order in any self-organizing system matters a great deal. By definition, an environmentalist can have little quarrel with the kind of order that ecosystems have produced by evolution (though he or she might wish for fewer deadly viruses and other living things that hurt human beings). That liberal democracy is a self-organizing system (as is the capitalist market) does not mean that it is at all defensible or adequate in the light of ecological criteria.

Ecosystems are self-organizing systems full of negative feedback devices that correct for disturbances to them. For example, a forest fire is normally followed by pioneer species of plants springing up in the burnt area, which in turn provide the growing conditions for more mature forest species to return. The idea of negative feedback also defines the metaphor of the thermostat. So what kind of "thermostat" does democratic pragmatism possess? The answer lies in the variety of individuals, organizations, parties, and movements which can bring pressure to bear in and on political interaction

94   Solving Environmental Problems

in response to environmental disturbances. For example, one would expect wilderness advocates to keep their eyes on old growth forests, so that if clearcutting threatens to get out of hand they can protest, lobby, hold press conferences, issue legal challenges, and so forth. Or if a proposal for a toxic waste incinerator in an urban neighborhood threatens life and health, the local community can organize against it. Survivalists would argue that these kinds of actions are all reactive and so incapable of anticipating limits before we hit them, though it should be noted that survivalist groups such as Zero Population Growth also participate in liberal democratic politics.

Whether or not these negative feedback devices are ecologically adequate depends crucially on the values of the people through whom the devices act. If people value tangible material goods above all else, then feedback will be impaired (though even these individuals might protest against any immediate environmental threat to their life and health). So is there anything in liberal democracy that is intrinsically conducive to ecological values? Let me take a look at two arguments which claim that there is.

Democratic pragmatism involves talk and written communication, not just strategizing and power-plays, and such communication works best when it is couched in the language of the public interest, rather than private interests. Steven Kelman (1987) believes that such talk is not cheap, and that people actually internalize public interest motivations. Adolf Gundersen (1995) applies this sort of analysis to public deliberation about environmental affairs. Deliberation is necessary for democratic pragmatism to work. Problem solving in democratic pragmatism, recall, is never a matter of individuals acting in isolation or under command from anyone else. Instead, problems always get discussed. Gundersen believes that the very act of discussion or deliberation about issues activates a commitment to environmental values, or, more precisely, "collective, holistic, and long term thinking." Long-term thinking might even extend to the wellbeing of future generations, who cannot of course participate directly in current debates. Gundersen's evidence is a series of 46 "deliberative interviews" which he conducts with a variety of people who did not in the beginning identify themselves as environmentalists. By the end of these discussions, all espoused environmental values more strongly. On this account, everyone has latent positive dispositions which only need to be activated into specific policy commitments. Discussion in liberal democratic settings forces people to scrutinize their own volitions and dispositions in a way that promotes such activation.

The idea that participation in democratic settings activates environmental values is shared by the environmental philosopher Mark Sagoff (1988). Sagoff believes that every individual has two kinds of preferences: as a consumer and as a citizen. These preferences may point in quite different directions for the same individual. His running example concerns the Mineral King Valley in California's Sierra Nevadas, where the Walt Disney Corporation wanted to build a ski resort. Confronting his students with this possibility, it turns out that many of them would enjoy visiting such a resort to ski and enjoy the après-ski nightlife. Few had any interest in backpacking into the existing Mineral King wilderness. But when asked whether they would favor construction of the resort, none did. The answer is that while as consumers they would love to ski there, as citizens they object to wilderness destruction. The implication is that citizen preferences are more concerned with collective, community-oriented values, as opposed to the selfish materialism of consumer values. While one might dispute the degree to which such public-spirited motivation pervades real-world liberal democratic politics, Sagoff's critique of economic reasoning and market rationality as applied to environmental policy is devastating. He also deploys his argument to excuse some of his more disgusting personal habits, notably driving a car that leaks oil everywhere which sports an "ecology now" bumper sticker (Sagoff, 1988: 53). The sticker proclaims his citizen preferences, the oil slick under his car his consumer preferences. The citizen in him would like the government to crack down on the consumer in him.

Discourse Analysis of Democratic Pragmatism

1. Basic Entities whose Existence is Recognized or Constructed

Like administrative rationalism, democratic pragmatism takes the structural status quo of liberal capitalism as given. However, the treatment of government is very different. Government is treated not as a unitary state, but rather as a multiplicity of decision processes populated by citizens. *Homo civicus* figures large, *homo bureaucratis* hardly at all. In short, government is carried out by liberal democracy, not the administrative state. Democratic pragmatism has little or nothing to say about ecosystems and the natural world; very different conceptions on this score are welcome in liberal democratic debate.

2. Assumptions about Natural Relationships

Both administrative rationalism and democratic pragmatism place nature as subordinate to human problem-solving efforts. Whether nature contains

96 **Solving Environmental Problems**

self-regulating ecosystems or is just a storehouse of brute matter and energy makes little difference here. The natural relationships within human society postulated by the two discourses are in contrast quite different. Democratic pragmatism celebrates equality among citizens (of course, the reality of liberal democracy may be very different). Everyone has the right to exert political pressure, be they scientists, elected officials, pressure group leaders, ordinary voters, or ordinary non-voters. Beyond this basic equality, political relationships are seen as interactive and far more complex than those in a bureaucratic hierarchy. Interactions feature a mix of competition and cooperation. Certainly cooperative problem solving can occur; but so can political conflict between partisans of competing interests (such as environmentalists and developers).

3. AGENTS AND THEIR MOTIVES

Agency in democratic pragmatism is for everyone, be they individual citizens and political activists or collective actors such as corporations, labor unions, environmentalist groups, community organizations, and government agencies. Motives are mixed. Many of these actors much of the time pursue selfish material interests, such as profit, increased property values, higher wages, more secure employment, or subsidized access to a favorite natural area. But the discourse also allows, indeed requires, that at key junctures agents can be motivated by the public interest. In the first instance, this public interest will have to be defined in plural terms. So what the Wilderness Society takes as being in the public interest will not necessarily be the same as for the Chamber of Commerce. Some democratic pragmatists would leave it at that, arguing that plurality here is irreducible, and that we can expect only piecemeal compromises across partisans of different views. But others I have discussed, such as Kelman, Gundersen, and Sagoff, hope for something more: reasoned public dialogue that will produce convergence on a common conception of the public interest (see also Williams and Matheny, 1995). If a single public interest does emerge through dialogue it is a very different matter from the unitary public interest that exists for administrative rationalists, for whom the public interest is something for analysts to discover, rather than the public to debate.

4. KEY METAPHORS AND OTHER RHETORICAL DEVICES

No vivid metaphors pervade democratic pragmatism in action. But two scientific metaphors are advanced by reflective defenders of this discourse. The first treats public policy as the resultant of forces acting upon it from different directions. These forces differ in the direction in which they want to pull public policy, and in their relative power, exercised by all the individuals and groups with the capacity to act. Such a metaphor is likely to be employed by those who think there can be no unitary conception of the public interest. Indeed, this metaphor was long a staple of pluralist accounts of the US political system developed by American political scientists.

A second metaphor is that of science in its entirety. As we have seen, Popperians believe that public policies are like scientific experiments, and that the proper attitude for scientists and policy makers alike is an open, critical, and democratic one.

Another metaphor I mentioned earlier is that of the thermostat, designed to trigger interventions (heating and cooling) as soon as temperature departs from a desirable range. Democratic pragmatism allows attention to a wide range of target variables analogous to temperature (economic and political as well as environmental ones), and many ways in which negative feedback can be brought to bear. Foremost among these is the possibility for aggrieved citizens and groups to mobilize when they perceive an environmental abuse.

BOX 5.1. DISCOURSE ANALYSIS OF DEMOCRATIC PRAGMATISM

1. **Basic Entities Recognized or Constructed**
   - Liberal capitalism
   - Liberal democracy
   - Citizens

2. **Assumptions about Natural Relationships**
   - Equality among citizens
   - Interactive political relationships, mixing competition and cooperation

3. **Agents and their Motives**
   - Many different agents
   - Motivation a mix of material self-interest and multiple conceptions of public interest

4. **Key Metaphors and other Rhetorical Devices**
   - Public policy as a resultant of forces
   - Policy like scientific experimentation
   - Thermostat

The Limits of Democratic Pragmatism

Democratic pragmatism has much to be said on its behalf. As an orientation to solving problems within the liberal capitalist political economy, it accepts

98   Solving Environmental Problems

many problems that baffle administrative rationalism. This transfer is often made for reasons relating to the need to legitimate policy decisions in the eyes of a broader public but, as we have seen, it can be justified in terms of more effectively resolving (or at least attacking) the problems too. If we look around today's world, we see that the countries that have progressed most in terms of environmental conservation and pollution control are the capitalist democracies (though it should be stressed that the most capitalist are not the best performers). The latter piece of evidence does not provide quite the comfort to democratic pragmatism than it might. For the acknowledged leaders in the environmental stakes include countries such as Germany and Japan (see Jänicke, 1996), whose policy-making structures impose substantial restraints on democratic pragmatism, especially on who can have access to policy making and under what terms. So in Japan policy making is monopolized by business and government elites; in Germany, labor union leaders also have a say. In each of these cases, usually described as corporatism, participation is through highly formalized channels, allowing little of the self-organizing give and take celebrated by democratic pragmatists. Moreover, some of the best-performing countries are adopting a discourse quite different from democratic pragmatism, as we will see in Chapter 8.

Skeptics might also argue that it is the prosperity of the capitalist democracies that allows them to cope better with their environmental problems than anyone else, as opposed to the intrinsic problem-solving qualities of democratic pragmatism. And there is always the possibility that they have succeeded in offloading many of their environmental problems onto poorer countries. So a clean and pleasant environment in Japan is purchased in part by the dirtier elements of manufacturing industry being transferred to other East Asian countries, not to mention deforestation of South East Asia to meet Japanese timber needs.

The main limit to democratic pragmatism is the simple existence of political power (which goes unrecognized by enthusiasts such as Gundersen and Sagoff). Politics in capitalist democratic settings is rarely about disinterested and public-spirited problem solving in which a variety of perspectives are brought to bear with equal weight. Often there are powerful interests with large financial resources at their disposal which will try to skew the outcomes of policy debates and decision-making processes in their direction. Now, sometimes that direction will coincide with ecological values. More often it will not, as the interests with by far the greatest amount of resources and the strongest incentives to deploy them in political interaction are business interests.

Business can influence the terms of debate by producing glossy advertising material to tout the environmental friendliness of its products. It can (and does) sponsor Earth Day festivities. It can produce television advertising to promote the corporate environmental image: so in the United States Weyerhauser promotes itself as "the tree growing company" with film of a bald eagle flying over a forest. The clearcutting of old growth forests which is also one of Weyerhauser's activities is unmentioned. Corporate actors also have greater access to expert counsel in public inquiries. Alternative dispute resolution can be manipulated by these actors and their sympathizers in government in order to co-opt and neutralize troublemakers from community and environmental groups. ADR can be oriented toward a "responsible development" gloss on projects which will generally go ahead, and toward treatment of environmental values as on a par with business's material interests (Amy, 1987). Participation by environmentalists in impact assessment might dissipate energies that would be better spent on other activities, if the impact assessment process merely legitimates decisions already made elsewhere on the basis of economic values or corporate profit (Amy, 1990: 60–4). Corporations can even offer employment to environmental activists. For example, leading British Green Jonathan Porritt signed on as an advisor to Sainsbury's, the food retailing giant, though this does not mean that the British Green Party has become the political wing of Sainsbury's.[5]

Such pressures do not go all one way; public opinion does exist as something more than the creation of business public relations departments, and public interest groups can mobilize expertise and support, even money. Still, so long as the structural status quo of the capitalist market economy is taken as given, business has a "privileged" position in policy making, for government relies greatly upon business to carry out basic functions such as employing people and organizing the economy (Lindblom, 1977: 171–5). Yet more fundamentally, the same state imperatives that constrain administrative rationalism, and which I discussed at the end of the previous chapter, also constrain democratic pragmatism, for as long as the latter remains a problem-solving discourse. These imperatives involve, first and foremost, maintaining the confidence of actual and potential investors. Any measures for environmental protection, conservation, or pollution control which threaten to undermine this confidence will be automatically punished by disinvestment. This possibility casts a long shadow over policy deliberations, however democratic they may be (see Press, 1994). And once business publicists realise this, they can make good strategic use of the disinvestment threat, even when there is no real intention to disinvest.

Democratic pragmatism as a discourse recognizes citizens as a basic

[5] This title was once held by the rump Social Democratic Party, when its main funding came from the Sainsbury family.

entity, and a natural relationship of equality across citizens. But this imagery of reasoned debate among equals is in practice highly distorted by the exercise of power and strategy, and by state imperatives lurking in the background. Matters appear still more doubtful in an ecological light when one further considers the character of actors and their interests. One advantage of democratic pragmatism stressed by its adherents is that it enables views on policy proposals to come from a variety of directions. Some directions represent conceptions of what is in the public interest. These conceptions may vary: to some, the public interest may involve mostly economic efficiency, to others distributional equity in society, to others still ecological integrity, to others social harmony. When liberal democratic enthusiasts such as Gundersen and Sagoff in an ecological context, and Dewey and Popper more generally, think of democratic debate, this is presumably what they have in mind.[6] But other interests involved are motivated mostly by their own material interests: corporations and industry associations concerned with maximizing profit and avoiding environmental controls on their operations, or labor unions concerned with the income and employment of their members, even if that means employment in unsustainable practices such as clearcutting of ancient forests. The pluralist aspect of democratic pragmatism treats all such interests and concerns as equally legitimate (see Williams and Matheny, 1995: 19–24). The mere fact of participation in liberal democratic settings does not lead actors to discard their motivations as consumers and producers in favor of more public-spirited citizen preferences, or to conclude that pursuit of their economic interests should be confined to the market place rather than allowed to enter politics.

More insidious still are special interests which masquerade as general principles. So, for example, the "Wise Use" movement in the American West in the 1990s has a name that connotes commitment to sensible use of resources, but in practice it seeks a regime of subsidized access for local communities and corporations to minerals, grazing rights, and timber located on public lands in the region.

Political rationality in democratic pragmatism means that all actors have to be mollified, pretty much in proportion to their ability to create difficulties for government officials, irrespective of whether they are motivated by conceptions of the public interest or more selfish material interests. This does not necessarily coincide with ecological rationality, which is concerned

---

[6] For a more explicit statement about the degree to which "public spirit" actually pervades even US politics, see Kelman (1987). According to Kelman, presidents, congresspersons, and bureaucrats alike are all motivated mainly by the desire to make an honest effort to achieve good public policy. But even Kelman recognizes that special interests will sometimes upset this happy situation.

with the integrity of natural life-support systems (see Dryzek, 1987: 118–20). So in 1993 the Clinton administration took a small step toward ecological rationality when Secretary of the Interior Bruce Babbit proposed reforming grazing law to end subsidized access for cattle ranchers to public land. It soon became evident that the politically rational thing to do was back off on these reforms for fear of the electoral weight of the Western states where these reforms would take effect, and where welfare ranchers and their sympathizers could tip the balance come election day.

Democratic pragmatism in some respects merits a similar summary judgement to administrative rationalism: plenty of achievements to look back upon, but limits to effectiveness increasingly apparent. This similarity applies mostly at the level of specific policies and institutions inspired or justified by the two discourses. But as a discourse, democratic pragmatism has one striking advantage: it is more conducive to an awareness of the limitations of its own institutional manifestations, and so to efforts to overcome these limits.

Democratic pragmatism as a political style developed mostly in the context of distributive issues, where the main task is to allocate the gains and losses of government activity. Thus when environmental issues reach the agenda, they too are treated in distributive terms, with the main question being how to strike a balance between winners and losers, such as economic and environmental interests. General interests in (say) the integrity of ecosystems or the quality of commons resources are less easily represented. As we shall see in Part IV, sustainability discourses dissolve such problems by dissolving the conflict between economic and environmental values. This raises the prospect of environmental values being assimilated in to, rather than overridden by, the economic imperatives of states in capitalist societies. But first, another problem-solving discourse merits examination.

References

Amy, Douglas J. (1987), *The Politics of Environmental Mediation*. New York: Columbia University Press.

—— (1990), "Decision Techniques for Environmental Policy: A Critique", pp. 59–79 in Robert Paehlke and Douglas Torgerson (eds.), *Managing Leviathan: Environmental Politics and the Administrative State*. Peterborough, Ontario: Broadview.

Anderson, Charles W. (1990), *Pragmatic Liberalism*. Chicago, Ill.: University of Chicago Press.

Bartlett, Robert V. (1990), "Ecological Reason in Administration: Environmental Impact Assessment and Administrative Theory", pp. 81–96 in Robert Paehlke and Douglas Torgerson (eds.), *Managing Leviathan: Environmental Politics and the Administrative State*. Peterborough, Ontario: Broadview.

Berger, Thomas (1977), *Northern Frontier, Northern Homeland: Report of the MacKenzie Valley Pipeline Inquiry*. Toronto: James Lorimer.

DiZerega, Gus (1993), "Unexpected Harmonies: Self-Organization in Liberal Modernity and Ecology", *The Trumpeter*, 10: 25–32.

Dryzek, John S. (1987), *Rational Ecology: Environment and Political Economy*. New York: Basil Blackwell.

—— (1996a), *Democracy in Capitalist Times: Ideals, Limits, and Struggles*. New York: Oxford University Press.

Fischer, Frank (1993), "Citizen Participation and the Democratization of Policy Expertise: From Theoretical Inquiry to Practical Cases", *Policy Sciences*, 26: 165–87.

Fukuyama, Francis (1989), "The End of History?", *National Interest*, Summer, 3–18.

—— (1992), *The End of History and the Last Man*. New York: Free Press.

Gundersen, Adolf (1995), *The Environmental Promise of Democratic Deliberation*. Madison, Wis.: University of Wisconsin Press.

Jänicke, Martin (1996), "Democracy as a Condition for Environmental Policy Success: The Importance of Non-Institutional Factors", pp. 71–85 in William M. Lafferty and James Meadowcraft (eds.), *Democracy and the Environment: Problems and Prospects*. Cheltenham: Edward Elgar.

Kelman, Steven (1987), *Making Public Policy: A Hopeful View of American Government*. New York: Basic Books.

Kemp, Ray (1985), "Planning, Public Hearings, and the Politics of Discourse", pp. 177–201 in John Forester (ed.), *Critical Theory and Public Life*. Cambridge, Mass.: MIT Press.

Lee, Kai N. (1993), *Compass and Gyroscope: Integrating Science and Politics for the Environment*. Washington, DC: Island Press.

Light, Andrew, and Katz, Eric (1996), *Environmental Pragmatism*. London: Routledge.

Lindblom, Charles E. (1959), "The Science of Muddling Through", *Public Administration Review*, 19: 79–88.

—— (1965), *The Intelligence of Democracy: Decision Making through Mutual Adjustment*. New York: Free Press.

—— (1977), *Politics and Markets: The World's Political-Economic Systems*. New York: Basic Books.

McFarland, Andrew (1984), "An Experiment in Regulatory Negotiation: The National Coal Policy Project", paper presented at the Annual Meeting of the Western Political Science Association.

Nelkin, Dorothy and Pollack, Michael (1981), *The Atom Beseiged*. Cambridge, Mass.: MIT Press.

Paehlke, Robert (1988), "Democracy, Bureaucracy, and Environmentalism", *Environmental Ethics*, 10: 291–308.

Popper, Karl R. (1966), *The Open Society and its Enemies*. London: Routledge and Kegan Paul.

Press, Daniel (1994), *Democratic Dilemmas in the Age of Ecology: Trees and Toxics in the American West*. Durham, NC: Duke University Press.

Pressman, Jeffrey and Wildavsky, Aaron (1973), *Implementation*. Berkeley, Calif.: University of California Press.

Rabe, Barry G. (1991), "Beyond the Nimby Syndrome in HazardousWaste Facility Siting: The Albertan Breakthrough and the Prospects for Cooperation in Canada and the United States", *Governance*, 4: 184–206.

Sagoff, Mark (1988), *The Economy of the Earth*. Cambridge: Cambridge University Press.

Torgerson, Douglas (1990), "Limits of the Administrative Mind: The Problem of Defining Environmental Problems", pp. 115–61 in Robert Paehlke and Douglas Torgerson (eds.), *Managing Leviathan: Environmental Politics and the Administrative State*. Peterborough, Ontario: Broadview.

Wildavsky, Aaron (1988), *The New Politics of the Budgetary Process*. Boston: Little Brown.

Williams, Bruce A. and Matheny, Albert R. (1995), *Democracy, Dialogue, and Environmental Disputes: The Contested Languages of Social Regulation*. New Haven, Conn.: Yale University Press.

[26]

THE ENVIRONMENTAL STATE AND THE FOREST: OF LOOKOUTS, LUMBERJACKS, LEOPARDS, AND LOSERS

Bianca Ambrose-Oji, Tim Allmark, Peter Buckley, Bindi Clements and Graham Woodgate

INTRODUCTION

Contemporary societies are facing the realisation that environmental changes are entering a new phase, one which challenges the old structural order. Whether viewed from the national, regional or international perspective, the modern technologies, institutions and systems of organisation that mediate relationships between people and the environment, have profoundly altered our relationship with the material world, at the same time as affecting how we perceive, understand and attempt to manage environmental resources and services. Consequently, modern life presents worrying contradictions; just as society begins to understand more about the consequences of anthropogenic environmental change, the alliance of science, technology and capitalism seem increasingly to multiply ecological risk.

As a result, we hear calls for bio-economic change by populations demonstrating against environmental degradation and social deprivation. Nevertheless, these same populations resist change to the lifestyle aspirations, which produce the environmental outcomes they fight against. Similarly, states continue to

The Environmental State Under Pressure, Volume 10, pages 149–169.

promote economic development and nurture corporate business as a source of wealth and power whilst, on the other hand, they adopt legislative frameworks designed to prevent ecological damage and foster environmental protection.

Correspondingly, while developing new perspectives to account for this contradictory 'modern condition', sociology has seen the re-appearance of its own epistemological fault lines and struggled to overcome the contradictions epitomised by the nature/culture and structure/agency debates. The emergent 'environmental sociology' has come some way in incorporating 'nature' into social analysis, and also recognised that the wider global configuration within which these society/environment relationships are ultimately embedded must also form part of the debate. Our aim in this paper is to harness some of the ideas coming from environmental sociology, to describe and examine the nature of the 'environmental state' and the contradictory role it plays in fostering and mitigating environmental problems.

Our discussion focuses on the issue of tropical forest destruction, which has both global and local dimensions and has become an important theme for states in the first and third worlds. Our specific concern with the 'environmental state' places the development of inclusionary governance and management of forest resources, at the heart of our analysis. Discussion throughout this paper is informed by extensive research conducted in the West African tropical forest region of South West Cameroon.

THE ENVIRONMENTAL STATE ...

The concept of 'globalisation' forces a re-examination of the concept of the state because, at one level, states are defined only in relation to other states, a situation which presupposes globalised relations and now prompts discussion about their power and autonomy relative to other modern global institutions. On a more fundamental level, if we agree that nation states are "either 'too small' to manage regional and global problems or 'too big' to deal with local environmental problems" (Bryant & Bailey, 1997, p. 52), we must also recognise the failings of social theories based on conventional nation state precepts in explaining the dynamic linkages between social phenomena and environmental changes experienced at a local level. How then might we reinterpret the idea of the state and present a more nuanced understanding of the environmental state? We begin by turning to Foucault for insight.[1]

Foucault identifies the emergence of biology as a science, as a defining moment, the "entry of life into history", which precipitated a cleavage from the situation where national polities were driven by "reasons of state", to one where they became driven by the need to control institutions relating to the material and administrative conditions sustaining production and reproduction: in other words, to life itself. In this way he suggests that biosciences have become the crucial instrumental knowledges. The result is a fundamental switch from the state's emphasis on the control of territory as land, to the control of territory as people, populations and resources.

Since the emergence of modern nation states on the global stage, state-sponsored bioscience has played a major role in driving the twin processes of industrialisation and capital accumulation, aiding the transformation of nature into ever more managed environments,[2] and reformulating traditional, nationally-bound relations of production into globally fluid conditions of production "where everything is treated as a commodity, even if it is not produced as a commodity" (Escobar, 1996, p. 54). Thus, what Foucault termed 'bio-power' grew out of the dual position of life as "outside history, in its biological environment, and inside human historicity, penetrated by the latter's techniques of knowledge and power" (Foucault, 1976, p. 146).

The role of the state in securing the material well being and reproductive capacity of its population has not changed. However, two of what Giddens (1990) identifies as the four central institutions of modernity, capitalism and industrialisation, have by and large been appropriated and dominated by global business. This changes the very nature of the state; not only does it become decentred, it is forced to consider a new dimension, transnational security threats in the form of ecological risk. The old order of state-based political, scientific and judicial institutions become impotent; the dividing line between domestic and foreign policies becomes fuzzy and the bio-political boundaries between states become blurred. The unpredictability of societal development, lead states to pursue strategies of ecological security which bring them into globalised conflicts over how ecological risks can be distributed, averted, controlled and legitimated (Beck, 1996).

In effect, nation states are transformed into the environmental state, which is far less "a collectivity existing within a clearly demarcated territory, which is ... subject to a unitary administration, reflexively monitored by both the internal state apparatus and those of other states" (Giddens, 1985, p. 11). Rather, it becomes much more of a complex and dynamically interdependent collectivity of national governments and civil societies that exists bound together *across* political territorial units, and is subject to a bio-political administration composed of national and suprastate economic and legislative agencies. Where the environmental state's concern switches from territory as land, to the control of populations and resources, it becomes more difficult to see a nation's boundaries restricted to geographical space. People are joined through their common utilisation and protection of resources; one person's environmental

152   B. AMBROSE-OJI ET AL.

conduct effects the limits of another's ecological freedom (Luke, 1999), regardless of the specific situation of actors, all form part of the same socio-ecological corpus.

The power of the environmental state does not necessarily diminish, rather it changes form. The structural properties of capitalism and industrialisation are patterned by agencies and organisations such as transnational companies, the World Trade Organisation and the United Nations. The state facilitates these processes at a local level because they remain tied to the material well being of populations. However, for the environmental state a bio-economic understanding of global systems ecology gives rise to new forms of biopolitics, that rely on bio-power "operating upon . . . the 'continuous and multiple relations' between the population, its resources and the environment" (Rutherford, 1999, p. 45). Maintaining dominance in this bio-political realm rests on the exercise of ecological governmentality; where "governmentality is the ensemble formed by institutions, procedures, analyses and reflections, the calculations and tactics that allow the exercise of this very specific albeit complex form of power, which has as its *target population*, as its principle form of knowledge *political economy*, and as its essential means *apparatuses of security*" (Darier, 1999, p. 22).

... AND THE FOREST

We turn now to consider the social relations surrounding tropical forests in Cameroon as a real-world example on which to base our theoretical abstractions. Cameroon has a long history of integration into European and global systems of trade and politics. Starting with Portuguese exploration in the Fifteenth and Sixteenth Centuries and then British and German mercantilism during the Eighteenth and Nineteenth Centuries, the forest represented an uncharted wilderness important in supplying slaves, ivory, wild rubber, palm oil, tannin, timber and forest spices to European and world markets (Ardener, 1996; DeLancy & Mokeba, 1990; Njeuma, 1989). During the late Nineteenth and early Twentieth centuries mercantilism was superseded by direct colonial rule. This period saw major changes to social power relations and laid the foundations for contemporary patterns of bio-power. Following Giddens's formulation, power is generated in the reproduction of structures of domination constituted by allocative and authoritative resources. "Any co-ordination of social systems across time and space necessarily involves a definite combination of these two types of resources" (Giddens, 1984, p. 258). For the colonial state the forest represented a significant part of a suite of allocative resources, which had associated with it a complex of authoritative apparatuses.

The conquest of territory in Cameroon saw the development of a system of tenure which declared that all land belonged to the Crown unless effectively occupied by 'natives' or private individuals (Anon, 1900; Ngwasiri, 1995). The test of occupation or ownership was conversion of 'virgin' forest into farmland; the forest effectively became state territory. Coinciding with the appropriation of land, the growing demands of first world industrialisation precipitated a symbolic reconstruction of the forest. Rather than a source of natural wealth, it became a resource ripe for conversion to plantation production (Epale, 1985; Konings, 1995). Economic dominance was assured by two means: trade in forest products was taken out of the hands of African businessmen, while new administrative procedures effectively made illegal native plantations of industrial commodities.

Authoritative dominance was consolidated through the application of rational knowledge and systems of bioscience. These explored, charted, measured, and inventoried the forest, and in many areas modified it as managed plantations. The forest's human populations were mapped, subjected to anthropological classification and incorporated into administrative management through the reinterpretation of social tradition and the invention of chieftancy (CNAB, 1916; CNAB, 1921; CNAB, 1923; CNAB, 1934; Geschiere, 1993). The importation of huge numbers of indentured labourers for the plantations, destabilised and further marginalised forest communities.

In the period covering independence from Britain and France, from the late 1950s to the early 1970s, the forest was symbolically transformed once more. This time it became the site of 'progress' and 'development', the seat of modern nationhood (Victoria Centenary Committee, 1958), and was subject to relatively intensive timber extraction as a source of foreign capital to fund the state's provision of basic infrastructure and welfare services. After 1972 the colonial administration was progressively replaced with a totalitarian regime, and society was urged to attain the goals of the five-year National Development Plans. Central to these was further forest clearance and the improvement of peasant agriculture to produce commodities for world markets.

However, the need to reserve the forest and forested land for public purposes was recognised from the earliest years; timber production reserves and 'conservation' areas were proposed and partially established between 1900 and the 1980s. Following the colonial approach, 'conservation areas' were located in mountainous areas (Kearns, 1997; Wiley, 1999). Systems of reservation servicing the needs of forest communities were also established during the British colonial period, where community control over land and forest resources was vested in the 'Native Authority'.

It is from these historical economic, political, social and conservationist roots that the most recent transformation of the forest, as a risk mitigating resource for the environmental state, has come into being. So, how does our concept of the environmental state equate with the current situation of Cameroon and its tropical forest resource?

THE ENVIRONMENTAL STATE IN THE FOREST

During the late 1980s and early 1990s, under the auspices of the World Bank and IMF the economic autonomy of Cameroon was lost to transnational corporations and the macro-economic policies of suprastate organisations. The instigation of a structural adjustment programme in 1992 pealed the death knell for the last of the government controlled parastatal plantation and processing agri-businesses and prompted a dramatic currency devaluation. Once again all eyes turned to the forest.

Whilst recognising the global importance of the forest's flora and fauna, the World Bank and ITTO[3] identified Cameroon's forests as natural capital ideally suited as security against the risks of debt repayment default.[4] Having projected the amount of income that could be generated from increased logging, the World Bank and the ITTO effectively laid plans to 'mine' the forest if the economic situation of the country worsened (Anon, 1991; Arentz, 1993). Facing declining terms of trade for agricultural commodities and reduced revenues from oil, the Cameroon government responded to external pressure, and promulgated a new Forest Law in 1994 (see Forje, 1993).

The environmental state signed up to forest destruction. The Cameroon government consequently became involved in supporting policies and projects that involved the transformation of natural capital into financial capital. In many cases it was assisted in realising forest policy by ex-colonial interests such as the U.K., French and German governments. The U.K. government was also instrumental in providing the largest employer in the country, the Cameroon Development Corporation, with expertise and materials to restructure and expand forest operations in the run-up to privatisation. Operationalisation of these economic risk mitigating activities was carried out by situated environmental professionals drawn from the relevant Cameroon line ministries, as well as expatriate representatives of business and government. For much of Cameroonian civil society the forest became a refuge from financial and other livelihood risks stemming from the harsh economic climate (Ndoye & Kaimowitz, 1998). For these situated actors the forest represents livelihood security: a 'free' source of land and exploitable resources (Demenou, 1997; Gockowski, 1997). For local community elites and entrepreneurs with larger capital endowments the forest presents development opportunities often by subcontracting to transnational companies.

In contrast to the ideology of 'globalism' (Beck, 1998, p. 28) that had driven structural adjustment, the parallel phenomenon of 'globality' produced a series of countervailing power effects that penetrated the social relations surrounding Cameroon's forests. According to Beck, globality represents the alternative politics of globalisation. It stands in stark contrast to the de-politicised economic dimension of globalism, and refers to global social order structured by social relations which are neither integrated in the politics of the nation state nor determinable by the politics of the nation state (Woodgate et al., 1999). The shared values of this 'world society' include ethnic diversity and environmental quality and resonate with the problematic of 'tropical deforestation', that had captured government and public attention in both donor nations and Cameroon. Constructed as problems of global environmental risk, 'climate change' and 'biodiversity loss' were quickly linked to forest destruction. Similarly, globality has helped to coach more sophisticated understandings of environmental issues, leading to the social construction of the environment in the third world as a livelihood issue, thus tapping into discourse around indigenous rights and the pursuit of sustainable forest livelihoods.

Reacting to these pressures, as well as those from suprastate organisations, such as UNCED and WWF, the environmental state conceded an important addition to Cameroon's new Forest Law. Clauses were introduced which allowed greater involvement in resource management for forest communities. The environmental state – the same expatriate government donor agencies and Cameroonian line ministries that were involved in forest destruction – began implementing or supporting participatory, Integrated Conservation and Development Programmes (ICDPs). These were to be implemented by environmental professionals drawn from the same pool of personnel involved in commercial exploitation.

Figure 1 illustrates schematically these dynamic connections and inter-relationships as they converge in participatory interventions. The environmental state is linked to situated actors as the 'risk population', which must be taken "into account in all its observations and savoirs, in order to be able to govern effectively in a rational and conscious manner' (Foucault, 1991 quoted in Burchell et al., 1991, pp. 144–145). Suprastate agencies and organisations of global capital are linked as the 'global agenda setting community'.

Each set of actors reflexively monitors changes in the social practices of the others, as well as environmental conditions in the material world. Perceived changes in either practice or conditions, prompt reactions from each group of actors, which in turn, alter patterns of agency and environmental possibilities. In this way the forest is refashioned physically as well as cognitively (c.f. Woodgate & Redclift, 1998).

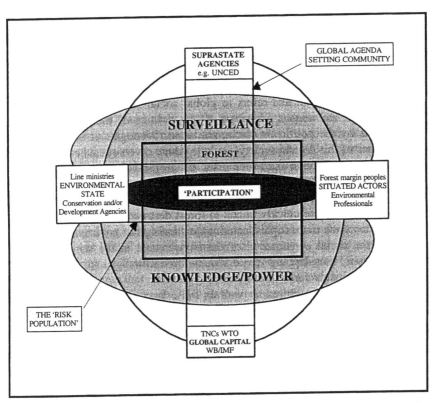

Fig. 1. Schematic of the Dynamic Social Interrelationships Surrounding the Forest.

The ability to monitor reflexively and initiate change depends on two crucial components of social practice. One of these is what Giddens (1990) identifies as a third institutional dimension of modernity – surveillance (control of information and social supervision), or what Foucault may have called apparatuses of state security (the essential means of governmentality). The other is what Foucault saw as the knowledge/power complex, a fused grid or network of relations expressed through action. Different capabilities concerning surveillance and the knowledge/power complex are associated with each set of actors. Each group employs these components of social practice to further its own agenda. For 'suprastate agencies' such as UNCED and GEF (a World Bank environment fund), the agenda is global ecological regulation as well as the promotion of sustainable livelihoods. For the institutions of 'global capital' e.g. transnationals and the World Bank, the agenda is the maximisation of profit based on neoliberal ideology. As for the situated actors, the forest margin communities are concerned with minimising livelihood risk and maximising security; and the environmental professionals, as representatives of nation states, have conservation and development agendas. The environmental state, Cameroon and donor country line ministries, and conservation/development organisations, aim to minimise ecological and livelihood risks, and build national economic security.

Having outlined how the global 'agenda setting community' and the 'risk population' come together within the wider material world and meet in the tropical forest, it is to this conjunction of the knowledge/power complex and surveillance we now turn to expose the power effects related to the operation of the environmental state.

OF LOOKOUTS

From our thumbnail sketch tracking the history and development of the environmental state in the forest, it becomes clear how previous modes of environmental protection have come under severe pressure. Reflexive monitoring by all actors of one anothers' activities, coupled with the shift of economic power to the hand of business, meant that old models of forest protection became untenable for two reasons. First, resources for maintaining 'quasi-military' style exclusionary conservation operations[5] disappeared, whilst at the same time civil resistance and incursion into the forests increased, making effective control impossible. Second, the environmental state was forced to minister to the risks perceived by the population (indigenous rights to self development and secure livelihoods), and those the state perceived as affecting the social body (global environmental quality and national economic capacity); whilst satisfying the edicts of the global agenda setting community (e.g. structural adjustment, ratification of UNCED's Forest Principles, Biodiversity and Climate Change Conventions, and Agenda 21 priorities).

Participatory approaches to conservation, in which communities were 'empowered' to direct their own 'development' were pushed forward as a credible alternative to exclusionary modes of conservation. The environmental state has adopted and normalised this discourse, and used it to legitimise the contradictory functions of forest protection and exploitation demanded by local and global interests. However, the discourse of 'participation' as theory and practice is subject to its own fundamental contradictions. As Brown (1997, pp. 13–14) explains, on the one hand populism suggests that the poor already have the qualities needed for their 'development' and the proper job of environmental professionals is to liberate them from structures of domination whilst, on the other hand, it also suggests that the structures of domination have so altered the consciousness of the poor that they no longer possess these qualities. Thus the task is to re-educate and re-instate a valid 'consciousness'.

A number of important points can be drawn from this contradiction. Both positions invest environmental professionals with an increased authority to monitor and investigate rural communities; tracking patterns of forest resource use, uncovering the political economy constituting their daily lives, and probing their environmental consciousness through the elicitation of indigenous knowledge (cf. Neumann, 1997, p. 560). Participatory techniques rely on the collection and exposure of large quantities of this kind of information, which environmental professionals then use to facilitate liberation or re-education projects.

These interventions at once claim to build the reflexive capacity of local communities, whilst continuing to vest authority in the environmental professionals who may themselves deny the ability of local communities to do this. Either way "the political and institutional dimensions of the situation are consistently discounted, and the argument is diverted from structural relationships to individual responsibilities" (Brown, 1997, p. 14), so that participatory processes facilitate the shifting of responsibility for bearing risk, from the state to individuals.

In this sense participation becomes a form of Foucauldian 'confession' and we can understand the emerging conservation orthodoxy as a form of surveillance. Rather like Foucault's 'panoptican' or watchtower, the environmental state constructs, through the discourse of 'participation', a lookout from which it can extend its gaze over the forest and its natural resources and into the lifeworlds of forest and forest margin communities. Through surveillance the knowledge/power complex is exposed as central to processes of participation. Following through Foucault's ideas of confession, he states that it is "not only confession of madness, but also the patient's own recognition of madness, [that are] the essential dimension[s] of the cure" (Foucault, quoted in Novellino, 1997, p. 55). In other words, once confessed, knowledge and lifeworld become objectified and subject to examination and appropriation by bioscience. Authority remains with the environmental professionals who control the process of analysis "stop[ping] short of advocating a full surrender of authority" to local people (Brown, 1997, p. 14). Therefore, as participatory conservation operates at global and local levels it raises important questions over whose environmental agendas and bio-power are being furthered.

OF LUMBERJACKS

The way in which surveillance and the knowledge/power complex are contained within the participatory process, satisfies the utilitarian projects of first world and third world elements of the environmental state. We have suggested that the environmental state is forced to minister to the 'risk population' whilst satisfying the edicts of the 'global agenda setting community'. Contradictions exist for the environmental state in that the risk population demands livelihood security predicated on forest development, and ecological security dependent upon forest conservation.

By and large, for the first world 'conservation-through-participation' serves a protective function by developing investments in 'risk-mitigating resources'. Here the environmental state focuses on the tropical forest as an 'sink' for CO_2 emissions, and as a source of novel species and genes with potential for mitigating risks inherent to industrially transformed and managed ecosystems. The financial investment by donors into Cameroon's forest conservation and management sector is not insubstantial, one estimate of bilateral aid alone, runs to over U.S.$100 million between 1990 and 1997. The first world is thereby afforded significant status whilst seeking a tangible return on its investment.

The processes of time-space compression that reorganise social relations and condition the permeable boundaries between first world and third world elements of the environmental state, depend, according to Giddens (1990), on 'disembedding mechanisms'. These 'lift out' social activity from localised contexts, and are mediated by two different kinds of encounter, what Giddens (*ibid.*) terms 'faceless commitments' and 'facework commitments'. The face-less commitments in our example relate to the structures, institutions and discourses which make up the agenda of the environmental state. Giddens shows how faceless commitments are dependent on the development of trust in abstract systems. Giddens makes the point that faceless commitments are either sustained or transformed by facework commitments at 'access points'.

Participation, and the surveillance/knowledge/power complex it encompasses, can be understood as a disembedding mechanism, where the expert knowledges of bioscience and risk constitute the abstract system. The expert system calculates benefits and risks of the actions of the environmental state, but also creates a universe of events by implementation of that knowledge. The access points of abstract systems involve individuals as representatives; in our example, the situated environmental professionals.

At these access points facework commitments directed by the environmental professionals tie the forest and forest margin communities into trust relationships. Even though the trust is with the abstract system rather than the individuals who represent it, "access points carry a reminder that it is flesh and blood people who are its operators. Face work commitments tend to be heavily dependent upon what might be called the *demeanour* of system representatives" (emphasis added Giddens, 1990, p. 85). Demeanour here relates to the neo-populist narrative of liberation. These encounters pull local communities into the first world project and into participatory conservation interventions.

Participation as praxis represents a semiotic conquest of local knowledges. 'Saving nature' demands the valuation of local knowledges of sustaining nature where "knowledge is seen as something existing in the minds of individual persons (shamans or elders) about external 'objects' (plants, species), the medical or economic 'utility' of which their bearers are supposed to transmit to us" (Escobar, 1996, p. 57). Participation separates out knowledge from power, and in the process of disembedding loses the context from which knowledge of resources emanates. Additionally, the philosophical base of participation assumes the possibility of self-development based on Habermasian views of consensus-seeking civil society. As Rutherford (1999, p. 44) stresses "not only is knowledge pivotal to practices of power; it is central to *the constitution of the objects upon which power operates* – that is to the making up of *both people and things*".

Sustaining faceless commitments also relies on re-embedding processes (Giddens, 1990). These processes complete the binding of people and institutions across space-time, and serve to hide the weaknesses, problems and uncertainties of the expert systems. The central concern of the first world for resources, identified by a 'gaze' that looks 'through' people, provides the channels not only for disembedding but also for re-embedding social relations. In this way knowledge and power are reinvented and reinserted into the forest milieu.

Through its focus on resources and its targeting of population, the environmental state of the first world is thus incorporated into social practice implying 'action at a distance' (Latour, 1992). The environmental state produces in essence, a situation that can be likened to O'Connor's (1989) notion of 'combined development' – or perhaps more accurately 'combined conservation' – where the first world's project of protecting risk mitigating resources relies on situated forest margin actors fulfilling a predetermined agenda. The environmental state as the Cameroon government, has the twin objectives of satisfying livelihood goals and facilitating national development. However, in bringing the surveillance and knowledge/power complex to bear on the forest, the spotlight on forest peoples and the extended gaze into the forest itself, create opportunities for coercive development of political capital, predicated on forest destruction.

What has to be impressed here is that, in Cameroon, the boundaries between the state as government, the state as line ministry, community elites, and civil society are not sharply defined. Civil organisations are often linked to state organisations, elites to government and so on. The practical consequence of this is that since Independence any relation involving the forest, *has to be* understood in terms of the power relations enmeshed within the national political economy.

We have already shown how at every major historical change of rulership the forest became a site of transformation, and how the forest's own history became part of political history. The strong ties between the forest and politics continue into the present day. The forest continues, for those competing for political position, to be a site to mobilise political support and achieve community representation. The economically well-to-do of forest and forest margin communities may also be representatives of line ministries, or agents of transnational companies. Participatory approaches provide an efficient means by which they can co-opt situated actors onto their personal agendas.

Those seeking political elevation often mediate between conservation/ development organisations and local communities, influencing the projects of the first world with demands for prerequisites (e.g. health facilities, new roads, etc.) to community participation. The same individuals may also become active in the NGO sector where they have sought control over the exploitation of particular forest resources and promised community benefits. In other areas they may be supporting logging companies, fixing terms between the community and business concerning royalties and the provision of services. For these local representatives of line ministries and government, knowledge of the discourse and discursive practices of local and global communities is vital. Local communities are engaged with the language of development and progress, whilst the same initiatives are presented to first world actors as 'sustainable community development', or 'indigenous rights' issues.

OF LEOPARDS

As we reach this point in the discussion, it is clear that the ecological discourse of the environmental state is not simply about the tropical forest environment, the key question concerns which social projects are furthered under the flags of resource and livelihood protection. The social relations surrounding the forest in Cameroon involve a number of powerful 'discourse coalitions' (Hajer, 1995), which struggle to stake their claims over forest resources and peoples.

This creates a situation that Burnham (1994) describes as the 'operational carve-up of zones of influence' between conservation and development interests, where each coalition effectively closes its eyes to the activities of the other, in return for being able to mark their territory successfully. In practice, vast swathes of the forest in Southern Cameroon have been identified as current and potential logging concessions, whereas in the South West conservation areas such as Korup National Park, vie for position with plantation agribusiness.

There is a further layer of contradiction introduced by the way that the discursive communities and policy coalitions, are overlain by epistemic fraternities subscribing to two different interpretations of what Hajer (1995) terms 'ecological modernisation'. One is based on institutional learning, the other on the creation of new institutions and political forms. The institutional learning perspective believes that ecological considerations should be treated as an added component for consideration within existing institutions. In contrast, the alternative view is that appropriation of ecological discourse by current institutions merely perpetuates the status quo, plunging the environmental state and the human species body into deeper crisis; the path to less destructive social practice lying in the emergence of new biopolitical institutions.

Putting all these elements of complexity and layers of incongruity together, it becomes easier to see how the environmental state remains in a position of constant tension, pressure and contradictory reality. It is easier to accept the means by which conventional and ecological forms of capitalization can "co-exist schizophrenically in the same geographical and cultural region" (Escobar, 1996, p. 56), where 'traditional', 'modern', and emerging institutions are caught in a maelstrom of contradictory, facilitative and exclusionary relationships.

OF LOSERS?

So what are the implications for the everyday people living in and around the forest on whom the environmental state focuses its gaze? Our starting point is that the notion of 'risk' is perceived differently by local populations compared with the other groups of actors in our discussion. As Jasanoff (1999, p. 150) puts it, risk is "experienced by experts and laypeople alike ... [but risk] ... is culturally embedded and has texture and meaning that vary from one social grouping to another". She goes on to say that "against this background, it makes very little sense to regulate risk on the basis of centralised institutional authority ... and claims to superior expertise" (*ibid.*).

The livelihood strategies of the local population are structured in response to different types and 'textures' of risk than those perceived by the groups that maintain authority over environmental discourse. It is the local populations themselves, who are the expertly skilled actors in interpreting and responding to the risks present in their own lifeworlds. Consequently, their agency may not easily be turned towards achieving the goals of forest conservation or forest development in the way envisaged by environmental professionals.

A second observation, supported by the historical analysis presented earlier in this paper, is that the discourse and praxis of 'participation' resembles many of the social practices and power relations of the colonial and post-colonial past. For many individuals in the forest zone of South West Cameroon suspicion of the motives of environmental professionals is real and tangible. Many people perceive and believe that the "new forms of intervention ... tend to represent a continuity with, rather than a cleavage from, past practices" (Neumann, 1997, p. 56). The trust so essential to the processes of disembedding and re-embedding social relations, and to the construction of the authoritative gaze, is not easily won. Access points remain places of extreme vulnerability for the environmental state.

Here we come back to Foucault, and underline how his notion of the 'panoptican', was very different to Weber's iron cage of subjugation and control. To Foucault liberty is not the absence of domination but "an expression of individuals' very own existence in the specificity of power relations" and that "liberation from 'oppression', ... is a delusion because power is not exclusively repressive, ... [but] 'capillary', diffused and everywhere" (Darier, 1999, p. 19). This position interprets power as 'constitutive' and 'enabling' (*ibid.*). In other words, the field of power may constrain the options open to the agency of individuals and groups, yet they maintain the capacity either to accept or challenge them. This idea of the limiting of options, accords with Giddens' analysis of the enabling and constraining features of social structure, and the " 'dialectic of control' – the space that exists, even when [authoritative and allocative] resources are not equally available to all parties in a relationship, for some sort of struggle to take place" (Craib, 1992, p. 50).

In the same way that participation presents opportunities for the environmental state to further its agenda of risk mitigation, it presents situated actors with similar reflexive means to pursue their goals and objectives of livelihood security. So, for the authoritative dimensions of the environmental state and the ontological security of environmental practitioners committed to the participatory project, the uncomfortable reality is that their "objectifying gaze at the black ... is haunted by the suppressed recognition that the glance could be returned" (Kearns, 1997, p. 451). Knowledge concerning forest resources and the local political economy, as well as expert knowledge held by environmental professionals exposed during participatory exercises, is open to scrutiny and exploitation by forest people.

Where conservation projects are perceived to further their own objectives, situated actors may subscribe to participatory interventions. They may also be willing to provide information as part of participation in practice but, nonetheless, what and how much information to provide is subject to skilled calculations concerning the risk of providing that information: the gaze of the state can be distorted by 'selected extracts'. The emphasis given to resources by those leading the participatory project provides a restricted rather than holistic view of the forest, which, when subjected to the power effects of the local political economy, means that participation is very often destructive rather than protective.

Individuals and groups may also agree to certain courses of protective action, and even develop systems of sanctions against offenders, whilst the reality of what they are actually doing 'backstage' outside the objectifying gaze may be very different. Resistance to the agendas of the environmental state comes in many forms. Many villages and individuals in the conservation zone of the South West have opted out of conservation interventions all together. In some examples not wishing to be 'emancipated' they simply choose not to confess. In other places the discourse of participation is reflected back at environmental professionals and used to expel them.

Around the Mount Cameroon area for example, there are a number of indigenous villages which, unwilling to countenance changes to livelihood security based on hunting, have resisted any meaningful contact with personnel from projects. Others have physically removed environmental professionals from their land, because they felt their objectives were being manipulated rather than facilitated by participatory projects concerning medicinal plants.

Acts of resistance also take more subtle forms. In another instance forest communities agreed to participate in inventorying the quantity, and mapping the location of a valuable species, with a view to what the project staff understood to be future sustainable exploitation directed by them. However, after the exercise was completed, replete with knowledge that strengthened their bargaining position, villagers negotiated exploitation concessions direct with an international company. Participatory inventories and forest mapping have also provided a route for people to identify and then open new areas for agriculture within the forest. Similarly, small scale community-based timber exploiters have been able to locate valuable trees and assess the extent of each others claims, moving in to cut trees ahead of their rivals in a race to realise profits. In all these instances; the benefits to either forest or biodiversity protection are debatable, but the importance in mitigating local risks and to local livelihood security is clear.

The protective and destructive contradictions inherent to 'participation', and the expert knowledge of local economy and risk held by situated actors, is nowhere more apparent that at Giddens' 'access points'. Keen to engender trust and elicit information, the agency of environmental professionals can be co-opted by situated actors. The vulnerability of facework has seen agency staff take an active role in supporting local livelihood activities, by transporting timber exploiters and their equipment into the forest to fell, or hunters into the forest to hunt, or by sharing meals of endangered species. The environmental professionals are helpless to shout out, fearing the collapse of the building of trust. Through all of this lies an implicit sanction by the environmental state, that people must secure their livelihoods at all costs, that the local political economy is the 'politics of the belly'.

Hence, there are unintended ecological consequences of action/resistance as well as unintended power effects of social knowledge, such that, "[t]he concept of normalisation/resistance cannot be understood as a fixed meta-narrative describing 'power' in the abstract, but, on the contrary, should be approached as a constant recontextualisation of power relations as lived and experienced by humans" (Darier, 1999, p. 18). This suggests that processes of 'modernization' and 'globalization' are woven together with local action to create institutions and practices which synthesize the 'traditional' and the 'modern' in previously unimagined ways.

TO CONCLUDE

The environmental state simultaneously employs a three-pronged strategy: it creates conditions favourable for capital accumulation and economic growth yet it maintains legitimacy by symbolically tending to the needs of the exploited and protecting the ecological capital on which we all depend. Participatory conservation is, in this sense, a process of symbolic legitimation which tends to the needs of the exploited 'peasant' as well as the exploited forest. However, it also provides the means whereby the target of the state, the population, exposes the knowledge/power complex constituting their political ecology, in a way that strengthens apparatuses of state security. Manipulating the allocative and authoritative resources implicated in the knowledge/power complex using diverse calculations, tactics, and manoeuvres, the environmental state furthers its risk mitigating agendas by seeing deeper into the forest and the lifeworlds of its inhabitants.

The ability of actors reflexively to monitor each other's actions, introduces the possibility of unintended outcomes arising from the exercise of either local or global agency. Participation is thus an activity which may transform social practice with protective functions into destructive consequences. In addition, aiming for forest protection through participatory discourse comes close to echoing historic patterns of social power relations, and creates conditions where "the overextension of post-modern ideas . . . could also be characterised as a kind of cryptocolonial discourse effectively masking the commercial exploitation of knowledge, culture and biotic resources (Gandy, 1996, p. 34); the danger being that communities are given symbolic stewardship over forest management only in so far as it meets the aims of the environmental state.

The environmental state will likely face increasing pressure to minister to risk populations in different geographic locales, bound together across permeable boundaries situated in compressed space-time. For the environmental state, the challenge remains one of developing institutional forms that can "accommodate the increase of cognitive reflectivity, argumentation and social choice" (Hajer, 1996, p. 266) of all those tied together as the risk population. Whether institutional learning, or the emergence of completely new biopolitical institutions is the route to fulfilling this challenge, the role of participation as a process and a discourse needs to be assessed critically. In whatever form, unintended consequences are likely to continue to produce contradictory effects on the material and social worlds. The fate of the forest and of 'nature' more generally are hard to predict. All we can be sure of are further surprises.

NOTES

1. We are aware of the difficulties in applying Foucault within sociological analysis and to environmental sociology in particular (for a useful critique see Fox, 1998). Foucault passed through three broad phases in his thinking and writing, which give rise to the contradictions in his work, as he continued to develop his ideas over time. Even though Foucault never looked at the question of the environment, some of his ideas concerning the nature of the state and of knowledge/power offer useful additions to any analysis of the environmental state.

2. For useful reviews see Giddens, 1990; Goodman and Redclift, 1991; Norgaard, 1994.

3. International Tropical Timber Organisation.

4. In 1991 Cameroon's debt as a percentage of GNP was 57.5% (World Bank, 1993).

5. This style of conservation has been popular the world over, but is particularly prominent in Africa. It is based on the demarcation of reserve boundaries and the action of Forest Department personnel patrolling sometimes vast tracks of forest, to prevent entry and resource exploitation by local populations.

REFERENCES

Anon (1900). All Highest Ordinance with regard to empowering the Governor of the Kamerun to issue Ordinances for the Protection of the Forest. *Imperial Gazette*.

Anon (1991). World Bank targets African greens. *Africa Analysis*.

Ardener, S. (1996). *Kingdom on Mount Cameroon; Studies in the History of the Cameroon Coast, 1500–1970*. Oxford, U.K.: Berghahn Books.

Arentz, F. (1993). Country Profile – Cameroon. *Tropical Forest Update*, 3, 18–19.

Bass, S., Dalal-Clayton, B., & Pretty, J. (1995). *Participation in Strategies for Sustainable Development*. London: IIED.

Batterbury, S., Forsyth, T., & Thompson, K. (1997). Environmental transformations in developing countries: hybrid research and democratic policy. *The Geographical Journal*, *163*, 126–132.

Beck, U. (1996). Risk Society and the Provident State. In: S. Lash, B. Szerszynski & B. Wynne (Eds), *Risk, Environment and Modernity: Towards a New Ecology*. London: Sage Publications.

Beck, U. (1998). *¿Qué es la Globalización? Falacias del Globalismo, Respuestas a la Globalización*. Barcelona: Paidos.

Brown, D. (1997). Professionalism, participation, and the public good: issues of arbitration in development management and the critique of the neo-populist approach. *Public Sector Management for the Next Century*. University of Manchester, Manchester, 29th June – 2nd July: University of Manchester.

Bryant, R., & Bailey, S. (1997). *Third World Political Ecology*. London: Routledge.

Burchell, G., Gordon, C., & Miller, P. (1991). *The Foucault Effect: Studies in Governmentality*: Harvester Wheatsheaf.

Burnham, P. (1994). The Cultural Context of Rainforest Conservation in Cameroon. *Thirty-Sixth Annual Meeting of the African Studies Association*. Boston, USA, December 1993: African Studies Association.

CNAB (1916). Qh/a/1916/1: Preliminary Report on the Forests of the British Sphere of the Cameroons. A.H. Unwin.

CNAB (1921). Ag4: Intelligence Report on the Clans and Village Groups in Victoria Division.

CNAB (1923). Ag7: Preliminary Assessment Report on the Bambuko People Victoria Division.

CNAB (1934). 1462/Ae22: Intelligence Report on the Bambuko Clan of the Kumba Division, British Cameroons Clans and Village Groups in Victoria Division : F. A. Goodliffe, Assistant District Officer.

Craib, I. (1992). *Anthony Giddens*. London: Routledge.

Darier, M. (1999). Foucault and the Environment. In: M. Darier (Ed.), *Discourses of the Environment*. London: Routledge.

DeLancy, M. W., & Mokeba, H., M. (1990). *Historical Dictionary of the Republic of Cameroon*. London: The Scarecrow Press.

Demenou, A. P. (1997). La Place du Bois de Fue dans un Sisteme Agroforestier: Rapport Final. Yaounde, Cameroon: CIFOR.

Dreyfus, H., & Rabinow, P. (1982). *Michel Foucault: Beyond Structuralism and Hermeneutics*. Chicago IL: University of Chicago Press.

Epale, S. J. (1985). *Plantations and Development in Western Cameroon, 1885–1975: A Study in Agrarian Capitalism*. New York: Vantage Press.

Escobar, A. (1996). Constructing Nature: Elements for a poststructural political ecology. In: D. Peet & M. Watts (Ed.), *Liberation Ecologies: Environment, Development, Social Movements*. London: Routledge.

Forje, J. W. (1993). *Legal and Policy Dimensions for Biodiversity Conservation and Resources Management in Cameroon*. Yaounde, Cameroon: Centre for Action Oriented Research on African Development.

Foucault, M. (1976). *The History of Sexuality*. New York: Panthenon Books.

Foucault, M. (1977). *Discipline and Punish: the Birth of the Prison*. London: Allen Lane.

Fox, N. J. (1998). Foucault, Foucauldians and sociology. *British Journal of Sociology, 49*, 415–433.

Gandy, M. (1996). Crumbling land: the postmodernity debate and the analysis of environmental problems. *Progress in Human Geography, 20*, 23–40.

Geschiere, P. (1993). Chiefs and Colonial Rule in Cameroon: Inventing Chieftancy, French and British Style. *Africa, 63*(2), 153–175.

Giddens, A. (1984). *The Constitution of Society: Outline of the Theory of Structuration*. London: Polity Press.

168   B. AMBROSE-OJI ET AL.

Giddens, A. (1985). *The Nation State and Violence.* Cambridge: Polity Press.

Giddens, A. (1990). *The Consequences of Modernity.* Cambridge: Polity Press.

Gockowski, J. (1997). *An Analytical Model of Deforestation Effects in Related Markets: the Case of Cocoa, Plantain, and Cocoyam Production in the ASB Cameroon.* Benchmark.

Goodman, D., & Redclift, M. R. (1991). *Refashioning Nature: Food, Ecology and Culture.* London: Routledge.

Hajer, M. A. (1995). *The Politics of Environmental Discourse: Ecological Modernization and the Policy Process.* Oxford: Clarendon Press.

Hajer, M. A. (1996). Ecological Modernisation as Cultural Politics. In: S. Lash, B. Szerszynski & B. Wynne (Eds), *Risk, Environment and Modernity: Towards a New Ecology.* London: Sage Publications.

Hughes, C., Hawthorne, W., & Bass, S. (1998). *Forests, Biodiversity and Livelihoods: Linking Policy and Practice.* London: Department for International Development.

Jasanoff, S. (1999). The Songlines of Risk. *Environmental Values, 8*(2), 135–152.

Kearns, G. (1997). The imperial subject: geography and travel in the work of Mary Kingsley and Halford Mackinder. *Transactions of the Institute of British Geographers, 63,* 450–472.

Konings, P. (1995). Plantation Labour and Economic Crisis in Cameroon. *Development and Change, 26,* 525–549.

Latour, B. (1992). *Science in Action.* London: Harvard University Press.

Luke, T. W. (1999). Environmentality as Green Governmentality. In: M. Darier (Ed.), *Discourses of the Environment.* London: Routledge.

Marshall, B. K. (1999). Globalisation, Environmental Degradation and Ulrich Beck's Risk Society. *Environmental Values, 8,* 253–275.

Messerschmidt, D. A. (1995). *Rapid Appraisal for Community Forestry: The RA Process and Rapid Diagnostic Tools.* London: IIED.

Ndoye, O., & Kaimowitz, D. (1998). Economics, Markets, and the Humid Forests of Cameroon. Research Mailing List, CIFOR.

Nelson, N., & Wright, S. (1995). *Power and Participatory Development: Theory and Practice.* London: Intermediate Technology Publications.

Neumann, R. P. (1997). Primitive Ideas: Protected Area Buffer Zones and the Politics of Land in Africa. *Development and Change, 28,* 559–582.

Ngwasiri, C. N. (1995). *Land Tenure in the Mount Cameroon Region?* Buea, Cameroon: University of Buea.

Njeuma, M. (1989). *Introduction to the History of Cameroon in the Nineteenth and Twentieth Centuries.* London: Macmillan.

Norgaard, R. B. (1989). The case for methodological pluralism. *Ecological Economics, 1,* 37–57.

Norgaard, R. B. (1994). *Development Betrayed: The End of Progress and a Coevolutionary Revisioning of the Future.* London: Routledge.

Novellino, D. (1997). *The Relevance of Social Capital in Theory and Practice: The Case of Palawan (The Phillipines).* Rome: Food and Agriculture Organisation of the United Nations.

O'Connor, J. (1989). Uneven and combined development and ecological crisis: a theoretical introduction. *Race and Class, 30,* 1–11.

Rutherford, P. (1999). The Entry of Life into History. In: M. Darier (Ed.), *Discourses of the Environment.* London: Routledge.

Scoones, I. (1997). The Dynamics of Soil Fertility Change: historical perspectives on environmental transformation from Zimbabwe. *The Geographical Journal, 163,* 161–169.

Stockdale, M., & Ambrose, B. (1996). Mapping and NTFP Inventory: Participatory Assessment Methods for Forest-dwelling Communities in East Kalimantan, Indonesia. In: J. Carter (Ed.), *Rural Development Forestry Study Guide: Recent Approach to Participatory Forest Resource Assessment.* London: Overseas Development Institute.

Victoria Centenary Committee (1958). *Victoria Southern Cameroons, 1858–1958.* Victoria, Southern Cameroons: Victoria Centenary Committee by Basel Mission Book Depot.

Wiley, L. (1999). Moving Forward in African Community Forestry: Trading Power, Not Use Rights. *Society and Natural Resources, 12,* 49–61.

Woodgate, G., Ambrose-Oji, B., Fernandez Durán, R., Guzmán, G., & Sevilla Guzmán, E. (1999). Alternative Food and Agriculture Networks: an Agroecological Perspective on Responses to Economic Globalisation and the 'New' Agrarian Question. Keynote paper to the European Union COST Social Science Working Group on Rural Innovations, Córdoba, Spain, June 1999.

Woodgate, G. R., & Redclift, M. R. (1998). From a "Sociology of Nature" to Environmental Sociology: Beyond Social Construction. *Environmental Values, 7,* 3–24.

World Bank (1993). *World Development Report.* Oxford: Oxford University Press.

Zarate Hernandez, J. E. (1998). Ethnography, Cultural Change and Local Power. *Journal of Historical Sociology, 11,* 138–149.

Zimmerer, K. S. (1994). Human Geography and the 'New Ecology': The Prospect and Promise of Integration. *Annals of the Association of Human Geographers, 84,* 108–125.

Part V
Agriculture, Food and Sustainable Rural Development

[27]

INCORPORATING NATURE

Environmental narratives and the reproduction
of food

Margaret FitzSimmons and David Goodman

INTRODUCTION

Forebodings of environmental crisis have lent a sense of urgency and of political relevance to the "greening" of social theory in recent years. The concerns of this increasingly widely accepted intellectual project are discernible in a broad range of scholarship in the social sciences and humanities. Contributors to this endeavour share an agenda: to bring "nature" "back in" to social theory by contesting its abstraction from "society." However, these reconstructive efforts have remained largely confined to separate academic fields and often imply different conceptions of nature–society intersections. With rare exceptions few have attempted to find a common ground among these perspectives or explored the implications of this scholarship for fields where dualist thought still holds sway. In this chapter, we propose to remap part of this shared terrain. Until recently, it has become a commonplace in social theory to ignore the specific "agency" and "materiality" of nature or, where that agency has been admitted, to conceive of it within the disabling binary logics that have for so long organised modern thought. Against this, we argue for a focus on *incorporation* – as metaphor and as process – as a useful way of bringing nature into the body of social theory and, more literally, into the social body of living organisms, including ourselves. More specifically, we bring this insight to bear on a subject of inter-disciplinary concern (and a long-standing concern of ours), which illuminates "society" and "nature" in their most intimate entanglement: the political economy of modern agriculture and agro-food networks.

We begin with a critical examination of two important bodies of thought – environmental history and Marxist political economy – that take issue with the Enlightenment ontology of nature as external, primordial and mechanistic and that seek to re-theorize the agency of nature. Additionally, each has focussed their critical energies on modern agriculture, a primary locus of metabolism

194

INCORPORATING NATURE

between society and nature. Following a critical appreciation of both bodies of thought, we suggest that the notion of *corporeality* provides an alternative means of theorizing nature's agency, one that evades the pitfalls of the "hostile" dichotomy of nature and society (Williams 1980) and avoids the modernist tendency to nominate either nature or society as ontologically prior (Latour 1993). How are the social practices and institutions of agriculture and food consumption theorized in recent environmental history and Marxist scholarship, and how do these theorizations assert conceptualizations of nature? More specifically, what are the implications for agrarian political economy if, within the metabolic relations which incorporate agricultural production and food consumption, we conceptualize nature as both internal *and* autonomous, as causal *and* contextual, and as always consequential?

Most work in agrarian political economy has been constituted in response to a discourse about capitalism and modernity that exalted manufacturing and addressed agriculture as a secondary locus, presenting the role of nature in agriculture as "exceptional." It has either failed to give theoretical weight to the metabolic relations which distinguish agro-food systems or has dismissed such approaches on the grounds of ecological or technological determinism. Here agriculture is routinely presented as just another industrial sector or branch of economic activity. This abstraction of nature has been applied *a fortiori* to the orthodox, modern disciplines of agricultural economics and rural sociology, but it also permeates more critical analyses based in political economy.

By positing the shared corporeality of agro-food practices – of nature into the human body and of humans into the complex life ways of the natural world – this chapter challenges the abstraction of agriculture as an economic activity. Our explanation of nature's agency places this corporeality at the forefront of the analysis. At any given conjuncture, the practice of agro-food is described by mutually constitutive practices and processes of metabolism and incorporation, which involve the dual and combined agency of biophysical processes and of social labour engaged in production and reproduction. This notion of shared corporeality speaks explicitly to a more general insistence that ecology and social relations, the production and reproduction of nature and society, be located within a unified analytical frame.

After reviewing environmental history (in the second section) and ecological Marxism (in the third section), we turn to our central theme of agro-food networks as the locus of metabolic incorporation between humans and nature (fourth section). The final section extends the notion of incorporation to the ingestion of "food" and considers metabolic, corporeal, social, and symbolic dimensions, both pleasurable and pathological, by focussing on the cases of BSE and anorexia. Although these are prelimary considerations, we hope that by reconceptualizing nature's agency we can begin to find progressive ways of remaking nature, ways which "commonsense" dualistic thinking currently disables.

MARGARET FITZSIMMONS AND DAVID GOODMAN

NATURE'S AGENCY IN ENVIRONMENTAL HISTORY

Nature as historical agent

Environmental historians are attempting to break social theory's long silence on the active material presence of nature in social life and social reproduction by reasserting nature's agency. This new field is a major current in the broad movement to redress the Enlightenment legacy of the ontological and historical abstraction of nature. Environmental historians have responded to this abstraction by reactivating the neglected side of the nature–society dualism to seek a new synthesis, what Worster (1984: 2) described as "an ecological perspective on history."[1] This ecological perspective is founded ontologically on the premise that societies arise within nature, tracing out multiple possibilities upon the grounds and landscapes laid out by nature's processes, nature's practices in time and space. Environmental histories thus begin with the material engagement of people and land. They practice "ecological thinking," constructing:

> Nature as an active partner . . . As parts of the whole, humans have the power to alter the networks in which they are embedded. Nature as active partner acquiesces to human interventions through resilience and adaptation or "resists" human actions through mutation and evolution. Nonhuman nature is an actor; human and nonhuman interactions constitute the drama.
>
> (Merchant 1989: 25)

This project to bring nature into history has been pursued in different ways and with varying narrative strategies. Here, we briefly review the recent evolution of this project, addressing changing views on how it should be prosecuted, to clarify the assumptions and meanings behind environmental historians' claim that nature is an independent actor on the stage. We engage selected canonical texts and commentaries which delineate "moments" of critical self-reflection on the field, its purpose, and prospects.

The first of these moments brings agriculture into the narrative tropes of the new environmental history. We identify this moment with the publication of Donald Worster's *Dust Bowl* in 1979. At this point, environmental history began to loosen its early ties with intellectual and political history, and its associated focus on the conservation movement and wilderness preservation as the antecedents of postwar American environmentalism.[2] Other landmarks of this transition include William Cronon's *Changes in the Land* (1983), and Carolyn Merchant's *Ecological Revolutions* (1989). Each signals a shift of attention, from wilderness to occupied landscape, from nature as primordial to nature as present and active in human affairs. How is this relationship delineated at this juncture, where the necessary human action of agriculture is brought into the narrative of

196

INCORPORATING NATURE

environmental history? Richard White (1985: 335) alludes to two aspects of this relationship that bear on the question of agency: physical limits and reciprocity. "Nature does not dictate, but physical nature does, at any given time, set limits on what is humanly possible. Humans may *think* what they want; they cannot always *do* what they want, and not all they do turns out as planned. It is in the midst of this compromised and complex situation of the reciprocal influences of a changing nature and a changing society that environmental history must find its home."[3]

The question of reciprocity is taken up explicitly in William Cronon's (1983) study of colonial New England. Cronon fully recognizes the reciprocal relations of nature and society in shaping this regional environment, but he also notes that "the period of human occupation in postglacial New England has seen environmental changes on an enormous scale, many of them wholly apart from human influence" (1983: 11). In short, "ecosystems have histories of their own" (p. 12). For Cronon, ecological history assumes that nature and society are entangled in "a dynamic and changing relationship," where "the interactions of the two are dialectical" (p. 13). In this "interacting system," culture and environment are reshaped dialectically in a continuing "cycle of mutual deter-mination." Accordingly, "changes in the way people create and recreate their livelihood must be analyzed in terms of changes not only in their *social* relations but in their *ecological* ones as well" (p. 13, original emphasis).

As a second "moment" of reflexive and programmatic analysis, we have selected a debate between leading environmental historians in *The Journal of American History* (1990). These exchanges revealed profound epistemological divisions and threw into question the moral certitude and political goals which, to paraphrase Cronon (1994), had nurtured "this child of environmentalism." In the lead paper, "Transformations of the earth: toward an agroecological perspective in history," Donald Worster (1990a: 1091) takes the "new" history to task for its "conceptually underdeveloped" analysis of interactions between the structure of production, technology, and the environment, which constitute the "techno-environmental base" of society. To rectify this omission, Worster proposes that environmental history should focus on "modes of production as ecological phenomena, and particularly as they are articulated in agriculture" (ibid.).[4]

Although he concentrates on the rise of the capitalist mode of production, Worster hastens to distance himself from Marxist conceptualizations which, he suggests, have neglected the possible causative role of ecological factors in the capitalist transition. These do not "acknowledge that the capitalist era in production introduced a new distinctive relation of people to the natural world. The *reorganization of nature*, not merely of society, is what we must uncover" (p. 1100, original emphasis). If, as White (1990) suggests, Worster's inspiration is Braudelian rather than Marxian, his program to comprehend the capitalist transformation of nature nevertheless has close parallels with ecological reformulations of Marxist theory, as we see below in the third section.

MARGARET FITZSIMMONS AND DAVID GOODMAN

Rather than giving greater unity and purpose to the field, Worster's attempt to set its agenda evoked strong dissent and exposed wide disagreement on the fundamental issues of causality and agency. Worster's sense of ecology is moral and holistic, following the views of nature of Clements and Odum. But his assertions of the authority of the ecological vision came at a time when this view had lost hegemony in academic ecology, where mathematical modeling of population dynamics and experimental manipulation of two- or three-species model systems now characterizes most research practice and where "scientific" ecology seeks to free itself from "natural history." At the "moment" of the 1990 debate, environmental historians were sharply divided on the epistemological implications of these conceptual disputes in ecology. As perhaps becomes the author of *Nature's Economy* (1977), which examines the cultural context and intellectual history of changing scientific paradigms of nature, Worster (1990a) is unimpressed by the latest "revisionist swing," and even less so by relativist interpretations of their significance (Worster 1990b).

However, Worster's colleagues are less sanguine about taking these ecological disputes in their stride. Thus, White (1990: 1114) believes that environmental historians are left without "a firm basis for their morality and causality." Cronon (1990: 1127) argues that new methodological tools are required to replace such outmoded concepts as equilibrium, community, and successional climax, which "underlie the old idea of the 'balance of nature' that so often supplies the analytical (and moral) scale against which we measure the environmental effects of human societies." White (1990: 1115) goes to the crux of the relativist critique when he states that "although ecology has been reified into nature, ecology is, in fact, only an academic discipline." But it is left to Stephen Pyne (1990: 1139) to spell out the implications of this reification when he argues that Worster "appeals to the laws of ecology to construct a nature that is external to humans and that provides a moral template against which to measure human behavior. This grants him, as author, a privileged omniscient position with which to view the spectacle." In rejecting this "implied claim to privilege," Pyne (1990: 1140) asserts that: "The laws of ecology become functional equivalents to other presumed 'laws' of human behavior and history and have, I believe, no more validity."[5]

Our third "moment" in the development of environmental history is the publication of William Cronon's acclaimed study, *Nature's Metropolis: Chicago and the Great West* (1991). Deservedly recognized as a milestone in the "new" history, this monumental work is considered here for what it has to say on the question of nature's agency, and particularly the distinction Cronon draws between "first" and "second" nature. Much of this theoretical terrain has previously been mapped by contributors to the "production of nature" debates, which followed Alfred Schmidt's *The Concept of Nature in Marx* (1971), and gained further momentum with the publication of Neil Smith's book *Uneven Development: Nature, Capital and the Production of Space* (1984).[6] However, in a more recent reconnaissance, David Demeritt (1994a) engages environmental

INCORPORATING NATURE

historians in a conversation with cultural geographers, which reveals the very different and irreconcilable worlds portrayed by their respective "metaphors of nature as agent and landscape as text" (p. 164). These metaphoric strategies, he argues, place environmental history and cultural geography at opposite poles of the nature/culture dualism "that fixes nature and landscape as either autonomous natural actors or absolute social productions" (p. 163).

Environmental history occupies its polar position because to make the analytical connection between the autonomous agency of nature and the consequences of that agency "requires an ability to step outside ourselves . . . to discover and acknowledge another, objective reality that we have not created nor ever fully controlled" (Worster 1990b: 1146); that is, external nature, primordial and originary, pre-human.[7] In short, what environmental historians assert as the "strong" criterion of nature's agency draws its explanatory power from the opposition between an external, pre-human nature and an historically subsequent state when nature and society have materially commingled. As we have just seen, recourse to the ontological categories of ecology, notably Clementsian ecosystems, with their putative "balance" and homeostatic properties, which are reified as nature "before" human disturbance, serves the same methodological purpose.

Similar considerations apply to Cronon's analytical scheme which, in much the same way, counterposes "first" and "second nature." "First nature" is identified with the vegetational geography – grasslands, hardwood and softwood forests, lakes and rivers – of the postglacial landscape of the Great West, in contrast to "A kind of 'second nature,' designed by people and 'improved' toward human ends, (which) gradually emerged atop the original landscape that nature – 'first nature' – had created . . . " (Cronon 1991: 56). "First nature," which is "the result of autonomous ecological processes," is the source of natural wealth or "natural capital" (p. 205), such as soil fertility, abundant forests: "this was the wealth of nature, and no human labour could create the value it contained" (pp. 149–50). Using the recurring metaphor of transmutation, "first" nature is transmuted into "second" nature, constructed nature, at the hands of humans and their technical devices, driven by the "logic" and "geography" of capitalism.

Cronon (1991) is fully aware of Schmidt's work and Neil Smith's critique and further elaboration of the concept of "second nature." However, in *Nature's Metropolis*, he chooses to ignore the warning that to treat "'first Nature,' primordial Nature as analytically and historically prior to 'second Nature,' social Nature" (Fitzsimmons: 1989a: 118, n. 2) risks falling back into the trap of Enlightenment ontology.[8] As Demeritt (1994a) notes, Cronon's use of the binary "first nature/second nature" framework displaces "the culture–nature dualism into a stratigraphy he can excavate" in order to reveal "the autonomous agency of nature" (p. 196). Echoing the misgivings expressed earlier by White (1990) and Pyne (1990) about environmental history's reliance on scientific ecology, Demeritt (1994a) argues that Cronon reifies the concept of ecosystem as nature, "first" nature, and "thus determines the essence of what nature 'really'

MARGARET FITZSIMMONS AND DAVID GOODMAN

is. In so doing, he reintroduces the problematic dualism between nature and culture that his book so effectively subverts" (p. 178).

In seeking to find a place for the autonomous agency of nature in its stories, environmental history continues to wrestle with the nagging question of causation and how this is to be resolved without depending on the received ontology of ecological science and .its binary categories. The methodological dangers of this position are appreciated by White (1990: 1114) when he observes that: "The field has a tendency to produce cautionary tales. But without a clear demonstration of causality, a teller's cautionary tale becomes a listener's just so story." Later, in the fourth section, we return to discuss the new "metaphoric tools" developed by Michel Callon, Bruno Latour and Donna Haraway that Demeritt (1994a) believes will release environmental history from Enlightenment antinomies by making "it possible to imagine nature as both a real material actor and a socially constructed object" (p. 163). First, however, we move from these general formulations of nature's agency to consider a more specific theorization – agency as ecological rules which set natural limits – as it is deployed in environmental histories of agriculture.

Agricultural narratives

The theorization of nature's agency as ecological processes that surround and constrain human action is a recurrent theme in the new environmental history and a key element in its methodological arsenal of causality. The most comprehensive statement of this view is to be found in the work of Donald Worster. We have already noted his advocacy of the concept of mode of production and his dissatisfaction with Marxist conceptualizations of the capitalist mode (Worster 1990a). These must be reformulated, he argues, to incorporate not only the "restructuring of *human* relations" (1990a: 1098), but also "The *reorganization* of nature" (p. 1100). Worster further recommends agriculture as a particularly appropriate arena for this research agenda, since it is through food production that "every group of people in history" has been "connected in the most vital, constant and concrete way to the natural world" (pp. 1091–2).

To investigate the capitalist reorganization of nature and human ecological relations, Worster (1990a) urges environmental historians to center their analyses on something like Polanyi's "great transformation." Correspondingly, in agriculture, the common bond uniting Worster's analysis of ecological restructuring and nature's agency, and the leitmotif of his narrative strategy, is the agrarian transition. This narrative, framed in vivid declensionist terms, describes the transformation of traditional agricultural landscapes – "carefully integrated, functional mosaics that retained much of the wisdom of nature" (p. 1096) – into highly specialized, ecologically risky and vulnerable capitalist monocultures. In one story, nature appears as a benevolently active partner, in the second, as a capricious, potentially revengeful presence, with the autonomy to expose the hubristic ambition of capitalist agriculture, and its dualistic Baconian–Cartesian foundations.

200

INCORPORATING NATURE

This analytical framework and narrative trajectory structure Worster's account of the US Dust Bowl in the 1930s, "one of the worst environmental catastrophes in recorded human experience" (p. 1106). This "disaster was due to drought, the most severe drought in some two hundred years. But it was also the result of the radically simplified agroecosystem the Plains farmers had tried to create" (ibid.). The moral to be drawn from this story, whether on the Great Plains or other places, involves humankind "knowing the earth well, knowing its history and knowing its limits" (ibid.).

Worster's "howling world of nature" that "has always been a force in human life" (p. 1096) is revealed when humankind transgresses its limits. In this framework of explanation, the agency of nature is made manifest through the narrative contrast between two 'second' natures or agroecological landscapes: pre-capitalist and capitalist. One is "based on close observation and imitation of the natural order" (ibid.), and the other on "a movement toward the radical simplification of the natural ecological order" (p. 1101). This natural order is represented by the laws of ecology to which all agroecosystems are subject. However, within this compass, since what distinguishes traditional agrarian landscapes from capitalist agroecosystems is precisely their "close observation" of these "laws," they are characterized as being "at once the product of nonhuman factors and of human intelligence, working toward a mutual accommodation" (p. 1097).

Merchant and Cronon also focus strongly on agriculture and the increasing exploitation of farming and natural resource economies under developing capitalism. Merchant (1989: 25) presents this transition as an ecological revolution, defined as "processes through which different societies change their relationship to nature. They arise from tensions between production and ecology and between production and reproduction. The results are new constructions of nature, both materially and in human consciousness." Cronon moves from the European occupation and later abandonment of the New England landscape as a core region of commercial agriculture (in *Changes in the Land*) to the integration and subordination of the West by urban and commercial institutions arising with the growth of capitalist agro-food systems (in *Nature's Metropolis*), setting up the modern dialectic between city and countryside which is mediated by agro-food institutions.

Thus, although ecological science speaks universally, to use Demeritt's phrase, "for what nature 'really' is," two dualistic or binary notions of agency and nature–society dialectics, each heavily charged with both moral and material ecological imperatives, are embedded on either "side" of Worster's analysis of agrarian transition, of Merchant's interrogation of ecological revolution, and of Cronon's city of the merchants of food. These are the premodern dialectic of "mutual accommodation," and the capitalist dialectic of accumulation, degradation and ecological catastrophe as humankind challenges nature's limits. We now turn to theorizations of the agency of nature encountered in "green" or ecological Marxism. Here again we will find that agriculture occupies a special

MARGARET FITZSIMMONS AND DAVID GOODMAN

position in the conceptualization of nature–society dialectics and the constraints to human activities of production and reproduction.

NATURE'S AGENCY WITHIN CAPITALISM

Nature as limits, nature as process

If nature as a constraint on human action is a recurrent theme in the new environmental history, it is also, but in quite different ways, a concept crucial to new work in "ecological Marxism." We use this term to review new engagements with the question of nature and society founded in Marxism in several disciplines. These formulations locate the point of analytic entry in society – in the laws of accumulation and the social relations and structures of modes of production, particularly of capitalism – rather than in the laws and processes of nature. This notion of the epochal specificity of nature–society dialectics, which has to be teased out of the analysis of the environmental historians, receives a more explicit, formal treatment in the discussions of ecological Marxism we review here. Using more emphatically the language of dialectics, rather than simply "interaction," nature is brought into the social world through the agency of labour in the extraction and transformation of use values, the industrial internalization of nature's processes, the instrumental knowledge and action structured by science and technology in the service of accumulation, and through the globalization of production and exchange mediated by the market for commodities. And it is here that we can begin to talk of nature as literally "incorporated."

But what "nature" is incorporated? Here we find that contributors to the discussions of ecological Marxism constitute nature quite differently in their theories. Some address nature as eco-physical, reading nature from within society as a physical nature of stocks and flows of potential use values (Martinez-Alier 1987; Altvater 1993) or as "conditions of production" (O'Connor 1988). Here nature remains external, inorganic. Others use a more supple dialectic to envision nature as biological, as life in process (Benton 1989, 1991, 1992, 1993; Harvey, 1982, 1996) within which human life is metabolically embodied through praxis. The implications of these two views for the incorporation of nature in ecological Marxist theory are quite distinct.

The concept of nature as physical nature leads inevitably to issues of limits: limits in nature's services, nature's stocks and flows, nature's reserves. Abstracting from limits in place to a grand global calculation of natural "accounts," this view presents nature through the lens of ecosystem ecology, in which life is a series of pumps and pipes for energy and materials. Thus Martinez-Alier and Altvater invoke the laws of thermodynamics to anticipate an ecological crisis of resource exhaustion and environmental pollution, while O'Connor, who also focusses on crisis, proposes a second contradiction of capitalism – the problem of reproduction of the conditions of production – which connects to and parallels Marx's first contradiction – that of reproduction of the forces of production

INCORPORATING NATURE

(human labour). This approach – nature as physical nature – presents a categorical conception which reduces nature to the inorganic. "Nature is man's *inorganic body* – nature, that is, insofar as it is not itself human body. Man *lives* on nature – means that nature is his *body*, with which he must remain in continuous interchange if he is not to die. That man's physical and spiritual life is linked to nature means simply that nature is linked to itself, for man is a part of nature" (Marx, in Benton 1993: 24). Though "man is a part of nature," the metaphor of metabolism that Marx presents here emphasizes action upon, not action within. Embodiment occurs through necessity, necessity mediated by the presence of class relationships of exploitation through which both labour and nature are subordinated to the service of capital. "The exploitation of the worker is simultaneously the exploitation of the soil." Nature's things, like people, are used and abused. As Harvey (1996) points out, this sense of nature as the subject of domination, as the location of exhaustible resources, connects some Marxist positions both to the "pessimism" of the Frankfurt School and to the dangerous straits of Malthusianism, in which nature (and nature in agriculture) becomes the transhistorical and universalized explanation of poverty and suffering.

From the publication of David Harvey's essay "Population, resources and the ideology of science" (1974), he has been a strong voice against this Malthusian position of universal limits. Those familiar with Harvey's writings on urbanization may not know that his early work was on agriculture. This grounds his sense of metabolism in the "form-giving fire" of the labour process in which "Labour is, in the first place, a process in which both man and Nature participate. . . . He opposes himself to Nature as one of her own forces, setting in motion arms and legs, head and hands, the natural forces of his body, in order to appropriate Nature's productions in a form adapted to his own wants" (Marx, in Harvey 1982: 101). The quotation continues: "By thus acting on the external world and changing it, he at the same time changes his own nature" (*Capital* I: 177). The sense of metabolism present in Harvey's (1996) work conceives nature as internal to the social species-being of people, as a part of the organic, not the inorganic body. Thus, the way people act is *within* not simply on nature, in the context of "socio-ecological projects" strongly structured by the modes of production within which that action is mobilized and constrained.

> What exists in "nature" is in a constant state of transformation. To declare a state of ecoscarcity is in effect to say that we have not the will, wit, or capacity to change our state of knowledge, our social goals, cultural modes, and technological mixes, or our form of economy, and that we are powerless to modify either our material practices or "nature" according to human requirements. To say that scarcity resides in nature and that natural limits exist is to ignore how scarcity is socially produced and how "limits" are a social relation within nature (including human society) rather than some externally imposed necessity.
>
> (Harvey 1996: 145)

MARGARET FITZSIMMONS AND DAVID GOODMAN

Harvey's sense of ecological nature returns us to a sense of possibilism, rather than determination. Instead of abstracting a universalized view of society and nature, Harvey recommends an "evolutionary" view, based on a "dialectical and relational schema for thinking through how to understand the dialectics of social–environmental change" (p. 190). This evolutionary view avoids the dissolution of socio-ecological projects into the abstractions of nature and society and thus allows for a necessary heterogeneity of outcomes and possibilities for transformation. As Harvey puts it, "The *general* struggle against capitalist forms of domination is always made up of *particular* struggles in which capitalists are engaged and the distinctive social relations they presuppose" (p. 201).

Agricultural narratives: ecoregulation and the labour process

Agroecological processes figure prominently in Ted Benton's formulation of an ecological Marxism (1989, 1992, 1993). Indeed, the distinctive "materiality" of nature in agriculture plays a pivotal role in the revision of Marxian economic concepts that Benton believes "constitute an indispensable starting point for any theory that would adequately grasp the ecological conditions and limits of human social forms" (1989: 63–4).

Benton's reconstructive analysis focusses on Marx's conceptualization of the labour process, both the abstract concept "as a transhistorical condition of human survival" and the forms labour takes under capitalism. In each case, Benton argues, "Marx under-represents the significance of non-manipulable natural conditions of labour-processes and over-represents the role of human intentional transformative powers vis-à-vis nature" (p. 64). Marx's abstract concept of the labour process, Benton suggests, is represented by a transformative intentional structure, possibly with some handicraft activity as a model, in which the "subject" of labour – products of nature or raw materials, variously defined – is transformed into use value. The difficulty with this conceptualization is its claim to be universally applicable to all types of human need-meeting interaction with nature. Benton (1989) contends that the transformative intentional structure is an inappropriate representation of the labour processes in extractive activities and agriculture. To overcome this lack of "independent conceptual specification," Benton uses the criterion of intentional structure to construct a broader taxonomy that distinguishes between productive, transformative labour processes, primary labour processes (hunting, mining, fishing), which directly appropriate nature, and eco-regulatory labour processes.

The last are exemplified by agriculture, where labour is "primarily deployed to sustain or regulate the environmental conditions under which seed or stock animals grow and develop" (Benton 1989: 67). The distinctive aspects of eco-regulatory labour processes include the deployment of labour to optimize conditions for organic growth and development, the corresponding orientation

204

INCORPORATING NATURE

of labour activities to sustain, regulate and reproduce these conditions, and spatio-temporal distributions of labour that are dependent mainly on these contextual conditions and on the rhythms of organic development (pp. 67–8). This dependence of eco-regulatory labour processes on naturally given contextual conditions means that: "For any specific technical organization of agriculture, these elements in the process are relatively impervious to intentional manipulation, and in some respects they are absolutely non-manipulable" (p. 68).

In the case of specifically capitalist forms, Benton suggests that Marx privileged instrumental transformative labour processes, and thus tended to under-theorize the extent to which capitalist industrial production "remained tied to eco-regulatory and primary-appropriative labours as the necessary sources of energy, raw materials and food, and so, also, to a range of non-manipulable contextual conditions" (p. 70). To capture these "footprints," Benton proposes an eco-logical reconstruction of Marx's conceptualization of capitalist labour processes that would give independent conceptual weight to naturally given enabling contextual conditions. In addition, this reconstruction would emphasize their continuing role in the sustainability of production, and recognize that naturally mediated but unintended consequences of production may undermine the persistence or reproduction of these contextual conditions (pp. 73–4).

Benton's further suggestions for an ecological Marxist political economy have some parallels with Worster's less formalized agenda for environmental history, notably Benton's insistence (which Harvey shares) on the historical, geo-graphical, and social relativity of nature–society interactions, and also of "natural limits" and the associated combination of enablement and constraint (positions with which Harvey 1996, disagrees). Benton suggests that each historical epoch or "form of social and economic life," with its own characteristic mode of production and labour processes, will present a "specific structure of nature–society articulation" (1989: 77). The dynamic of each historically articulated structure, in turn, produces correspondingly distinctive ecological problems and interrelations with its own specific contextual conditions and limits. It follows that "since natural limits are themselves theorized, in this approach, as a function of the articulated combination of specific social practices and specific complexes of natural conditions, resources and mechanisms, what constitutes a genuine natural limit for one such form of nature/society articulation may *not* constitute a limit for another" (p. 79).

Benton thus offers "a genuinely dialectical concept of society–nature relations" (Castree 1995: 24), and an historically contingent theorization of natural limits. He also provides the foundations for a rigorous, historicized analysis of modes of production and their characteristic structures of nature–society articulation. By stressing articulation rather than binary opposition, Benton avoids the pitfalls of Worster's moral rhetoric and teleology, with its normative opposition between a (pre-capitalist) dialectic of reciprocity and a capitalist dialectic of over-exploitation and degradation.

205

MARGARET FITZSIMMONS AND DAVID GOODMAN

Benton (1989) makes two proposals for further reconstructive work that deserve careful consideration, not least by environmental historians. The first would extend the typology of labour processes and their intentional structures in order to emphasize their character "as modes of social appropriation of nature" (p. 80). The second proposal would "reconceptualize the Marxian typology of modes of production" so that each mode would be specified in terms not only of its social–relational elements, but also its form of nature–society interaction. "Each mode must be conceptualized in terms of its own peculiar limits and boundaries, and its own associated liabilities to generate environmental crises and environmentally related patterns of social conflict" (p. 81).

Benton provides a partial yet significant development of this first proposal in his book, *Natural Relations* (1993), which is concerned primarily to convene an "encounter" between traditions of socialist thought, ecological politics and philosophies of animal rights. In this discussion, Benton argues for the specificity of agricultural labour processes, which he attributes, following Goodman and Redclift (1991), to the constraints associated with biological processes that have created distinctive historical patterns of capital accumulation and labour process organization. Adapting his earlier formulation, he emphasizes the importance of analyzing socio-economic relations and non-human nature, in this case livestock, within a single interpretive framework.

Many Marxist approaches to the capitalist transformation of agriculture have relied heavily on the concept of "formal subsumption" to analyze the processes underlying the emergence of an agricultural wage labour force. Benton (1993: 156) would extend this concept to encompass the "whole complex of wage-labour, stock animals, and ecological conditions, whose interrelations are reorganized and subjected to distinctive forms of regulation under commercial pressures." Suggesting that "we should, perhaps, speak of the ecologico-socio-technical organization of the labour process" (p. 156), he refers to the capitalist reorganization of this complex as "material subsumption." Benton invokes his concept of eco-regulatory labour processes to insist that the distinctive character of agricultural labour practices is preserved even into the intensive regime of the factory farm and animal confinement systems, and "continues to operate as a limit to the full subordination of the labour-process to the prevailing mode of economic calculation" (ibid.).

Benton goes on to discuss the tension between pressures to treat animals instrumentally as mere "things" and countervailing limits "to the full realization of these pressures, which derive from the organic, psychological and social requirements of the animals themselves" (p. 157). Benton's analysis here is limited to different regimes of animal husbandry, and he denies that he is attempting an historical account or periodization of agricultural labour processes and their reorganization. Nevertheless, the promise of this theoretical framework for an ecological history of agro-food systems is clear.

INCORPORATING NATURE

AGRI-CULTURE AS A NATURE–SOCIETY HYBRID

Relationship more than system should be our starting point.

(Cronon 1990: 1130)

All of culture and all of nature get churned up again every day.

(Latour 1993: 2)

Many of the theorizations of nature–society relations reviewed above rely heavily on interactive or else dialectical concepts, whether framed in terms of natural limits, reciprocity or mutual accommodation. Yet even posing the issue as one of a dialectical relationship between nature and society – with its Hegelian lineage of dissolving dualisms – seems still to reproduce the dualism which we are seeking to resolve. If nature and society are active partners locked in an irreversible, continuing process of mutual determination, how is the materiality of these conjoined natures to be theorized? On many different temporal and spatial scales, nature and society are active contingent categories, mutually determined and constituted in endless cycles of reproduction and production. To portray these co-productions as nature–society dialectics is to risk, to loosely paraphrase Donna Haraway, trying to balance on both poles at once. It is this balancing act that persuades Demeritt (1994a: 183) that new metaphors are needed "for framing nature as both a real material actor and a socially constructed object."

For this purpose, Demeritt recommends the work of Bruno Latour and Donna Haraway. Latour (1993: 51) closes the Kantian "Great Divide" between nature and culture by analyzing these interactions in terms of symmetrical processes that create hybrids, which, following Michel Serres, he calls "quasi-objects, quasi-subjects" that "are simultaneously real, discursive and social" (p. 64). Haraway (1991) develops the metaphor of the cyborg to reveal the partnerships, though not always equal, between human and nonhuman actors joined in the mutual construction of artifactual nature. Since it is currently more prominent in agro-food studies, we concentrate below on actor network theory (ANT) formulated by Latour in collaboration with Michel Callon.[9]

In seeking to retie the Gordian knot between nature and society, Latour (1993) advances the notions of mediation and network. The work of mediation "creates mixtures between two entirely new types of beings, hybrids of nature and culture" (p. 10), which are mobilized and assembled into networks. The practices of mediation, mobilizing things and assembling hybrids correspond, in Latour's metaphor, to "a delicate shuttle" weaving the natural and social worlds into "a seamless fabric." This "socialization of nonhumans" (p. 42) prompts Latour to "use the word 'collective' to describe the association of humans and nonhumans" (p. 4), which forms the "Middle Kingdom" between the nature–society poles of modernity.

MARGARET FITZSIMMONS AND DAVID GOODMAN

Latour's exploration of this middle territory of collective associations poses an incisive, frontal challenge to the notion of autonomous agency that is so central to the environmental history project. In his account, the ever-problematic modern duality has collapsed under its own weight, unable to withstand the increasing scale and scope in the mobilization of networks and multiplication of hybrids. This "third estate" is not "faithfully represented either by the order of objects or by the order of subjects"; the practice of mediation has, in essence, conflated the two poles (Latour 1993: 49–50). Agency in these associative networks is conceptualized as the collective capacity of humans and nonhumans to act; it is an effect of these heterogeneous networks. Nonhuman agents also are endowed with active properties in the conceptualization of collective agency formulated recently by Michel Callon and John Law, based on the notion of hybrid *collectifs* (Callon and Law 1995).[10] Donna Haraway (1992) develops a related perspective when she argues that nature and society have imploded, and calls for formulations in which nature can be "a social partner, a social agent with a history, a conversant in a discourse where all of the actors are not 'us'" (p. 83).

These conceptualizations of collective agency reveal the limitations of formulations which, in the words of Callon and Law (1995: 502), "localize agency as singularity – usually singularity in the form of human bodies." While environmental historians also are seeking to correct "singular" notions of agency based on human intentionality and praxis, their "strong" formulation of nature as an autonomous actor, for all its usefulness, runs the risk of repeating the same error at the opposite pole. To paraphrase Latour (1993: 106–7), if the concept of agency is not centered on the "productions of natures-cultures" he calls collectives, we risk falling back into the binary categories in which nature is construed as external "things-in-themselves" and society as "men-among-themselves." As Demeritt (1994a: 180) observes, Latour's "metaphors make it possible to follow environmental historians in talking about the agency of nature without appealing to a transcendent nature beyond (society)."

The analytical framework articulated by Latour (1993: 107) of heterogeneous associations "of elements of Nature and elements of the social world" also provides a "common matrix" for a "comparative anthropology" of contemporary societies and others. "All collectives are different from one another in the way they divide up beings, in the properties they attribute to them, in the mobilization they consider acceptable" (ibid.). However, although all collectives obey the common principle of symmetry, that is, of being co-productions of nature–society, they may differ in size, in the scope of the mobilization, which offers an understanding of "the practical means that allow some collectives to dominate others" (pp. 107–8).

Increases in size, scope and power of collectives, "like the successive helixes of a single spiral," thus require increasing enlistments of quasi-objects, of "both forms of nature and forms of society" (p. 108). Respecting the common principle of symmetry, differences in the complexity, intricacy and length of networks are

INCORPORATING NATURE

explained by the capacity to recruit these hybrids. It is for this reason that modern "Sciences and technologies are remarkable . . . because they multiply the nonhumans enrolled in the manufacturing of collectives and because they make the community that we form with these beings a more intimate one" (ibid.).

A history of agricultural quasi-objects: the corn collective

This analytical perspective of mediation and the creation of heterogeneous collectives, allied to an understanding of their differences or asymmetries – "The extension of the spiral, the scope of the enlistments . . . the ever-increasing lengths to which (modern science) goes to recruit" quasi-objects – offers some intriguing insights into agro-food systems. (Latour 1993: 108) This potential can be glimpsed if we recognize the intricate ways in which the "seamless fabric" is continually refashioned over space–time in production and reproduction. For example, as hunting and gathering practices, already highly selective, gave way to agrarian communities with "domesticated" animals and plants, those "quasi-objects, quasi-subjects" co-produced over the centuries become the "traditional" livestock bloodlines and landraces, the "heirloom" varieties whose history as quasi-objects is conveyed to the present in genetic materials and situated farmer knowledges. This history clearly can be described by Latour's metaphor of collective associations of humans and nonhumans, differentiated by the "scope of the enlistments," and extending through time and space to form international networks.

In the case of corn, for example, such a history might encompass, selectively, the agricultural origin story of the corn mother told by Indians in eastern North America, and associated with corn planting in forest clearings (Merchant 1989), the place of corn in meso-American cultures, the Columbian exchange (Crosby 1972), botanical expeditions, and the expansion of corn as a commercial crop, supported in the USA by an extensive institutional infrastructure. Subsequent mappings of corn following the rediscovery of Mendelian genetics are perhaps even more revealingly portrayed as collective enlistments of widening scope, emphasizing Latour's contribution as co-founder with Michel Callon of the so-called "Paris School" of science studies (Pickering 1992). These mappings, again selectively, would include early research into hybrid vigor, or heterosis, parent corn lines, hand pollination, the double-cross technique of hybridization, and the development of the Burr-Leaming hybrid (Bogue 1983). This highly innovative quasi-object permitted the production of seed corn on a commercial scale, the enabling condition for the introduction of locally adapted hybrid varieties to the Mid-West.

The increasing scope of this collective mobilized, *inter alia*, the offspring of parent corn lines, private philanthropy, public agricultural research stations, state land-grant colleges, cosseted experimental seedbeds, and a private hybrid seed industry. In this collective, we can see the origins of the modern agro-food

209

complex as mechanical and chemical innovations converged toward, and are inscribed on, the new seeds, transforming the economic, social and techno-ecological foundations of agriculture and accelerating the processes of industrial appropriation and substitution (Goodman *et al.* 1987). These inscriptions produced a new plant architecture as hybrid varieties were designed for yield responsiveness to intensive fertilizer use, greater photosynthetic efficiency, higher plant density and whose strong stems, uniform height and simultaneous ripening facilitated mechanized harvesting. The "translation" of this collective to the tropics and sub-tropics,[11] extending its real, social and discursive elements, enlisted the Rockefeller Foundation, Mexican agricultural research and policy institutions, large-scale public irrigation programs, multinational corporations, and strategies of agricultural modernization, discursively and geo-politically propagated as the "Green Revolution."

This skein later enrolled new human and nonhuman recruits as it extended to the Ford Foundation and a system of international agricultural research centers, subsequently coordinated by the Consultative Group on International Agricultural Research representing governments, private agencies, and multilateral funding institutions. The hybrid corn collective and its multiplying quasi-objects are easily discerned in current practices of gene prospecting, gene banking, the mapping of plant genomes, and the gene-mixing networks of agri-biotechnologies. It may be fruitful to consider these collectives, at least in part, as a productive force (Yoxen 1981), constantly shaped and reshaped by translation and mediation.

Returning to the hybrid corn collective, this quasi-object is also metabolized industrially and in human stomachs as, for example, corn flour, tortillas, bread, corn starch, and as an ingredient of many thousands of food products. Corn as animal feed similarly is metabolized in the double gut of feedlot cattle and dairy cows, and by factory-farmed chickens and hogs, before its secondary metabolism as animal protein for human consumption. This indirect consumption of grain, reflected in the monocultural practices supporting the livestock-feed complex, is the hallmark of modern agro-food networks. So, this collective becomes *corporeal*, incorporated into a social body of multiple quasi-objects.

In effect, the real, social and discursive character of the hybrid corn collective is literally ingrained in the spatio-social structures and practices, the political ecology, for example, of Mid-Western corn-hog production and the broiler industry of the American South, and their international translations. Finally, the increasing scope of collectives enlisting the new quasi-objects of industrial metabolism is exemplified by the biotechnological production of high fructose corn syrups, single cell microbial proteins using corn starch as the feedstock, and a variety of new feed and food byproducts. Again, the notion of translation or network is a useful metaphoric device which, in this case, captures salient characteristics of the industrial substitution processes that are transforming modern agro-food production networks.

This brief discussion of actor network theory, particularly when infused with an

INCORPORATING NATURE

awareness of human metabolism, also suggests potentially fruitful avenues for the analysis of food habits and practices. These habits can be seen as incorporations of, constituents of, and constituted by, collectives of varying scope, which enroll practices of food provision. That is, these collectives "translate" or mediate the personal. This approach may thus offer a way to integrate the ethnography of the personal, the familiar, everyday experience, with different collectives of quasi-objects varying in size and scope. Some reflections along these lines are presented in the following section.

FOOD AND EVERYDAY METABOLIC STORIES

The quasi-objects which appear within "food" allow us to examine the location of metabolism and incorporation at multiple sites along a dimension which connects nature, agriculture, the food system and its produced commodities and human needs, and the social constitution of the body as both actor and medical object. "Food has shifted from being something that people see in its nutritional values and its appetite appeal and pleasure, to something that they have to be careful of because it will do them harm. . . . This opens the opportunity to market many, many new foods" (NPR, 1996).

The two short stories we provide to illustrate the possibilities of this approach have various elements in common: both require the decomposition of organisms (humans and others) into elements of nature/science, culture, and power; and both allow the translation of certain material elements, practices and meanings from eaten to eater in ways mediated by particular intervening industrial metabolisms. Yet each is deaf to parallel anti-narratives that communicate power relations more clearly. The first story, that of BSE (bovine spongiform encephalophy) transforms animals into cannibals; the second, that of Redux or fen/phen, recomposes anorexia, a lethal disease of the social body, into "oral anorectics," now a pharmaceutical cure for the metabolic "disease" of obesity.

BSE: a co-production denied

The saga of bovine spongiform encephalophy (BSE) – mad cow disease or *la maladie de la "vache folle"* – is full of metaphorical possibilities and invites multiple "readings." It can be represented as a grotesque consequence of the hubris of modern industrial farming, with its subtext of "nature" striking back against wanton human interference. The story can be told as an archetypal "food scare," those episodic occurrences that expose the co-productions and collective associations of non-human and human "actants" that make up the human food chain. The BSE controversy also illustrates beautifully Latour's notion of the translation of actants into different collectives, which variously struggle to deny, recognize, contain or extend the scope of the mobilization. That is, translation as the creation of links between agents that did not exist previously and which

211

MARGARET FITZSIMMONS AND DAVID GOODMAN

modify the agents involved. The politics of the BSE saga can also be interpreted, somewhat freely, in terms of another meaning Latour (1994: 36) gives to mediation, that of "blackboxing," or "a process that makes the joint production of actors and artifacts entirely opaque." In this paper, a brief chronology of BSE in Britain only hints at the rich analytic and metaphoric material awaiting further exploration.

Spongiform encephalopathies are an extremely rare group of neuro-degenerative diseases that includes scrapie in sheep and several human forms, such as Creutzfeldt-Jakob Disease (CJD), whose incidence is under one case per million people per year. The existence of scrapie has been known since the nineteenth century, and there is no evidence of its transmission to humans through the food chain. Although some experts assert that a very rare spongiform encephalopathy may have previously existed in cattle, the crisis began when BSE was identified in a dairy herd in Kent, England, in November 1986. For the public, the "scare" factor arises from the belief that BSE can be transmitted to humans as a form or variant of CJD as the result of eating infected beef products.

The political and scientific crisis that accompanied and greatly exacerbated the BSE scare was based on the persistent rejection by the public authorities, despite circumstantial evidence to the contrary, of any possible link between BSE and CJD. This position reflected scientific doubts, later modified in the 1990s, that spongiform encephalopathies could cross species barriers: from sheep to cattle and thence to humans. This skepticism was born of ignorance, however, since there is no convincing explanation of how either BSE or CJD is transmitted, although there are hypotheses involving misshapen proteins called prions and viral agents (Radford 1996; *The Economist* 30 March, 1996: 25–7).

While systematically denying any conceivable link between BSE and CJD, the British government took a number of steps that were directly at odds with its public pronouncements. In 1988, the government banned the use of meat and bone meal from rendered sheep and cattle carcasses as protein feed for cattle. This gave consumers a rare glimpse into the "black box" of the food chain to reveal the industrial conversion of ruminants into both carnivores and cannibals. With ruminant tissue used in cattle feed now apparently identified as the proximate cause of BSE, attention then focused on the British rendering industry. For a variety of reasons, rendering processes were modified in the early 1980s as companies abandoned the use of powerful chemical solvents and carcasses were "cooked" at lower temperatures for shorter periods than previously. In the party political arena, these findings prompted attacks on the neo-liberal deregulation policies implemented by the Conservative governments of Margaret Thatcher and John Major. In an extravagantly dubious gesture of patriotic confidence in British beef, John Gummer, the Minister of Agriculture and Fisheries, appeared on television to feed his daughter with a beefburger!

While still vigorously denying the transmissibility of BSE to humans, the government took a further contradictory step in 1990, when it removed specific kinds of bovine offal from the food chain. As Radford (1996) notes, this measure

INCORPORATING NATURE

came one year after pet food manufacturers had taken this same step independently. This pattern of rumor and consumer suspicion, government denials and damage limitation continued until late 1995, when ten cases of a new variant of CJD were reported, strengthening the circumstantial evidence of a transmissible encephalopathy. Moreover, the victims of this new variant were young people rather than the old, as with classical CJD. With this news, the "mad cow" collective began its pan-European "translation."

The European Commission, on 17 March 1996, imposed a ban on the international sale of all meat and other products of British cattle, which subsequently provoked the so-called "beef war" following the British government's decision, on 21 May 1996, to adopt a policy of "non-cooperation" with its European partners, urged on by bellicose Euroskeptics and the tabloid press. Awkward questions have followed about shipments of ruminant-based cattle feed to Europe after the 1988 ban in Britain, as well as exports of calves to France and other countries. Although some experts had rejected the possibility of "vertical" or maternal transmission of BSE to calves born to infected cows, circumstantial evidence again indicated that this was indeed conceivable, as the British government acknowledged in August 1996.

As the BSE crisis has deepened, lower beef consumption has brought sharp falls in beef prices throughout Europe, threatening rural livelihoods and raising the specter of widespread farm bankruptcies. French farm unions have organized a series of protests, including a national road blockade on 28 August 1996, to check the provenance of beef carcasses and live cattle in trucks and at abattoirs (*Le Monde* 30 August 1996). In France, beef producers, processors and distributors have instituted an "identity card" scheme to track individual animals through the beef commodity chain. This scheme, under the label "Viande Bovine Française," creates new conventions of quality assurance and a preference for local beef at the expense of imported meat.

Consumers in Europe have been exposed to complex debates over the rates of selective culling and the length of time needed to eradicate BSE from cattle herds. In Switzerland, for example, the government plans to slaughter 230,000 cattle, representing one in eight of its total herd (*Financial Times* 17 September 1996). Between May and October 1996, over 500,000 cattle were slaughtered in Britain following the decision to remove cattle aged over thirty months from the food chain. Newspaper readers have become aware of the shortage of special incinerators for infected cattle and a host of other macabre details, such as an estimated backlog of cows awaiting slaughter in October 1996 of 400,000. Moreover, since the rendered down carcasses of cattle will no longer enter the food chain as animal feed for their fellow species, schemes are afoot to use these remains for fuel in British power stations. As Radford (1996) wryly observes, the nutritionists' adage of food as fuel will now take on a literal but entirely different meaning.

The BSE crisis and its trajectory fits nicely with Latour's notion of agency as "productions of natures-cultures" or collective associations. In this respect, a

MARGARET FITZSIMMONS AND DAVID GOODMAN

food scare of this magnitude opens the "black box" of the modern agro-food system to wider scrutiny, revealing the scope of enlistment of human and non-human actants in prosaic decisions of everyday life. Yet, this is a co-production of the most intimate kind: of food and human metabolism. Ultimately, it is a question of identity, and most pointedly so in the case of BSE, since human forms of spongiform encephalopathy take over the victim's proteins bringing loss of memory, dementia, and death.

Anorexia/anorectic redux: hunger and metabolism

Another co-production of food and human metabolism appears internal to the human body. It is incorporated in the intersection of intention, culture and metabolism as expressed in the apparently individual construction of the body itself. Here, food is dangerous because it is food, and may accumulate. Obesity has been formally characterized as a social (as well as a medical) disability. "The US Equal Opportunity Commission, responding to complaints of widespread discrimination against obese persons, has now declared obesity a protected category under the federal Americans with Disabilities Act" (Medical Sciences Bulletin 1997: 1). The stigmatization of obesity is closely socially coupled with the simultaneous construction of social food, offering pleasure, pain, health, and illness as co-productions.

Anorexia nervosa – self-starvation – is increasingly recognized among the eating disorders with which modern society has become concerned. Anorexia and the related disorders of bulimia and binging occur most frequently in young women, though occasionally in men. Anorexia refers to "want of appetite," even to "lack of desire." Current readings of anorexia discover the agency of this phenomenon in both the social construction of women's bodies and the individual's need to master that little left to her own control. In a recent review of two books on anorexia, Susie Orbach reflects on what "is so fundamental in the anorexic's plight: *the struggle for human agency*. For women who starve themselves, there is always the attempt to create out of the material of the body a self that they can find acceptable – a self that, in its very essence, questions the one that has been given" (Orbach, *TLS* 8/9/96, emphasis added).

Susan Bordo (1985) provides us with a remarkable interrogation of the cultural and social axes on which anorexia is constructed: mind–body dualism, control, and gender/power. She writes: "the anorexic's 'protest,' like that of the classic hysterical symptom, is written on the bodies of anorexic women and *not* embraced as a conscious politics, nor, indeed, does it reflect any social or political understanding at all. . . . The anorexic is terrified and repelled, not only by the traditional female domestic role – which she associates with mental lassitude and weakness – but by a certain archetypal image of the female: as hungering, voracious, all-needing, and all wanting. It is this image that shapes and permeates her experience of her own hunger for food as insatiable and out-of-control, which makes her feel that if she takes just one bite, she won't be able to stop" (p. 44).

INCORPORATING NATURE

This "intimate" collective now enlists the quasi-objects of pharmacology, with its technological triumphalism. Metabolism can be defeated; the desire to incorporate food can be overcome. "Molecular biology will ultimately provide the 'cure' for obesity. . . . Obesity is a chronic disease that requires lifelong management. Drug treatment can play an important role in any management strategy, and combination therapy with two anorectic drugs may be the best approach. . . . Physicians who prescribe appetite-control drugs should plan to continue therapy for at least 5 to 10 years' (Http://pharminfo.com/pubs/msb/obesity.html). The world wide web becomes a frame within which to promote this strategy, and its implements, and to contest it. The mechanism for this transformation is a set of drugs called oral anorectics, drugs which induce anorexia by design.

These drugs are revolutionizing the diet industry, which each year collects several billion dollars from consumers of networks of quasi-objects (of drugs, alternative diets, exercise programs, and psychological support) which provide antidotes to the dangers of food. Fen/phen (fenfluramine and phentermine) and Redux (dexfenfluramine, the dextro-isomer) apparently act on the production of serotonin in the brain. Serotonin is an important neurotransmitter, and concerns about the impact of these drugs under long-term administration are now surfacing, but the commercial possibilities of these proprietary medications are immense. Some research suggests that these medications, if taken over a long period, can lead to the death of serotonin-producing cells or to primary pulmonary hypertension, a lethal disease of the lungs. Supporters of these medications find flaws in this research, and argue that the experience of thousands of Europeans who have taken these drugs proves their safety. Enthusiasts, such as Dr Pietr Hitzig (http://www.fenphen.com/hope.html) promote fen/phen as "a major paradigm shift in modern medicine." Hitzig writes: "Beyond weight management, when properly administered, FEN/PHEN can eliminate craving disorders such as severe obesity, nicotine longing, and drug or alcohol addiction. It can manage psychoneuroses, affect immune disorders like asthma and hives, and rein in obsessive/compulsive conditions such as nailbiting and bulimia. It can control attention deficit disorders, even those with hyperactivity, and it can eliminate sexual addiction, rage, and depression." What more could any body want?

Metabolism and incorporation link the corporeality of the social body to the agro-food system and its discontents. Rather than addressing the transgressions of social justice incorporated in (real) starvation at the Malthusian margin of the global market, the agro-food system finds new markets in social fears, incorporating (pharmacological) starvation into the commodities of food. Food is now a drug for which the antidote can be found.

In both of these short stories, incorporation is tied to transgression. Our use of actor-network theory encourages us to take our analysis of the dialectical composition of nature and culture, and of the hybridities that appear reflected in the facets of that dualism, into the social composition of the commodity itself.

MARGARET FITZSIMMONS AND DAVID GOODMAN

For it is in commodities, including the commodity body of a woman (or a steer), that the natural and social worlds are mutually incorporated, through the intertwined agency of "eco-regulatory process" and the "form-giving fire" of labour, not in circumstances of our own choosing.

CONCLUSION

The "greening" of social theory has coincided with a growing awareness that modern, asymmetric formulations of nature–society relations are profoundly problematic. Often, the nonhuman realm is "blackboxed" and agency is conceptualized as the "singular" property of human intentionality, which acts on, and in opposition, to a passive, mechanistic nature. In this chapter, we have focused on environmental history and Marxist political economy as two privileged theoretical sites where the abstraction of nature is taken seriously, and have critically examined the strategies deployed to redress this asymmetric treatment: the autonomous agency of nature as ecological limits, and nature–society dialectics. Yet these proposals are still infused, to varying degrees, with the polarities of modernism, both in their general articulation and more specifically when extended to the case of agriculture.

This ontological "discontinuity problem," in Val Plumwood's (1991) elegant phrase, can be addressed more productively, we suggest, by applying the alternative metaphorical tools of actor-network theory. With interactive symmetry as its basic premise, agency is conceptualized as the collective capacity of associative, and most importantly, relational networks. The principle of symmetry, and its importance in overcoming modern polarities and silences, is that consideration is given to non-human and human entities equally, with no prior assumption of privilege, rank or order. This concept of collective agency, of active relational materiality, offers fruitful new ways to theorize the processes of production and reproduction that describe, conjoin, and mutually constitute the natural and social worlds into Latour's "seamless fabric."

In addition to its promise as a general framework of analysis of nature–society interactions, the actor-network perspective of relational symmetry between nonhuman and human worlds underlies the notion of corporeality developed in this chapter. This concept is used here to theorize agency in agro-food networks and to reject a more local ontological "discontinuity": the abstraction of nature in mainstream agrarian political economy. The notion of corporeality is proposed to capture the relational materiality of ecologies and bodies that characterizes agro-food networks. In other words, those collective associations constituted by the prosaically complex, recursive metabolic exchanges that define the social reproduction and production of agro-food nature and humans.

Explorations of this kind, moving between general and specific theorizations of nature–society relations, illustrate the conceptual challenges and potential pitfalls that lie behind the seemingly simple task of bringing nature "back in." Yet this

INCORPORATING NATURE

reconstructive analytical work has much to contribute to the articulation of political projects to overcome the environmental despoliation and social asymmetries of late modernity and create more ecologically sensitive, egalitarian societies.

NOTES

1 As a corrective to the erasure of the materiality of produced nature that he detects in some Marxist geographical accounts, Castree (1995: 21) approvingly quotes Donald Worster that "nature itself is 'an agent and presence in history.'" This reference is more than convenient coincidence since, in this particular respect, Castree's project for Marxist geography has some affinities with the epistemological foundations of environmental history.

2 Worster (1984) observes that in 1972, when the *Pacific Historical Review* devoted an issue to environmental history, "the main themes . . . were conservation, water development, wilderness, national parks, and the Department of the Interior" (2, note 3).

3 The existence of physical limits to human possibility and the elemental role of environment in shaping society are stressed by John Opie (1983) in an essay on method which appeared at the same "moment." Opie cites the *Annales* school and particularly the work of Fernand Braudel in support of this position.

4 Worster advocated this conceptual innovation in his 1982 presidential address to the fledgling American Society of Environmental History, arguing that the new field should give analytical prominence to the ecological origins and impacts of modes of production. This ecological perspective on the development of social institutions and social change, which Worster (1984) attributes to Wittfogel's extension of Marx, is more fully elaborated in Worster's *Rivers of Empire* (1985). Additional discussion of modes of production also can be found in Worster (1987, 1988).

5 With the notable exception of William Cronon (1992, 1994b, 1995), engagement with the social constructionist challenge to the moral authority and normative stance of environmental history has been dismissive and slight. David Demeritt (1994b) provides a fuller formulation of the constructionist position, building in part on Cronon's discussion of the fundamental role of narrative or "stories" and narrative strategy in environmental history, but Cronon (1994b) so far has been his only interlocutor.

6 These debates are reviewed by Redclift (1987) and Castree (1995).

7 Demeritt (1994a) traces this explanatory framework to the ways in which environmental historians have read the narrative strategy of Carl Sauer and H. C. Darby in cultural geography, which uses sequential landscape cross-sections to evaluate the impacts of human–nature interaction on landscape change. However, Sauer never begins with a pre-human landscape, but with "the reality of the union of physical and cultural elements" (1925: 325). He quotes Vidal de la Blache: "Human geography does not oppose itself to a geography from which the human element is excluded; such a one has not existed except in the minds of a few exclusive specialists."

8 In response to critical commentary, Cronon (1994a: 173) acknowledges "his analytical compromises in the service of . . . writerly rhetoric. 'First' and 'second' nature are not completely successful because they appear to reintroduce the very dualism they seek to undermine, but I was unwilling to introduce 'third' nature to label a dialectic that already seemed inescapably implied by 'second' nature." Cronon identifies his central question in *Nature's Metropolis* as being about "human alienation from nature" (p. 171).

MARGARET FITZSIMMONS AND DAVID GOODMAN

9 For actor network theory in agro-food and rural studies, see Murdoch (1995), Long and van der Ploeg (1994, 1995), Lowe and Ward (1997), and Whatmore and Thorne (1997).
10 We are indebted to Sarah Whatmore and Lorraine Thorne for this reference to Callon and Law (1995). The notion of hybrid *collectifs* is used by Whatmore and Thorne (1997) to analyze alternative international circuits of food production, distribution, and consumption.
11 Latour (1994) clarifies the concept of translation by noting that like Michel Serres and following the sociological usage of Michel Callon (1986), "I use *translation* to mean displacement, drift, invention, mediation, the creation of a link that did not exist before and that to some degree modifies two elements or agents" (p. 32).

REFERENCES

Altvater, E. (1993) *The Future of the Market: An Essay on the Regulation of Money and Nature after the Collapse of "Actually Existing Socialism,"* London: Verso.
Benton, T. (1989) "Marxism and natural limits," *New Left Review* 178: 51–86.
—— (1991) "Biology and social science: why the return of the repressed should be given a (cautious) welcome," *Sociology* 25: 1–29.
—— (1992) "Ecology, socialism and the mastery of nature: a reply to Reiner Grundmann," *New Left Review* 194: 55–74.
—— (1993) *Natural Relations: Ecology, Animal Rights and Social Justice,* London: Verso.
Bogue, A. G. (1983) "Changes in mechanical and plant technology: the corn belt, 1910–1940," *Journal of Economic History* 43(1) 1–25.
Bordo, S. (1985) "Anorexia nervosa: psychopathology as the crystallization of culture," in D. Curtin and L. Heldke (eds) *Cooking, Eating, Thinking: Transformative Philosophies of Food,* Bloomington: Indiana University Press.
Callon, M. (1986) "Some elements of a sociology of translation: domestication of the scallops and the fishermen of St. Brieuc Bay," in J. Law (ed.) *Power, Action, and Belief: A New Sociology of Knowledge?,* London: Routledge & Kegan Paul.
Callon, M. and Law, J. (1995) "Agency and the hybrid *collectif,*" *South Atlantic Quarterly* 94: 481–507.
Castree, N. (1995) "The nature of produced nature: materiality and knowledge construction in marxism," *Antipode* 27: 12–48.
Cronon, W. (1983) *Changes in the Land: Indians, Colonists, and the Ecology of New England,* New York: Hill and Wang.
—— (1990) "Modes of prophecy and production: placing nature in history," *Journal of American History* 76(4): 1122–31.
—— (1991) *Nature's Metropolis: Chicago and the Great West,* New York: W. W. Norton.
—— (1992) "A place for stories: nature, history, and narrative," *Journal of American History* 78: 1347–76.
—— (1994a) "On totalization and turgidity," *Antipode* 26: 166–76.
—— (1994b) "Cutting loose or running aground," *Journal of Historical Geography* 20: 38–43.
—— (1995) (ed.) *Uncommon Ground: Toward Reinventing Nature,* New York: W. W. Norton.
Crosby, A. W. (1972) *The Columbian Exchange: Biological and Cultural Consequences of 1492,* Westport, CT: Greenwood Press.

INCORPORATING NATURE

Demeritt, D. (1994a) "The nature of metaphors in geography and environmental history," *Progress in Human Geography* 18: 163–85.
—— (1994b) "Ecology, objectivity and critique in writings on nature and human societies," *Journal of Historical Geography* 20: 22–37.
FitzSimmons, M. (1989a) "The matter of nature," *Antipode* 21: 106–20.
—— (1989b) "Reconstructing nature," *Society and Space* 7: 1–3.
Goodman, D. and Redclift, M. (1991) *Refashioning Nature: Food, Ecology and Culture*, London: Routledge.
Goodman, D., Sorj, B. and Wilkinson, J. (1987) *From Farming to Biotechnology: A Theory of Agro-Industrial Development*, Oxford: Blackwell.
Haraway, D. (1991) *Simians, Cyborgs, and Women: The Reinvention of Nature*, New York: Routledge.
—— (1992) "Otherworldly conversations; terran topics, local terms," *Science as Culture* 3: 64–98.
Harvey, D. (1974) "Population, resources, and the ideology of science," *Economic Geography* 50: 256–77.
—— (1982) *The Limits to Capital*, Chicago: University of Chicago Press.
—— (1996) *Justice, Nature, and the Geography of Difference*, Oxford: Blackwell.
Latour, B. (1993) *We Have Never Been Modern*, Brighton: Harvester Wheatsheaf.
—— (1994) "On technical mediation, philosophy, sociology, genealogy," *Common Ground* 3: 29–64.
Law, J. (1992) "Notes on the theory of actor-network: ordering, strategy, and heterogeneity," *Systems Practice*, 5: 379–93.
Long, N. and van der Ploeg, J. D. (1994) "Heterogeneity, actor, and structure: towards a reconstitution of the concept of structure," in D. Booth (ed.) *Rethinking Social Development, Research and Practice*, Harlow: Longman.
—— (1995) "Reflections on agency, ordering the future and planning," in G. E. Frerks and J. H. B. den Auden (eds) *In Search of the Middle Ground*, Wageningen: Wageningen Agricultural University.
Lowe, P. and Ward, N. (1997) "Field-level bureaucrats and the making of new moral discourses in agri-environmental controversies," in D. Goodman and M. Watts (eds) *Globalising Food: Agrarian Questions and Global Restructuring*, London: Routledge.
Mann, S. (1990) *Agrarian Capitalism in Theory and Practice*, Chapel Hill, NC: University of North Carolina Press.
Mann, S. and Dickenson, J. (1978) "Obstacles to the development of a capitalist agriculture," *Journal of Peasant Studies* 5: 466–81.
Martinez-Alier, J. (1987) *Ecological Economics: Energy, Environment and Society*, Oxford: Blackwell.
Merchant, C. (1989) *Ecological Revolutions: Nature, Gender, and Science in New England*, Chapel Hill, NC: University of North Carolina Press.
Murdoch, J. (1995) "Actor-networks and the evolution of economic forms: combining description and explanation in theories of regulation, flexible specialization and networks," *Environment and Planning A* 27: 731–57.
NPR (National Public Radio) (1996) "Morning edition, September 27", interview with George Rosenbaum (Bob Edwards, interviewer).
O'Connor, J. (1988) "Capitalism, nature, socialism: a theoretical introduction," *Capitalism Nature Socialism* 1: 11–38.

219

MARGARET FITZSIMMONS AND DAVID GOODMAN

Opie, J. (1983) "Environmental history: pitfalls and opportunities," *Environmental Review* 7: 8–16.

Pickering, A. (1992) "From science as knowledge to science as practice," in A. Pickering (ed.) *Science as Practice and Culture*, Chicago: University of Chicago Press.

Plumwood, V. (1991) "Nature, Self, and Gender: Feminism, Environmental Philosophy, and the Critique of Rationalism" in K. J. Warren (ed.) Ecological Feminism, *HYPATIA* 6, Special Issue: 3–27.

Pyne, S. (1990) "Firestick history," *Journal of American History* 76: 1132–41.

Radford, T. (1996) "Poor cow," *London Review of Books* 5 September: 17–19.

Redclift, M. (1987) "The production of nature and the reproduction of the species," *Antipode* 19: 222–30.

Sauer, C. O. (1925) "The morphology of landscape," in J. Leighly (ed.) (1963) *Land and Life: A Selection from the Writings of Carl Ortwin Sauer*, Berkeley: University of California.

Schmidt, A. (1971) *The Concept of Nature in Marx*, London: New Left Books.

Smith, N. (1984) *Uneven Development: Nature, Capital, and the Production of Space*, Oxford: Blackwell.

Unger, R. (1987) *False Necessity: Anti-Necessitarian Social Theory in the Service of Radical Democracy*, Cambridge: Cambridge University Press.

Walker, R. (1994) "William Cronon's *Nature's Metropolis*: a symposium," *Antipode* 26: 113–76.

Whatmore, S. and Thorne, L. (1997) "Nourishing networks: alternative geographies of food," in D. Goodman and M. Watts (eds) *Globalising Food: Agrarian Questions and Global Restructuring*, London: Routledge.

White, R. (1985) "American environmental history: the development of a new historical field," *Pacific Historical Review* 54: 297–335.

—— (1990) "Environmental history, ecology, and meaning," *Journal of American History* 76: 1111–16.

Williams, R. (1980) *Problems in Materialism and Culture*, London: Verso.

Worster, D. (1977) *Nature's Economy: A History of Ecological Ideas*, San Francisco: Sierra Club Books.

—— (1979) *Dust Bowl: The Southern Plains in the 1930s*, New York: Oxford University Press.

—— (1984) "History as natural history: an essay in theory and method," *Pacific Historical Review* 53: 1–19.

—— (1985) *Rivers of Empire: Water, Aridity, and the Growth of the American West*, New York: Oxford University Press.

—— (1987) "New West, true West: interpreting the region's history," *Western Historical Quarterly* 18: 141–56.

—— (1988) "Appendix: doing environmental history," in D. Worster (ed.) *The Ends of the Earth: Perspectives on Modern Environmental History*, New York: Cambridge University Press.

—— (1990a) "Transformations of the earth: toward an agroecological perspective in history," *Journal of American History* 76: 1087–1106.

—— (1990b) "Seeing beyond culture," *Journal of American History* 76: 1142–7.

Yoxen, E. (1981) "Life as a productive force," in L. Levidow and R. Young (eds) *Science, Technology and the Labour Process*, London: CSE Books, pp. 66–122.

[28]

NOURISHING NETWORKS

Alternative geographies of food

Sarah Whatmore and Lorraine Thorne

[T]he capitalism of Karl Marx or Fernand Braudel is not the total capitalism of the Marxists. It is a skein of somewhat longer networks that rather inadequately embrace a world on the basis of points that become centres of profit and calculation. In following it step by step, one never crosses the mysterious lines that divide the local from the global.

(Latour 1993: 121)

INTRODUCTION

The spatial imagery of a 'shrinking world' and a 'global village' are the popular hallmarks of an understanding of the limitless compass and totalising fabric of contemporary capitalism that has become something of a social science orthodoxy, known as *globalisation* (Featherstone 1990, Sklair 1991). No less heroic than the institutional complexes which it depicts, such an understanding perpetuates a peculiarly modernist geographical imagination that casts globalisation as a colonisation of surfaces which, like a spreading ink stain, progressively colours every spot on the map. This spatial imagery suffuses the political economy of agro-food through analytical devices like 'global commodity systems' (Friedland *et al.* 1991); 'agro-food regimes' (Le Heron 1994) and 'systems of provision' (Fine *et al.* 1996). In the most cogently argued versions, globalisation is animated as a political project of world economic management orchestrated by a regiment of capitalist institutions including transnational corporations (TNCs), financial institutions and regulatory infrastructures (McMichael 1996: 112). But the most potent agro-food expression of this spatial imagery must surely be George Ritzer's notion of 'McDonaldization'. He coins the term to describe a process of social rationalisation modelled on the fast-food restaurant which he argues has 'revolutionised not only the restaurant business, but also American society and, ultimately, the world' (Ritzer 1996: xvii). This is social science at its most triumphant – a rhetorically seductive best-seller which serves up the world on a plate.

That some markets indeed have global reach is not in dispute. What we want to emphasise is that this reach makes the corporations and

SARAH WHATMORE AND LORRAINE THORNE

bureaucracies that fashion such markets both powerful and vulnerable, being woven of the same substances as the more humble everyday forms of social life so often consigned to the 'local' and rendered puny in comparison. One of the most serious consequences of orthodox accounts of globalisation, whether of the more rigorous or the more populist varieties identified above, has been the eradication of social agency and struggle from the compass of analysis by presenting global reach as a systemic and logical, rather than a partial and contested, process (Amin and Thrift 1994). TNCs and associated regulatory bureaucracies become magnified into institutional dinosaurs whose scale and mass overwhelms the paltry significance of their social fabric, at the same time as the life practices and milieux of lesser social agents are dwarfed and overshadowed in this colossal landscape. But size, as the dinosaurs discovered, isn't everything.

Our point then, is that there is nothing 'global' about such corporations and bureaucracies *in themselves*, either in terms of their being disembedded from particular contexts and places or of their being in some sense comprehensive in scale and scope. Rather, their reach depends upon intricate interweavings of *situated* people, artefacts, codes, and living things and the maintenance of particular tapestries of connection across the world. Such processes and patterns of connection are not reducible to a single logic or determinant interest lying somewhere *outside* or *above* the social fray. This distinction is the difference between systems and networks; a shift in analytical metaphor which takes up critiques of the globalisation orthodoxy, notably within geography and anthropology, as a failure of both social and spatial imagination (Strathern 1995, Thrift 1996).

Two complementary influences on the elaboration of these critiques are particularly important for our purposes here, the one concerned with rethinking *political economy* and the other with recognising *space-time*. In the first case, economic sociology and institutional economics have emphasised the embodied and routinised social practices which constitute markets, corporations and regulatory bureaucracies against accounts (Marxist and neoclassical) which tend to treat these institutional complexes as abstracted presences, or the product of some historically teleological process (Underhill 1994, Thrift and Olds 1996). Economic institutions and practices are conceived of not as some separate, and still less determinant, 'sphere' of activity which articulates with other 'spheres' of civic society or governance but as socially embedded and contingent at every turn (Smelser and Swedberg 1994, Murdoch 1995). In the second case, poststructuralist ideas have informed theoretical efforts to deconstruct the geometric landscapes – what Barnes (1996) has called the 'Enlightenment view' – of political economy. By fashioning the modern world as a single grid-like surface, such landscapes make possible the encoding of general theoretical claims as omnipresent, uni-versal rationalities. In contrast, critics point to the *simultaneity* of multiple, partial space-time configurations of social life that are at

288

ALTERNATIVES GEOGRAPHIES OF FOOD

once 'global' and 'local', and to the *situatedness* of social institutions, processes and knowledges as always contextual, tentative and incomplete (Thrift 1995).

Such critiques, especially that derived from institutional economics, have been taken up already by those working in agrarian political economy (see Goodman and Watts 1994, Whatmore 1994). While it remains 'against the grain', such work marks the beginnings of an understanding of globalisation as partial, uneven, and unstable; a socially contested rather than logical process in which many spaces of resistance, alterity, and possibility become analytically discernible and politically meaningful. In this paper we want to extend these lines of critique, particularly that concerned with spatial re-cognition, as a basis for exploring alternative geographies of food that have been eclipsed by mainstream political economy accounts. Little work in this vein has made its way into the agro-food literature as yet (but see Arce and Marsden 1993, Cook and Crang 1996 for related forays).

The title phrase 'alternative geographies of food' signals an effort on our part to see the world differently in (at least) two senses. We begin by taking up the geographical implications of *actor-network theory* (ANT) which both of us have been exploring in work elsewhere (Thorne 1997, Whatmore 1997) and which resonates with other contributions to this volume (notably, the chapter by Ward and Lowe). As the opening quotation suggests, this involves the elaboration of a *topological* spatial imagination concerned with tracing points of connection and lines of flow, as opposed to reiterating fixed surfaces and boundaries (Thrift 1996, Bingham 1996). In particular, we draw on the work of Bruno Latour (1993, 1994) and John Law (1986, 1991, 1994) to elaborate an understanding of global networks as performative orderings (always in the making), rather than as systemic entities (always already constituted). We then go on to explore some of the analytical and political spaces which such an understanding opens up, by means of a case study of *fair trade coffee networks*. This case study illustrates the fashioning of social and environmental configurations of agro-food production and consumption that coexist with those of industrial food corporations but which in some way counter, or resist, their institutional values and practices.

GLOBAL NETWORKS OR 'ACTING AT A DISTANCE'

> The two extremes, local and global, are much less interesting than the inter-mediary arrangements that we are calling networks.
>
> (Latour 1993: 122)

The work of Latour and Law, and their respective notions of 'hybrid networks' and 'modes of ordering', provide ways of reconceptualising power relations in space from the flat, colonised surfaces of globalisation to the fric-tional lengthening of networks of remote control. In so doing, the key question becomes not that of scale, encoded in a categorical distinction

SARAH WHATMORE AND LORRAINE THORNE

between the 'local' and the 'global', but of connectivity, marking lines of flow of varying length and which transgress these categories. To put this question in the terms of ANT, what are the conditions and properties of 'acting at a distance'? Formulating inquiry in this way refuses the privileged association *a priori* between particular kinds of social institutions (notably TNCs) and global reach and, by implication, the pervasive mapping of the conventional sociological binaries of 'macro–micro' and 'structure–agency' onto that of the 'global–local'. Our account builds on the early efforts of geographers to explicate the spatial dimensions of ANT and their import for understanding power as a thoroughly relational process (Murdoch 1995, Murdoch and Marsden 1995) and for recognising the active part of non-humans in the fabric of social life (Thrift 1995, 1996).

Where orthodox accounts of globalisation evoke images of an irresistible and unimpeded enclosure of the world by the relentless mass of the capitalist machine, ANT problematises global reach, conceiving of it as a laboured, uncertain, and above all, contested process of 'acting at a distance'. Law illustrates this conception with the example of Portuguese efforts to expand the reach of European trade in the fifteenth and sixteenth centuries by capturing the spice route to India (1986). This achievement required the Portuguese to refashion contemporary navigational complexes in ways which, as Law puts it, addressed not only the question of social control but also that of

> how to manage long distance control *in all its aspects*. It was how to arrange matters so that a small number of people in Lisbon might influence events half-way round the world and thereby reap a fabulous reward.
>
> (Law 1986: 235, original emphasis)

Law's evocative case study of 'acting at a distance' centres on the technological metaphor of 'remote control' which tends to conjure the dynamics of networking in the rather conventional geographical binary of core (transmitter) and periphery (receiver). Nor are the implications of this metaphor restricted in his work to this particular case study. The imprint of 'remote control' marks his elaboration of ANT more widely. Thus, for example,

> heterogeneous socio-technologies open up the possibility of ordering distant events from a centre . . . [in which] the centre is a place which monitors and represents the periphery and then calculates how to act on the periphery.
>
> (Law 1994: 104)

A rather different, and to our mind more promising, exposition of the spatial configuration of actor-networks is that derived from Latour's notion of 'network lengthening'. Reminiscent of the nomadic cartographies of Deleuze and Guattari (1983), the idea of 'lengthening' not only problema-

ALTERNATIVES GEOGRAPHIES OF FOOD

tises the process of 'acting at a distance' but also disrupts the bi-polarities of 'core' and 'periphery'. These generic spaces, like those of 'local' and 'global', enshrine a geometric vocabulary concerned with the geography of surfaces. The unilinearity encoded in their relationship makes less sense in a topologic vocabulary concerned with the geography of flows. Here, a network's capacities over space-time represent the simultaneous performance of social practices and competences at different points in the network; a mass of currents rather than a single line of force. In these terms, actor-networks are best understood as 'by nature neither local nor global, but [only] more or less long and more or less connected' (Latour 1993: 122).

By implication, the size, or scale, of an actor-network is a product of network lengthening, not of some special properties peculiar to 'global' or 'core' actors – the 'dinosaurs' of our earlier analogy. Furthermore, the power associated with global reach has to be understood as a social composite of the actions and competences of many actants; an attribute not of a single person or organisation but of the number of actants involved in its composition (Callon and Latour 1981, Murdoch and Marsden 1995). How, then, is this network lengthening achieved?

The answer advanced in ANT is that network lengthening requires the mobilisation of larger numbers and more intricately interwoven constituents, or *mediators*, to sustain a web of connections over greater distances. In so doing, it focuses analytical attention on describing this process of mediation and its agents in ways which force a challenging, and sometimes disconcerting, shift in the horizons of social research. As Law notes in relation to his Portuguese case study,

> if these attempts at long-distance control are to be understood then it is not only necessary to develop a form of analysis capable of handling the social, the technological, the natural and the rest with equal facility, though this is essential. It is also necessary that the approach should be capable of making sense of the way in which these are fitted together.
>
> (Law 1986: 235)

At once it becomes essential to talk of network mediators other than people, that is other than the human actors on whom the whole compass of conventional theories of social agency (including other social network theories) is built. To be sure, people in particular guises and contexts act as important go-betweens, mobile agents weaving connections between distant points in the network; for example, the sailors in Law's Portuguese study, or the managerial elites of corporate business today. But, insists ANT, there are a wealth of other agents, technological and 'natural', mobilised in the performance of social networks whose significance increases the longer and more intricate the network becomes. Latour calls these agents 'immutable mobiles', such as money, telephones, computers, or gene banks; objects

SARAH WHATMORE AND LORRAINE THORNE

which encode and stabilise particular socio-technological capacities and sustain patterns of connection that allow us to pass with continuity not only from the local to the global, but also from the human to the non-human. The more they have proliferated in everyday life the more, it seems, these 'objects' have been effaced in social theory leaving us awed by the subsequently fantastic properties of social entities like TNCs. By taking such objects into account 'one can follow the growth of an organisation in its entirety without ever changing levels and without ever discovering "decontextualised" rationality' (Latour 1993: 122).

It should by now be apparent that a move from 'globalisation' to global networks as a basis for understanding the conditions and properties of 'acting at a distance' is no small step. Tracing the process and agents of mediation in the way suggested by ANT implies a pretty radical re-cognition of social agency. It is worth rehearsing three major, mutually reinforcing, elements of the theory as it is advanced, in different ways, by Latour and Law (and Callon) before illustrating their implications for the analysis of agro-food networks. These elements can be identified for the sake of brevity as the qualities of hybridity, collectivity, and durability.

Breaking down the global–local binary through the idea of the lengthening of networks is intricately tied up with breaking down the nature–society binary through the idea of *hybridity*. Just as the global–local distinction serves to purify processes and entities that are not of themselves confined to any particular spatial scale, so the ontological separation of society and nature purifies the messy heterogeneity of life. Overlaid, these binaries creates four distinct regions between which nothing is supposed to take place but in which most things are happening (Latour 1993: 123). Actor-networks mobilise, and are constituted by, a multiplicity of different agents, or 'actants', human and non-human; technological and textual; organic and mechanic. More radically still, networks build and enmesh differently constituted entities/actants which combine these properties in varied and dynamic ways. These hybrids represent states of being which fall somewhere between the passive objects of human will and imagination which litter the social sciences, and the autonomous external forces favoured in natural science accounts. Following Michel Serres (see Serres and Latour 1995), Latour designates these in-between states of being as *quasi-objects* which are as 'real as nature, narrated as discourse, collective as society [and] existential as being' (Latour 1993: 89).

Returning to the Portuguese study, Law shows how a composite of agents are enjoined as emissaries of network lengthening, including documents, devices, and people fashioned in particular ways. For example, a document called the 'Regimento' inscribed a distilled and simplified instruction for navigating by stars which permitted the navigator to pass beyond the established envelope of North European travel. Devices included the 'carreira', a ship designed for carrying cargo and avoiding plunder, and 'a kind of simpli-

ALTERNATIVES GEOGRAPHIES OF FOOD

fied black box', the astrolabe. Similarly, this effort to act at a distance mobilised people with very particular kinds of skills or embodied social practices, including navigators, sailors, and merchants.

This example picks up and illustrates a second key step in understanding the process of network lengthening, the fundamentally relational, or *collective* conception of social agency that characterises ANT. Thus, the significance of the 'documents, devices and drilled people' in Law's Portuguese study is the way in which they hold each other in position. 'The right documents, the right devices, the right people properly drilled – put together they would create a structured envelope for one another that ensured their durability and fidelity' (Law 1986: 254). Yet the full implications of this conception of social agency are relatively underdeveloped in this early case study. It is in Law's later work and, more particularly, in the notion of the *hybrid collectif* (Callon and Law 1995) that the importance of the active properties of non-human agents in the lengthening of networks is most fully explored. For Latour, these agents are a vital part of a network's collective capacity to act 'because they attach us to one another, because they circulate in our hands and define our social bond by their very circulation' (1993: 89).

But this represents the point of greatest tension between ANT and conventional theories of social agency which centre on notions of intentionality and, by implication linguistic competence, as a peculiarly human capacity. In what sense then, are the 'agents' of the hybrid collectif to be understood? The answer provided by Callon and Latour makes the break with conventional social theory explicit. Agents in ANT are

> effects generated in configurations of different materials. Which also, however, take the form of attributions. Attributions which localise agency as singularity – usually . . . in the form of human bodies. Attributions which endow one part of the configuration with the status of prime mover. Attributions efface the other entities and relations in the collectif or consign these to a supporting and infrastructural role.
>
> (Callon and Law 1995: 503)

In short, the logocentric bias of social theory which links agency (the capacity to act or to have effects) to language-based intentionality is refused. The agency of the hybrid collectif is a bold attempt to shift the (considerable) weight of this discursive privilege to recognise other, material, forms of signification by which the specific capacities and properties of entities from x-rays to viruses make their presence felt.

Thus far we have outlined hybridity and collectivity as necessary corollaries of the process of mediation by which networks are sustained over greater distances. Of equal significance is the question of how such networks are strengthened and stabilised over time or, in ANT terms, how they are made *durable*. In Law's book *Organizing Modernity*, he adapts Foucault's

SARAH WHATMORE AND LORRAINE THORNE

notion of 'discursive practices' to propose *modes of ordering* as a way of conceptualising the durability of networks. Modes of ordering are both narrative,
'ways of telling about the world . . . what used to be, or what ought to
happen', and material, 'acted out and embodied in a concrete, non-verbal,
manner in a network' (Law 1994: 20). He shows how organisations perform
multiple 'modes of ordering', which influence the ways in which agents are
enrolled in global networks. While these organisational patternings or
habits are invariably plural rather than singular, Law argues that 'only a relatively small number of modes of ordering may be instantiated in the
networks of the social at a given time and place' (ibid.: 109). In other words,
the durability of long distance networks requires strong fabrics of social
organisation at all points in the network, making the patterning of social
and environmental practices in *particular* times and places integral to the
business of network enrolment.

To return to the Portuguese example, a significant 'ordering' which can
be identified in the reconfiguration of the spice trade is that associated with
'reaping a fabulous reward'. This example is an antecedent to one of the
most significant modes of ordering observed by Law in his later work on the
organisation of laboratory science in the UK today – that of 'enterprise',
which celebrates 'opportunism, pragmatism and performance'. In addition
to 'enterprise', Law identifies 'vocation', 'administration' and 'vision' as
orderings shaping the performance of science. Parallel modes of ordering can
be imputed with respect to the activities of networks of enrolment by TNCs.
Their implication is that global networks, including those of TNCs, are
performative rather than structural; (de)stabilised through the creative,
collective practice of inter-dependent capacities, intentionalities and relationships by numerous actants. As ANT insists, this understanding of global
networks seeks to avoid the reductionism of saying that networks, however
long their reach, stand outside their performances. So, for Law, organisational modes of ordering

> are patterns or regularities that may be imputed to the particulars that
> make up the recursive and generative networks of the social. They are
> nowhere else. They do not drive those networks. They aren't outside
> them. Rather, they are a way of talking of the patterns into which the
> latter shape themselves.
>
> (Law 1994: 83)

FAIR TRADE COFFEE: AN ALTERNATIVE NET-WORKING

In this context, alternative geographies of food are located in the political
competence and social agency of individuals, institutions, and alliances,
enacting a variety of partial knowledges and strategic interests through
networks which simultaneously involve a 'lengthening' of spatial and insti-

ALTERNATIVES GEOGRAPHIES OF FOOD

tutional reach *and* a 'strengthening' of environmental and social embeddedness. Such networks exist alongside the corporate and state networks of orthodox accounts of globalisation, sometimes overlapping them in space-time; sometimes occupying separate sites and establishing discrete lines of connection; and sometimes explicitly oriented towards challenging their associated environmental and social practices. In the case of food, the 'devices, documents and drilled people' of Law's Portuguese example translate into a broader compass of material concerns than that associated with traditional agrarian political economy. These include the encoding of particular agricultural and dietary knowledges in the form of various technologies; the legal inscription of agro-food practices, from patents to health criteria; and the disciplining of bodies, from obese and skeletal people to industrial animals and plants.

Using this collection of ideas, and working to avoid the bias of scale in structuralist accounts (which inscribe a macro–micro division and then reify the former), we propose that modes of ordering which spin documents, devices, and living creatures (including people) as other than passive agents through multiply sited networks are both possible and extant. In the case study we discuss one such patterning explicitly oriented towards enacting an alternative commodity network, which we have identified as *a mode of ordering of connectivity*. In this mode of ordering, stories are told of partnership, alliance, responsibility and fairness, but performed in very different ways to the neoliberal encoding of these terms (Barratt-Brown 1993). This is a mode of ordering concerned with the empowerment of marginalised, dismissed, and overlooked voices, human or non-human. Implicit in this empowering performance is the knowledge that 'some network configurations generate effects which, so long as everything else is equal, last longer than others' (Law 1994: 103). The mode of connectivity therefore not only tells and performs but also tries to concretely embody a recursive effect of social, and sometimes environmental, embeddedness.

With roots in nongovernmental organisations dedicated to alleviating poverty in the 'Third World', the fair trade 'movement' has grown in the UK over the past twenty-five years. The charity Oxfam established a wholly owned trading company in 1964 with other organisations gradually emerging as fully-fledged trading companies from solidarity markets (for example, Equal Exchange Trading Limited), or educational functions (for example, Twin Trading and the Third World Information Network – TWIN). The recently formed British Association of Fair Trade Shops (BAFTS) consists of shops committed to principles of fair trade. Other organisations do not trade at all but provide support in the form of campaigning and lobbying (for example the World Development Movement). The point here is that fair trade organisations in the UK are diverse and numerous, with the physical transactions of trading only one of their component activities. The institutions, transactions, and technologies

SARAH WHATMORE AND LORRAINE THORNE

of fair trade serve to illustrate some of the key concerns highlighted by an analysis of agro-food patterns as hybrid networks. In particular, it shows how the global reach of so-called alternative agro-food networks (or their capacity to 'act at a distance') enrols coincident actants and spaces to those of 'main-stream' commercial networks. It is the modes of network strengthening (or making durable) that are analytically distinctive between the orderings of fair trade and capitalist commerce and that open up economic and political possibilities for configuring alternative geographies of food.

In this case study we discuss a hybrid network of four UK fair trade organisations and a Peruvian coffee exporting cooperative, although there are many other agents in this network, as becomes clear. In the late 1980s 'Oxfam Trading', 'Twin Trading', 'Traidcraft' and 'Equal Exchange Trading Limited' came together to create a consortium called *Cafédirect* which procures, imports, and markets a brand of coffee of the same name, available in ground and freeze-dried forms. The four partners are located in different cities in the UK – Oxford, London, Newcastle-upon-Tyne, and Edinburgh respectively. In the early days, the hybrid network of Cafédirect operated with no central office. Instead, partners had designated responsibilities, for example the buyer working for one organisation, the wholesale administration handled by another and so on, with one of the partners, 'Twin Trading', acting as the operational focal point. In 1993 the consortium became registered as a private company which has recently appointed a managing director, and the partners are now 'shareholders'. Cafédirect was the second fairly traded product in the UK to receive the Fair Trademark, which legitimises the product as fairly traded according to criteria set out by the Fairtrade Foundation, an independent organisation recently given charitable status but originally established by several fair trade organisations, including Oxfam and Traidcraft. Thus the product of the Cafédirect network is given institutional legitimacy by a hybridised form of itself.

Cafédirect's southern partners are small-scale farmers whose coffee trees cling to steep mountain slopes in Costa Rica, Peru and Mexico, in the case of the Arabica component of the brand, while the Robusta component comes from similar producers in Tanzania and Uganda. In this case study we restrict our discussion to some of Cafédirect's partners in Peru, namely the exporting cooperative of CECOOAC-Nor, located in Chiclayo on the northern coast of Peru. CECOOAC-Nor is the central cooperative of nine individual coffee producing cooperatives dotted through the northern Andean mountains. They were all established in the 1970s during a period in which the then military government supported farmers cooperatives through an Agrarian Bank. But during the 1980s subsequent governments relinquished support and the bank became defunct, leaving farmers vulnerable to commercial bank interest rates and the purchasing strategies of commercial traders (*comerciantes*).

In the 1970s cooperatives were able to provide services to their members,

296

ALTERNATIVES GEOGRAPHIES OF FOOD

including medical and educational services. Since then, these support services have been eroded, adding to the exposure of the cooperatives to renewed economic pressures. As access to cheap credit dried up the cooperatives have struggled to pay for their members' coffee. The situation worsened in 1989 when the International Coffee Agreement collapsed, leaving prices unregulated. Embedded in a political, economic, and social climate of considerable turmoil, the small-scale coffee producers in the northern Andes were buffeted by the vagaries of the Cocoa, Sugar, and Coffee Exchange in New York (CSCE), which regulates the Arabica futures and spot markets, and the powerful *comerciantes* for whom credit access was not a problem.

In 1990 CECOOAC-Nor made its first sale to a fair trade organisation, a key event for its survival. The buyer was a roaster belonging to Max Havelaar, a Dutch-based hybrid network of mainstream coffee roasters who, in exchange for paying a fair price, are able to carry the Max Havelaar trademark on their coffee packaging. Sales to Cafédirect followed, the contracts negotiated with both the Cafédirect buyer and the CECOOAC-Nor export manager paying close attention to the daily market prices in New York. The key difference between fair trade buyers and commercial dealers is that the former pay a guaranteed minimum price (which protects farmers should the market go into free-fall), and a standard number of points above the CSCE price when the market price exceeds the minimum (in effect, a 10 per cent premium). The CSCE is therefore one of many coincident actants and sites in the hybrid network of fairly traded coffee and the commercial coffee networks (see Figure 11.1). Other such coincidences include the export and import authorities for whom documentation must be in order for goods to be granted passage.

Cafédirect pays CECOOAC-Nor using the international financial system (although there may be delays in the release of payments from Peruvian banks for other reasons). The stock exchange, customs officials, and banking clerks are all actants of the hybrid network of fair trade, so too are their computers, telephones, and fax machines. Just as there are coincident actants and spaces between fair trade and commercial coffee networks, so too is there a coincident mode of ordering – that of *enterprise* – pragmatic, opportunistic, and canny (Law 1994: 1). The 'Third World' partners of Northern fair trade organisation are not insulated from the disciplines of the market – delivery deadlines, contracts, and quality conditions all have to be met. Northern fair trade organisations employ the same 'just-in-time' rationale as commercial companies, importing green coffee into the UK in accordance with the statutory trading regulations. The processing of ground coffee is also carried out in the UK, while the freeze-dried coffee is processed in Germany.

However, while the mode of ordering of enterprise is present throughout the fair trade hybrid network, it is mediated and re-articulated by another mode of ordering – that of *connectivity*. The raison d'être of Cafédirect, and

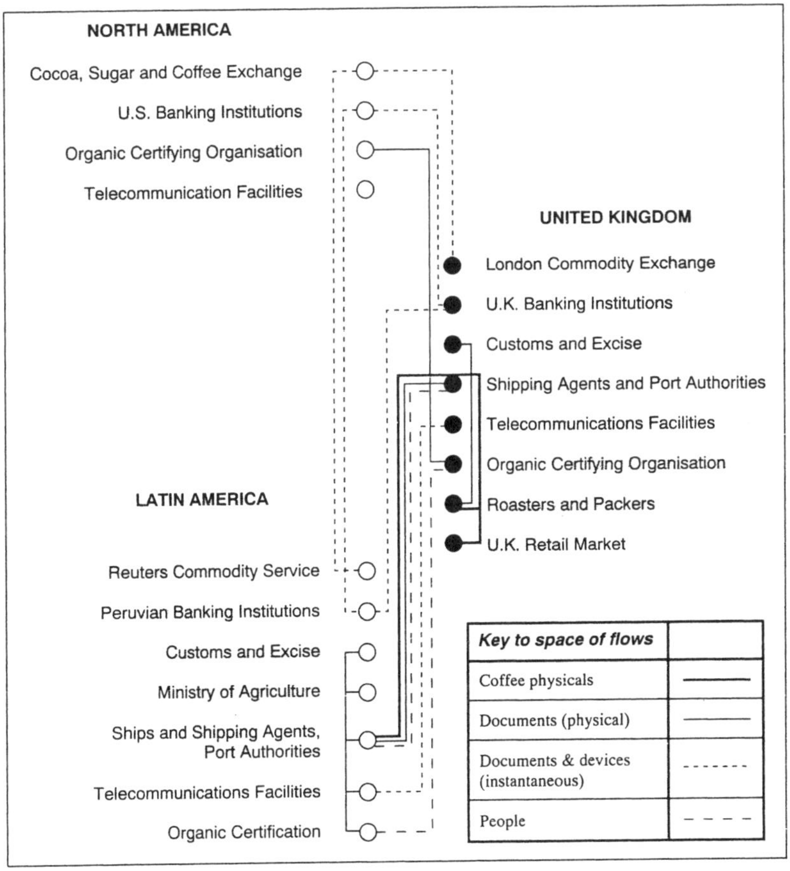

SARAH WHATMORE AND LORRAINE THORNE

Figure 11.1 Network 'lengthening': coincident spaces of a fair trade and commercial coffee network

the social agency of the fair trade network as a whole, rests on the mobilisation of a mode of ordering of connectivity different from that of the cost-minimising, self-interested individual of neoclassical economic theory. The packaging of Cafédirect coffee products makes the discourse of connectivity explicit.

> 'This is a fair trade product. More of the money you pay for Cafédirect freeze-dried goes directly to the small-scale coffee farmers in Latin America and Africa. Fair trade means coffee growing communities can afford to invest in healthcare, education and agriculture'.

These words establish a connection between those who grow and those who buy Cafédirect coffee. *Connectivity* as a mode of ordering establishes the

ALTERNATIVES GEOGRAPHIES OF FOOD

performance of 'fairness', rather than charity, in which the farmer gets a 'fair price' and the consumer 'gets excellent coffee'. In order to strengthen the network, fair trade organisations must make concrete the telling and performing of connectivity and fairness in the hybrid network. The farmers theoretically get a higher price for their coffee when they sell it to the cooperatives and this additional income gives them opportunities they otherwise would not have.

But the story is more complicated because another actant in this network, the coffee, is fraught with variabilities that reverberate through the network as a whole. In order to provide consumers of Cafédirect with 'excellent coffee', the cooperatives must submit only the highest quality beans. If the coffee is of low quality (reasons may include rainfall, 'pests', fermentation) it will not be suitable for the fair trade contracts negotiated by the cooperative export manager and the Cafédirect buyer, and farmers will sell to the *comerciantes*. If the price on the stock exchange is high *comerciantes* will pay well even for this low quality, and they will pay in cash. When the CSCE price is high – if, for example, the coffee harvest in Brazil is devastated by frost – farmers may see little benefit in selling to the cooperative. In such circumstances tensions between the modes of ordering of enterprise and connectivity become immediate and tangible as, for example, the warehouse goes unfilled.

At each point in the hybrid network there is instability and uncertainty, so that strengthening the embeddedness of the cooperatives is as important to the fair trade network as strengthening consumer support for fair trade coffee through marketing strategies and educational campaigns. Network strengthening is a process performed both locally and globally (see Figure 11.2). 'Strengthening' social and environmental habits of association amongst producers involves the enhancement of essential services – agricultural, medical, and educational. At the present time in the cooperatives of CECOOAC-Nor it is mainly agricultural services which are provided, facilitated by a full-time organic technician who travels between the cooperatives.

The second key aspect of the mode of ordering of *connectivity* evidenced in this case study, that of sensitivity to interactions between human and nonhuman actants in the network, is accomplished through organic farming practices. Making the soil fertile by cultivating earthworms (*lombrices*) and mulch, interplanting with shade trees and not burning-off makes coffee growing practices less environmentally destructive. Six of the cooperatives have organic certification granted by the Organic Crop Improvement Association (OCIA International), drawing into the hybrid network yet other actants and sites across the US, Germany and the UK. The whole process of organic certification is now regulated in law under European Union legislation (yet another coincident actant and space of fair trade and commercial networks offering organic products). The issue of environmental embeddedness, while a key part of the practices associated with the

SARAH WHATMORE AND LORRAINE THORNE

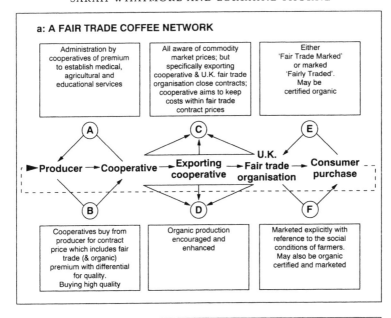

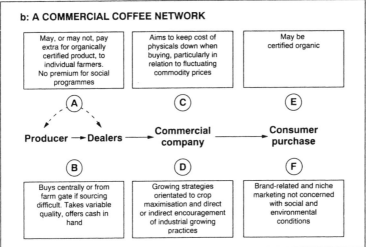

Key
A - Premium
B - Buying strategy
C - Relation to
   commodity market
D - Bean
E - Certification
F - Marketing

Figure 11.2 Network 'strengthening': fair trade
and commercial coffee networks exhibit
distinctive 'modes of ordering'

300

ALTERNATIVES GEOGRAPHIES OF FOOD

strengthening of alternative food networks, is no less dynamic than their institutional and technological aspects. For example, the land occupied by the farms of CECOOAC-Nor were pristine forest only fifty years ago, the habitat of bears and tigers.

This brief description of a fair trade network is partial not least because there are other coffee growing organisations selling to Cafédirect, creating more heterogeneity than this example is able to convey. Nonetheless, it serves to illustrate how alternative geographies of food lengthen their reach using many of the same actants and spaces as their commercial counterparts. What is analytically distinctive, however, is *how* they strengthen relationships amongst formerly 'passive' actants in commercial networks – the producers and consumers – through a mode of ordering of connectivity which works for non-hierarchical relationships framed by 'fairness'.

ALTERNATIVE GEOGRAPHIES OF FOOD

> What is to be done, then, with such sleek, filled-in surfaces, with such absolute totalities? Turn them inside out all at once, of course; subvert them, revolutionise them. The moderns have invented at one and the same time the total system, the total revolution to put an end to the system, and the equally total failure to carry out that revolution.
>
> (Latour 1993: 126)

The tendency to transform the lengthened networks of modern social life into systematic and global totalities generates heroic accounts of globalisation which do not recognise their own partiality (Thrift 1995: 24). For Latour, such accounts of the relentless logic of social rationalisation belie 'a simple category mistake, the confusion of one branch of mathematics with another' (Latour 1993: 119). Where the concepts 'local' and 'global' work well for surfaces and geometry, they mean little for networks and topology. While Latour's own style of writing is too supercilious for some – there is nothing simple about this category mistake – it should not detract from the importance of recognising the power of metaphor and language in shaping economic, as much as scientific, understandings of the world (Mirowski 1995, Barnes 1996); a power that is made flesh in numerous ways. In one sense, such vocabularies become embodied in the performance of individual and collective social identities and practices, both amongst corporate managers and oppositional political movements. In another sense, they become encoded in the authoritative texts and devices of law and science or in the engineered bodies of plants and animals (including humans).

In outlining an alternative understanding of global networks, the main points that we take from actor-network theory are that networks, unlike systems, are not self-sustaining; they rely on hundreds of thousands of people, machines, and codes to make the network. They are *collective*, that is their length and durability are woven between the capacities and practices of

301

SARAH WHATMORE AND LORRAINE THORNE

actants-in-relation. They are *hybrid*, combining people and devices and other living things in intricate and fallible ways in the performance of social practices. They are *situated*, inhabiting numerous nodes and sites in particular places and involving their own particular frictions (cultural and environmental) to network activity. And, finally, they are *partial* even as they are global, embracing surfaces without covering them, however long their reach.

Our treatment of 'global agro-food systems' as hybrid networks – partial and unstable orderings of numerous practices, instruments, documents, and beings – is a provocative one for those brought together under the hallmark of political economy in this book. The workshop from which this collection of papers derives provided a rare, perhaps unique, opportunity to air such ideas in an atmosphere of creative engagement. In the much less forgiving spirit of print, we are aware that we have probably overstated our case in places and have certainly left our own difficulties and qualms about ANT for another time. But if this exploratory piece has succeeded in conveying something of the possibilities for the field of agro-food research that have excited us about this theoretical project it will have served its purpose.

Rather than conceptualising the spatial orderings of economic activity in territorial terms – a globalisation of surfaces – this approach implies a conception of the spatial orderings of economic activity in mobile terms – a lengthening of flows. It shifts concern from a predictable unfolding of social structures in space to the means whereby networks of actors construct space by using certain forms of ordering which mobilise particular rationalities, technological and representational devices, living beings (including people), and physical properties. More than this, unlike the filled-in surfaces of globalisation, this approach opens up space-time to the coexistence of multiple cross-cutting networks of varied length and durability, for example in the many coincidences between the institutional spaces and geographical places inhabited by commercial and fair trade coffee networks. TNCs emerge as no longer unique in their substantive capacity for global reach. By exploring the role of the unspoken presences (or immutable mobiles) which hold such connections in place we can begin to talk about 'alternative geographies' of food in the same register, not as some pale spectre in the colossal landscape of 'capital'. It is the political competence and social agency expressed through the mode of ordering of connectivity in the fair trade network – including Cafédirect, the exporting cooperative CECOOAC-Nor, and the 3,000 small coffee farmers – which effects the difference.

ACKNOWLEDGEMENTS

We are indebted to the organisers and participants of the 'Berkeley Workshop' for intellectual (and financial) support, to colleagues in the Geography Department at the University of Bristol (particularly the 'Nature and Society reading group') who worked through many of these ideas with

ALTERNATIVES GEOGRAPHIES OF FOOD

us, to Nick Bingham and Jon Murdoch for their comments, and to Simon Godden, the department's cartographer, for the diagrams. Finally, we should like to acknowledge the funding provided for the empirical work by a University of Bristol Scholarship, and the cooperation of people at Cafédirect and CECOOAC-Nor.

BIBLIOGRAPHY

Amin, A. and Thrift, N. (1994) *Globalisation, Institutions and Regional Development in Europe*, Oxford: Oxford University Press.

Arce, A. and Marsden, T. (1993) 'The social construction of international food: a new research agenda', *Economic Geography* 69, 3: 291–311.

Barnes, T. (1996) *Logics of Dislocation: Models, Metaphors and Meanings of Economic Space*, London: Guilford Press.

Barratt-Brown, M. (1993) *Fair Trade*, London: Zed Books.

Bingham, N. (1996) 'Objections: from technological determinism towards geographies of relations', *Society and Space* 14, 6: 635–57.

Callon, M. and Latour, B. (1981) 'Unscrewing the big leviathan', in K. Knorr-Cetina and A. Cicourel (eds) *Advances in Social Theory and Methodology*, London: Routledge and Kegan Paul.

—— and Law, J. (1995) 'Agency and the hybrid collectif', *South Atlantic Quarterly* 94, 2: 481–507.

Cook, I. and Crang, P. (1996) 'The world on a plate. Culinary culture, displacement and geographical knowledges', *Journal of Material Culture* 1, 2: 131–53.

Corbridge, S. (1993) 'Marxisms, modernities and moralities: development praxis and the claims of distant strangers', *Society and Space* 11, 4: 449–72.

Deleuze, G. and Guattari, F. (1983) (English translation) *Anti-Oedipus*, Minneapolis: University of Minnesota Press.

Featherstone, M. (ed.) (1990) *Global Culture: Nationalism, Globalisation, And Modernity*, London: Sage.

Fine B., Heasman, M., and Wright, J. (1996) *Consumption in the Age of Affluence: The World of Food*, London: Routledge.

Friedland, W., Busch, L., Buttel, F., and Rudy, A. (1991) *Towards a New Political Economy of Agriculture*, Boulder: Westview Press.

Goodman, D. and Watts, M. (1994) 'Reconfiguring the rural or fording the divide?: capitalist restructuring and the agro-food system', *Journal of Peasant Studies* 22, 1: 1–49.

Latour, B. (1993) *We Have Never Been Modern*, Brighton: Harvester Wheatsheaf.

—— (1994) 'Pragmatologies', *American Behavioral Scientist* 37, 6: 791–808.

Law, J. (1986) 'On the methods of long-distance control: vessels, navigation and the Portuguese route to India', *Sociological Review Monograph* 32: 234–63.

—— (ed.) (1991) *A Sociology of Monsters: Essays on Power, Technology and Domination*, London: Routledge.

—— (1994) *Organising Modernity*, Oxford: Basil Blackwell.

Le Heron, R. (1994) *Globalized Agriculture*, Oxford: Pergamon.

Lupton, D. (1986) *Food, the Body and the Self*: London: Sage.

McMichael, P. (1996) *Development and Social Change: A Global Perspective*, California: Pine Forge Press.

Mirowski, P. (1995) *Natural Images in Economic Thought*, Cambridge: Cambridge University Press.

SARAH WHATMORE AND LORRAINE THORNE

Murdoch, J. (1995) 'Actor-networks and the evolution of economic forms: combining description and explanation in theories of regulation, flexible specialisation and networks', *Environment and Planning A* 27, 5: 731–57.

—— and Marsden, T. (1995) 'The spatialization of politics: local and national actor-spaces in environmental conflict', *Transactions of the Institute of British Geographers* 20, 3: 368–80.

Ritzer, G. (1996) *The McDonaldization of Society*, California: Pine Forge Press (revised edn).

Serres, M. and Latour, B. (1995) *Conversations on Science, Culture, and Time* (translated by R. Lapidus), Ann Arbor: University of Michigan Press.

Sklair, L. (1991) *Sociology of the Global System*, Baltimore: Johns Hopkins University Press.

Smelser, N. and Swedberg. R. (eds) (1994) *The Handbook of Economic Sociology*, Princeton: Princeton University Press.

Strathern, M. (ed.) (1995) *Shifting Contexts*, London: Routledge.

Thorne, L. (1997) *Towards Ethical trading space?*, unpublished PhD thesis, University of Bristol.

Thrift, N. (1995) 'A hyperactive world', in R. Johnston, P. Taylor, and M. Watts (eds) *Geographies of Global Change*, Oxford: Basil Blackwell.

—— (1996) *Spatial Formations*, London: Sage.

—— and Olds, K. (1996) 'Refiguring the economic in economic geography', *Progress in Human Geography* 20, 3: 311–37.

Underhill, G. (1994) 'Conceptualising the changing global order', in R. Stubbs and G. Underhill (eds) *Political Economy and the Changing Global Order*, Basingstoke: Macmillan.

Whatmore, S. (1994) 'Global agro-food complexes and the refashioning of rural Europe', in A. Amin and N. Thrift (eds) *Globalization, Institutions and Regional Development in Europe*, Oxford: Oxford University Press.

—— (1997) 'Dissecting the autonomous self: hybrid cartographies for a relational ethics', *Society and Space* 15, 1: 37–53.

[29]

Alternative Food and Agriculture Networks: an agroecological perspective on responses to economic globalisation and the 'New' Agrarian Question

Graham Woodgate, Bianca Ambrose-Oji, Ramón Fernandez Durán, Gloria Guzmán and Eduardo Sevilla Guzmán

'The collapse of the global market will be a traumatic event with unimaginable consequences. However, I find it much easier to imagine that scenario than the continuation of the present system' (George Soros).

Abstract

The 'agrarian question' has been a key topic for debate in rural sociology throughout much of the 20th century. Its subject of concern has been the fate of the peasantry in the context of the development of capitalism, with a clear distinction between those who foretold processes of differentiation leading to the disappearance of the peasantry and those who considered the special characteristics of peasant modes of production capable of continued reproduction at the margins of the capitalist world. Since the 1980s, however, it has become increasingly obvious that the agrarian question is beginning to take on a new dimension. Today we are forced to ask questions concerning the (re)productive capacity of underlying ecosystems as well as small-scale producers in the context of economic globalisation. Given the increasing evidence that the negative externalities of capitalist industrialisation reside in the ecological as well as the socioeconomic sphere, we are prompted to remember Marx's famous prophesy that progress in the development of capitalist agriculture represents progress 'not only of robbing the labourer, but of robbing the soil'.

This paper seeks to address this 'new' agrarian question and, in particular, issues surrounding the production, distribution and consumption of food. It does so by presenting an initial analysis of the impacts of economic globalisation and then considering social responses to such processes. The analyses are then related to a conceptual model of socioenvironmental relations, in order to demonstrate that while structuralist analysis may highlight important meta issues it is unable to shed much light on the diverse ways in which different groups and individuals perceive and respond to the world around them.

Rehearsing the main impacts of industrialised food systems provides important background information for the subsequent identification and analysis of five distinct forms of agriculture that have arisen in response to different perceptions of these impacts on agriculture and the production, distribution and consumption of food. From here, our attention is directed to a consideration of some of the institutions, people and processes that are involved in the day to day (re)construction of alternative food and agriculture networks, highlighting the idea that ecological and technological, as well as human agents can be understood as socioenvironmental actors. This is followed by an examination of the ways in which European policy has responded to agricultural and agrarian issues through the instrument of the CAP and how these policies have been taken up within the sector.

The lessons learnt from this mixture of theoretical, conceptual and the empirical materials are then incorporated into a proposal for a more appropriate, holistic and pluralistic approach to socioenvironmental processes and relationships, which we equate with the emerging theoretical orientation of agroecology. The final section of the paper indicates the relevance of the agroecological approach and agenda to the understanding and maintenance of important socioenvironmental spaces within which the cultural and ecological diversity that is so crucial to the future health and vitality of rural life can thrive.

Introduction

In looking to understand 'new food networks' as spaces of resistance to 'economic globalisation', it is important to come to terms with the concept of economic globalisation, in order to know something about what it is that the networkers are attempting to resist. Perhaps not surprisingly, most work on globalisation approaches the topic from structuralist perspectives, offering analyses concerning the general dynamic of what Wallerstein (1974, *inter alia*) would have called the world capitalist system. The following paragraphs are an example of the sort of interpretation that one might expect to see.

A Cameo of Capitalist Catastrophe

In recent decades the sovereignty of the capitalist economic system has been extended on an ever more global scale, until today there are very few areas of the world, or groups of people, that escape its predatory logic. The continuing commoditisation of different facets of daily life already affects practically all the spheres of our existence, especially in the countries of the Centre. Transnational capital, especially speculative finance capital, seems to operate virtually without restrictions across the globe, fashioning suprastate institutional structures (the IMF, IBRD, WTO, OECD, G-7, EU, NAFTA, OPEC, Mercosur, etc.) in accordance with its logic of profit and accumulation. This new global mode of operation is organised around neoliberal economic philosophy which gives little consideration to the wider human, social or ecological aspects of life. Everything is subordinated to the logic of competition and the market: the victims of this 'new order' are legion.

In the Periphery more than a billion people exist in absolute poverty, excluded from the benefits of modern society. Most of the remainder of those living in the South and East, with the exception of small, affluent elites, languish under the burden of structural adjustment programmes that impose stringent economic restrictions in attempts to tackle increasing levels of external debt. The rural/ agrarian populations of the South see their social structures, their traditions and their forms of production and consumption systematically degraded, as the result of the expansion of agribusiness and continued penetration by the products of transnational companies.

Meanwhile, in the countries of Centre, the hard won achievements of decades of social struggle are being rapidly dismantled through the deregulation of labour markets and the parallel disassembling of the social support provided by the welfare state. As a result, unemployment and social exclusion are on the increase and life for the poor becomes ever more precarious as public goods and services (housing, health, education, etc.) are privatised and access comes to depend on the logic of the market and private benefit.

The disparity in the distribution of wealth is daily more extreme in both the Centre and the Periphery. Increasing indebtedness of people, small-scale enterprises and even societies as a whole is the result of a perverse mechanism that pumps wealth from the bottom of the socioeconomic hierarchy upward to a tiny minority at the global scale. In these conditions formal democracy becomes a masquerade, as civil rights are drained of social and political content. As protest grows, police and repressive instruments of all types are developed to tackle increasing crime and public disorder.

All of the social misery entailed in the development of global capitalism is accompanied and contributed to by increasingly numerous and severe ecological impacts. Widespread, large scale, capitalist production does not just involve the intensive use of unrenewing resources with its related degradation and pollution of ecosystems. The processes of economic globalisation and the struggle for competitive advantage are also stimulating progressive environmental deregulation on a worldwide scale. Paradoxically, at exactly the moment when problematic ecological changes have acquired a planetary dimension, the logic of globalisation promotes the dismantling of the few instruments of environmental regulation that have recently been established in order to ameliorate environmental impacts. The term 'sustainable development', promoted as a *sine qua non* for social justice and ecological harmony at the Rio Summit in 1992, is simply an exercise in camouflage, painting a 'green' complexion on the face of capitalism's demands for continued profit and accumulation.

Something to protest about indeed, and the preceding image of the impacts of economic globalisation is not without substance. Beck (1998), for example, identifies the universalisation of the industrial economy as a primary phase in a wider process of globalisation. According to Beck, the concept of 'economic globalisation' refers to 'the economy, its markets, competition for employment, production processes, services, finance, information and life in general'. Beck suggests that the ultimate political consequences of the triumph of globalisation – what he terms 'globalism as ideology', which reduces globalisation to the economic dimension – may include the total destruction of what were once considered key institutions of 'civilised' society (such as fiscal justice, public spending, state pensions, social welfare, the autonomy of local authorities and self-determination of organised labour) in the face of the 'global reach and power of the institutional complexes of transnational capital' (*ibidem*; pp. 15, 27).

Although not the thesis his work presents, Beck's description of the ultimate triumph of globalisation is chilling, presenting a picture of an unstoppable process. Nevertheless, any seemingly unstoppable process requires a motive force; the exercise of power by real people in real places and, as Darier (1998: 18) points out, while disciplinary mechanisms can restrict what collective or individual identities can be or become, 'the existence of disciplinary mechanisms with a right of sovereignty also enables individuals or groups to take on an identity which might be the condition for subsequent... actions'. In short, the exercise of power in the process of economic globalisation involves a dialectic between the normalisation of global capitalism as a mode of existence and resistance to it. As Foucault (1988: 12) points out, '[i]f one or the other were completely at the disposition of the other and became his thing, an object on which he can exercise an infinite and unlimited violence, there would not be relations of power... In order to exercise a relation of power, there must be on both sides at least a certain form of liberty'.

Thus, as we can so clearly identify the losers in the process of economic globalisation we must surely find groups and individuals that are prepared, whether openly or as part of more clandestine movements, to demonstrate their resistance. In reality, recent years have witnessed the establishment of a range of social movements, promoting alternative economic structures and models of social and environmental security. Just like the spectre of economic globalisation which they seek to resist, these social responses may also be analysed in terms of their structure and functions. The following paragraphs provide some examples.

Resistance to Neoliberal Economic Globalisation: A Brief Narrative

In 1988, questions posed to the General Assembly of the IMF and the IBRD in Berlin promoted the coming together of a variety of social movements in opposition to the objectives of these financial institutions, allowing them to forge a common critique of neoliberal policies. Their critique of neoliberalism encompassed both the social and the ecological, stressing the inextricable links between the two. Such critical reflection was later enriched by similar responses to meetings of the G-7 nations, in particular the establishment of The Other Economic Summit.

Later, in response to preparations for the celebration of the 500th Anniversary of the so-called 'Discovery' of the Americas in 1492, there was contact between organisations of the Centre and the Periphery, especially between groups from western Europe, the USA and Latin America. In the Americas themselves, particular emphasis should be given to the organisation and coordination that these events provoked among indigenous American organisations, while in Nicaragua, in 1991, a meeting of peasant farmers from around the world led to the establishment of a new forum, the *Vía Campesina* or Peasant Road, as a means of coordinating their resistance to the progressive domination of rural life by the agribusiness sector.

Preparation for activities that ran parallel to the Earth Summit at Rio in 1992, likewise contributed to the flourishing of critical thought with respect to scientific and technological 'progress', the seemingly unstoppable development of productive forces and, in general, what was characterised as the 'myth' of development. While the Rio Summit can be seen as a massive marketing campaign to get the world 'on message' in terms of the concept of sustainable development, the parallel activities signified the crystallisation of new forms of organisation in opposition to continuing globalisation. The international network 'A SEED' (Action for Solidarity, Ecology, Equity and Development) emerged from these encounters as one of the most lucid voices in opposition to the processes and consequences of globalisation, achieving an important presence in various locations in the Centre, the Southern Periphery and also, for the first time, in the East.

New solidarities were formed among very different organisations and social movements from Canada, the USA and Mexico in opposition to the signing of the North American Free Trade Agreement (NAFTA), for example. These led to the establishment in the USA of the campaign '50 Years Are Enough' which protested against the impacts of half a century of the IMF and IBRD. The campaign produced a raft of opposition activities in different countries of the world and culminated in the alternative forum 'The Other Voices of the Planet', which convened in Madrid, in the autumn of 1994.

More violent opposition to the NAFTA exploded on 1 January, with the uprising of the indigenous Zapatista rebellion in Chiapas, Mexico. From the heart of the Lacandon rainforest, in the summer of 1996, the Zapatistas announced the First Intergalactic Encounter against Neoliberalism and for

Humanity. This meeting and the subsequent one in Spain the following summer accelerated networking at an international scale and paved the way for the establishment at the beginning of 1998, in Geneva, of the People's Global Action (AGP) network against 'free' trade: the first truly global network in opposition to economic globalisation and neoliberalism.

The first meeting of the AGP, attended by some three hundred representatives of activist groups worldwide, demonstrated the great variety of movements in opposition to economic globalisation. There were representatives from groups as diverse as: indigenous people's movements from countries including New Zealand, Ecuador and Nigeria; peasant movements from India and Nepal and the landless people's movement of Brazil; urban dwellers against structural adjustment programmes from Buenos Aires and Mexico City; new, mainly clandestine, unions of assembly plant workers in Central America; the European network against unemployment and social exclusion; the 'Food not Bombs' group from the USA; new organisations in defence of workers threatened by privatisation programmes, such as Canadian postal workers and the new French union – SUD (Solidaires Unitaires Democratiques); various European squatters' movements; the British group, Reclaim the Streets, whose activities have now spread on a more global basis; different groups and networks in opposition to the Maastricht Treaty – the European face of globalisation; and radical ecological groups like the Rainbow Warriors and Earth First! The list is indeed long.

The most recent manifestations of international resistance to economic globalisation have seen: Europe-wide marches against unemployment converging in Cologne at the end of May, 1999; Caravan 99 – a series of events coordinated by the AGP in which hundreds of Indian farmers and members of the Landless Movement of Brazil will tour Europe staging debates and demonstrations, campaigning against GMOs and the penetration of transnational agribusiness; the campaign for the writing off of Third World debt by the year 2000; and Abolition 2000, which will march from Amsterdam to Brussels to promote the abolition of all nuclear weapons before the end of the millennium. In the words of Reclaim the Streets, all such activities are aimed at making resistance to economic globalisation as transnational as capital.

Thus, in the face of the continued prosecution of economic globalisation, resistance movements are emerging and beginning to cause considerable concern to those whose interests are bound up with the successful development of truly global free trade. It was not by chance that during the September 1998 meeting of the International Chamber of Commerce in Geneva, discussions turned to what was termed the growing 'globalphobia' and calls were made for actions to combat the propaganda generated by those opposed to continued globalisation.

Modelling Development Dynamics and Popular Resistance

The preceding sections of this paper have provided a critique of economic globalisation and demonstrated the growing resistance to its further progress. At the level of abstract metatheory, the international expansion of the logic and practice of neoliberal market economics, or what Beck (1998) has called globalism, contradicts or threatens people's ability to enjoy healthy and fulfilling lives (see Figure 1).

The impacts of the globalisation of the capitalist/industrial way of life or mode of existence, are revealed not only in the contradictions involved between the forces and social relations of existence, but also in the deterioration of the diversity and innate (re)productive capacity of species, ecosystems and human cultures, at the same time as the consumption of industrial products has implications for human health. In other words, as well as influencing the ways in which we perceive and understand ourselves and the world, the industrial mode of existence affects the conditions of our existence, or what O'Connor (1998) terms the conditions of production. As the mode and conditions of existence change, so do ideology and social institutions, and we attempt to modify the way we live in response to changed conditions and consciousness. Indeed, there appears to be a multidirectional, multi-layered coevolutionary (c.f. Norgaard, 1984, 1987, 1994 and 1997) relationship between the conditions of our existence, our mode of existence, and our social institutions and consciousness.

The diagram in Figure 1[1] depicts the dialectical tensions among and within the socioenvironmental structures that are, as Giddens (1984, *inter alia*) might say, both the medium and the outcome of the practices that (re)constitute the world. Through the day to day (re)production of social and ecological structure, in the dialectical processes of existence, people demonstrate their ability, whether by design or caprice, to (re)fashion the world in which they live.

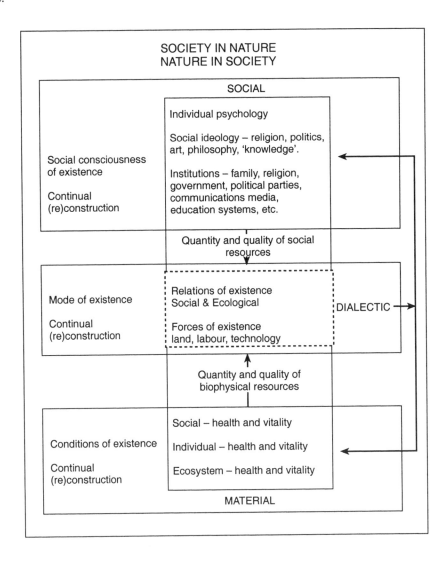

Figure 1:   *Framework for the analysis of socioenvironmental relations*

Agency (or the ability to (re)fashion the world) is an ecological as well as social attribute. Society and nature are themselves dialectical partners so that social agency is also ecological agency and ecological agency has social impacts. Norgaard (1994) demonstrates this through the example of agricultural pesticides, showing how the introduction of a new chemical technology can lead to the development of pest resistance or the elimination of pest predator populations, prompting the development of new technologies and/or new attitudes to address pest problems in continually restructuring agroecosystems. Nature and society continually (re)fashion each other and, in the process, (re)fashion themselves.

This conceptualisation of socioenvironmental relations is important, but if our theory is to be of value in practical and policy terms, we need to shed light on the detailed practices and processes through which history is made. By refocusing our attention on the day to day activities of real people, in real places, at specific times, we can perceive the multi-layered, temporally and spatially contingent ways in which different groups and individuals experience and exist in the world and the strategies and tactics they adopt in pursuit of their objectives. We become aware that different groups and individuals experience the world differently and that there are unforeseen as well as planned outcomes of policy and practice that are also of great importance to the unfolding of history. We recognise that at any given moment in time and space, the prevailing mode, conditions and social consciousness of existence, represent a temporary synthesis of who and what we have been, and who and what we want to become. We recognise that what 'is', is contingent on who, when and where we are, and how we see the world. In this context all notions of determinism, equilibrium and teleological process have to be set aside. Rather than a universal reality in which the seemingly 'limitless compass and totalising fabric of contemporary capitalism' (Whatmore and Thorne, 1997: 287) deny all alternative modes of existence, we can perceive multiple realities and how certain aspects of globalisation provide important spaces of resistance.

The threats to social and ecological welfare inherent in the ideology of globalism are counterposed, according to Beck (1998) by what he terms 'globality'.[2] Beck (1998: 28) claims that 'globality' refers to a perceived and reflexive 'world society' structured by social relations that are neither integrated in the politics of the nation state nor determined or even determinable by the politics of the nation state. The shared values of this 'world society' include gender equality, ethnic diversity and environmental quality: globality represents the alternative politics of globalisation, indicating cultural, ecological and social dimensions as well as the de-politicised economic dimension of globalism.

Alternatives to the Global Industrial Food System

The social and ecological impacts of globalism are perhaps most frequently associated with manufacturing and the provision of services such as transport, although industrialised agriculture is also a key area of social and ecological concern. In turning our attention to the diversity of alternative production systems that have arisen in opposition to the socioenvironmental threats implied by industrial agriculture, it is first necessary briefly to review what economists would call the negative externalities of industrial agriculture on what we have termed the conditions of existence. Table 1 identifies impacts in both the biotic and abiotic environment, from physical erosion and chemical contamination, to genetic erosion through the loss of

Table 1   *The negative externalities of industrial agriculture on the resource base including wildlife and humans*

Resource	Externality	Activities	Examples
Soil	–Wind and water erosion	–Loss of flora on cultivated land –Excessive deep cultivation –No replacement of organic matter –Burning of crop residues	–The USA loses more than 1,000 mt of top soil each year, equivalent to 300,000 ha of agricultural land[1]
	–Chemical degradation and the build up of salts	–Over grazing –Irrigation with salty water –Salt water intrusion due to over-extraction from aquifers –Application of chemical fertilisers and biocides	–About 100 m ha, or half the global total of irrigated land is thus affected[2]
	–Biological and physical degradation	–Excessive deep cultivation –No replacement of organic matter –Burning of crop residues –Application of chemical fertilisers and biocides	–Beneficial soil microbes are destroyed, leading to the long-term reduction of soil fertility[3]
Atmosphere	–Greenhouse effect and climate change	–Internal combustion engines –The conversion of forests to agriculture	–Possible shifting of agroecological zones
	–Loss of stratospheric ozone	–Application of chemical fertilisers and biocides	–Damage to crops and livestock from excessive ultraviolet radiation
	–Acid rain	–Burning of crop residues	–Around 30% of the trees in the Black Forest are dead or dying[4]
	–Generalised atmospheric pollution	–Accumulation of manure in intensive livestock enterprises	
Water	–Pollution of marine and freshwater resources	–Application of chemical fertilisers and biocides –Accumulation of manure in intensive livestock enterprises	–In Spain, 40% of reservoirs are subject to processes of eutrophication[5]
Genetic Resources	–Loss of genetic diversity and local agricultural knowledge	–Use of exotic and hybrid varieties and GMOs and the use of livestock breeds with narrow genetic bases that are maladapted to local ecosystems	–50% of the livestock breeds present in Europe at the beginning of the 20th century are now extinct[6]
Wildlife	–Physiological abnormalities –Death	–Application of chemical fertilisers and biocides –Burning of crop residues –Introduction of GMOs	–In Belgium pesticides have contributed to the loss of 60 wild plant species and the death of numerous birds[7]
People	–Social exclusion – Physiological abnormalities –Death	–Loss of employment and increasing financial hardship in rural communities –Application of chemical fertilisers and biocides	–In Britain, less than 2% of the population is directly employed in agriculture. –Organo phosphates and chlorines cause a variety of problems for reproductive systems[8]

Sources: 1. Myers, 1987; 2. Arnold et al., 1990; 3. Doran et al., 1987 and Parr, 1974; 4. French, 1993; 5. Avilés, 1992; 6. FAO, 1993; 7. Roelants du Vivier, 1988; 8. Misch, 1994 and Bellapart, 1996.

uncommoditised and less financially rewarding species, to problems of human health and unemployment.

Issues such as those highlighted in Table 1 represent barriers to continued capitalist accumulation, leading to what O'Connor (1998) has called the second contradiction of capitalism, which involves a crisis of under rather than overproduction. As resources have been depleted and contaminated, as the conditions of existence have deteriorated, while industrial agriculture has either had to intensify the level of external inputs such as fertilisers and pesticides or even to abandon large areas of formerly productive land, other people have sought to develop new or resurrect old, socially- and environmentally-friendly styles of agriculture with which to produce nourishing foods and healthy living and working environments.

Alternatives to resource-degrading, industrial agriculture, based on very different sets of agricultural practices have begun to appear since the beginning of the twentieth century. Without attempting to produce a definitive list, the people that may be considered central to such projects include: Albert Howard, Rudolf Steiner, Hans Muller, Lady Eve Balflour, J.I. Rodale, and Masanobu Fukuoka.[3] However, the take up and implementation of these alternative natural resource management practices has been slow due, fundamentally, to opposition from the emerging industrial agriculture lobby (Tate, 1994). It was not until the 1960s and 1970s, that agricultural practices linked to assuaging environmental concerns in industrialised countries, began to gain support (Lemkow and Buttel, 1983). Towards the end of the 1970s interest in traditional forms of agriculture, practised by indigenous and peasant farmers in the South, especially Latin America, also began to attract interest (Gliessman, 1978). By the end of the 1980s traditional agricultural, and new, environmentally-friendly, technologies were being brought together within the framework of agroecology (Altieri, 1987).

Although there is a great variety of alternative environmentally- and socially-friendly agricultures today, these variations can, we would suggest, be reduced to five main styles. In the following paragraphs we identify and differentiate these responses to industrialised food production.

Organic Agriculture[4]

Organic agriculture is generally understood as the form of production defined and promoted by the International Federation of Organic Agriculture Movements (IFOAM); as agriculture that aims to produce high quality products by working with, rather than dominating natural systems. It also aims to reduce agricultural pollution to a minimum and maintain biodiversity, while producing adequate economic returns (IFOAM, 1989). Organic agriculture tends to enhance biological cycles and processes through the use of local and renewable, rather than non-renewable, industrial resources, in order to improve the long term fertility of soils. Organic agriculture has arisen in response to the second contradiction of capitalism, to the degradation that industrial agriculture has visited upon ecosystems and the concerns about the risks to human health involved in consuming industrially produced foodstuffs.

IFOAM's definition of organic agriculture, while theoretically sound at the ecological and agronomic level, tends to deal with the establishment and promotion of standards for organic production. National organic agricultural associations, such as the Soil Association in Britain, have developed norms and standards of production, with which producers must comply in order to register their produce as 'organic' and obtain premium prices. Such standards are also 'exported' and applied to agricultural commodities produced in other countries for export to the UK. Furthermore, the Soil Association also works in conjunction with fair trade organisations and producer co-operatives, as a key actor in alternative food production and trading networks (see, for example, Whatmore and Thorne, 1997).

Nevertheless, in general terms, the application of organic standards offers a reductionist vision, confined to processes of production, processing and preservation of agricultural products which do not employ synthetic chemicals or genetically modified organisms. While the aims and objectives of members of IFOAM may be to provide consumers with authoritative and verified standards of organic produce, free from the genetic and chemical contamination associated with industrial foods, there is limited engagement with the socioeconomic and cultural contexts within which more sustainable forms of agriculture and rural resource use must develop. There are no limits to the scale of organic production operations either, which has meant that in recent years increasing numbers of transnational food conglomerates have bought up the most successful organic product lines, weakening any claims that might be made supporting organic production as inherently more socially just than chemical-intensive production. The first contradiction of capitalism does not appear to figure as part of organic agriculture's raison d'être.

Biodynamic Agriculture

Biodynamics originated from Rudolf Steiner's school of 'anthroposophy' or 'spiritual science' in the 1920s (Steiner, 1985). Steiner worked on the development of a worldview which would serve as a framework to guide practical agricultural tasks on the farm, in order to avoid the degeneration of both food quality and ecological systems. From the biodynamic perspective the farm is understood as a living organism, sharing the same attributes as all other living beings (Wortmann, 1977). The farm as 'organism' is considered to have three essential elements, the farmer, the soil and the cosmos, which must be maintained in equilibrium by applying specific biodynamic preparations to the soil and plants, and timing cultural activities to harmonise with cosmic events and cycles.

Although biodynamic agriculture incorporates a high degree of holism, with farms integrating crops, livestock and forestry, its lack of a basis in any systematic form of science, makes its functioning somewhat difficult to comprehend. Perhaps more problematic is the way in which, like the conventional science it seeks to replace, it proposes a universal remedy for agricultural problems. The biodynamic creed dictates the precise manner in which agricultural production should be carried out. Thus, while it addresses cultural issues, it does so in terms of defining how people *should live*, rather than seeking to understand how they *do live*. Furthermore, the biodynamic movement is highly individualistic, proposing that the lack of sustainability in agriculture can only be overcome by personal transformation through conscientious and responsible consumption, such that the individual becomes the protagonist of global transformation towards a biodynamic society (Lievegoed, 1977). In short, it dictates the use of universal biodynamic preparations to balance ecological and cosmic forces, and defines appropriate social behaviour, whilst like organic agriculture, it tends to ignore the important socioeconomic and cultural contexts within which any alternative style of food production must function.

Permaculture

A contraction of 'permanent agriculture', permaculture originates from Australia and the work of Bill Mollison at the University of Hobart, Tasmania (for an introduction to permaculture see Mollison and Slay, 1991). According to Mollison, permaculture represents a response to two phenomena of urban industrial societies. The first relates to the dependence of urban centres on rural areas for their supply of food and the high energy demands in terms of production and distribution that this implies. The second is linked to the phenomenon of urban to rural migration by sectors of urban society that have become disenchanted with urban living. Permaculture thus seeks to design agricultural production systems for both urban dwellers and for those who have moved out of the cities into marginal rural areas and wish to practice 'sustainable' agriculture on a part time basis, with the objective of achieving food self-sufficiency and a healthier, more fulfilling lifestyle. Scientifically speaking, permaculture has a strong basis in ecology, landscape design and architecture, which are applied to the design of highly biodiverse and integrated systems, not only of agricultural production but also of human settlement (Mollison and Holmgren, 1978, 1979). Thus, permaculture represents an interesting and useful project for disenchanted urban dwellers burdened by the risks of modern living.

More recently, permaculture projects have also been established in less industrialised countries, notably India, working with peasant communities to engage in development processes, based on existing cultural and ecological resources. Overall then, permaculture provides both a critique of the globalising impact of the market economy and agribusiness, as well as techniques for designing more stable, environmentally-friendly production systems and living arrangements. Unlike organic and biodynamic frameworks, however, permaculture does not engage in the promotion of production standards.

Natural Agriculture

The fourth style of environmentally friendly agriculture to which we turn our attention was developed in Japan by Masanobu Fukuoka. Fukuoka suggested a method of cultivation 'without doing anything', which arose from field work spanning more than 50 years. Over time, his experimentation aimed at eliminating unnecessary labour and reducing costs, equipment and practices that were not compensated adequately when the long term externalities of their use were taken into consideration.

The practice of agriculture without doing anything is based on: a) not cultivating the soil; b) not using fertilisers; c) not weeding and; d) not using pesticides. For Fukuoka, 'not cultivating' did not mean that 'it would not be necessary to loosen the soil and improve its porosity', because he recognised the importance of maintaining 'an abundance of air and water in the soil', nevertheless, suggested Fukuoka 'the land lives by itself and cultivates itself' (1995: 139–45).

Although the empirical basis of his claims was founded on his experiences in Japan, the generalisations that Fukuoka claimed constitute a global proposal arising from a critique of the 'Laws of Modern Agricultural Science', which are substituted by the 'Principles of Natural Cultivation' that are found in nature. Fukuoka's proposal also possesses a philosophical basis, starting with the principle that people are part of nature, it challenges the atomistic ontology of modern industrial society. From this basis Fukuoka proceeded to identify three types of agriculture: a) 'Natural Mahayana' – the form of agriculture practised when people are 'united with nature: the form of agriculture which transcends time and space and achieves the zenith of understanding and wisdom'; b) 'Natural Hinayana', a form of agriculture that represents a transitional phase from conventional scientific agriculture towards 'Natural Mahayana'; and c) Conventional or 'scientific agriculture' within which people 'live in a state of contradiction, virtually separated from nature'.

The interesting thing about Fukuoka's exposition is how he situates b) and c) in the same plane, because despite type b) moving against the current of industrial 'progress', rejecting conventional scientific diagnoses and prescriptions, it still pertains to the world of science so that both can be compared directly. In our opinion, this is a specially valuable aspect of Natural Agriculture since although one would 'differentiate fundamentally between Natural and Scientific agricultures due to the diametric opposition between their perceptions, thinking and research orientation', in order to explain the methods of Hinayana cultivation we can still employ the 'terminology and methods of modern science' (*Ibidem*, pp. 125–29).

Traditional, Peasant or Indigenous Agricultures

One of the key elements in the development of peasant and indigenous production strategies is the control that the household exerts over the means of production, over the land, over knowledge and in general over the labour process. That is to say, they exercise control over the mechanisms of production and through these over all, or most of, the mechanisms of reproduction.

For several decades now, there has been a systematic collection of information about diverse indigenous groups, which, in general, display a profound wisdom with respect to the soil, climate, vegetation, animals and ecosystems, that translates into 'multidimensional production strategies (diversified ecosystems with multiple species and products) which generate, within certain limits, ecological technologies' (Altieri, 1991). Indigenous farmers have thus developed important understandings of local biological and edaphological taxonomy, that have allowed them to predict climatic oscillations through the use of indicators and generate appropriate forms of management for specific problems such as the erosion of steeply sloping land, flooding, drought, pest and disease outbreaks and the low fertility of soils (Bulmer, 1965; Berlín, Breedlove and Raven, 1973; Williams, 1980; Christany et al., 1986; Chambers et al., 1989; Woodgate, 1991; Cooper, Vellve and Hobbelink, 1992; de Beof, Amanor, Wellard and Bebbington, 1993; and Scoones and Thompson, 1994). In attempting to reproduce such systems and introducing into others new but appropriate technologies, an interesting proposal has arisen which deserves mention.

Low External Input Sustainable Agriculture (LEISA) has been established and developed by the Centre for Low External Input, Sustainable Agriculture in Leusden, Holland. According to Reijentjes, Haverkort and Waters-Bayer (1992), LEISA refers to those forms of agriculture that seek to optimise the use of locally available resources by combining the different components of the farm system so that they complement each other and have the greatest possible synergistic effects. In addition, LEISA systems seek ways of using external inputs only to the extent that they are needed to provide elements that are deficient in the ecosystem and to enhance available biological, physical and human resources. Where external inputs are used, close attention is paid to maximising recycling and minimisation of detrimental environmental impact (op. cit.: 21).

LEISA is less concerned with the wider factors that compromise agricultural sustainability, however and, like permaculture, it does not promote specific production standards. Nevertheless, in addition to the general principles for sustainable agricultural systems which it maintains, LEISA also places emphasis on the need to engage in participatory rural development processes. In this sense LEISA includes an important element for achieving more sustainable agricultures, which, with the possible exception of permaculture, is largely missing from the other styles of alternative agriculture that are mentioned above, and reflects an important component of the agroecological approach developed towards the end of this paper.

Taken as a whole then, the alternative styles of agriculture that we have briefly reviewed demonstrate the demand for alternatives to industrial production and how such demand is being met. While organic, biodynamic and natural agricultures deal mainly in the technical aspects of more sustainable production systems and thus respond to the second contradiction of capitalism, permaculture and traditional production are less prescriptive and more sensitive to cultural contexts, they represent responses to the social consequences of economic globalisation as well as its impact on the conditions of existence. Each deals with elements that are important to the development of more appropriate modes of food production, consumption and distribution, although none incorporates the full range of variables that are implicated in the perceived threats of globalisation. This is perhaps not surprising given the subjective and partial way in which different people and cultures construct and experience the impacts of industrialisation and globalisation. Nevertheless, the appearance and institutionalisation of alternative agricultures and food networks certainly demonstrates demand for non-industrial foods as well as a desire on the part of producers for more ecologically and culturally relevant production systems. These practical experiences in alternative styles of agriculture have much to contribute to the intellectual framework of 'agroecology'.

The largely structural approach taken so far in this paper, however, does not permit us entry into the lifeworlds of the real people that engage in alternative food production and distribution activities in opposition to the global, industrialised food system. Whatmore and Thorne (1997) suggest that it is rather unhelpful to construct transnational corporations and their bureaucracies as 'global' entities following a logical process towards a predetermined destination, and the same criticism can clearly be levelled at similar representations of resistance activities. But let us not reject structuralist interpretations of historical processes at the same time as we dismiss teleological visions of the future. We can add to, rather than replace, the foregoing analyses by refocusing our attention on the real people whose daily lives (re)produce the structural characteristics of resistance to economic globalisation.

As Whatmore and Thorne point out, it is important to understand structural properties as dependent upon intricate networks of '*situated* people, artefacts, codes, and living things' (288, emphasis in original). Understanding globalisation, despite its evident, often negative, impacts as partial, uneven, unstable and socially contested rather than ubiquitous and logical, brings into focus 'many spaces of resistance, alterity, and possibility, [which] are analytically discernible and politically meaningful' (op. cit.: 289). Darier (1998) is in agreement when he suggests that:

> the concept of normalisation/resistance ... should be approached as a constant recontextualisation of power relations as lived and experienced by humans ... In brief, social change, revolution and

environmental activism is a never-ending activity in which tactics and goals are constantly re-evaluated and adapted to changing circumstances.

Thus in the following section of this paper we move to investigate some of the artefacts, codes, and living things that situated people employ in their strategies of resistance to the globalisation of food production, distribution and consumption.

Alternative Food Networks from the Bottom Up

The factors that stimulate a given individual to seek to resist the normalisation of a particular social paradigm are many, varied and in a constant state of flux. Identifying exactly where the germ of resistance emerges at the level of individual lifeworlds is likely to be difficult if not impossible. Nevertheless, we can say that when a certain social or ecological condition becomes worrisome, issues are formulated and contested discursively. As we saw in earlier sections of this paper, resistance has emerged to both the social and ecological contradictions of the globalisation of neoliberal economic philosophy and markets. But exactly what prompts any given individual to act must have some significant material or symbolic impact in their own lifeworld. Those of us that would identify ourselves as environmentalists might expect, for example, that the large numbers of farmers that are currently seeking advice on organic production techniques from the British Government's Organic Conversion Information Scheme (OCIS), were doing so because they had experienced the impact of industrial production on the conditions of their existence; on the land, crops, livestock and ecosystems that they manage. Anecdotal evidence from those providing the advice through the OCIS, however, suggests that the main incentive is economic, stemming from: depressed prices for industrially produced food stuffs, unmet demand for organics, price premia and financial support from the Government's Organic Farming Scheme, during the period of conversion (Boden, 1999 and Morrish 1999, personal communication). Once the interest and motivation to explore alternative production methods are established, however, new socioenvironmental spaces of resistance, what Allen (1996) calls 'possibility space', begin to come into focus.

Possibility space represents a multidimensional socioenvironmental space in which there is potential for social and ecological innovations to arise. It is 'explored' when human individual and group activity is influenced by new knowledge and ideas, or information and perceptions concerning the behaviour of others and the character of socioenvironmental structure (Woodgate and Redclift, 1998).

'In the real world', writes Allen, 'competitors, allies, clients, technologies, raw materials, costs, and skills all change. Any group or firm that fixed its behaviour would sooner or later be eliminated, having no adaptive or learning capacity with which to respond'. Thus, socioenvironmental structure (underlying motive forces as well as surface appearances) can best be understood as a *'temporary balance between exploration and constraint'* (Allen, op. cit.: 89, emphasis added). Allen's ecological understanding of structure reflects Giddens' (1979) assertion that social structures both enable and constrain the human agency through which they are (re)produced. And Ingold (1992) is referring to a similar model when he argues that 'the dialectics of the interface between persons and environment should be understood in terms of a dichotomy between effectivities and affordances – *between the action capabilities of subjects and the possibilities for action offered by objects*' (Ingold, 1992: 51–52, emphasis added).

The dynamics of this dialectic can be understood as involving the employment, generation, transfer and transformation of natural, human, social, physical and financial capitals. The diagram in Figure 2 represents an attempt to map out some of the artefacts, codes and living things that individuals might seek to employ to their advantage in pursuit of livelihood or lifestyle aims and objectives. The interaction of these networked institutions depends upon the day to day activities of socioenvironmental actors from the representatives of government agencies and financial insitutions, community groups and family members, to agricultural crops and wildlife species, landscape and climate. Individuals entering and (re)constructing a presence

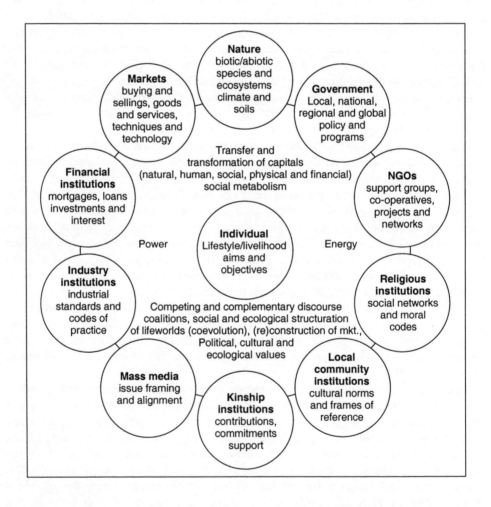

Figure 2:   Socioenvironmental Networking

within networks, employ their own human capital – psychology, personality, knowledge and understanding – to integrate or network other forms of capital (symbolic and instrumental value). Social capital relates to the interpersonal relationships between and among individuals, to the institutional complexes that structure the social world and the symbolic values which society places on the various phenomena of the prevailing socioenvironmental reality. Financial capital is the abstract market value of resources, while natural capital relates to the health and vitality of the people, species and ecosystems, landscapes, soils and climates, which inhabit and structure the external world. The benefits derived from successful networking are reflected in: the augmentation of political power; improvements in socioeconomic status and increased access to energy and material resources for network members.

All of us rely on the external world for our health and welfare, Marx described nature as our inorganic body, suggesting that we had to maintain a constant dialogue with it in order to live healthy and fulfilling lives. For most people living in highly industrialised societies, however, their dialogue with nature occurs at a distance, mediated through the institutions of the market and public policy. For the producer, however, and especially the producer wishing to resist the forces of globalisation, aspects of nature are incorporated into their personal resistance networks as actors and structures that either enable or constrain their lifestyle/livelihood aims and objectives. The presence or absence of different landforms, habitats, and species of plants and animals in and around an agricultural holding is brought to bear on the process of developing alternative production and living strategies. The absence of severe weather conditions, pest populations and weed species and the presence of favourable soils, good supplies of water and appropriate crop species, structure the (re)productive strategies of indivuduals and institutions. While the instrumental value of such ecological capital is employed directly by the producer, its symbolic value can also influence his or her possibility space.

Taking another example from the British context, the assessment of applications for the Department of Environment Food and Rural Affairs' (DEFRA) 'Countryside Stewardship Scheme' (CSS), involves the Farming and Rural Conservation Agency's assessors in completing a checklist of environmental features. Each application is scored in relation to the existence, quantity and quality of features which the CSS aims to conserve. The higher the score the more likely the application is to proceed. This feature of the CSS carries recognition of the roles and agendas of other actors within different socioenvironmental institutions. The values implicit in the scoring system depend on the work of other government and non-government organisations such as the regional nature conservation agency, English Nature and the County Wildlife Trusts. The local or bioregional context is also of great importance as scoring for features of ecological importance is linked to the location of such features in relation to the list of conservation priorities set out by English Nature for the different 'natural areas' (or bioregions) of the country.

Geographical and cultural context can also be important actors in alternative food networks, when local or regional identity is attached to particular products – regional cheeses and wines are good examples. A farmer may produce one of the world's best sparkling white wines, if they do not produce it in the Champagne region of France, however, the product cannot be marketed as Champagne. In Spain, the indigenous black pig or *cerdo iberico* enjoys a great reputation for producing the very best *pata negra* ham, but this can only be accomplished through traditional, extensive production in the *dehesa* of southern Spain. Within alternative food networks, the cultural resonance of particular species, products, landscapes or geographical regions can be a key to the success of alternative enterprises.

Activities associated with the establishment and functioning of alternative food networks are influenced by, and influence, the media. At the level of the individual producer, a brief glance through any of the farming press will soon reveal particular frames of reference through which specific issues are aligned with more persistent areas of agricultural interest. Biological pest control methods, for example, can be aligned with current debates on the pesticide treadmill and the fate of regional wildlife. Rare breeds and organic production may be linked into strategies for overcoming public scepticism about the safety of eating certain products. While the individual may not, initially, show any particular interest in specific aspects of their mode and conditions of existence, when an aspect is framed in the context of a more persistent social issue, receiving a good deal of media and thus public attention, benefit may be had from emphasising, or in some cases glossing over, the resonance of the particular with the general. In this way, over time, the media can both enable and constrain the activities of networks and their members, through their (re)construction of discourse.

We have already covered the role of industry institutions through the example of national organic standards bodies such as the Soil Association. Registering with the Association as an organic producer entitles the farmer to employ the Soil Association's organic standard symbol as a powerful actor in his or her strategy of resistance. In the context of growing public concern about issues of food safety, the organic standard symbol has come to be seen by many as a reliable assurance of safety and quality. We have also noted, however, that the organics network is not immune to penetration by large scale capital, that while it may respond to deteriorating conditions of existence it offers no refuge from the social impacts of economic globalisation.

Here, we must also mention the fact that some of the central institutional complexes of the global economy may also be enrolled as facilitative actors in the personal networks that producers construct in pursuance of their strategies of resistance. Of growing importance is the 'information superhighway', where the global and local are fused in the virtual world of computers and digital communications technology. Computerised networking, a lynch pin in the (re)productive strategies of global finance capital, also links together institutions and individuals involved in alternative networks, creating space for the discourse and organisation of resistance.

The contradictions involved in incorporating the institutions of economic globalisation into networks of resistance are perhaps most obvious in the financial sector. Banks often provide the necessary start-up capital for alternative food enterprises, so that a portion of the production must be devoted to the payment of interest. Similarly, for those that have grown tired of the industrial way of life and have the means to opt out of the industrial mode of existence, interest on investments may play a significant role in producing a viable and fulfilling lifestyle. In this situation, the profits from other activities – perhaps activities occurring at a great distance, under socially dubious production relations with problematic environmental impacts – act in support of what is claimed locally to be a model of social and ecological propriety. On the other hand, there are other actors and networks available to the producer, which may not entail such compromise.

Charities, trusts, support groups and co-operatives are all represented in the growing array of alternative food networks. Some may constitute alternative food networks in and of themselves. These and other NGOs also play supporting roles in producers' networks, as do religious, kinship and community institutions, the latter being particular important in the periphery, where access to state or market institutions and actors is usually limited. Reciprocal labour and equipment sharing agreements and village- or church-based community infrastructural projects may all figure highly in the alternative networks of producers in the periphery. In the Centre, experiments in community supported agriculture may allow farmers to improve their cash-flow and financial viability, through the receipt of up-front payments for regularly delivered produce in the coming season. Box schemes make it easier to budget with regular income to offset expenditure, while Local Exchange and Trading Schemes (LETS) may greatly reduce the necessity for a wide range of cash transactions.

Besides the obvious economic benefits of schemes such as those just mentioned, the interpersonal and inter-group contact involved in the process of networking also implies space for the development of discourses of resistance. While discourse is continually transforming and transformed, for the individuals and groups that involve themselves in the process, discourse coalitions can provide ontological security (though, of course, also insecurity) that acts as a kind of 'social glue' (Shackley, 1997), holding together networks of people with diverse livelihoods/lifestyles, yet a common interest in disassociating themselves from the production, distribution or consumption of industrially produced, ecologically and socially damaging, globally sourced food.

While the preceding review provides an insight into some of the actors that may be brought together in networks of resistance, it is far from exhaustive. Nevertheless, it does provide an initial guide as to some of the constituents and dynamics of alternative food networks. The complexion of alternative food networks will vary from person to person, place to place and time to time. The uneven development that results from the successes and failures of all networks of existence, imparts particular characteristics to regions and cultures, which may prove useful in developing more appropriate, culturally and ecologically resonant public policy (see Grove-White, 1996 and Marsden et al., 1997, *inter alia*).

So what are the roles that we as academics can play in understanding alternative food networks and socioenvironmental spaces, and promoting them as important options for an uncertain future? To answer this question we can draw on the insights already revealed by the theoretical, conceptual and empirical discussion so far. Before we do so, however, it will be useful to take a brief look at the development and current status of agricultural policy in Europe and some of the options for change that are being discussed.

Sustainable Agriculture and the European Union

The European Common Agricultural Policy was established with two key objectives in mind: European food self-sufficiency and the maintenance of a vibrant rural society. These objectives were to be achieved through pricing policy. However, in the context of significant contrasts among the agrarian structures of member states, the lion's share of subsidies were reaped by the largest farms of the most highly industrialised nations. Under the influence of production subsidies, such enterprises embarked on a period of rapid industrialisation.

In the first ten years of the CAP, the then European Economic Community achieved virtual self-sufficiency in terms of cereal production, due largely to an average annual price increase of 14 per cent (Parra Orellana, 1993). However, by the end of the 1970s production and storage costs were so high that surpluses had to be subsidised before they could be sold on the world market, which led to serious distortions in world market prices for the subsidised commodities.

As a result, production subsidies came to be seen as the central issue of concern during the Uruguay round of the GATT negotiations. The end of the 1970s and early 1980s also brought recognition of the increasingly severe impact of intensive, industrialised agriculture on the European environment, which, when added to the concerns of farmers surrounding possible cuts in price subsidies and those of consumers concerning continual price rises, prompted the reform of the CAP in the early 1990s.

In 1991, the European Commission published a document on the evolution and future of the CAP which recommended that reform should take account of the following issues:

- the double role of farmers as producers and environmental stewards
- the need to maintain a sufficient number of family farms in order to preserve the unique nature of the farmed environment
- alternative economic activities should be promoted to achieve rural development
- extensification and environmentally-friendly farming should be further promoted
- CAP funds should go directly to support farming incomes.

The final reforms, implemented in 1992, involved: important reductions in cereals and dairy product prices; control of production through the institution of compulsory set-aside; premia for extensive production and the conservation of landscape, flora and fauna; and compensation payments for income lost due to price reductions. Nevertheless, the de-coupling of subsidies from production was far from completed, an issue likely to be pressed during current World Trade Organisation negotiations, which will seek further significant reductions in all barriers to global free trade. In addition, while set-aside is taking significant amounts of land out of production, it appears to pay little attention to the nature conservation potential of the land which is actually set aside.

One of the premises of the Commission's 1991 recommendations for reform referred to the 'socially and ecologically integrating' character of small family farms, yet the 1992 reforms provide only quantitative environmental instruments, aimed at securing a reduction in the hectarage under cultivation. The quality, or nature conservation potential, of the land set aside from cultivation appears almost an irrelevance and as a result set-aside schemes, like earlier production subsidies, have been monopolised by large, highly intensive holdings, where the nature conservation potential is often limited due to the cumulative impact of years of deep cultivation, chemical inputs and field consolidation.

Today the pressure for further reforms is increasing. External pressure will be exerted during the 1999 WTO meeting. Urgency is also imperative because of the proposed Eastern Enlargement of the European Union to include states with even greater numbers of small-scale land holdings, which would require significant and possibly unfundable subsidies given the current character of the CAP. Internal pressures are also on the increase, with production estimates beyond the year 2000 indicating large surpluses for commodities that remain unregulated. In addition, the growing importance of issues associated with rural development such as the environment, loss of community and unemployment cannot be ignored as concern extends from those living with such problems in rural areas, to the wider society at large. Indeed, as has been noted, we have already witnessed the emergence of environmental social movements responding to issues such as the perceived cruelty of animal exports from the UK, for example, or the discourse of distrust surrounding the risks of genetically modified organisms and antibiotics in agriculture.

Thus, it is not surprising that some commentators have suggested that member states will only agree to continue funding the CAP if it delivers values or services of interest to the European public at large (Zeeuw and Sanchez, 1997).

Proposals were suggested in 1996 for the transformation of the CAP into a Common Agricultural and Rural Policy for Europe, aimed at promoting economically viable and environmentally sustainable agriculture and the integrated development of the Union's rural areas (Buckwell, 1996). The policy mechanisms for achieving this included: market stabilisation, environmental and cultural landscape payments, rural development incentives and transitional adjustment assistance. However, the Commission's own report was less radical, representing a continuation of the 1992 reforms, reducing prices further and involving cross compliance for environmental initiatives (European Commission, 1998). The reforms finally agreed by member states in March 1999 were even less far reaching.

How then might an alternative approach to rural development informed by the preceding discussion differ from that taken to date by the European Union?

Agroecology

In previous publications we have sought to define agroecology as more than just another scientific discipline. We see it more as a theoretical orientation, following in the footsteps of previous intellectual endeavours aimed at counteracting the perceived negative impacts of capitalist expansion (Sevilla Guzmán and Woodgate, 1997). Stemming from a critique of modern industrial society and its bases in conventional, disciplinary science and capitalism, agroecology represents an attempt to break free from the fossil-fuel trap in which modern society has become ensnared and promotes ecological – rather than industrial – management of natural resources and agricultural production. It represents a political endeavour as well as an intellectual challenge and draws on both 'red' and 'green' traditions in constructing its agenda for progress.

As a point of departure from conventional agricultural research and development approaches we have defined agroecology as promoting:

> the *ecological management* of biological systems through *collective forms of social action*, which pursue *coevolutionary pathways* that address the needs of society/nature without jeopardising the integrity of society/nature. This is to be achieved by *systemic strategies* that promote the development of more equitable and flexible forces and relations of production, and modes of consumption and distribution. Central to such strategies is the local dimension where we encounter *endogenous potential* encoded within landscapes and knowledge systems (local, peasant or indigenous) that demonstrate and promote both *ecological and cultural diversity*. Such diversity should form the starting point for alternative agricultures and for the establishment of dynamic yet sustainable rural societies.

As we have already detailed, the modern, industrial context in which agroecology has arisen, has seriously degraded the bases and mechanisms of renewability of many pre-industrial agroecosystems, whether locally and directly through the development of high chemical input, energy intensive monocropping systems, the fragmentation and isolation of habitat and the acculturation of ecologically adapted cultures or, more globally, reflected in phenomena such as acid precipitation, climate change and the loss of biological and cultural diversity. At the same time, however, as we saw in our review of alternative styles of agriculture and as demonstrated by the resistance of many indigenous cultures to the imposition of industrial imperatives through government policies and market forces, globalisation does create spaces for the maintenance, rehabilitation and development of more sustainable rural livelihoods. The objective of agroecology then, should be to work together with grassroots communities and relevant governmental and non-governmental organisations in order to identify and support alternative food network initiatives, starting from an analysis of the ways in which situated people in traditional and alternative cultures capture the agricultural potential of both social and biological systems in the course of their coevolution. Such potential is represented within knowledge systems.

Local, peasant or indigenous knowledge systems tend to differ from scientific knowledge in that they are practical and encoded in culture, rather than theoretical and abstract. Agroecology should aim to help people rescue, revitalise and develop local, peasant or indigenous knowledge systems in order to re-empower themselves to take control of their own (re)production. To achieve this, it will also be important to demonstrate the wisdom[5] of such systems in the context of their specific biophysical and social settings and, we believe, to seek suitable mechanisms for their defence in the face of capitalist development, both in respect of its negation of local knowledge and, ironically, its co-optation such as in the registration of genetic property rights by transnational corporations or what has been called 'bio-piracy', for example.

Every agroecosystem has an endogenous potential in terms of the production of materials and information (knowledge and genetic codes) that arises from the historical trajectory of society/nature in the locality (coevolution). Such potential tends to have been masked and degraded both in its social and ecological aspects by processes of industrial modernisation. Agroecology should therefore seek to utilise and develop further this endogenous potential rather than negating it and replacing it with industrial structures and processes. The social aspects of endogenous potential may be brought to light in the struggles of local groups to resist global processes of industrial modernisation, while the ecological dimensions are to be found in the genetic diversity and ecological dynamics of the agroecosystems that such groups seek to maintain or reclaim. It is our belief that the role of agroecology is not only to investigate the technical aspects of endogenous potential, but also to engage with the political and ethical struggles of local groups that seek to maintain it together with their cultural identity.

The further development of endogenous potential depends upon the ecological management of biological systems. This differs from the industrial model as it tends to reinforce rather than override or replace the mechanisms which provide for the (re)production of nature/society. One of the prime characteristics of agroecology should be its respect for the ecological structures and processes from which, as an associated species, we may achieve social reproduction through collective forms of social action. In the context of the pursuit of alternative pathways for the development of food and agriculture networks, collective forms of social action relate to the relationships we enter into with those social groups that are attempting to come to terms with industrial modes of production, consumption and distribution. As we have noted, such groups include citizens of the centre as well as the periphery: the urban and the rural and the emerging networks which link them and their hopes for the future. They also include the enlightened policy makers and institutions that may form part of alternative food networks.

Collective forms of social action that link rural communities, local consumers, academics and relevant policy-related institutions, can be employed in the generation and deployment of systemic strategies in pursuit of socioenvironmentally beneficial coevolution. The social factors that we need to take into account include: ethnic, gendered, epistemological, ethical, religious, political and economic elements of agroecosystems. Similarly, we need to take account of a broad range of biophysical factors such as water, soil, solar energy and plant and animal species, in terms of the ways in which they interact not only among themselves but also with human actors and social institutions. Systemic strategies require an holistic approach to understanding the energy, material and information flows generated in processes of production, consumption and circulation within and between systems and networks, while attempting to guide coevolutionary processes in a more beneficial direction implies making ethical decisions.

The current fashion for participation, while recently criticised as an instrument of globalisation, has opened up small but significant spaces for promoting the agroecological agenda and, in this context, agroecology must engage with enlightened policy makers and authorities in order to promote more integrated, holistic and pluralist approaches to rural development, which respond to the opportunities and constraints of specific people and places, rather than imposing blanket models for 'sustainable development' which respond to the needs of capital. We must be able to communicate effectively with the people responsible for policy formulation and implementation, as well as with farmers.

A Final Discussion and an Agenda for Agroecological Research

Given our appreciation of the implications for agriculture and natural resource management of the further, unchecked development of the global economy in the context of European policy indecision, we offer the following proposal for an agroecological research agenda for Europe.

Analysis of emergent social structures in the different spheres of human activity and experience relating to agrarian life show, as a result of the globalisation process, a clear tendency to organise their key functions and processes around networks of actors held together by the social glue of shared dissatisfaction with the dominant paradigm of industrialised food production, processing, distribution and consumption. The multidimensionality of globalisation produces internal contradictions, which we seek to employ politically in our proposal, following the formulation of Beck (1998: 28–32). The power structures generated around the agro-food complexes of highly industrialised agricultural commodities are substantially modifying production processes towards styles of agriculture which are highly prejudicial to the material conditions of our existence while, at the same time, they are also leading to the erosion of local knowledge concerning the management of natural resources, prejudicing the accomplishment of traditional agricultural tasks, fragmenting traditional social institutions and diminishing collective social action.

The threats to the future of rural livelihoods presented by globalisation are clearly linked to the ideology of globalism (Beck, 1998): a kind of liberalism writ large, which reduces – through monocausal economistic methods – the multidimensional character of globalisation to the single dimension of the economy. Nevertheless, as Beck has pointed out, there is another phenomenon of globalisation: the social construction of a global consciousness: thinking globally as part of a 'global village'. Beck suggests that analysis of the multiple dimensions of globalisation cannot be understood as a unified phenomenon unless they are first understood individually and in terms of their inter-relationships (1998: 29). In this way, we can open up spaces and perspectives for political activity in order to confront the de-politicising infatuation with globalisation which is central to the ideology of globalism. In terms of agroecology and sustainable rural futures for Europe, we believe it important to identify an agenda which promotes the following activities:

- Involvement with networks of producers, communities, government agencies and NGOs in order to identify and support alternative food and agricultural initiatives
- Defending the concepts of ecological and cultural diversity as an important inheritance for future generations
- Becoming involved in the ethical and political struggles of marginalised local groups which are attempting to maintain endogenous potential and local identity
- Helping in the revitalisation and development of local, peasant or indigenous knowledge systems
- Utilising and developing endogenous potential, instead of negating it and substituting it with industrial structures and processes, by employing the agroecological perspective through participatory action research techniques
- Participation in the on-farm development of ecological techniques and demonstration of their potential for extension through the identification and support of 'agroecological beacons' – working examples of locally appropriate rural resource management systems and food networks
- Promoting self-sufficient systems with the capacity for generating and integrating fair trading networks
- Demonstrating the fallacy of genetic engineering as an element of ecological management.

What agroecology lays bare is the fact that sustainable rural innovations or development can only proceed from a sound understanding of the continual (re)production of the social, cultural, political and ecological, as well as the economic structure of the European reality and from a basis in the ecological, rather than industrial, management of natural resources. The framework of agroecology is suggested as a first step in this direction.

Notes

1. The diagram draws on ideas from historical materialism and more recent Green Marxist approaches (Marx, *Economic and Philosophical Manuscripts of 1844* and *A Critique of Political Economy* (1859); Parsons, 1977; O'Connor, 1998; Benton, in Benton and Redclift, 1994; Dickens, 1997).
2. We have translated this concept from the Spanish text, where it is termed '*globalidad*'. We might also use the word 'globalness', however, the concept is perhaps best summed up in the notion of 'thinking globally' in the context of the green maxim 'think global act local'.
3. In the bibliography some of the key works of these authors are listed. Nevertheless, there are many scholars linked to this type of work, such as Ehrenfield Pfeiffer, Hans Rush, Faould Lamaire, Jean Boucher, Claude Aubert, Mokiti Okada and Francis Caboussou, that have developed partial proposals for more effective resources management or which complement aspects of the more holistic works identified above. Few if any offer global proposals however (cf. Tate, 1994: 11–26, and Bonilha, 1992: 15–26).
4. Also known as 'ecological' or 'biological' agriculture.
5. This should not be taken as a signal that all aspects of local knowledge systems are ecologically and socially sound. Agroecology should view all claims to truth in a critical light.

Bibliography

Allen, P.M. (1996), 'Evolution, Sustainability and Industrial Metabolism', in Robert Ayers and Udo Simonis (eds), *Industrial Metabolism: Restructuring for Sustainable Development*, Tokyo, New York and Paris: UN University Press, pp. 78–100.

Altieri, M.A. (1987), *Agroecology: the Scientific Basis of Alternative Agriculture*, Boulder, Colorado: Westview Press.

Altieri, Miguel A. (1991), 'Por qué estudiar la agricultura tradicional', in *Agroecología y Desarrollo*, **Año I** (1), 16–24.

Archetti, E.P. and S. Aass (1978), 'Peasant Studies: An Overview', in Howard Newby (ed.), *International Perspectives in Rural Sociology*, New York: John Wiley.

Balfour, E. (1943), *The Living Soil*, London: Faber and Faber.

Barahona, R. (1987), 'Conocimiento campesino y sujeto social campesino', in *Revista Mexicana de Sociología*, **49**, 167–90.

Bartra, R. and G. Otero (1988), 'Crisis Agraria y Diferenciación Social en México', *Revista Mexicana de Sociología*, **Año L** (1), Enero–Marzo, 13–49.

Beck, U. (1998), *¿Qué es la Globalización? Falacias del Globalismo, Respuestas a la Globalización*, Barcelona: Paidós.

Berlín, B., D.E. Breedlove and P.H. Raven (1973), 'General Principles of Classification and Nomenclature Folk Biology', in *American Anthropologist*, **75**, 214–42.

Boden, R.F. (1999), OCIS consultant, Mrow Organic Farm Services, personal comment.

Boeringa, R. (1980), *Alternative Methods of Agriculture*, Amsterdam: Elsevier.

Bonilha, J. (1992), *Fundamentos da agricultura ecologica: sobrevivência e qualidade de vida*, Sao Paulo: Nobel.

Brown, L.R., C.H. Flavin, H. French, J.N. Abramovitz, C. Bright, S. Dunn, G. Gardner, J. Jacobson, J. Mitchell, A. Platt McGinn, M. Renner and J. Tuxill (1998), *The State of the World 1998*, Spanish edition, Barcelona: Icaria.

Bryant, B. (ed.) (1995), *Environmental Justice: Issues, Policies and Solutions*, Washington DC: Island Press.

Buckwell, A. (1996), *A Common Agricultural and Rural Policy for Europe*, Wye, Kent: Wye College Press.

Bulmer, A.R. (1965), 'Review of Navajo Indian Ethnoentomology', in *American Anthropologist*, **67**, 1564–66.

Canuto, J.C. (1998), *Agricultura ecológica en Brasil. Perspectivas socioecológicas*, Ph.D. thesis, ISEC, University of Cordoba, Spain.

Chambers, R. (1983), *Rural Development: Putting the last first*, London: IT Publications.

Chambers, R., A. Pacey and L.-A. Thrupp (1989), *Farmer First: Farmer Innovation and Agricultural Research*, London: Intermediate Technology Publications.

Christany et al. (1986), 'Traditional Agroforestry in West Java: The Pekarangan (Homegarden) and Kebun-Talun (Annual Perennial Rotation) Cropping Systems', in G. Marten (ed.), *Traditional Agriculture in Southeast Asia*, Boulder: Westview Press, pp. 132–56.

Collier, G.A. (1994), *Basta! Land and the Zapatista Rebellion in Chiapas*, Oakland CA: Food First.

Cooper, D., R. Vellve and H. Hobbelink (1992), *Growing Diversity: Genetic resources and local food security*, London: IT Publications.

Darier, É. (1998), *Discourses of the Environment*, Oxford: Blackwell.

de Boef, W., K. Amanor, K. Wellard and A. Bebbington (1993), *Cultivating Knowledge: Genetic diversity, farmer experimentation and crop research*, London: IT Publications.

Dobson, A. (1992), *Green Political Thought*, London: Routledge.

Esteva, G. and I. Illich (1986), 'El Desarrollo: Metáforo, Mito, Amenaza', *Tecno-política*, Mexico DF: Sorremans.

European Commission (1998), *Agenda 2000: the Legislative Proposals*, Brussels: European Commission.

Fukuoka, M. (1995), *La senda natural del cultivo. Teoría y práctica de una filosofía verde*, Valencia: Tarapión.

Fernández Durán, R. (1993), *La Explosión del Desorden: La metrópoli como espacio de la crisis global*, Madrid: Fundamentos.

Fernández Durán, R. (1996), *Contra la Europa del Capital*, Madrid: TALASA.

Foucault, M. (1988), 'The Ethic of Care for the Self as a Practice of Freedom', in James Bernauer and David Rasmussen (eds), *The Final Foucault*, Cambridge MA: MIT Pres, pp. 11–20.

Gauthier, R. and G. Woodgate (1998), 'Coevolutionary Agroecology: a policy-oriented analysis of socioenvironmental dynamics, with special reference to the forest margins of North Lampung, Indonesia', *INTECOL 98*, 19–24 July, Florence.

Giddens, A. (1979), *Central Problems in Social Theory*, London: Macmillan.

Gliessman, S.R. (ed.) (1978), *Seminarios Regionales Sobre Agroecosistemas con Enfasis en el Estudio de Tecnología Agrícola Regional*, Cárdenas, Tabasco, Mexico: CSAT.

Gliessman, S.R. (ed.) (1989), *Agroecology. Researching the Ecological Basis for Sustainable Agriculture*, New York: Springer-Verlag.

Gonzalez de Molina, M. and J. Martinez-Alier (eds) (1992), *Historia y Ecología*, Madrid: Marcial Pons.

Grove-White, R. (1996), 'Environmental Knowledge and Public Policy Needs', in S. Lash, B. Szerszynski and B. Wynne, *Environment and Modernity: Towards a New Ecology*, London: Routledge.

Guha, R. and J. Martinez-Alier (1997), *Varieties of Environmentalism: Essays North and South*, London: Earthscan.

Hecht, S. (1987), 'The evolution of the Agroecological Thought', in M.A. Altieri, *Agroecology: the Scientific Basis of Alternative Agriculture*, Boulder, Colorado: Westview Press.

Hechter, M. (1977), *Internal Colonialism: The Celtic Fringe in British National Development, 1536–1966*, Berkley and Los Angeles: University of California Press.

Howard, A. (1940), *An Agricultural Testament*, London: Oxford University Press.

IFOAM (1989), *Basic Standards of Organic Agriculture*, Ouagadougou, Burkina Faso: IFOAM.

Ingold, T. (1992), 'Culture and the Perception of the Environment', in E. Croll and D. Parkin (eds), *Bush Base-Forest Farm: Culture, Environment and Development*, London: Routledge.

Latour, B. (1993), *We have never been modern*, Brighton: Harvester Wheatsheaf.

Latour, B. (1994), 'Pragmatologies', *American Behavioral Scientist*, **37** (6), 791–808.

Law, J. (1986), 'On the methods of long-distance control: vessels, navigation and the Portuguese route to India', *Sociological Review Monograph*, **32**, 234–63.

Law, J. (ed.) (1991), *A Sociology of Monsters: Essays on Power, Technology and Domination*, London: Routledge.

Law, J. (1994), *Organising Modernity*, Oxford: Blackwell.

Leff, E. (1986), *Ecología y Capital*, México: Siglo XXI.

Leff, E. (1994), *Ecología y Capital. Racionalidad ambiental, democracia participativa y desarrollo sustentable*, México: Siglo XXI, pp. 320–21.

Lemkow, L. and F. Buttel (1983), *Los Movimientos Ecologistas*, Madrid: Mezquita.

Lievegoed, B.J.C. (1977), *La Espiga*, Madrid: Editorial Rudolf Steiner.

Marsden, T., J. Murdoch and S. Abram (1997), 'Rural Sustainability in Britain: the social basis of sustainability', in M. Redclift and G. Woodgate (eds), *The International Handbook of Environmental Sociology*, Cheltenham, UK and Northampton, MA, USA: Edward Elgar.

Martinez-Alier, J. (1995), *De la Economía Ecológica al Ecologismo Popular*, 1st edition, Montevideo: REDES. Barcelona: Icaria.

Mollison, B. and D. Holmgren (1978), *Permaculture I: a perennial agriculture for human settlements*, Tyalgum, Australia: Tagari Publications.

Mollison, B. and D. Holmgren (1979), *Permaculture II: practical design for town and country in permanent agriculture*, Tyalgum, Australia: Tagari Publications.

Mollison, B. and R.M. Slay (1991), *Introduction to Permaculture*, Tyalgum, Australia: Tagari Publications.

Morrish, C. (1999), OCIS consultant, c/o Elm Farm Research Centre, personal comment.

Norgaard, R.B. (1984), 'Coevolutionary Agricultural Development', *Economic Development and Cultural Change*, **32** (3), 525–46.

Norgaard, R.B. (1987), 'The Epistemological Basis of Agroecology', in M. Altieri (ed.), *Agroecology: The Scientific Basis of Alternative Agriculture*, Boulder, Colorado: Westview Press, pp. 21–27.

Norgaard, R.B. (1994), *Development Betrayed: the end of progress and a coevolutionary revisioning of the future*, New York and London: Routledge.

O'Connor, J. (1998), *Natural Causes: Essays in Ecological Marxism*, New York and London: Guilford.

Palerm, A. (1980), 'Antropólogos y campesinos: los límites del capitalismo', in *Antropología y Marxismo*, México: Nueva Imagen.

Parra Orellana, J. (1993), *Estudios de viabilidad de sistemas agroecológicos en la provincia de Cádiz*, Córdoba, Spain: ISEC y CEPA.

PRATEC (1993), *Afirmación Cultural Andina*, Lima, Perú: PRATEC.

Rangan, H. (1996), 'Forma Chipko to Uttaranchal', in R. Peet and M. Watts (eds), *Liberation Ecologies*, New York and London: Routledge.

Reijentes, C., B. Haverkort and A. Waters-Bayer (1992), *Farming for the Future: an Introduction to Low-External-Input and Sustainable Agriculture*, London: Macmillan Press.

Rodale, J. (1945), *Farming and Gardening with Compost*, New Delhi: Adair.

Rostow, W.W. (1960), *The Stages of Economic Growth. A Non-Communist Manifesto*, Cambridge: Cambridge University Press.

Sachs, W. (ed.) (1992), *The Development Dictionary: A Guide to Knowledge as Power*, London: Zed Books.

San Martín, J. (1997), *Uk"amäpi. Así nomás es pues*, La Paz, Bolivia: AGRUCO.

Scoones, I. and M. Thompson (1994), *Beyond Farmer First*, London: IT Publications.

Sevilla Guzmán, E. (1983), 'Una breve incursión por la otra sociología rural', in Howard Newby and E. Sevilla Guzmán, *Introducción a la Sociología Rural*, Madrid: Alianza.

Sevilla Guzmán, E. and K. Heisel (eds) (1988), *Anarquismo y Movimiento Jornalero en Andalucía*, Córdoba: Ediciones del Ayutamiento.

Sevilla Guzmán, E. and ISEC Team (1995), 'The Role of Farming Systems Research/Extension in Guiding Low Input Systems towards Sustainability: an Agroecological Approach for Andalusia', in J.B. Dent and M.J. McGregor (eds), *Rural and Farming Systems Analysis: European Perspectives*, Wallingford: CAB International.

Sevilla Guzmán, E. and G. Woodgate (1997), 'Sustainable Rural Development: Forma industrial Agriculture to Agroecology', in M. Redclift and G. Woodgate (eds), *The International Handbook of Environmental Sociology*, Cheltenham, UK and Northampton, MA, USA: Edward Elgar.

Shackley, S. (1997), 'Trust in Models? The mediating and transformative role of computer models in environmental discourse', in M. Redclift and G. Woodgate (eds), *The International Handbook of Environmental Sociology*, Cheltenham, UK and Northampton, MA, USA: Edward Elgar, pp. 237–60.

Shanin, T. (1971), *Peasant and Peasant Societies*, Harmondsworth: Penguin.

Shanin, T. (1990), *Peasant Societies*, Oxford: Blackwell.

Steiner, R. (1985), *Geisteswissenschaftliche Grundlagen zum Gedeihen der Landwirtschaft. Landwirtschaftlicher Kurs*, (Koberwitz bei Breslau 1924) Dornoach, Switzerland: Rudolf Steiner Verlag.

Sunkel, O. and N. Gligo (eds) (1980), *Estilos de desarrollo y medio ambiente en la América Latina*, Mexico DF: Fondo de Cultura Económica.

Tate, W. (1994), 'The development of the organic industry and international perspective', in N. Lampkin and S. Padel (eds), *The Economics of Organic Farming: An International Perspective*, Wallingford: CAB International, pp. 11–26.

Toledo, V.M. (1985), *Ecología y autosuficiencia alimentaria*, México: Siglo XXI.

Toledo, V.M. (1986), 'Vertientes de la Ecología Política', in *Ecología Política*.

Toledo, V.M. (1989), 'The Ecological Rationality of Peasant Production', in Miguel Altieri and S. Hecht (eds), *Agroecology and Small-Farm Development*, Boca Raton, FL, USA: CRC Press.

Toledo, V.M. (1990), 'The Ecological Rationality of Peasant Production', in M.A. Altieri and S. Hecht (eds), *Agroecology and Small-farm Development*, Boca Raton, FL, USA: CRC Press.

Toledo, V.M. (1991), 'La resistencia ecológica del campesinado mexicano', in Memoria de Angel Palerm, *Ecología Política*, **1**.

Toledo, V.M. (1993), 'La racionalidad ecológica de la producción campesina', in E. Sevilla Guzmán and M. González de Molina (eds), *Ecología, Campesinado e Historia*, Madrid: Ediciones la Piqueta, pp. 197–218.

Wallerstein, I. (1974), *The Modern World System*, New York: Academic Press.

Warman, A. (1988), 'Los Campesinos en el Umbral de un Nuevo Milenio', *Revista Mexicana de Sociología*, **Año L** (1), Enero–Marzo, 3–12.

Whatmore, S. and L. Thorne (1997), 'Nourishing Networks: Alternative geographies of food', in D. Goodman and M. Watts (eds), *Globalizing Food*, London and New York: Routledge.

Wilken, G.C. (1987), *Good Farmers*, Berkeley: University of California Press.

Williams, B. (1980), 'Pictorial Representation of Soils in the Valley of Mexico: Evidence from Codex Vergara', *Geoscience and Man*, **21**, 51–60.

Williams, R. (1980), *Problems in Materialism and Culture*, London: Verso.

Wolf, E.R. (1982), *Europe and the People Without History*, Berkeley: University of California Press.

Woodgate, G. (1991), 'Agroecological Possibilities and Organisational Limits: some initial impressions from a Mexican case study', in D. Goodman and M. Redclift (eds), *Environment and Development in Latin America: the politics of sustainability*, Manchester: Manchester University Press.

Woodgate, G.R. and Redclift, M.R. (1998), 'From a "Sociology of Nature" to Environmental Sociology: Beyond Social Construction', *Environmental Values*, **7**, 3–24.

Wortmann, M. (1977), *Konventionelle und Biologisch-dynamische Landwitz-schaft*, Darmstadt: Verlag Lebendige Erde.

Zeeuw, A. de and B.K. Sanchez (1997), *European Agricultural Policy: Between Reform and Enlargement*, Centre for European Policy Studies.

[30]

Conclusions: rural development as 'real' ecological modernisation?

Introduction

Section 3 of the book has taken a markedly different perspective in examining the character of rural development. It has placed emphasis upon the ways in which rural and agricultural 'natures' *may* be more effectively incorporated into our understanding of rural change, and, particularly how this might lead to more sustainable rural development in the future. The exploration has attempted to bring together an appreciation of rural development practices and prospects on the one hand with theories of agro-ecology and ecological modernisation on the other. There has been a tendency for the latter bodies of theory to be far too restrictive, with agro-ecology often too readily associated with organic producer movements, and with ecological modernisation being associated with either industrial sectors and/or simplistic market-based assumptions of win-win environmental outcomes. I would contend, having taken the particular analytical journey displayed in this volume, that a focus upon rural development has much to benefit from the critical development of both bodies of theory. In addition, both bodies of theory, when examined critically can help to design a more effective and engaging rural development paradigm. One which progresses the intellectual and well as practical 'condition' of rural sustainability.

In the foregoing chapters of this last section of the book, moreover, I have been attempting to focus as much upon the obstacles now inherent in the rural development paradigm, as upon the real opportunities. In the chapter on short supply chains (Chapter 10) we see the evolutionary risks associated with alternative food supply chain developments; and in the case of organics in the UK (Chapter 11) we see that the overall contribution of the rise of organics and its relationships to sustainable rural development and agro-ecology are still contingent upon the reorganisation and regulation of supply chains more generally. There are, in short, obstacles and pitfalls in progressing *real* rural and sustainable development benefits, even where there is a growth of demand and supply of more sustainable food and other rural products and services.

238   *The Condition of Rural Sustainability*

These alternative rural development activities (as outlined in chapter 9) have to compete with the professional, economic, political and scientific logics explored in the earlier two sections of the book- the agro-industrial and the post-productivist logics. We have seen, for instance, that even when the post-productionist logic adopts a more environmental protectionist agenda (Chapter 8), the particular ways it does this both in compartmentalising the environmental problems and solutions and in restricting its appreciation of the role of agriculture, tends to continue to fragment the establishment of real and more viable alternatives from taking root in the countryside. In short we have to be critically aware of the rhetoric of sustainable development and ecological modernisation. And we have to apply an equivalent level of intellectual rigour to these discourses, as to those associated with the agro-industrial, post-productivist and post-modernist perspectives. This is a rich intellectual 'battleground.' To borrow Norman Long's phrasing: a 'battlefield of knowledge' (Long and Long 1992).

In this final chapter, I will explore a series of integrating concepts which begin to build a more rigorous and critical rural development perspective through the theoretical prism of what I term 'real' ecological modernisation.

Over recent years the sub-disciplines of rural sociology, development studies and the newly emerging social science of the environment have been attempting to address many of the same types of theoretical and empirical questions albeit from different starting points. The rural sociology of advanced economies has for a long time now drawn very productively from the field of development studies, even if both have remained quite distinct sub-disciplines with their own communities of interest and professional publication outlets. Similarly, the growth of work on the sociology of the environment, particularly in the European and North American context, has attempted to very much set its own broad agenda, but has done so in ways which have overlapped with the theoretical agenda of the more traditional rural sociology. The latter's increasing ecumenical concern for aspects of rural nature, as almost a 'last refuge' in the process of urban-based modernisation, has meant that it has been the originator of significant theoretical and conceptual impulses into the wider and growing debates which have encapsulated environmental social science. While the latter, it might be argued has taken on a more industrial and urban basis – addressing questions of ecological modernisation for instance – it has also needed to refer to key authors in the older, sister disciplines of rural and development sociology. Indeed, all three sub-areas witness the creative engagement of several key authors who have their origins in rural sociology and anthropology. None of these authors would just regard themselves as rural sociologists; rather they are contributing to wider sociological and geographical debates concerning nature, space and environmental policy (see, for instance, the contributions the Environmental Sociology Handbook, edited by Redclift and Woodgate 1998).

While many may suggest, in a tidy-minded fashion, that these developments represent something of a chaotic and disparate set of conditions which tend to diminish, rather than enhance, the true innovative character of rural sociology of advanced economies; I want, in this chapter, to demonstrate how I beg to differ. Rather, I want to begin to demonstrate how a wider theoretical and conceptual landscape can help to assist contemporary rural sociology in progressing its agenda. I note particularly here the recent assessment of rural sociology by Buttel (2001), where he makes the point that the past decades work on aspects of regulation and globalisation, for instance, has tended to be quite the reverse of the earlier developments of the 1970s and 80s (what was then termed the 'new rural sociology'). He argues for more theoretical innovation to be undertaken. While the past decade or so has demonstrated quite a flurry of rich empirically engaged work (on areas of globalisation for example), actual theoretical development has reached something of a hiatus; with various 'schools' tending to adopt a position along the actor-oriented political-economy axis. Moreover, as Buttel also alludes, this can lead to the rather random/chaotic choice of micro-empirical case studies; with the suggestion that this can begin to lose sight of 'the big picture'. A key question here then is how can a more theoretical agenda be established?

Ecological modernisation, and more sustainable rural development: towards new rural eco-realities.

However critical one might be about arguments associated with the rhetoric of sustainability, it is also the case that writers have pointed to the development, albeit fledgling in some cases, of a more ecologically modernising agenda. This is centrally associated with a European perspective on the development of clean industrial technologies, and the ways in which environmental coalitions and movements begin to affect reluctant state agencies. As I have suggested in the concluding section of this book, these ideas at least deserve some attention with regard to rural development. Indeed, the degree to which we might be entering a new phase of modernisation which would be much more ecological is becoming a central theme in rural and agro-food studies (see Goodman 1999, for instance); and the rural domain is becoming a central field for exploring the role and meaning of social nature debates. Also, as I argue above, many leading writers in the field are also contributing to the development of environmental social science, through publishing in their more recent bespoke journals and research collections.

240   *The Condition of Rural Sustainability*

Now taking Buttel's challenge seriously, and at the same time as the arrival of more effective debates about a new modernisation process, it is necessary in my view to address a central theoretical question. This in macro terms is: *to what extent are we seeing the arrival of a more ecologically modernising process operating in advanced societies, and as part of this, through rural development trends specifically?* Second, if we believe that this is a viable question, then what conceptual development and empirical realities does it suggest with respect to the rural sphere? Taking some empirical and theoretical avenues in the three resource areas of agricultural restructuring, food supply chains and forestry, I want to suggest that the answer to the first question is positive; and then demonstrate, through the definition of some conceptual parameters how we might address the challenge this creates for us in the second.[1] What I suggest we are witnessing is the development of an ecological modernisation process which is significantly different in its character from the early industrial modernisation process. As we saw in the first two sections of this book, the latter, which has by no means completely disappeared is, arguably, less in the ascendancy and is subject to internal and external crisis tendencies (such as food scares, legitimisation and ethical concerns), as well as deep structural tendencies which are seen as increasingly contradictory. Meanwhile social-ecological debates - albeit in a complex and diverse way - are gaining ground in different guises and through different types of social, political and economic practices. While these may confront the former structural changes, associated with globalisation of corporate capital, for instance, they are not, I will argue, simply marginal or subject to the marginalisation effects of corporate states, firms and their established social and political logics. Rather, they may suggest a new centrality for many of the features of rural life that the earlier industrially-based modernisation process tended to marginalise. For instance, aspects of agro-ecological development as part of rural development; the development of decentralised and more sustainable rural communities as a central part of settlement hierarchies; and more mobile and ICT-based sharing of experiences in rural and urban areas. Indeed, we might suggest that one central element of ecological modernisation is the very re-definition of the spatial and social balances between urban and rural living experiences, and about the re-alignment, more specifically, between nature, quality, region and locale producers and consumers for a more ecological rural resource base.

Some may see these notions as going too far. However, I think that we need to at least debate them in such a way as to re-build a more viable and robust rural development perspective which at least begins to suggest how such notions might be more effectively progressed. Indeed, just as with the industrial mode of modernisation, a new ecological paradigm also needs a viable, critical and normatively-engaging social science. This is particularly the case with EM given, as we shall see below, the spatially variable and context dependent ways in which it actually expresses itself. What seems clear is that there is a lack of coherence in EM, one which can be partially or contradictorily adopted and pursued by national, regional and local governments; and one which may need particular confluences of strategic and local interests and actors to operate in new and innovative ways.

Looking at the recent rural sociological, and particularly the environmental social science literature over recent years, one begins to see this tendency being reported. One further key question is how far and fast will it travel, and how do we best equip ourselves as scholars to develop a growing relevance in understanding and mediating its required and contested knowledges?

There are some large questions here. If we are to meet Buttel's challenge it would seem necessary that we have to start looking at these bigger pictures. The 'new rural sociology' and political economy that was established and developed throughout the 1980s and 1990's was built upon the development of an intense and very effective critique of the industrialisation modernisation project (particularly as it related to the agro-food complex). Now we should recognise that the challenge has begun to change; for it is no longer sufficient to critically examine the problems of such ageing 'regimes'. As I suggested in the introduction to the book, and then pursued at various points in it, we need to be reconstructing as well as de-constructing models and frameworks which suggest *how things could work in different and more socio-ecological ways over space and time.* We need to see better how actions and cases at one level can build up into significant projects of change more broadly.

In conclusion, here I will explore a series of key concepts and theoretical formulations which will hopefully begin to build not so much on the diffusion of effort that some might argue we have witnessed, but on some useful integrative themes which will, I believe, yield a more robust and theoretically engaging rural sociology with environmental sociology. This involves, I will argue, the need to re-problematise space and spatial relations (as socio-natural constructions) in our analyses, but to do so in ways which re-engage with the somewhat traditional concepts of *community, regulation, consumption, exclusion, justice, bureaucratisation, professionalisation and expertise, associationalism and responsibility.* By doing this I believe we can build upon the somewhat false, and dare I say now, somewhat futile and oversimplified dualisms between structures and actor strategies and networks, social constructivism and realism, globalisation and localism, economistically determined productionism and culturally confined consumptionism. I will argue that we need more engaging conceptual and theoretical formulations which help and guide us to not only make sense of the 'new ruralities' which confront us, but also allow us to play a more *reconstructivist* as well as *critical interpretive* role in both rural and environmental social science.

Key conceptual starting points: empowering social ecologies

Most recently, I have been engaged in three rather long term projects, which while linked have concerned themselves with quite distinct areas of activity and arenas of natural resource.[1] These are associated with agro-food developments, farming and rural development, and thirdly, and more recently with the forestry sector. In conducting this work with a variety of colleagues I have been made increasingly aware how aspects of what we might term, ecological modernisation are contestably taking hold; albeit interfacing and competing with more established and conventional modernising models. New alternatives, for instance, in food supply chain development – socio-natural networks – are clearly establishing themselves which I would argue are new (although I recognise that a conceptual and empirical challenge here is very much to persuade some of our close colleagues that this is little more than 'old wine in new bottles'). Similarly in the farming field, detailed investigations in England and Wales, as well as in other European regions, exhibit a variable shift toward what we have termed the 'broadening, deepening and regrounding of conventional agricultural practices'. In the forestry sector too, with the slow adoption of common property resource concepts in some European regions, and even in the UK now some recourse to sustainability and social inclusion discourses, we see the traditional, narrow definition of the forestry as productivist rural space beginning to be challenged (Mather 2001; Bishop *et al.* 2002).

Emerging out of these three theoretical and empirical explorations we see, moreover, the need to conceptually progress a rural and environmental sociology which can accommodate and facilitate ecological modernisation. What are then some of these conceptual and theoretical coordinates for a more socio-natural rural sociology? I outline here six such theoretical coordinates making reference to the three rural resource areas of food, farming and forestry.

Environmental and territorial justice

One key feature of current patterns of rural development concern what seems to be greater amounts of economic and geographical uneven development. This is partly exacerbated by the gradual shift, on the part of many nation states, away from explicitly fostering more convergent, balanced, regional economic development. A key feature of extant rural and environmental arenas comes then in needing to address aspects of both territorial and environmental justice. The adoption of sustainable development goals cannot really be progressed unless it begins to deal with spatial uneven development, and particularly how local and regional people's conditions are incorporated into the analysis of how those broader and long term conditions could be improved. A central question to consider, is the extent to which scholars engage with the debates and assumptions of territorial and environmental justice. That is, having identified injustices in the uneven risk, distribution and quality of resources in space, how far should we go in formulating ways of reducing or compensating for this unevenness (see SDRN 2002)? For instance, it is quite clear from our work on forestry and community in South Wales that any attempts by the Forestry Commission to encourage more participation and inclusion in the forested areas is constrained by the quite long history of growing social and spatially based deprivation of the nearby communities, for which the withdrawal of other state services and support structures has played a full part (see Marsden *et al.* 2001b). Similarly, the growing social science research in the areas of food scarcity, and the identification of 'food deserts' – often themselves hidden enclaves in larger, prosperous cities and regions – demonstrates, on the one hand, the acute unevenness of rights to food consumption that the now corporate retailer-led supply chains have reproduced (see Carley *et al.* 2001). The question is, however, not simply the issue of the simple empirical identification of these disparities. It also concerns how an engaging social science of rural development and food formulates alternatives which reduce and combat these. In the rural development field, while many of the grant-aided funding schemes emanating out of the EU still have a strong territorial justice philosophy behind them (e.g. Structures funding, LEADER etc), the emphasis of a social capital and capacity logic governing local and regional allocations systems inevitably means that many rural groups and localities are failing to develop the critical mass to establish and capture such funding benefits.

Hence, we can see here that progressing environmental and territorial justice questions are almost unavoidable in addressing these new developmental trends. It these cases we need to do so explicitly. For instance what are the consequences of the further concentration of resources and economic development? What sort of trade-offs are possible or legitimate? How can injustices be compensated, monetarily and non-monetarily? How can a more multi-level governance system in the rural development sphere (i.e. combinations of EU, national, regional and local policy platforms) progress a renewed set of regional and local convergence policies? Moreover, what are the social and political effects of persistent injustices in and through different rural spaces?

Community and Association

Much of the social science of the environment literature (see Irwin 2001) and rural social nature debates, for instance, have tended to so far underplay one of the traditional strengths of rural sociology: community. It is somewhat surprising then that notions of community and association

244 *The Condition of Rural Sustainability*

have so far failed to intervene as important working and active mechanisms between the 'social' and the 'natural'. Two examples illustrate this from our work on farming and rural development, and from the forestry and community work.

Alternative supply chains and rural development activities are, as we saw in Chapter 10, it built upon new sets of associations and associational capacities of actors to engage in ways which shape both the social and the natural. Associational interfaces (often as emerging and contingent networks and chains) are both informal but highly significant in establishing trust, common understandings, working patterns, and forms of co-operation and co-optation between different actors in the supply chain. These differ from institutional interfaces which include state regulations and the support and services offered by rural economic development agencies (see Long 2001). And, they are often crucial in generating and facilitating supply chain interfaces at a regional level – a key new spatial platform for the development of agro-food alternatives to take hold (Chapter 9). However, such interfaces are vulnerable to internal and externally generated disruptions. There is no inevitability that strong and mutually reinforcing associational interfaces will be reproduced over time. Furthermore, where they do not exist, or have broken down, it may take many years to re-build relationships and working trust relationships to a point where regional or local actors – or actors operating at a distance across a supply chain – can create the conditions necessary to effectively and efficiently meet and relate to consumer demands. In many cases, in what I have termed 'short supply chains' these new associational competences are formed across the traditionally recognised producer/consumer arena. Indeed, re-connecting associational capacity across this former divide is part of a new set of innovations that mark out the new modernisation projects from the old. Our evidence from European case studies suggests that sustaining rural development through the evolution of reconfigured supply chains must be based upon new combinations of both institutional support and associational development. Furthermore, these relationships must be able to adapt to internal and external shocks and pressures over time and space. Here, and again distinctively, there is no one model. A key question then is the degree to which these features will need to become more widespread if real aggregated rural development impacts are to be achieved, and how, if they are not apparent, could they be generated?

In the local context of residential forest communities in South Wales, we also see how deep-seated local interpretations and impressions of community, and particularly of the marginalisation effects of the State as part of community life, have a critical bearing upon the constructions and shapes of socio-natural relations and practices in that community. In short, the social character and construction of the community – in this case a socially rich place, but marginalised and peripheralised by the State – provides an important social prism through which nature is perceived and used (see Bishop *et al.* 2002). Hence socio-natural perceptions and practices emerge as an expression of the social construction of the community; and in this case, the particular incision of the state in this construction. In this sense what we can infer from this is that particular types or sets of socio-natural relations and practices cannot be simply 'read-off' from the prevailing sets of *realist* social and economic regulatory conditions. Neither, however, as social constructionists may propose, can they just be rendered as varyingly 'co-constructed' within environmentally related practices and social contexts' (Irwin 2001). The residents in the community are not just free agents in their constructions of natural relations. Neither is the forest a neutral natural actant operating in a completely natural setting. Both nature (in this case the forest) and the people are actively engaging in broader socio-political conditions which, in turn help to shape the particular types of socio-natural relations in this type of local context. Such a postulate suggests that there is an inherent partiality about the two earlier approaches. What needs to be added to both conceptions is an empirically embedded understanding of how the natural becomes an active ingredient in the continual process of community construction.

Exclusion and empowerment

While aspects of rural social exclusion have become a vibrant topic of concern, especially amongst rural geographers (see Cloke *et al.* 2000; Shucksmith 2000); the emphasis of this work has thus far been largely upon the identification of exclusionary practices in different social, economic, institutional and domestic arena. One further and important aspect – as agro-ecological frameworks suggest – concerns the ways in which communities, different actors and agencies can become more empowered; and to do so in contexts which are ecologically as well as socially sustainable. In our forestry communities we witness a long historical process of disempowerment brought about by both the productivist priorities of the mining and forestry sectors, and in addition, the gradual marginalisation of much of the community by labour markets and the state authorities (see Chapter 6). Here disempowerment is multi-faceted, and it is the combination of these marginalisation histories which provide the backdrop for any change of Forestry Commission policy in terms of enhancing community and sustainable development. The exclusion-empowerment equations operate differently between and through communities and they provide a key mechanism in establishing the social landscape upon which new, potentially more ecological forms of modernisation could take hold. Indeed, they provide a major way in which ecological modernising principles can in themselves become marginalised and obscured in the face of what are seen to be more short-term employment imperatives.

A further, if separate element of exclusion and empowerment comes in terms of the market and consumer exclusions operating in the conventional food supply system. Here we see two key processes at work which deserve much more attention in progressing a more ecologically modernising agenda. These concern the exclusionary tendencies based both upon price, quality and location encouraged by the corporate retailers in the operation of their food chains (see Competition Commission 2000). This is generating a major feature of the 'new food politics' with consumer agencies adopting exclusionary arguments as well as food quality arguments in their political articulations with government authorities. The operation of what is called in the trade as 'price flexing' – whereby the corporate retailers purposely vary their grocery prices in the light of local competitive conditions rather than being related to actual costs- has become widespread in the UK. Even the conservatively written recent Competition Report of the national government concluded that where the big corporate retailers were practising this, it tended to operate against the public interest. Customers tend to pay more at stores that do not face particular competitors than they would do if those competitors were present in the area. In many of the marginalised working class areas of urban and rural UK these monopoly retailing arrangements are now common place. Hence we see here that there is a real need to link the particular corporate and institutional practices with local empowerment and exclusionary conditions – in space. In many of the debates so far – both academic and public policy – these linkages in space have been at best blurred. Indeed, the spacing of exclusionary practices and their links to corporate strategies has been neglected. It is not so much about the identification of 'food deserts' as understanding the interfaces of corporate strategy and local consumption in their varied spatial contexts. As this example shows, what we witness in many areas are competition practices going in reverse. With major retailers being able to create almost 'monopoly consumption spaces' in which they can raise prices, beyond their relationships with 'true' costs. Keeping other retail competitors *out* as well as harnessing loyal and recurrent consumers *in* to their stores becomes a central mechanism *in* the territoriality of exclusive food consumption in the British context.

A third arena of exclusion/empowerment concerns those at the other end of the food supply chain-the primary producers. Despite government policy rhetoric about the need to abide by the laws of fair trading and European competition policy, many farmers and many processors find themselves excluded from the often more lucrative retailer – led food markets. For those that do gain entry, the degree of informal control over their operations severely constrains their 'room for manoeuvre'. In many ways these are the newly created forces of subsumption operating in the retailer-led chains; whereby pricing and conditions can be placed upon producers and processors in ways which are seen to be 'consumer-led', but really emerge from the day-to day management of these supply chains by the category managers of the retailers. With exclusion or relative empowerment in this regard, therefore, we see also the creative development of social and economic dependencies operating between different sets of actors in the supply chain. Local rural and agricultural spaces are, therefore, no longer controlled at a distance by the corporate input suppliers (i.e. associated with concepts of appropriation, substitution and subsumption of production). Now it is more variably conditioned by the down-stream retailers who engage groups of consumers and governments in their powerful networks. Hence, primary production becomes something of a backwater and 'dirty' activity which needs to be 'cleaned up' by the state and corporate retailers on behalf of the public.

We see here, then, through these examples how exclusion and empowerment strands are a critical integrating mechanism for bringing together the social, economic and institutional construction and allocation of power, both in and through rural (as well as urban) spaces. This is cross-cutting, both vertically through supply chains and laterally through community / institutional interfaces.

Consumption and production: socially and culturally reconstructing the 'quality' commodity

While considerably more emphasis has been placed upon understanding the relationships between production and consumption; and particularly the ways in which the very fabric of food fuses both natural and social hybridities, there needs to be more attention given to the ways in which the hybrid social and natural relations surrounding food are governed, empowered and used. While accepting that there has been something (although I think somewhat overdrawn) of a conceptual distinction made between the more political economy-inspired analysis of production and the more culturally-inspired consumption studies, there is a clear need to explore how new alliances and relationships can be brought together in ways which progress the understanding of alternative food networks or chains. Also, we need to know much more about how these both use and travel through space. Our recent European evidence suggests high levels of spatial variability between different rural regions in the setting up and sustenance of alternative supply chains. These variabilities are particularly affected by the type and degree of institutional support, via, not just the national state, but regional knowledge and skill-based agencies; and by the highly context dependent types of associational involvement from a variety of different actors. It is clear that the innovation patterns, the skills bases and the degree to which such initiatives can utilise and exploit the 'territorial worth' of their localities and regions are all critical factors. These factors show that aspects of space, quality convention, nature, and agricultural and food socio-technical practices (e.g. the particular ways of cutting, curing, salting and carving of meats, for instance) come together in rural spaces. Moreover, many of these initiatives also reconstruct important new co-locational alliances with specific groups of consumers. Many consumers, for their part are increasingly searching for 'something else' other than the standardised or indeed mass-produced specialised types of food product. The consumption experience, often involving direct contact with the producer or the seller becomes an important ritualistic consumption practice.

However, what marks these alternative food chains out from the conventional system, is by no means their face-to-face nature necessarily. In some of the more mature quality supply chains we see the development of spatially extended networks, which are selling brands, labels and seriously commodifying their culinary repertoires (e.g. Parmigiano Reggiano Cheese). They are still categorically alternative, however, in that that have and do re-align nature, space, socio-technical practices, and quality conventions in ways which make it impossible to replicate these outside that network. These then are the new ecologically-deepened supply chains, and to describe and understand them requires much more than a recourse to such generalised notions of mutual or reciprocal hybridities or metabolics. Rather, it requires a concerted effort to understand the *theory and practices of the actors* – both producer, consumers and exchange actors – who mobilise and animate/demarcate such networks (see Verschoor 1998, for instance). These new food networks are now a common occurrence and in many regions are by no means marginal to the conventional system. In Northern Italy, we see a concentration of quality food networks, while in Germany and the Netherlands, new alliances are more associated with agri-tourism ventures and nature and landscape management. Food as a culturally hybrid entity, which becomes unevenly embedded into the fabric of new rural development practices; and new synergies become developed between food, agricultural practice, consumption practices and associational and institutional arrangements.

Understanding the wealth and worth of these series of micro-social practices, and still more, assessing what in more generalised terms they 'add up to' is a major empirical and theoretical task to which Buttel (2001) alludes, and for which scholars have only recently embarked. It is clear, however, that the volatilities in the consumption/production relations associated with the conventional systems, will have pervasive effects and interactions upon the competitive spaces that these alternative food supply chains operate in. This is highly contingent, not just upon some vague notions of consumer culture or sovereignty. It is also centrally conditioned by the contested and institutional ways in which the 'consumer interest' is continually constructed – and by whom. Such analytical progress will not simply rely upon a realisation that nature and society are hybridised in food. The issue is how, where and by which powerful/ non-powerful actors? Food as a realm of governance and social and political regulation is not contradicted by more socially constructivist processes. These need to be put together; not least because institutional actors and agencies are part of that constructed and contested process. Somehow, we need to understand how alternative food networks not only get formed, but then get demarcated and maintained as a socio-competitive dynamic. They are not static events.

Corporate responsibility and accountability

The past two decades have witnessed a significant growth in research work on the agro-industrial globalisation and regulation of agribusiness and the workings of multi-nationals (see Friedland 2001 for review of the commodity systems approach). This has been a major development of the discipline of rural sociology, and it has emerged as a clear critique of industrial modernisation in the agro-food sector. In postulating aspects of ecological modernisation, however, we also now need to consider and critically assess how business relationships (both with each other, with consumers, and with local communities) are changing as a result of a number of significant forces. These include: changes in the regulatory frameworks; the globalisation of supply chains and the increasing mobility of capital and knowledge; the application of ICT to radically restructure certain markets, industries and places; changing patterns of consumption and falling consumer trust in existing forms of corporate and government communications; the emergence of civil society groups and global protest movements and a realisation that companies may be more vulnerable to pressure for change than entrenched or undemocratic governments; the fragmentation of local communities and constructions of community; the pressure from the investment community in the form of the growing ethical investment movement; and the pressure from insurers who see the reduction of environmental damage and social conflict as an important way for companies to reduce levels of risk.

These reconstituting forces are, in turn, reshaping the relationships between firms, governments and 'communities of interest'. Amongst the actors there are key constituencies who will help to shape the dynamic and developing relationships both within their actor-spaces and between themselves and other actors. From the point of view of business it is now more essential (albeit to varying spatial and sectoral degrees) that these changing relationships are constructed and constantly reconstructed in ways that help to ensure its longer-term survival. These can be depicted in

250   *The Condition of Rural Sustainability*

the Figure 12.1. However, neither the effects on businesses of the processes of change that I identify here will not be even, and nor will be the impacts on the 'communities of interest'. *What is necessary in research terms then is to theoretically and empirically understand the richness, complexity and contestability of business responses to, and the management of, its wider environment.*

Figure 12.1 Changing relationships between key actors

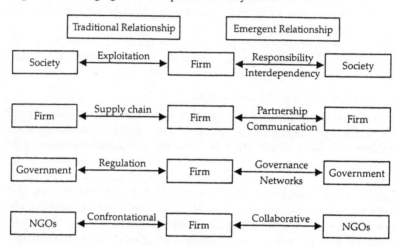

In short, we need new constructed models of business behaviour and relationships which are embedded in the social, environmental and political contexts, which they are also attempting to shape. So far environmental and rural sociologists have tended to avoid these ventures; leaving it to the environmental economists and ethical marketing specialists to engage in the tracing of these new patterns. For instance, such discipline-specific research is pursuing the following lines:

- the inclusion of sustainability and social responsiveness within corporate accounting and reporting practices, and its relationships to the growing ethical investment industry is typically being researched within the accounting and finance disciplines (e.g. Gray *et al.* 1995).
- changing consumer demand for ethically and environmentally acceptable products and the response of companies to demands for such products, new information and new marketing approaches is typically being researched by the marketing and economics disciplines (e.g. Menon and Menon 1997).
- the evolution of environmental and social regulation and its impact on firms is typically researched within the legal and public policy discipline (e.g. Garrod 2000)

- the implications of sustainability in terms of industry structure and infrastructure is typically a focus of research in the planning, geography and public policy disciplines – and, the influence of global capital flows and governance standards is primarily researched within the law, finance and international relations disciplines (see Brack 1995).

Yet, in all these areas environmental social science, and more specifically rural social science, has a potentially important role to play, particularly in understanding how these changing business, government, community relationships are spaced and re-spaced. In the food sector, for instance, the contested competitive spaces between conventional and alternative supply chains is occurring in a broader context of a reduced reliance simply upon legal compliance as a justification and legitimisation of actions. In this sense de *jure* regulation is not enough. Also there is a broadening amongst many firms of the 'stakeholder concept' whereby companies are increasingly having to respond not just to customers and investors, but also those with a physical stake in their actions, including the communities within which they operate and NGO's representing a myriad of interests (Polonsky 1995). We see this empirically, for instance in the redefinition of UK forestry commission policy and the new sets of relationships developing with government agencies. Moreover, consumer groups and governments have traditionally championed consumer rights in terms of choice, value and safety of products. Yet concerns over the sustainability and social responsiveness of businesses has led to an increased interest among stakeholders about the methods and consequences of production (Peattie 1999). This is most easily observable within the food industry, where concern is centred on issues relating to production practices – such as the use of chemicals, the use of GM and the constituents of animal feedstuffs, pollution and the destruction of habitats.

These trends suggest, at the very least a set of key research questions:

- how are changing patterns of demand leading to the development of more sustainable and socially responsible strategies, products and technologies?
- what types of new market and institutional structures (e.g. supply loops and networks) will develop in response to product take-back, as businesses are required by legislation and consumer pressure to become even more accountable for the life-cycle of their products?
- what opportunities will arise for the restructuring of industries around new business models and types of production systems and technologies?
- how will business to business and business to consumer relationships change if a service based economy (i.e. through leasing, take-back and

service arrangements) begins to replace the traditional exchange of physical goods?

To begin to answer some of these questions will require the development of new social and regulatory 'designs' around which we can begin to explore the richness and complexity of business/ environment relationships. Such an endeavour will need to take us far beyond the much more established and somewhat retrospective 'tracking' of the agro-industrial multi-national commodity flows. Moreover, we should put aside the rather binary question of whether firms will or will not ecologically modernise. Rather, we should explore both *what is* and *what might be*.

Regulation and bureaucratic professionalisation

As I argued in Chapter 8, it is important to recognise that the story of environmentalisation over the past two decades in the rural field has been one in which a particular form of Webarian bureaucracy has been increasingly prevalent. We need to recognise, both why this has been the case, and conversely, why it is not necessarily the only model in town. In the context of the agricultural and food sector in Europe (post BSE) termed this more specifically the *hygienic mode of regulation*. As the industrial mode of food supply has become even more crisis-ridden, the state has attempted to largely 'correct' this by setting up highly professionalised and bureaucratised forms of environmental safeguards and instruments. This has also been conducted in ' the interests of the consumer', as a way of governments seeking to protect their interests at the same time as allowing corporate industry the ability to exploit new markets. For instance, one recent expression of this is the advocation by some corporate supermarkets and government officials that eventually *all* farmers will have to old some form of quality licence to operate. The growth of a profound regulatory burden, as a response to the crisis in the industrial mode of agro-food, tends therefore, only to strengthen the economic and political power of established agro-industrial interests (including the large retailers and manufacturers). Both private and public forms of regulation are used to 'clean-up' the industrial system in the ostensible 'public interest'. Such *schematisation* holds the added consequence of further constraining the real potential of integrated agricultural development as well as providing new regulatory barriers to market entry for many smaller producers and processors. For consumers, it allows the disconnections and distanciations between production and consumption to conveniently continue: with an encouragement that 'safety' comes before (or gets conflated with) sustainability.

These processes have tended to break, or at least 'fracture' the environmental and rural development question into specific boxes, projects and schemes; making it more difficult to make holistic connections (as associated with agro-ecology for example ; see Guzman and Woodgate 1999). As a result it has been difficult for many actors to construct viable and integrated alternatives, or to harness the necessary spatial, natural, regional and knowledge-based resources necessary to progress *real* rural development options.

The broader field of rural development, as well as that of agro-food, has also become increasingly populated with project managers, consultants, exchange agents etc. such that a profession has been established to which some are excluded. Moreover, current priorities of national governments as well as emerged EU food quality policy concern the reconciling of the demands and risks of the 'careful consumer'. In the agro-food sector this is largely done by assembling a bureaucratic-hygienic apparatus-itself something of a new compromise between governments and capital-in order to stave off further and potentially deeper consumer-led legitimisation crisis in the old industrial system as a whole.

There is a need, therefore, for rural social scientists to contest these regulatory modes and to apply other, for instance, agro-ecological and food supply-chain ecological models to rural realities. This will require us to explore the contradictions and practices embedded in the different modes of environmental policy discourse, and for us to challenge the specificity of environmental expertise and professionalisation. How can a more holistic food ecology be created? And, what novel forms of regulation would this require? Is the bureaucratic/hygienic mode sustainable over time and space? And what barriers does it place upon achieving real ecological modernisation? For instance, as I argued in Chapter 1, while the current agro-environmental policy and rural development discourse continues apace in the European Commission, at the very same time we see, for instance in Finland, the rapid structural concentration of farms occurring as a result of continued policies of CAP. The surface waves of ecological modernisation discourses often seem to obscure the deeper countervailing currents of structural changes in the agro-food sector.

Conclusions: looking through the environmental maze and broadening politial economy

Past analyses in rural, and to a large extent in environmental sociology more generally, have to a great extent been built upon sophisticated and critical interpretations of the industrial modernisation project. In rural development terms, for example, this has focused upon challenging the economistic notions of scale, critical mass, centralisation, globalisation and marginalisation that this model has clearly engendered. Ecological modernisation, in all of its shades, nuances and theoretical flaws, at least brings forth a new question. That is, how could/should the relationships between civil society, the state and the market be re-arranged in ways which would usher in different types of more sustainable development which would incorporate ecological worth? A 'new age' of ecology, however, has begun in a slow, fledgling and uneven way. I have argued here that it does have some real intellectual purchase and potential, that part of this allows us to overcome some of the theoretical rigidities of the past, and that part of its value is that it brings spatiality into a central arena in rural political economy. In addition, it opens the door to more theoretical pluralism, debate and progress (as I have tried to explore in the three sections of this book); moving beyond social constructivist versus realist debates, structure and action and macro and micro. Here, in conclusion, I have attempted to set out here some of the cardinal conceptual reference points which have emerged as I have conducted three different research projects in the food, farming and forestry sectors. These are then partly empirically grounded as well as theoretically constructed arguments and, as such they deserve much more expansion, debate and consideration than is feasible here.

However, one of the fruitful opportunities such an exercise begins to explore, is the possibilities of re-assembling conceptual frameworks in ways which integrate nature and space within the broader political economy of national and international ruralities. As I have argued above, many of the current environmental discourses and regulatory frameworks tend to fracture such integrative endeavours in such ways as to create false divisions of professional labour between different communities of interest (including academics, policy officials environmental NGO's, consultants, and a whole range of 'project managers' who are now engaged in competitively progressing rural development initiatives). This makes integration in policy development and implementation all that more difficult, and it leads to the driving out of a radical consideration of alternatives by the urgency of meeting bureaucratically applied performance measures and indicators. Hence the critical development of environmental and rural social science is now a more central task in creatively engaging with what might be, as well as what is. The conceptual starting points I have outlined here are middle level concepts which can start to address this task. We should remember that the agro-industrial modernisation project has developed an elaborative and justificatory social science with which to legitimise itself; yet an equivalent social science for ecological modernisation is still very much in its infancy and liable to marginalisation. In undertaking these explorations it will be necessary, as most of the conceptual parameters suggested here demonstrate, to embed our conceptions of 'producers' and 'consumers' much more into the fabric of the contested worlds of industrial and ecological modernisation currently being applied in the advanced economies.

Conclusions: Rural Development as 'Real' Ecological Modernisation?   255

Note

The arguments developed here draw upon three research projects being conducted by the author and several colleagues (including, Jo Banks, Paul Milbourne, Jon Murdoch, Kevin Bishop). The first was entitled *Innovation and Quality in the Food chain: strengthening the regional dimension'* (funded by the Economic and Social research Council). The second is entitled *'The Socio-economic impact of rural development policies: realities and potentials'* funded by the EU; and the third related to an ethnographic study, *'Forestry, community and land in the South Wales Valleys'* funded by the UK Forestry Commission. The early results ideas emanating from these projects are contained in recent articles (see Murdoch *et al.* 2000; Marsden *et al.* 2001b; Bishop *et al.* 2002).

References

Bishop, K., Kitchen, L., Marsden T. K., Milbourne, P. (2002) *Forestry, Community and Land in the South Wales Valleys*. Final Report to the Forestry Commission (Department of City and Regional Planning, Cardiff University, Cardiff).

Brack, D. (1995) Balancing trade and the environment *International Affairs* 71, 497–514.

Buttel, F. H. (2001) Some reflections on late twentieth century agrarian political economy *Sociologia Ruralis* 41, pp. 165–182.

Carley, M., Kirk, K., McIntosh, S. (2001) *Retailing, sustainability and neighbourhood regeneration* (Joseph Rountree Foundation, York).

Cloke, P., Milbourne, P., Widdowfield, R. C. (2000) The hidden and emerging spaces of rural homelessness *Environment and Planning A* 32, pp. 77–90.

Competition Commission (2000) *Supermarkets. A Report on the Supply of Groceries from Multiple Store in the United Kingdom* (3 vols) (HMSO, London).

Garrod, N. (2000) Environmental contingencies and sustainable modes of corporate governance *Journal of Accounting and Public Policy* 19, pp. 237–261.

Goodman, D. (1999) Agro-food studies in the 'age of ecology': nature, corporeality, bio-politics *Sociologia Ruralis* 39, 17–38.

Gray, R., Walters, D., Bebbington, J., Thompson, I. (1995) The greening of enterprise: an exploration of the (NON) role of environmental accounting and accountants in organizational change *Critical Perspectives on Accounting* 6, pp. 211–239.

Guzman, E., Woodgate, G. (1999) Alternative food and agriculture networks: an agro-ecological perspective on the responses to economic globalisation and the 'new agrarian question'. Paper presented at EU COST Workshop.

Irwin, A. (2001) *Sociology and the Environment* (Polity Press, Oxford).

Long, N. (2001) *The Power of Music. Issues of Agency and Social Practice* (Wageningen University, Wageningen).

Long, N., Long, A. (eds.) (1992) *Battlefields of Knowledge: the Interlocking of Theory and Practice in Social Research and Development* (Routledge, London).

Marsden, T. K., Milbourne, P., Kitchen, L., Bishop, K. (2001b) Communities in Nature: the construction and understanding of forest natures in South Wales Valleys Communities. Paper at the XIX European Congress for Rural Sociology, Dijon, September, 2001.

Mather, A. S. (2001) Forests of consumption: postproductivism, postmaterialism, and the postindustrial forest *Environment and Planning C: Government and Policy* 19, 249–268.

Menon, A., Menon, A. (1997) Entreprenuerial marketing strategy: the emergence of corporate environmentalism as market strategy *Journal of Marketing* 61, pp. 51–67.

Murdoch, J., Marsden, T. K., Banks, J. (2000) Quality, nature, and embeddedness: some theoretical considerations in the context of the food sector *Economic Geography* 76, pp. 107–125.

Peattie, K. (1999) *Environmental Marketing Management: meeting the green challenge* (Pitman Publishing, London).

Polonsky, M. J. (1995) A stakeholder theory approach to designing environmental marketing strategy *Journal of Business and Industrial Marketing* 10(3), pp. 29–46.

Redclift, M., Woodgate, G. (1998) (eds) *The International Handbook of Environmental Sociology* (Edward Elgar Publishing, Cheltenham).

SDRN (Sustainable Development Research Network) (2002) *A New Agenda for UK Sustainable Development Research* (Policy Studies Institute, London).

Shucksmith, M. (2000) Social Exclusion in Rural Areas (Joseph Rowntree Research Trust, York).

Name Index